LOUIS I. KAHN THE NORDIC LATITUDES

FAY JONES SCHOOL OF ARCHITECTURE + DESIGN
UNIVERSITY OF ARKANSAS PRESS
A COLLABORATION

Other Titles in This Series

Interpreting Kigali, Rwanda:
Architectural Inquiries and Prospects
for a Developing African City

Shadow Patterns:
Reflections on Fay Jones
and His Architecture

Barns and Portrait Paintings

Of the Soil:
Photographs of Vernacular Architecture
and Stories of Changing Times in Arkansas

Architects of Little Rock: 1833–1950

Just Below the Line:
Disability, Housing, and Equity in the South

Sacred Spaces:
The Architecture of Fay Jones:
The Life of AIA Gold Medal–Winning
Architect Fay Jones (HD DVD)

LOUIS I. KAHN THE NORDIC LATITUDES

Per Olaf Fjeld and Emily Randall Fjeld

UNIVERSITY OF ARKANSAS PRESS Fayetteville 2019

Printed in Korea by Four Colour Print Group, Louisville, Kentucky

ISBN: 978-1-68226-112-5
eISBN: 978-1-61075-681-5

23 22 21 20 19 5 4 3 2 1

♾ The paper used in this publication meets the minimum requirements of the American National Standard for Permanence of Paper for Printed Library Materials Z39.48-1984.

Library of Congress Control Number: 2019939498

CONTENTS

FOREWORD

The Fay Jones School of Architecture and Design, in collaboration with the University of Arkansas Press, is pleased to bring forward into publication *Louis I. Kahn: The Nordic Latitudes*, authored by the Norwegian architect and educator Per Olaf Fjeld together with his wife and partner, the American-born artist Emily Randall Fjeld. This book builds upon the series of publications that the Fay Jones School has undertaken over the last ten years in partnership with the University of Arkansas Press—a collaboration initiated by Professor Jeff Shannon during his tenure as dean and developed subsequently in his role as executive editor of the collaborative publications. *Louis I. Kahn: The Nordic Latitudes* expands this legacy and, by extension, celebrates the school's namesake, the internationally renowned architect and educator Fay Jones, himself a former dean of the school. The example Jones set—intertwining the ambitions and ideals of professional practice with the ambitions and ideals of a professional education in architecture—remains fundamental to the perspectives, curricula, and overall educational character of the school that now proudly bears his name. Highlighting the life and work of another internationally renowned architect, *Louis I. Kahn: The Nordic Latitudes* may be seen as an emblem of the school and of the school's place in architecture culture more generally.

The book at hand, whose diverse components coalesced over many years, weaves together cultural histories, architectural histories, and personal histories—all intertwined by the exceptional interpretive voice of Per Olaf Fjeld. Fjeld presents an explicit agenda from the outset: to position, or indeed, reposition, the thought and work of Louis Kahn within a distinctly Nordic context, in a Nordic "light," so to speak, at a Nordic latitude. This, of course, is a counter-history of sorts, given that Kahn is most often presented as an architect shaped more by his exposure to the Mediterranean "light"—the culture of forms and principles to be found especially at the latitudes of Rome and Athens—rather than that of sixty degrees north, the latitude of Kahn's birthplace in Estonia. Such a proposition is one of effective surprise and one that, at the very least, asks the reader to question their preconceptions and the conventional presentations of Kahn.

While Kahn's identity as a "man of the North" may well have been intimated by Kahn to the then-young Norwegian during his first days as a student in the now-fabled masterclass studio at the University of Pennsylvania, its full significance only emerged for Fjeld as he moved through his own development as an architect and educator in the years that followed. Fjeld's understanding of Kahn in a Nordic light was illuminated by his nearly lifelong engagement with the Pritzker Prize–winning Norwegian architect Sverre Fehn. But perhaps even more significantly, Fjeld came to realize that Kahn's life and work paralleled those of Fehn's mentor, Arne Korsmo, a Norwegian architect and educator whose legacy has generally been underappreciated in scholarship, especially within English-language architecture circles. The year that Fjeld spent in Kahn's masterclass studio can now be understood retrospectively as "the last masterclass," but for the author this period was already suffused at the time with wonder. The history and atmosphere of that magical year is embodied by the talismanic presence in this book of Fjeld's journals, capturing his daily encounters with Kahn.

All of this to say that *Louis I. Kahn: The Nordic Latitudes* narrates a fascinating set of overlapping, even laminated, histories: the life and work of Louis Kahn set within the longer, rich history of Nordic architecture; the experience of Per Olaf Fjeld and his classmates in the Kahn masterclass studio (in particular, the day-to-day pedagogy of the architect in concert with his collaborators); and Per Olaf Fjeld's work in education and in architecture culture more generally, extending the legacy of Kahn into the contemporary moment. Throughout this account—populated by the vital figures of Kahn, Sverre Fehn, Arne Korsmo, Giancarlo De Carlo, and so many others of this important period of late modernism—the voice of Per Olaf Fjeld remains constant: it is the voice of a passionate, reflective educator, always searching for more and more complete reconciliations with his own experiences, with the legacies of his mentors, and with his deeply felt ethical obligations to architecture.

A book of this character is ever a collaborative project, and there are numerous individuals to acknowledge with gratitude. Here in Fayetteville, Mike Bieker, director and publisher of the University of Arkansas Press, and David Scott Cunningham, editor-in-chief at the press, understood its value immediately and guided its progress. Tim Walker, principal of DoXA Design, established the initial cover and page design templates, giving visual definition and refinement to the book's intentions at a critical juncture in development. From these initial design concepts, Liz Lester, designer at the press, developed and extended this visual character to encompass all aspects of the book's design and typeset the entire manuscript. Molly Rector, project editor at the press, oversaw the production process. At the Fay Jones School, the book took shape with the encouragement and editorial observations of Professor Jeff Shannon, and with insight and counsel from Fay Jones Distinguished Visiting Professor Juhani Pallasmaa. Lane Schmidt, executive assistant to the dean, coordinated editorial, design, and production meetings. The final manuscript emerged through the tireless, attentive, and sensitive efforts of Janet Foxman, the school's special publications editor, who then led the editorial and production process through to completion.

This book has a personal significance for me. In the spring of 1984, while serving as coeditors of *Perspecta: The Yale Architectural Journal*, Issue 24, my colleague David

Thompson and I approached Sverre Fehn and Per Olaf Fjeld with a proposal to contribute to the issue, a proposal spurred by the publication of their compelling collaboration titled *The Thought of Construction*. As graduate students in architecture, we spent almost all our days in Paul Rudolph's Art and Architecture Building looking out on, in some sense, the alpha and omega of Louis Kahn's life work: the Yale University Art Gallery of 1953 and the Yale Center for British Art, completed after his death. We saw in Sverre Fehn's work a clear inheritor of the legacy of Kahn and we read in Fjeld's words a clear stance on the substance and meaning of architecture. After a period of time, Fehn and Fjeld responded to our proposal, and we were gifted with a dialogue between the two that was published in 1988 as the essay "Has a Doll Life?" To work with Per Olaf Fjeld and Emily Randall Fjeld, to extend the legacy of Sverre Fehn and the legacy of Louis Kahn after some thirty-five years, to participate in the publication of this book—all of this is testimony to the resonances of life.

We look forward to further publications of this character, both in collaboration with the University of Arkansas Press and in collaboration with other exceptional architectural practitioner-educators.

Peter MacKeith
Dean of the Fay Jones School of Architecture and Design
University of Arkansas, Fayetteville

ACKNOWLEDGMENTS

Emily and I would like to express our gratitude to the many colleagues and friends who made this book possible. Though we were not able to reconnect with all my fellow classmates from the 1972–73 masterclass, many responded to our outreach, and we are very thankful for this. In particular, we are grateful for the effort that Robert Couch, Timothy Spelman, Chiaki Arai, and Farrokh Sabouri put into sharing their pictures, drawings, and other materials so essential to this book.

We would like to thank the Oslo School of Architecture and Design, which supported this project from the start. The school's former dean, Karl Otto Ellefsen, and its present dean, Ole Gustavsen, have both been very generous. We thank the many colleagues who have contributed images, and my teaching team at the Oslo School of Architecture, Lisbeth Funck and Rolf Gerstlauer, who have been openhanded with their time and help. A very special thanks goes to architect and former student Jon Reksten for his work producing many mock-ups of the manuscript as well as his inspiration throughout the project.

It is with gratitude and great respect that we thank Dean Peter MacKeith at the Fay Jones School of Architecture and Design, University of Arkansas, for his interest and courage to take on this project. We are appreciative of the support and effort from the Fay Jones School of Architecture and Design; its former dean, Jeff Shannon; and the University of Arkansas Press. In relation to this, we have been very fortunate to have Janet Foxman to edit and advise during the last stages of manuscript preparation, which has been inspiring and vital to the end result.

We thank William Whitaker, the curator and collections manager of the Architectural Archives of the University of Pennsylvania School of Design, and the Louis I. Kahn Collection at the University of Pennsylvania for all their help and guidance.

A very personal thanks goes to Nathaniel Kahn for his generosity and our conversations together regarding the content of this book.

Per Olaf Fjeld

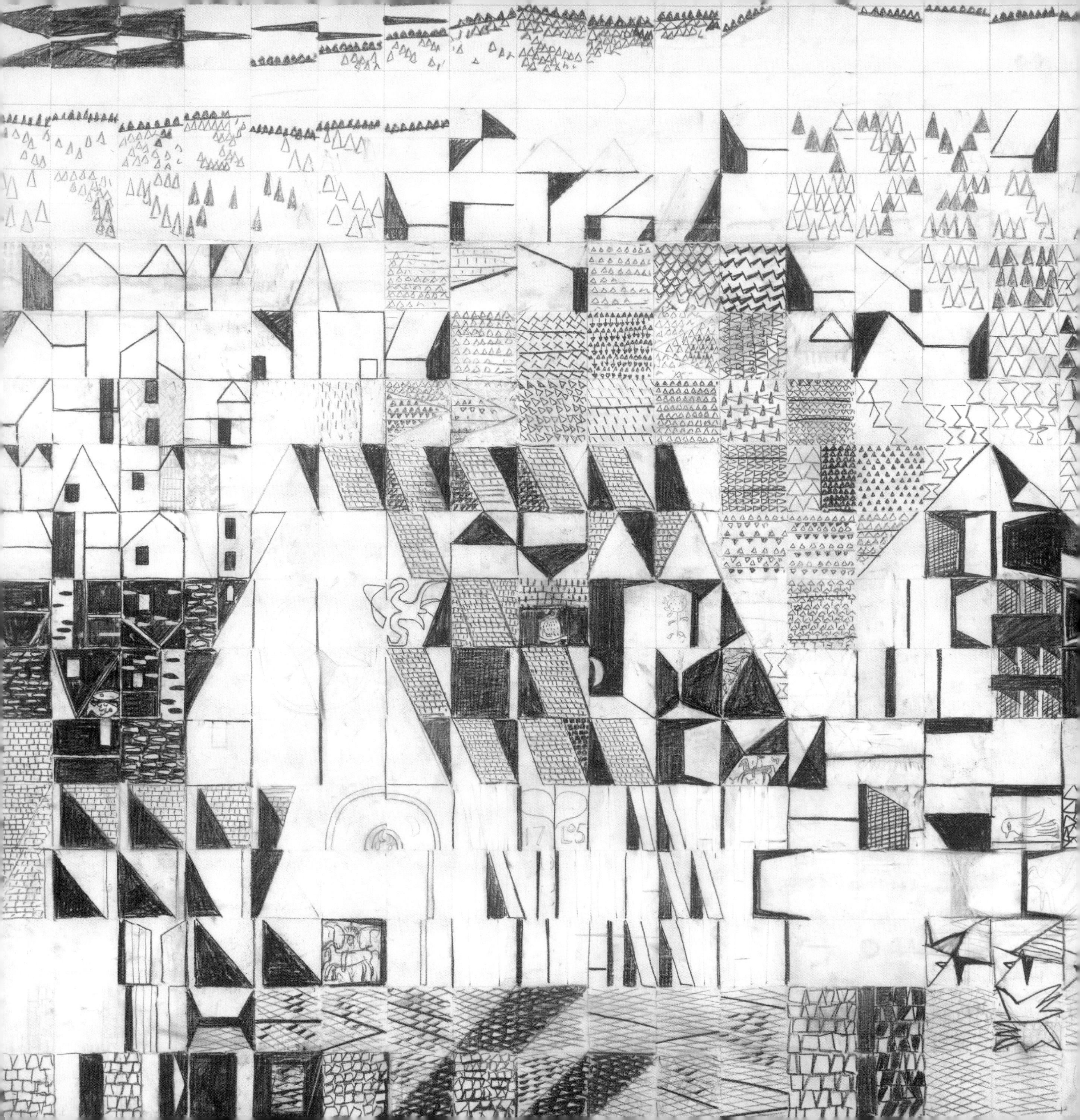

INTRODUCTION

Everyday circumstances in life leave traces, and inside this web of events some imprints are deeper and more profound than others. My lifelong practice of taking notes and keeping a journal is the thread that pieces together the diverse contents of this book. During six years as a student in the United States I kept notebooks I called "architectural capsules," which were not diaries of events but of thoughts and observations concerning everything I perceived as important in architecture at that moment. Central to these notebooks is the time I spent in Louis I. Kahn's masterclass at the University of Pennsylvania—an education that impacted the choices I made as an architect and teacher in all that followed.

I kept a regular journal of the Monday and Friday classes with Kahn and his team. From the start I was conscious of my notebooks' value as firsthand recordings; but at the close of the masterclass, with my journals carefully packed and shipped home, I could not foresee the long-term influence that Kahn's teachings would have on my career decisions, nor how returning to practice in Norway would be pivotal in my understanding Louis Kahn's teaching anew. My motivation to write this book begins here—as a personal story. But my life after graduation—which has inspired me to rethink Kahn, his creative base, his Nordic connections, and his legacy—also animates this text.

I received all my formal architectural education in the United States; prior to Kahn's masterclass, I earned a professional degree at Washington State University. There, during my last year, Kahn was scheduled to lecture—but he never made it, sending an assistant in his stead. The presentation captivated the audience, but as students we were not yet able to fully appreciate Kahn's work on its own terms. His approach and his built work and their deceptive spatial simplicity seemed foreign to the current architecture my class admired at the time.

Some months earlier I had applied specifically to Kahn's masterclass along with a couple of other graduate schools, and though I was advised that one of the other schools would be a better springboard to a future career, I made up my mind.

I felt very fortunate when I entered Kahn's classroom in the early fall of 1972, and I know my new classmates experienced the same emotion. For all our expectations, though, we soon realized no tickets to success were on offer, no answers, just questions. As it was not a homogeneous class, Kahn was not the perfect teacher for every student, and at times this was a sensitive issue. Yet I think most students felt a personal connection with him on some level.

My first personal exchange with Kahn related directly to his Nordic ties. Within weeks of the first day, he pulled me aside and asked if I knew the Norwegian architect Arne Korsmo, and he also commented that I was the only Norwegian student who had ever attended his

Mural study from Louis Kahn's Weiss House (1944–50) depicting elements reminiscent of a Nordic landscape. *Nathaniel Kahn Collection.*

masterclass. His remarks stayed with me throughout the first semester, but I was unable to put this conversation into any perspective before I returned home. There another side of Kahn's story began to take form. In the late August after my graduation in 1973, I landed a job with the future Pritzker Prize–winning architect Sverre Fehn. He had been an early student of Arne Korsmo's and, at the time of my return home, was a professor at the Oslo School of Architecture. He also knew many of the architects who had attended the International Congresses of Modern Architecture meeting (CIAM) in Otterlo in 1959, the year Kahn participated. From the beginning, Fehn was generous in introducing me and my wife Emily—whom I had met during my second semester in Philadelphia, and who joined me in Oslo in 1974—to many of his international colleagues and friends. He also encouraged me to take an active part in ILAUD, the International Laboratory of Architecture and Urban Design, which was initiated by Giancarlo De Carlo not long after Kahn died. In the laboratory environment of De Carlo and a number of his former Team 10 colleagues and friends, new perspectives on Kahn emerged—acquired slowly, summer after summer.

Now, though my professional life as a teacher and architect is based in Scandinavia, I often find myself caught between two perceptions of Kahn's work and creative approach: one tied to the United States, the other Nordic. But Kahn's contemporaries and influences from Europe and the Nordic countries are perhaps the least explored. Much of what I later discovered and understood about Kahn was entwined with the activities that Emily and I experienced together over the years from our base in Oslo. As I continued to keep journals, including during my time with Fehn and my years in ILAUD, I began to see other connections between what was developing out of Nordic and European architectural discourse and past discussions from the masterclass. Over time I met individuals who knew Kahn from his early visits to Europe, and some of these acquaintances became close friends. Our conversations about Kahn were open and contextual. All of this has shaped a more nuanced picture of Kahn's teaching than the one I originally took home with me as a young graduate.

To connect Kahn to the Nordic region and cultural values gives greater insight into his architectural focus and vocabulary. When perceived through a twentieth-century Nordic sensibility, some of his most iconic phrases, terms, and ideas gain new meaning and, in many ways, greater clarity. For this reason, in the first section I present a short history of the Baltic/Nordic area as a backdrop to Kahn's family history, and then I move on to various events and people important to Nordic architectural history in the first half of the twentieth century. From there, the section focuses on the friendship between Louis Kahn and Arne Korsmo, from their first meeting in 1928 to Korsmo's death in 1968.

The second section, "The Masterclass," contains three parts, beginning with an account of the studio class, the teachers, the guests, the elective courses, and a description of the four projects Kahn assigned that year. The second part is a condensed presentation of the notebooks in which I recorded Kahn's insights during our masterclass studio. A complement to my journal notes, the third part is an investigation of the various terms Kahn used in our classroom discussions.

Ten years after finishing the masterclass, I was awarded a Fulbright–Hays grant to conduct research in the Kahn Collection at the University of Pennsylvania. This effort forms the backdrop of much of the third section. In the time span building up to my return to the University of Pennsylvania, Emily and I set up a small practice, I published my first book on Sverre Fehn, and I taught with Fehn on a regular basis at the Oslo School of Architecture. Before setting out for Penn, I met with Fehn several times in preparation for an article we were then writing together. The topic of mass was central to our discussions and inspired me to revisit Kahn's thinking on the matter in advance of my research at Penn.

When I returned to Penn, the Kahn Collection was in an early stage of organization and its future economic backing was still uncertain. Most days I was the collection's only visitor, and I spent my time reading Kahn's correspondence and taking a closer look at his writings, drawings, and sketches. By chance, I ran into Gabor Szalontay, Esther Kahn, and Dean G. Holmes Perkins, and I made a note of all of these encounters.

In conclusion, I explore Kahn's legacy in the context of the present architectural discourse, but I keep the content here within the realm of firsthand knowledge. Toward the end of Kahn's career there was a dramatic change within architecture, and this was not merely a generational shift. New technologies, a rapidly expanding media, and a changing social awareness transformed the profession throughout most of the world in a very short period of time. These changes affected how Kahn's legacy has been perceived over the last decades, influencing what has been appreciated and what has been forgotten, including in his teaching and creative approach. For this reason, I have focused on the issues that concerned Kahn in class, particularly his "institutions of man" and his definitions and interpretations of nature, which I feel are more than ever relevant to the future of architecture and architectural education.

This book has required maturity, thus it took years before I was able to decipher, with Emily's input, Kahn's Nordic link. It begins and ends as a personal story; with keen respect for my teacher, this is all I can offer.

Per Olaf Fjeld

NORDIC CONNECTIONS

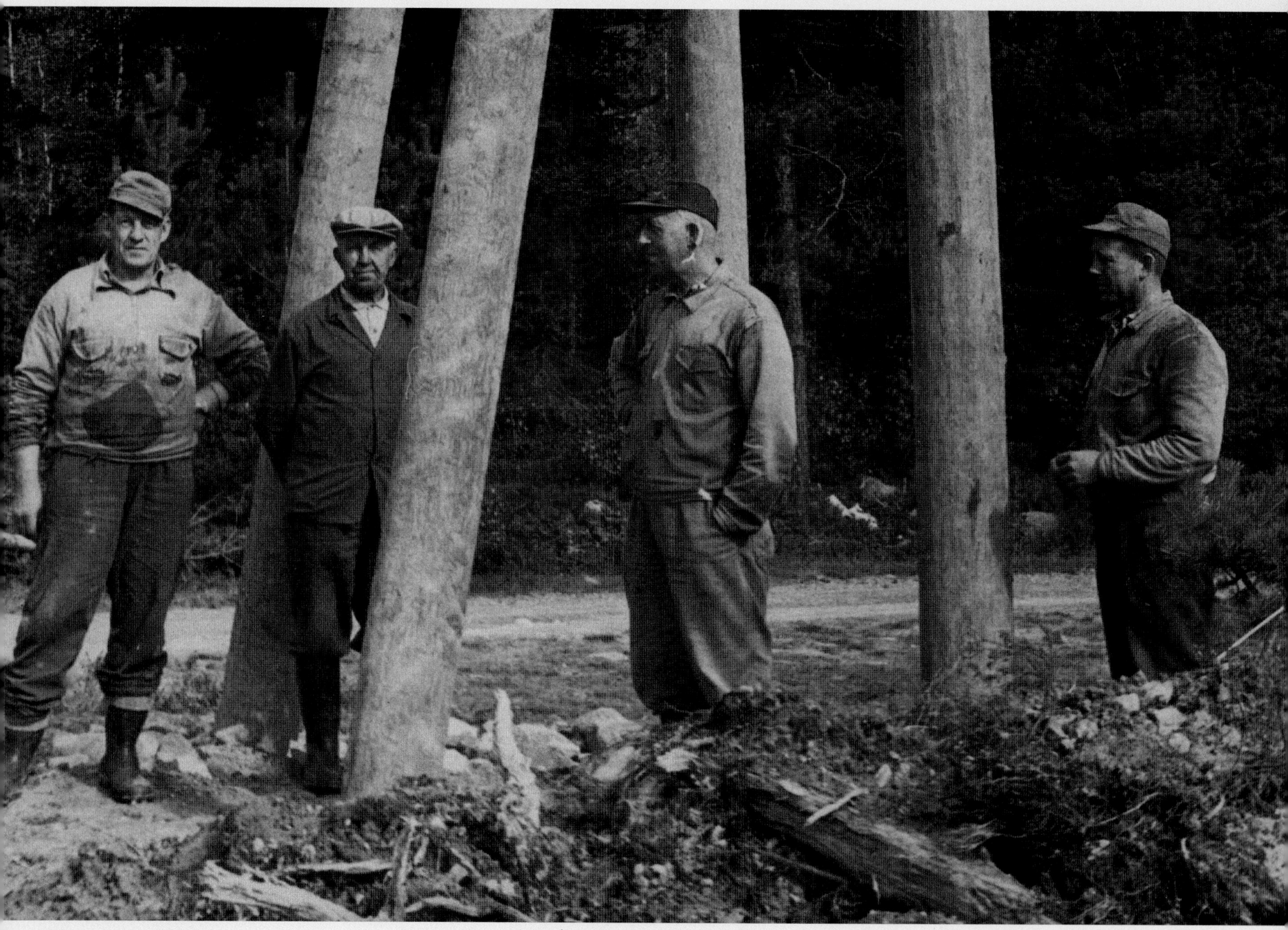

My father's crew erecting poles for new electrical lines along the Norwegian–Swedish border, 1955. *P. O. Fjeld.*

1 NORDIC CONNECTIONS

When I first entered Louis Kahn's masterclass at the University of Pennsylvania, I intuitively felt a connection. Probably the same feeling many students had, since no one really escaped Kahn's charisma; but for me this feeling was rooted in something that preceded our first meeting by many years: a connection by way of a childhood landscape and its light.

My father was an engineer in charge of developing and overseeing the electrical supply for a district in Norway along the border with Sweden. Here there are dense forests, lakes, rivers, and few inhabitants. One of my strongest memories is tagging along with my father to isolated farms that were about to be hooked up to the electrical power grid. For the families on these farms the first flip of the switch was almost a miracle, and they would deck out their kitchen tables in celebration. From that day onward, these families' daily chores and winter evenings were never the same.

Sometimes in the summer I would accompany my father while he checked the lines, the old concrete transformer stations, and small power plants, picking berries or fishing along the way; and though it could be quite late when we finally returned home, the sun had not set. In the winter these same trips were usually conducted in a dim midday light or darkness that had a soft lulling silence from a deep layer of snow that covered the ground and dense forest. In all of these childhood memories, nature and its light have a clear presence, and this influences how I perceive the world today.

Louis Kahn's earliest experiences of nature were on the Baltic island of Saaremaa, Estonia. The island of his childhood was a flat landscape of fields, forests, farms, pebbled shorelines, the sea, and the small, sleepy resort town of Kuressaare, with its simple one- and two-story buildings of timber and masonry and a castle ruin at its center. Saaremaa is almost as far north as the landscape of my childhood, thus they share the same light, the same seasonal changes and immediacy of nature's forces. Within weeks after entering Kahn's class, I sensed there was something basic I intuitively understood about him: I knew his landscape and light. In many ways, Kahn's early years on Saaremaa were his personal "knowing," as he called it; but as a young student, I knew very little of this. For me at that time he was foremost an American from Philadelphia.

In class, Louis Kahn often talked about how circumstances or chance plays into how one lives or perceives the world and how these unknown factors may overturn the best-laid plan. A few weeks into the first semester Kahn pulled me aside and asked, "Do you know Arne Korsmo?" I answered no and was too shy to follow up the question, so the conversation ended there. I could see he was disappointed and sensed I had missed something, a puzzle piece or a key—and this feeling lingered in me for the rest of the year. Over time I have come

750 Two early Viking ship burials at Salme, Saaremaa, ca. 750.

793 Viking raid on Lindisfarne.

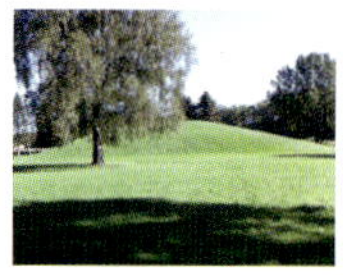

Oseberg Viking burial mound, Norway, dated 834. *P. O. Fjeld.*

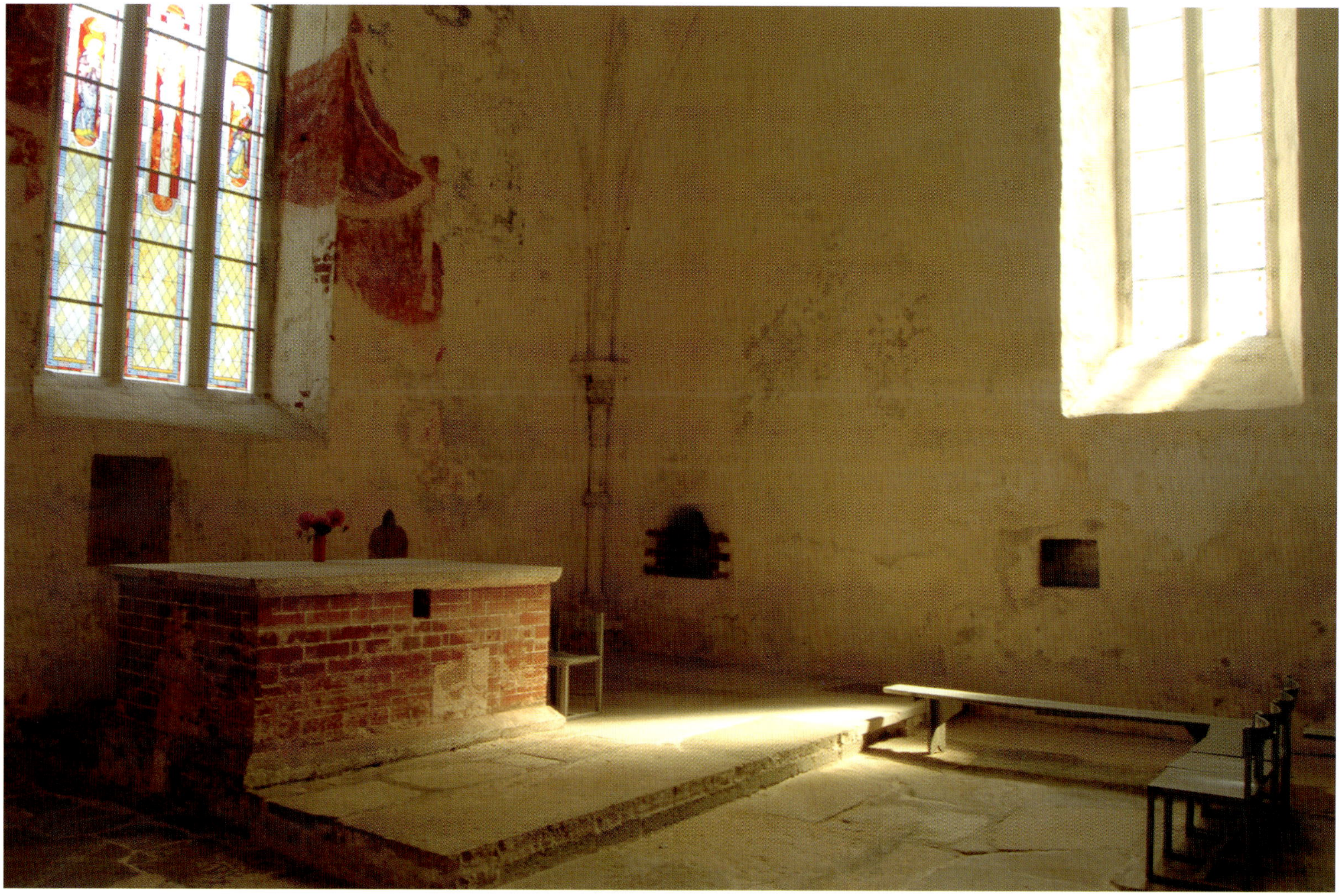

Interior of a church at Pöide on the island of Saaremaa, Estonia. As a child, Kahn lived on this island in the town Kuressaare. *Paulis Gibze.*

to understand that life is full of chance events and overlapping acquaintances and influences. Kahn's friendship with the Norwegian architect Arne Korsmo and the circumstances of his question to me that day set in motion a long process of my understanding Kahn's Nordic link.

My formal architectural education was in its entirety American, thus my knowledge of Nordic architectural heritage was rather limited when I arrived in Philadelphia, and what I learned during my six and a half years in the United States was filtered through an Anglo-

960–1013 The slow Christianization of the Nordic region: Denmark, 960; Sweden, 995; Iceland, 1000; Norway, 1013. (The Baltic coastal areas were Christianized 1193–1387.)

988 Vladimir I of Kievan Realm (modern-day Belarus, Russia, Ukraine) baptized into the Greek Orthodox Church in 988.

1025 Kingdom of Poland established.

1098 The first extensive Jewish immigration from central and southern Europe to Poland occurs under the rule of Boleslaw III.

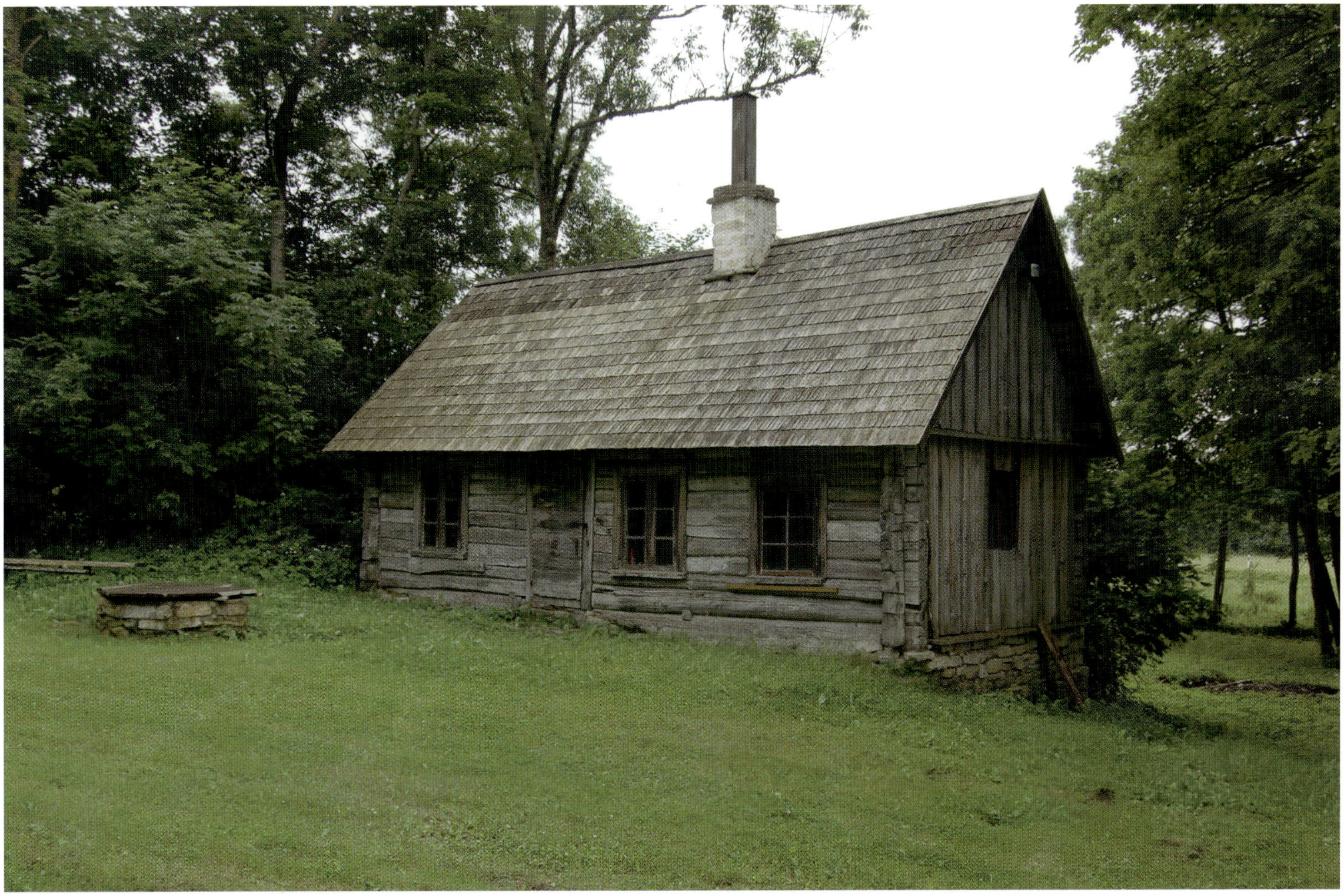

Nordic vernacular architecture—a house near Kuressaare. *Paulis Gibze.*

American perspective. After I returned home to Norway, Arne Korsmo's name came up within weeks after starting my first job with architect Sverre Fehn, and his name would pop up over and over again in the years that followed. Korsmo clearly made a strong impression on his early postwar Norwegian students and friends; and his numerous activities, travels, and contacts—including Kahn—were inspirational for many. When I returned home in 1973, many of Korsmo's students comprised much of the teaching staff in Norwegian architectural

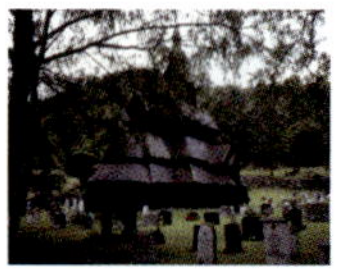

Borgund Stav Church built ca. 1180. Stav churches were built throughout the Nordic region. *P. O. Fjeld.*

1201 Riga proclaimed the seat of the Livonian bishopric. The Livonian Brothers of the Sword established to safeguard control and Christianization.

1206 The Danish king Valdemar II and the bishop of Lund invade Saaremaa. (The Danish are unable to defend their fortress there over time.)

1227 The Livonian Brothers of the Sword invade Saaremaa during the Livonian (Nordic) Crusade and establish a bishopric (Ösel-Wieck) on the island. The local population periodically resists foreign rule and forced conversion to Christianity.

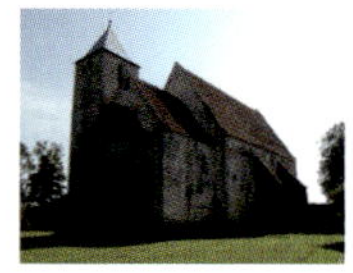

St. Martin's Church in Valjala, Saaremaa (built 1227–40) is the oldest stone church on the island. *Paulis Gibze.*

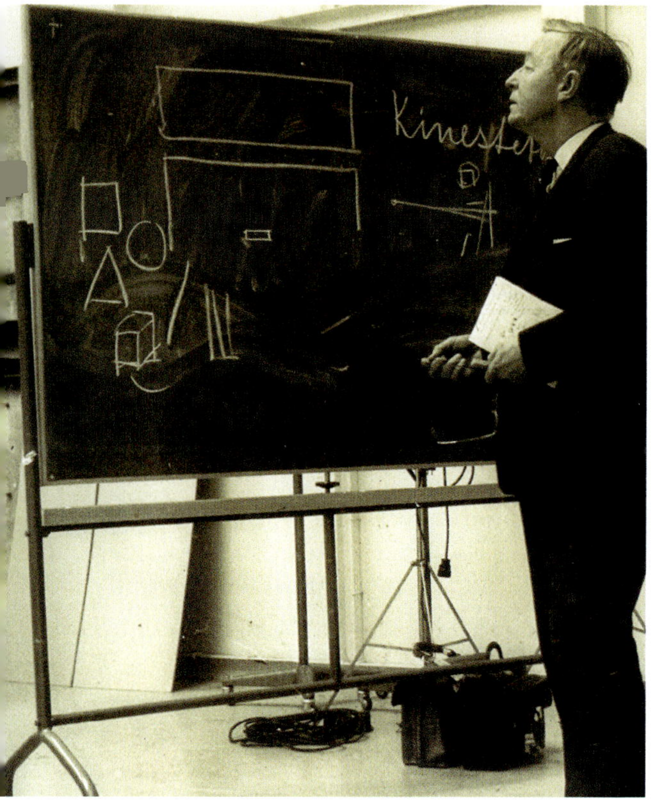

Arne Korsmo in front of his studio blackboard. Odd Østbye recalled his first day as a student in Korsmo's class: "We sat down in the classroom and Korsmo entered for the first time, looked at us and said, 'I am going to teach you about form.' Then he looked at us again with that funny look of his and said, 'I haven't any idea what that is so can you help me?' And with that, we began to do the most absurd things." *Property of Astrid Skjerven.*

schools, and many others were involved in the more interesting offices. Over the years, conversations with Fehn or his classmates and friends often seemed to come back to things Korsmo said or did. In time, after establishing my own small practice in Oslo, gaining a greater familiarity with Scandinavian architecture in general, teaching, and establishing a growing network of European architects and scholars, I acquired a broader perspective on Kahn's forty-year friendship with Korsmo and on his Nordic ties.

In this chapter I use this friendship to investigate some events, influences, people, and certain key Kahn terms such as "nature" and "institution" from a Nordic perspective. Kahn's friendship with Korsmo was just one of many, but it began at a very early stage in both men's careers, which is in itself noteworthy. Though very cosmopolitan, Korsmo practiced and lived his entire life in Scandinavia; what brought the two men together throughout their lives was not proximity. They were just two friends who met when circumstance allowed and who shared an interesting mix of acquaintances and an intensely motivated relationship to teaching and architecture. Before describing their first meeting in the fall of 1928, it is necessary to detail a few Nordic architectural and political events from the period surrounding the Kahn family's emigration from Estonia.

Geography and History

A line drawn across Norway, Sweden, Finland, and Russia at the 60-degree latitude cuts just above or below a number of major cities: Oslo, Stockholm, Helsinki, and St. Petersburg. Pärnu, Estonia, where Kahn's birth was registered, and the island of Saaremaa, where he lived, are only slightly further south. A hundred fifty years ago this region stretching from Norway to St. Petersburg was, outside of its few urban centers, made up of small farms, fishing villages, some mining communities, and a substantial timber industry. Thus the region was primarily an important exporter of raw materials. For the most part, this area escaped the first wave of the Industrial Revolution and the environmental, health, and social issues that came with it. This is not to say there were no problems or poverty—quite the opposite—but those generally stemmed from geographical and climatic conditions. For centuries, the tough climate of short summers and dark, cold winters formed a natural barrier, not just from the rest of Europe, but even from the nearest urban centers. This isolation forced the people of this region to develop a broad range of handicraft skills, a good understanding of and respect for their natural environment, and a straightforward pragmatic attitude to survival and coexistence.

Also important to understanding this region's cultural development is that the Roman

1240–41 First wave of the Mongol invasions reaches current-day Belarus and eastern Poland.

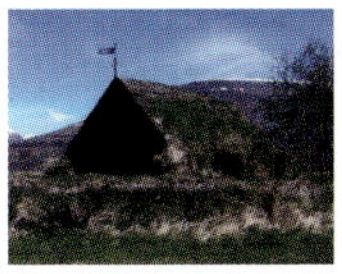

Chapel at Gröf, Iceland's oldest turf church, first mentioned in 1240.
P. O. Fjeld.

1249 The Swedish achieve control over much of western Finland after the Second Swedish Crusade.

1253 Kingdom of Lithuania established.

Empire never reached this far north, nor had any real influence or direct impact here outside of trade. A European architectural heritage built on a Latin inheritance—with all its symbolic references concerning civic participation, philosophy, religion, and education—was far more a collateral and, at times, even an exotic layer in the North. The Christian faith took hold very late in the Nordic region, thus its cultural and social impact was a slow, uneven process relative to that in the rest of Europe. In 1198, a papal decree sanctioned a Crusade to Christianize the Baltic area, and the Teutonic Knights quickly established Christian strongholds along the coast. At the same time, western Russia turned to Constantinople and the Orthodox Church. The Christianization of the three Scandinavian countries was equally late and uneven, but also entangled in the region's relationships to England, Scotland, and Ireland, which were under the domain of the Roman Catholic Church. For all of these countries, the transformation away from earlier beliefs and traditions was in many ways a political and military move to unify power, thus many pre-Christian attitudes and values were retained and incorporated into the new reality.

This mixed inheritance ensured that how one perceived the human being on earth would inevitably differ slightly here from the rest of the European continent. Some elements of earlier beliefs, language, and rune script, as well as social and political attitudes and ties, lingered on for another two centuries. Later, even the German Hanseatic League, with its tight grip on trade, was confined for the most part to urban centers. Sweden, Denmark, Russia, and, at its height, the Hanseatic League dominated the Baltic and Nordic areas for centuries. Parts of Estonia, Kahn's birth country, were ruled at one point or another by each.

From czarist Russia west to the Scandinavian countries, objects and influences from central Europe arrived periodically, usually through trade or with individuals returning home after a stay abroad. These new styles and ideas from the Continent were subject to the region's deep-seated pragmatism. The focus centered on the incoming style's physical attributes, especially those that allowed for a transformation of the materials at hand and adjustments in relation to the terrain, climate, energy requirements, and the local workforce's skills. The symbolism, philosophy, and attitudes that propelled a style originating from central or southern Europe were not necessarily interpreted from the same perspective in this region. For example, while the nineteenth-century revival of classicism in city planning and in the fashioning of public institutions was understood by a broad European and North American public as representing a shared cultural and civic inheritance, this understanding was not as widespread within the Nordic region. Likewise, while other nineteenth-century style movements were imported into the area, their primary motivations did not necessarily reflect Nordic

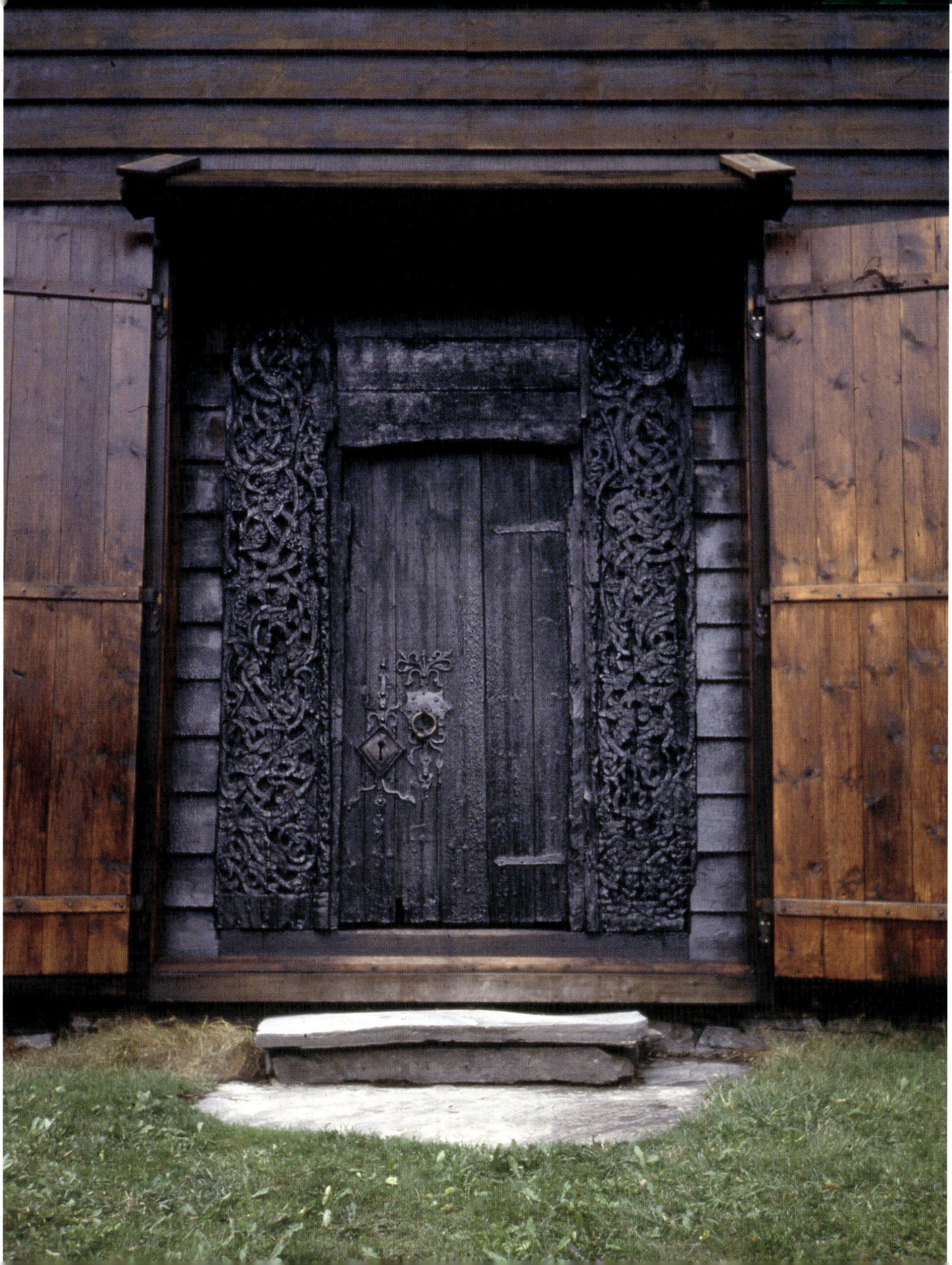

1344–45 | St. George's Night Uprising on Saaremaa. The local population rebels against the Livonian Order killing German inhabitants and drowning priests.

1349 | Bubonic plague outbreak in Norway. It spreads to Sweden and Denmark by 1350, and eastern Russia and the Baltic by 1351.

1380s | Construction of the Kuressaare Fortress, a landmark that Kahn remembered from his childhood, begins.

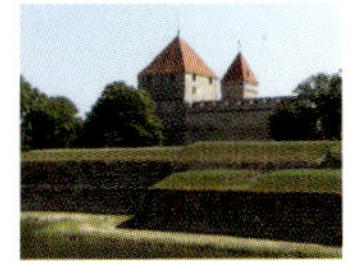

Kuressaare Fortress. *P. O. Fjeld.*

1397 | The Kalmar Union, which would last until the early 1500s, joins the kingdoms of Denmark, Sweden, and Norway, including areas along the Baltic coast, Iceland, Greenland, Faroe, Shetland, and the Orkney Islands.

society, so a certain freedom or independence in relation to modifications arose. Abroad, without consideration of fundamental social and cultural differences, these adjustments were simply deemed "provincial" or "idiosyncratic."

Meanwhile, by the end of the nineteenth century, artifacts and archaeological research throughout the Nordic area—along with a renewed interest in the few Nordic sagas that had survived early Christianization—propelled a growing focus on the region's own early history, languages, and way of life. In Norway, the first of the Viking ships was excavated in 1905; in Sweden, archaeological work began on the mound graves in Birka as early as 1870; and during the same period, Denmark began to uncover interesting settlements and artifacts. On Saaremaa, among other projects, efforts to restore the Kuressaare fortress that Kahn's father claimed to have worked on were underway. While the first archaeological discoveries directly influenced what was later termed "National Romantic style" or "National Realism," these finds also fanned a sense of belonging to a particular history, language, and landscape and inspired a sense of cultural legitimacy.

In 1901 Louis Kahn was born on the island of Saaremaa, where he would live until the late spring of 1906. At the time of Kahn's birth, most of Estonia's population, like the rest of the Nordic population, was still involved in agriculturally related work. However, unlike its close neighbor Finland, which retained some autonomy, Estonia was by the end of the nineteenth century completely absorbed into the Russian Empire, and with this came Russian law, language, and administration—changes that also affected the other Baltic nations. Despite the czarist government's efforts and forced relocations of various groups of people to other areas in Russia, in Estonia a sense of nationhood and indigenous culture survived. The Estonian-speaking Finno Ugric population who were the majority began to move into urban areas and inspired an academic interest in their own culture and language. There were also active Estonian Swedish- and German-speaking populations.

To the west, Norway became a sovereign nation in 1905. It had undergone centuries of Danish rule; Hanseatic trade dominance; shifting borders in relation to Sweden; and finally, at the close of the Napoleonic Wars, a forced union with Sweden. Toward the end of the nineteenth century, in parallel with the political movement for independence, an interest in Norwegian cultural identity emerged—encompassing history, literature, language, architecture, customs, and folklore—much like what was developing in Estonia during the same period. The nation's capital, called Christiania under Danish and Swedish rule, was eventually renamed Oslo, in reference to an earlier name from the Middle Ages. With independence came new institutions and a focus on forming a Norwegian identity and language. At the same time, the

Kravik Farm, Norway. A detail from an early medieval farmhouse, which was later paneled and modernized. Inspired by the saga of Sigurd Favnesbane, the woodcarver of this preserved doorway drew from pre-Christian imagery. The left side of the portal depicts Gunnar in the Ormegården (snake/dragon yard), while a carving of the head of Odin hides in the shadow above the door. *P. O. Fjeld.*

1559 | Livonian Order sells Saaremaa to Denmark.

1567 | Construction begins on Andrea Palladio's Villa Rotunda in Vicenza, Italy.

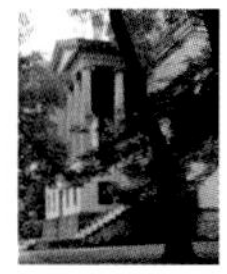

Villa Rotunda. *P. O. Fjeld.*

1569 | Union of Lublin establishes a Polish-Lithuanian Commonwealth.

1570 | Palladio publishes *I quattro libri dell'architettura* (*The Four Books of Architecture*).

population was gravitating toward the nation's urban centers, bringing with them all the knowledge, skills, and independent thinking of isolated rural life. These expanding urban centers proved a vital connection to the changes unfolding abroad.

A Family Background

To Kahn's family, Latvia's and Lithuania's history are as relevant as that of Estonia's. In one generation, Kahn's mother's family lived in all of the Baltic nations—moving from Lithuania to Latvia and finally settling on the island of Saaremaa, Estonia. Kahn's parents' early life, their educations, and the decisions they made with regard to the future were a consequence of decades of Russian policy concerning the Baltic region. The couple started their married life in a period of economic and social strife, but they were not without education, skills, and culture. Kahn's father's position in the paymaster's office in the Russian army would have required education, but advancement in the army was very difficult for Jewish citizens. Meanwhile, Kahn's mother's proficiency and interest in German language, literature, and music was typical of the secular Jewish middle class in the region. The Jewish population in Kuressaare was very small (111 people in 1881, down to 35 in 1913).

Despite the tough and almost paranoid efforts of the czarist government to Russianize the Baltic population in the nineteenth century, many small German- and Swedish-speaking communities survived. A leftover from earlier Hanseatic rule, German continued to be the mother tongue for some in all three of the Baltic provinces—often the language of local administrators, large landowners, academics, and elite urban milieus. The overlapping histories of the region explain why so many languages, including the Nordic languages, were so active.

Toward the latter half of the nineteenth century, very old, established Jewish communities within the Russian Empire faced displacement, increased harassment, and pogroms. Lithuania, with its strong historical ties to Poland and parts of Belarus, was home to a number of these established communities. But by the mid-nineteenth century, many families from these communities were on the move. Some emigrated to North America; others moved northwest into Scandinavia; still others moved further north along the Baltic coast, out of their ancient tight-knit communities into a more anonymous and secular situation where there was a greater possibility of employment. With the lifting of Riga's residency restrictions in 1840 and a positive outlook for employment, the city's Jewish population grew rapidly. In 1869 the Great Choral Synagogue was erected in Riga, and within a year of its completion Kahn's mother's family had moved there from Lithuania. (Birth records document that Kahn's paternal grandfather was also from Lithuania.) In 1872 Kahn's mother, Bertha (Beila-Rebecka Mendelowitsch), was born in Riga, but around 1880 her family moved once again, now to the Estonian town of Kuressaare (Arensburg) on the island of Saaremaa (Ösel), where four of her younger siblings were born between 1881 and 1890. Toward the end of the century, some of the family, including Bertha, moved back to Riga; but clearly, based on these dates, Kahn's mother spent a considerable part of her childhood on the island. A number of her siblings' families were still residing in Kuressaare when, newly married, Bertha returned there with her husband from Riga in 1900. Louis Kahn was born in the island town the following year.[1] Since the island population was small, much official administration, including the registry of births outside the officially recognized churches, took place in a designated administrative town on the mainland, Pärnu, and this explains why Kahn's birth is registered there. This practice of registering island births on the mainland continued on and off throughout the twentieth century.

A pleasant town of four and a half thousand citizens, Kuressaare had an active cultural life with opportunities for a good basic education at the turn of the century. About 63 percent of its population spoke Estonian as their first language; about 30 percent, German; and the remaining, Russian, Swedish, or Latvian. It was a truly multilingual population. Exactly what Kahn spoke as a child at home or in public remains somewhat unclear, as his day-to-day experience was probably far more diverse than existing paperwork reveals. Considering Kahn was a little over five years old when his family emigrated, his language skills would have then been in place. Perhaps the timing of this move also influenced how he later expressed himself in English—his choice of words, metaphors, and phrases. Though he lost the multilingualism of his childhood, he certainly demonstrated a sensitivity to the polyglot layers of language and cultures in the masterclass.

Because Kuressaare's main income came from health resort–related activities in the latter half of the century, it adapted as necessary to visitors' needs—supplying health services, transportation (car service and, from 1920, a small train from the ferry), photographers, entertainment, parks, and easy access to the natural surroundings. By 1875 telegraph service was available, and in 1907 the town acquired its first telephone. A regular ferry traveled to and from Riga most of the year, so it is easy to understand how the Kahn family maintained ties to that city.

What attracted well-heeled visitors from central Russian and Baltic cities was not luxurious accommodations or service but rather a magical simplicity—a belief in the positive effects of sea air and mud cures and direct contact with the natural surroundings. The simplicity and relatively diminutive size of the town's public buildings and housing for all economic classes

1710 | During the Great Northern War, Riga becomes part of the Russian Empire.

1721 | At the close of the Great Northern War, Sweden cedes Saaremaa and the eastern part of Finland (Old Finland) to Russia.

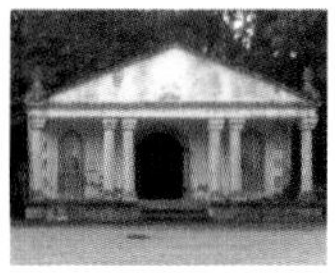

Kudjape Cemetery, Kuressaare, established in 1787. The family tombs and headstones reveal a mixed Nordic population. The Jewish section was demolished during World War II. *P. O. Fjeld.*

1772–95 | Partition of Poland. Many of the freedoms first established in 1098 for Jewish immigrants diminish greatly during this twenty-year period.

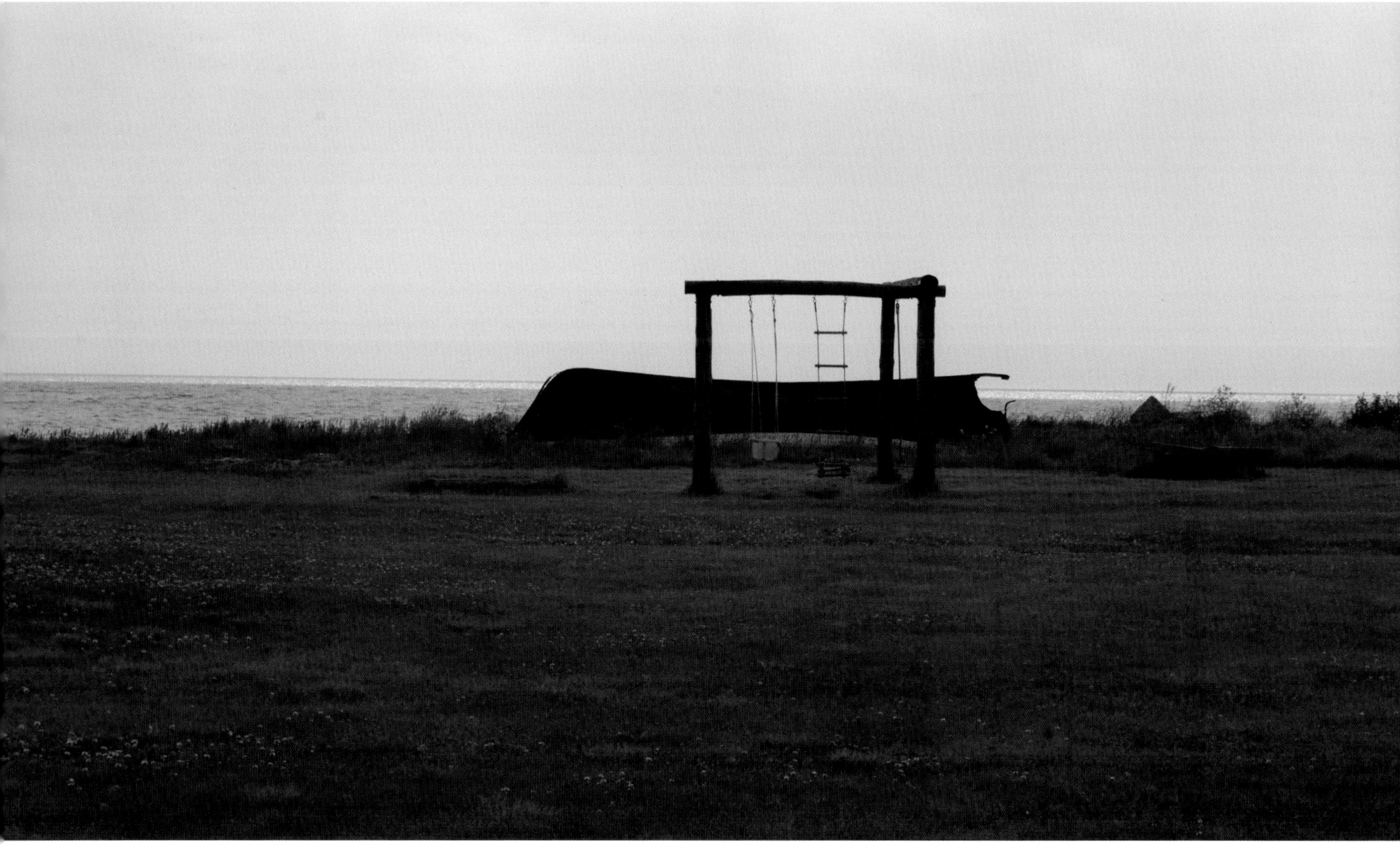

For the most part, Saaremaa's coastline is low and shallow; in the summer, the transition from the green pasture to the blue sea is soft and hazy. Saaremaa is the largest island in Estonia. *Paulis Gibze.*

1809 Sweden cedes its remaining portion of Finland to Russia with the Treaty of Fredrikshamn in connection with the Napoleonic Wars.	**1814** With the Treaty of Kiel, Denmark is forced to cede Norway to Sweden, in part as a trade-off for Swedish territory ceded to Russia in 1809.	**1825** Charles Garnier born.	**1853** P. V. J. Klint born.	**1856** Hendrik P. Berlage born.	**1860** Ferdinand Boberg born.	**1866** Ragnar Östberg born.	**1867** Frank Lloyd Wright born.	**1868** Peter Beherens born.	

created a sense of returning to and taking part in something basic. This was analogous to the concurrent interest among Scandinavian urban dwellers for a very minimal, primitive cottage as a second home, a retreat into nature. Like all the Nordic nations, Estonia and Latvia have an almost mythical reverence for the natural landscape, light, and seasonal changes that permeates deep into their cultural identities—and such a reverence would have informed Kahn's childhood experiences. Indeed, a number of Kahn's observations and comments from lectures echo this mythical reverence.

One other small, curious detail, from Kahn's last year on the island: In 1905, gas lighting was finally installed along a central street and the market square in Kuressaare. This was a major event for the town that inspired much celebration—and it occurred only two blocks from the house where Kahn is assumed to have lived.

There were clearly economic and political problems at the time of the Kahn family's emigration to the United States in 1906. As noted in many accounts, the first decade of the Kahn family's life in Philadelphia was difficult, likely in no small part because of what they brought with them in terms of expectations, language, education, skills, social position, and cultural identity, all of which were now under pressure in their new situation. Both what Anne Tyng recounts in her book *The Rome Letters, 1953–1954* and what Alexandra Tyng was able to glean of family history in her book *Beginnings: Louis I. Kahn's Philosophy of Architecture* indicate the Kahns had been part of an educated Jewish middle class. The authors' descriptions of family life, the Kahns' proficiency in German and other languages, their interest in literature, even Kahn's mother's very skilled needlework and musical abilities—all have to be understood in the context of the Baltic/Nordic society of the time. Though there was a lack of money, and Kahn's father probably underestimated the importance of speaking English to finding work, the family did not arrive in the United States culturally empty-handed. But the difficulties and losses associated with the move to Philadelphia must have been traumatic. And with the onslaught of World War I and the Russian Revolution, any possibility for the family to return home vanished.

In parallel to the events unfolding in the Russian Empire, the entire Nordic area was also in transformation, with new laws enacted there regarding land, labor, class, and broader voting rights. As a young child, Arne Korsmo experienced dramatic changes in the social structure of life in Oslo that would positively affect his family's prospects. The enfranchisement of women quickly followed for the whole region—first in Finland in 1906, then in Norway in 1910 and Estonia in 1918. As people gravitated toward urban centers, a large skilled middle class was beginning to take form and have a voice. A technical industrialization also took hold,

1870 Lars Sonck born.

1871 Great Choral Synagogue in Riga completed. Archeological excavations begin on the Birka site in Sweden.

1872 John Molitor (Kahn's first employer) born.

1873 Eliel Saarinen born.

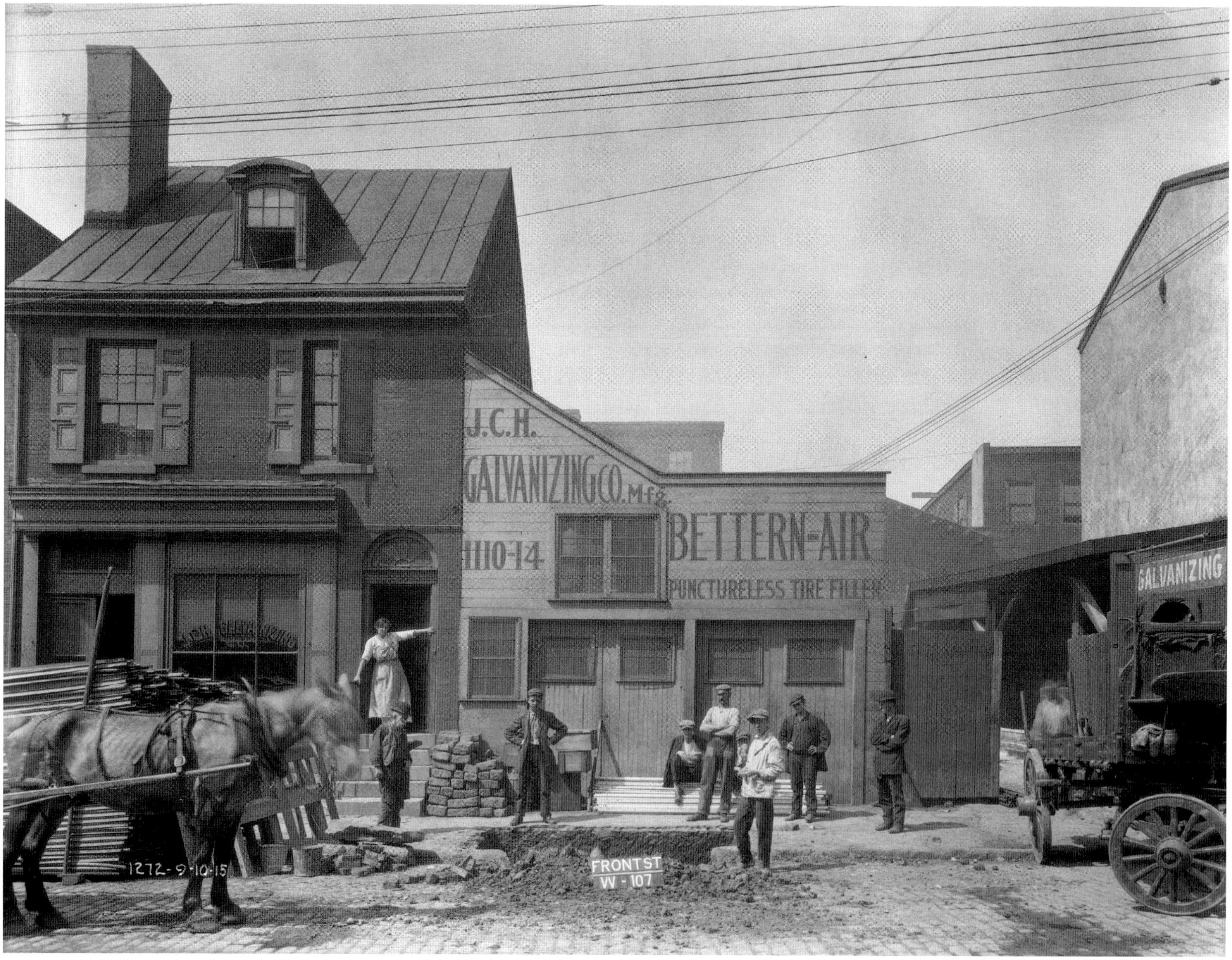

bringing new interpretations and experimentation to industrial building, particularly within the hydroelectric industry. Though Kahn's family did not experience this period of change in the Nordic region firsthand, they took with them to the United States the cultural mind-set that had helped bring about these changes. Estonia became an independent nation in 1918 (only to fall under Soviet rule in 1940). At the time, Louis Kahn was seventeen years old and a student at Central High School in Philadelphia. On his first return trip to Europe, in 1928, he visited Estonia and Latvia as independent nations.

At the start of my masterclass year, the Baltic nations were part of the Soviet Union—almost invisible, caught up in East-West tensions. The island of Saaremaa had been off-limits to foreigners for years; Finland was still carefully balancing its politics between the Soviet Union and its Nordic neighbors. Thus as a student I had difficulty placing Kahn's background outside of his early years in Philadelphia. Today, the Baltic countries are active participants in all the main Nordic cultural organizations, perceiving themselves as clearly Nordic in sentiment while prizing their independence and individual identities.

Nordic Architectural Developments

For the 1889 Paris World Exposition, a young Swedish architect, Ferdinand Boberg, was asked to provide drawings for a reconstruction of an old Nordic dwelling for the French architect Charles Garnier's exhibition L'Histoire de l'habitation humaine. Unlike the other entries, Boberg's final contribution was not a form of stage setting. He delivered a timber cabin that was built with traditional methods true to its material, structure, size, and openings for light. It was sited at the foot of the newly erected Eiffel Tower—a simple dwelling at the foot of a technical and political demonstration. Dismayed over the exposition committee's placement of his exhibition, Garnier attacked the Eiffel Tower's viability as a landmark, but Boberg was fascinated and inspired by the structure. He would continue in the years that followed to search for the core attributes of materials and traditional methods, while at the same time exploring new technologies and sidestepping the constraints of style.

Most contemporary Nordic architecture at this time was regarded from abroad as provincial modifications of existing Continental styles, but this perception overlooked some regional developments that were beginning to have an impact. In Scandinavia, new ideas for housing and public facilities—adapted to the local urban landscape, industrial production, and population density—were quite unlike the examples from England or Germany that had inspired them. The poetry and prose that had propelled the Continental architectural developments

Turn-of-the-century Philadelphia: Front St. south of Girard, 1915. Kahn would have been fourteen years old when this photograph was taken. By Kahn's account, "A city is a place where a small boy, as he walks through it, may see something that will tell him what he wants to do his whole life." *Photo courtesy of PhillyHistory.org, a project of the Philadelphia Department of Records.*

were quickly available in the North and admired in relation to the observation of natural phenomena, but these expressions were at the same time perceived as foreign. There was an affinity for the end products of the style movements from abroad, but the reactionary idealization of life was a difficult fit.

In May of 1914 a large exhibition in Malmö, Sweden, was mounted to showcase architecture, new industrial technology, and design objects produced in the Baltic region. The Baltic Exhibition's head architect was Ferdinand Boberg, the same architect who had placed the timber house under the Eiffel Tower twenty-five years earlier. The exhibition's theme was oriented toward the region's future potential and was clearly influenced by new architectural ideas and technologies found in earlier exhibitions from the United States, England, and France. The exhibition reflected the building traditions of the region, emphasizing the materials and features inherent to the various nations along the Baltic coast. Initially, Boberg felt the exhibition should face the sea to reflect the region's history, but the chosen site was inland, along an old medieval dam reservoir. The layout of the exhibition took inspiration from a careful study of Malmö's natural surroundings and influenced the development of the city for decades. The exhibition's overall focus was straightforward: it illuminated how things were made and who was making them and showcased innovations in both handicrafts and large-scale industry. It was a strange mix of highly technical German industrial products, elements from the growing Nordic hydroelectric industry, Russian and Nordic jewelry, glass and ceramics from large industrial fabricators, and smaller-studio design production. The Russian pavilion was designed by Boberg and included work from the Baltic provinces of Russia.

The commercial, historical, and cultural ties among Nordic urban centers, the coastal regions of Poland, Northern Germany, and St. Petersburg were still active at this time, but shortly after the opening of the Baltic Exhibition, World War I broke out. Germany pulled out, and Russia, due to internal politics, left half of its contribution to the exhibition behind in Malmö. This marked the beginning of the deterioration of a shared perception of Baltic history and identity that would not reappear until the end of the twentieth century.

The exhibition also marked a turning point in Scandinavian architecture, since there were now clear signs of discord in the architectural establishment. In spite of the exhibition's regional theme, Boberg received tough criticism from slightly younger but established Stockholm colleagues, including Ragnar Östberg, who contended that this "Baltic sensibility and material choice" were not necessarily what they considered Swedish and did not promote a proper unified national style. This wave of criticism would culminate in the response to Boberg's Nobel Festival Hall project, after whose completion the fifty-five-year-old architect

1900 Arne Korsmo born.

1901 Louis I. Kahn, Junzo Sakakura, and Jean Prouvé born.

1902 Arne Jacobsen born.

1903 Norman Rice born.

1905 Norway's union with Sweden is dissolved. Lars Sonck's Eira Hospital completed in Helsinki.

Franco Albini, Oskar Stonorov, and Esther Kahn born.

1906 Kahn family emigrates from Estonia to the United States, settling in Philadelphia.

August Komendant born.

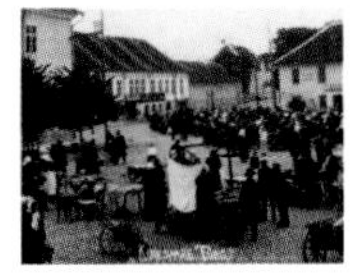

Kuressaare marketplace ca. 1920. Two of Kahn's uncles opened a butcher shop in the second building from the left in 1914. *Saaremaa History Museum Archive.*

1907 Charles Eames born.

soon quit his practice and moved to Paris. He stayed true to his interest in the core essence of materials and traditional building methods, while eschewing historicism and imitation.

During a visit to the Baltic Exhibition, two young architects, Sigurd Lewerentz and Erik Gunnar Asplund, decided to enter the competition for the Woodland Cemetery in Stockholm as a team. Lewerentz's proposal for a funerary chapel in Helsingborg was included in the Baltic Exhibition, and the project received many positive reviews. At the time, Lewerentz was also working on a proposal for the Malmö Eastern Cemetery, which would be realized later. Kay Fisker—who would be a pivotal figure in early modern Danish architecture and education—saw the exhibition as a young student. Struck by Lewerentz's chapel project, he applied to work for both Lewerentz and Asplund on the Woodland Cemetery once he completed his architectural studies in Copenhagen.

By the time of Kahn's first European visit as a young architect in 1928, most of Boberg's public buildings were still in use; Ragnar Östberg's influence was beginning to fade; Asplund and Lewerentz had completed some of their most important early works; and Kay Fisker and Poul Henningsen's Hornbæk Housing Complex had been built.

After the close of World War I, Finland was an independent nation but had suffered a short civil war in the midst of all the turmoil. The Baltic nations were also independent and grappling with the social and economic aftermath of World War I. St. Petersburg, despite all the confusion brought on by the revolution, enjoyed a brief interval of remarkable architectural creativity. New design work there set a clear agenda directed toward a broad spectrum of users where cold climate, light conditions, and social issues all directly influenced the brief. In the small window of time predating Stalin, St. Petersburg continued to have cultural and economic ties with its Nordic neighbors; visitors to the 1930 Stockholm Exhibition would have noticed sensibilities that were reminiscent of design work coming out of Russia. From St. Petersburg to Oslo, quite a few concrete functionalist buildings were already completed or under construction by the late 1920s. Considering the relatively small size of most Nordic urban populations, the number of functionalist/modernist buildings that were constructed in Nordic cities by that time is noteworthy.

On the Continent, modernists like Walter Gropius and Le Corbusier endorsed the use of prefabricated materials and promoted greater collaboration with large-scale technological industries—and in many ways they took for granted that the general public would embrace their new approach. In the Nordic countries there was little centralized industrial development to support this transformation; instead, small and often very skilled local workshops that had been involved in the construction of many Beaux Arts buildings fifteen years earlier were now

1910 Adolf Loos presents his Ornament and Crime lecture (published in 1913).
Eero Saarinen and Felix Candela born.

1911 Marshall McLuhan born.

1912 Ray Eames born.

1913 Kenzo Tange born.

1914 Baltic Exhibition, Malmö, Sweden. Start of World War I.
Ralph Erskine born.

1915 Ferdinand Boberg's Nordisk department store opens in Stockholm. Gunnar Asplund and Sigurd Lewerentz begin work on Woodland Cemetery, Stockholm.
Abel Sørensen born.

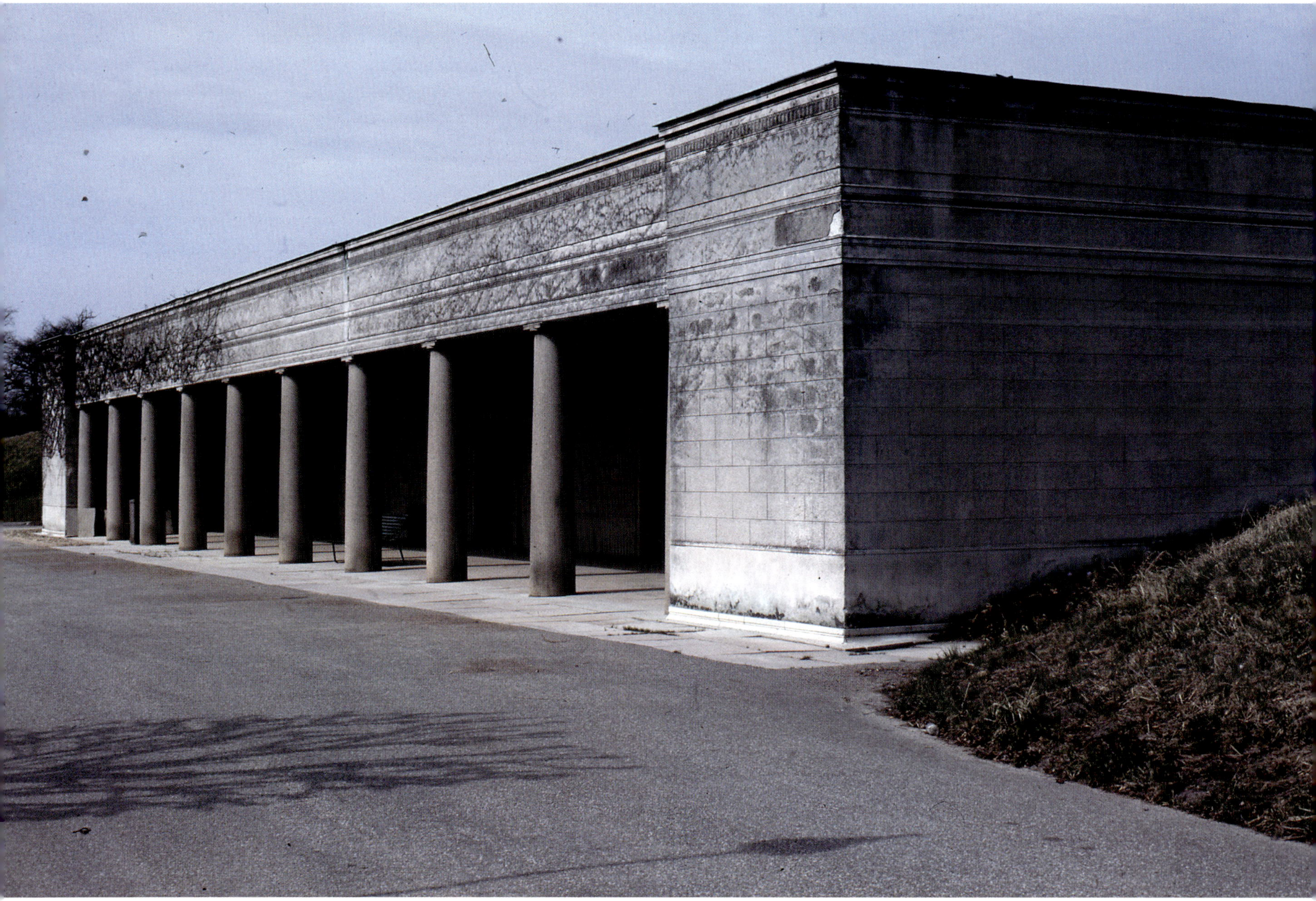

1916 Lewerentz begins work on the Malmö Eastern Cemetery (1916–69).

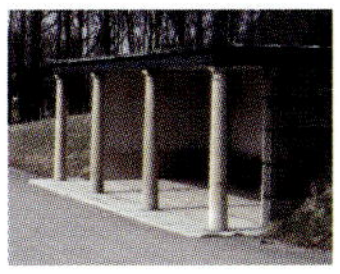

An early pavilion at the Malmö Eastern Cemetery. *P. O. Fjeld.*

1917 Russian Revolution. Finland declares independence.

Grete Prytz (Kittelsen) born.

1918 End of World War I; Finnish Civil War; Estonian independence.

Jørn Utzon and Aldo van Eyck born.

1919 Eliel Saarinen's Helsinki Central Station inaugurated.

Giancarlo De Carlo born.

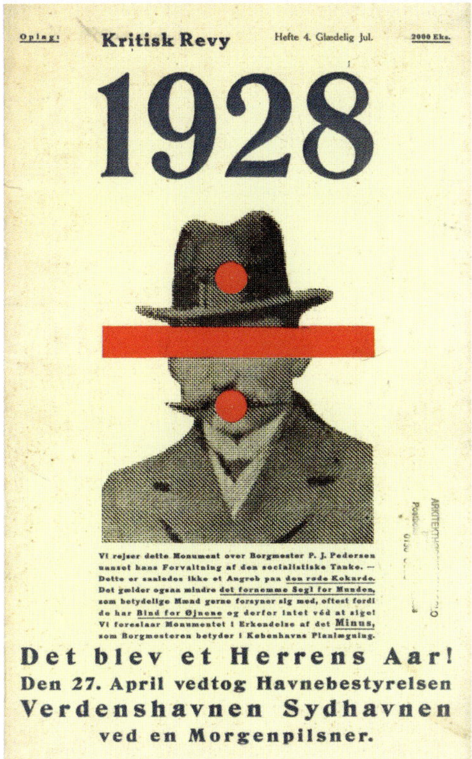

ABOVE: The cover of the last issue of *Kritisk Revy*, 1928. The magazine was published in Copenhagen in 1926–28, with Poul Henningsen as its editor in chief. According to its manifesto, the journal's main goal was to eliminate neoclassicism and to do away with the academy and its instruction. *Kritisk Revy 1928, Copenhagen editor in chief Poul Henningsen.*

LEFT: A Nordic reinterpretation of classicism: The first chapel built in the Malmö Eastern Cemetery by Sigurd Lewerentz. Lewerentz worked on this cemetery complex from 1916, when he won the competition for it, until 1969, when he completed the last of his buildings, the Flower Kiosk. *P. O. Fjeld.*

erecting the new modernist works, and the general public was receptive to the new approach. During this same period, the hydroelectric-power industry spread rapidly throughout the region and brought with it—to both urban and rural sites—concrete industrial structures such as the small transformer huts I visited with my father as a child. It is from this background that Nordic Modernist architecture evolved.

During this era of cultural exchange, architectural books and magazines principally from Germany, France, and the Netherlands were quickly translated and published in all the Nordic countries. There were ongoing discussions concerning the impact of new work and ideas coming out of the United States, Germany, and France, particularly in relation to their possible adaptation to Nordic society. Continuing the centuries-long tradition of adapting outside influences to their specific situation, the era's thinkers were selective and pragmatic in their choices; the radical, short-lived Danish magazine *Kritisk Revy* (1926–28), edited by Poul Henningsen, exemplified such thinking. Its core message was a clear rejection of the hegemony of existing nineteenth-century styles (especially neoclassicism) and the endorsement of modernism as an alternative. But the magazine was nonetheless critically explorative and open to conflicting opinions. The publication was notably tough, unafraid of local political debates, and went straight to the heart of fundamental architectural and planning issues concerning Copenhagen and the Nordic region as a whole. The last issue of *Kritisk Revy* came out just months after Kahn's first visit to Copenhagen—and Arne Korsmo would certainly have been familiar with the magazine.

The harsh climate and the rapid migration to urban areas in the North had a direct influence on how and why modernism was applied and broadly accepted by the general public. Modernism was capable of addressing the constraints of the northern climate with an economy of space and materials by adapting its spatial approach to local conditions. Also, the social changes so clearly manifested in the first years of modernism were already embedded in early twentieth-century Scandinavian work despite the constraints imposed by imported styles. The Nordic urban transformation encompassed changing perceptions of privilege and public institutions and broader and more inclusive definitions of a building's users—and all of these human factors greatly inspired the architecture of the time. On some deep level, the modernist approach was compatible with Nordic culture, and on an abstract level, already familiar.

For instance, the Nordic mind-set toward nature was an essential quality in both turn-of-the-century buildings and modernist work of the 1930s. This mind-set understood the human as in nature, part of it—not an observer elevated from nature's processes, cycles, or transformations. As Kahn would say in class, "We cannot separate ourselves from nature's laws."

1920 Ian McHarg and Anne Tyng born.

1920–25 Le Corbusier and Amédée Ozenfant edit the magazine *L'Esprit Nouveau.*

1921 Bengt Edman born.

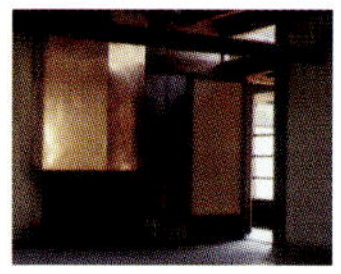

The Schindler Chace House (1921–22) in West Hollywood was of great interest to many Nordic architects visiting the United States. *P. O. Fjeld.*

1923 Ragnar Östberg's Stockholm City Hall completed. Le Corbusier publishes *Vers une Architecture* (*Toward an Architecture*), translated into English four years later.

Peter Smithson and Reima Pietilä born.

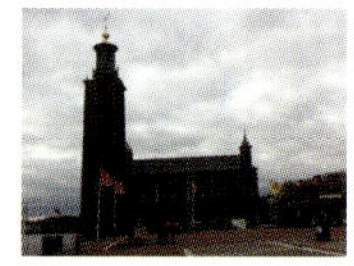

Stockholm City Hall. *P. O. Fjeld.*

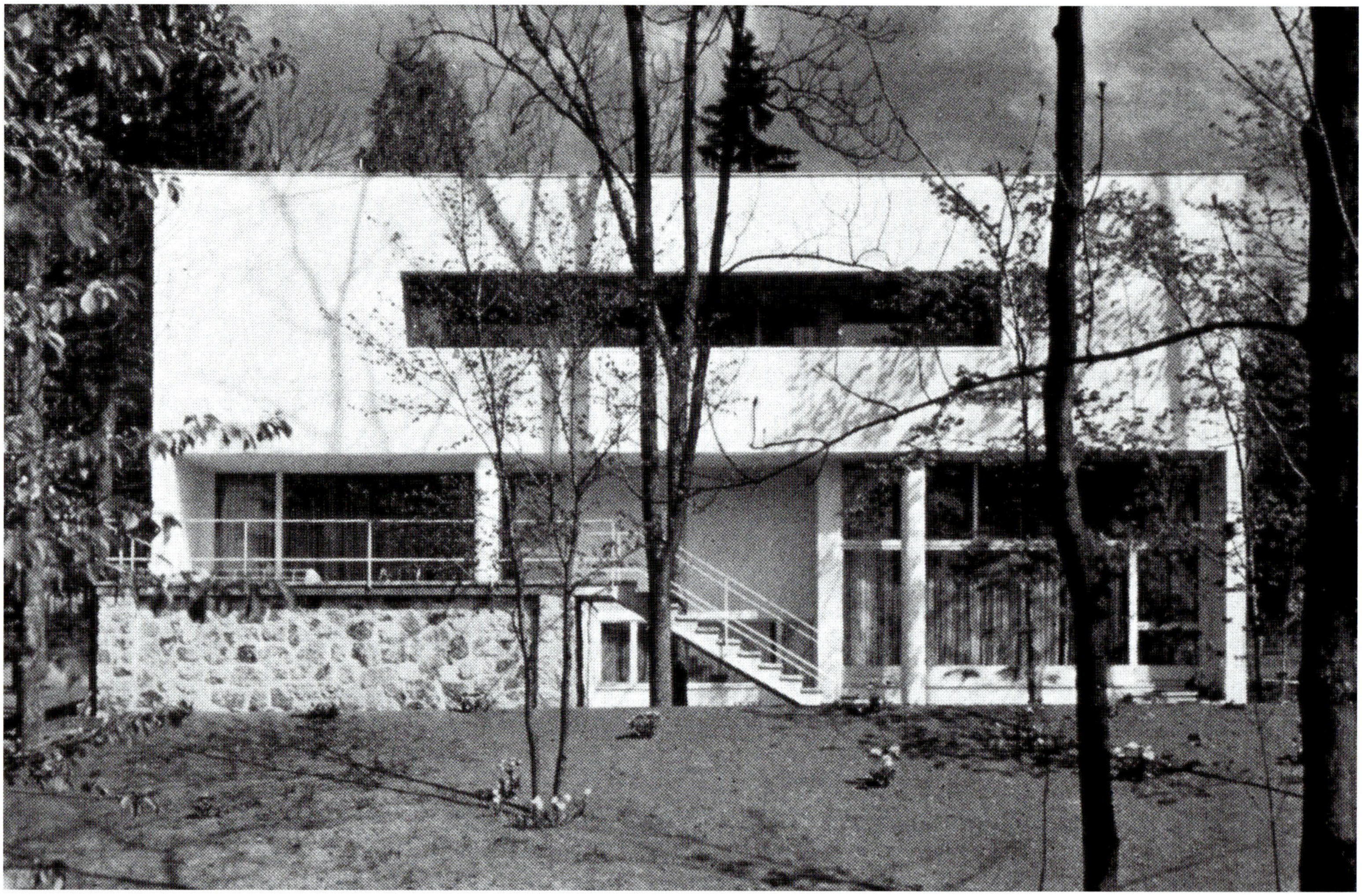

Ove Bang's Ditlev-Simonsen House, Oslo, 1937. Sigfried Giedion praised the house for being more hospitable to living than Le Corbusier's designs. *The Oslo School of Architecture and Design Photo Archive. Photo by Teigen.*

How much of this attitude to nature he picked up from his childhood, family, or visit in 1928 is hard to say; but his focus on daylight and the imagery he derived from it, as well as the language and syntax of his lectures and writings, have a far greater meaning when his birthplace is taken into account. Once in class when talking about the threshold from inside to outside, he commented, "In the North you will immediately face the sun." It was meant as a general

1924 | Hack Kampmann's Copenhagen Police Headquarters completed.

Sverre Fehn born.

1925 | L'Exposition Internationale des Arts Décoratifs et Industriels Modernes in Paris includes Esprit Nouveau pavilion by Le Corbusier.

Charles Moore and Robert Venturi born.

1926 | Sesquicentennial Exposition in Philadelphia (whose design Kahn worked on in the office of John Molitor). Walter Gropius's Bauhaus School in Dessau completed.

Christian Norberg-Schulz born.

1926–28 | Poul Henningsen edits *Kritisk Revy.*

1927 | Weissenhof Estate housing exhibition in Stuttgart. P. V. J. Klint's Grundtvig Church inaugurated in Copenhagen. Nicolsky and Krestin's School for the Tenth Anniversary of the Revolution in St. Petersburg completed. Lars Backer's Skansen Restaurant in Oslo completed.

Balkrishna Doshi born.

remark, but that spring day it seemed to be an image so tied to Scandinavia that I felt it was directed toward my Swedish American classmate and me.

This Nordic perception of the human as in and part of nature—versus the prevailing notion in central Europe of greater separation and abstraction—was apparent on many levels in architectural discourse. The friendship between the Swiss architectural historian Sigfried Giedion and Alvar Aalto is very revealing on this point. During a lecture at the Oslo School of Architecture in 1990, the historian-theorist and one-time partner of Arne Korsmo, Christian Norberg-Schulz, recounted a visit Giedion made to Oslo in 1950. Stopping to look at a functionalist house by the Norwegian architect Ove Bang, he commented, "This is as good as anything of Corb . . . but you can live in it."[2] On one level, Giedion placed the work clearly within the realm of Corbusier's influence and a central European context, but at the same time he admitted there was a key difference. As Norberg-Schulz later elaborated, nowhere in Le Corbusier's five points is there anything about "to live in." In the Scandinavian languages, unlike French, there is a very clear differentiation between "home" and "house," with an implicit understanding of "to live in." When Giedion made his remark in 1950, he had already traveled to Scandinavia many times and had been a friend of Aalto's for years. He had pondered the differences between Nordic and Continental perceptions of value. Aalto fished and found essential value in being in nature. Giedion collected art; in a sense, his notion of value originated with the manmade.

In the same lecture, Norberg-Schulz pointed out that early Nordic Modernist architects like Ove Bang had a very solid education in the Beaux Arts tradition, but one that was interpreted through Nordic sensibilities. The base from which these early modernists tested and understood the potential of new materials, ideas, and social changes of the time carried elements of their earlier Beaux Arts education, particularly in relation to nature and the substance of mass. They distinguished between a feeling of "*romfölelse*" (room) and a concept of space, and they connected humanness to this feeling of "room."

Giedion's remark—"but you can live in it"—brings me to the Swedish architect Erik Gunnar Asplund. His influence as an architect, teacher, and mentor was felt throughout the Nordic countries, but it took a long time before the depth of this impact was truly understood abroad; even as late as 1955, an English publication on his work by Eric de Maré described him as an insignificant teacher. His training was classical, and his early work reflected this training, but he also revealed a talent that went beyond the mastering of style. Asplund was committed to core human issues in his work, and like Kahn he insisted on starting each project from its bare beginnings to uncover the essential. At the start of a new project he did not refer to drawings

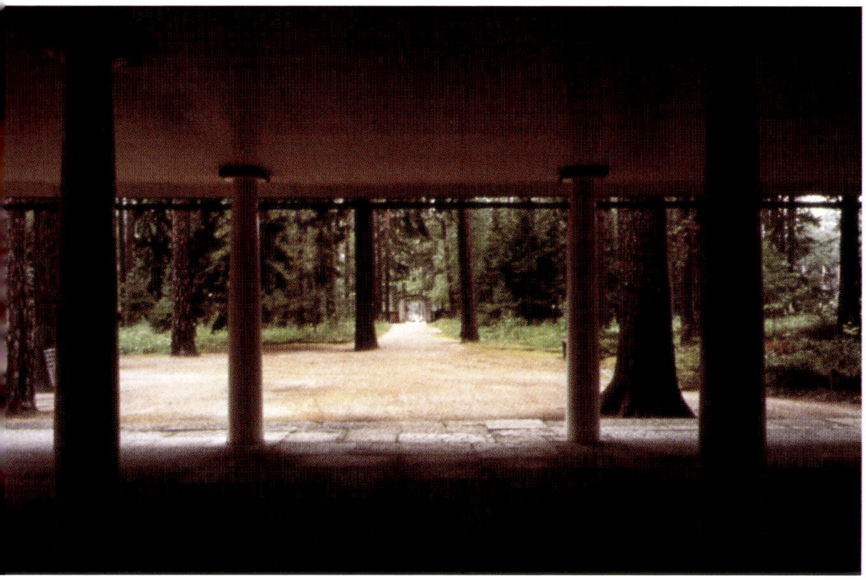

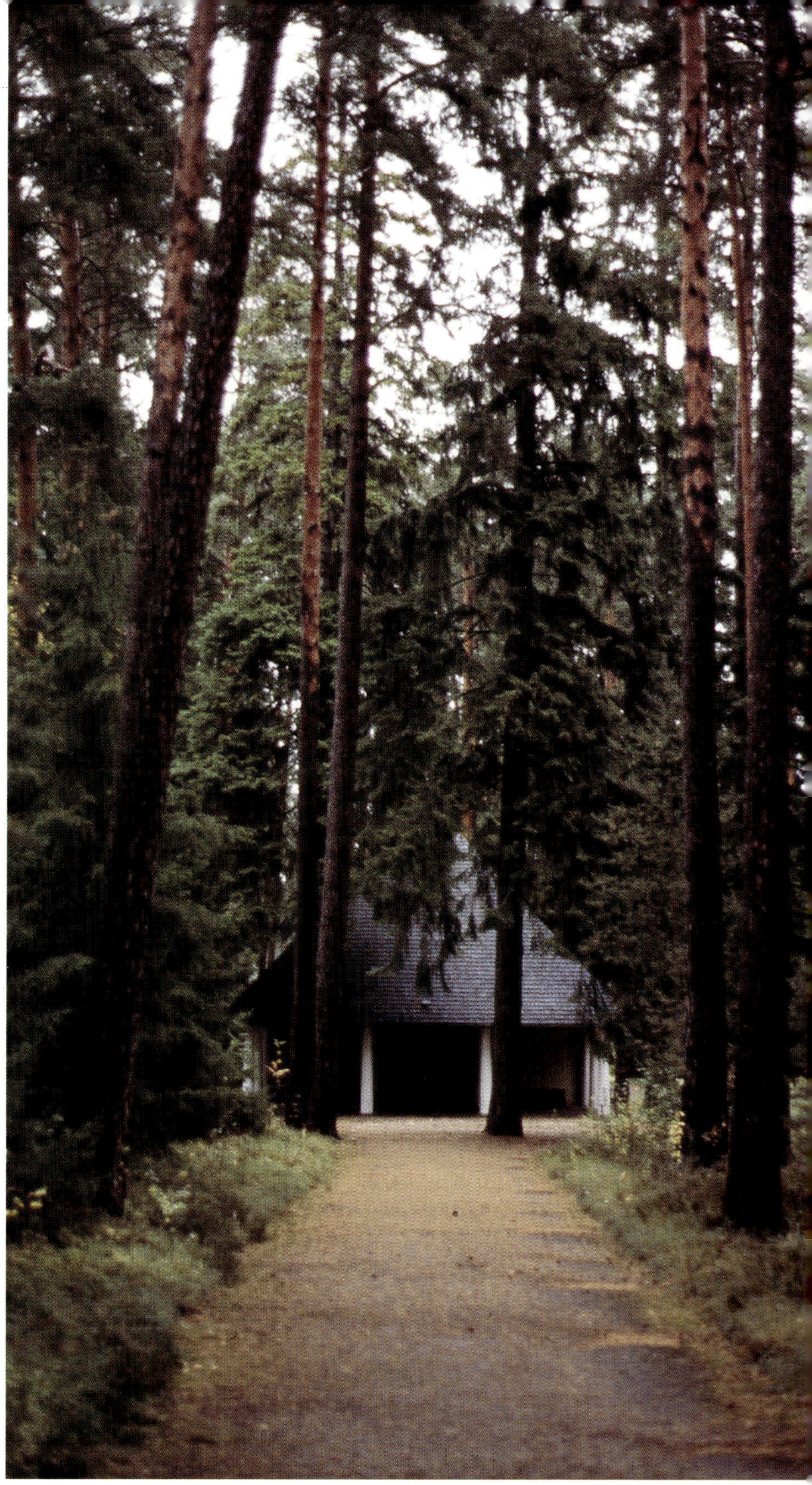

ABOVE: The Woodland Chapel's open entrance hall, with its painted Ionic wood columns, supports a pyramidal roof. The site is an integral part of the spatial experience of the chapel. *P. O. Fjeld.*

RIGHT: Gunnar Asplund and Sigurd Lewerentz, Woodland Chapel at the Woodland Cemetery. The entrance as the final destination of a walk through nature. *P. O. Fjeld.*

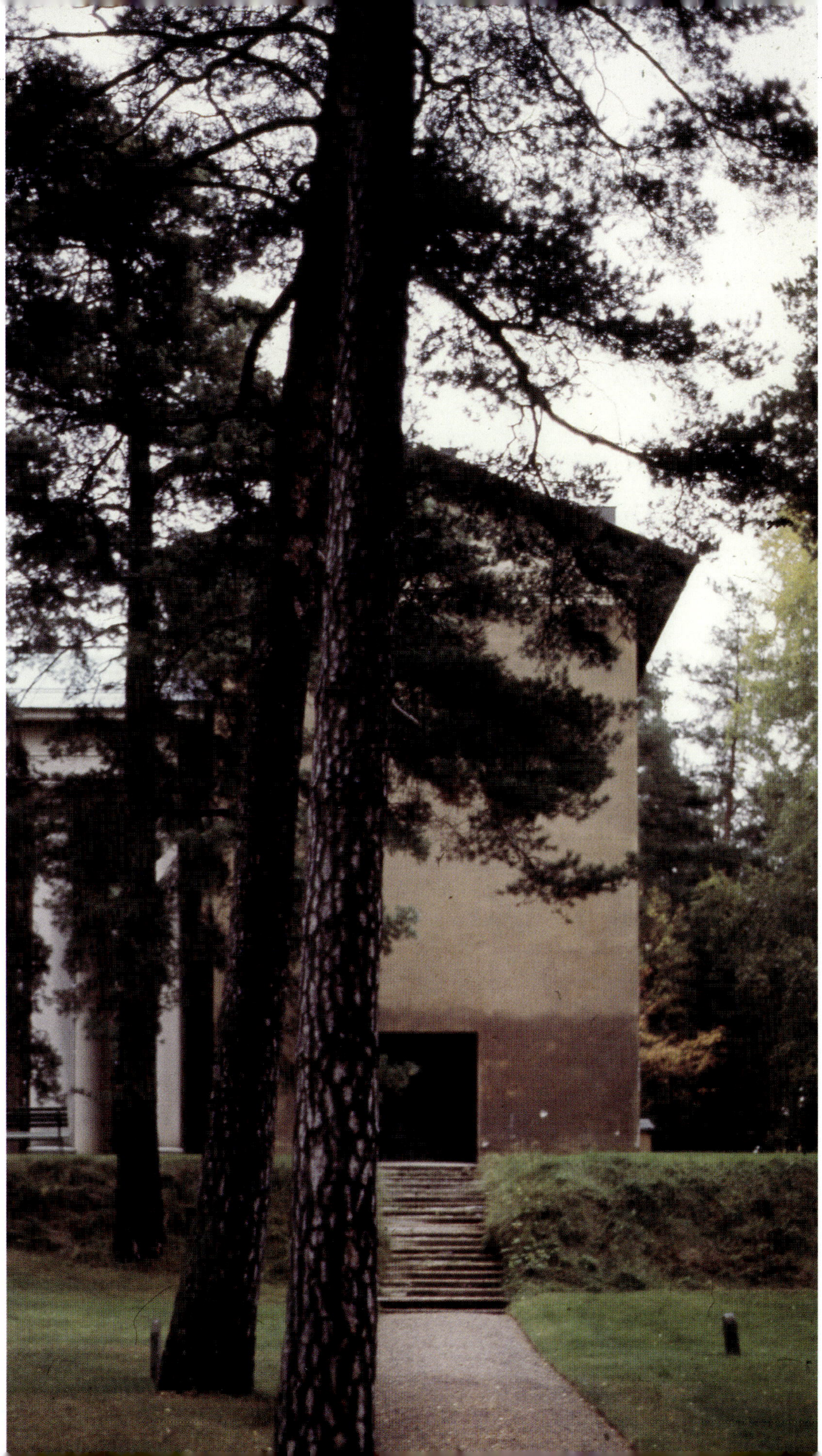

Sigurd Lewerentz, Resurrection Chapel at the Woodland Cemetery, 1925. West facade, with exit door and stair as part of the landscape leading down to the graveyard. The chapel is an important example of Swedish neoclassicism, but on close examination it nevertheless reveals great freedom and abstraction in relation to the principles of classicism. *P. O. Fjeld.*

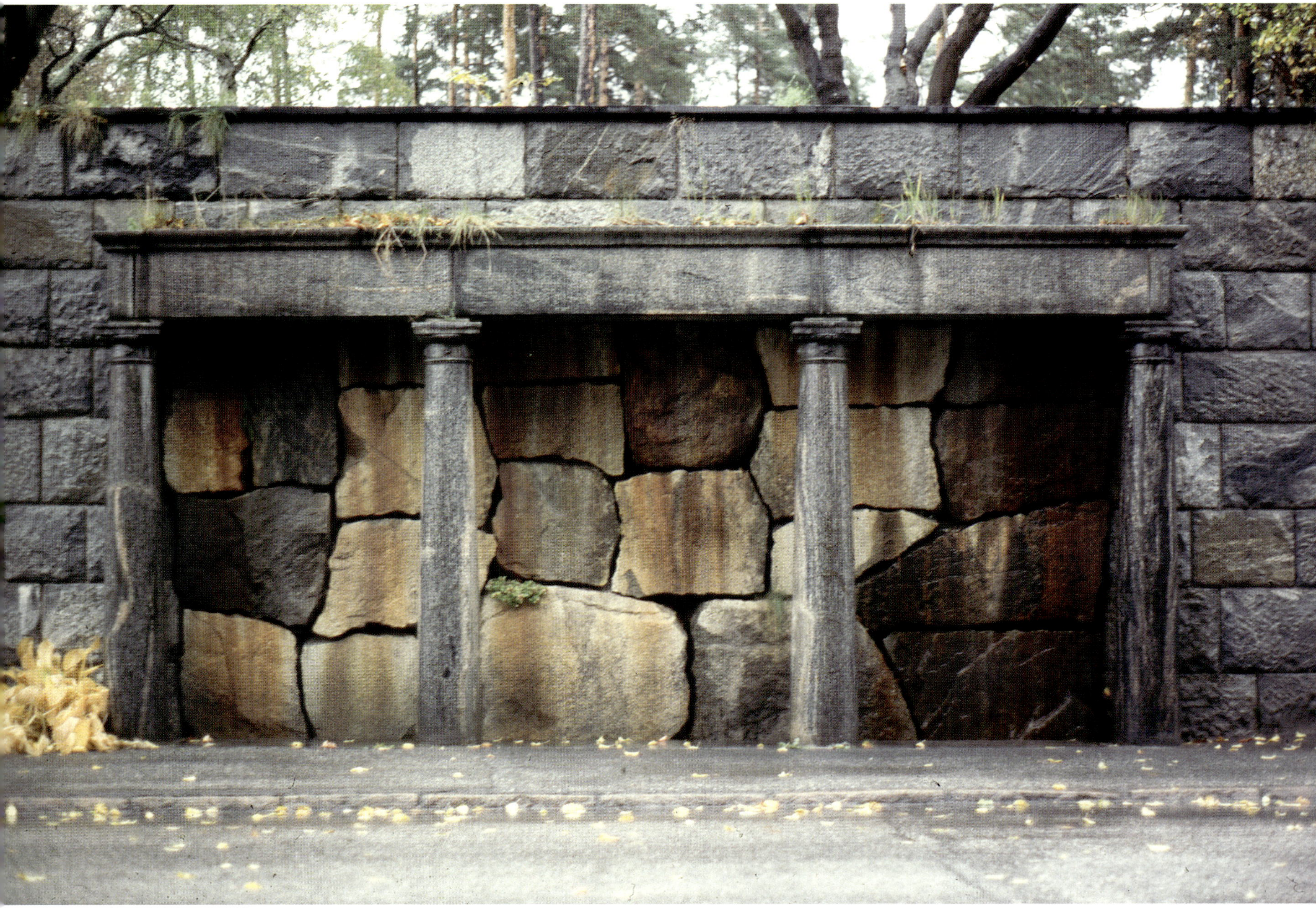

or material from his earlier work, as he felt each new project deserved a clean-slate mentality. He was not a vibrant public speaker—keeping very much to structural, material, and practical issues when giving a lecture—but his one-on-one conversations with students were intense and closer to what occurred in his office. He would often sit beside his assistants and sketch with them as a way of communication and discovery. All sketch material, good or bad, was kept for further discussion during a project, and working with models was considered an essential part of gaining a spatial understanding of each task. The relationships between room and person as the result of social issues, nature, and the connection between structure and daylight were central to both his smallest and largest projects. There was no set formula, but a positive skepticism in relation to dogma, style, and academic analysis. Issues concerning light and space—such as how daylight enters a room in relation to an individual who enters this same room simultaneously, and how in this situation space is challenged by the scale of an opening—were an ongoing office topic and also filtered into his pedagogy. Such conversation was complex enough to interest him as well as students, as it encouraged individual interpretation.

Asplund's clean-slate approach influenced the next generation's attitudes and pedagogy. His office was small, but the number of prominent Nordic architects who worked for him over the years or studied under him at the Stockholm Technical University is noteworthy. As a mature young architect, Arne Jacobsen had close contact with Asplund from about the time of the Stockholm Exhibition of 1930 until Asplund's death ten years later. In 1920, a young Alvar Aalto traveled to Stockholm hoping to work in Asplund's office, but without luck. However, he continued to visit Asplund when possible and developed a deep lifelong friendship with him. Upon hiring two Norwegian architects in 1928, Aalto insisted they visit Asplund's newly finished Stockholm Public Library on their way to Finland; twenty years later, Korsmo insisted his students visit the same library along with the Woodland Cemetery.

Asplund's influence also set a clear ethical and social stance within the profession. His extension of the old Gothenburg Town Hall, finished in 1934, exemplifies this stance, and in many ways is a built example of Kahn's term "institutions of man." For this project he struggled to find a precise relationship between the new addition, the old city hall, and the city square; in the end, the building was essentially drawn from the inside out. The entire sequence moving into the main hall flooded with natural light, the building's generous slow stair up to the offices encircling the hall above with their furnishings—all work toward a spatial equality and respect for the users, whether the defendant in a court case, the judge, the administrative staff, or the janitor. Hierarchy and privilege were held to a minimum, and Asplund was adamant on this issue.

For me, Kahn's concept of "serving and served spaces" comes to mind in connection

Detail of the main entrance of the Woodland Cemetery, Stockholm, designed by Gunnar Asplund and Sigurd Lewerentz in 1920. *P. O. Fjeld.*

1928 | Kahn and Korsmo first meet in Italy. CIAM I held in La Sarraz. Alvar and Aino Aalto and Erik Bryggman design the Turku seven-hundred-year-anniversary fair. Willem Marinus Dudok's Nassau School and Asplund's Stockholm Public Library open.

Kiyonori Kikutake, Alison Smithson, Fumihiko Maki, and Harriet Pattison born.

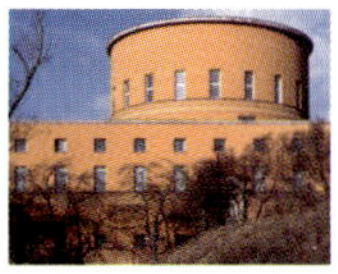

Stockholm Public Library. *P. O. Fjeld.*

1929 | Great Depression begins. CIAM II held in Frankfurt am Main. Alvar Aalto's Turun Sanomat office building completed in Turku, Finland. Mies van der Rohe's German Pavilion for the Barcelona Exposition erected. Richard Neutra's Lovell House, Los Angeles, completed.

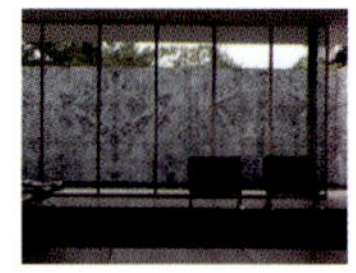

Mies van der Rohe's German Pavilion for the Barcelona Exposition. *P. O. Fjeld.*

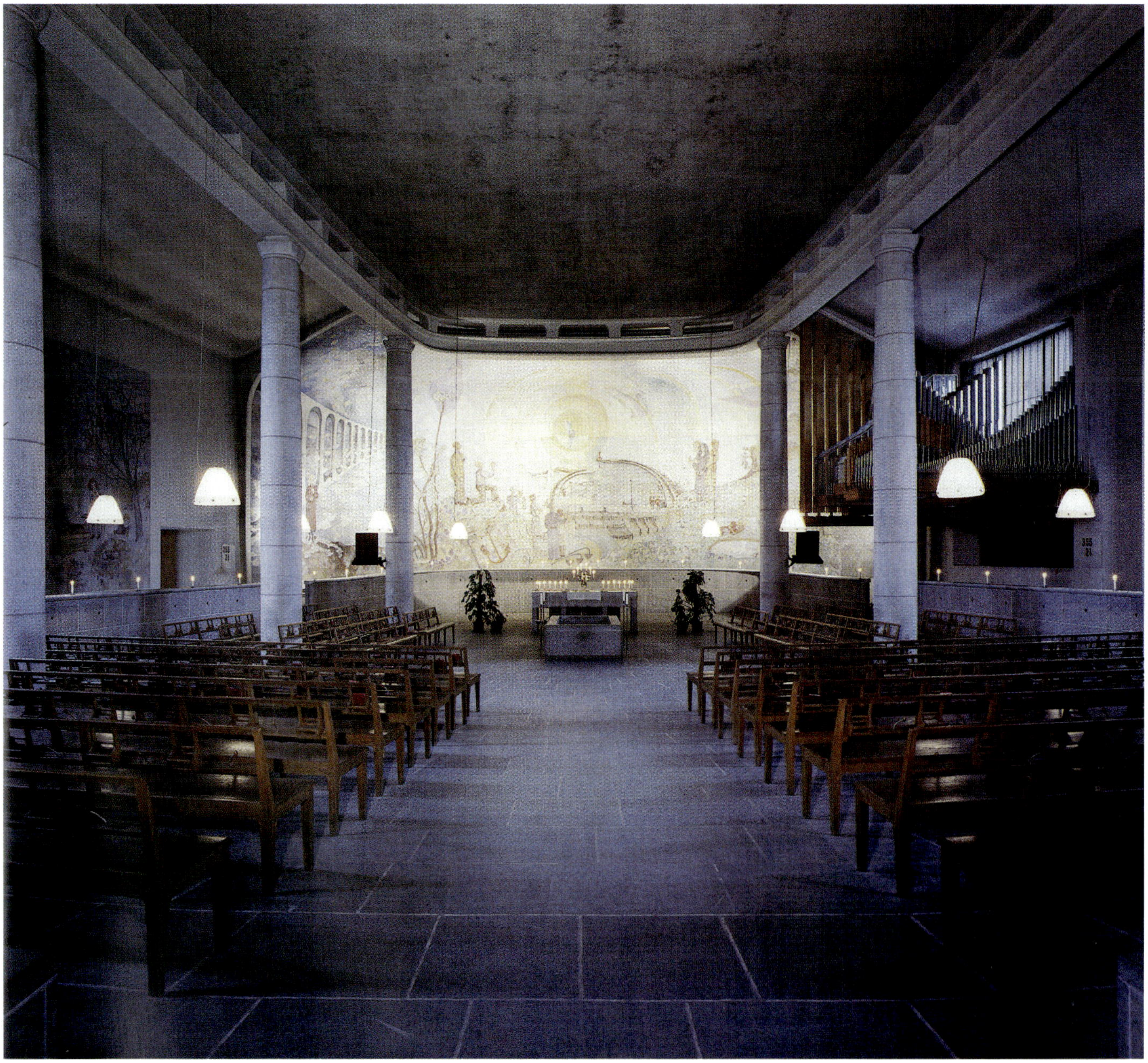

1930 CIAM III held in Brussels. Asplund-designed Stockholm Exhibition takes place. Erich Mendelsohn's Krasnoye Znamya power station in St. Petersburg and Mies van der Rohe's Villa Tugendhat completed. Arne Korsmo and Sverre Aasland complete houses on Lille Frøens vei and begin houses along Havna Allé.

P. V. J. Klint and Lars Backer die.

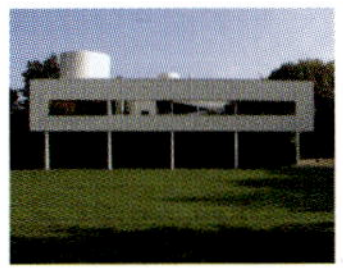

Le Corbusier and Pierre Jeanneret's Villa Savoye completed in 1931 in Poissy, France. *J. Reksten.*

1931 Sven Markelius and Uno Åhrén's Student Union building opens. Jan Duiker's Zonnestraal Sanatorium completed. W. M. Dudok's Hilversum Town Hall completed.

1932 Henry-Russell Hitchcock and Philip Johnson present the International Style in an exhibit at the Museum of Modern Art, New York, and in a concurrent publication.

Herman Hertzberger born.

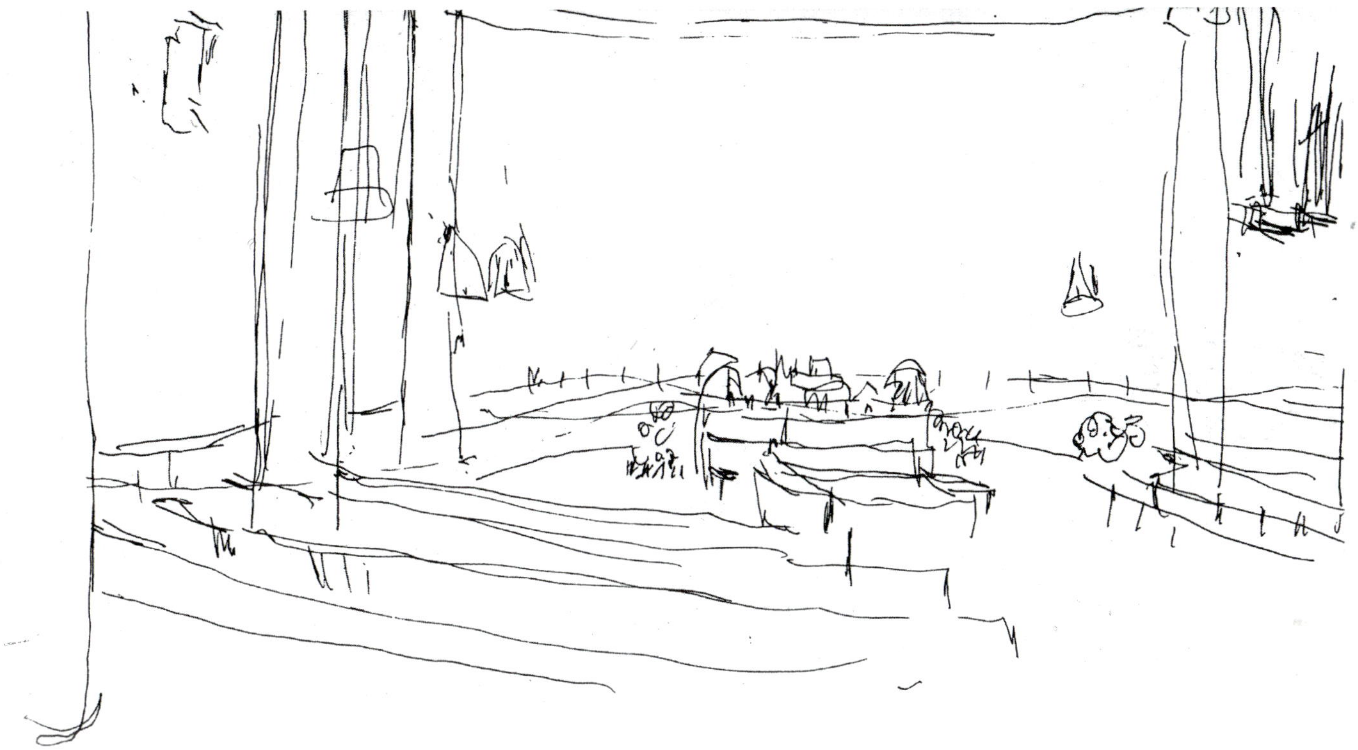

ABOVE: Sverre Fehn's student sketch of the interior of the Holy Cross Chapel at the Woodland Cemetery, 1947. *The National Museum, Oslo, Sverre Fehn, student notebook 1947.*

LEFT: Gunnar Asplund, interior of the Holy Cross Chapel. The tilted floor is as an extension of the landscape, a reminder of the nature connecting life and death. *P. O. Fjeld.*

with this building. Here all spaces are of equal importance, a collective sequence and effort of serving and being served. Asplund made a clear attempt to emphasize spatial accessibility for all, to reach an understanding of communality, of consensus, thus reducing the sense of privilege and position. Each space has an identity and importance both as a spatial singular and as a spatial collective. In many ways, the approach reflected modern Sweden and how its citizens were beginning to perceive public institutions. Asplund was tough and consistent in what he felt were primary motivations in architecture. He put the human first, and thereby influenced an entire generation of Nordic architects.

Among the most gifted Norwegian architects of this period was Lars Backer, who first studied in Oslo and then completed his architectural degree in Stockholm just as Asplund began to teach part time. (Backer was invited personally by Giedion to the first CIAM meeting, held in La Sarraz in 1928.) Soon after his stay in Stockholm, Backer took an internship at the Architect's Association in London; upon returning home, he immediately began

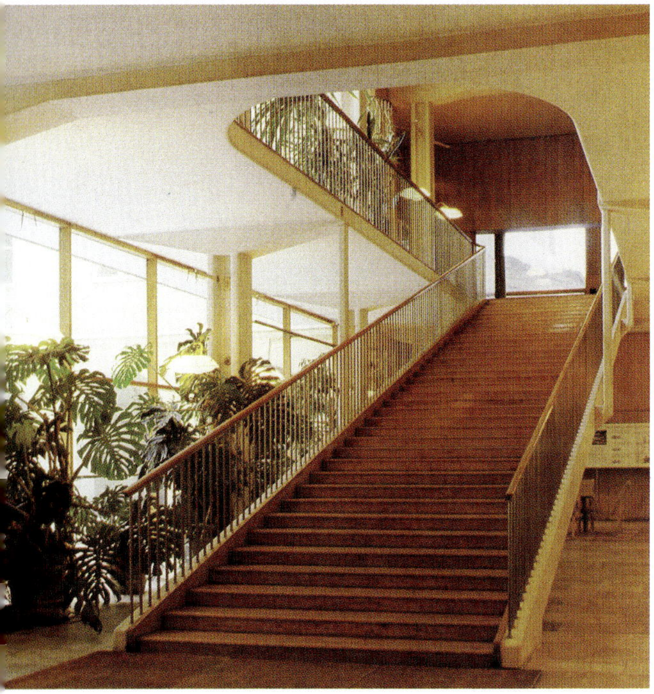

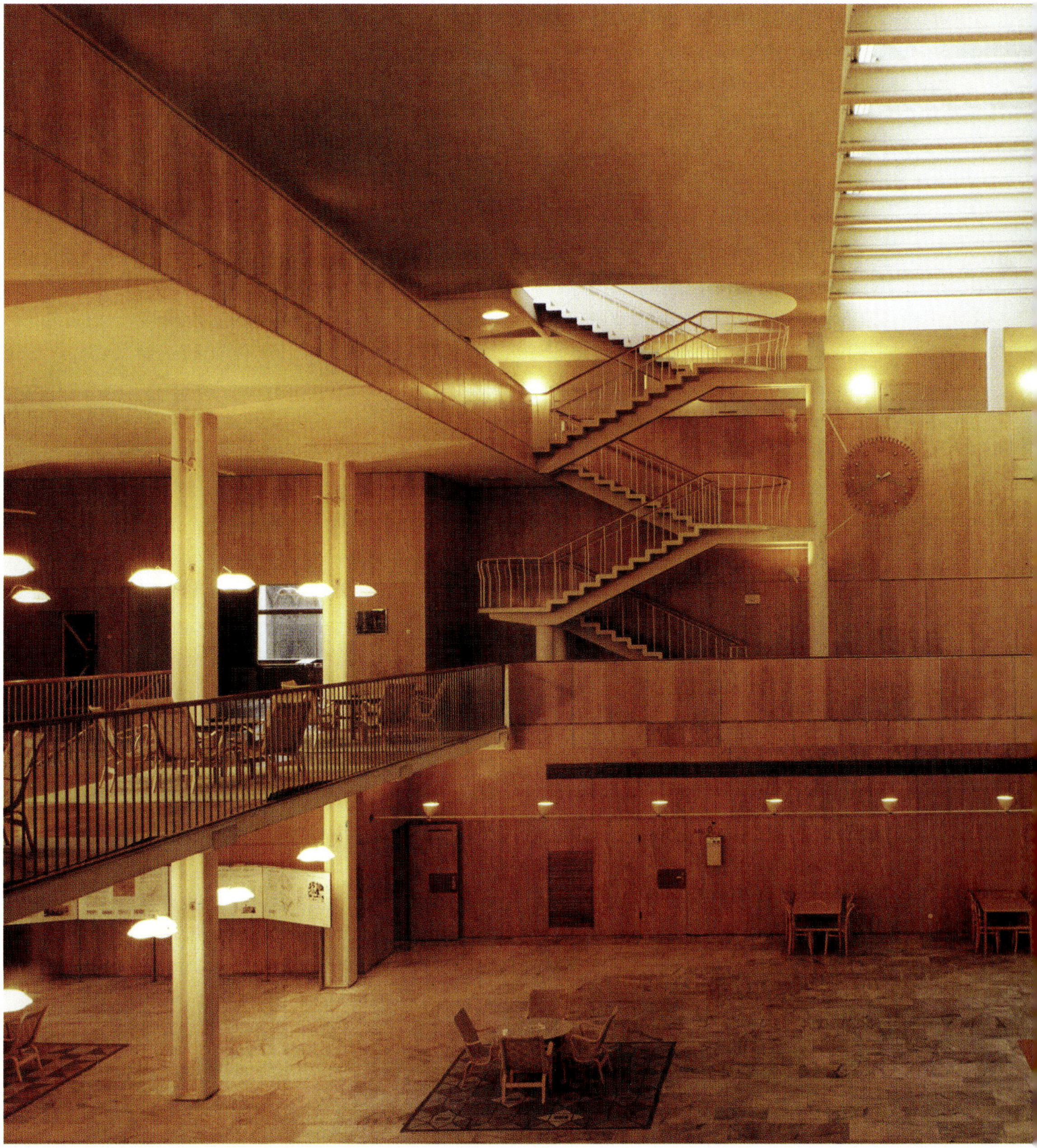

ABOVE: Gunnar Asplund, Gothenburg Town Hall addition, 1935. The main stairwell, as seen from the entrance level. The slow pace of the stair allows time for reflection for those making their way to the courtrooms on the second floor. *Swedish Arkitektur Förlag. AB. Stockholm. Photo by Jaạn Tomasson.*

RIGHT: In Asplund's addition to the town hall, the courtrooms and offices open on to a second-floor balcony that skirts the main public entrance hall, providing equal, nonhierarchical access to the courtrooms and other parts of the building. *Swedish Arkitektur Förlag. AB. Stockholm. Photo by Jaan Tomasson.*

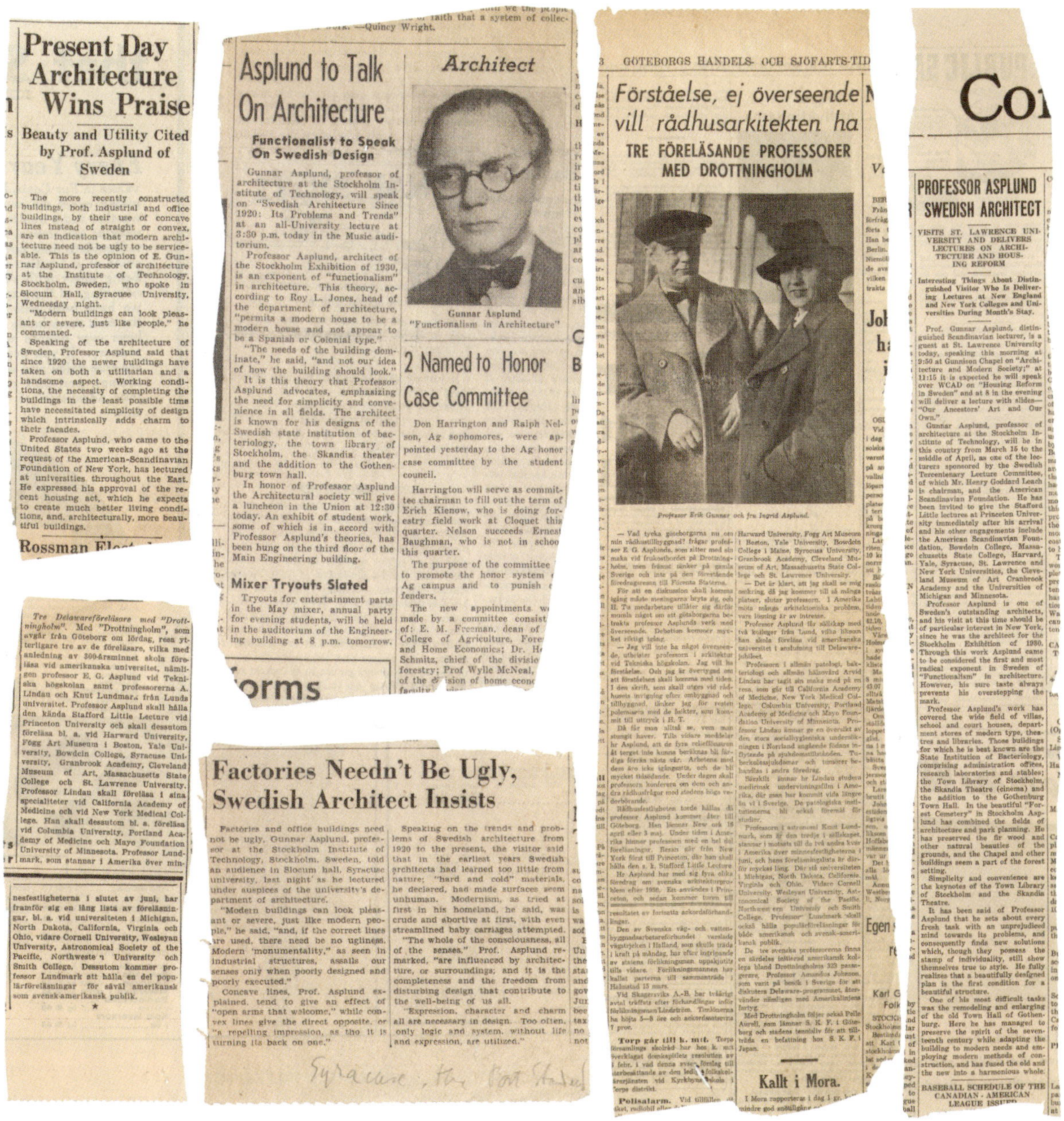

Present Day Architecture Wins Praise

Beauty and Utility Cited by Prof. Asplund of Sweden

The more recently constructed buildings, both industrial and office buildings, by their use of concave lines instead of straight or convex, are an indication that modern architecture need not be ugly to be serviceable. This is the opinion of E. Gunnar Asplund, professor of architecture at the Institute of Technology, Stockholm, Sweden, who spoke in Slocum Hall, Syracuse University, Wednesday night.

"Modern buildings can look pleasant or severe, just like people," he commented.

Speaking of the architecture of Sweden, Professor Asplund said that since 1920 the newer buildings have taken on both a utilitarian and a handsome aspect. Working conditions, the necessity of completing the buildings in the least possible time have necessitated simplicity of design which intrinsically adds charm to their facades.

Professor Asplund, who came to the United States two weeks ago at the request of the American-Scandinavian Foundation of New York, has lectured at universities throughout the East. He expressed his approval of the recent housing act, which he expects to create much better living conditions, and, architecturally, more beautiful buildings.

Rossman El...

Tre Delawareföreläsare med "Drottningholm". Med "Drottningholm", som avgår från Göteborg om lördag, resa ytterligare tre av de föreläsare, vilka med anledning av 300-årsminnet skola föreläsa vid amerikanska universitet, nämligen professor E. G. Asplund vid Tekniska högskolan samt professorerna A. Lindau och Knut Lundmark från Lunds universitet. Professor Asplund skall hålla den kända Stafford Little Lecture vid Princeton University och skall dessutom föreläsa bl. a. vid Harward University, Fogg Art Museum i Boston, Yale University, Bowdoin College, Syracuse University, Granbrook Academy, Cleveland Museum of Art, Massachusetts State College och St. Lawrence University. Professor Lindau skall föreläsa i sina specialiteter vid California Academy of Medicine och vid New York Medical College. Han skall dessutom bl. a. föreläsa vid Columbia University, Portland Academy of Medicine och Mayo Foundation University of Minnesota. Professor Lundmark, som stannar i Amerika över minnesfestligheterna i slutet av juni, har framför sig en lång lista av föreläsningar, bl. a. vid universiteten i Michigan, North Dakota, California, Virginia och Ohio, vidare Cornell University, Wesleyan University, Astronomical Society of the Pacific, Northwestern University och Smith College. Dessutom kommer professor Lundmark att hålla en del populärföreläsningar för såväl amerikansk som svensk-amerikansk publik.

★

...faith that a system of collec-...
—Quincy Wright.

Asplund to Talk On Architecture

Functionalist to Speak On Swedish Design

Gunnar Asplund, professor of architecture at the Stockholm Institute of Technology, will speak on "Swedish Architecture Since 1920: Its Problems and Trends" at an all-University lecture at 3:30 p.m. today in the Music auditorium.

Professor Asplund, architect of the Stockholm Exhibition of 1930, is an exponent of "functionalism" in architecture. This theory, according to Roy L. Jones, head of the department of architecture, "permits a modern house to be a modern house and not appear to be a Spanish or Colonial type."

"The needs of the building dominate," he said, "and not our idea of how the building should look."

It is this theory that Professor Asplund advocates, emphasizing the need for simplicity and convenience in all fields. The architect is known for his designs of the Swedish state institution of bacteriology, the town library of Stockholm, the Skandia theater and the addition to the Gothenburg town hall.

In honor of Professor Asplund the Architectural society will give a luncheon in the Union at 12:30 today. An exhibit of student work, some of which is in accord with Professor Asplund's theories, has been hung on the third floor of the Main Engineering building.

Mixer Tryouts Slated

Tryouts for entertainment parts in the May mixer, annual party for evening students, will be held in the auditorium of the Engineering building at 8 p.m. tomorrow.

Architect

Gunnar Asplund
"Functionalism in Architecture"

2 Named to Honor Case Committee

Don Harrington and Ralph Nelson, Ag sophomores, were appointed yesterday to the Ag honor case committee by the student council.

Harrington will serve as committee chairman to fill out the term of Erich Kienow, who is doing forestry field work at Cloquet this quarter. Nelson succeeds Ernest Baughman, who is not in schoo[l] this quarter.

The purpose of the committee [is] to promote the honor system [on] Ag campus and to punish [of]fenders.

The new appointments w[ere] made by a committee consist[ing] of: E. M. Freeman, dean of [the] College of Agriculture, Fore[stry] and Home Economics; Dr. H[...] Schmitz, chief of the divisio[n of] forestry; Prof Wylle McNeal, [...] of the division of home econ[omics] ...

...orms

Factories Needn't Be Ugly, Swedish Architect Insists

Factories and office buildings need not be ugly, Gunnar Asplund, professor at the Stockholm Institute of Technology, Stockholm, Sweden, told an audience in Slocum hall, Syracuse university, last night as he lectured under auspices of the university's department of architecture.

"Modern buildings can look pleasant or severe, just like modern people," he said, "and, if the correct lines are used, there need be no ugliness. Modern 'monumentality,' as seen in industrial structures, assails our senses only when poorly designed and poorly executed."

Concave lines, Prof. Asplund explained, tend to give an effect of "open arms that welcome," while convex lines give the direct opposite, or "a repelling impression, as tho it is turning its back on one."

Speaking on the trends and problems of Swedish architecture from 1920 to the present, the visitor said that in the earliest years Swedish architects had learned too little from nature; "hard and cold" materials, he declared, had made surfaces seem unhuman. Modernism, as tried at first in his homeland, he said, was crude and abortive at first, with even streamlined baby carriages attempted.

"The whole of the consciousness, all of the senses," Prof. Asplund remarked, "are influenced by architecture, or surroundings; and it is the completeness and the freedom from disturbing design that contribute to the well-being of us all.

"Expression, character and charm all are necessary in design. Too often, only logic and system, without life and expression, are utilized."

Syracuse, the Post Standard

3 GÖTEBORGS HANDELS- OCH SJÖFARTS-TID...

Förståelse, ej överseende vill rådhusarkitekten ha

TRE FÖRELÄSANDE PROFESSORER MED DROTTNINGHOLM

Professor Erik Gunnar och fru Ingrid Asplund.

— Vad tycka göteborgarna nu om min rådhustillbyggnad? frågar professor E. G. Asplunda, som sitter med sin maka vid frukostbordet på Drottningholm, men främst tänker på gamla Sverige och inte på den förestående föredragsresan till Förenta Staterna.

...

Harward University, Fogg Art Museum i Boston, Yale University, Bowdoin College i Maine, Syrocusa University, Granbrook Academy, Cleveland Museum of Art, Massachusetts State College och St. Lawrence University.

— Det är klart, att jag skall se mig omkring då jag kommer till så många platser, slutar professorn. I Amerika möta många arkitektoniska problem. ...

Kallt i Mora.

Co...

PROFESSOR ASPLUND SWEDISH ARCHITECT

VISITS ST. LAWRENCE UNIVERSITY AND DELIVERS LECTURES ON ARCHITECTURE AND HOUSING REFORM

Interesting Things About Distinguished Visitor Who Is Delivering Lectures at New England and New York Colleges and Universities During Month's Stay.

Prof. Gunnar Asplund, distinguished Scandinavian lecturer, is a guest at St. Lawrence University today, speaking this morning at 9:50 at Gunnison Chapel on "Architecture and Modern Society;" at 11:15 it is expected he will speak over WCAD on "Housing Reform in Sweden" and at 8 in the evening will deliver a lecture with slides—"Our Ancestors' Art and Our Own."

Gunnar Asplund, professor of architecture at the Stockholm Institute of Technology, will be in this country from March 15 to the middle of April, as one of the lecturers sponsored by the Swedish Tercentenary Lecture Committee, of which Mr. Henry Goddard Leach is chairman, and the American Scandinavian Foundation. He has been invited to give the Stafford Little lectures at Princeton University immediately after his arrival and his other engagements include the American Scandinavian Foundation, Bowdoin College, Massachusetts State College, Harvard, Yale, Syracuse, St. Lawrence and New York Universities, the Cleveland Museum of Art Cranbrook Academy and the Universities of Michigan and Minnesota.

Professor Asplund is one of Sweden's outstanding architects, and his visit at this time should be of particular interest in New York, since he was the architect for the Stockholm Exhibition of 1930. Through this work Asplund came to be considered the first and most radical exponent in Sweden of "Functionalism" in architecture. However, his sure taste always prevents his overstepping the mark.

Professor Asplund's work has covered the wide field of villas, school and court houses, department stores of modern type, theatres and libraries. Those buildings for which he is best known are the State Institution of Bacteriology, comprising administration offices, research laboratories and stables; the Town Library of Stockholm, the Skandia Theatre (cinema) and the addition to the Gothenburg Town Hall. In the beautiful "Forest Cemetery" in Stockholm Asplund has combined the fields of architecture and park planning. He has preserved the fir wood and other natural beauties of the grounds, and the Chapel and other buildings seem a part of the forest setting.

Simplicity and convenience are the keynotes of the Town Library of Stockholm and the Skandia Theatre.

It has been said of Professor Asplund that he sets about every fresh task with an unprejudiced mind towards its problems, and consequently finds new solutions which, though they possess the stamp of individuality, still show themselves true to style. He fully realizes that a beautifully designed plan is the first condition for a beautiful structure.

One of his most difficult tasks was the remodeling and enlarging of the old Town Hall of Gothenburg. Here he has managed to preserve the spirit of the seventeenth century while adapting the building to modern needs and employing modern methods of construction, and has fused the old and the new into a harmonious whole.

BASEBALL SCHEDULE OF THE CANADIAN - AMERICAN LEAGUE ISSUED

Newspaper clippings from Asplund's American lecture tour, which took place while his office was working on the addition to Gothenburg Town Hall. He lectured at a number of schools, including Princeton, Yale, Harvard, and Cranbrook Academy. *Property of the Swedish Centre for Architecture and Design, Stockholm.*

introducing new work and writings from the Continent to the Oslo milieu. (As a young student, Arne Korsmo would have undoubtedly been aware of this architect, who was eight years his senior.) Unfortunately, Backer died young, just as his work began to have an impact, and his loss was keenly felt by many young Nordic progressive architects.

Aalto's correspondence concerning the Athens CIAM meeting of 1933 indirectly reveals the significance of Backer's early death, as Aalto expressed concern about who would fill Backer's role in representing Norway at the meeting.[3] At this time, Aalto had contact with a number of important young Swedish architects, and his network of Nordic colleagues was growing rapidly. In 1930, immediately following the opening of the Stockholm Exhibition, Aalto and the Swedish architect Sven Markelius drove from Stockholm to Trondheim, Norway, through a remote mountainous area to attend the first Nordic Functionalist Congress. Here, despite the significant travel distance for many participants, Aalto and Markelius were joined by progressive architects from all over the Nordic region, and architectural magazines from Finland, Denmark, Sweden, and Norway all reported on the meeting. This was the start of a lively exchange within the Nordic region that developed parallel to the various modernist movements and organizations on the Continent. Thus Aalto's involvement in the CIAM meeting of 1933 in Athens was not a solo act from the North. He had a good grasp of and support from the Nordic progressive architectural milieus, and a number of individuals representing these attended the meeting with him.

Why are these people and events relevant to Kahn? Already at the time of Kahn's visit in 1928, a new direction was emerging within Nordic architecture and education, and Korsmo experienced this development and its architects firsthand. Their focus was not on style but core human issues and the realization that human well-being was a reflection of the social changes within society. Many of the fundamental priorities of twentieth-century Nordic work were closely related to the core issues that came up in Kahn's masterclass. Foremost among those priorities was the greater egalitarianism that had unfolded in the Nordic countries through a grassroots transformation. The various Nordic architectural schools had addressed these changes within their curriculums by the time Arne Korsmo and Kahn met in 1928.

The 1928 European Study Tour

The young Arne Korsmo, the son of a well-known biology professor at the University of Oslo, was exposed to many strong and influential individuals in 1920s Oslo. Korsmo, whose first jobs were with progressive architects, moved to the prestigious office of Arneberg & Poulsson about nine months before he met Kahn in 1928. Arneberg & Poulsson at the time was working on the new Oslo City Hall, with its distinctive brick twin towers. Over the years, Korsmo recounted a story to his students about how his bosses Arneberg and Poulsson, along with Ragnar Östberg, who was visiting from Stockholm at the time, looked out of the office window toward the nearby Akershus Castle and ramparts and with great indignation discussed Lars Backer's new modernist building, the Skansen Restaurant. Östberg exclaimed, "It looks like something unmentionable fouling its own city."[4] Only months after this outburst, Kahn would visit Östberg's office in Stockholm and soon after meet Korsmo for the first time.

Louis Kahn lived in a city of nearly two million people. After graduation from the University of Pennsylvania in 1924, he worked on the Sesquicentennial Exposition in the office of John Molitor and lived with his parents to save money for his trip to Europe. By the early 1930s Philadelphia boasted a few modern works, such as the PSFS Building by Howe and Lescaze, finished in 1931; but at the outset of Kahn's European visit of 1928, much of the new construction there, though expertly crafted, was fairly conventional for the time.

Kahn's school friend Norman Rice was already working in Le Corbusier's office in Paris by the time Kahn departed in May. Arne Korsmo was also getting ready for a longer study tour of the Continent. He applied for a travel grant, which revealed an informed emphasis on new projects in Europe; Erich Mendelsohn, Willem Dudok, and new Dutch architecture were particularly noted. While in Germany, he planned to focus on Mendelsohn's work in Berlin, but he would also visit Dessau and the Weissenhof exhibition, then Prague and Vienna, and then slowly move south to Venice and Rome.

In May of 1928 Louis Kahn landed in England, which he spent several weeks exploring. He then crossed the Channel, stopping in the Netherlands and Belgium before heading to Scandinavia, where he visited Copenhagen, Stockholm, and Helsinki. From there he made his way to family in Riga and then to the island of Saaremaa. Kahn's sketches from his stay in the Netherlands reveal an interest in the new Dutch modernist work, as well as in buildings more in line with his Beaux Arts education. Kahn visited many of the same Dutch modernist buildings—including Duiker's Zonnestraal Sanatorium and works by J. J. P. Oud—that Alvar Aalto visited just a month later. There is seemingly little physical proof to indicate what contemporary architecture Kahn saw in Denmark and Sweden. Nor is there any evidence of a stop between Copenhagen and Stockholm, but it's certainly possible he saw the first stage of Lewerentz's Malmö Eastern Cemetery and his Resurrection Chapel in Stockholm, which were both included in an exhibition of Lewerentz's work in New York in 1931.

Considering the length of Kahn's stay, why were there so few sketches from Scandinavia?

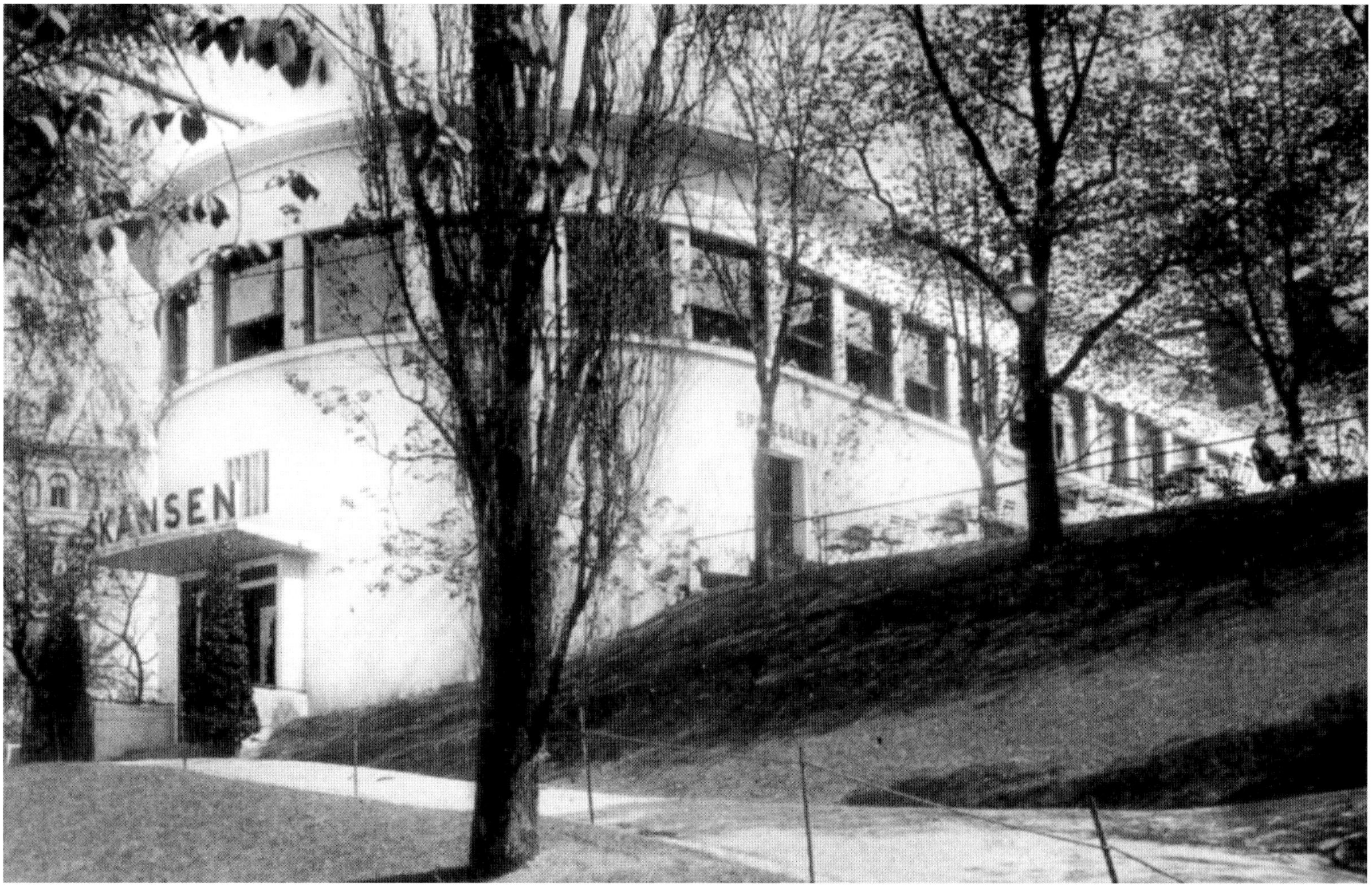

Lars Backer, Skansen Restaurant, Oslo, 1927 (demolished). The restaurant was the subject of a heated conversation between Arneberg, Poulsson, and Östberg that Korsmo overheard in 1928. *The Oslo School of Architecture and Design Photo Archive; photo by O. Væring.*

I was fortunate to have a conversation with Nathaniel Kahn about the lack of Nordic sketches, and he directed me to the backside of one of the drawings that Kahn made in the Netherlands, revealing a quick sketch of P. V. Jensen-Klint's Grundtvig Church, and a small, very primitive plan of the Copenhagen Police Headquarters. In addition, there is an attempt by Kahn to phonetically understand the meaning of the name "Copenhagen" in semi-Danish, and in the top corner, in someone else's handwriting, a list of the names "Berlage," "Alexander Kropholler," "Kromhaut," and "Moldo Krop (Beeldhouver)." Clearly Kahn was straddling what was familiar

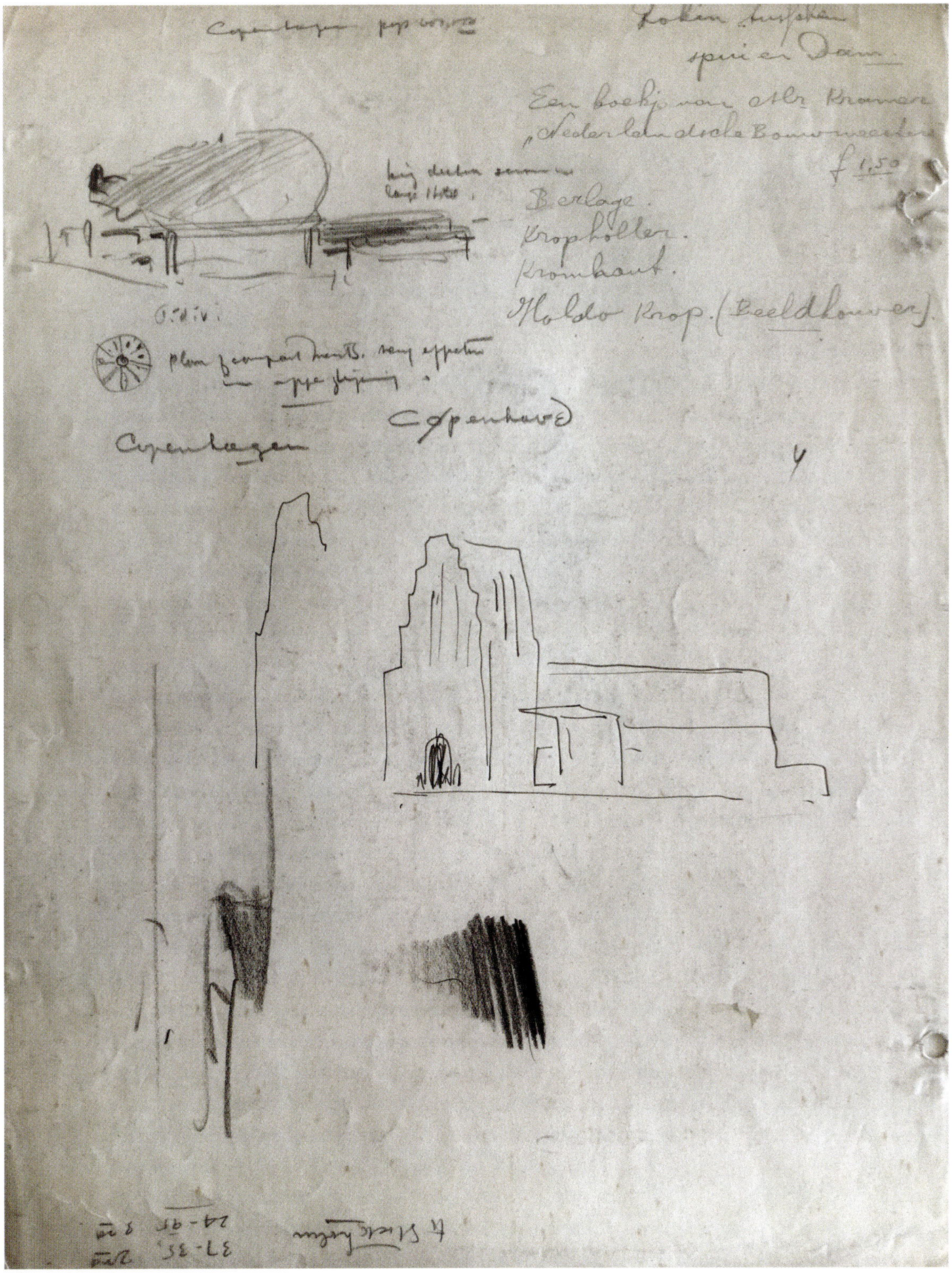

A page of sketches that Kahn made during his visit to Copenhagen in 1928. It shows a very rudimentary sketch of Grundtvig Church and a plan of the Copenhagen Police Headquarters, which had just opened before his visit. On the same paper, he attempted to transliterate "Copenhagen" (København). *Nathaniel Kahn Collection.*

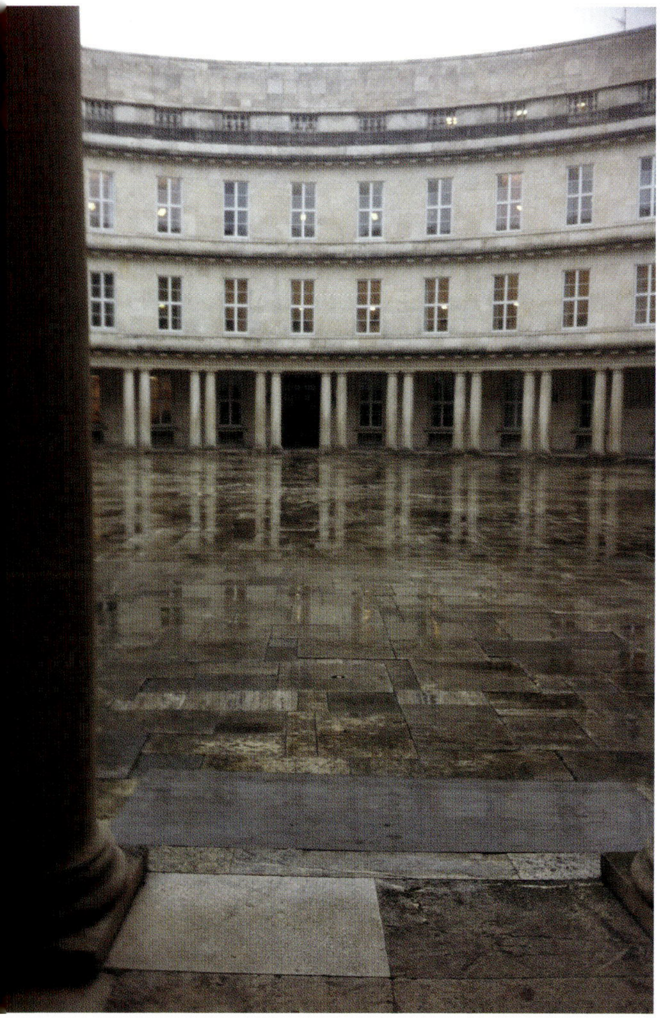

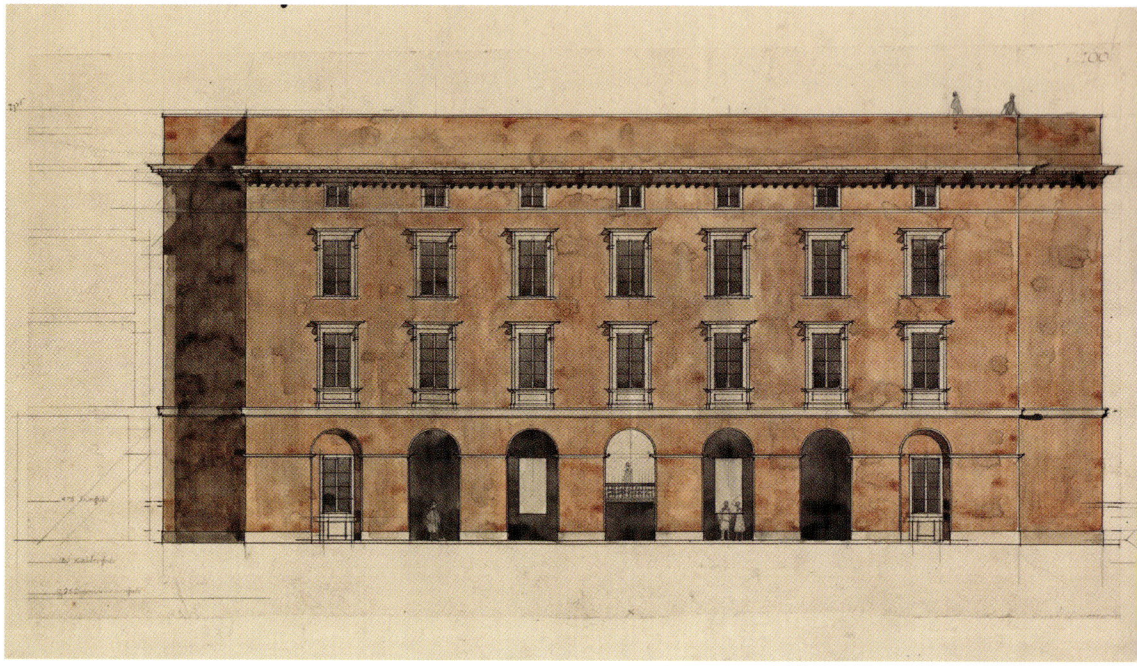

ABOVE: Hack Kampmann and Aage Rafn, Copenhagen Police Headquarters, 1918–24. Forty-four column pairs form a circular inner courtyard, providing an opportunity for pause before proceeding further into the building. *P. O. Fjeld.*

UPPER RIGHT: Early exterior drawing of the Copenhagen Police Headquarters. Notice the structural change in regards to the inner court. *The Danish National Art Library, Copenhagen.*

from his education in Philadelphia and what was now evolving. The small sketches from Copenhagen suggest he was architecturally informed, as the first phase of Jensen-Klint's Grundtvig Church had just been completed less than two years earlier. Kahn was in Sweden for ten days, but there is little to indicate what he saw, but his pastel of the interior of the Stockholm City Hall's Blue Room (1911–23) by Ragnar Östberg, plus a small booklet signed by Östberg, give some idea.

Just months before Kahn's visit to Stockholm, Asplund's Stockholm Public Library opened to the public; at this time, both its modernist wing of commercial spaces and its landscaping were nearly complete. So centrally located, it would have been almost impossible for Kahn to miss. In addition, Asplund's Woodland Chapel, with a gate and graveyard landscaping by Lewerentz, and the nearby neoclassical Resurrection Chapel by Lewerentz had already been in use for several years before Kahn's visit. All of these sites were well known in the Nordic countries, but it is nevertheless difficult to know with certainty what Kahn visited.

In Finland, he used Eliel Saarinen's Helsinki Central Train Station and sketched the Eira Hospital by Lars Sonck. At this point in time, the Turun Sanomat office building (1928–30), the Viipuri Library (1927–34), and the Paimio Sanatorium (1929–33) were on Alvar Aalto's drawing board. In addition, Aalto and Erik Bryggman were working on the modernist exhibition planned for the following spring to commemorate Turku's seven-hundred-year history.

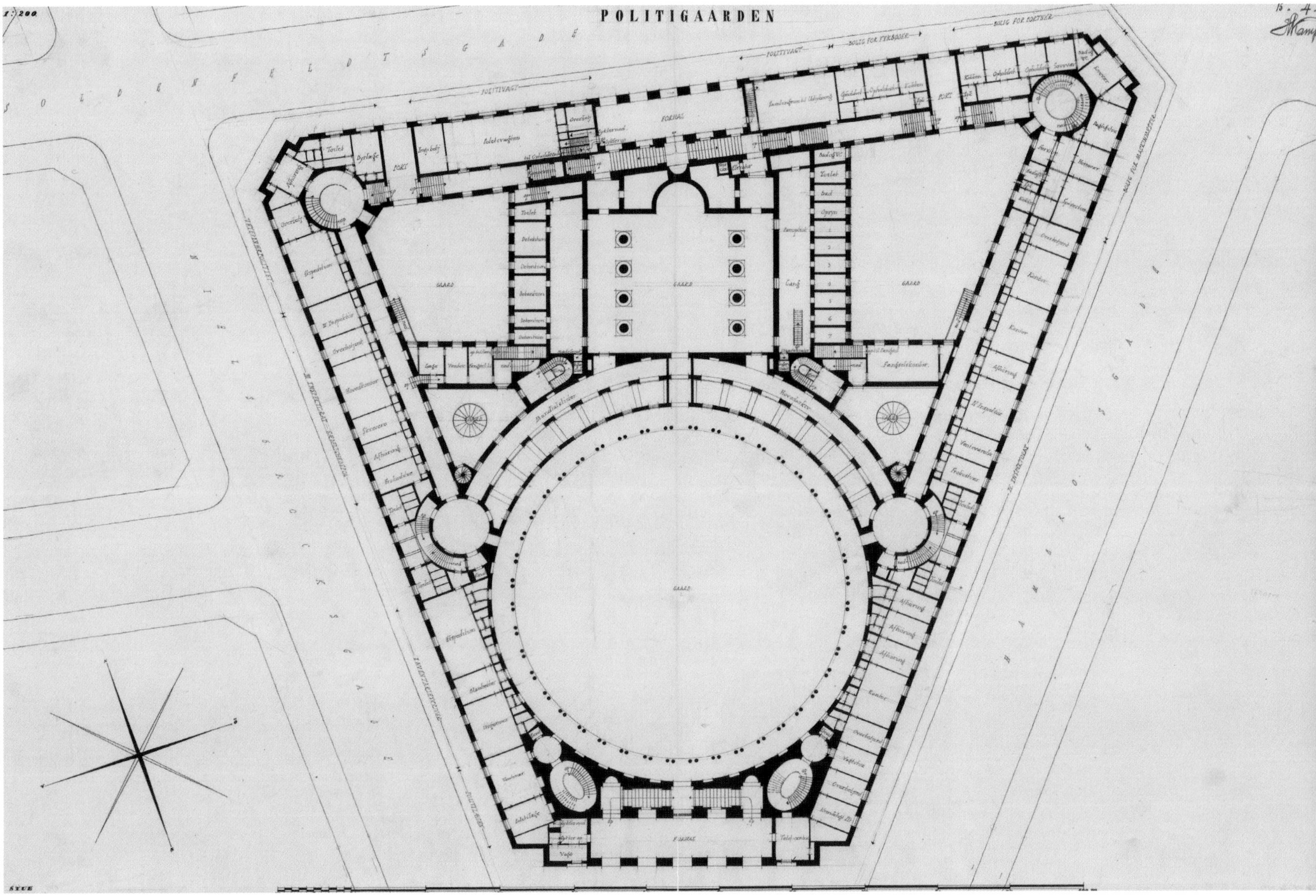

The striking geometrical order in this plan of the Copenhagen Police Headquarters reflects a building that is neither static nor monolithic. The building's precise relationship between mass and void, open and closed, generates a strong spatial awareness. *The Danish National Art Library, Copenhagen.*

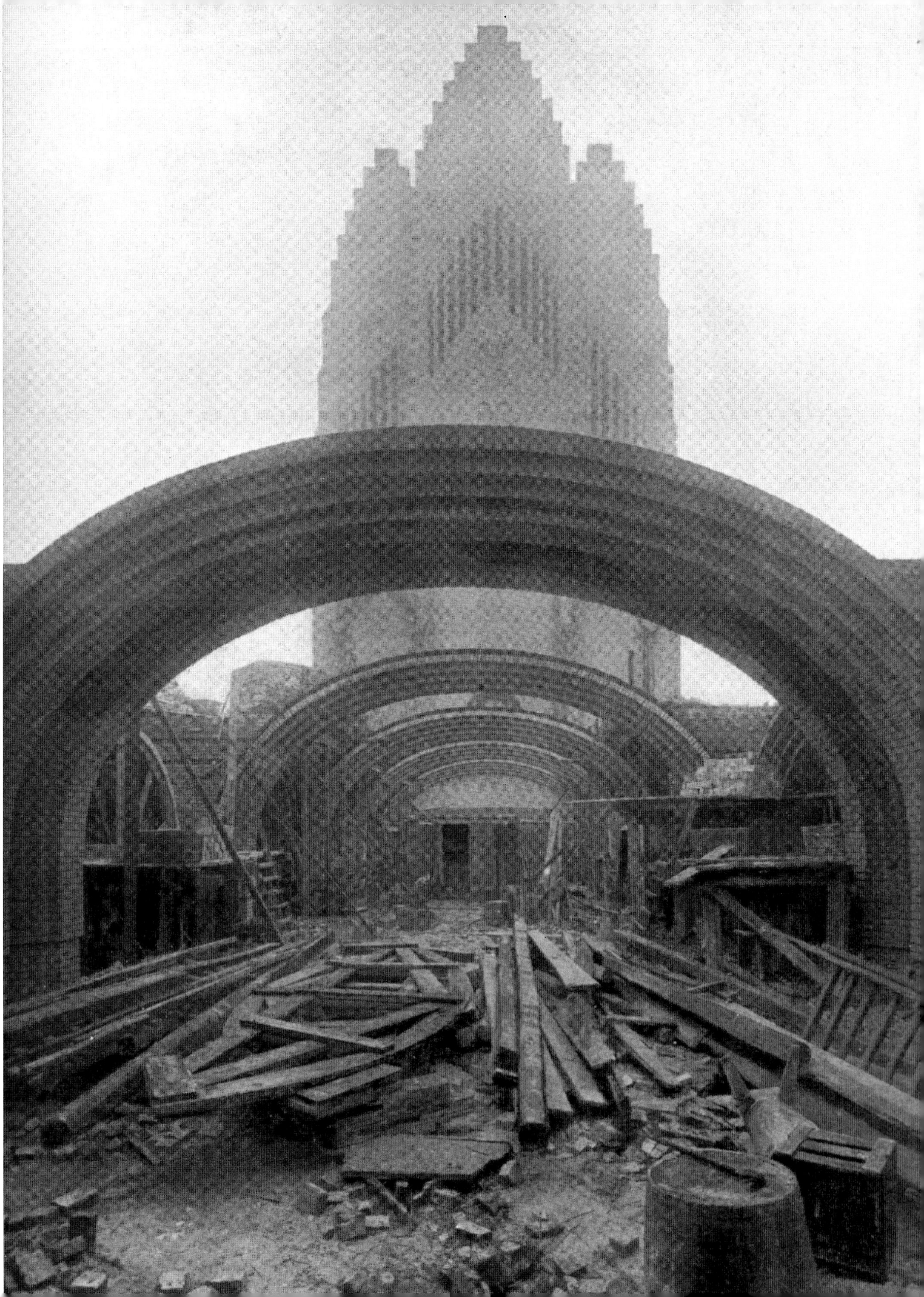

P. V. Jensen-Klint and Kaare Klint, Grundtvig Church, Copenhagen, 1921–40. Steen Eiler Rasmussen noted how closely the final building resembled the first sketches of this project. He also remarked that human activity appears subordinated, almost abstracted, by the building's strong spatial expression.
The Danish National Art Library, Copenhagen.

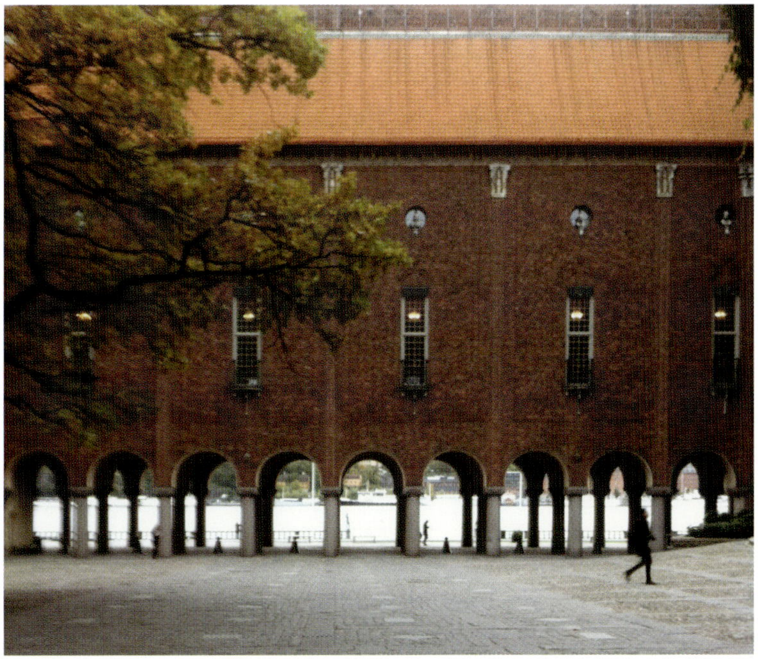

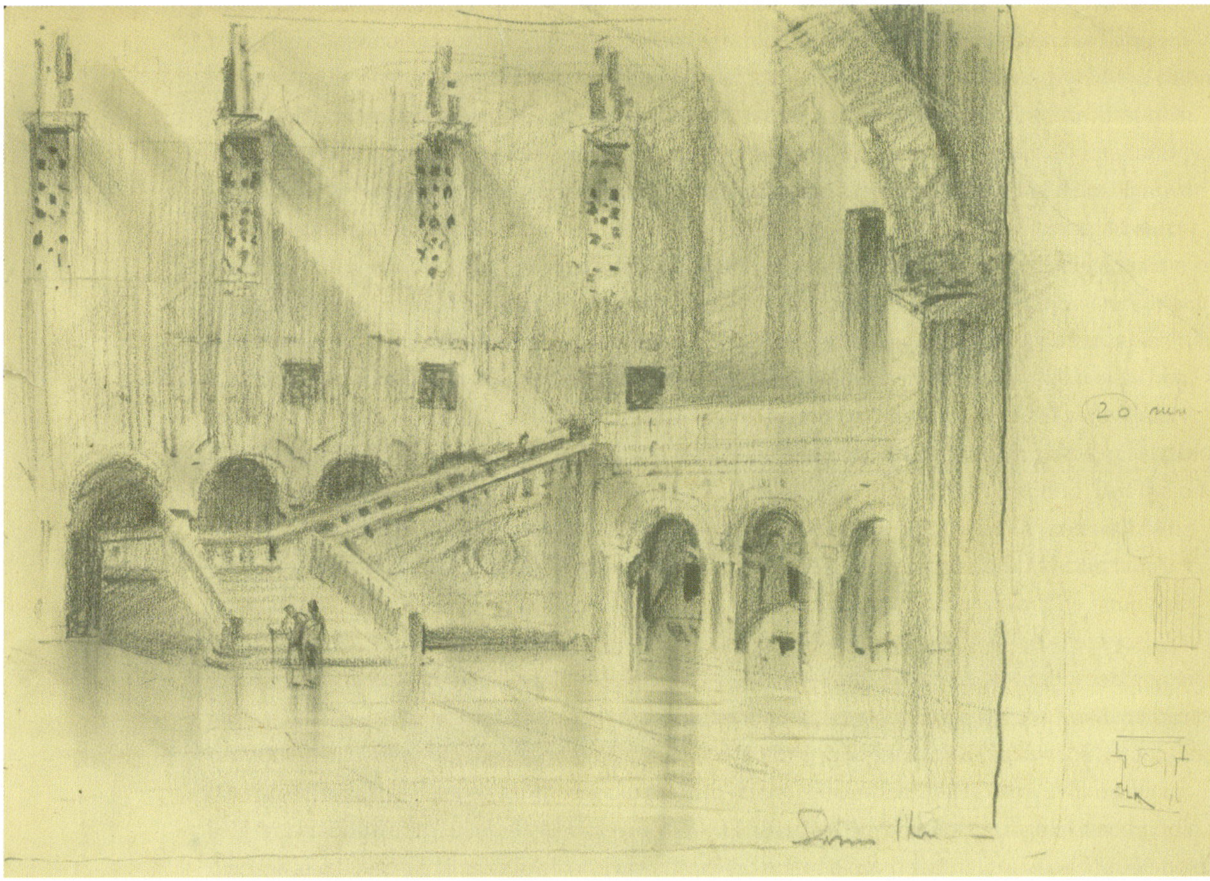

TOP: Stockholm City Hall, Ragnar Östberg, 1925. Facade of interior courtyard facing the water. The large red-brick wall articulates a meeting with the granite column row. A single "munck" brick used in some areas of the building weighs about eight kilos. *P. O. Fjeld.*

RIGHT: Kahn's 1928 sketch of the Blue Room inside Ragnar Östberg's Stockholm City Hall. Östberg's original intention was to keep the Blue Room open to the sky. *Nathaniel Kahn Collection.*

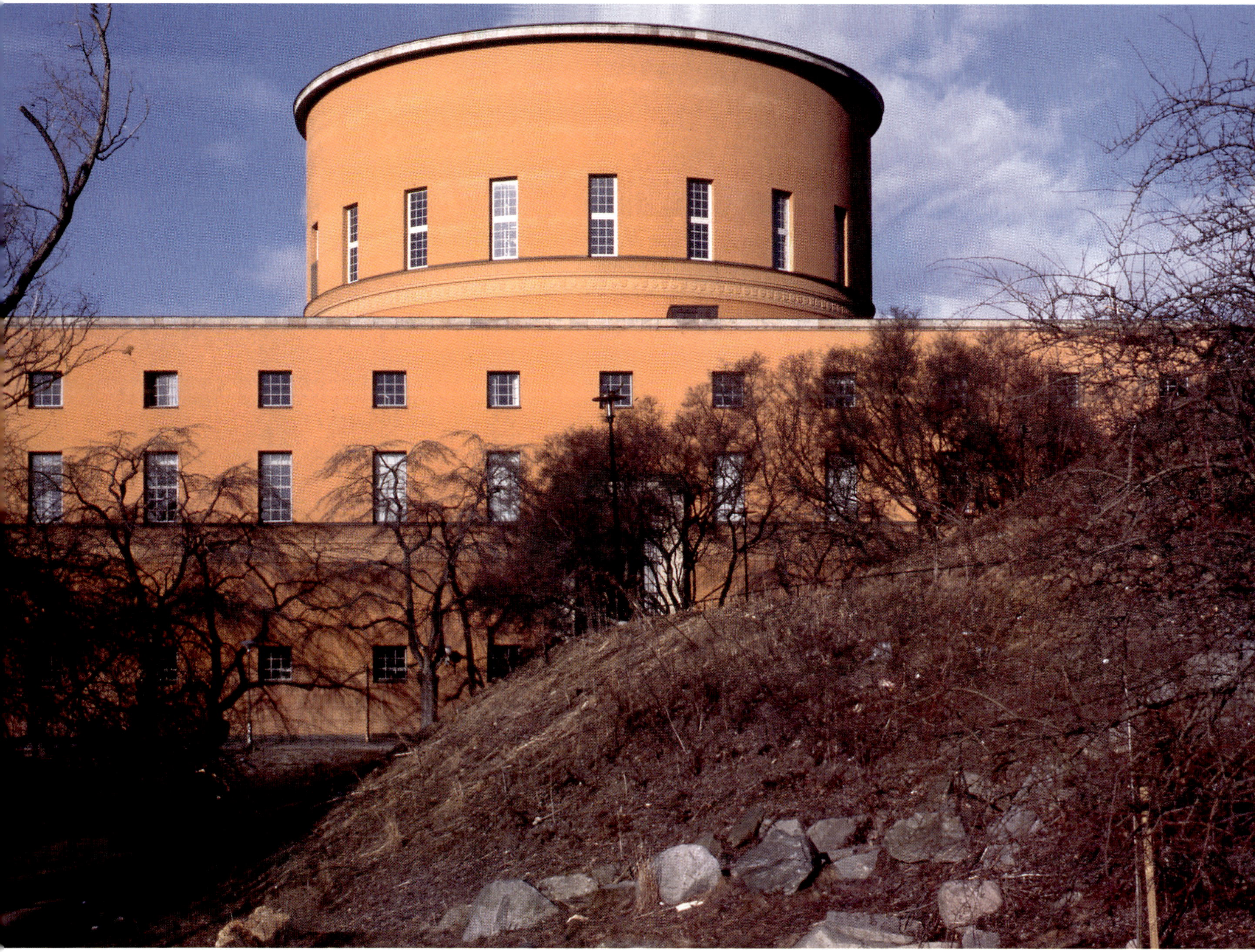

OPPOSITE: Exterior of Gunnar Asplund's Stockholm Public Library, 1919–28. The geometrical shapes that characterize this building appeared in much European work around 1920. Though the main building was finished earlier, the modern wing and landscaping, also by Asplund, were nearly complete at the time of Kahn's visit in 1928. *P. O. Fjeld.*

RIGHT: "Bokhallen," the book shelves encircling the main reading room of the Stockholm Public Library. *P. O. Fjeld.*

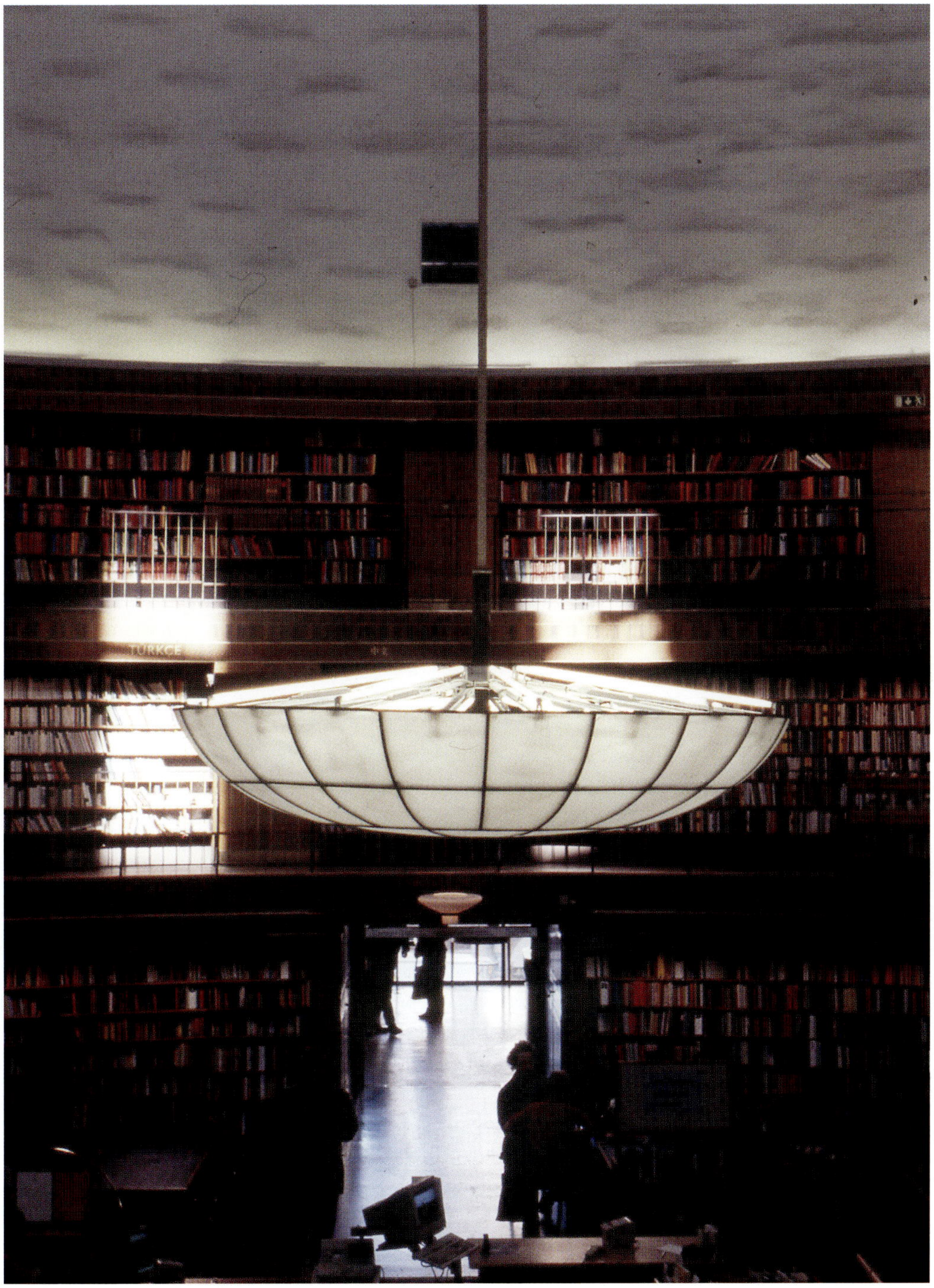

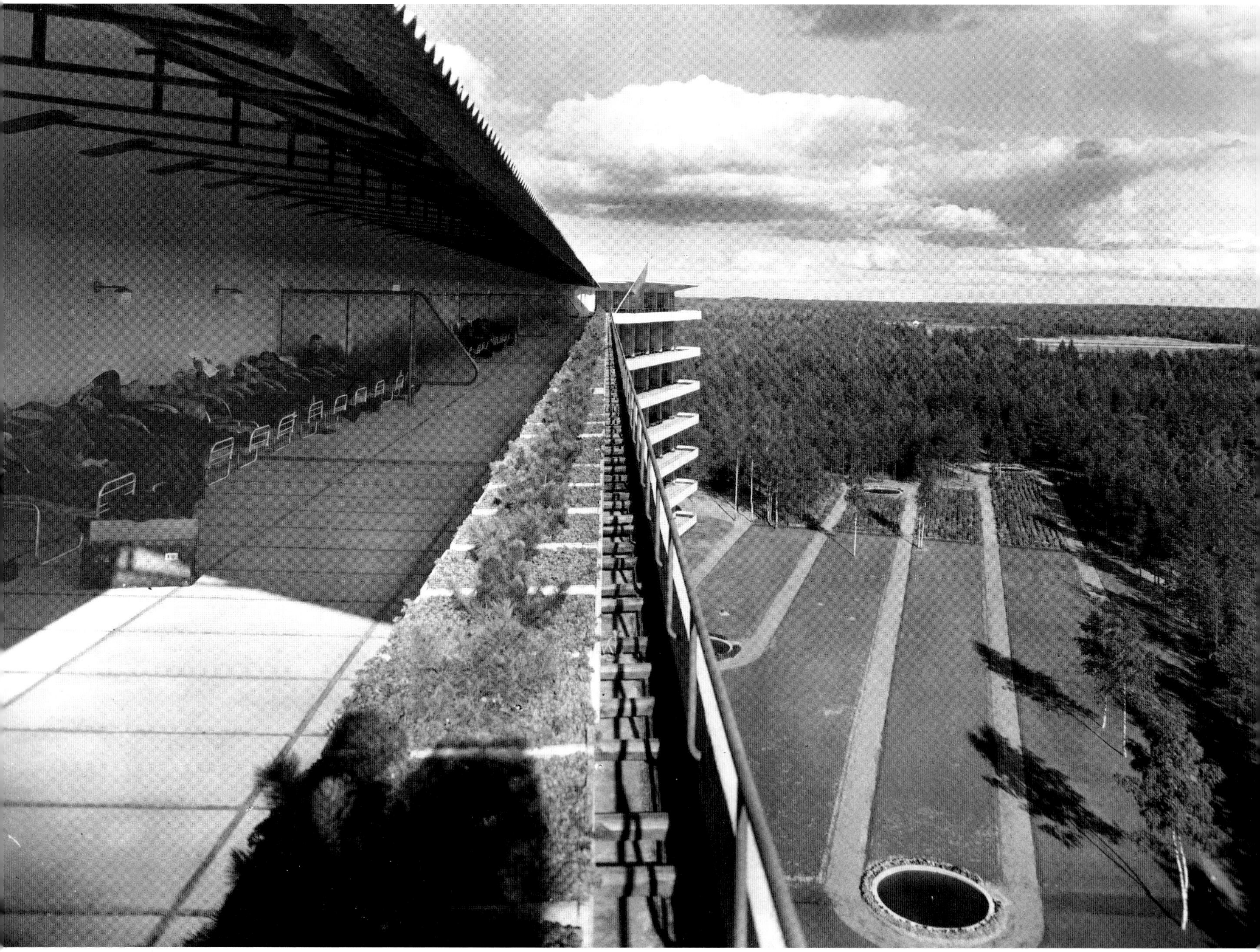

During this project they communicated regularly with Asplund, who was then working on the Stockholm Exhibition.

From Helsinki, Kahn moved on to Riga to visit his maternal grandmother, and from there, to the island of Saaremaa. How he divided his time between Riga and Kuressaare is somewhat unclear, but considering that much of his mother's family still lived and worked in Kuressaare it is likely that he had an extended stay there. In many ways Kahn's later comments on the sparse living conditions he experienced with his extended family need to be understood in relation to the general Nordic standard of living at the time as well as the limitations set by climate. The building types, materials, and the sizes of rooms on Saaremaa and in Riga were not unlike what was found throughout the Nordic region. The size of living spaces was limited by climate as well as heating costs; while food selection, which continued to be an issue for many well into the middle of the century, was limited by transportation costs. One of Kahn's few recorded memories of Saaremaa features a meal of plaice and small red potatoes, a traditional spring or early summer meal.[5] It was not an easy life, but within its simplicity was a precision connected to survival, and thus also joy in small seasonal pleasures.

Even in hard times, Riga was still an active trading and cultural center, and beautiful with its unusually numerous Art Nouveau buildings, which were constructed under czarist Russia and drew from St. Petersburg's architectural and craftwork milieus as well as German influences. In 1928 many of these buildings were in fairly good shape, as were the older sections of the city. After his stay in Riga, Kahn traveled down through the Continent, slowly working his way to Rome, by chance stopping in much the same places as Arne Korsmo at about the same time. The two-month period from when Kahn landed in the Netherlands until he boarded a train headed south in Riga has been summed up in a few sentences by most scholars; but in retrospect this part of his tour can be interpreted as an important factor in how he would later perceive and develop the concept of the "institutions of man." Both the Netherlands and the Nordic countries were undergoing profound grassroots political and social transformations that were inspirational for their architectural development, and this shift required a deeper questioning about the role of public institutions. In these countries, the resulting architectural transformations found easy acceptance from the general public and were quickly implemented into the existing built fabric, which was not necessarily the case further south on the Continent or in Great Britain. It is noteworthy that at this time, Nordic architectural publications' references to new projects abroad were not solely focused on German, French, or American production. That Nordic architects found a particular resonance in modern Dutch work is very relevant to modern Scandinavian architecture's later developments and concerns.

Alvar Aalto's Paimio Sanatorium, Finland, 1928–32. For Aalto, the orientation of the sanatorium played an essential role, since at the time of the building's construction there was a clear awareness of the importance of sunlight to health. His sophisticated placement of balconies and windows likewise took this into account. During the coldest months, daylight can last as little as five and a half hours at this latitude. *Alvar Aalto Museum. Photo: Gustav Welin.*

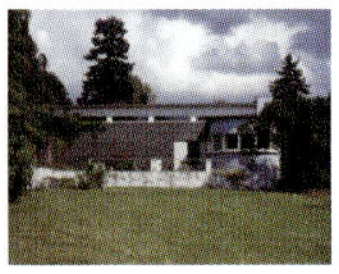
Villa Dammann designed by Korsmo and Aasland completed. *P. O. Fjeld.*

1933 CIAM IV held in Athens. Alvar Aalto's Paimio Sanatorium completed.

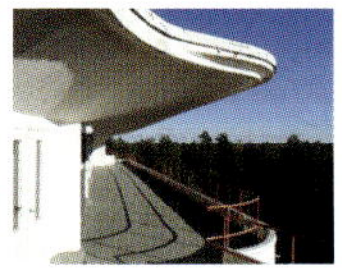
Paimio Sanatorium. *G.Welin, Alvar Aalto Museum.*

1934 John McAllister born.

Hendrik Berlage dies.

1935 Alvar Aalto's Viipuri (Vyborg) Library completed.

Jan Duiker dies.

Early German functionalist work and Le Corbusier's pavilion in the 1925 Paris Exhibition and his writings of the time were debated, admired, and adapted on some level throughout the Nordic region, but there was clearly hesitancy on the part of Nordic architects to adopt their formalist approach.

Not long after my return home to Norway in 1973, Christian Norberg-Schulz recounted how Louis Kahn and Arne Korsmo first met, and over the years he would return to that moment whenever we talked about Kahn. In the fall of 1928, the two young architects sat together on a train headed for Rome. By the time they had arrived, they decided to meet up again and visit sites together. Kahn had his sketchbook, and Korsmo also kept a diary. One of Korsmo's entries describes their shared visit to the temple at Paestum: "The yellow columns stood majestically side by side. Then the sun sank into the sea. The clouds turned green and the columns blazed a deep crimson. The sea was on fire, the sand golden—a last greeting from the sun god before the night fell. Far away across the plain lay the snow-covered mountains"[6] Korsmo's prose connected architecture to nature, pinpointing a fleeting moment within a sense of permanence.

During their time together, the two would have undoubtedly discussed their own architectural work and future aims, what was being built in the United States and Scandinavia, and probably their plans for the remainder of their trips. Korsmo's stay in Rome ended earlier than Kahn's; he left for Amsterdam with the primary goal of visiting Hilversham and Dudok. Like Aalto and Kahn months earlier, Korsmo visited the Zonnestraal Sanatorium; and his itinerary reflected Kahn's Dutch sketches, as he saw works by J. J. P. Oud and Henrik Berlage, the Olympic Stadium by Jan Wils, and an apartment block by J. Zietsma. As he left Rome, Korsmo recorded in his diary, "I was fascinated by all this history, but kept wondering if it would be possible to smuggle the same joy into the logic of our time." It is remarkable that the idea of joy in architecture had already entered his thinking, since both Korsmo and Kahn would return to this notion later in life.[7]

The Next Stage

In May of 1930, a year after Kahn returned home to Philadelphia, the Stockholm Exhibition opened, with Gunnar Asplund as its head architect and Gregor Paulsson as its director.[8] Asplund's modernist approach to the project was flawless and genuine, a straightforward expression of the social changes and the economic struggles of the time. The main buildings were open, light, and approachable, with a clear ambition to achieve a spatial and functional

1937 CIAM V held in Paris. Paris International Exposition includes pavilions by Korsmo, Aalto, Sakakura, and Sert. Frank Lloyd Wright inaugurates Taliesin West.

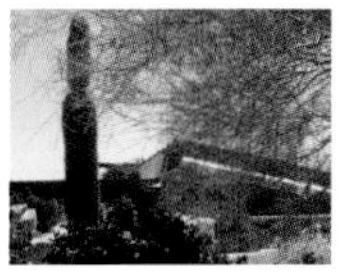

Taliesin West.
P. O. Fjeld.

1938 Aino and Alvar Aalto exhibition at the Museum of Modern Art in New York. Frank Lloyd Wright's Fallingwater completed.

1939 New York World's Fair. Aalto's Villa Mairea, designed for Harry and Maire Gullichsen, completed. Start of World War II. Finland invaded by Soviet Union.

clarity that could support daily life as an expression of joy—an ambition similar to what Kahn impressed upon us as students years later. There was an effort to reach out to and engage a large and varied public through architecture and objects that supported everyday living; the exhibition was not aimed at one specific group, nor shackled by pressure to appease a rigid formalized doctrine. Asplund and his team of architects were able to synthesize a modern Nordic sensibility with elements and tendencies from abroad; they were selective in choosing elements and brought forward spatial properties that had the capacity to respond to the transformations within Scandinavian society. A great deal of skepticism had preceded the exhibition's opening, but most criticism faded away quickly as the project's broad appeal and immediate impact was felt not just in Sweden but the Nordic region as a whole.

Lewerentz, Asplund's partner during the first stage of work on the Woodland Cemetery, designed all the lettering for the exhibition programs and other text material; its signage, including the much-published signposts; and a café, Gröna Udden. He also contributed two interesting, provocative housing entries. In addition, and to the benefit of all his colleagues involved in the exhibition, he set up a company to produce specialized windows to fulfill the new design criteria, as well as a workshop that experimented with electric signs. His contributions were clearly essential to the success of the event.

A large section of the exhibition addressed the need for inexpensive housing for a growing urban population. This area attracted many visitors, but the built, full-scale housing entries were widely criticized, since several works simply downscaled or minimized existing criteria found in the middle-class housing of the time. Aalto picked up on this problem in his reviews of the exhibition, but he nevertheless commented positively on the low-cost housing projects submitted by his friends Sven Markelius and Uno Åhrén. He noted that these works had "balanced forms of radicalism for a housing exhibition opposite of the artistic radicalism which is quite normal in a commercial world." He further commented that "they did not follow an action/reaction situation rather these projects developed."[9] In short, Aalto stressed, just as Kahn would point out later, the importance of finding the core of a project more than relying on newness as a catalyst.

Aalto ends his critique of the Stockholm Exhibition by noting that:

> *Kritisk Revy* once published a Tivoli photograph of a paper lantern in the branches of a tree over a café table. The caption was: eternal world. It is the same—that Stockholm Exhibition contains in all its outer physiognomy. "As a total effect there is no exhibition that competes with this," said Sigfried Giedion to me. "I consider Weissenhof as

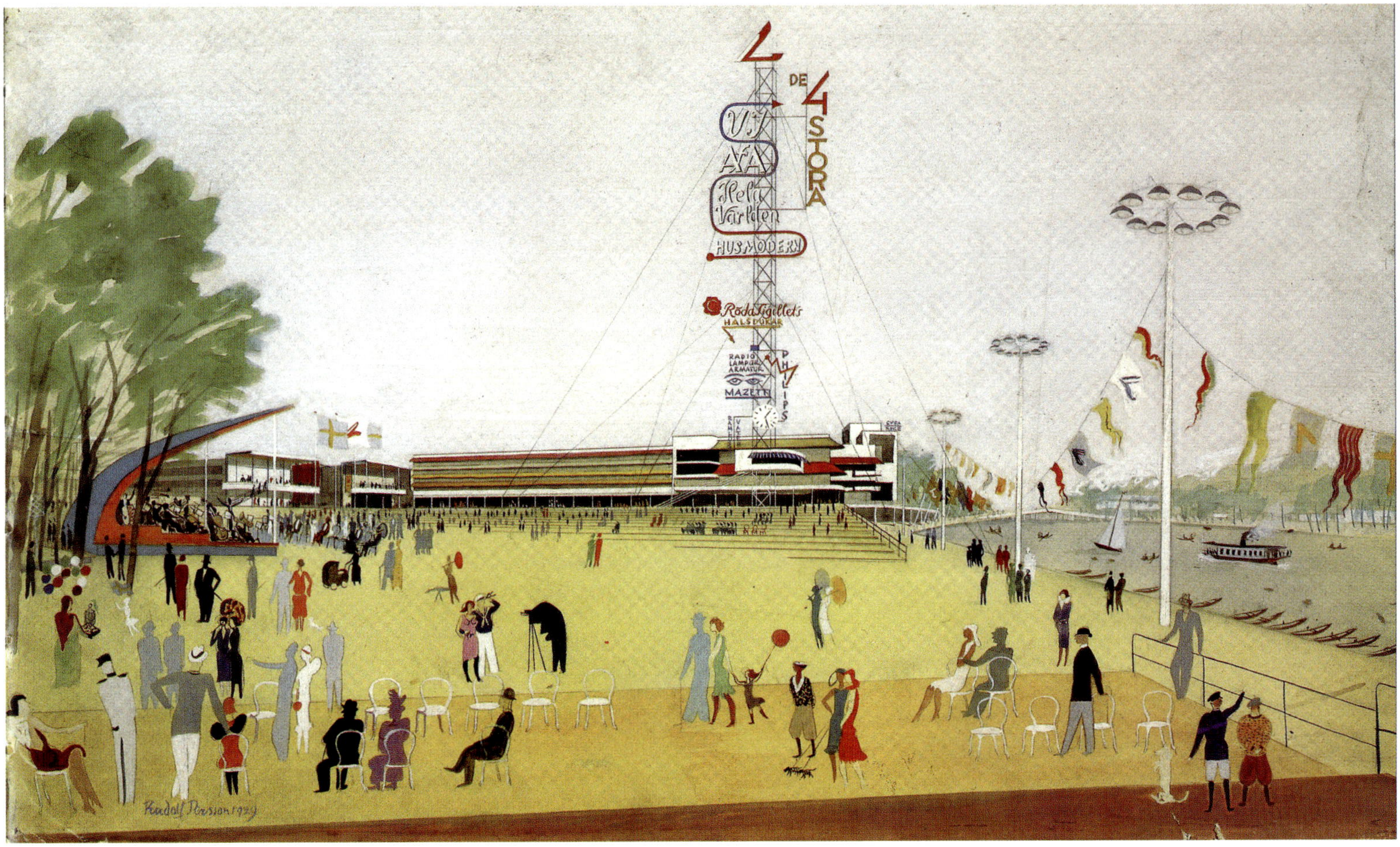

ABOVE: Painting of the Gunnar Asplund–designed Stockholm Exhibition of 1930. *The Swedish Centre for Architecture and Design, Stockholm.*

OPPOSITE: The main exhibition street of the Stockholm Exhibition of 1930 titled "Akseptera." *The Swedish Centre for Architecture and Design, Stockholm.*

> historically more important and perhaps also some of the Werkbundutställningar, but Stockholm . . ." I agree.[10]

Two years later, in 1932, the Museum of Modern Art in New York held an exhibition presenting the "International Style" to a broader American public. Its curators, Henry-Russell Hitchcock and Philip Johnson, had traveled throughout Europe deciding which works to include. They had visited many cities, including Stockholm, but their final selections were heavily biased toward a few individuals and countries considered frontrunners of the International Style. Åhrén's Flamman Soundfilm Theatre (1929) and Student Union Building (with Sven Markelius, 1930), a small housing development (siedlung) by Eskil Sundahl (1930), and Asplund's pavilions for the Stockholm Exhibition (1930) comprised Sweden's representation; notably, Lewerentz's café, Gröna Udden, was omitted. From Finland, Erik

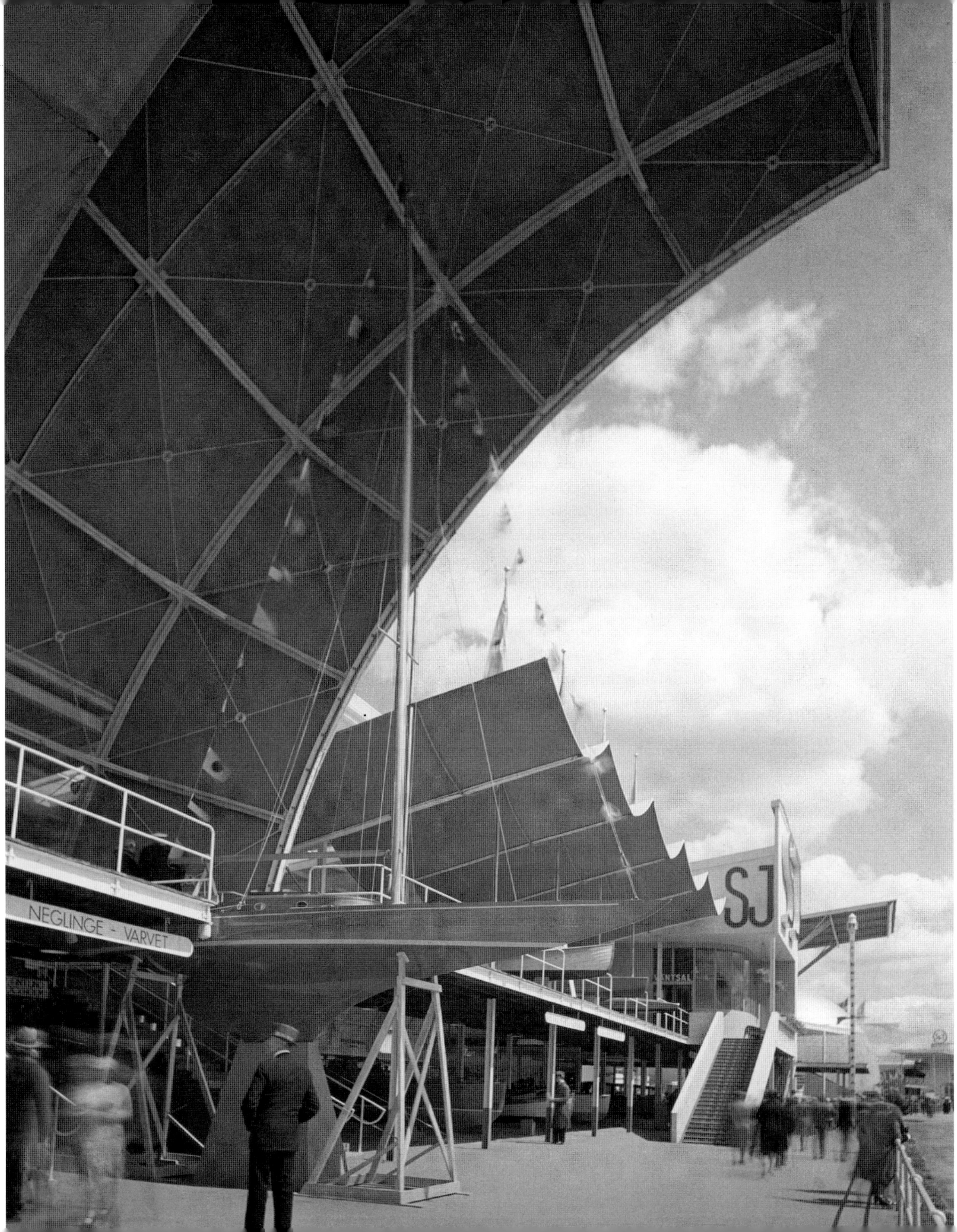
NEGLINGE - VARVET
SJ

Bryggman's pavilion in Antwerp (1929) was accepted, and Aalto's Turun Sanomat building (1930) was included at the last minute. But nothing from St. Petersburg, Denmark, or Norway—nor any modernist Nordic work made prior to late 1929—was included. Considering the breadth and quality of work, the Dutch representation was also somewhat limited. Meanwhile, Kahn expressed disappointment regarding the American projects that were selected.

Hitchcock and Johnson clearly prioritized style: the facade, the visual sensation of materials, and what they termed "volume." But in evaluating the works from a somewhat two-dimensional perspective, they undervalued the spatial integrity tied to material and tactile impact. In consequence, the curators' discussion was far more concerned with how the various works fulfilled their rather vague criteria in relation to style and visual appearance. Markelius's Student Union Building was therefore criticized for the thickness of its wood window frames, ignoring that it was a practical response to the use of glass in the Nordic climate; the curators indicated metal frames would have been stylistically more correct. Aalto's Turun Sanomat office building was also interpreted through a rather narrow visual focus, thus some essential features were overlooked and a broader discussion never materialized. Just the same, the exhibition had a profound effect on American architectural education and the American public's concept of what was being built in Europe and why. Unfortunately, since the exhibit presented the projects as the result of a few very influential architects, it left little possibility to appreciate parallel developments in other areas of Europe and the rest of the world. It was perhaps more telling in what it left out than in what it included.

Around the time of the exhibition, Kahn, through his activities in the Architectural Research Group, entered a city-planning competition for Stockholm's Lower Nøremalm district during the winter of 1932–33. His project did not attract notice, but due to his participation, one can infer he was aware of some developments in Scandinavia. Le Corbusier also submitted an entry, simply disregarding the brief by proposing to move the entire project further south of Stockholm. There was also an entry from Lewerentz, who, unlike most, did not focus on movement to and from the district, but rather on the district's core content—the reason for its existence.

Two Careers, Two Paths

At the time Louis Kahn returned home to Philadelphia in 1929 and Arne Korsmo returned to Oslo, the two architects' careers shared many concerns. But while Kahn was coping with the effects of the 1930 economic depression, Korsmo's small practice had a number of commissions and his future looked bright. He embraced a modernist approach and was considered an important young talent not only in Scandinavia, but also in Europe as a whole. Abreast of all that was changing both in relation to approach and materials, Korsmo was full of vigor and optimism as he translated many influences into his work yet retained a Nordic sensibility and expression that was his own. Not long after returning home he began work on Villa Dammann (which would become Sverre Fehn's home many years later). Sadly, in 1935, he contracted tuberculosis and had a lung removed. His long recovery took a toll on his office, and he began to teach at the Arts and Crafts School in Oslo in 1936. Just the same, he was actively involved in competitions and various national and international organizations and was able to secure interesting commissions for his small office.

In 1937 Korsmo was responsible, along with the architects Knut Knutsen and O. L. Schistad, for the Norwegian Pavilion at the World Exhibition in Paris. In the midst of growing international tension, many of the most powerful, politically influential nations reverted back to a monumental neoclassicism for their pavilions, while the smaller nations, including those from the Nordic community, presented work that revealed further interpretations of modernism, new technology, and an awareness of the specifics of their natural and cultural situations. This was the very exhibition where Aalto's Finnish Pavilion gained much international attention, which in turn led to the Aino and Alvar Aalto exhibition at the Museum of Modern Art the following year.

Despite the prewar tensions, the Paris event was a crossroads of new influences and architects—and this would have an impact on Korsmo's later work. During the event, Korsmo became better acquainted with Aalto and other Nordic architects; and the combined effect of the Finnish, Swedish, Norwegian, and Danish pavilions manifested a clear regional modern expression and cemented friendships and professional contacts. The impact of the Japanese Pavilion by Junzo Sakakura on the Nordic architectural milieu was apparent in the number of Nordic publications concerning Japan in the year that followed. In addition, Gio Ponti and other young Milanese architects had previously voiced admiration for modern Swedish design; the Paris exhibition was a starting point for the first initiatives toward a greater exchange between designers and architects from the Nordic region and Northern Italy. This exchange would bear fruit after the war.[11]

Aino and Alvar Aalto's exhibition at the Museum of Modern Art in 1938 and their Finnish Pavilion at the World's Fair in New York a year later were experienced as new and fresh relative to much of the modernist work that had been presented earlier in North America. Finland's nature and history and the expectations of a modern Nordic society, with its clear

1940 | Germany invades Norway and Denmark.

Peter Beherens and Gunnar Asplund die.

1941 | Nazi occupation of Saaremaa. Århus City Hall by Arne Jacobsen and Erik Møller completed.

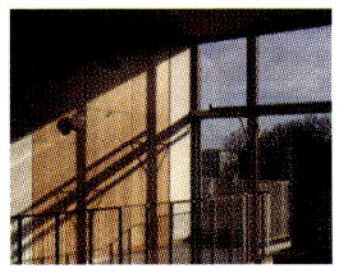

Interior of Århus City Hall. *P. O. Fjeld.*

1943 | Howe, Stonorov, and Kahn's Carver Court housing in Coatesville, PA, completed.

1945 | End of World War II.

Ragnar Östberg dies.

focus on public institutions, both influenced and gave precision to their work. All of this was appreciated by the visiting public, but perhaps only partially understood. Unfamiliar elements in their work were termed "individualistic," but in fact their Nordic background was the root of their inspiration and their link to the final expression.

Alvar Aalto and William Lescaze, one of the architects of the PSFS Building in Philadelphia, had been friends from about 1933; not long after, Kahn's friend George Howe, Lescaze's collaborator, was also an acquaintance. Howe, along with Wharton Esherick, presented the Pennsylvania Hill House at the exhibition America at Home in the same New York World's Fair of 1939. As with the Finnish Pavilion, a wooden interior set Howe and Esherick's project apart. Esherick's furniture for the pavilion has an interesting Nordic connection. A trip to Scandinavia in 1930 influenced Esherick's approach to furniture design, as he was struck by the pared-down simplicity and directness of early vernacular timber housing and furniture. Later, in 1956, Kahn designed an alteration and addition to Esherick's workshop.

Just prior to World War II, exhibitions and publications related to modern Nordic architecture were sporadic and somewhat limited in scope in North America. Work from Eliel Saarinen's office—which was in the odd position of being considered Nordic in America and American in Finland—and Aalto's projects toward the end of the 1930s were the only well-publicized new Nordic architecture at the time. Yet many influential universities and schools were strengthening their teaching staff with talent from central Europe, and these individuals set a new pedagogical agenda promoting their "international" relevance. Still, in a sense they arrived with only half a suitcase: they brought with them modernist expressions and new pedagogical ideas, but left behind the social and physical environments that had fostered their thinking and work.

During this period of economic depression, Kahn struggled to keep a job and make ends meet. He would stay active through various organizations such as the T Square Club. His commitment and support in relation to shared social values concerning architecture were recognized by many, but not always appreciated. In 1938 he worked on a competition to rehabilitate an impoverished area in Philadelphia; this was the basis of a partnership and friendship with George Howe and the start of his materializing ideas around social and low-income housing. Later, in collaboration with his partners Howe and Oskar Stonorov, he designed the Carver Court Housing, completed in 1943. The project gained recognition and new commissions for their office, and as a team the architects actively promoted social housing and community participation.

In 1944 Kahn published his article "Monumentality," and though its title may be somewhat

1946 | Saaremaa becomes a restricted zone in the Soviet Union.

Ferdinand Boberg dies.

1947 | CIAM VI, Bridgwater meeting. Ehle House project designed by Kahn and Abel Sørensen.

1948 | Alvar Aalto's MIT Baker House Dormitory completed. Aldo van Eyck initiates design for Nagele village. Jean Prouvé designs Ferembal Demountable House.

1949 | CIAM VII held in Bergamo. Ray and Charles Eames House completed. Korsmo's Fulbright trip begins in late fall.

Aino Aalto dies.

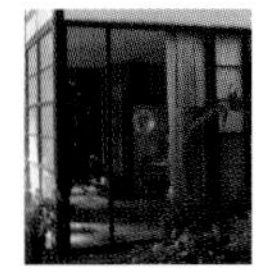

Eames House. *P. O. Fjeld.*

misleading, he used the term "monumentality" to search for an architecture that goes beyond functional program requirements. In the text he focused on the potential of new materials and new technologies and their capacity to release another form of monumentality, considering this a means to reach an architecture with a collective identity. One can see early developments here of what he later termed "the institutions of man." Kahn presented a reliance on structure as a key instrument for spatial identity, one that also carries an aesthetic integrity and an abstract dimension. This approach was related to much Nordic architectural discourse of the same period, as were the article's demands for new relationships between symbolism, representation, and abstraction in a changing society. Within the various Nordic publications of the time, there was no lack of interest in discussing how one should architecturally address the open, flat social structure of Nordic society and its institutions. In these discussions, the question of a new monumentality embedded in structural clarity as vital to spatial identity was often addressed.

Kahn expressed an admiration for ancient buildings and their inherent monumentality, but for him it was not a question of imitation but of learning from the past. Therefore he was concerned about the lagging position of architectural history as well as modernism's tunnel vision regarding functional aspects to verify value. Such concerns were likewise voiced by the Swedish architect Uno Åhrén only a few years after the Stockholm Exhibition of 1930. An adamant supporter of functionalism, Åhrén was nonetheless concerned that some elements within the new movement could potentially compromise integral Swedish attitudes in relation to society, culture, and the natural environment in order to meet questionable "functional" requirements. These same concerns were voiced by many Nordic architects, and Kahn must have been aware of this discussion on some level. In the North, style and the application of rigid definitions are not much to hold on to in a snowstorm. To put it as Aalto once did—the functionalists were not functional enough, in that they had not gone to the heart of the matter: *nature*.

Toward the close of World War II, Kahn's office was gaining momentum, but George Howe left the partnership in 1943 and Stonorov followed some years later. However, Anne Tyng stayed on, and her talent and structural intelligence were important to the work that followed. In 1947, Kahn was offered a teaching post at Yale at the last minute. Oscar Niemeyer had been the first choice, but political difficulties arose concerning his work visa. It was not an auspicious start for Kahn, but his talent as a teacher was soon recognized, as the student response was immediate and invigorating. The war years constituted a positive turning point for Kahn, quite different from Korsmo's experience of a fast-track career brought to an abrupt halt.

Finland was the first of the Nordic countries to feel the effects of the political changes just prior to World War II due to its precarious situation with the Stalinist Soviet Union. Soon after, Germany began its occupation of Norway and Denmark, and the political situation became much entangled. Even Sweden's fragile neutrality had an effect on the Nordic architectural community. Many public institutions were closed or severely controlled. Certain areas of the building industry were very active as a result of the war, but others came to a halt, and communication between the Nordic nations was difficult. Although Aalto was tempted by the prospect of teaching in the United States in 1939, he cut his engagement short and returned home to Finland. Scandinavian students and architects abroad were forced to return home or risk being stranded.

Like many other Nordic architects, Korsmo saw his bright career turned upside down. Having moved out of Oslo, he was finally forced to flee Norway to neutral Sweden, and he remained in Stockholm until 1945. This was unfortunate for his practice, but during his exile he met a number of influential Scandinavian architects and designers in the same situation. Perhaps the most important of his new acquaintances was his soon-to-be second wife, Grete Prytz (Kittelsen), an important postwar Norwegian designer. She was a good friend of Maire Gullichsen, who along with her husband Harry had engaged Aalto to build the Villa Mairea. Prytz's friendship with the Gullichsens began during the Paris exhibition of 1937, years before she married Korsmo, thus the couple had independent relationships to various groups and individuals in Finland. Another important contact who worked with Korsmo in the office of modernist Paul Hedquist was the Danish architect Jørn Utzon, also in exile. During this period Utzon, Korsmo, and a number of other Nordic architects formed a lively social network where much was discussed, including a growing interest in Asian architecture, in particular Japanese. The Danish Arne Jacobsen, another war refugee in Sweden, had been interested in certain aspects of Japanese architecture and gardens prior to the war, but upon returning home intensified and renewed this focus particularly in relation to gardening. It is said that the introduction just after the war of a certain bamboo species adapted to the Nordic climate was due to his efforts; some of the first bamboo used in landscaping projects in Norway, including those of Korsmo, arrived via Denmark. At the close of the war, Utzon and Korsmo agreed to meet at the teahouse of Stockholm's Ethnological Museum, and this occasion resulted in a number of articles on Japan. One of the most memorable, titled "Japan and the West's Architecture," includes their reflections on their meeting in the teahouse. Their shared captivation with Japanese architecture was now filtering into both men's postwar work. The Nordic region's attraction to Japan was not the result of a Parisian or Californian influence, but a direct response to and sense of kinship with the Japanese respect for materials at hand, daylight, and the relationship to the site as nature. Utzon soon made the first of his many visits to the East, but it would take some time before Korsmo visited Japan—and his travel companion on that trip would be Louis Kahn.

For Korsmo, exile in Stockholm was a period of reflection. Once home, his work shifted, became more experimental, with a greater focus on spatial and material investigations. Unfortunately, he never regained the steady activity that had characterized his office before the war. Shortages of materials beset all levels of society, and the acute need for architects and the lack of necessary funds meant that politically there was not much room for experimentation. In this early postwar period Korsmo and Utzon designed a number of projects and competitions together, but the political mood in Scandinavia moved toward something termed locally as "realism." The public, recovering from the trauma of occupation, sought familiar architectural images, approaches, and solutions to commissions. Though earlier Nordic social attitudes and motivations were still intact, project decisions were now directed by a narrow definition of basic needs, and this required quantifying and measuring the process and end results. An issue for many architectural milieus throughout Europe, this was the cause of a deep division inside CIAM once the meetings resumed. Also, because many talented European architects, often in search of better opportunities, had emigrated to the United States prior to or just after the war, many countries lacked the necessary architectural capacity and expertise for reconstruction work. The four-to-five-year gap in the education of new architects posed another challenge; but when finally in place, this young generation possessed a strong voice—a reaction, almost a skepticism, toward all past theory and dogma. Already in the first postwar CIAM meeting, it was apparent this new generation of young architects was searching for its own architectural content.

Sweden suffered far less economic and physical damage than the other Nordic nations, but the architectural community there experienced similar aftereffects of the war. There, essentially to jump-start the country's production, the surge to rationalize and systemize the building industry trickled down to the smallest details. Parallel with the efficiency upswing was a growing unease concerning the quality and inventiveness of this highly regulated work, and this duality affected both architectural education and the profession. All the same, the Nordic community came out of the war experience with their architectural institutions somewhat intact, since most architects had managed to survive and remain within the region and thus ensure that educational institutions retained a form of continuity.

In the fall of 1945, Korsmo returned to his teaching post in Oslo, and his classes were more experimental than ever. As Sverre Fehn recalled about Korsmo's class,

> We were tossed back and forth through art history with reckless subjectivity. Without dates. Without a plan. The way to Africa was via Leo Frobenius. The journey from Egypt to Neo-Classicism was never undertaken. Thirty years after Arne Korsmo's great lecture on Sumerian sculpture, I find myself standing in front of a display case in the Altes Museum in East Berlin. All of these Persian statues are suddenly mine.[12]

Over the years, several of Fehn's classmates recounted Korsmo's many comments and discussed his approach to teaching with me, and some elements are so similar to Kahn's terms and phrases that I never read them without thinking of the masterclass studio. Two better-known comments from Korsmo's teaching are: "The young child sees the dog before he is able to distinguish one dog from another" and "I am not able to teach within the differences of beautiful and ugly, neither can I discriminate the Renaissance over the Gothic."[13]

Korsmo's first class after the war consisted of a remarkable group of students who would later have a profound effect on Norwegian architecture. During this period Jørn Utzon traveled between Copenhagen and Oslo to work on various projects, including a chair for a competition held by the Museum of Modern Art in 1948 and various Norwegian architectural competitions and planning commissions. Some of Korsmo's early students were involved in this work and thus also acquainted with Utzon. In 1948 Utzon published an article titled "Arkitekturens Væsen" (The Nature of Architecture). The article touched upon issues close to Kahn's remarks on nature and materials but also reflected some very basic attitudes important to many Nordic architects of the time. Utzon's ambition was to reach an architecture that responded directly to the site—a connection that would be the origin and catalyst for its poetic simplicity. These architectural aims also placed the human clearly within the realm of nature, not outside it as an observer remote from its processes. Utzon's friend Sverre Fehn would say, "the animal in man," indicating that embedded in architecture is also an understanding of and respect for nature. This is remarkably close to "the laws of nature" and "the rules of man" that Kahn repeatedly brought up in the masterclass.

In the first years after the war, many young Scandinavian architects visited North America. Common among the travel reports and articles they produced upon returning home was a great enthusiasm for new work in the Midwest and California, but their impressions were otherwise somewhat reserved. One Swedish architect went so far as to suggest that perhaps so many Bauhaus stars heading the important North American architectural schools with almost no theoretical opposition was a problem. The Nordic interest in North America had stemmed for the most part from a need to redefine architecture in relation to the postwar situation, in light of growing dissatisfaction with job possibilities at home and the pressure to systemize all aspects of building production. This led to a somewhat naive notion that the situation in the United States was different. In general, Western building industries were quick to see the financial benefits of systemization, with the potential to control building processes, investment, creative input, and the workforce. These changes brought about greater formalization within the architectural curriculum, which both Kahn at Yale University and Korsmo at the Oslo School of Architecture experienced firsthand.

The Postwar Situation

Gropius appointed Korsmo to the education committee for the 1949 CIAM meeting in Bergamo. Korsmo decided to make the long drive to Bergamo, which gave him the opportunity to visit various projects along the way. Reconstruction was now well underway throughout Europe; work on Le Corbusier's Unité d'habitation had begun, and new attitudes and inventiveness in relation to housing and public buildings were surfacing everywhere, including Northern Italy. Meanwhile, the meeting's location ensured that many important Italian postwar architects and teachers were actively involved in the event. A number of these architects would soon become acquaintances of Korsmo and, within the next ten years, of Kahn. The ideas that surfaced at Bergamo arrived fresh with Korsmo when he visited Kahn in Philadelphia only months later.

The architects on CIAM Bergamo's education committee represented a mix of generations and nationalities, as well as competing agendas. One group endorsed loyalty to prewar ideas and icons, while architects from a younger generation demanded changes in attitudes within the profession and a different type of collective openness. Some called for greater conformity in architectural education. It was at this meeting that Gropius presented his Twelve Points on education, which were published and reviewed in some form by most of the attending nations. Although Korsmo and Gropius shared many ideas about education, their philosophies were not entirely aligned. Now, as a committee member appointed by Gropius and labeled a rationalist, Korsmo was caught in the middle of growing tensions, and his position between two generations of architects would affect his relationship with Team 10 (the group

1950 Kahn leaves for the American Academy in Rome in late fall. Kahn's Weiss House completed. Kenzo Tange commences work on the Peace Center in Hiroshima. Mies van der Rohe begins work on Crown Hall at the Illinois Institute of Technology. Bengt Edman and Lennart Holm complete the "New Brutalist" Villa Göth in Uppsala. Josef Albers begins work on his series *Homage to a Square*. Eliel Saarinen dies.

1951 CIAM VIII held in Hoddesdon. Korsmo returns to the United States. Mies van der Rohe's Farnsworth House completed. Franco Albini's Municipal Gallery of Palazzo Bianco completed. Junzo Sakakura's Kamakura Museum of Modern Art inaugurated. Steen Eiler Rasmussen's *Towns and Building* first published in English (two years after the Danish edition).

1952 Le Corbusier's Unité d'habitation completed. Franco Albini begins work on the Municipal Gallery of Palazzo Rosso (1952–62). Sven Markelius designs the interiors for the United Nations Secretariat Building.

of architects who created a schism within CIAM beginning in 1953) and his position at the CIAM Otterlo meeting later.

To illustrate the complexity and tension within the Nordic discussions and tie these to certain aspects of the debate happening within the United States at the time, the activities of the Swiss historian Sigfried Giedion are again interesting to follow. Prior to the CIAM Bergamo meeting, Giedion gave a heated lecture in Oslo, the bulk of which concerned the postwar situation. New architectural influences from abroad were visible within the Nordic region, but as had been the case earlier, Nordic architects adapted and transformed these influences in relation to their own natural environment and regional cultural/social situation. New work that evolved out of this was not merely a provincial interpretation, but rather a parallel development with a different architectural premise at its core.

Giedion opened his Oslo lecture by calling the new Swedish architecture "a charming, beautiful girl who can commit any sin and be forgiven because she sins so charmingly, and it would be a break with etiquette to measure her with a common yardstick."[14] He went on to discuss an article in the *Architectural Review* from 1948 concerning "New Empiricism," in which "coziness" was the byword. Giedion also made a reference to Lewis Mumford's notion of the "Bay Region Style" and his call for a more human approach to modernism. Giedion then proceeded to read Marcel Breuer's curt rebuttal to Mumford's Bay Region Style. In the end, Giedion turned to the 1947 Bridgwater CIAM meeting and the input from the British MARS group that pressed for a more sociological approach. Giedion was caught between prewar functionalist ideals and the evolving mind-set of postwar realities.

There were a number of rebuttals to Giedion's speech, from both local Oslo and Swedish architects, but in the context of Uno Åhrén's prewar concern in relation to functionalism, this discussion was not new to the Nordic region. A few weeks after Giedion's speech, Richard Neutra was the guest lecturer in Oslo. The event, sponsored by the Oslo Chapter of the Norwegian Architects Association, was so packed that many were turned away for lack of space. The audience was eager to hear Neutra's lecture, but not within the context Giedion had presented two weeks earlier. It was Neutra's lightweight structures and relationship to the landscape that were of interest.

In a discussion with Sverre Fehn about the upstart PAGON—the Norwegian group for CIAM in which Giedion was heavily involved in its initial phase in 1950—Fehn commented about the divisions, the different groups, and various roles influential architects played in CIAM. He mentioned Korsmo's enthusiasm and interest in CIAM, and how he shared his experiences and acquaintances with the young members of PAGON. He talked about the

Dutch groups De 8 and Opbouw (and in particular the Nagele project that Aldo van Eyck designed while involved in De 8) and the young French groups Les Jeunes and ASCORAL. Important in the context of Kahn, Fehn's early knowledge and admiration of van Eyck's work stemmed from Korsmo.

When I first read the many postwar travel reports by Nordic architects, the various articles concerning the need for a new pedagogical approach in both architecture and planning, and, not least, Giedion's Oslo lecture, I was reminded of all the contention that evolved over the years in CIAM prior to the Otterlo meeting. I reflected on Kahn's friend and former partner George Howe, who as chair of the Yale School of Architecture in the early 1950s oversaw changes in pedagogy and curriculum; and on Dean G. Holmes Perkins's situation at the University of Pennsylvania. Perkins was influenced as a planner by the doctrines he encountered at Harvard under Gropius and Breuer, and yet as the new dean at the University of Pennsylvania, the first person he hired was Lewis Mumford. Not long after, he hired Kahn.

New Connections

In the fall of 1949 Arne Korsmo received a Fulbright–Hays grant for an extended visit to the United States, with the primary goal of researching new teaching methods. The pedagogical output of the late László Moholy-Nagy, who founded the Institute of Design in Chicago (now part of Illinois Institute of Technology), constituted one main focus of his trip. After stopping first in New York, Korsmo and Grete Prytz went straight to visit Kahn in Philadelphia, staying for a number of days. From there the couple followed Kahn up to Yale, where an exhibition by Josef Albers made a deep impression and, by chance, Korsmo met Eero Saarinen. The couple continued north to Boston, visiting Gropius at Harvard and stopping to see Adelbert Ames Jr.'s perception studies in New Hampshire.

From New England the Korsmo couple traveled to Chicago with an invitation from Edgar Kaufmann Jr., who introduced them to Mies van der Rohe and Frank Lloyd Wright. Another highlight of the trip was an invitation from Edith Farnsworth to stay in the nearly completed house that Mies had designed for her. Grete Prytz was scheduled to participate in a course at the Institute of Design, and she ended up teaching and giving a guest lecture there as well. Korsmo made a stop at Saarinen's office, and at some point, Jørn Utzon, also on a Fulbright–Hays grant, and his wife, Lis, joined him and Grete Prytz. The two couples bought a used car and continued the trip together, stopping at Taliesin and Taliesin West and hiking with Wright in the desert. Then they moved on to California to see Neutra's and Schindler's work among

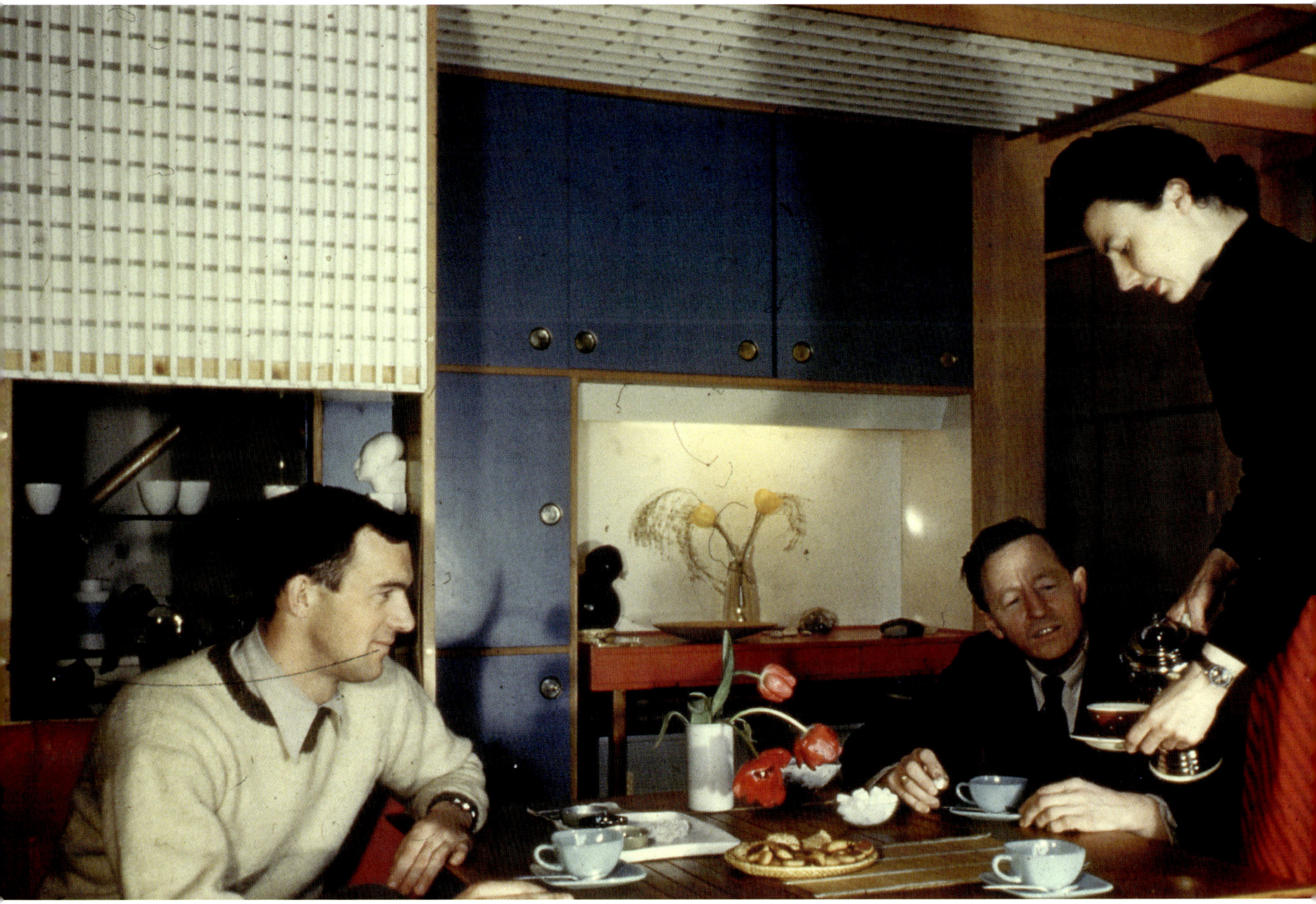

others', and, finally, to visit the newly finished home of Charles and Ray Eames. This last stop in the United States was the beginning of a lifelong friendship between the three couples. They spent the remainder of their trip in Mexico and Guatemala visiting ancient sites. Utzon would later refer to the impact of these buildings in relation to his understanding of the platform.

A curious circle of overlapping acquaintances was formed, and Kahn was part of the story. At this point, these connections were still somewhat loose, but the trip would have a great influence on Korsmo's creativity and teaching in the coming years. Along with Josef Albers's work at Yale and his new pedagogical approach to color, which Korsmo later phased into his own courses, and a genuine interest in Mies van der Rohe's new work in Chicago—what made a lasting impression on Korsmo was not the Bauhaus masters' work in the United States, but rather his visits with Kahn and the Eames couple and new work built in the West of the United States. These impressions gave new vitality and direction to both his work and pedagogy once home.

Korsmo's visit to Philadelphia and New Haven raises some interesting questions related to Kahn's three-month stay at the American Academy in Rome. Toward the end of 1950, a few months after Korsmo returned home, Kahn departed for Rome and then received the commission for the Yale University Art Gallery while he was abroad. George Howe, then dean at the Yale School of Architecture, had also recently spent time at the American Academy in Rome, so it is reasonable to assume some discussion of sites and interesting new work in advance of Kahn's trip. There is no doubt that the ancient ruins and architecture depicted in Kahn's sketches were deeply inspirational, but it is difficult to believe that Kahn remained solely focused on ancient works during this formative trip, especially since he received the Yale University Art Gallery commission toward the end of his stay. During Korsmo's time in Philadelphia, did he and Kahn discuss the new postwar architecture then unfolding in Northern Italy?

Just after Kahn's arrival in Rome, he wrote back to his office:

> What is necessary is the interpretation of the architecture of Italy as it relates to our knowledge of building and needs. I care little for the restorations (that kind of interpretation) but I see great personal value in reading one's own approaches to the creation of space modified by the buildings around as the point of departure. I find it quite difficult translating the masonry construction into steel and concrete and I intend to talk to the Fellows, explore their reactions as to what they see into similar aims. They are quite excited about my idea.[15]

Jørn Utzon (left) visiting Grete Prytz and Arne Korsmo in their Oslo apartment after their return from the United States in the early fall of 1950. Many of the interior elements first tested here would later reappear in their home on Planetveien. *Property of Margrete Refsdal.*

At the time he sent this letter, Kahn had not yet traveled north in Italy, nor to Egypt and Greece. Le Corbusier's Unité d'habitation is often mentioned as a possible influence on his work once he returned home, but the complex was a building site at the time of his trip, though it had been published very early in the building process and commentary about it spread quickly. In light of this speculation, it is important to note that the same postwar situation that fostered Unité d'habitation was unfolding elsewhere in Europe due to the same housing needs and scarcity of materials. Also, in Northern Italy at the time of Kahn's trip there were several very interesting new exhibitions, gallery reconstruction work, and new buildings within close proximity to Rome.

At about the same time as Kahn's Academy stay, a concerted effort was made to encourage the Nordic countries to participate in the Milan Triennale. Finland, Denmark, and Sweden entered in 1951; and in the following Triennale of 1954, Norway was represented by Korsmo and Grete Prytz, who won the prestigious Grand Prize. In the Triennale of 1957, Aalto was involved in setting up the exhibition through his connection with Gio Ponti; Arne Jacobsen won a gold medal for his FH4130 stacking chair; and Korsmo and Prytz exhibited work that likewise earned a gold medal. (Interestingly, Kahn received an invitation to present his Mill Creek housing project at this Triennale, but it appears his office did not follow up on the invitation.) The push for Nordic participation in the Milan Triennale resulted in a network that included, among others, Aalto, Luigi Nervi, Ignazio Gardella, Franco Albini, and Gio Ponti. This connection would result in the exhibition New Italian Architecture in Stockholm and Helsinki in 1953. Albini's work, which clearly influenced Korsmo's design work after the war, was presented in this Nordic exhibition.[16] A push to establish a center for Italian culture in Stockholm coincided with these events: the Italian Culture Institute by Ponti and Nervi was inaugurated in 1958.

All these activities were unfolding during the time frame of Korsmo's visit to the United States, Kahn's trip to Rome, and Anne Tyng's Rome stay in 1953–54. Nervi's work was well published in the United States, so it is not surprising that Tyng originally intended to work in his office on a Fulbright–Hays grant. Meanwhile, Kahn's Rome letters to Tyng indicate that he was clearly familiar with the postwar developments in Milan and Northern Italy and the impact of Nervi's work. In his correspondence with Tyng, he notes that the new approach to space and structure found in Nervi's designs was not necessarily reflected in the schools in Rome.

At the time of Kahn's Rome Academy visit in 1951, Franco Albini's office had completed a number of interesting projects, including several exhibition and museum interiors; both the Venetian exhibition at Brera Gallery in Milan and the Municipal Gallery of Palazzo Bianco in Genoa were completed by this time. Kahn's Yale University Art Gallery echoes sensibilities

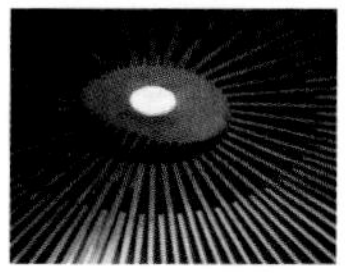

Roof structure from the interior of the Museum of the Treasury of San Lorenzo by Franco Albini. *Courtesy of the Municipality of Genoa, dir. Musei di Strada Nuova.*

present in Albini's exhibition work—a parallel approach in relation to primary structure, light, and material. This influence is further apparent in work in Genoa of a slightly later date—the Municipal Gallery of Palazzo Rosso and the Museum of the Treasury of San Lorenzo. These works reflect much of what Kahn mused over in his first letter to the office from Rome. His original plans for the Yale University Art Gallery, with their lack of secondary walls and their introduction of "pogo" display structures, reflect his intention for a clear separation between a primary structure and any type of additional structural elements. He articulated a concern for such separation in my masterclass over twenty years later. Albini, like Kahn, was very sensitive to how different spaces connected to create a spatial integrity, and to this end, in a 1954 lecture on architecture and exhibitions, he commented,

> To achieve this result one must, in my view, employ spatial solutions rather than plastic solutions: one must create architectural spaces, or underline existing ones, connecting them in absolute unity with the works exhibited. It is in my opinion that what must be constructed are precisely the voids, because air and light are construction materials. The atmosphere should not be still and stagnant, but vibrant, and the audience should feel immersed and stimulated, without noticing what is happening.[17]

Another interesting connection related to Kahn's development in the latter half of the 1950s also began with the 1949 CIAM Bergamo meeting. Korsmo met the Dutch architect Aldo van Eyck there, and he was very impressed by van Eyck's plan for the Nagele project. He was quick to share what van Eyck discussed at the meeting with his students back in Oslo, as Fehn later noted to me. Kahn and Korsmo's brief visit in Philadelphia in the late fall of 1949 indicates the possibility of a robust sharing of ideas and acquaintances between the two men. (An exhibition the following year in Chicago brought Korsmo back to the United States, and he returned again in 1954 to attend the opening of a design exhibition that included some of his and Grete Prytz's work; but it is uncertain whether the two friends saw one another during these visits.)

At the time of Korsmo's first American trip and Kahn's stay in Rome, the generational shift in architectural work and education was quite apparent. The older, established CIAM leadership, aware of the dissatisfaction of the younger architects, partially conceded the organization was faltering. Kahn and Korsmo belonged to the generation caught between these two factions: they were fifteen or twenty years younger than the original CIAM members, and about twenty years older than most of the future Team 10 members. In 1950, Giedion contacted Korsmo about setting up a national subgroup for young architects similar to the

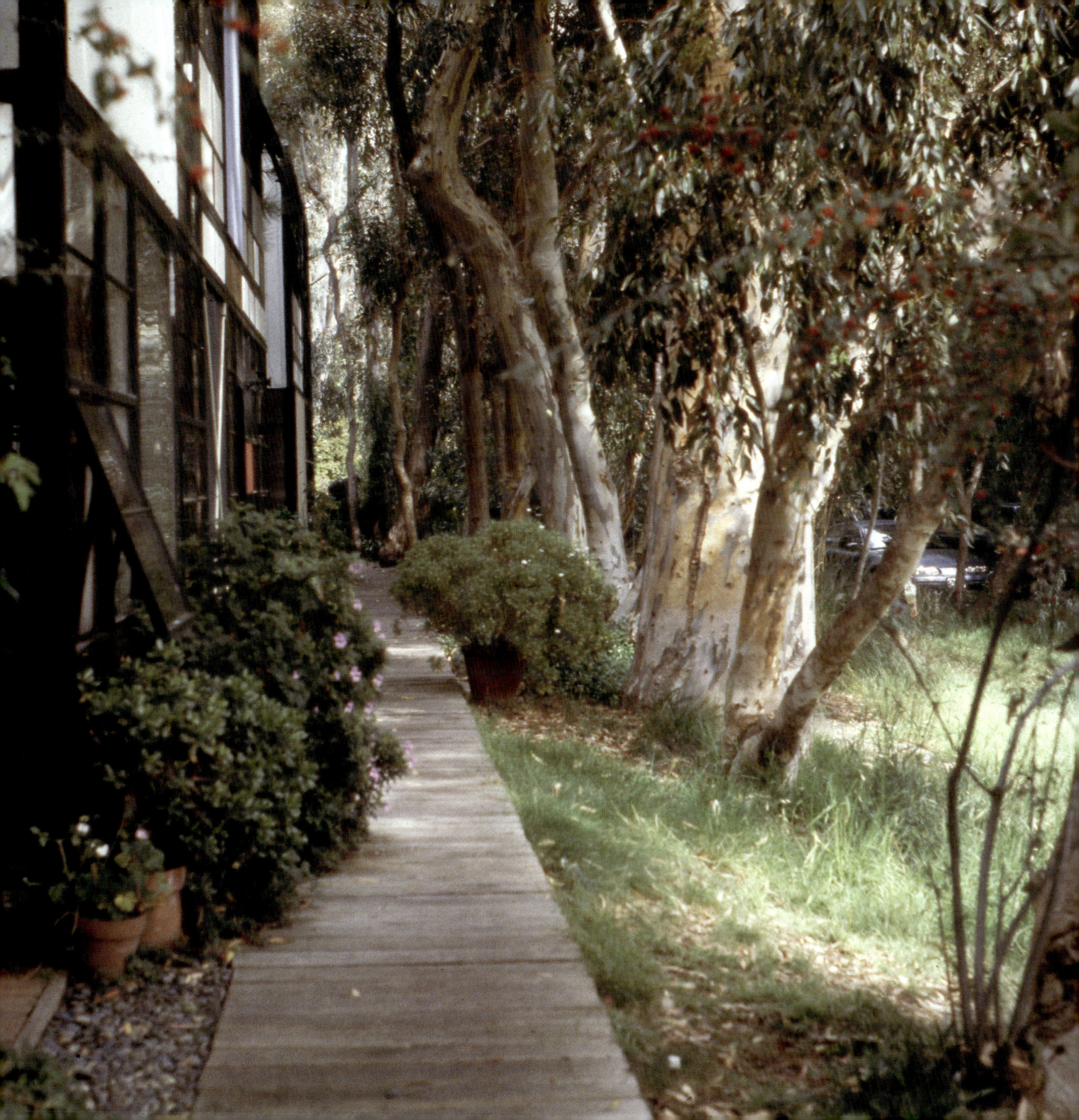

groups in Great Britain (MARS), Holland (De 8 and Opbouw), and France (Les Jeunes). The Norwegian group (PAGON) mentioned earlier included, among other progressive young architects, Christian Norberg-Schulz; Sverre Fehn and his early partner Geir Grung, an original Team 10 member; and Odd Østbye, a close friend of Fehn's. Utzon was also a supporter of PAGON and joined the group whenever possible (although he did not attend any of the CIAM meetings nor later Team 10 events, despite invitations).

In 1952 PAGON published a statement concerning CIAM's aims. The statement flippantly asked, "What difference does it make that one saves a housewife two steps when she has in the meantime divorced?"[18] This comment questioned the validity of some of CIAM's prewar criterion in a postwar reality, particularly in relation to functionalism's tenets. Korsmo, who continued to attend CIAM meetings throughout the decade, remained caught in the middle: on the one hand, he was concerned with ideas and work promoted by the earlier generation; on the other, he questioned CIAM's future if it did not face the evolving social and economic changes. Curiously, the changes that Korsmo's first American trip had brought about in his late work never seemed to override the perception of him as a functionalist or rationalist in the narrowest of definitions. (Kahn's work would suffer similar trend-oriented interpretations: in relation to New Brutalism in the mid-1950s and then postmodernism toward the end of his life and posthumously.)

When Kahn returned home from Rome, work on the Yale University Art Gallery began at once, and his reputation as an important teacher was established. When the gallery was completed, this work propelled Kahn into an international focus. A half year earlier, Korsmo had returned home from the United States full of new impressions and vigor, but the Norwegian postwar economy was slow to recover. In this period of transformation, a younger generation was beginning to fill the void created by the loss of architectural mentors like Asplund, and new connections between the Nordic nations were forming.

Before his trip, Korsmo's small apartment near the Oslo School of Architecture had been packed with students experimenting with small spatial installations; when he returned from the United States, he moved into a larger apartment and set up an experimental course over two years with a focus on light and color, complemented by 1:1 test models built at the school. But despite all of Korsmo's international activities, professional connections, and enthusiasm, his situation at the Oslo School of Architecture was becoming more and more strained and open to attack. His programs were explorative, impossible to measure, and often at odds with the attitudes of his colleagues—altogether, a situation remarkably similar to that of Kahn's later years at Penn.

Charles and Ray Eames House, Pacific Palisades, California. With Grete Prytz and Jørn and Liz Utzon, Korsmo visited the Eames House during his first trip to the United States in 1950. The house was clearly a strong inspiration for Korsmo's own house on Planetveien in Oslo. *P. O. Fjeld.*

1958 Kiyonori Kikutake's Sky House completed. Kenzo Tange's Kagawa Prefectural Government Hall completed. Eero Saarinen's David S. Ingalls Rink in New Haven completed. Jørn Utzon's Kingo Houses completed. Mies van der Rohe's Seagram Building completed.

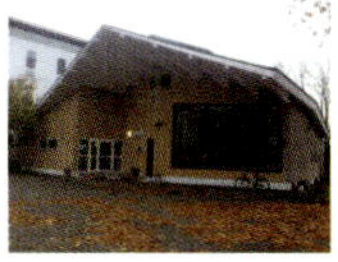

Ponti and Nervi's Italian Culture Institute in Stockholm inaugurated in 1958. *P. O. Fjeld.*

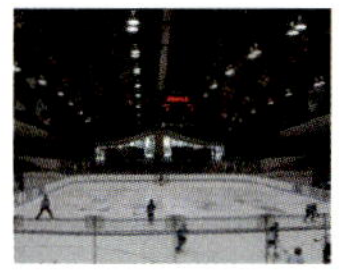

David S. Ingalls Rink. *Elisa Grindland.*

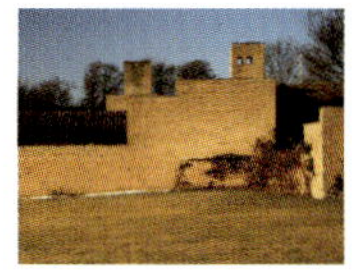

Kingo Houses, Denmark. *Arne Eggen.*

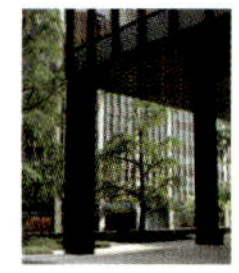

Mies van der Rohe's Seagram Building. *Elisa Grindland.*

About Korsmo's work of the time, critics remarked on a Japanese influence and affinities with the Eames House; but there were also elements from Kahn's Weiss House, which was just finished when he visited Philadelphia. Sverre Fehn noted to me several times that when returning to Paris by train with Korsmo after Le Corbusier's opening of the Unité d'habitation at the Aix-en-Provence CIAM meeting in 1953, Le Corbusier was not the topic of their conversations: Korsmo talked only about the Eames couple the entire trip home.

By the mid-1950s, Korsmo and Grete Prytz had won a number of international design prizes and exhibitions and were at a peak of international exposure. During this period Korsmo completed his last commissions in Oslo, including a row-house complex that incorporated a design for his own home (1953–56). In this project, he developed what he called a Mekano House, which deployed an Erector Set–like flexibility. Many have connected this aspect to principles from Mies van der Rohe, in whom Norberg-Schulz, one of Korsmo's collaborators on the project, had a great interest as a student a Harvard. Indeed, the row houses include some clear reapplications of Miesian details and ideas. But when understood through Korsmo's own comments, this Erector Set–like flexibility can also be seen as a way to physically involve the user, in that the size and weight of all the building's parts are combined with regard to what an individual can physically manage and what was feasible in relation to the climate and specific site conditions. Norberg-Schulz remarked that the project constituted three variations on a single theme; each unit addressed a living, active situation—"work as an expression of living," as Korsmo would say. The interplay between the "workrooms," the inhabitants' comings and goings, and the direct and indirect physical interaction with the natural surroundings was essential. In this light, Charles and Ray Eames, Prouvé, and Albini seem far more relevant as possible influences. Korsmo had a fundamental interest in how things were made and how they worked, but this did not override his deeper concern for core human issues. While far-flung influences are certainly apparent in the project, it also reflects a Nordic sensibility and way of living.

More Connections

Throughout the 1950s, several architects who would later be active in Team 10, and also a number of Nordic architects, lectured or taught in the United States. The Danish architect and historian Steen Eiler Rasmussen, for instance, made several visits to teach and lecture in the United States—at MIT and Harvard in 1953, Yale in 1954, and the University of Pennsylvania as a guest professor in 1958. In a 1965 article for *Perspecta 9/10: The Yale Architectural*

Journal, Kahn would recall a later meeting in which Rasmussen provided feedback concerning his plans for the Citadel of Assembly in Dhaka:

> I spoke to Mr. Steen Eiler Rasmussen about the deliberate separation of the two citadels and he has inspired me to look into this decision and sense whether the two can be brought together and have a greater meaning than the meaning of looking across the separating park at each other. I felt that their being separate was good, living on different planes of inspiration. But Mr. Rasmussen knows the beginnings of towns in their essence so beautifully that I feel that this plan needs a thorough review before I can feel confident about the belief which is in back of it.[19]

Ushering in another cross-cultural endeavor, Eero Saarinen began work on the American Embassy in Oslo in 1954. Saarinen's second wife wrote fondly of a family stay in the city during the embassy's construction and stated that this trip was one of the few actual vacations the couple had had together. Saarinen commented on the positive public acceptance of his embassy in Oslo compared to the reception of his similarly designed chancellery in London; he was impressed by the broad acceptance of modern work in Norway. Kahn and Saarinen maintained fairly regular, though brief, correspondence throughout this period. Any concrete record of contact between Korsmo and Saarinen during this time is difficult to trace, but the local architects responsible for the on-site work in Oslo were well known to Korsmo.

Kahn's work on Wharton Esherick's studio (1955–56) and, later, Margaret Esherick's house (1959–62), likewise brings to mind the Nordic connection, albeit slight, of Wharton Esherick's visit to Norway with the German artist Hanna Weil in 1930. He recalled with enthusiasm "those old Norse log house(s), filled with tools, tables, beds, tankards wonderful in their simplicity and variety yet over it I felt a great love, the workman's love of materials, love of the use of objects, love of the family for which they were made, how they loved a log, loved the grain house which kept their food."[20] These same timber houses intrigued Kahn for the same reasons during his visit to Oslo in 1966.

Adding to this Nordic American mixture was the Danish American architect Abel Sørensen, who worked in Kahn's office while Stonorov was still a partner, and who later collaborated on the design for the Ehle House project (1947–58). Meanwhile, Sørensen was designing furniture and gaining some recognition and commissions. In this capacity his path may have crossed with Grete Prytz's and Korsmo's, as they seemed to have had many shared acquaintances. Kahn appears to have kept in touch with Sørensen after he left the office, particularly while he worked in the United Nations Planning Office in New York; in this capacity

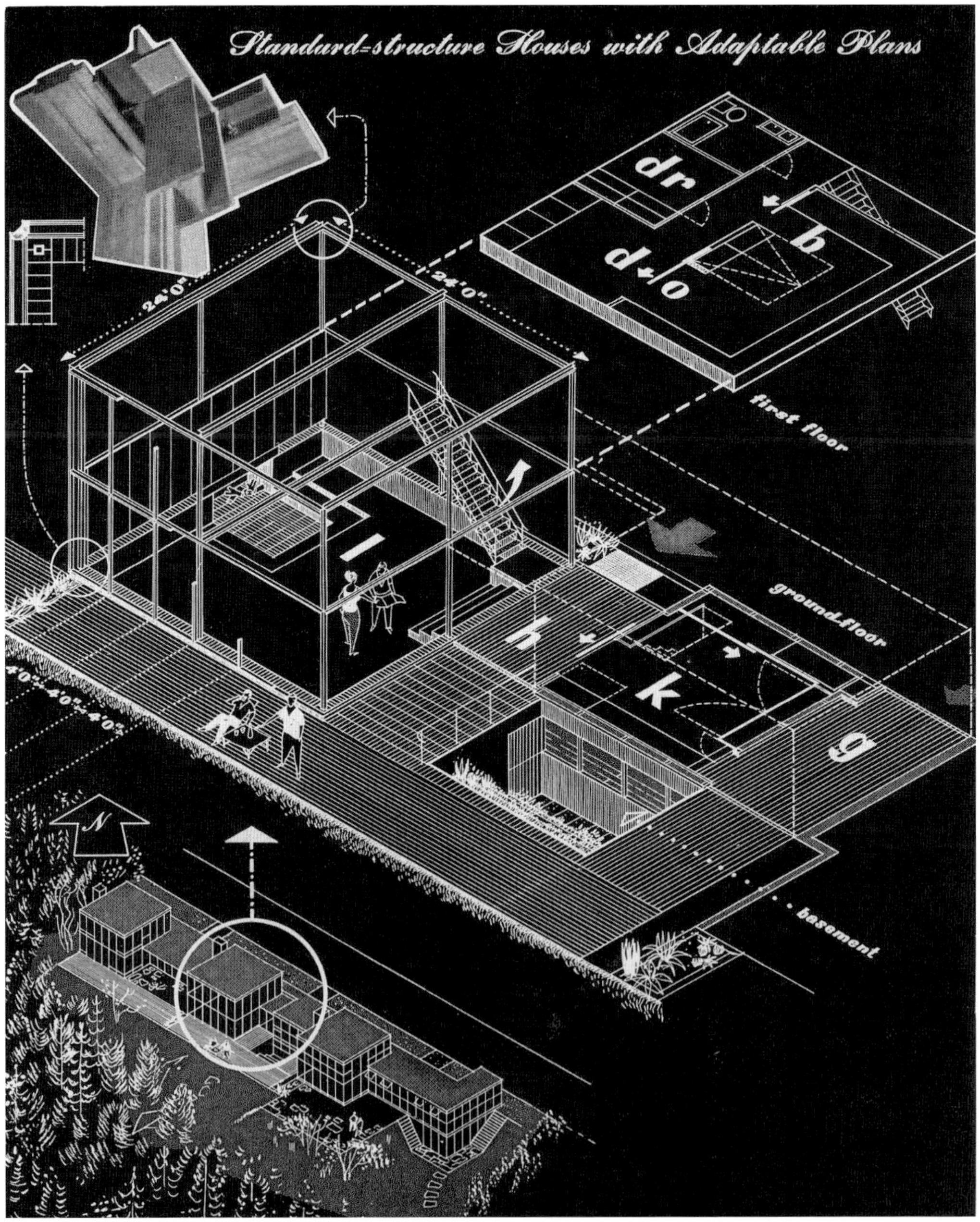

RIGHT: Korsmo's Mekano House diagram. The modular Mekano building system promoted creative use of space and a lively interplay between the inhabitant, everyday tasks, and the house. Korsmo's own house on Planetveien served as a live-in laboratory for testing these possibilities. *Property of Margrete Refsdal.*

OPPOSITE: The sunken court of Korsmo's house on Planetveien becomes an extension of the interior work-space. *The Functionalist Arne Korsmo, Universitets Forlaget 1986, pg. 105. Photo: Guillemot.*

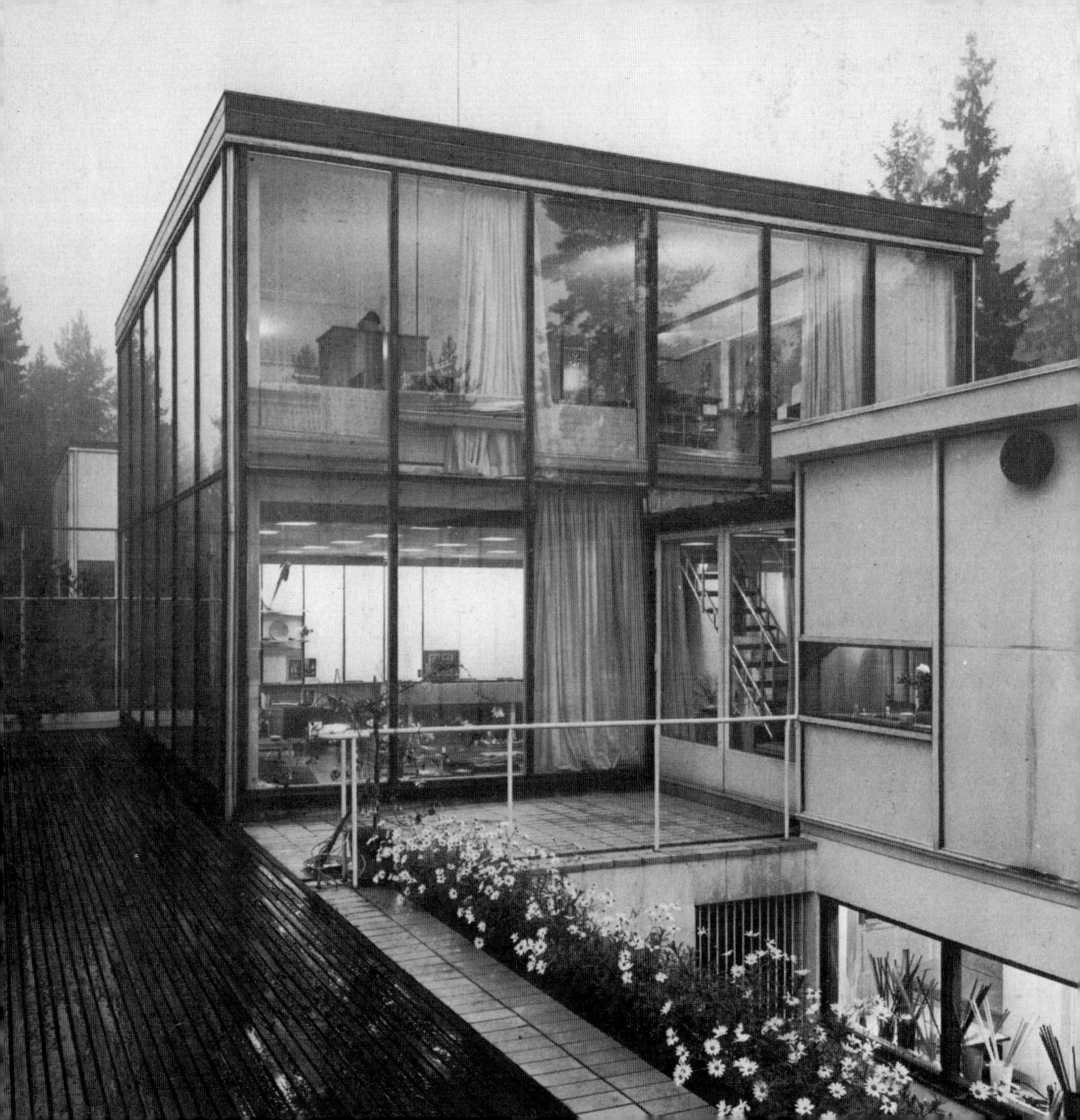

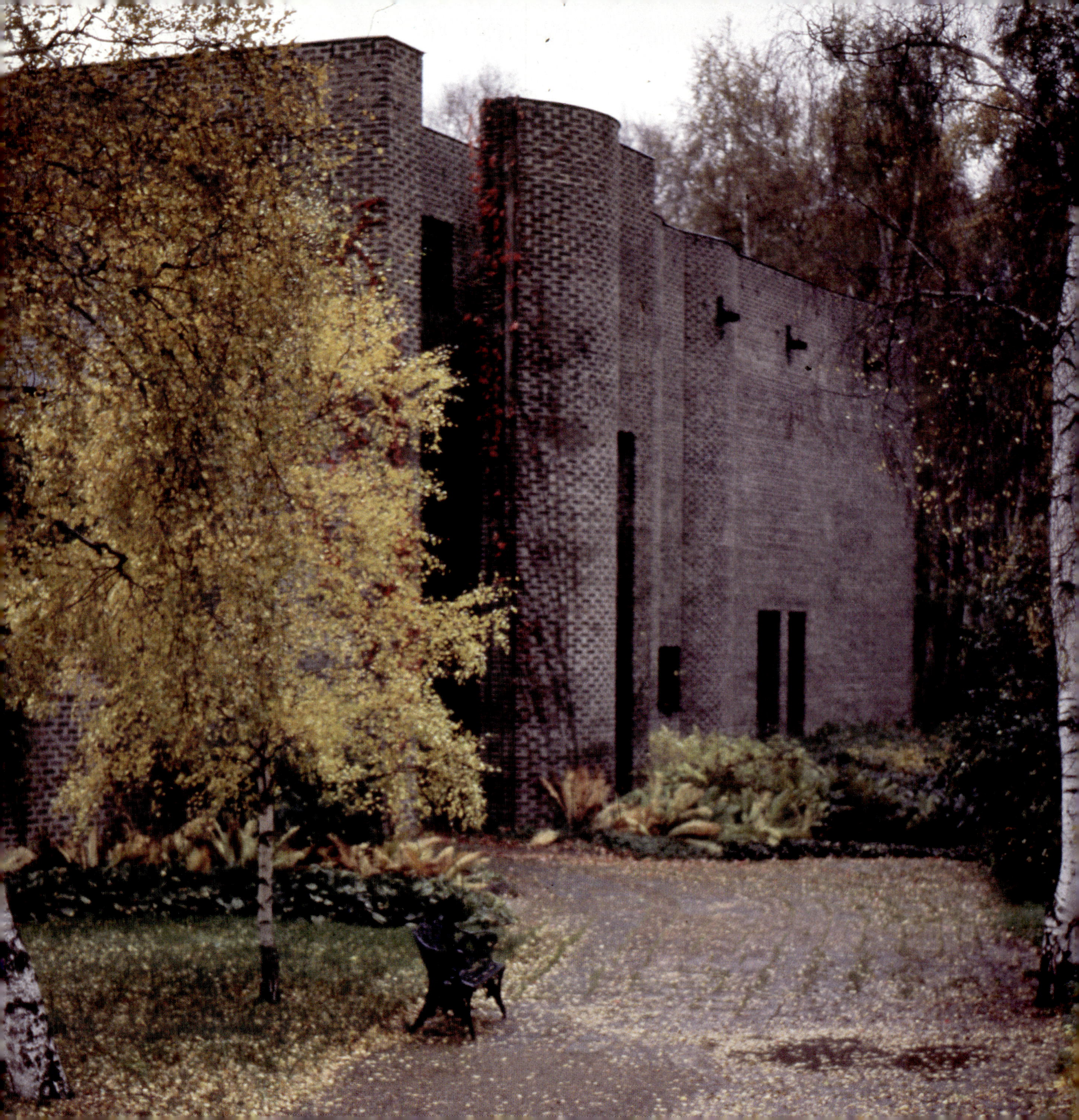

Sørensen also had renewed contact with Scandinavian architects as well as Danish furniture designers. In their correspondence Kahn and Sørensen discussed some design choices made in the new United Nations building. Whether or not they touched upon the selection of Nordic architects for the interiors is unclear, but the choices concerning the interiors did cause some contention and involved people Kahn knew.

Just as Korsmo completed his Mekano House, Kahn began working on the Richards Medical Research Laboratories at the University of Pennsylvania. By 1957, Kahn was teaching at Penn and Korsmo was a professor at the Norwegian Institute of Technology in Trondheim. Though Korsmo moved his practice north, and though his nearly ten-year period teaching in Trondheim would have a profound effect on the department of architecture, he was to a certain extent isolated from his friends, colleagues, and all that unfolded in Oslo. The situation toward the end of his life is best illustrated by Fehn's bittersweet comment that Korsmo kept his office in the breast pocket of his jacket. To counterbalance some of the alienating effects of his move, Korsmo remained active abroad, including in his obligations to CIAM. So by the time Kahn attended the Otterlo Meeting of 1959, Korsmo was already well acquainted with many who attended, including Peter and Alison Smithson and Aldo van Eyck.

By 1959, Kahn's stature as an architect was gaining momentum; his masterclass at Penn was established; and the Yale University Art Gallery, Trenton Bath House, and Richards Medical Research Laboratories were finished and published. His plans for downtown Philadelphia had caught the interest of many young European architects, but at home he experienced both anxiety and frustration in relation to this project. His commission to build the First Unitarian Church in Rochester, NY (1959–65), which would generate much positive energy and provide guidance for the future direction of his work, was in a very early phase. His "form drawing" (a search for the architectural core in a project) and focus on daylight were soon central issues in his creative process, lectures, and teaching.

In relation to Kahn's commission for the First Unitarian Church, it is interesting to return to Scandinavia and consider some developments in Sweden before discussing the 1959 CIAM meeting. The architect Sigurd Lewerentz, seventy-four years old at the time of the Otterlo meeting, had finished St. Mark's Church in Björkhagen outside Stockholm during the winter of 1958–59, just as the planning phase of the First Unitarian Church began. Typical of much of his career, Lewerentz faced problems and setbacks with this commission. He had completed all of the working drawings and prepared them for implementation by 1956, but the project was put on hold due to economic issues.

This church and Lewerentz's St. Peter's Church in Klippan (1963–66) embody many of the concerns Kahn outlined in the masterclass. Lewerentz was not a teacher in the formal

Sigurd Lewerentz, St. Mark's Church in Björkhagen, 1959. Lewerentz demonstrated a great sensitivity to the almost untouched site. The tone, texture, and color of the brick walls beautifully contrast with the white birch trees in both winter and summer. The church was completed just as Kahn began work on the First Unitarian Church in Rochester. *P. O. Fjeld.*

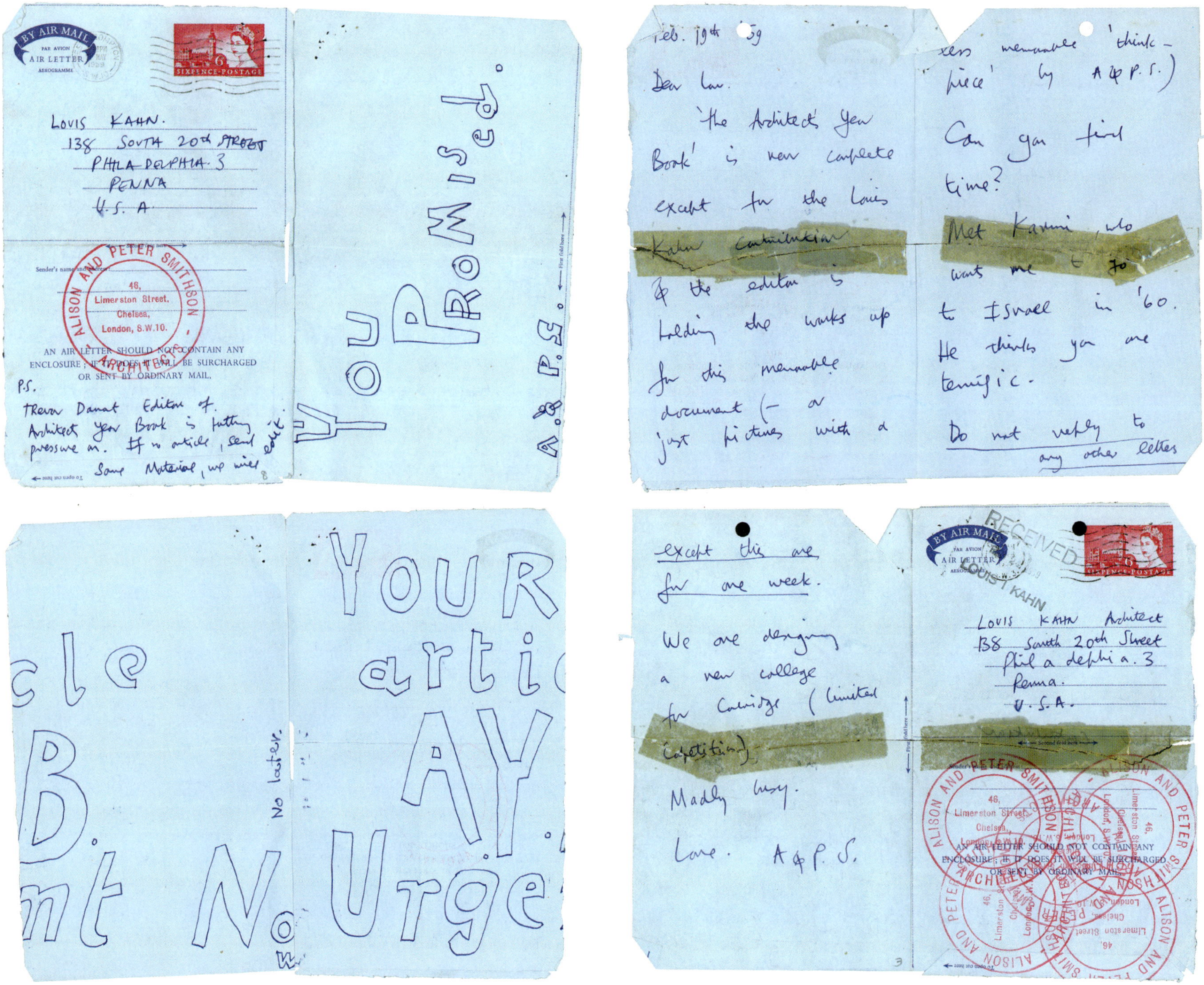

BY AIR MAIL
PAR AVION
AIR LETTER
AEROGRAMME
SIXPENCE POSTAGE

LOUIS KAHN.
138 SOUTH 20th STREET
PHILADELPHIA 3
PENNA
U.S.A.

ALISON AND PETER SMITHSON - ARCHITECTS
46, Limerston Street, Chelsea, London, S.W.10.

AN AIR LETTER SHOULD NOT CONTAIN ANY ENCLOSURE; IF IT DOES IT WILL BE SURCHARGED OR SENT BY ORDINARY MAIL.

P.S.
Trevor Danat Editor of Architect Year Book is putting pressure on. If no article, send some material, we will edit.

YOU PROMISed.

A.&P.S.

Feb. 19th '59

Dear Lou.

'The Architect's Year Book' is now complete except for the Louis Kahn contribution & the editor is holding the works up for this memorable document (– or just pictures with a less memorable 'think-piece' by A&P.S.)

Can you find time?

Met Kahmi, who wants me to go to Israel in '60. He thinks you are terrific.

Do not reply to any other letters except this one for one week.

We are designing a new college for Cambridge (limited competition)

Madly busy.

Love. A&P.S.

YOUR article

AY. B.

Urgent No.

No later.

RECEIVED
LOUIS I KAHN

Louis Kahn Architect
138 South 20th Street
Philadelphia 3
Penna.
U.S.A.

1959 | CIAM XI held in Otterlo. Kahn begins work on the Salk Institute for Biological Studies. Eero Saarinen's U.S. Embassy in Oslo completed. Sigurd Lewerentz completes St. Mark's Church in Björkhagen. Alison and Peter Smithson win competition to design The Economist Building in London.

Frank Lloyd Wright dies.

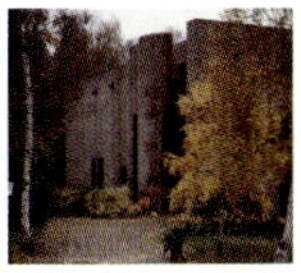

St. Mark's Church in Björkhagen. *P. O. Fjeld.*

1960 | World Design Conference in Tokyo. Aldo van Eyck's Amsterdam Municipal Orphanage completed. Eero Saarinen's U.S. Embassy in London opens. At the University of Pennsylvania, Kahn's Richards Medical Research Laboratories and Eero Saarinen's Hill College House are completed.

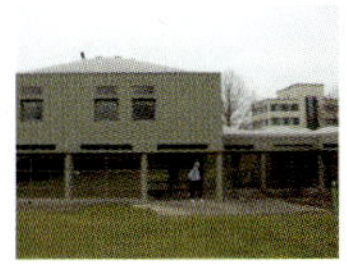

Amsterdam Municipal Orphanage. *Kaia Opstad.*

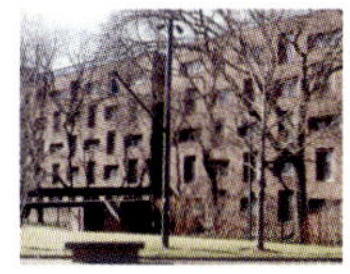

Hill College House. *P. O. Fjeld.*

sense. He was reserved, gave few interviews, and wrote very little; but those few who were lucky enough to work in his modest office regarded him as a remarkable teacher. His work spanned many decades of architectural change—from the pared-down Scandinavian neoclassicism of the Resurrection Chapel in the Woodland Cemetery; to his remarkable modernist café, Gröna Udden, in the Stockholm Exhibition of 1930; to the churches in Björkhagen and Klippan; to the concrete Flower Kiosk (1969) he designed for the Malmö Eastern Cemetery at the very end of his career.

Like Kahn's Yale University Art Gallery, Lewerentz's last works were categorized for a period under what was being termed "New Brutalism" in Great Britain. Reynar Banham as well as Alison and Peter Smithson wrote several articles defining this architectural category, and all of these commentators at first ascribed Lewerentz's late work to it. By the time I met Peter Smithson in the International Laboratory of Architecture and Urban Design (ILAUD) in 1986, he was still referring to the Flower Kiosk as an example of the New Brutalist style. In the magazine *Architectural Design* (1957), Peter and Alison Smithson argued that at its core Brutalism is an attempt to be "objective about reality; the cultural objectives of society, techniques" and what they termed "urges." Perhaps in an effort to distance themselves from Banham's increasing focus on New Brutalism as a set of formal principles, they went on to argue that up to this point the term had only been discussed stylistically and that Brutalism was in fact an ethical category. Here again cultural differences in relation to nature arise when referencing Nordic work. In discussing Brutalism as initiating a movement, it is implicit that one is moving from one interpretation to another, but in the Nordic region this objective reality (as the Smithsons termed it) was by necessity always present, style or no style. Within their interpretation the human appears slightly outside the realm of nature, reflecting a more Continental sensibility and cultural inheritance. The inclusion of Lewerentz's late work in New Brutalism as a style thus derailed a more fundamental discussion, and this was possibly true for other Nordic work of the same period. It was not style, theory, or method that motivated Lewerentz, but rather his intense personal search into daylight, structure, and material as mass. This was understood through a very measured, reflective inquisitiveness tied to the social concerns of the society and the nature he inhabited.

Was Kahn familiar with Lewerentz's work? Probably, since a number of his European friends and colleagues were deeply inspired by his late work. St. Mark's Church in Björkhagen was completed only months before the opening of the CIAM meeting in Otterlo.

Airmail letters from Alison and Peter Smithson first asking, then begging, Kahn to send material for the *Architect's Year Book. Louis I. Kahn Collection, the University of Pennsylvania and the Pennsylvania Historical and Museum Commission.*

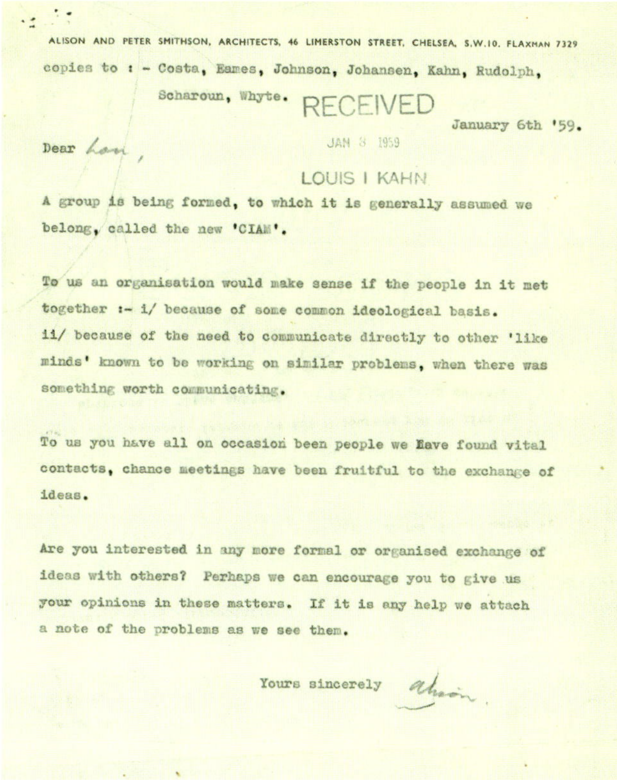
ALISON AND PETER SMITHSON, ARCHITECTS, 46 LIMERSTON STREET, CHELSEA, S.W.10. FLAXMAN 7329

copies to : - Costa, Eames, Johnson, Johansen, Kahn, Rudolph,
Scharoun, Whyte.

RECEIVED
JAN 8 1959
LOUIS I KAHN

January 6th '59.

Dear Lou,

A group is being formed, to which it is generally assumed we belong, called the new 'CIAM'.

To us an organisation would make sense if the people in it met together :- i/ because of some common ideological basis.
ii/ because of the need to communicate directly to other 'like minds' known to be working on similar problems, when there was something worth communicating.

To us you have all on occasion been people we have found vital contacts, chance meetings have been fruitful to the exchange of ideas.

Are you interested in any more formal or organised exchange of ideas with others? Perhaps we can encourage you to give us your opinions in these matters. If it is any help we attach a note of the problems as we see them.

Yours sincerely Alison

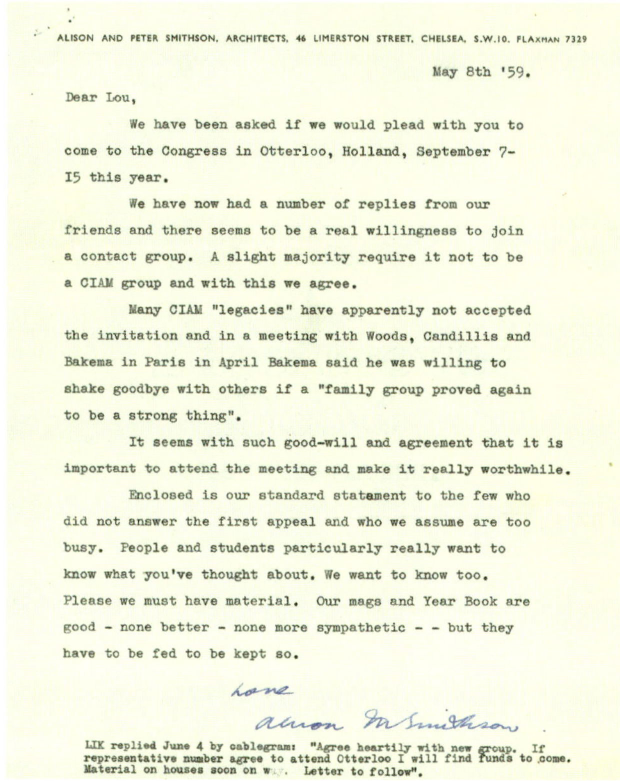
ALISON AND PETER SMITHSON, ARCHITECTS, 46 LIMERSTON STREET, CHELSEA, S.W.10. FLAXMAN 7329

May 8th '59.

Dear Lou,

We have been asked if we would plead with you to come to the Congress in Otterloo, Holland, September 7-15 this year.

We have now had a number of replies from our friends and there seems to be a real willingness to join a contact group. A slight majority require it not to be a CIAM group and with this we agree.

Many CIAM "legacies" have apparently not accepted the invitation and in a meeting with Woods, Candillis and Bakema in Paris in April Bakema said he was willing to shake goodbye with others if a "family group proved again to be a strong thing".

It seems with such good-will and agreement that it is important to attend the meeting and make it really worthwhile.

Enclosed is our standard statement to the few who did not answer the first appeal and who we assume are too busy. People and students particularly really want to know what you've thought about. We want to know too. Please we must have material. Our mags and Year Book are good - none better - none more sympathetic - - but they have to be fed to be kept so.

Love
Alison M Smithson

LIK replied June 4 by cablegram: "Agree heartily with new group. If representative number agree to attend Otterloo I will find funds to come. Material on houses soon on way. Letter to follow".

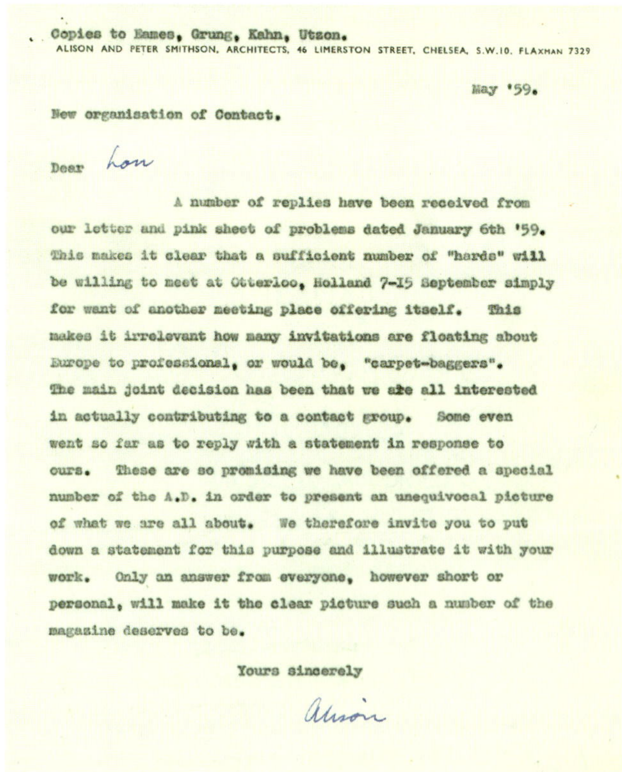
Copies to Eames, Grung, Kahn, Utzon.
ALISON AND PETER SMITHSON, ARCHITECTS, 46 LIMERSTON STREET, CHELSEA, S.W.10. FLAXMAN 7329

May '59.

New organisation of Contact.

Dear Lou

A number of replies have been received from our letter and pink sheet of problems dated January 6th '59. This makes it clear that a sufficient number of "hards" will be willing to meet at Otterloo, Holland 7-15 September simply for want of another meeting place offering itself. This makes it irrelevant how many invitations are floating about Europe to professional, or would be, "carpet-baggers". The main joint decision has been that we are all interested in actually contributing to a contact group. Some even went so far as to reply with a statement in response to ours. These are so promising we have been offered a special number of the A.D. in order to present an unequivocal picture of what we are all about. We therefore invite you to put down a statement for this purpose and illustrate it with your work. Only an answer from everyone, however short or personal, will make it the clear picture such a number of the magazine deserves to be.

Yours sincerely

Alison

Correspondence between the Smithsons and Kahn. The letter of January 6 is a general letter concerning a "new CIAM" (later called Team 10). The letter dated May 8 is the Otterlo invitation to Kahn. Copies of the letter dated May 1959, which refers to the new CIAM, were also sent to Eames, Grung, and Utzon. *Louis I. Kahn Collection, the University of Pennsylvania and the Pennsylvania Historical and Museum Commission.*

Otterlo

Just before Kahn received the commission to build the First Unitarian Church, Alison and Peter Smithson contacted him about publishing his work in the British *Architect's Year Book*. Like many others, they encountered obstacles to their requests for Kahn to send materials. Their correspondence about this went back and forth for a while; by 1959, the Smithsons' requests finally gave way to conversation about the upcoming CIAM meeting in Otterlo and an invitation for Kahn to attend.

The title for this CIAM meeting—"Research Group for Social and Visual Relationships"—was a clear signal of changes to come, indicating that a break from the old-guard CIAM members was now inevitable. The meeting and discussions that followed were electric. Many participants considered it one of the most important architectural events of the last century, and it was not unusual that references to this meeting came up twenty-five years later in ILAUD discussions. Kahn's speech toward the end of the closing session was later described as an essential turning point in relation to all that had been presented. Kahn noted:

> I have the good fortune to observe the plans and work of the men here, and have seen that almost everyone started with the solution of the problem, given the conditions upon which design was made. But I think I may say freely that very few started with a kind of sense of realization of the problem and then inserted design as its natural extension—a circumstantial thing, because I really do believe that design is a circumstantial thing. I believe that a man must realize something before he has the stimulation within himself to design something. I believe that there are many in our profession who rely entirely upon the actual design and very little on the way of thought as to what a thing wants to be, before they try to develop the design—the solution of the problem.[21]

Both Arne Korsmo and the English Swedish architect Ralph Erskine presented projects dealing with subarctic conditions, including daylight or the lack of light and how this affects inhabitants. Both architects focused on the importance of a communal acceptance of a project and the crucial relationship between the interior and exterior spaces in a setting where nature is so demanding. They argued for a better understanding of shared outdoor space, seasonal changes, and extreme light conditions, and a stronger focus on pedestrian movement in a subarctic winter landscape. However, many were critical of what they perceived as a spatial exaggeration in relation to polar conditions. In Oscar Newman and Jakob Bakema's final publication from the 1959 CIAM meeting, the project of the younger Erskine received a

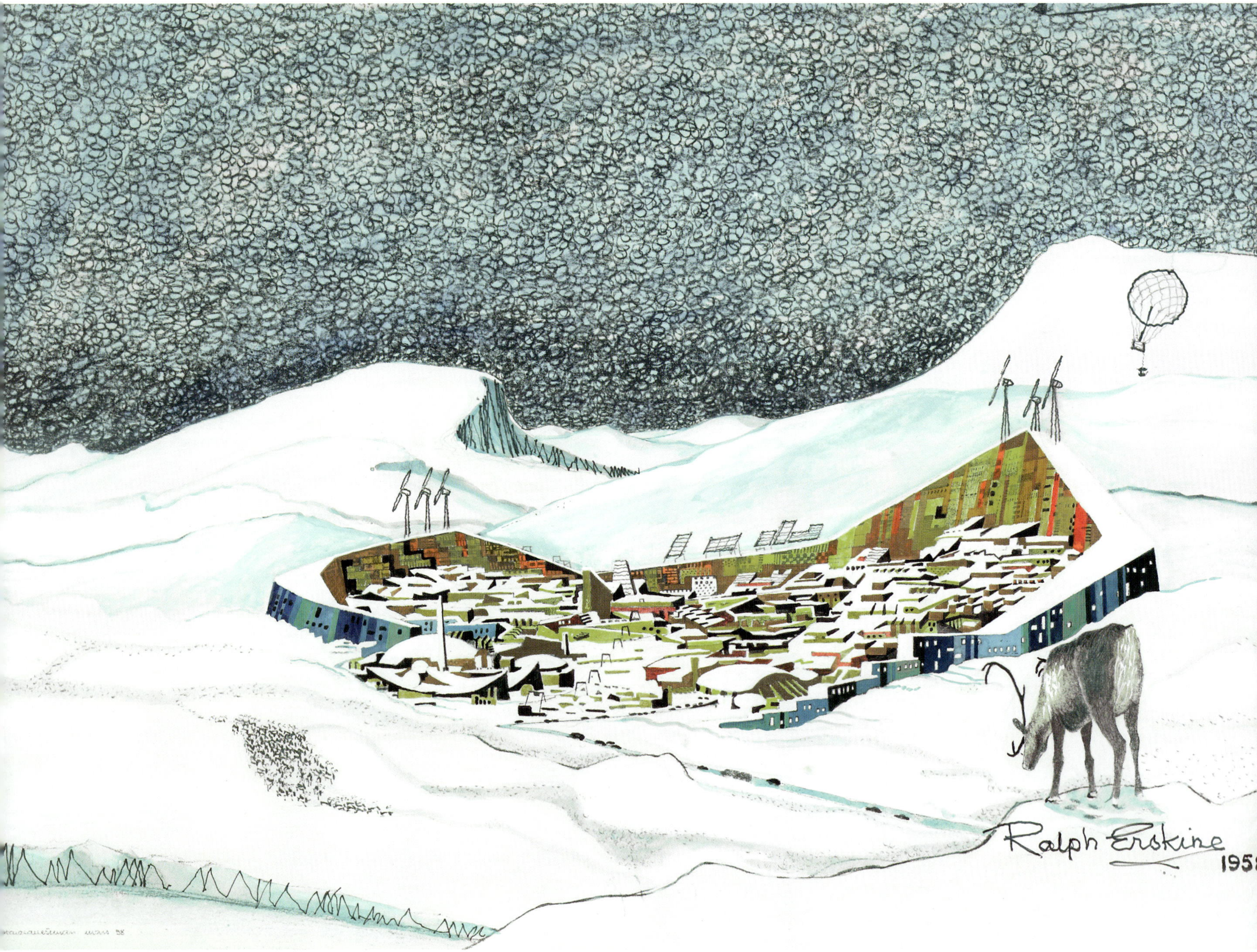
Ralph Erskine

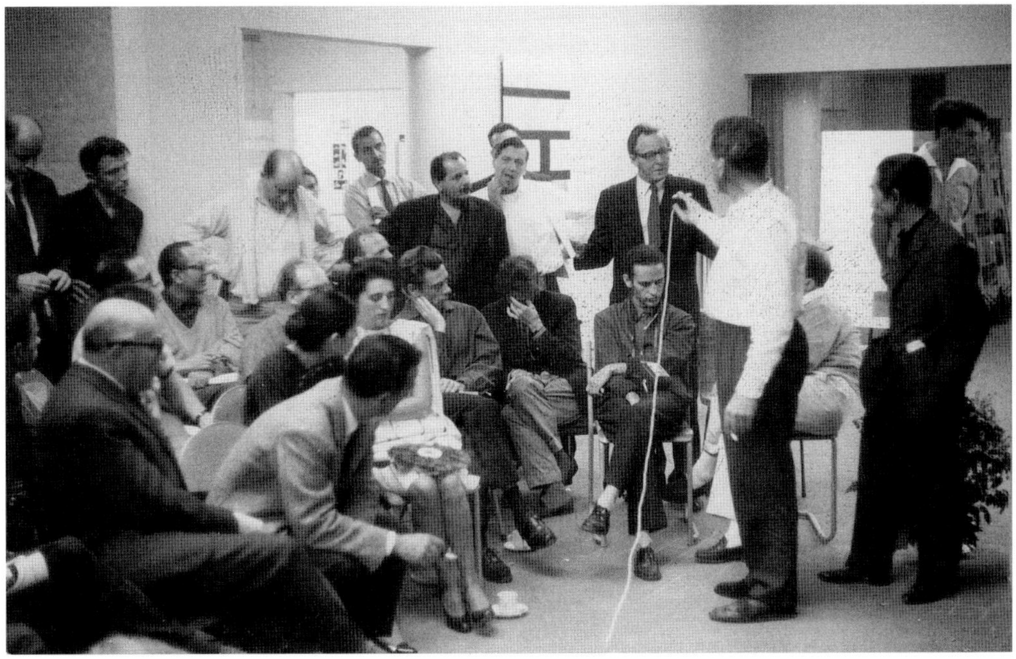

TOP: Session from the CIAM Otterlo conference: Korsmo, standing, is pictured in reading glasses and holding some papers; in front of him, holding the microphone, is Herman Haan. Kenzo Tange is behind Haan. Franco Albini (who was not a registered conference participant) is standing against the back wall (fifth from the left). Also in this photo are Peter and Alison Smithson, De Carlo, van Eyck, Bakema, Candilis, Woods, Ernesto Rogers, and Erskine. *Photographer unknown; Collection Het Nieuwe Instituut archive.*

OPPOSITE: Ralph Erskine, study for an ideal town in a subarctic environment, 1958. Aspects of this drawing, presented at the CIAM Otterlo meeting, would inform Erskine's Svappavaara project in Sweden. *Ralph Erskine Collection, the Swedish Centre for Architecture and Design, Stockholm.*

far more extensive presentation than that of the "rationalist" Korsmo. Curiously, the few times Peter Smithson later referred to Korsmo in articles, it was always as a functionalist or rationalist, thus almost excluding him from any postwar relevance. In relation to Team 10 discussions, Korsmo all but disappears; yet his friend and former student Geir Grung was one of the group's founding members, and the group continued to extend invitations to both Kahn and Utzon for several years.

In a letter to Kahn shortly after the meeting, Erskine wrote, "I am still thinking about the congress at Otterlo, and I still find, looking back that some of the discussions, some of the people and some of the movements were most fascinating, and I would not have missed it for anything—in spite of the quarrels!" He then goes on to ask if Kahn would contribute to the magazine *Carré Bleu*: "I wondered if, for example, you would write something about your conception of space? Your talk to us at Otterlo made such an impression on me."[22] *Carré Bleu*—always abreast of new thinking, inquisitive, and quite independent of commercial pressure in its choice of subjects and attitudes—served an important role in helping Nordic architects get exposure abroad. André Schimmerling and Aulis Blomstedt cofounded the magazine along with the much younger Reima Pietilä. All three of these individuals attended CIAM or Team 10 meetings at some point and maintained active correspondence with some of the Team 10 participants as well as various Norwegian PAGON members.

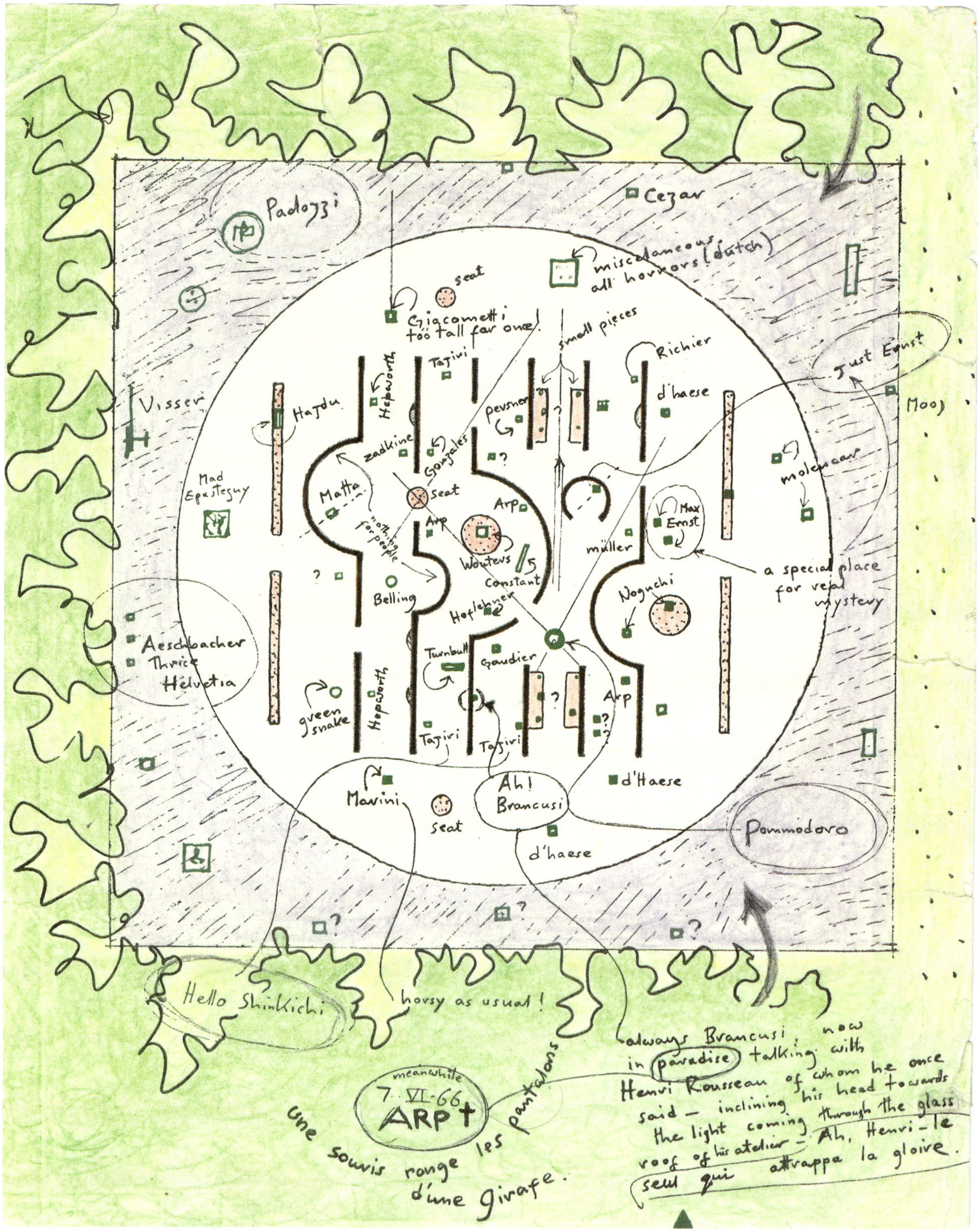
Padozzi
Cezar
miscellaneous all horrors (dutch)
seat
Giacometti too tall for once
small pieces
Richier
Just Ernst
Moo
Visser
Hajdu
Hepworth
Tajiri
zadkine
Gonzales
pevsner
d'haese
molenaar
Mad Epsteinery
Matta
seat
nothing for people
Arp
Wouters
Constant
müller
Max Ernst
a special place for real mystery
Belling
Hoflehner
Noguchi
Aeschbacher Thrice Helvetia
Turnbull
Gaudier
green snake
Hepworth
Tajiri
Tajiri
Arp
d'Haese
Marini
seat
Ah! Brancusi
d'haese
Pommodoro
Hello Shinkichi
horsy as usual!
always Brancusi now in paradise talking with Henri Rousseau of whom he once said – inclining his head towards the light coming through the glass roof of his atelier – Ah, Henri – le seul qui attrappa la gloire.
meanwhile
7. VI. 66
ARP †
une souris ronge les pantalons d'une girafe.

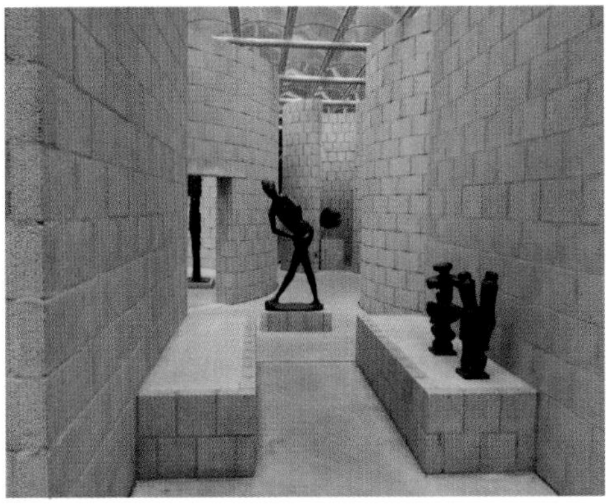

ABOVE: Aldo van Eyck, Sonsbeek Sculpture Pavilion, Arnhem, 1965–66. The pavilion was demolished at the end of the exhibition but later rebuilt. *Earon Matthew.*

OPPOSITE: Drawing of the Sonsbeek Sculpture Pavilion by Aldo van Eyck. The relationship between the straight and curved line, between the concave and convex, gives an imprint of a spatial energy field. *Aldo+Hannie van Eyck Stichting/Foundation.*

In retrospect, one of the more remarkable occurrences at the CIAM Otterlo event was Aldo van Eyck and Kahn meeting for the first time. Their concurrent work and reflections about architecture were now in the same room, and it became apparent there were similarities in their creative thinking. The interview with Herman Hertzberger for the Vitra Kahn Exhibition of 2013 is, in all its simplicity, the most telling about the architects' unique connection to each other. In it Hertzberger recalled:

> There was talk about Kahn and I remember that there was some competition between Aldo van Eyck and Kahn. Not openly, but I felt that. Particularly because Aldo van Eyck at the time was making his Orphanage building that was really a startling example of something you had never seen before. All these equal elements in a configuration—that was a new thing! And then I found out Kahn also did that in his Jewish Community Centre. There must have been a sort of equal feeling of Kahn and van Eyck. This is actually the moment that these things start. You can see his intention to make, as it were, settlements, or even cities, out of elements. And in that way he also made buildings as cities. The idea of difference between a building and a city didn't exist anymore from that moment on.
>
> And in a sort of naive way I sometimes said, "Hey Aldo, I saw these sorts of things also in Kahn." Well there would always be an answer like, "H'mmm, yes, I know that but . . . well, it's not important . . ." But he never said, "I was first!" And he also never said, "Yes, I took that from Kahn." But I'm absolutely sure that they were influenced by each other.[23]

Hertzberger's interview must be appreciated in the context of his activities, his pivotal role in the magazine *Forum*, his deep interest in architectural issues, and his many professional contacts at the time of the meeting.

Some areas of Kahn's and van Eyck's thinking overlapped, but one of the difficulties in discussing similarities almost sixty-five years later lies in how one interprets their work and approach—where one puts the emphasis of meaning. Francis Strauven's important book, *Aldo van Eyck: The Shape of Relativity* (1989), gives some depth to this challenge, but his interpretation of Kahn's vocabulary was influenced by the period in which he wrote the book and the tacit hold postmodernist interpretation had at the time. As a result, some interesting parallels between the two architects' work were overlooked, especially in relation to Kahn's concepts of "the laws of nature" and "the rules of man." At the time of Strauven's publication, concepts like "spaces that serve or are served" tended to be critics' prevailing focus, but without their fully taking into account the importance of how Kahn perceived nature and the "institutions of man." This interpretation assumed a spatial hierarchy that, as Strauven pointed out, was far from van Eyck's thinking. However, if Kahn's concept of "served and servant" is interpreted in the vein of Asplund's thinking, more similarities emerge between Kahn's and van Eyck's design philosophies.

Another area of misunderstanding was the assumption that Kahn approached his projects from an a priori or formal perspective. In fact, Kahn's main interest was uncovering what he called "knowing"—a condition without shape, before an idea, a "volume zero." Van Eyck worked toward concepts that would gradually take shape through a process of exploration, working his way through elementary human relationships. In returning to my class notes about Kahn's "form drawing," it became apparent how close Kahn's and van Eyck's thinking were on many levels, despite their different vocabulary, expressions, and personalities. Van Eyck made a clear differentiation between art (including architecture) and nature, emphasizing that art has its own logic. On this point, Kahn's comment that "nature's order does not imply beauty" reveals an interesting but challenging connection between the two architects.

In Kahn's closing speech at Otterlo he referred to van Eyck's lecture the day before:

> Aldo who simply talked about a door. I think it is a wonderful thing to review the aspects of architecture from that sense. The mere fact that one can get to be totally preoccupied with this sort of thing is wonderful, because from it can grow many wonderful things, it could lead a man to a realization which goes far beyond the problem of a door or gateway.[24]

Van Eyck's elaborating on the role of a door must have made an impression, because Kahn also mentioned this moment in our class, in reference to how, independent of scale, one can never be sure what will spark an idea.

During the meeting, van Eyck invited some of the attendees to visit the Amsterdam Municipal Orphanage, which at that time was still under construction. Both Kahn and Korsmo visited the site. The orphanage would have a profound influence on work and architectural discourse during the following decades. I visited the orphanage in the mid-1970s with Sverre Fehn. I remember he asked me to keep in mind the original drawings and van Eyck's brief for the project:

> Our house must be a friendly house in every aspect, both inside and outside. It must be a home, a home for children who for shorter or longer time—for years, maybe—will not be living with their parents, who will miss their own home. It is up to us to try to make up

> for that deficiency. On approaching our house, the child must enter gladly: its outward appearance should ooze friendliness, becoming to the child, as it were, to enter.[25]

This echoed Kahn's discussion about our first project in the masterclass, the orphanage at Girard College.

CIAM had been faltering for some time and its future was at stake. Many hoped that the Otterlo meeting would give clarity to the situation. Both van Eyck and Kahn made critical observations about the meeting and CIAM's future, remarking on the great possibilities of the past decade and the failure to act on them. In addition, there were critical comments from other prominent participants, including the Japanese architect Kenzo Tange, whose speech tied into Kahn's concerns. The decision to dismantle CIAM was made toward the end of the session the day after most participants had returned home, thus the final blow to the organization appeared to some to be an internal resolution. This situation troubled many, including Korsmo, who did not take part in any Team 10 activities.

Shortly after this meeting, invitations went out to a number of participants to attend the World Design Conference headed by Kenzo Tange and Junzo Sakakura in Tokyo the following spring. About two hundred fifty architects from twenty-seven countries were invited, including Louis Kahn and Arne Korsmo, both of whom were asked to participate in discussion panels and give a lecture. A number of interesting international figures were present at the conference, including Jean Prouvé, Jacob Bakema, Ernesto Rogers, Ignazio Gardella, Franco Albini, Peter Smithson, Paul Rudolph, Balkrishna Doshi, Ralf Soriano, and Ralph Erskine. Along with Tange and Sakakura, Fumihiko Maki, Minoru Yamasaki, and Kiyonori Kikutake were among those representing the Japanese delegation; a younger Japanese contingent arrived in the form of a new group called the Metabolists. During the conference, Kikutake presented his Sky House, which he invited participants, including Kahn and Korsmo, home to see; Kahn gave a lecture at Waseda University and was on a discussion panel with Tange and Smithson; and Korsmo was one of the main speakers the following day. Finally able to visit Japan, Korsmo planned a longer stay to study vernacular architecture after the conference, but Kahn's visit was relatively short. Nevertheless, the two friends clearly had a lively couple of days together at the close of the convention before Kahn returned to Philadelphia.[26] Importantly, this trip forged a Japanese connection to Kahn's masterclass: many Japanese students would study at Penn over the years that followed.

Several other meaningful contacts were made or reaffirmed during the conference. By 1960 Kahn had definitely met Franco Albini, as they both attended the conference in Tokyo and possibly met at Otterlo. In 1963 Kahn was awarded an honorary professorship from the

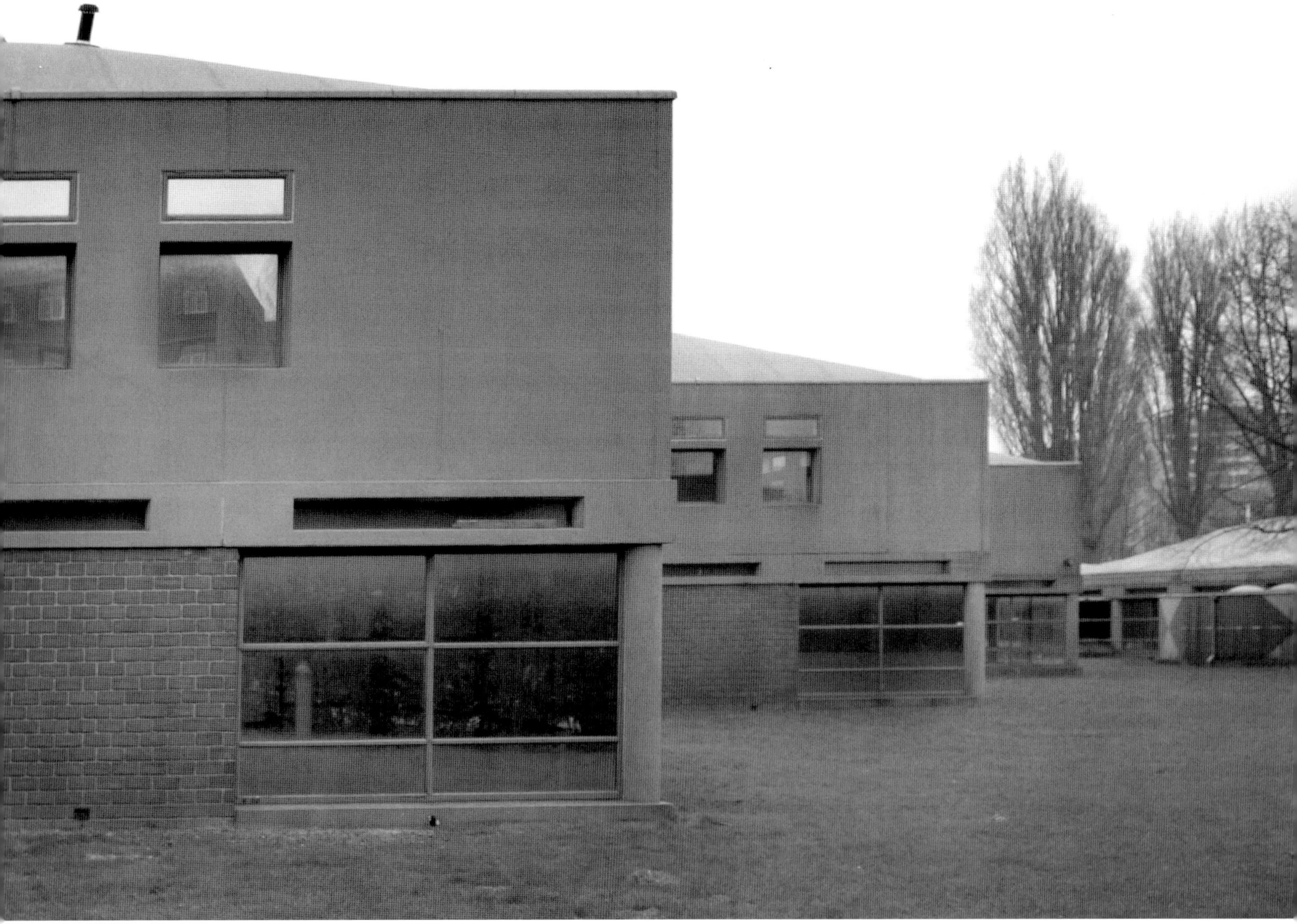

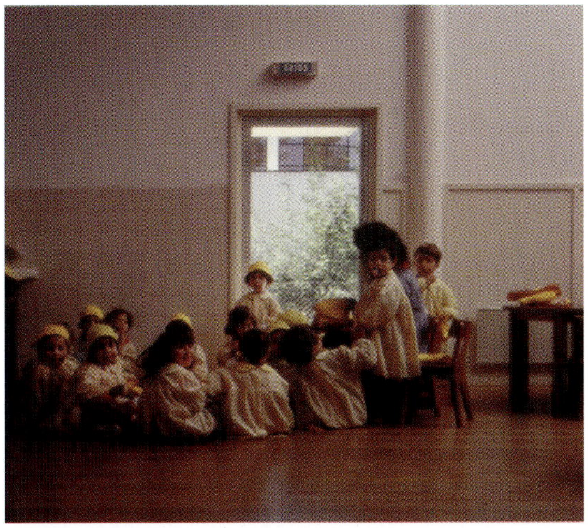

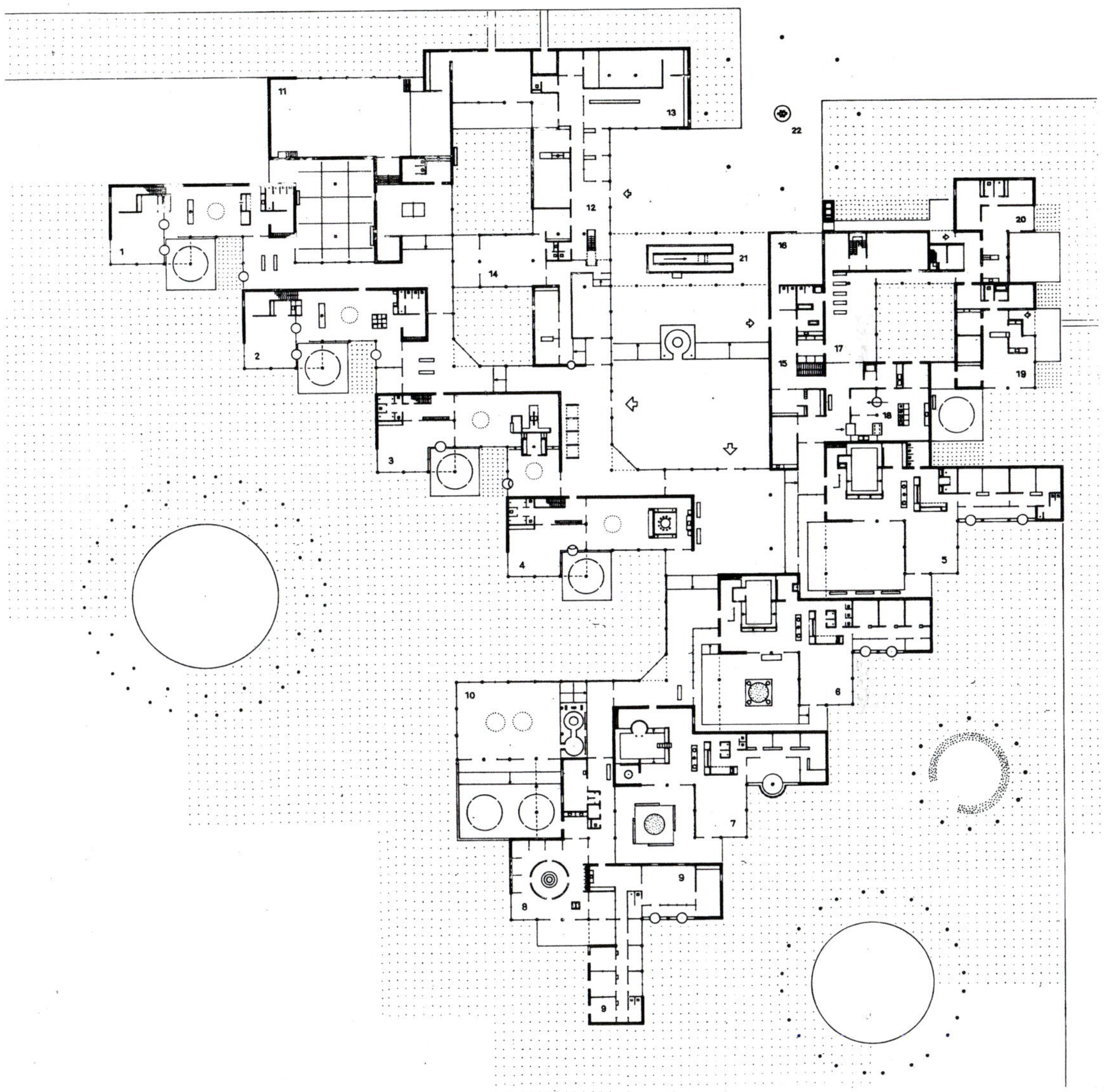

OPPOSITE: The Amsterdam Municipal Orphanage (1955–60) was nearly complete by the time of the CIAM Otterlo meeting. Van Eyck invited a number of CIAM attendees, including Kahn and Korsmo, to visit the site. *Kaia Opstad Sæbø.*

RIGHT: Aldo van Eyck, plan of the orphanage. *Aldo+Hannie van Eyck Stichting/Foundation.*

ABOVE: Children's story hour at the orphanage. *P. O. Fjeld.*

1961 Korsmo visits the Salk Institute for Biological Studies. Carlo Scarpa begins work on the Fondazione Querini Stampalia. Ponti, Nervi, and Danusso's Pirelli Tower completed.

Eero Saarinen dies.

1962 Kahn completes Margaret Esherick House and begins work on the National Assembly Building in Dhaka and the Indian Institute of Management. Ralph Erskine's housing project in Svappavaara completed. Sverre Fehn's Nordic Pavilion for the Venice Biennale completed. Balkrishna Doshi founds the Centre for Environmental Planning and Technology in Ahmedabad.

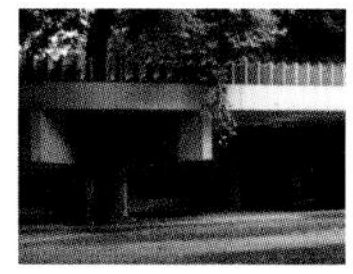

Nordic Pavilion for the Venice Biennale completed in 1962. *P. O. Fjeld.*

May/11/Wed Sankei Hall	Opening Ceremony 9:30 11:00		Lectures by Guest Speakers Herbert Bayer Max Bense Shinichiro Tomoaaga 1:00 4:00
	SEMINAR SESSION 9:30 12:00		PANEL DISCUSSIONS 1:30 4:30
May/12/Thu Cycle I "Personality" Kokusai Hall	Chairman: Ernesto N. Rogers(A) Vice-chariman: Isamu Kenmochi(I.T.) Speakers: Carl Auböck(I.C.) Yusaku Kamekura(G) Joseph Muller-Brockmann(G) Minoru Yamasaki(A) Reporters: Morning Ko Yanome Afternoon Kiyoshi Awazu Ken Harada Namio Nozaki	Individuality Rm B	Panelists: Franco Albin: (A) Yusaku Kamekura(G) Joseph Muller-Brockmann(G) Bruno Munari(G) Kohei Sugiura(G) Moderator: Takashi Kono(G)
		Regionality Rm A	Panelists: Daisaku Cho (I.T.) B.V. Doshi(A) Ralph Erskine(A) Kiyonori Kikutake(A) Minoru Yamasaki(A) Moderator: Hiroshi Ohe(A)
		Universality Rm C	Panelists: Carl Auböck (I.D.) Eric Herlow(ID) Yki Nummi(I.D.) Riki Watanabe(I.D.) Kazumi Yotsumoto(I.D.) Moderator: Kiyoshi Seike(A)
May/13/Fri Cycle II "Practicability" Kokusai Hall	Chairman: Will Burtin(G) Vice-chairman: Masaru Katsumi(C) Speakers: Saul Bass(G) Hans Gugelot(I.D.) Christopher Tunnard(L) Sori Yanagi(I.D.) Reporters: Morning: Afternoon Hideo Mukai Hidehiko Saz anami Shinya Iwasaki	Environment Rm B	Panelists: Yoshinobu Ashiwara(A) Walter Granville(Color) Kenichiro Ikehara (L) Paul Rudolph(A) German Samper (A) Moderator: Fumihiko Maki(A)
		Production Rm C	Panelists: Sergio Asti(I.D.) Hans Gugelot(I.D.) Tatsumi Kato(Craft) Sori Yanagi(I.D.) Walter Landor(I.D.) Moderator: Shutaro Mukai(I.D.)
		Communication Rm A	Panelists: Otl Aicher(G) Saul Bass (G) Hatsuhiko Ga (C) Herbert Pinzke(G) Ryuichi Yamashiro(G) Moderator: Hiroshi- Hara(G)

May/14/Sat Cycle III "Possibilities" Kokusai Hall	Chairman: Tomas Maldonado(C) Vice-chairman: Shoichi Kawai(A) Speakers: Max Bense(Ph) Jean Prouve(I.D.) Hans Schleger(G) Kenzo Tange(A) Reporters: Morning: Shinichi Segi Afternoon Noriaki Kurokawa Sen Okamoto Masahiro Yonekura	Society Rm C	Panelists: Yoshio Hayakawa(G) Max Huber(G) Uzo Nishiyama(A) Raphael Soriano(A) Moderator Noboru Kawagoe(C)
		Technology Rm A	Panelists: Alfred A therr(A) Shinya Izumi(I.D.) Masato Otaka(A) Jean Prouve(A) Alberto Rosselli(I.D.) Moderator: Kazuhiko Hongo(A)
		Philosophy Rm B	Panelists: Max Bense (Ph) Kenji Ekuan(I.D.) Louis Kahn(A) Peter Smithson(A) Kenzo Tange(A) Moderator: Ryuichi Hamaguchi(A)
May/14/Sat 7:00-9:00 Evening Education Seminar Kokusai Hall	Chairman: Iwataro Koike Speakers: Otl Aicher(G) Jupp Ernst(I.D.) Arne Korsmo(A) Hans Schleger(G)		May/15/Sun free Sight-seeing of Tokyo
May/16/Mon Closing Session Kokusai Hall	Resume by Ernests Rogers Will Bartin Tomas Maldonado Iwataro Koike Declaration: Junzo Sakakura Closing address: Hisaakira Kano		

ABREVIATION: G - Graphic designer
A - Architect
I.D. - Industrial designer
C - Critic
Ph - Philospher

The schedule for the list of speakers for the World Design Conference in Tokyo, 1960. Kahn was on a discussion panel with Peter Smithson and Kenzo Tange. Korsmo gave a lecture the following day. *Louis I. Kahn Collection, the University of Pennsylvania and the Pennsylvania and the Pennsylvania Historical and Museum Commission.*

Polytechnic University of Milan along with Alvar Aalto and Kenzo Tange. In a conversation I had with the Italian architect Francesco Gnecchi Ruscone, who was present at the award ceremony and had the task of translating various speeches, he noted the difficulties in translating Kahn's acceptance speech; but more importantly, he confirmed that Kahn, Albini, and Tange were clearly friends from an earlier time. The award ceremony in Milan is interesting especially in light of the overlapping professional connections. Albini and a number of other important Milan architects, including Ernesto Nathan Rogers and Ignazio Gardella, were present. In one photograph from the awards ceremony, Tange and Kahn are sitting beside Aalto and Gio

1963 | Sigurd Lewerentz begins work on St. Peter's Church in Klippan. Robert Venturi completes Guild House in Philadelphia.

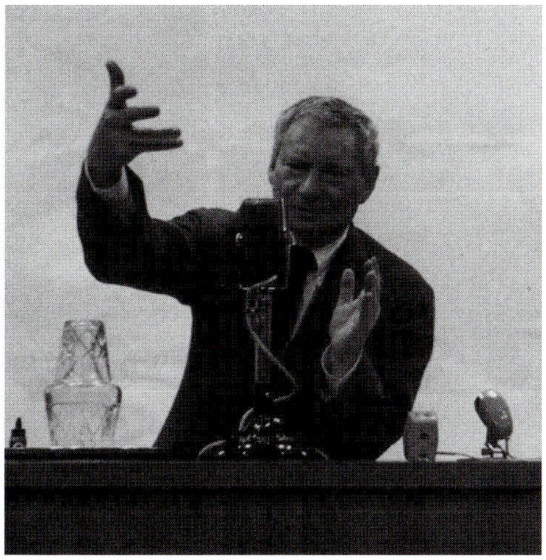

ABOVE: Kahn lecturing at Waseda University in Tokyo during the World Design Conference. *Louis I. Kahn Collection, the University of Pennsylvania and the Pennsylvania Historical and Museum Commission.*

RIGHT: Free time in Tokyo: Kahn and Korsmo socializing after some intense days at the conference. Jørn Utzon later noted that the Japan visit constituted a very intense reunion for the two friends. *The Oslo School of Architecture and Design Photo Archive.*

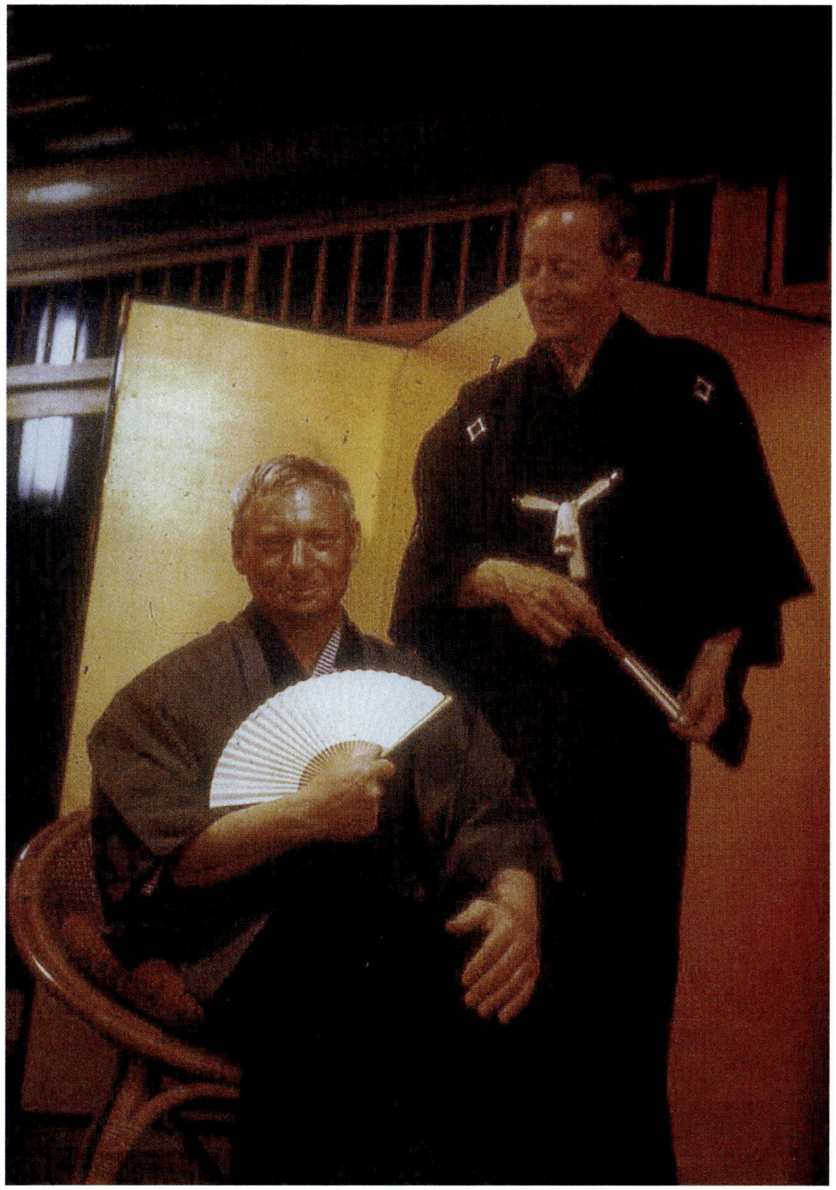

1964 | Korsmo visits Kahn. Kenzo Tange's Tokyo Olympic Arenas completed. Venturi completes the Vanna Venturi House.

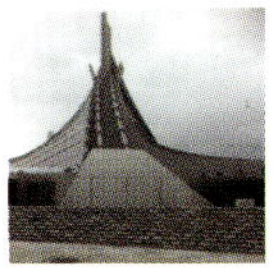

Tokyo Olympic Arena. P. O. Fjeld.

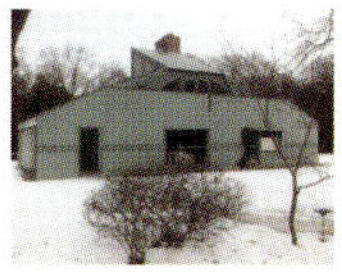

Vanna Venturi House. *P. O. Fjeld.*

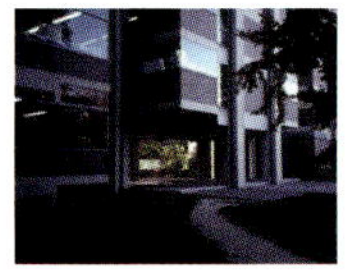

Kahn's David Goddard Laboratories completed in 1965. *P. O. Fjeld.*

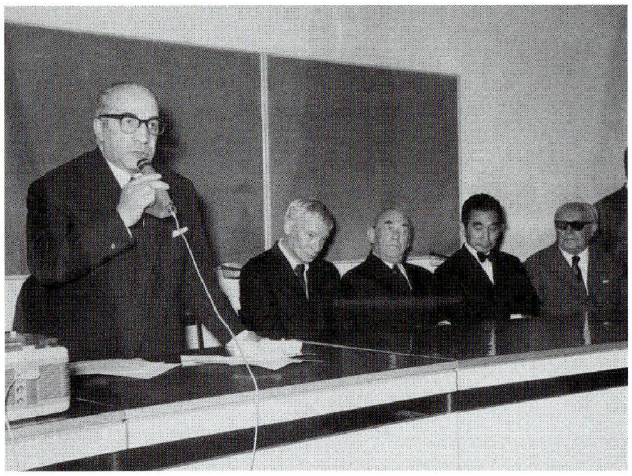

Photo from the ceremony for honorary professorships from the Polytechnic University of Milan, 1963. From left to right: the speaker and dean of the faculty Luigi Dodi, Louis Kahn, Alvar Aalto, Kenzo Tange, and (wearing sunglasses) Gio Ponti. Franco Albini was also present at the award ceremony. *Louis I. Kahn Collection, the Architectural Archives: University of Pennsylvania.*

Ponti, who had known one another for some time through their efforts to establish a Nordic–Italian cultural exchange. This event, along with the Otterlo meeting and the Tokyo conference, sheds a different light on Kahn's connections and knowledge of contemporary Italian architecture, as the network of overlapping friends and acquaintances was more extensive than often presented. Kahn's Palazzo dei Congressi project in Venice unfolded almost five years after this award ceremony in Milan.

It is Nordic

Korsmo made a visit to the West Coast on a second Fulbright grant sometime between his Japan trip and a later New York trip in 1964, and he had clearly seen Kahn's Salk Institute by the time of his New York stay. During his visit to New York, he sent a letter to Kahn while attending a design conference, mentioning John McAllister, who was project manager for the Salk Institute at the time. Korsmo wrote:

> The newspaper *Aftenposten*, Oslo wanted very eagerly when they saw your name in the program for the congress as a panelist—to get an interview. They asked me to contact you about this matter. I don't like to trouble you, but I certainly would like to meet you as an old friend. I had hoped perhaps it was possible to meet you in Philadelphia close to your work and working place. I remember your words from our last meeting in Philadelphia, "Next time I shall have so much to do so it will not be easy for anybody to take my time." But even then I hope to have the opportunity to meet both you and John. My warmest greetings, Arne.[27]

The contents of this note seem straightforward—but in fact the only time I can confirm Korsmo was in Philadelphia was fifteen years earlier, during the trip of 1949–50. The letter's humor is in what is not said, and at the same time it is so direct. It is Nordic. I am reminded of the short notes from Eero Saarinen to Kahn's office over the years; and of Kahn's letter to Anne Tyng complaining over the lack of complimentary words in Saarinen's recommendation for Venturi's Rome Academy application and how Saarinen replied, "I couldn't think of any more." Some have interpreted Saarinen's notes as slightly cold, but there is also something of the same directness and dry humor found in Korsmo's letter.

Earlier in 1959, a few months before the Otterlo meeting, Kahn accepted an invitation to lecture in Oslo through one of Korsmo's former students, a PAGON member. Unfortunately this fell through due to lack of funds, but there was clearly a desire that he visit Oslo, and

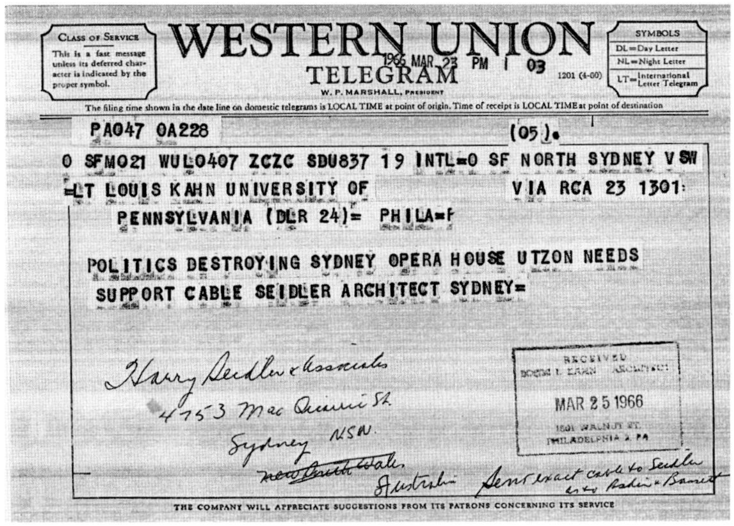

WESTERN UNION
TELEGRAM
W. P. MARSHALL, PRESIDENT
1966 MAR 23 PM 1 03

PA047 OA228 (05).

0 SFM021 WUL0407 ZCZC SDU837 19 INTL=0 SF NORTH SYDNEY VSW
=LT LOUIS KAHN UNIVERSITY OF VIA RCA 23 1301:
PENNSYLVANIA (DLR 24)= PHILA=F

POLITICS DESTROYING SYDNEY OPERA HOUSE UTZON NEEDS
SUPPORT CABLE SEIDLER ARCHITECT SYDNEY=

Harry Seidler & Associates
4753 Mac Quarrie St
Sydney NSW
New South Wales
Australia

RECEIVED
LOUIS I. KAHN ARCHITECT
MAR 25 1966
1501 WALNUT ST.
PHILADELPHIA 2 PA

THE COMPANY WILL APPRECIATE SUGGESTIONS FROM ITS PATRONS CONCERNING ITS SERVICE

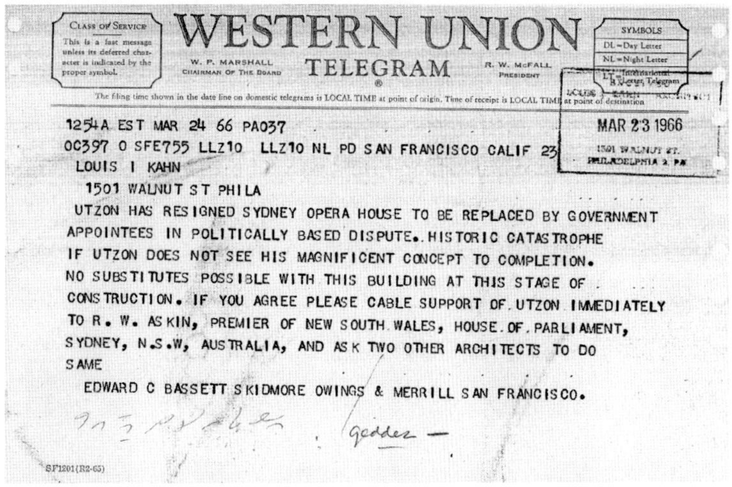

WESTERN UNION
TELEGRAM
W. P. MARSHALL, CHAIRMAN OF THE BOARD
R. W. McFALL, PRESIDENT

MAR 23 1966
1501 WALNUT ST.
PHILADELPHIA 2 PA

1254A EST MAR 24 66 PA037
OC397 O SFE755 LLZ10 LLZ10 NL PD SAN FRANCISCO CALIF 23
LOUIS I KAHN
1501 WALNUT ST PHILA
UTZON HAS RESIGNED SYDNEY OPERA HOUSE TO BE REPLACED BY GOVERNMENT APPOINTEES IN POLITICALLY BASED DISPUTE. HISTORIC CATASTROPHE IF UTZON DOES NOT SEE HIS MAGNIFICENT CONCEPT TO COMPLETION. NO SUBSTITUTES POSSIBLE WITH THIS BUILDING AT THIS STAGE OF CONSTRUCTION. IF YOU AGREE PLEASE CABLE SUPPORT OF UTZON IMMEDIATELY TO R. W. ASKIN, PREMIER OF NEW SOUTH WALES, HOUSE OF PARLIAMENT, SYDNEY, N.S.W, AUSTRALIA, AND ASK TWO OTHER ARCHITECTS TO DO SAME
EDWARD C BASSETT SKIDMORE OWINGS & MERRILL SAN FRANCISCO.

Geddes —

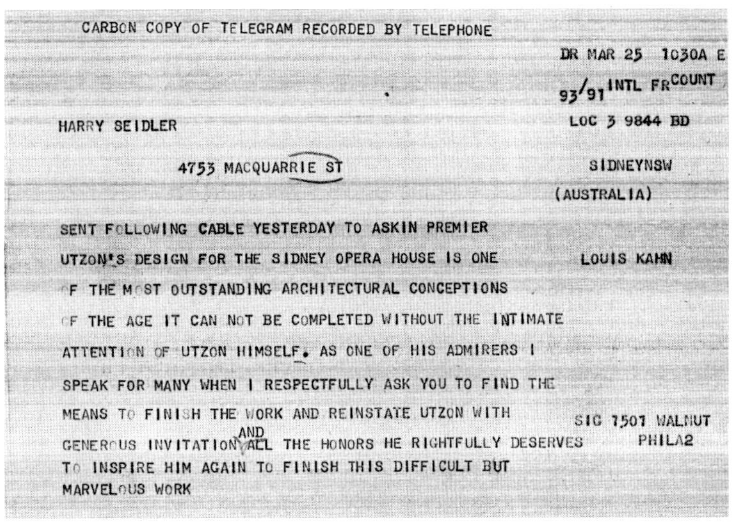

CARBON COPY OF TELEGRAM RECORDED BY TELEPHONE
DR MAR 25 1030A E
93/91 INTL FR COUNT
HARRY SEIDLER LOC 3 9844 BD
4753 MACQUARRIE ST SIDNEYNSW
(AUSTRALIA)

SENT FOLLOWING CABLE YESTERDAY TO ASKIN PREMIER
UTZON'S DESIGN FOR THE SIDNEY OPERA HOUSE IS ONE OF THE MOST OUTSTANDING ARCHITECTURAL CONCEPTIONS OF THE AGE IT CAN NOT BE COMPLETED WITHOUT THE INTIMATE ATTENTION OF UTZON HIMSELF. AS ONE OF HIS ADMIRERS I SPEAK FOR MANY WHEN I RESPECTFULLY ASK YOU TO FIND THE MEANS TO FINISH THE WORK AND REINSTATE UTZON WITH GENEROUS INVITATION AND ALL THE HONORS HE RIGHTFULLY DESERVES TO INSPIRE HIM AGAIN TO FINISH THIS DIFFICULT BUT MARVELOUS WORK

LOUIS KAHN
SIC 1501 WALNUT
PHILA2

Telegrams dated March 1966 requesting Louis Kahn's support for Utzon during disputes about his work on the Sydney Opera House. Kahn's Nordic lecture tour and Utzon's return to Denmark occurred about the same time. *Louis I. Kahn Collection, the University of Pennsylvania and the Pennsylvania Historical and Museum Commission.*

1965 | Louis Kahn's Erdman Hall and Salk Institute for Biological Studies completed. MLTW's Sea Ranch Condominium completed.

Le Corbusier and Kay Fisker die.

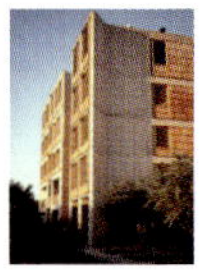

Salk Institute for Biological Studies. *P. O. Fjeld.*

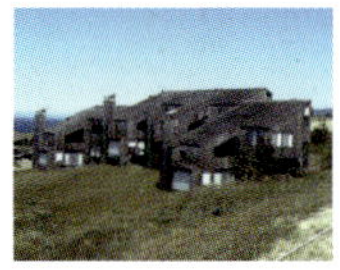

Sea Ranch Condominium. *P. O. Fjeld.*

finally in 1966 a lecture was scheduled. This trip evolved out of an invitation to be the main speaker for the sixtieth-anniversary celebration of the Danish Architects Association in Copenhagen, and in conjunction with this Louis Kahn was pressed into an extremely ambitious Scandinavian tour. Kahn would lecture in Denmark, Norway, Sweden, and Finland in six days. Svend Wohlert, who was involved with supplying furniture for the Salk Institute, extended a personal invitation for him to meet cabinetmaker Poul Hansen and architect Hans Wegner during his stay in Copenhagen. Arne Jacobsen sent a personal note with his regrets that he would not be able to attend the lecture due to ill health. At some point during this Nordic visit, Norberg-Schulz received a panicked phone call very early in the morning about Kahn not being at his hotel when a colleague arrived to drive him to the airport. He had last been seen the night before with Korsmo; rumor had it that the two, up all night and consuming a fair amount of aquavit and pickled herring, had managed to get to the airport on their own. Considering the tough lecture schedule, it is remarkable that a few hours later Kahn would once again give another lecture, and with the same vigor. The sixty-five-year-old Kahn had received requests to lecture all over the world, but the schedule for the Scandinavian tour was one of the toughest.

After a successful visit to Denmark, Kahn arrived in Oslo in the early morning and embarked on a whirlwind tour that included the Norwegian Museum of Cultural History, lunch in a timber restaurant overlooking the city and fjord, and a visit to the Oslo City Hall—that same city hall with two towers that Korsmo had worked on briefly just before leaving for his 1928 tour of Europe. Kahn felt the city hall was the best building in town and jokingly commented, "These architects have copied my work." In his lecture that night to the Oslo Chapter of the Norwegian Architects Association, Kahn referred to the old vernacular timber buildings at the museum (the same museum Wharton Esherick had visited earlier) and the Viking ships nearby, remarking, "I do not know any better architecture. [. . .] The building is really a way of life, and I don't know of anything greater to achieve than to express your building as a way of life. Not a way of living . . . a way of living is a personal choice."[28] Harald Hille, then chairman of the Oslo Chapter of the Norwegian Architects Association, later recalled not only how uplifting and inspiring Kahn's visit had been for many of his generation, but also the satisfaction he felt that Kahn had finally made a visit to Oslo.

Early the next morning Kahn was off to Stockholm to give a lecture and open a small exhibition of his work. Architect Carl Nyrén had extended the invitation on behalf of the Swedish Architectural Association, and parallel with Kahn's exhibition, Nyrén's students mounted an exhibition of their work in town planning. Kahn's lecture at Stockholm's Museum of Modern

1966 | Kahn lectures in Denmark, Norway, Sweden, and Finland. Kahn begins work on the Kimbell Art Museum. Reima Pietilä's Dipoli Student Assembly Building completed. Robert Venturi's *Complexity and Contradiction in Architecture* is published. Aldo van Eyck's Sonsbeek Pavilion completed. Jørn Utzon resigns from the Sydney Opera House project.

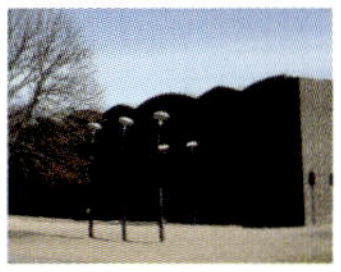

Lewerentz's St. Peter's Church in Klippan completed in 1966. *P. O. Fjeld.*

1967 | Kahn's Fisher House completed. Sverre Fehn begins work on the Hedmark Museum, Norway.

Poul Henningsen dies.

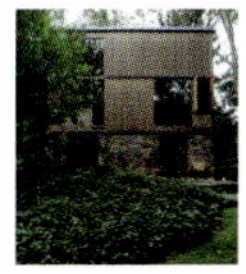

Fisher House from the garden. *P. O. Fjeld.*

1968 | Korsmo dies in Peru.

Art was packed; as in Copenhagen and Oslo, many were turned away for lack of space. The preparation for the Stockholm lecture and exhibition had faced many challenges, best characterized by a Swedish journalist who attempted to put together a presentation of Kahn's work for a magazine ahead of the visit. The journalist traveled back and forth to Kahn's office in the hope of gathering pictures, but to no avail, despite the efforts of some of Kahn's assistants to help. The pictures arrived with Kahn the day of his speech along with some material for the exhibition. This predicament was not unlike the challenges Alison and Peter Smithson had faced in their attempt to publish his work.

All four of Kahn's Scandinavian lectures were unique. In Finland, his lecture was part of a conference titled "The Planning of Helsinki Metropolitan Area." Aalto lectured the following day, and the content of his talk seemed to be a response to what Kahn had presented earlier. In Helsinki, Kahn was offered a variety of possible sites to visit; apparently when Reima Pietilä's newly finished Dipoli project was suggested, he ungraciously declined and chose instead to visit the Seurasaari Open-Air Museum (similar to the Norwegian Museum of Cultural History). I have always found this story surprising considering that Pietilä and Kahn had many Nordic friends in common, but Kahn could be curt at times, and he must have been exhausted.

In late August of 1968, two years after Kahn and Korsmo had last seen one another, Korsmo traveled to Peru for a design conference in Cuzco. At its close he made his way to Machu Picchu, a trip he had dreamed of making for years. He suffered a stroke at the main gate and died a few days later.

Among his numerous accomplishments, Arne Korsmo had opened a window for many young Scandinavian architects into some of Kahn's universe. And so Korsmo and Kahn's friendship belonged not just to both of them but also to Nordic architectural history.

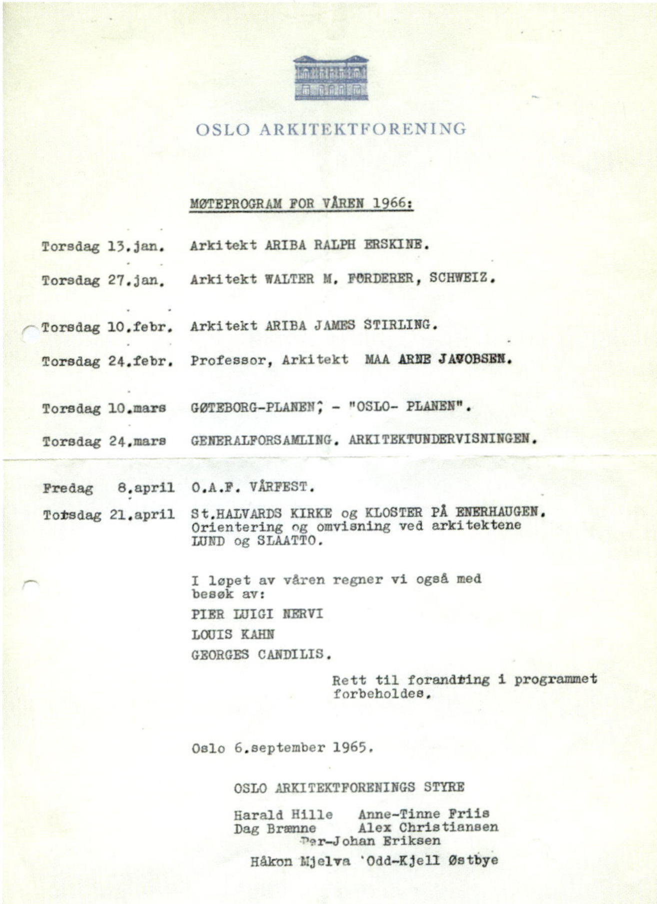

OSLO ARKITEKTFORENING

MØTEPROGRAM FOR VÅREN 1966:

Torsdag 13.jan.	Arkitekt ARIBA RALPH ERSKINE.
Torsdag 27.jan.	Arkitekt WALTER M. FØRDERER, SCHWEIZ.
Torsdag 10.febr.	Arkitekt ARIBA JAMES STIRLING.
Torsdag 24.febr.	Professor, Arkitekt MAA ARNE JACOBSEN.
Torsdag 10.mars	GØTEBORG-PLANEN; - "OSLO- PLANEN".
Torsdag 24.mars	GENERALFORSAMLING. ARKITEKTUNDERVISNINGEN.
Fredag 8.april	O.A.F. VÅRFEST.
Torsdag 21.april	St.HALVARDS KIRKE og KLOSTER PÅ ENERHAUGEN. Orientering og omvisning ved arkitektene LUND og SLAATTO.

I løpet av våren regner vi også med besøk av:

PIER LUIGI NERVI

LOUIS KAHN

GEORGES CANDILIS.

Rett til forandring i programmet forbeholdes.

Oslo 6.september 1965.

OSLO ARKITEKTFORENINGS STYRE

Harald Hille Anne-Tinne Friis
Dag Brænne Alex Christiansen
Per-Johan Eriksen
Håkon Mjelva Odd-Kjell Østbye

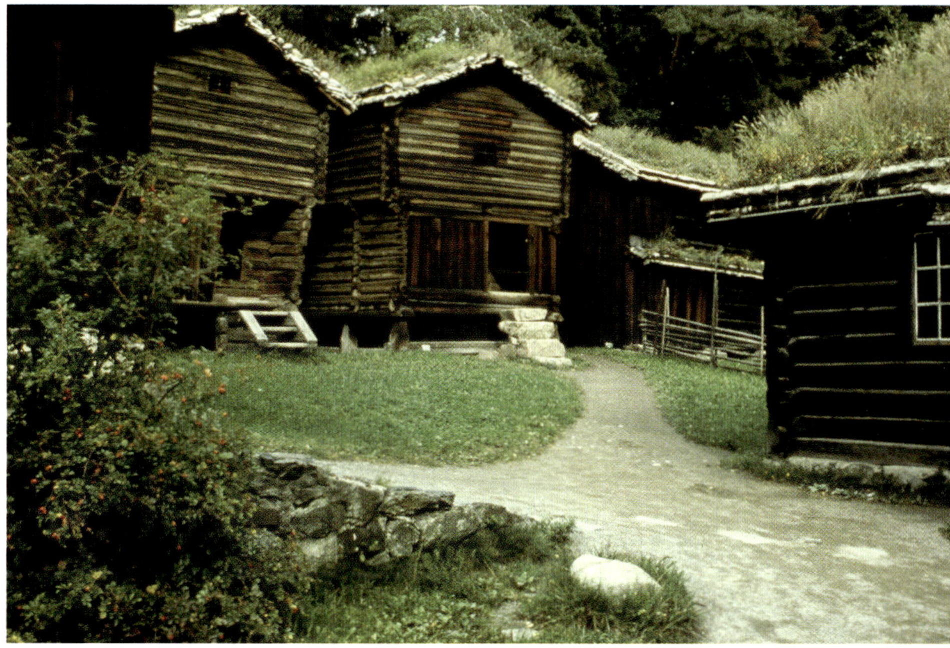

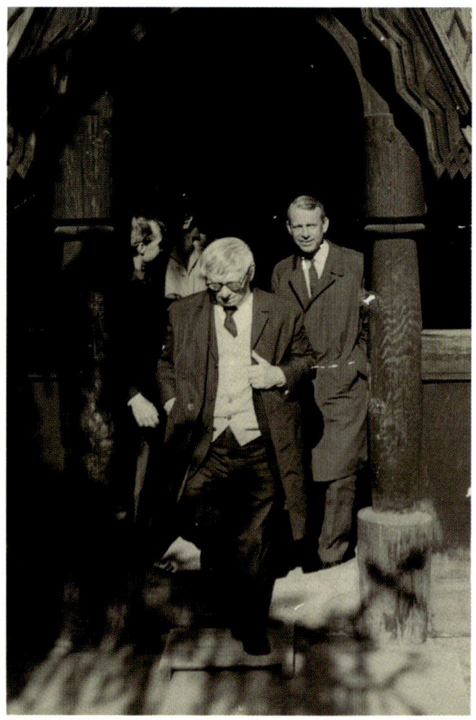

ABOVE: The Oslo Chapter of the Norwegian Architects Association's 1966 spring program. Note that the other lecturers that spring included Ralph Erskine, Walter Förderer, James Stirling, and Arne Jacobsen. *Property of the Oslo Chapter of the Norwegian Architects Association.*

TOP RIGHT: The vernacular timber houses at Oslo's Norwegian Museum of Cultural History that Kahn praised during his speech in Oslo. *The Oslo School of Architecture and Design Photo Archive.*

RIGHT: Kahn on the steps of the stav church at the Norwegian Museum of Cultural History. *Property of the Oslo Chapter of the Norwegian Architects Association.*

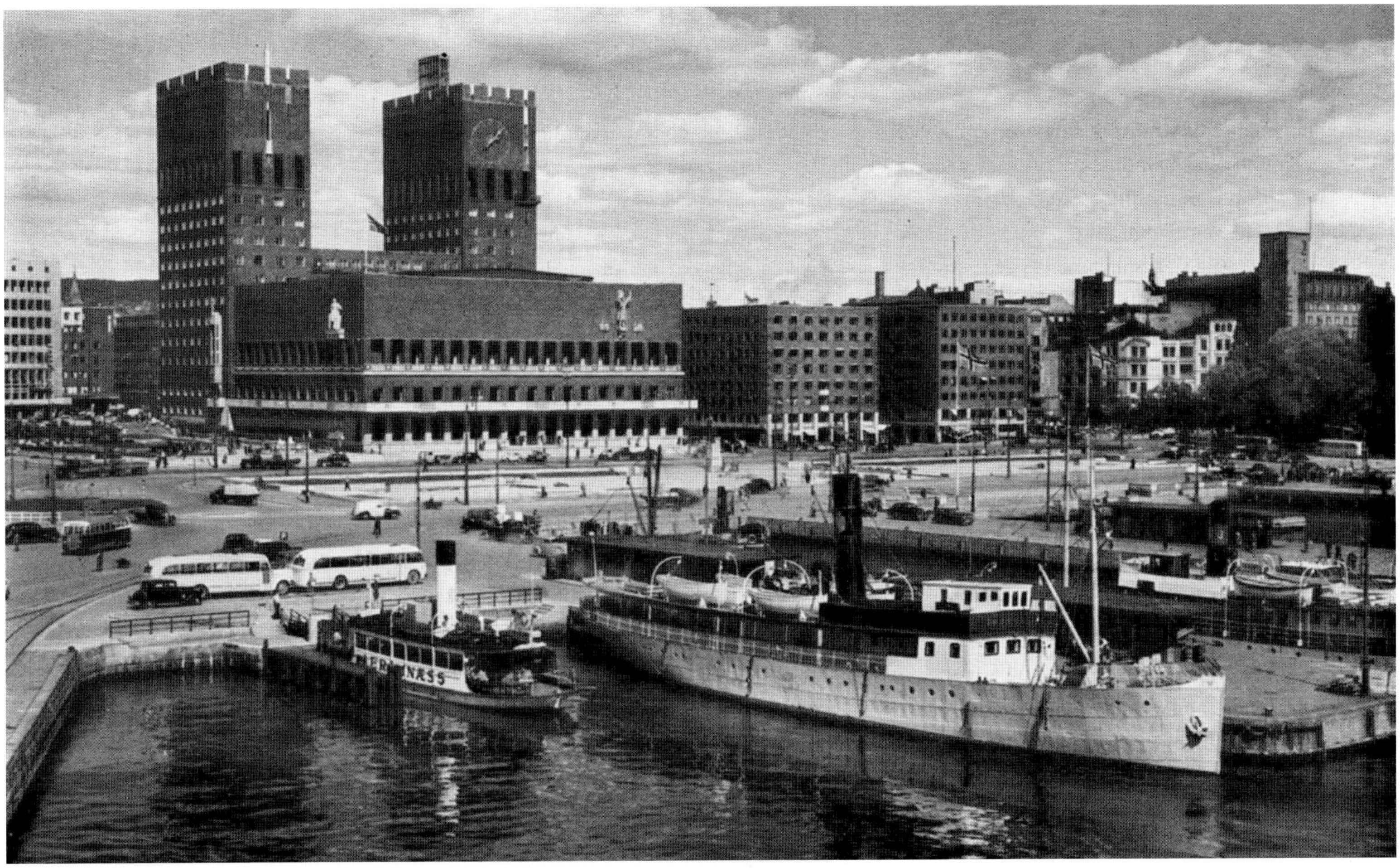

Oslo's central harbor and the adjacent city hall by Arneberg & Poulsson pictured about the time of Kahn's visit in 1966. Kahn exclaimed that the Oslo City Hall was the best building in town and joked that the architects had copied him. *Bonytt; photographer unknown.*

Kahn's Oslo Lecture, Scandinavian Lecture Tour April 20, 1966

Authors' Note: Transcription from archival recording. Brackets indicate indecipherable text.

I want to introduce my mind to you, which is trying to distinguish between the measurable and the immeasurable, and it gravitates, as it should, towards the immeasurable [. . .]. I want to justify that the measurable in man is a servant of the immeasurable. Whatever nature makes man cannot make. Whatever man makes nature cannot make. It seems as though man at the very beginning of things hammered at the door of nature to make an instrument which would express the immeasurable: the immeasurable of hate, of love, of integrity, and nobility. I believe the *raison d'être* of living is just to express. Everything in nature makes a record of what it is made of and how it was made. In man there is a record of how he was made. The fetus is a living record of how he was made. Nature makes things non-consciously, whereas man makes things consciously. Nature cannot build a house, nor build an airplane, nor write a book. These are all instruments man has found to express the immeasurable.

When you read a great writer like Gogol you realize he is a chooser of incredible things. He chooses mountains, a serpent, and the child. He composes a kind of symbolism of man. Architecture falls in this area of inspiration which guides our life. You might say the inspiration to live makes us want to have the promise it takes to live. The inspiration to learn only stems from the way we were made, because everything that was made in nature must be answerable to the laws of nature. This is true of the smallest thing as well as the largest thing.

Architecture does not exist. Architecture itself is a spirit. It is a miraculous thing that man has found a way of expression which has made architecture—*architecture*. But architecture knows no style. It knows no particular way. Architecture is big enough to take on the Gothic and the Renaissance, Egyptian and Greek architecture, all at once. It has no preferences, so therefore the architect, when he does a work, offers it to architecture. This is his greatest act: he can come to the point where his work is worthy to be offered to architecture. *Architecture* is a spirit. It would be well not to consider that you are doing modern architecture, because architecture does not understand this. It only understands architecture. So, it is not modern. It is not ancient. It is not traditional, nor conventional. It is simply an expression of that which is an enclosure, an environment which you offer architecture in all modesty. The search for principles is a wondrous thing and it comes from these primitive ideas, not something that is very complicated.

I saw the early houses in wood today [. . .] at the museum [the Norwegian Museum of Cultural History], and the ships [at the Viking Ship Museum in Oslo]. I don't know of any better architecture. I don't know of any! When you walk in you could actually sense the life, you could reconstruct the life of the people. It is a terrific offering to architecture. Everything including the furniture is a part of architecture. You don't call in the expert to tell you how to do the furniture. If you go through the building it is all part of it. The building is really a way of life, and I don't know of anything greater to achieve than to express your building as a way of life. Not a way of living [. . .], a way of living is a personal choice. When you build a house for a client, you must build it so that the client after the client will enjoy the house, not only the client that ordered the house. Architecture is never worth anything if it just satisfied the person you built it for.

Now, these inspirations of man—the inspiration to live, to learn, to question, and to express—that are the greatest inspirations of all, bring about the institutions of man. The institutions of man, whose desires on the part of man express a way of life, establish supports for the activities of man. The institutions of learning come from the inspiration to learn, which as I said, is only a reflection of how we were made, since everything that we make must be answerable to the laws of nature—every one of them, whether it is a microbe or a man. All the laws of nature are involved. [. . .] Science deals with what is.

Art deals with what is not and trying to find the answers in the atmosphere of ideas, of nature, and of man. Now I know it is a very hard goal to say it's wrong to be working only as a draftsman, but believe me, it is terribly important to be in touch with architecture even if you are not immediately able to translate what you are struggling over. [. . .] I think people live only when they are involved in their minds. Living with that mind is magnificent.

I think everybody is the same [. . .] essentially, that is, they are the same as far as their souls, but their minds are different because the brain is different. You get the brain from nature, but you get your soul from some unbelievable thing. It cannot be measured. It is the center of all measurements. And, in that combination of the immeasurable and the brain which is measurable, you have the mind. [. . .] This is why everyone is a singularity. Everyone is different from one another. This sounds as if you are in the realm of the inaccessible, but I will bring it back to the realm of the accessible.

Let us go back to the wall—an old wall, a good solid wall. A man could watch it, very pleased that he has the protection of the wall. He lives for many years behind the wall perfectly satisfied that he is safe until at last, long enough for him to question, he asks, "Is it worthwhile being so safe?" And so he punches a hole through the wall, and the wall cries, "Look, I am a wall, don't do this to me. I am supposed to protect you. What kind of man are you?" "Protection or no protection, I have to look out." The wall still cries but knows it can't do anything about it because, after all, the wall is stupid. But the next time, the man builds a wall because he finds it is pleasant to look out at the sharpness of the sun. He sees through it, and he pleases the wall by incorporating the opening in the wall as part of the order of making a wall. He makes the opening clean instead of ragged because he gets more light out of it. He put a lintel over the opening so that the wall is pleased that it does not lose its integrity and is still able to make an opening. [. . .] And it so happens that the wall has found an order which can include an opening, and it feels very proud and honored. But out of all this comes the great discovery of the column. The column is really a musical expression of an opening in which the solid and the void are in rhythm with each other, and this is the beginning of architecture. I believe this also is what we are still living off of today. We are not fundamentally different from the very time when the column came out of the wall and this musical rhythm of openings and solids gave rise to the arch and the dome. Everything follows, and it should teach us that structure is the maker of light. The light of a vault is a choice of structure. When you choose a vault you are already choosing the light. When you choose the column you are choosing a kind of light. Today the columns can be so far apart that the rhythm becomes less musical. You can disrespect the beginning in not striving to make it musical. The column must then be considered as a station. It is no longer a column as a concentrated load, but one that takes loads from many different directions. The column becomes something very different. The opening should be the expression of the amount of light you need. The privilege is there. I know that no client would support this idea, but to turn your mind towards your rights. In your own way, turn to what every country needs and you will produce a sense of architecture. I never lose sight of this stuff myself, though the struggle is enormous, and I make many mistakes. I am tempted to do many things which are not according to the principles [. . .]. But it pains me very much if I cannot point to something that does not belong to me essentially, because it belongs to the principle, and the only thing that belongs to me is the way I express it. [. . .] You can say, for instance, the first man that invented a waltz had to prove it by his own composition. But the waltz belongs to all musicians—the same with a symphony. In the same way, I think architecture needs a constant realization that what belongs to every architect is the biggest contribution. What Mozart did and what Beethoven did was to open the mind to new realizations. All other musicians following them were made to compose through them. But all that Mozart can claim, really, is his own compositions, which are magnificent. Now every building that an architect does or makes is answerable to the institutions of man, as I said, in the home, in the government, in health, in learning, in research.

In old institutions, many times you find them trying to emerge into new expressions—trying to find a realm of spaces which is good to be in within the environment of these activities.

I will tell a story about my class in the university. I gave the problem of the search for the meaning of a new institution: I gave the problem of a monastery. I told the class that this is the first monastery that has ever been. I told them also that I was a hermit who thought of this idea: I came out of a rock somewhere, and tried to convince the other hermits around that it was good to have a community of monks. But I did not know exactly what it really was, except I knew we had to meet somewhere, of course. Otherwise, what kind of community is it? Each one would have a place of their own, because already they had a place of their own. It was out of the very nature of things, and I tried to describe it as abstractly as I could—the position, its placement—in talking to my class, who were future monks. The class was stunned because they had nothing to work on. I have a class of half foreigners and half from the United States. Out of them an Indian girl said, "I believe that the cell is the most important element of the monastery, and the right for the chapel to exist comes from the cell. The retreat is a limitation of the cell, and workshops come from the cell." The class was startled because it realized there was this power in the cell. An Indian boy, either from jealousy or ambition, said, "I agree with you, but I believe each part must be equal to each other." This seemed like a very simple and innocent thing, but that thought was tremendously powerful. An English student, who was by far the most talented, was extremely inspired by these two, who had a much more transcendent view of things than some that are racing back and forth in their Mercedes. He designed something that was very remarkable, and in this design he showed the retreat a half a mile away from the refectory. He said, and believed, that the retreat is an honor for the monastery, and it should surrender one of its most important parts. This is thinking in terms of a certain monastery—not looking at a program, but looking at the sense of it. I was thrilled with this turn, you see, but all the time, the clock was ticking away, because we must show what we do at school and, after all, we must finish the problem. We invited a monk from Pittsburgh to come and tell us something about it. He listened and said, "The cell can be a central idea. It is a small room, but to a monk a small room is a large room. But I am a painter and the monastery gave me a studio, so I have a great big room, and when I come back to the cell I feel tired, I feel restrained. I see the design, which is nice, but I don't think there is a monk alive that would walk a half a mile to the refectory because it does not work out with his time system." [. . .] We were defeated. Then [after] three weeks of reconsidering things, he returned as a juror. He had thought about this during his three weeks away and became a total supporter of an idea which he had previously never dreamed of, because he realized what was happening: a reconsideration of the institutions of man, which is part of man's heritage. You cannot take a previous answer and use it modified without tremendous thought almost equal to the thought of its beginnings.

The beginning is so remarkable [. . .] that any architect can take from a "monk conception" and produce the first monastery, as in Certosa di Pavia, in which each part had never been conceived before. A cell, if you think of it, is nothing but remarkable, and a cell has also—because it was thought of so humanely—its own garden. After all, it was man, and he had to have some association with nature—his own way and the way he did architecture in those days. There was little residuary, like an extra column or an extra space. A part of the world was your domain. You could imagine mountains, fields, and a house, anything you wanted. He was given that privilege. Not a hard thing, but something that came out of soft pliability, plasticity of stone. Then the arcades came, which gave you the connection with the small garden that lead to a larger garden with a chapel, which lead to an even larger garden with a church. But all this was thought of without a program. It was thought of as nature coming into being—something that belongs to man, that is, expressing the coming of a new institution of man, expressing it as nature.

The new principle of the same conception is when you do a program. Rethink as nature—not taking it as it comes, because a program that comes from a client is an area program. You have got to make it a space building. The difference is like day and night. You have got to change areas into space. What it means, you have got to pause, you must think of form, you must think of arches, you think of space. You must think of the character of light. All of this comes in—though where does this come in the program? [. . .] You must take all the corridors and make them into galleries, because who wants a corridor? Nobody, except as a secret passage from here to there. Actually, it is completely unnoble as architecture. It is a mouse's building, but not man's building. Then, you have got to change the budget into economy, which is the biggest job of all, because the clients think in terms of budget, which is based purely on what was miserably done before. This is not all: you have got to change it into economy, which may cost much money if the attitude is not right.

And so you can go on to change a lobby into a place of entrance, which is a very important part of the building, which can mean the difference between a stairway and an elevator. A building, in my opinion, should add to the treasury of spaces of a city, town, or a country place. It must be part of the treasury and not considered as a temporary or momentary decision.

Architects are worried because they don't do all the buildings—in the United States, 15 percent [. . .]. Why do architects worry so much about that? Why don't they worry about making the 15 percent exemplary—something that becomes an example to architecture? But no, they want to make 20 percent of some mediocre stuff? Is it because architects do not really believe that they have the power that they really have? I don't think they do. I think it would be much better that they did only 5 percent instead of 15 percent, if everything they did belonged to architecture and everything everyone else did just belonged to building. That is a different thing. All buildings are not architecture. Architecture is a noble thing that has a transcendent thought. Think of the wonder of a temple. The seeds of order of a building which is formed have honored use, where no religion is pointed out, where every religion can have its space. And think of the marvel of the architect who thinks of a round building so he does not have corners where a ritual can be expressed, any kind of ritual. And then he puts a window on top, so you don't even have direction in a round building. Unfortunately, he has to put a door in, which he must have cried like anything about—after all, he has to have a door. But this is the spirit that is the Pantheon. The Pantheon is a terrific building, because it emerges as a true expression of a treasury of spaces. And what is architecture but the thought of making a space—a space that leads to the development of the institutions of man, the will to live and learn. If you instead consider corridors galleries, then you have given the value of this room that of the gallery, which belongs to the students, since classes are held there. The students have their own classroom if this is associated with the garden and not the internal air system or the recipient of lockers.

The most important space in a building is often that which your client does not talk about at all. It is the connection, the architecture of connections, in which you forget for a moment your duties. You are in a mood, you are in yourself, in preparation for what may be expected. The building is a tremendous psychological instrument.

In an architectural space I believe that how a space is made must be evident in the space itself, in the same way that whatever nature makes it records in how it was made. We as architects are involved in [the] making of spaces and their connections, and we must make spaces where how space is made is evident in the space itself.[29]

Kahn's Address to Architecture and Planning, SAFA Conference, Finland

Authors' Note: Transcription from archival recording. Brackets indicate indecipherable text.

It seems to me that there is a need to reconsider the scope of architecture. I have not studied city planning nor residential planning, but simply from looking back to the beginning, which somehow fascinates me, know that there are in the air many more aspects of architecture than one can imagine. I believe that in the making of a city and considering regional problems, that we could consider water itself, aqua, as architecture. I think that there is architecture in the movement of a car. A plane flying around is actually architecture. It is not just a flat thing on a piece of paper. The utilities have architecture. Then we can also say that light has architecture. They are all, in a way, strong elements. We have to agree that getting the opportunity to express the importance of water is a great thing. In some places water is not fit to drink and there are no ways of making it drinkable. Maybe you have not thought of this, but in many places it is necessary to get water from various sources and distribute it through long pipes, which always have to be replaced by new ones after some time.

When considering the architecture of movement, you must consider stopping as important as going. The garage should be considered as an extension of the street. The street is different. It must be designed for stopping and going. A railway station is also not a building. It is merely an extension of the street, and its architecture is really a street architecture. It is "via" architecture. The same is true of the terminal, which is a building with its shape expressed as street architecture. These buildings are more like the street than buildings. A fire station does not have to be a building. The same with the police station: it does not have to be a building. It is part of the street. If you have a contrast between movement and service, if you regard the street as movement and the different stations as services, you can go on with other architectures. You might say then that you are trying to put the garage out in the street. A street just finds itself in places where it is needed. Maybe you are going to build a gas station. It should just be part of the street.

It is general to make a new road from one that was once one for the horse and wagon. We are still making things in principally the same way as Romans and Greeks did. We are just using new expressions.

The architect has to be inspired when designing something, and the building has to inspire too. Man wants to find out how we are made. Once we know that, we know all the laws. There is no mystery when things come from deep inspiration. If you are inspired and you are going to provide for a desire, then you have a great thing going on. The greatest inspiration of all is the inspiration to express, and I believe that to express is the reason for existence; there is no other reason. I believe that this distinguishes us from other forms of life.

Being original is a very important thing. I think that those men who made the first city did a great thing. It is always hard to create something new and unknown. Here is a story about a man and a wall. The man was inside surrounded by walls and he wanted to see out. That is why he dug a hole in the wall. The wall cried, “What are you doing to me?” And the man answered, “I must see out.” The wall was very unhappy. But the man built the hole again, knowing the value of the opening. He made the wall with better stone, and the wall felt pretty good. Nature has inspired us to do all kinds of different things. Man could not fly, but he saw the birds fly and so he decided he wanted to do it too. So now we have airplanes. Man saw a fish swim, and so we have boats.

Light is an important thing in architecture too. The shape which the structure gives must be sympathetic to the shape of light. The light must be so planned that it designs the same thing when you have an oblong shape. If you have a square shape then the light is square, and so on.

An architect must not be a builder. It is not important that the architect does all the work. It is important that one distinguishes between the architect and builder.

When a program comes from a client, there will no doubt be a lot of changes. When you, the architect, might change the corridors into galleries, he might change the places of the rooms, taking into consideration the time of day, the season of the year, and so on. Light is very important in designing.

I believe if you consider the inspiration to express the greatest, then I would say science is the same. The scientist compares himself with what is not. The comparison of yourself with what is not gives you an opportunity to create new things. That is life.[30] ■

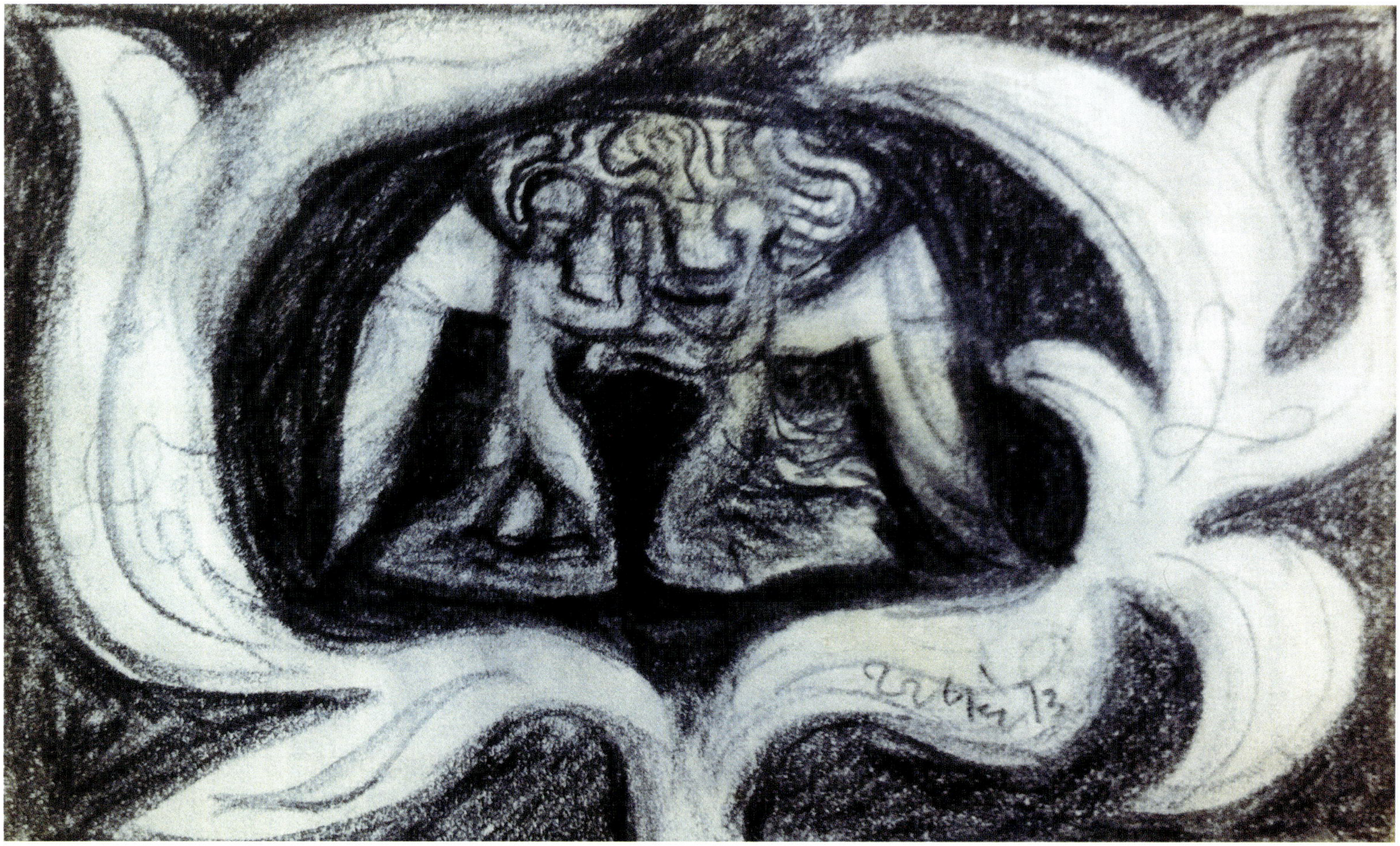

Drawing Kahn made in the year of his death, 1973. The blue, frosty color and strong framing of the couple reflect a Nordic sensibility. *Nathaniel Kahn Collection.*

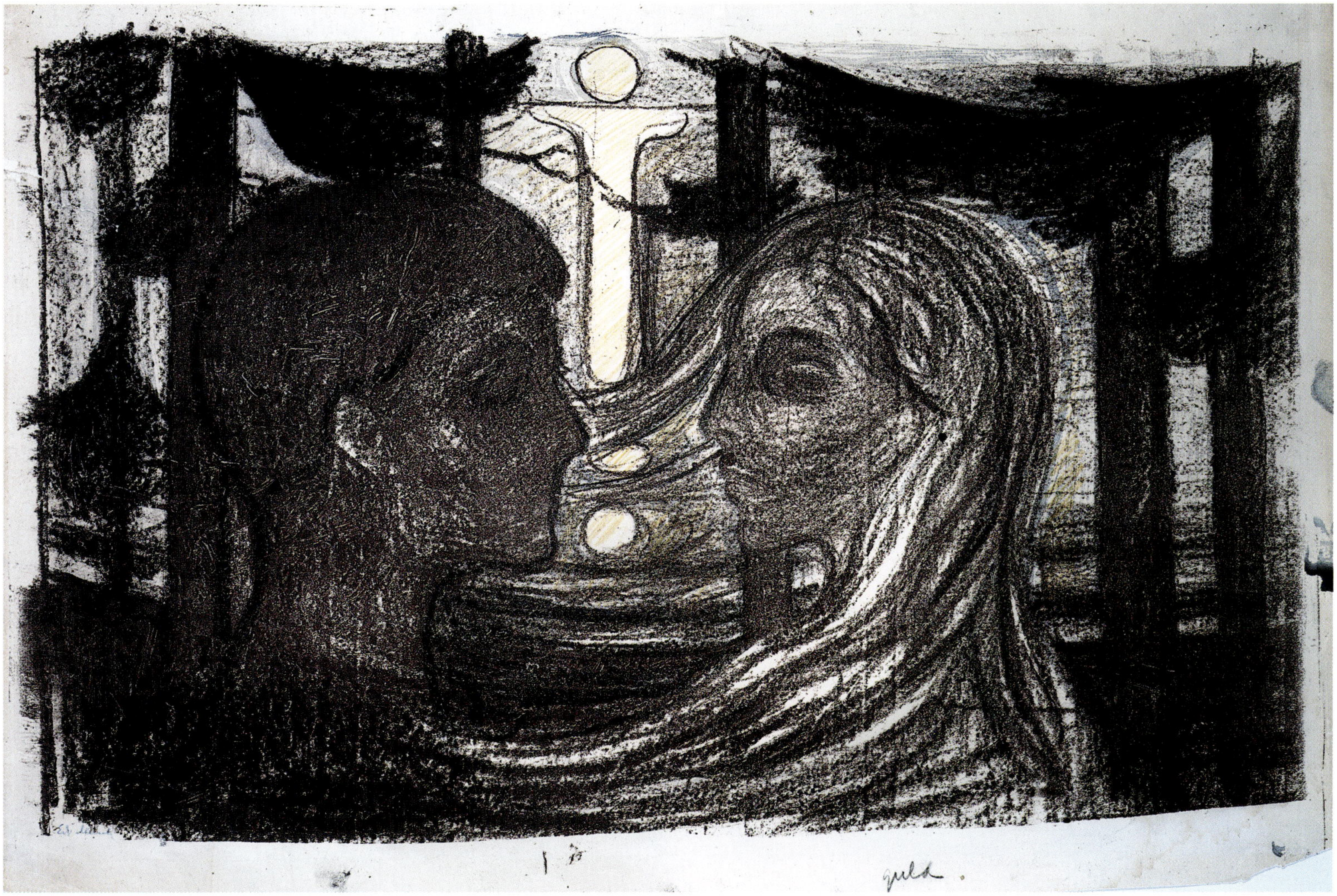

Attraction, 2 by Edvard Munch. Kahn's 1973 drawing of the couple shares similarities of composition, tone, and mood with this rendering. Some of Munch's Nordic sensibility seems to be present in Kahn's drawing as well. *The Munch Museum Archives, Oslo.*

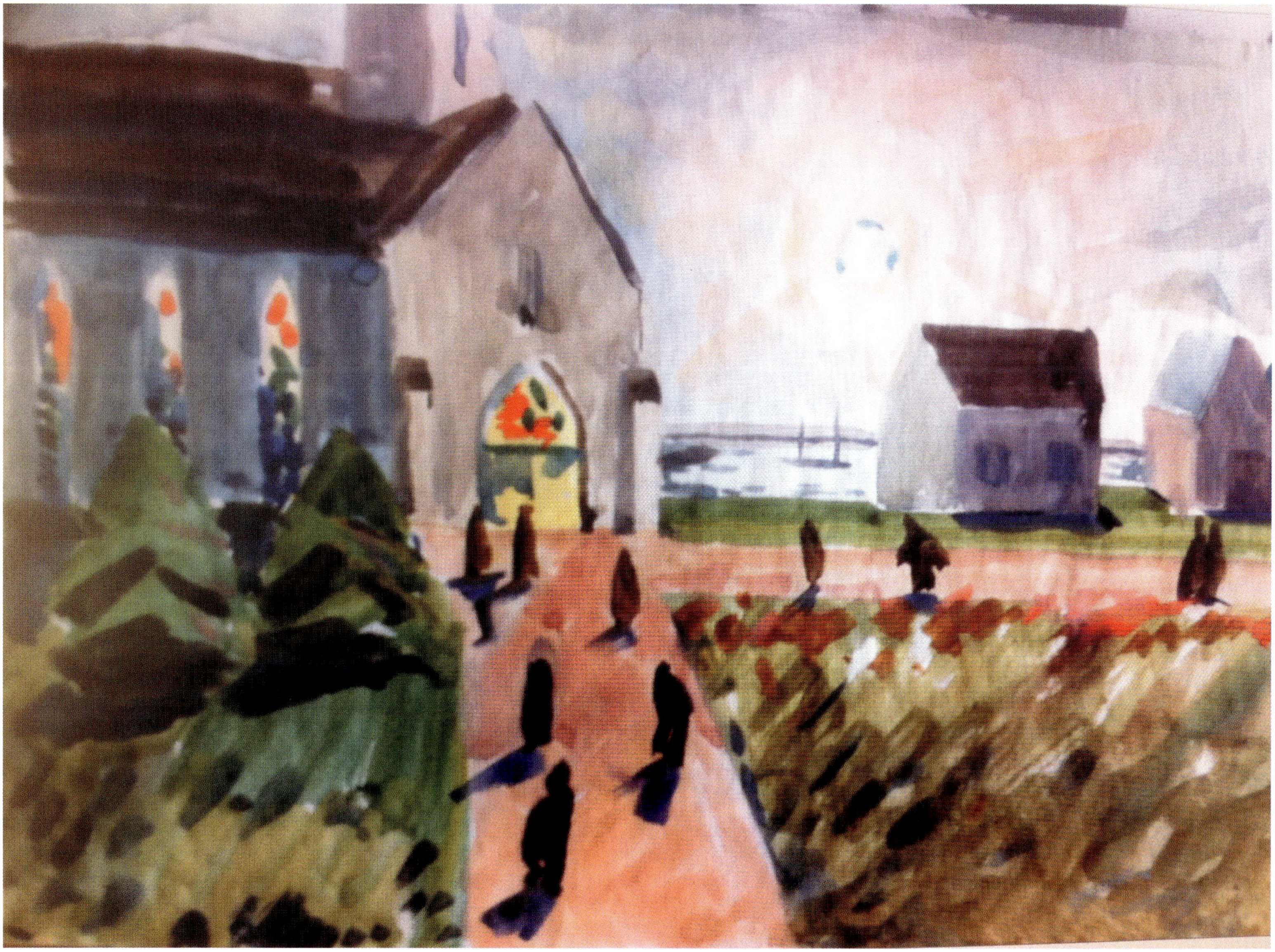

Watercolor by Louis Kahn. This study of light in Canada seems to capture the same light present in the Nordic region. *Nathaniel Kahn Collection.*

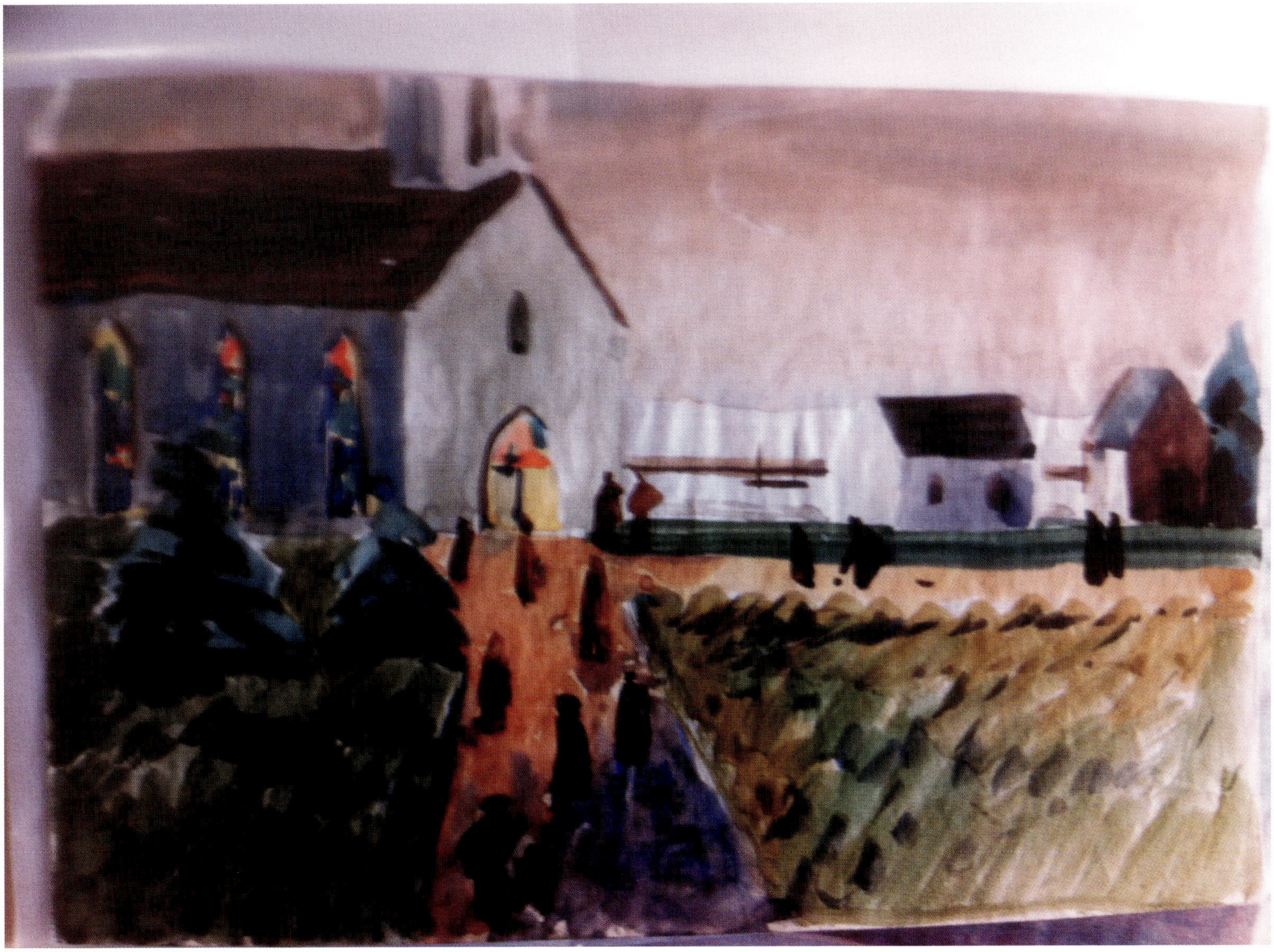

Watercolor by Louis Kahn. This study of light pictures the same church in Canada slightly later in the day than in the corresponding image. *Nathaniel Kahn Collection.*

THE MASTERCLASS

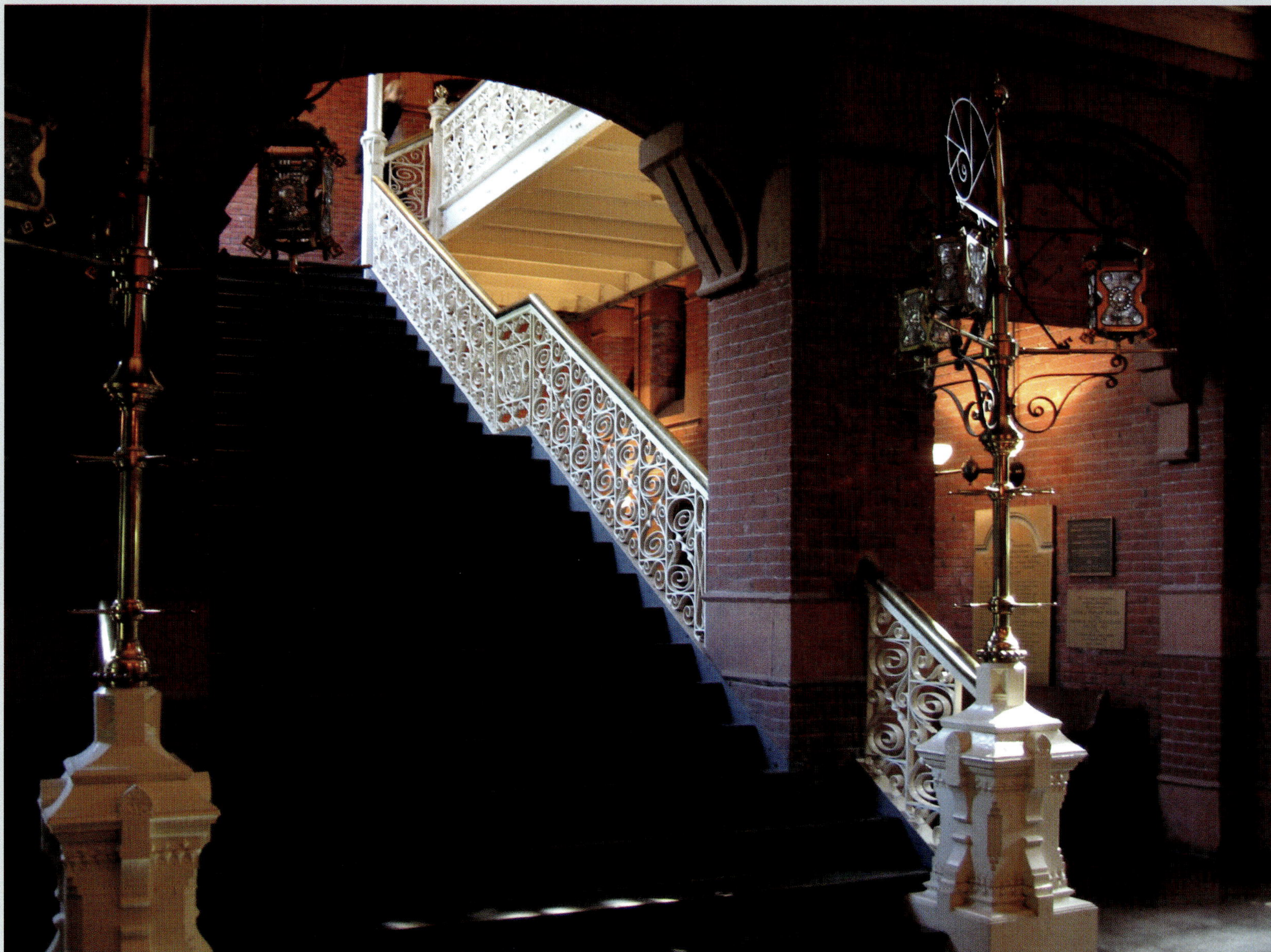

The cast-iron stair leading up to the masterclass studio in Frank Furness's Fine Arts Library at the University of Pennsylvania. *P. O. Fjeld.*

2 THE MASTERCLASS

When I entered the Louis I. Kahn masterclass at the University of Pennsylvania in 1972, the studio was located on the second floor of the Fine Arts Library by Frank Furness. Furness's building lent a unique identity to the class. Opposite the then-new architectural school, the library with its grand exterior entrance was, for all its formality, strangely welcoming. Its first-floor lobby opened directly on to the main reading room, and a wide cast-iron staircase led up to the half-circular room of Kahn's studio. Large vertical windows gave plenty of light, and a narrow interior balcony that encircled the studio formed a viewing platform for both students and visitors. It was a great place to work—intimate, crammed with models and drawings. My class consisted of students from all over the world, a small group of seventeen men and one woman. Despite our different backgrounds, ages, and experience, we soon formed a tight bond.

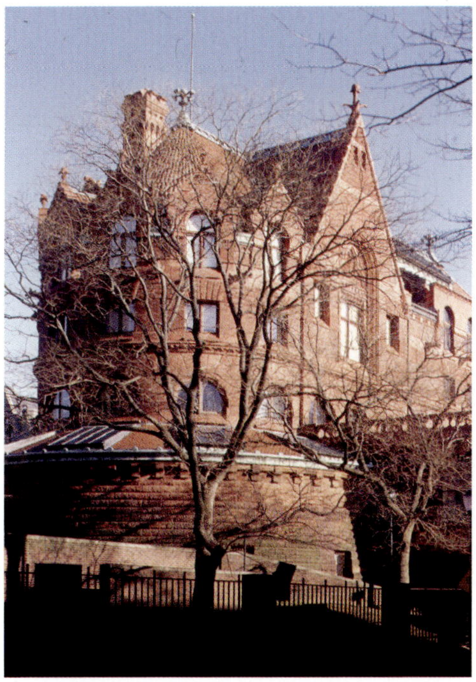

Kahn's masterclass studio was located on the second floor of the Fine Arts Library. Daylight entered the studio room from the top two sets of windows. *P. O. Fjeld.*

The teaching team consisted of Kahn, architect Norman Rice, and engineer Georges Robert Le Ricolais. Rice, Kahn's classmate at both Central High School in Philadelphia and the University of Pennsylvania, had been the first American architect to work in Le Corbusier's office. The French engineer Le Ricolais had come to the United States late in his career as a visiting professor at Yale and, within a short period, had joined the Penn architecture department about the same time as Kahn. At the start of our studio Kahn was seventy-one; Le Ricolais, seventy-eight; and Rice, the youngest of the team, had just turned sixty-eight. Kahn and Le Ricolais would tease Rice that he was still too young to have a clear personal opinion.

Even at seventy-one, Louis Kahn was a very striking, energetic figure. From the studio windows we could see him walking full speed toward the library building, his dark blue suit jacket flapping, and his white hair in all directions. An architect, yes—but I sometimes sensed his self-image was more that of a sportsman. In the studio he always sat on the edge of his chair, if he sat down at all. That posture kept him alert, never too comfortable. In general he was the last to take a seat, often joking with Rice and Le Ricolais to please sit down, they were too old to remain standing. We knew we were dealing with a mature teaching group; no one complained even when Rice or Le Ricolais took a small nap in the middle of it all. When the projects were not challenging enough to keep their interest or when Kahn went off on a long, personal argumentation, they would fade out. Just the same, a word or a sentence from Kahn's monologue could suddenly spark their interest, and they would rejoin the discussion all over again.

From a student's perspective, the team appeared tightly knit and their disagreements seemed to be an extension of their friendship. Yet each clearly had his allotted time and expertise. We arrived in awe of the idea of studying with Kahn, but it did not take long to grasp the

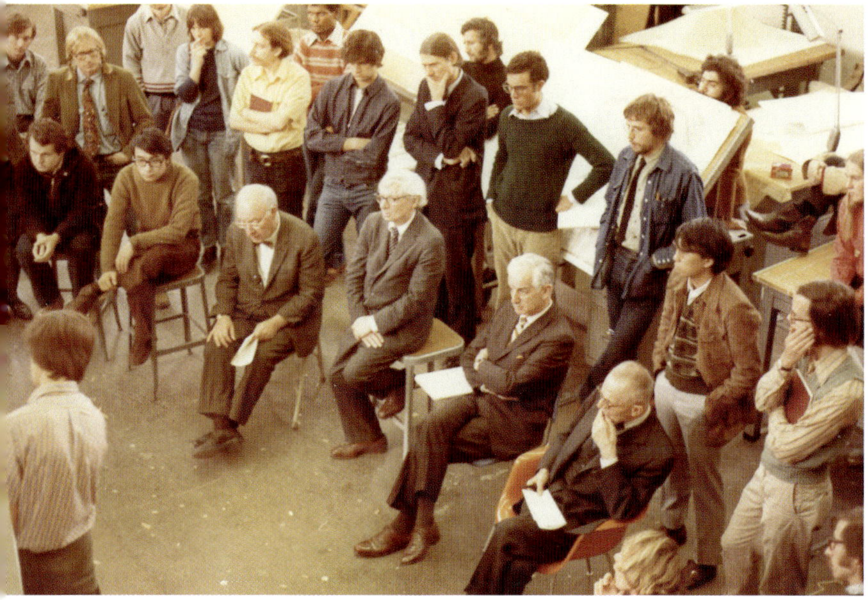

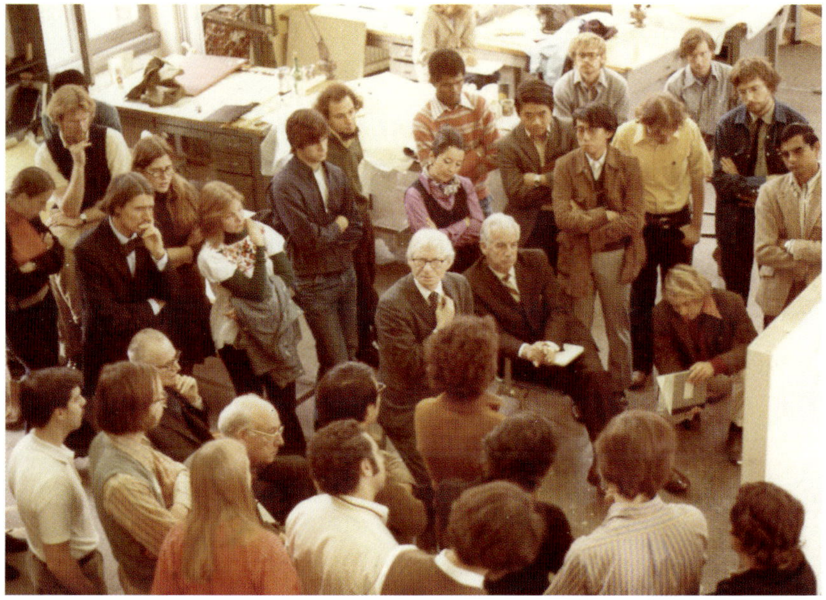

ABOVE LEFT: One of the first sessions of our masterclass during the fall of 1972. Louis Kahn is at the center, sitting on a stool in his characteristic "edge position." Norman Rice is seated to his right. Robert Le Ricolais, in his usual pose with his hand on his chin, is sitting comfortably in an Eames chair. *Robert Couch Private Collection.*

ABOVE RIGHT: A pin-up discussion. Whether or not we had advanced our work since the last pin-up, we had to share our latest sketches and drawings. *Robert Couch Private Collection.*

RIGHT: Close-up: Kahn and Le Ricolais. *Robert Couch Private Collection.*

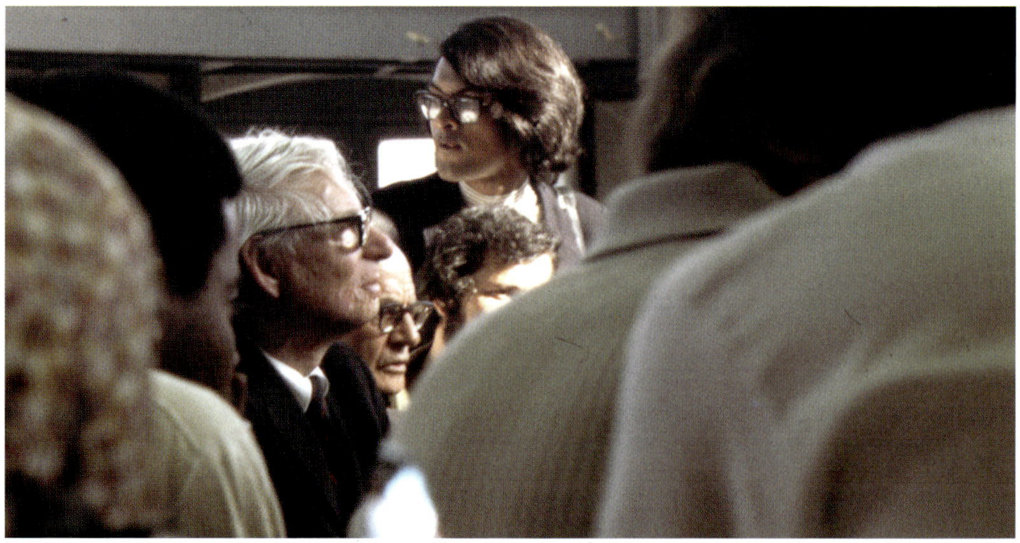

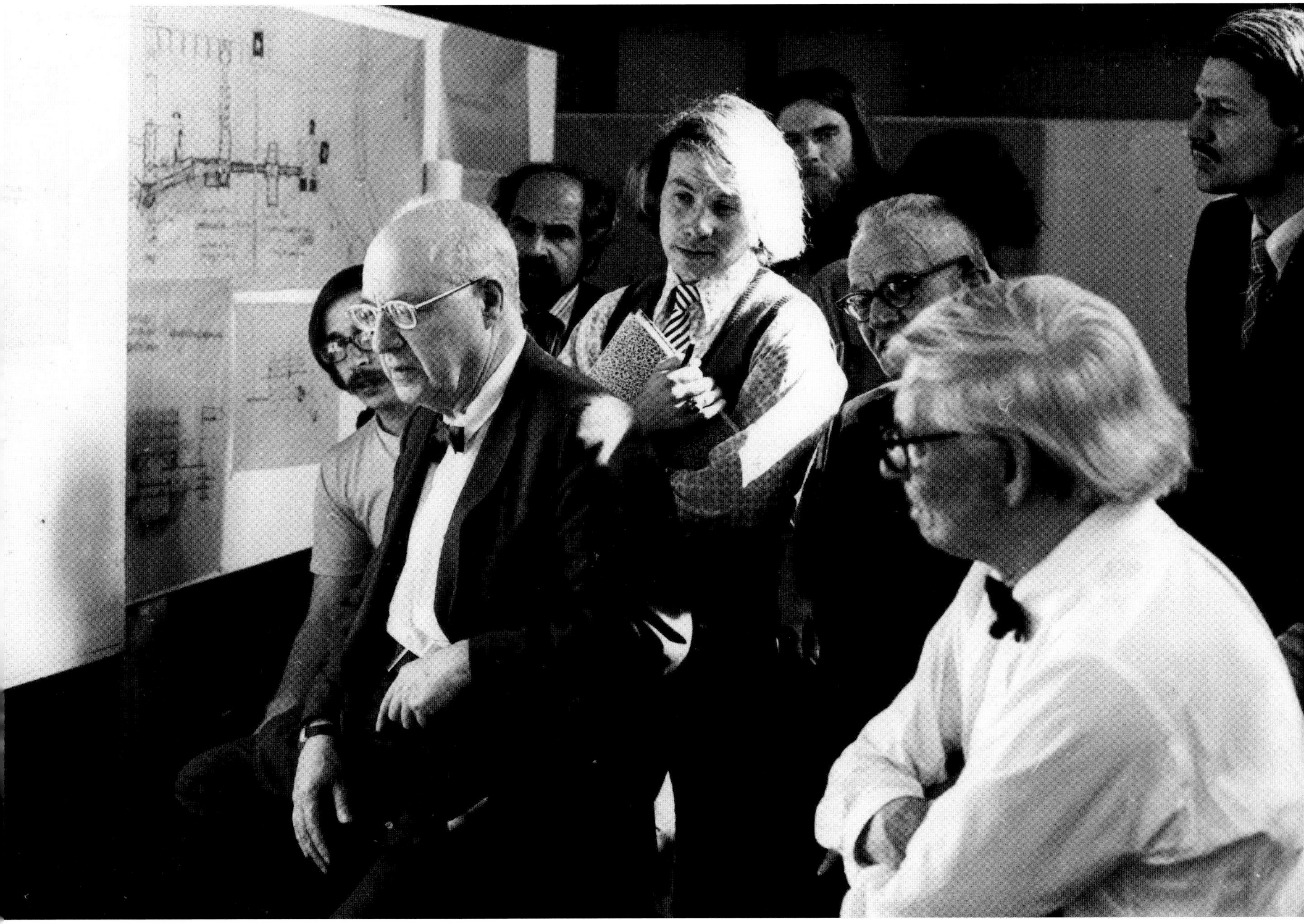

Class in session: Kahn and Norman Rice contemplating a student project before sharing their feedback. I am behind Rice with my notebook. Le Ricolais is to my left. *P. O. Fjeld.*

importance of Rice and Le Ricolais. There was no question that Kahn was the leader and driving force, but the team was a unit.

Kahn's stature as a famous architect and the growing recognition of his built work certainly influenced the studio. His capacity to inspire students and filter his enthusiasm, curiosity, and creative energy back into the class was unique. Everything that had no obvious or immediate answer seemed to appeal to him. He would respond with, "I do not understand what you are saying, but this interests me," and from there his imagination would vitalize and expand the project discussion. None of us were able to escape his charisma, a positive energy that seemed to capture and lure everyone into his world. Rumors that Kahn was exhausted by his work and that he was almost blind, even when wearing his thick glasses, trickled in; but in class we sensed very little of this, and we rather believed the opposite—that he could see through each one of us.

Kahn's studio teaching was based on the idea of holding on to what he called the "immeasurable dimension" for as long as possible, to prolong and feed the intuitive awareness of a spatial situation. Kahn believed that the process of developing an idea from the first faltering thoughts and observations to a more concrete idea could solidify a project's direction too soon, before its underlying architectural potential could be truly discovered and understood. He therefore taught us to have patience with intuitive content, to allow wonder to mature gradually—and then, once we grasped its potential, to allow this understanding to give tenor and direction to the project. To rely on the immeasurable (a spatial awareness that was outside a tangible set of facts), and through this prolonged process find direction toward the measurable (the project and its physical conditions), was a difficult enterprise for many in the class. For most of us, our prior training and progression through projects had been guided by a detailed program. So at the start of each masterclass assignment we felt there was very little to work out from or hold on to. But over time, we learned that this challenge was the same that Kahn set for himself with each new project, seeing himself as a student all over again.

Kahn would talk about the "incompleteness of knowledge" and "the importance of knowing." He regarded knowledge as something one learned or attained, and knowing as a deep-rooted, intrinsic comprehension or personal insight, a wisdom essential to the creative process. Few of us had reflected on these concepts before entering his class, but gradually we were able to apply the distinctions within our work. Nevertheless, much of Kahn's thought process remained mysterious to us. For instance, he might follow up an observation that "You can only learn that which is already within yourself" with the statement that "Knowledge is as important, as it can keep you in touch with your knowing." His tendency to go in several direc-

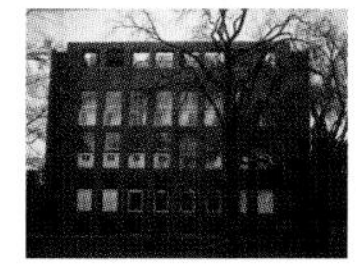

Phillips Exeter Academy Library. *P. O. Fjeld.*

tions at once generated a certain amount of pressure in the studio, as we were trying to make sense of all the pieces while also contributing our own interpretations. In the background, Rice and Le Ricolais could suddenly help reframe the discussion with a few precise comments, but that was not always sufficient to get us back on track.

The atmosphere was intense. It was a day-and-night studio, in that all project work in this precomputer age was very time-consuming and physically tied to the classroom. Some students with families would leave in the evening to work at home, but most of us were tied to our studio desks. We pressed ourselves close to our limits, and the hidden competition between us generated energy. One Japanese student hardly left his desk for a year. A teacup, a small teapot, and a rice cooker were always mixed in among his papers and drawing equipment. He had no time for sleep. His intense work ethic, along with a highly motivated class, also added to the pressure. When Kahn was away, either on a site visit or to deliver a lecture somewhere in the world, the studio continued full speed. We knew he would be back for the next pin-up, and there was no opening for not being prepared. Our ambitions were all-consuming and seemed to overpower everything else.

The given program was the same for all, but the individual critiques at the drawing table were highly personal. Kahn seldom talked directly about a project or the drawings so carefully laid out on the table, as these often ended up as a support to the conversation rather than its focus. Through his stories, which turned the conversation to everyday things tangential to the project at hand, he kept each one of us alert. Gradually we came to understand our project's breadth, as our sensitivity to the task shifted with each discussion. The architectural awareness emerging from these one-on-one sessions was contingent upon the situation and impossible to prepare for in advance. Kahn never openly guided a project in a particular direction. After he finished his one-on-one discussion with you and moved on to another student, there was often an underlying feeling of being alone with the task. Each of us had to unravel the content of his particular feedback and interpret it for our own work, and at times this process would backfire. When that individual work process faltered, several days could pass before all of the students were on track again. I remember slowly comprehending my architectural aims, but the lack of a clear physical expression persisted to the end.

For all the group spirit in the studio, we could not really help each other. Finding creative energy was individual; and all the skills, knowledge, and constructive criticism from our earlier studies and training seldom seemed enough, in that Kahn's approach required another type of concentration. Knowledge as such was no longer regarded as the primary content, as we were constantly reminded of Kahn's differentiation between "knowing" and "knowledge." The uncertainties and dualities that surfaced in Kahn's language never abated, and not everyone experienced this shift of focus as positive. The process was an ongoing struggle for all of us on some level. Some students had difficulty translating Kahn's teaching approach, vocabulary, and ambition into a direction or platform of their own. Others questioned the validity of his core concerns. His teaching was not a neat package of set answers that ensured future professional success.

In class you were more or less left to invent your own program, and the given project information was far more open for personal interpretation than most of us had experienced prior to Kahn's studio. In the coursework for my professional degree, a student's ability to address the spatial program was an important criterion for grading, and I think this was true at most schools of architecture at that time. By contrast, Kahn challenged us by explicitly stating that he had little trust in any fixed or given program, arguing that the most important spaces in a building were seldom described in the brief. We knew he was referring to spaces such as the central open court at the Salk Institute and the main interior room in the Phillips Exeter Academy Library, but he never mentioned them by name, so the idea of "a core space" remained abstract, open for interpretation. His push to rely on intuition alone at the start of a new project was an ongoing challenge for most of us. He had an almost naive belief in our capacity to start a project from zero and in our ability to face a given program without any preconceived content or image. The critical early stages of a new project generated frustration; but the reflective pause we ultimately found in this fragile start gave room for intention to mature, and Kahn never gave up on our ability to reach this concentration. The creative pause was a skill I had to learn. It quickly became clear that the potential embedded in this type of reflection would not necessarily surface through merely satisfying the precepts of the set program assignment. In retrospect I can see the reflection was a form of training: exercising and exploring the limits of our creative stamina.

This open pedagogy also presented problems for the teaching team. I remember overhearing during my first semester the three teachers discuss their frustration over the slow pace of student progress and the lack of adequate drawings and models. Their real concern was probably how the department would react to what could be perceived as a meager output. In the Kahn Archives, correspondence between the team from other years reveals concerns over the slow pace of work and how the department would react, so this must have been a recurring problem.

When the class was struggling, Kahn would respond with comments such as "We are all born with a sense of what to do, but how to do it . . . we are not born with. You can only learn that which is already within yourself." As a young graduate student full of yourself, accepting this type of encouragement was uplifting, but it was also brutal. There was no set answer, no platform for comparison, no place to hide. We were expected to present our work to the others regardless of our progress relative to the last review. Despite the individual nature of the feedback we received, we were primarily learning and sharing as a group, so there was no point of withholding work or feeling jealous. If someone attempted to copy an idea, Kahn would let it pass; the original idea had long since transformed, and the copy was already stale. That said, he would not let arrogance slide. Once full of myself, I criticized a fellow student's project section. Kahn reacted at once, leveling me with, "*Do you think your opinion belongs to eternity*?" Painful as it was, I learned a lot that day. What gave me the right to judge? It was not a matter of the quality of the section but of respecting the individual creative act. We never heard Kahn speak disparagingly of another colleague. Likewise, I do not recall him ever complaining about a building process, project, or client in front of the class. After class when the three friends would occasionally have a drink together, what was said then stayed with them.

Twice a week we had a pin-up discussion where each student would present his or her project to the team. (Notations from these sessions form the bulk of my class notes.) During the critiques, some of which could last for hours, each of the three teachers had a specific role: Le Ricolais would address material and its structural capabilities; Rice, use and functional aspects; and Kahn, everything else. On more general topics, each would make his opinions very clear, and the discourse that followed had no limitations. These sessions were often crowded, not just with drawings and models but also with people. We gained inspiration and a broader perspective from architects, philosophers, poets, and painters from outside the school who would suddenly appear in the studio. These guests were of all ages and nationalities, and some were friends and colleagues Kahn had met during his numerous trips. Many attended just to listen; but some actively participated in our discussions, and this usually gave the class, and particularly Kahn, even more momentum and energy.

During the course we were given four assignments: an orphanage, a shopping center, a library, and an urban intervention in the center of Philadelphia. The projects varied in program complexity and scale, but we could not escape the social challenges or concerns embedded within the programs' intentions. We were from the very start dealing with what Kahn termed "institutions of man." This dimension always surfaced in the discussions, and our different backgrounds, language skills, and life experiences gave rise to a variety of interpretations. Each assignment had specific challenges, but the library project was perhaps the most unique

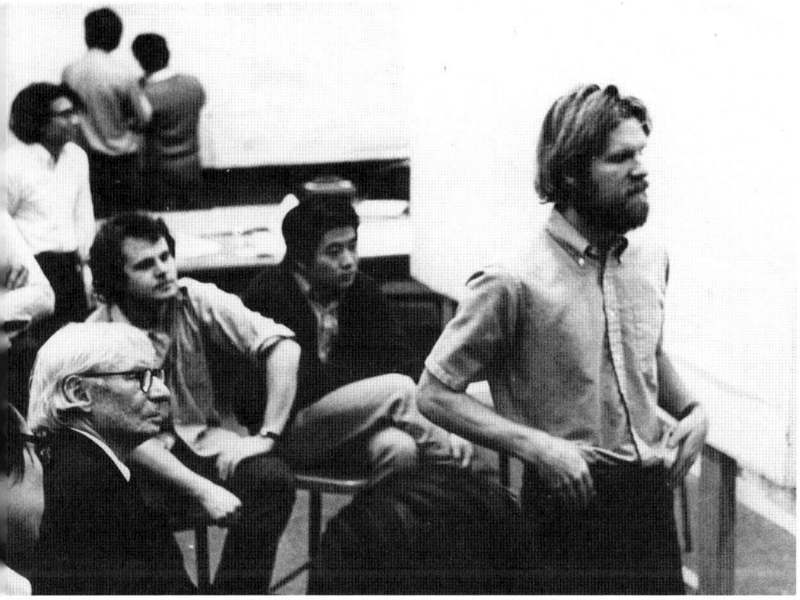

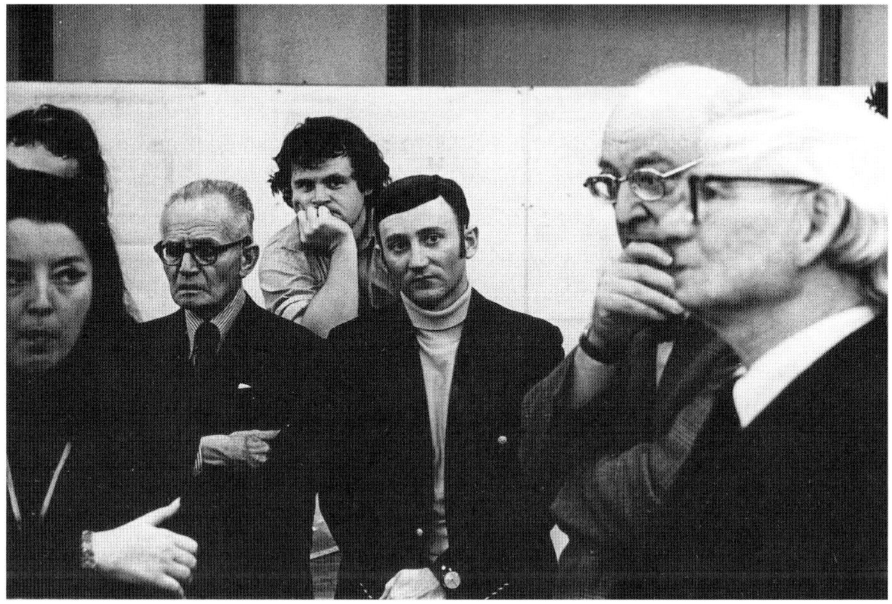

ABOVE LEFT: Buzz (Leland) Kimball presenting his work. *Tim Spelman.*

ABOVE RIGHT: The only woman in the class, Svetlana–Kana L. Radevic, presenting her work. Le Ricolais is pictured to her immediate left. *Robert Couch Collection.*

RIGHT: Tim Spelman standing next to Kahn. *P. O. Fjeld.*

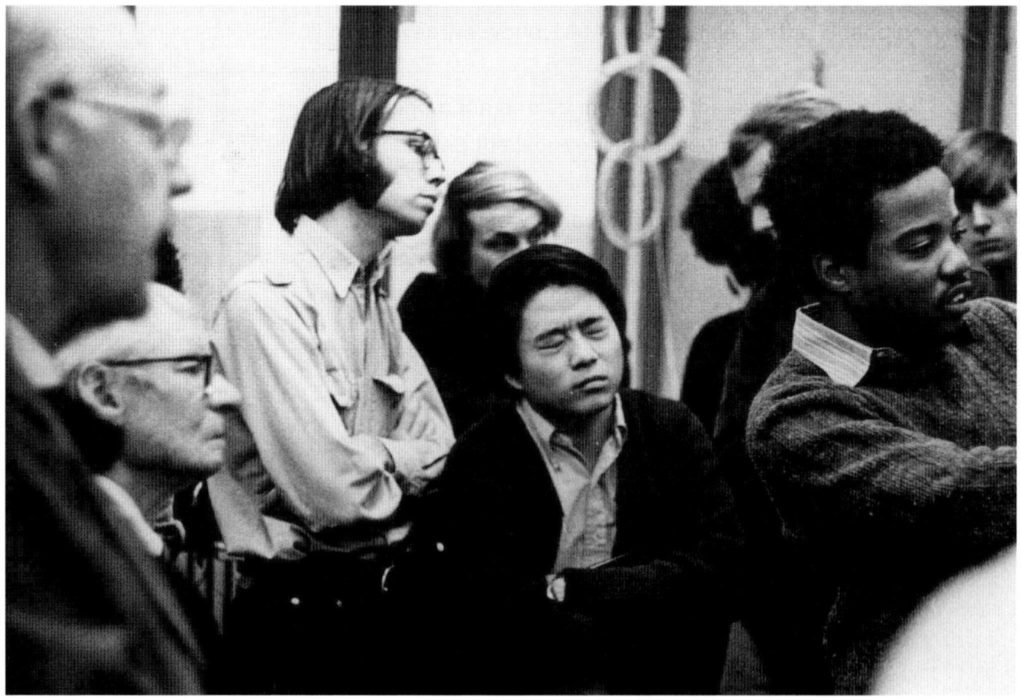

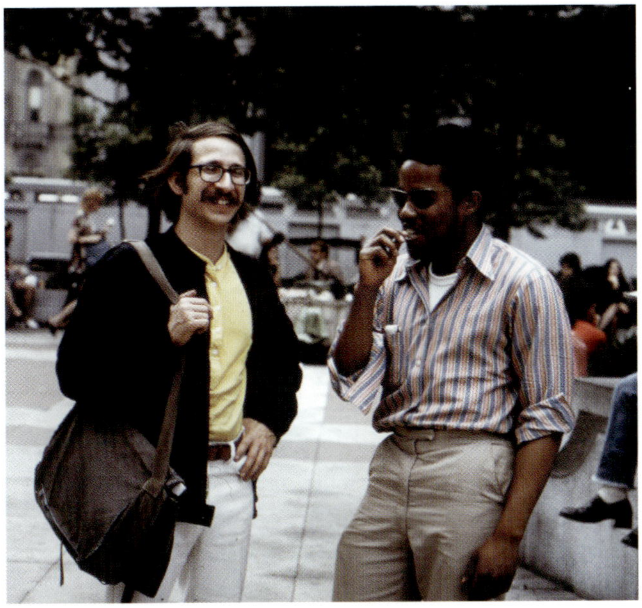

ABOVE: Masterclass classmates Jackson L. Burnside from the Bahamas (right) and Alberto Oliveira from Portugal (left). *Robert Couch Collection.*

RIGHT: Per Olaf Fjeld and Emily Fjeld in the studio. Emily was a student at the Philadelphia College of Art at the time. *P. O. Fjeld.*

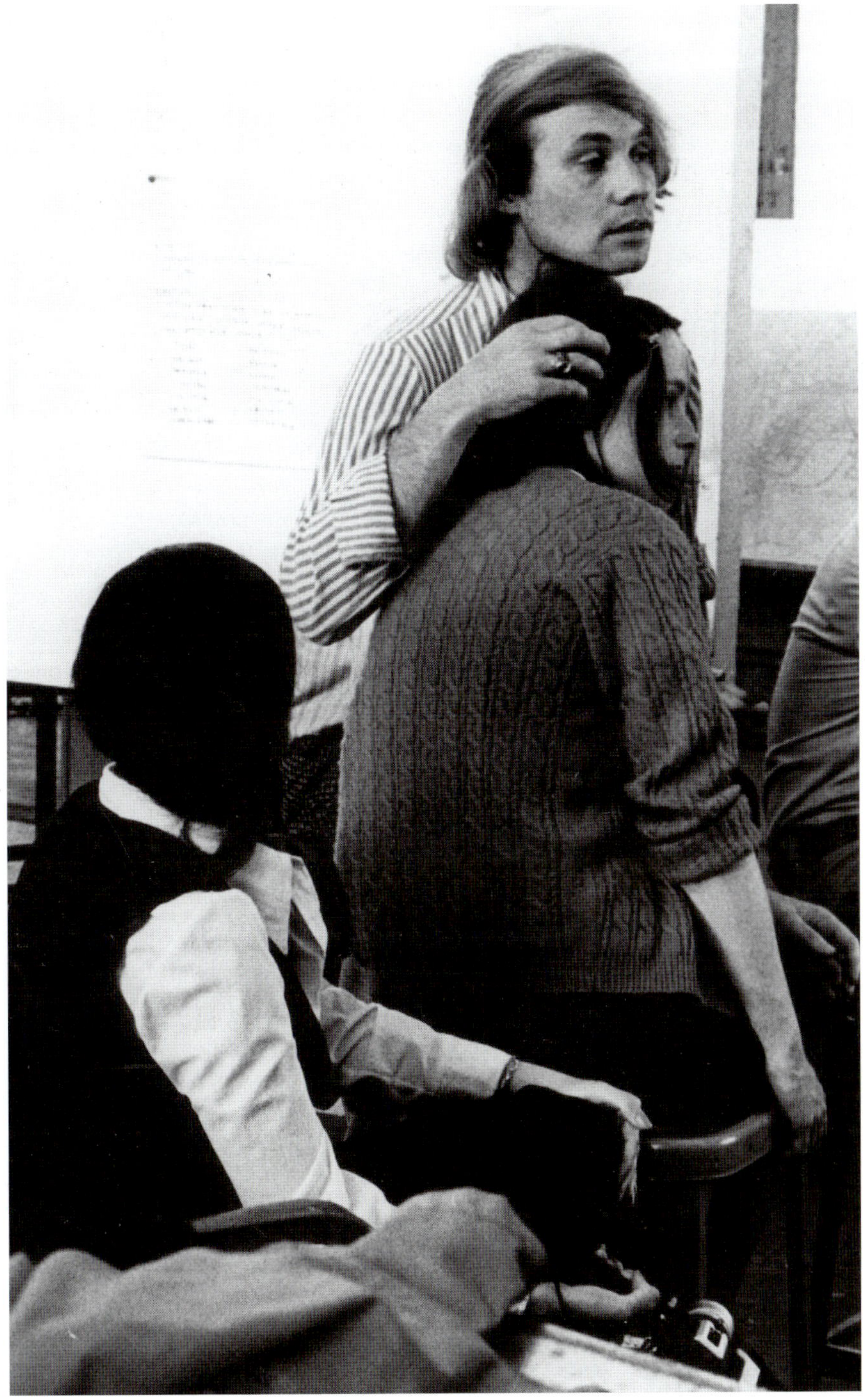

experience, since Kahn's library at Phillips Exeter Academy had just been completed that fall and the entire work process behind the drawings was still fresh to him. (He joked about that library as "a doughnut concept with the most important room in the middle.") A week before he presented the library assignment to the class, he was featured in a six-page article in *Time* magazine, which caused quite a buzz on campus. When we deliberately placed the magazine around the studio, we recognized that he was clearly flattered by the attention, but shy at the same time.

The most memorable event was when Kahn brought in a full set of his Exeter library working drawings for us to study. This unusual gesture was important for the class, since the drawings made a link between his personal vocabulary and the physical building in New Hampshire. All year we had been striving to connect what Kahn discussed in class to our individual projects, and the introduction of the blueprints into the studio seemed to ease that effort. Yet characteristically, he did not talk about the drawings, nor did he ever formally present his work or other architects' work. Instead, he talked about the everyday or general aspects of libraries—their "nature." He zeroed in, for instance, on the librarian and challenged us to imagine what type of person the librarian in our project would be; he felt we should be able to understand the specific space a librarian would require. This approach made us confront our own preconceptions about libraries and helped us work to ensure the relationship between the books, the users, and the room came first.

The Exeter drawings also broadened our perspective on Kahn's unpredictability, vocabulary, and what we had perceived as the lack of direction in class discussions. It now crossed our minds that his curiosity and roundabout questioning, so essential to his creative approach, had materialized the very precise technical working drawings he brought to the studio that day. Within the architecture school we had been confronting skepticism about the studio almost daily; the blueprints seemed to confer an odd sense of security against that talk. Their appearance injected us with new energy and a sense of being on track.

There were few of us who escaped the influence of the Phillips Exeter Academy Library in our work, and I was certainly not one of them. Kahn's built work and creative approach was always present in our thoughts. The challenge was to avoid filtering his expressions directly into our own projects. In the beginning most of us behaved like "mini Kahns"—and this approach was popular neither with the teaching team as a whole nor, in particular, Kahn. To mimic his work could only end in mediocrity.

In class Kahn stressed that every line in a plan or section should indicate a desired relationship between structure and daylight, and no secondary walls should disturb this relationship. Structure, material, and daylight alone completed a room, and yet each room's individual identity needed to be understood as part of a spatial sequence—the plan as "a society of rooms." In addition, each room required its own unique structure, not one borrowed from an adjacent room. This spatial integrity was of course difficult for us to achieve in our own projects, especially if we had not experienced firsthand the exceptional spatial energy that most of his work generates. Sometimes, when his words alone were not enough to convince a skeptical student, visiting his buildings helped illuminate his classroom guidance. The major works students could access in the vicinity of the university were the Richards Medical Research Laboratories on campus, the dormitory at Bryn Mawr College, and several houses on the outskirts of Philadelphia. Kahn never personally suggested we visit them. Perhaps he just took for granted that we had seen some of his built work; but when one of his buildings came up in a class discussion, he never followed up the mention with any detail. Strangely, for all the attention his architecture received at that time, it stayed more or less outside our studio.

I remember being very surprised when I arrived in Philadelphia to hear that Kahn's laboratories and dormitory had been severely criticized by a number of his colleagues on campus. They asserted that the laboratories did not function well; or that the dormitory was too rigid, that its interior expression was overly simplified or brutal for women's housing. There were many competing agendas to appease at the time, as well as an upcoming generation of teachers in search of position and new ideas and pedagogical programs. In this early 1970s soup of on-campus contention, Kahn's personality, work, and teaching approach were a target for scrutiny, but in class, departmental contentions seemed to vanish.

Aware of his audience, Kahn always made an effort to introduce visitors to the class. Robert Venturi, Buckminster Fuller, August Komendant, Romaldo Giurgola, Felix Candela, and Anne Tyng were a few I made note of at the time. (I can still remember his introduction of Komendant to the class: "We have pessimists, and we have pessimists on top of pessimists. May I introduce my longtime collaborator, Mr. Komendant.") The discussions among the teaching team and the guests could be rather intense, fairly convoluted, and long. To us students, it appeared as if they all were rather eager to challenge one another's positions and thoughts. Not all the conversations were necessarily in line with what Kahn was advocating on a particular day, but miraculously, he always managed to ride like a wave on top of it all.

During his visits Komendant gave each of us a structure-related critique. The sessions were interesting and quite straightforward, as he spoke directly about each project's structural identity and capacity. This approach appeared to worry Kahn, who soon expressed a concern that the work was in too early a stage for such a detailed evaluation. He believed that

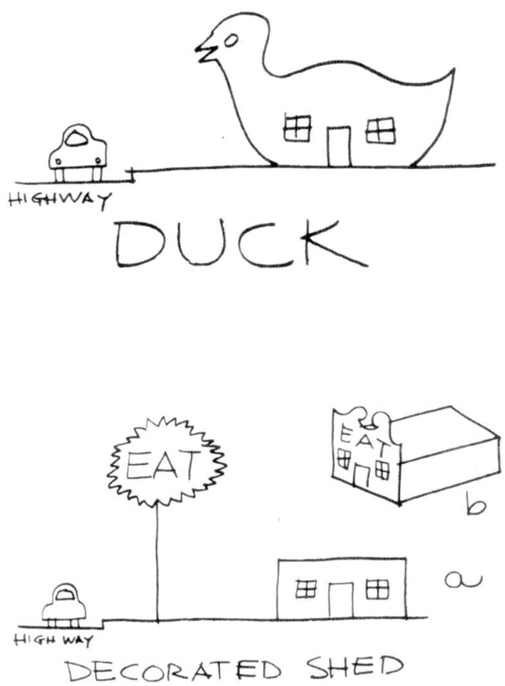

Robert Venturi's drawing "Duck vs. Decorated Shed" (1968) was known to most in the class. *Robert Venturi Collection, The Architectural Archives, University of Pennsylvania.*

at that stage such a critique would serve only to incrementally improve rather than to support a deeper search into the core of the project. Komendant replied, "You are never satisfied with anything." I sensed the two men shared a deep mutual understanding, although at the time I was unaware that Komendant was also born in Estonia, a connection that would not have held so much significance for me then.

We were all excited when Robert Venturi visited, as we knew he had worked and taught with Kahn. In many ways Venturi breathed a youthful presence into the studio because he was closer to us in age. His built work and writings had a strong hold on young architects during this period, and it was not unusual then for Kahn and Venturi to be mentioned together in articles or to be compared as if their work shared a common platform beyond their affiliation. However, in class we experienced their interaction as two paths that appeared to be going in opposite directions. Venturi's books and built work gave him a certain position that seemed to require Kahn to fight for his opinions during their intense discussion. I think it was the tension in the confrontation that surprised us. The two men seemed far apart—and it was far more than a mere difference of opinion that separated them.

The relationship between the car and the house was the principal focus of their debate. Kahn argued vehemently that the car did not belong to the house. Venturi took the opposite position, and his comments in support of it were both challenging and provocative. In one corner, Kahn was concerned with the pedestrian situation and the activation of urban areas by public transportation, and he believed that citizens having easy access to public spaces gave life to the city. Kahn did not have a car, or even a driver's license for that matter, and yet he had been very engaged in urban planning issues in Philadelphia where the car had been a major element. Most of us had come across his movement plans in our earlier studies. Also, many of us were taking landscape architect Ian McHarg's elective course, so environmental concerns were also in the mix.

In the opposite corner, Venturi embraced the car as part of daily life. Venturi did not believe there was much separation between living and driving in daily life, and he wanted the car to enter the plan of the house. Kahn, who clearly disliked this argumentation, faced his old collaborator with the remark, "Why? . . . After all, you are not such a bad architect." Kahn's comment did not seem to bother Venturi, as he was probably accustomed to this kind of talk from Kahn, but I remember being very agitated over the whole experience. (Even Emily, my girlfriend then, recalls how upset I was when I saw her later that evening.)

It was not a clearly argued exchange between the two architects, and the intransigence on both sides created a discussion that went in circles. The situation got even more intense when a Kentucky Fried Chicken restaurant became the center of contention. Venturi argued that in this case the building as a sign was more important than the building as a space—an assertion that was like throwing a torch into an already tense situation. Kahn argued vehemently that the room, no matter what, was always of primary importance. At that moment I got a foretaste of the many changes facing us as the upcoming generation.

Buckminster Fuller, a frequent presence on campus, would make short, drop-in visits to the studio. His reason for visiting was mostly to say hello to and have a chat with Kahn and the other teachers; but just the same, his visits were an event from the students' point of view, and the antithesis of his open lectures on campus, which could last up to six hours nonstop. These long, almost performance-like lectures were not unusual. Just being present at them, even more than listening attentively to them, seemed paramount.

When Spanish-born architect Felix Candela visited the class during my first semester, his work was already well known and appreciated by many architecture students. I had fond memories of sitting as a teenager with friends atop one of his structures in Oslo, sharing our dreams for the future. Candela had a rather humorous dialogue with Kahn about Buckminster Fuller's dome that engaged the entire class. For Candela, a geodesic dome was just a structural volume, not what he considered architecture. Candela also gave a lecture and participated in a pin-up discussion. The time he spent with us was short but rewarding, since he sent Kahn into an exuberant performance mode. The next day he took part in Le Ricolais's class.

An early and important collaborator of Kahn's, Anne Tyng dropped by the studio in the fall, but I did not I know who she was so early in the year. Fortunately, she reappeared for our last review, the urban intervention assignment, and gave intense critiques of a few projects. Uncharacteristically, Kahn was fairly quiet when she was in the studio. Unfortunately, in the discussions that followed her comments, the architectural object seemed to be the focus more than the core challenge of the assignment: the relationship between context and the architectural object. One student put his main entranceway through an old oil refinery in South Philadelphia partially in response to Kahn's comment in class that "a polluted river is still a river,"[1] but the impact of his decision was not debated in the review.

Gabor Szalontay was a regular participant in Kahn's masterclass. Known simply as Gabor, he at times played a catalyst role in setting the atmosphere of the studio, since he could interject a word or sentence into the discussion that would shift its entire focus. Gabor was a uniquely reflective person who, as I understood at the time, Kahn engaged as a conversation partner in his office, a role he clearly served in the classroom as well. Gabor was a man of words always searching for a deeper or more specific meaning in each phrase or word that

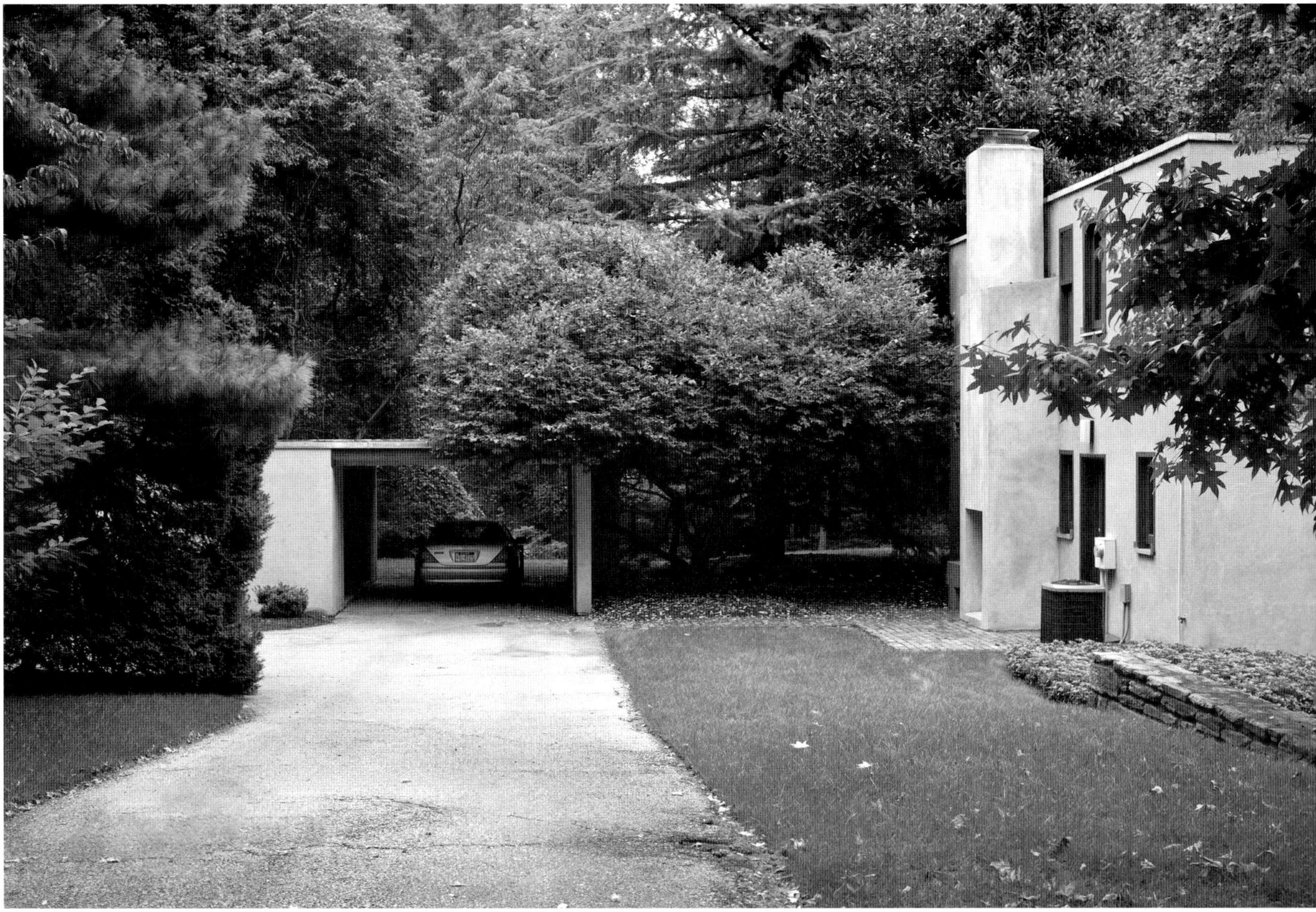

The carport and east facade of Kahn's Esherick House, 1959–61. The relationship between the car and the house generated a heated discussion between Kahn and Venturi. *Jon Reksten.*

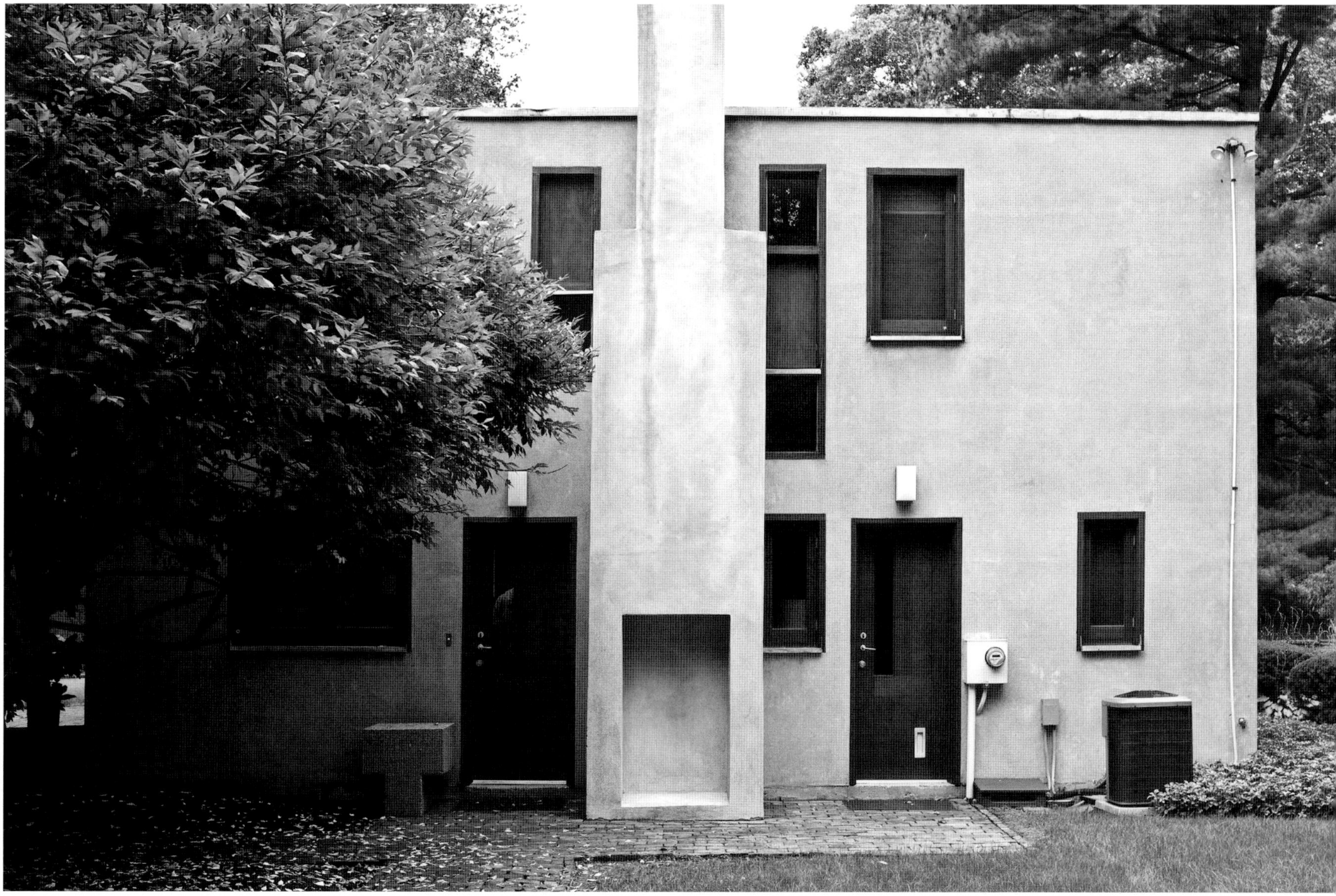

East facade of the Esherick House. *Jon Reksten.*

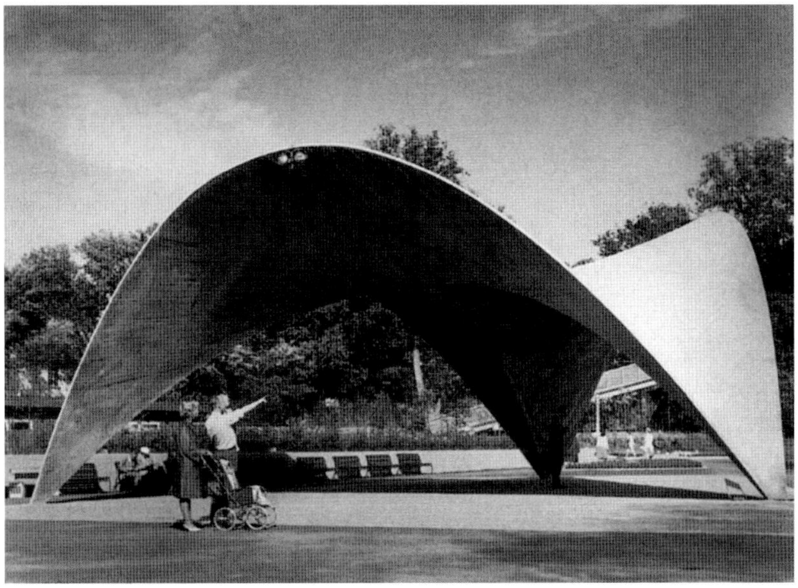

ABOVE: Felix Candela's Concrete Roof Shell, Frogner Park, Oslo (1962). Not long after it was in place, the structural shell became a popular climbing spot for children and teenagers. *Byggekunst NR 7–1965.*

RIGHT: Drawing of R. Buckminster Fuller's canonical geodesic dome for the American Pavilion for Expo 1967 in Montreal. Felix Candela remarked in the studio that "Everybody thinks Bucky invented the dome. He invented the name of a dome. When you come up with a new name, you become famous." *Courtesy of the Estate of R. Buckminster Fuller.*

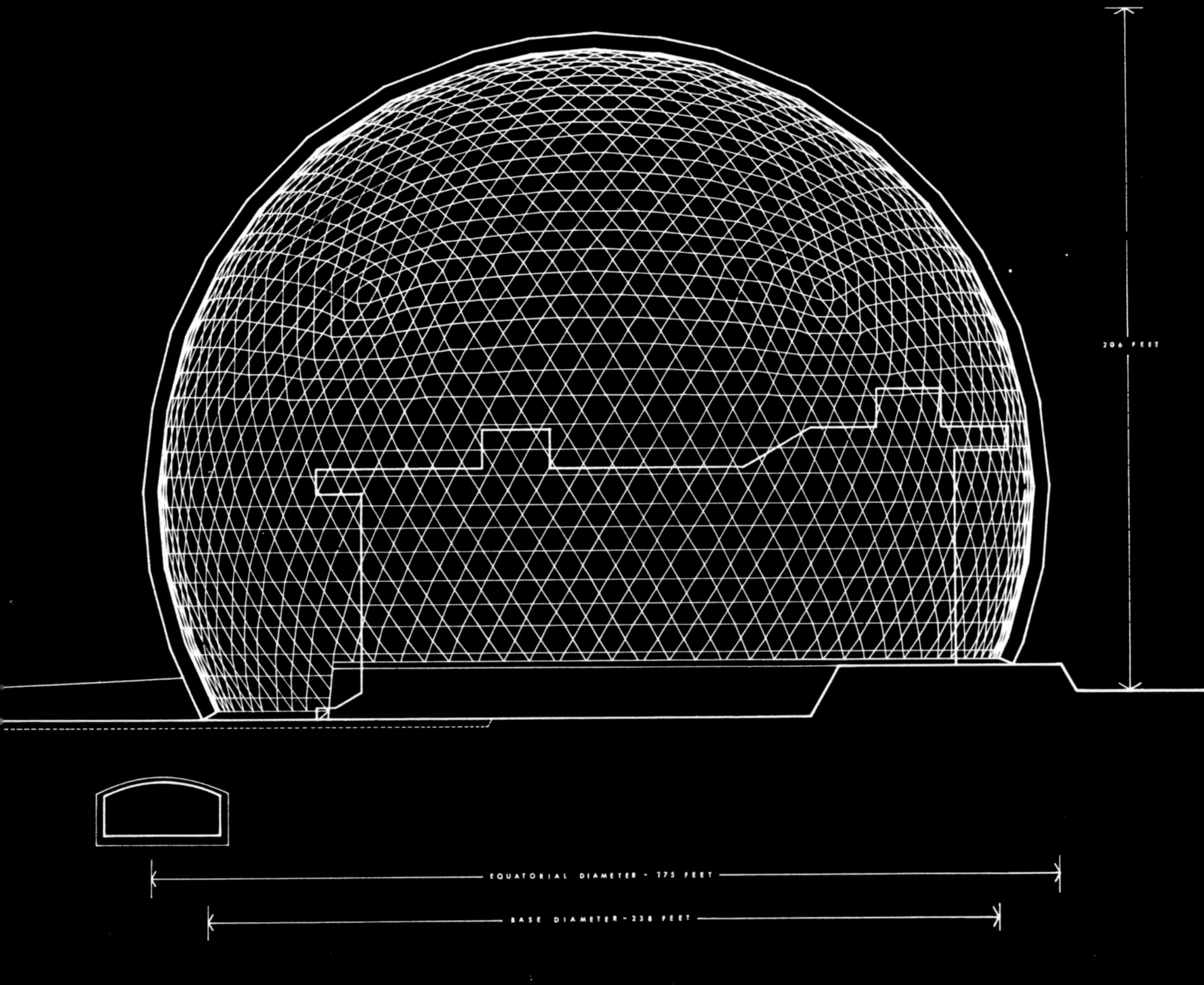
206 FEET
EQUATORIAL DIAMETER - 275 FEET
BASE DIAMETER-238 FEET

passed into his realm. It was as if he smelled or tasted each sentence he was in the process of constructing, and if one suited, he seemed to spell it out in the air, where Kahn would catch it. A long discussion would inevitably follow.

For the class these were exciting as well as exasperating exchanges. Gabor's initial comments were always enigmatic, and the members of the teaching team seldom agreed with one another. In this whirlwind of opinions, one's own thoughts needed to be very strong and well-constructed to survive the discourse. Norman Rice was usually the first to give in, perhaps because he was tired or not particularly interested in the topic. Le Ricolais was stubborn and never gave in, but I had the feeling that it was not important for him to win the debate or to make Kahn see the issue at hand from another angle. The discussions set off by one of Gabor's sentences could go on forever, for as long as Kahn sensed a discovery was still in the air. I think Kahn hated to concede, so in this situation there was seldom a conclusion or agreement. But while the debate would remain unsettled, it had nevertheless served to draw inspiration from everyone. By the end of each session, despite all the open questions, a new layer of awareness had in fact entered our projects.

We picked up very early in the year that Kahn's "Silence and Light" talk was an annual event for all his masterclasses, so there was some anticipation as to when this would take place. One afternoon during the second semester the oak-framed blackboard, cleaned for Kahn's session, was wheeled out from its corner. What followed was a performance. I think we were all very conscious of experiencing something rare, and of the intimacy of Kahn's presenting perhaps his most famous lecture topic just to us. We were all already familiar on some level with his silence and light material, but each of us brought our own interpretation, since at that time its content was relatively untouched by academic research and appraisal.

Slightly self-conscious, Kahn walked in front of the blackboard. The entire class gathered around with an intensity of expectation. I do not know exactly why, but the two words—"silence" and "light"—struck a deep, familiar chord within me. His focus was on the human being's unique ability to express, and as his talk unfolded, it gave more personal insight into how Kahn envisioned the beginning of a creative act. Afterward a student asked him to draw simultaneously with both hands. Slightly embarrassed, he did so, impressing and delighting all of us. He laughed and got a little carried away, but it was also a celebration of drawing and our own creative abilities as humans.

That afternoon in his usual roundabout way, he made it clear that curiosity and keeping alive an eagerness to discover at the start of a project would give depth to its conclusion. It was a glimpse into his world of teaching himself while teaching others—the most valuable insight he could offer. He revealed something of his inner complexity, admitting that even for him, limitations and the possibility of failure lurked within the creative process. He was a master architect, but that afternoon he too was vulnerable. In that moment, he helped us see him as one of us—as a seventy-two-year-old student—and this made him an incredible teacher.

Once during our library project in the second semester Kahn took us down to the first floor of the Fine Arts Library to visit the rare book collection. It was an event. Kahn wanted to show us some large architectural volumes from the collection. I do not remember the titles, but what I clearly recall was his passionate admiration for the large hand-drafted plan, section, and facade drawings. He never mentioned his student days at Penn or his Beaux Arts training under Paul Cret, but that afternoon together in the library we understood that this material was familiar and dear to him. Very slowly, page by page, he went through the drawings, commenting on each. Like the Silence and Light lecture, this event revealed another side of Kahn: he was intense, but also strangely alone in the midst of his students. We listened attentively to all he said, nodding our heads. The mood of that moment, even though it was just a little interval, changed and gave depth to the semester.

It always surprised me that so few architecture students from the other classes partook in Kahn's open studio discussions. This was due in part to the move into the new architecture building at Penn in 1965. For years Kahn had conducted his studio in a large open room that extended the entire length of what was originally the dental school. This was a large gallery space into which the different studio classes were packed together with minimal division. McHarg, Holmes Perkins, Le Ricolais, Buckminster Fuller, Kahn, and the rest of the faculty had shared the same room. But when the studios and faculty offices moved into the new building, Kahn chose instead the second floor of the Fine Arts Library building. During the first years after the move his students protested over their isolation from the main school and its activities; even as late as 1972 many of us still felt a slight disconnect. Our studio only partially interacted with the rest of the architecture department, so some students in the masterclass had little interaction with students from other classes. The separation did not seem to bother Kahn, but he was certainly aware of it. The growing division within the department was clearly felt by the students who had studied at Penn prior to entering Kahn's masterclass. On a few occasions—after these students had to recalibrate their relationships with former classmates and teachers—their uncomfortable situation produced outbursts of frustration and criticism after class. There was little open discussion about all of this, but a latent tendency to criticize the validity and innovativeness of Kahn's methods lingered in the background throughout the year.

Fortunately, there were many people from other parts of the university and the rest of the architectural world who visited the studio. The class was an event, an international architectural forum open to all. The studio was clearly Kahn's domain, but I never sensed that he closed the door to anyone.

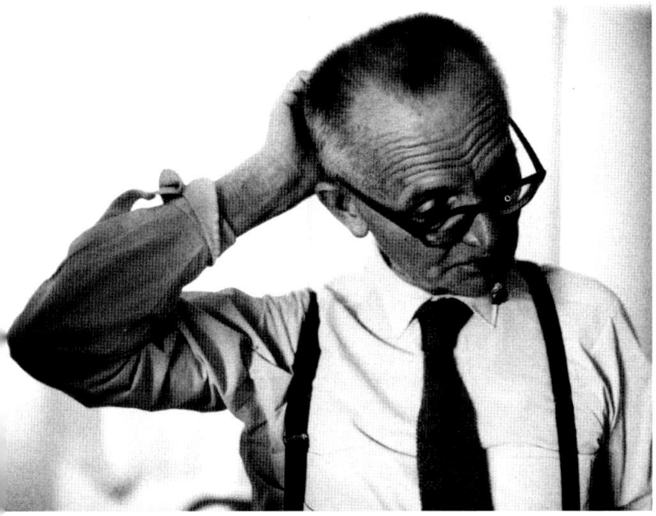

ABOVE: Robert Le Ricolais had two educational objectives: to provide students with a broader understanding of natural laws and to give them a working knowledge of the scientific method. *Robert Le Ricolais Collection, The Architectural Archives, University of Pennsylvania.*

OPPOSITE: Part of Le Ricolais's model collection at the University of Pennsylvania, as pictured in 1972. *Robert Le Ricolais Collection, The Architectural Archives, University of Pennsylvania.*

Elective Courses

Along with Kahn's masterclass we enrolled in elective courses, which all took place in the new building. Their agendas and pedagogical approaches were different but not necessarily in conflict with the studio's; rather, they offered a counterbalance that both broadened and, to a certain extent, defined possible future directions and challenges. Robert Le Ricolais's experimental structural course, taught with his assistant of the time, Peter McCleary, truly complemented Kahn's studio. It was great to experience Le Ricolais outside the masterclass, to understand his intellectual and creative capacity in the peace of his own class. Reading Le Ricolais's correspondence with Kahn years later, I sensed the same poetic sensibility and warmth that we observed in Le Ricolais's own studio but seldom encountered in the team-taught masterclass. Though it was not obvious to me at the time, I realize now that Le Ricolais's principal contribution to the masterclass was a deeply felt, supportive friendship along with a well-intentioned counterbalance.

Early in his career in France, Robert Le Ricolais was best known for his written work on structural theory; but in the United States, research funds and support encouraged him to focus his energies on testing the relationship between structure and form through physical inventions. His approach of applying mathematical theories to physical models generated numerous spatial discoveries. This was one reason Kahn was so interested in his work and had invited him to become part of his teaching team. Le Ricolais was an unusual person—reserved, methodical, and possessing a sense of humor that surfaced occasionally in the studio. He was able to make his ideas and, at times, very complicated calculations comprehensible for most of us. With an almost poetic sensibility, this scientist's many numbers and symbols would come alive on the blackboard.

Le Ricolais opened his class with the following sentence: "In my mind, to teach is not to learn something together. You have to learn from yourself."[2] He usually started each session with a talk related to a principle of structural geometry that we would later test through a model. It was a very physically active studio, and yet advanced theoretical discussions between Le Ricolais and McCleary were also a key feature. At times their discussions left us behind, as their calculations surpassed our mathematical knowledge.

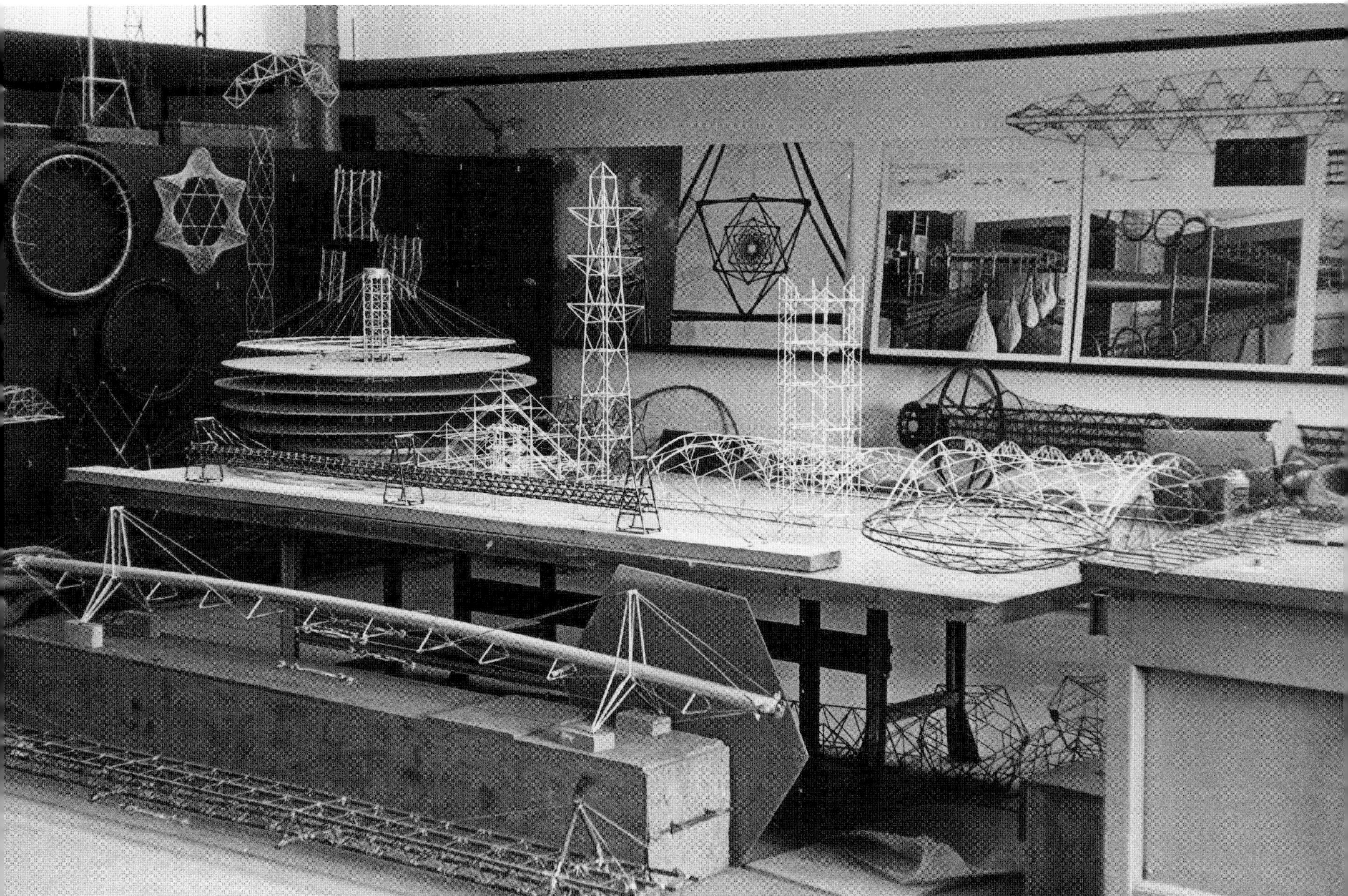

My professional degree from Washington State University had focused on developing engineering abilities: calculating structures and understanding their limitations, rules, statistics, and history. As at most architectural and engineering schools of the time, we had learned about structure from the desk only. We had not really practiced materializing engineering concepts firsthand, so physical resistance forces had remained abstractions. Of course, we were without computers, and slide-rule work was time-consuming. So I had come to understand this part of my studies as important but not architecturally motivating. Le Ricolais, making a connection that I had been striving to attain for years, changed all of this for me. In his class, through experimentation, I began to understand more about each structure's physical resistance forces; the structural knowledge that I had been exposed to in my earlier education was now finally activated. We gained a more complete comprehension of structure through a new awareness of structural capabilities in different materials; learning to transform a calculation into a material presence; and learning to directly sense physical force. It was exhilarating—and these activities also influenced and stimulated our work in the main studio.

Le Ricolais insisted that a structure had to be tested through models and drawings with the same intensity and concentration as a direct spatial search. From the start he encouraged us to work in teams. For one project, I was assigned to model the hull of a ship with a classmate who had come from Sweden as a young adult. Left on our own, we quickly returned to our mother tongues, and Le Ricolais allowed us to enjoy that freedom undisturbed in our little Scandinavian bubble. In the masterclass, by contrast, Kahn always seemed very alert to when Claes and I lapsed out of English.

We would generally work in steel and became fairly proficient at welding by the end of the year. Our various models seemed quite precise from our student perspective, and we were all very proud of having transformed a raw material into a spatial object that embodied theory. When the testing began, it was sometimes hard to see the models deform.

Le Ricolais's class also introduced me to a structural vocabulary that took time to fully comprehend. One of my notebook entries from September 1972, in which I recorded several statements that Le Ricolais made to the class, encapsulates that language:

> "The art of making light structure is to use heavy members."
> "As soon as you reduce the size of its members you will increase the number of joints."
> "To search for a structure concerns numbers and not areas."
> "When dealing with volumes, the boundaries are the most important."
> "As soon as you have a tension system you have elongation."[3]

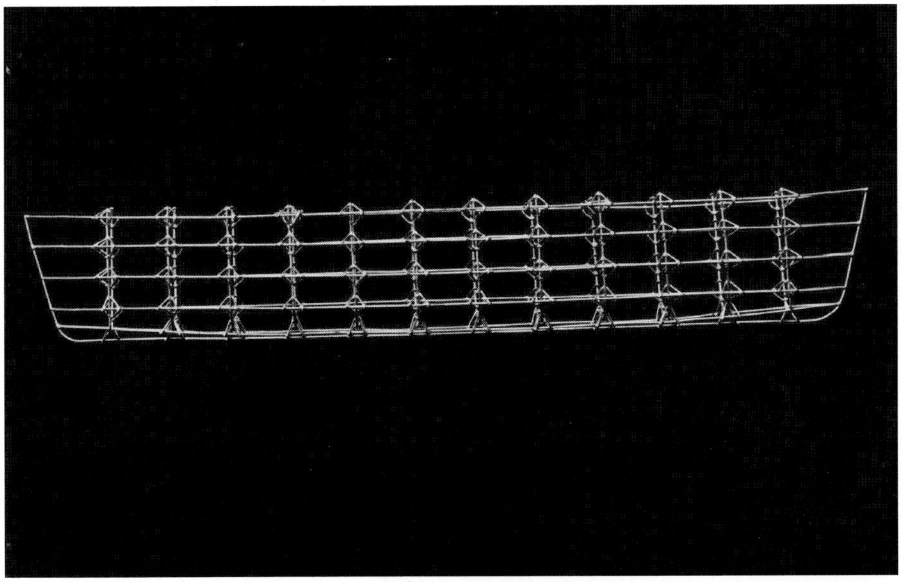

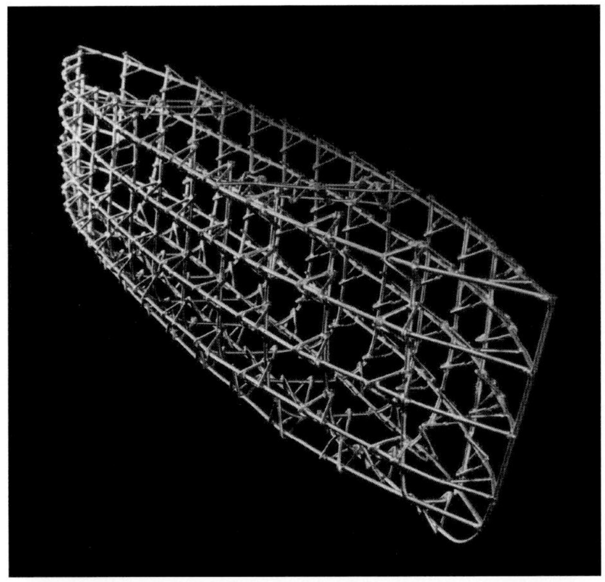

ABOVE LEFT: Material and structure as a boat. Model by Claes Erikson and Per Olaf Fjeld. *Robert Le Ricolais Collection, The Architectural Archives, University of Pennsylvania.*

ABOVE RIGHT: Boat structure model as photographed from above. *Robert Le Ricolais Collection, The Architectural Archives, University of Pennsylvania.*

RIGHT: One of the structural models ready for testing in Le Ricolais's class. *Robert Le Ricolais Collection, The Architectural Archives, University of Pennsylvania.*

FAR RIGHT: The model after the test. It was always moving to see our structures distorted. *Robert Le Ricolais Collection, The Architectural Archives, University of Pennsylvania.*

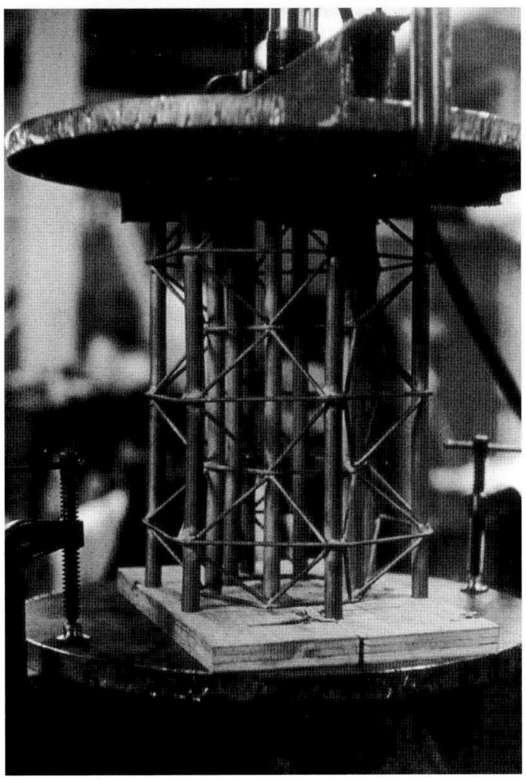

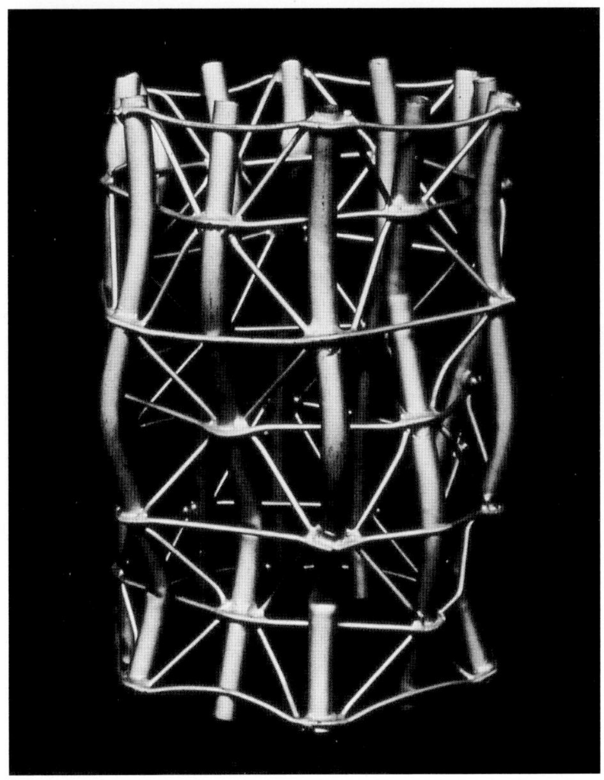

We learned to have respect for structure and to regard it as a crucial instrument in distinguishing between physical truths and physical lies. This lesson became particularly apparent when Le Ricolais would firmly redirect our focus during pin-up discussions when we would find ourselves arguing for a structural identity that had little real spatial presence. There was always a scientific base at the core of his teaching. Further into the semester, we realized that his teaching method was supported by the same open, creative search that undergirded the masterclass studio. No matter how demanding Le Ricolais's course was at times, I looked forward to each session.

I made a short visit to Penn just as the school was closing down Le Ricolais's studio. The shop assistant who had been there for years was packing and was clearly moved by the experience. Despite the commotion of the move, he rummaged around until he found the ship-hull model I had made in class. Somehow, for me this incident embodied the dedication of the entire team inside Le Ricolais's studio. I was moved that the shop assistant found the model, well aware that hundreds of students had worked on projects in the studio over the years.

I also enrolled in a landscape architecture course taught by Ian McHarg. McHarg's book *Design with Nature* had made a deep impression on many students at that time. He was a very engaged and popular teacher, always drawing a crowd with his lectures. Unfortunately, having just attended his elective class and not his studio, I never really got to know him. Most students supported his concerns over environmental issues and admired the energy and focus of his work. With our youthful optimism, it was easy to envision his ecological propositions materializing a stronger relationship between nature and architecture. Though concerns related to the built environment's impact on nature had entered mainstream architectural discourse by this time, they were still peripheral to other considerations and were often expressed merely in terms of efficiency and new technology. In a sense, this prevailing attitude had been handed down from an earlier generation: the built object remained primary in architectural discourse. McHarg was at the forefront of his generation working toward a change in such attitudes.

He therefore offered yet another interpretation of the relationship between architecture and nature than the one we encountered in the masterclass. Kahn did not really regard the connection between nature and the human as a project, but rather as an everlasting relationship in which nature wins in the end. That said, I never really felt a distinct difference between what was discussed in McHarg's class and what came up in the masterclass. In many ways, McHarg's course was an extension, although with its own unique approach, to Kahn's ideas about "the laws of nature" and "the rules of man."

In the early 1960s Ian McHarg hosted a local television program called *The House We*

Live In, for which he interviewed many prominent people of the time, such as the anthropologist Margaret Mead and the biologist Julian Huxley. The series investigated various scientists' views on major topics, including the cosmos and evolution. The exuberance and earnestness of McHarg's work outside the school was akin to what he brought to the classroom. His elective course was in many ways a discussion forum supported by a reading list that included such books as Rachel Carson's *Silent Spring*, Aldo Leopold's *A Sand County Almanac*, and B. F. Skinner's *Walden Two*. After McHarg's lectures there were often heated debates. Some students were quite hard-core in their perception of the architectural object as a threat to nature, while others regarded McHarg's opinions as politically speculative; thus there was always an element of agitation. McHarg's class stirred the pot with its attack on the architecture profession and its close connections with commercial interests—connections that many felt limited the development of a better relationship between architecture and nature.

McHarg required a term paper at the end of the semester. Mine, titled "The Japanese Garden," dealt with an integrated cultural relationship between nature and architecture over a long time aspect. My choice of topic was not as arbitrary as it may seem, since, as I mentioned earlier, a renewed interest in Japanese culture had emerged throughout Scandinavia just after the war and had remained a source of inspiration in the Nordic region throughout my adolescence. (Though much of this interest among architects in Norway related in part to Korsmo, I was unaware of the connection at the time.) Kahn also talked about the garden as a unique mixture of nature and culture—and about the garden and the room as the beginning of architecture.

A required elective in the masterclass program was a course on architectural psychology and urban design taught by John Lang. This was an odd match with the studio, as Lang's lectures often contradicted what Kahn said in class. In retrospect, I can see that the content of Lang's course was more in line with studio courses at other influential graduate schools at the time, as his pedagogical approach relied more on a design method and program content guided by structured studies of human behavior. Edward T. Hall's *The Hidden Dimension* constituted one core source for our discussion.

Lang promoted the idea that the development of a general work method would enhance the possibilities for different design alternatives, which in turn could be tested and evaluated. In his opinion, an assessment of method would serve most architects as well as society, since it would mitigate the possibility of failure. Lang also introduced us to different perception theories related to physical space, as well as to new research on what was feasible and acceptable in regard to social behavior. In general, Lang criticized the lack of a

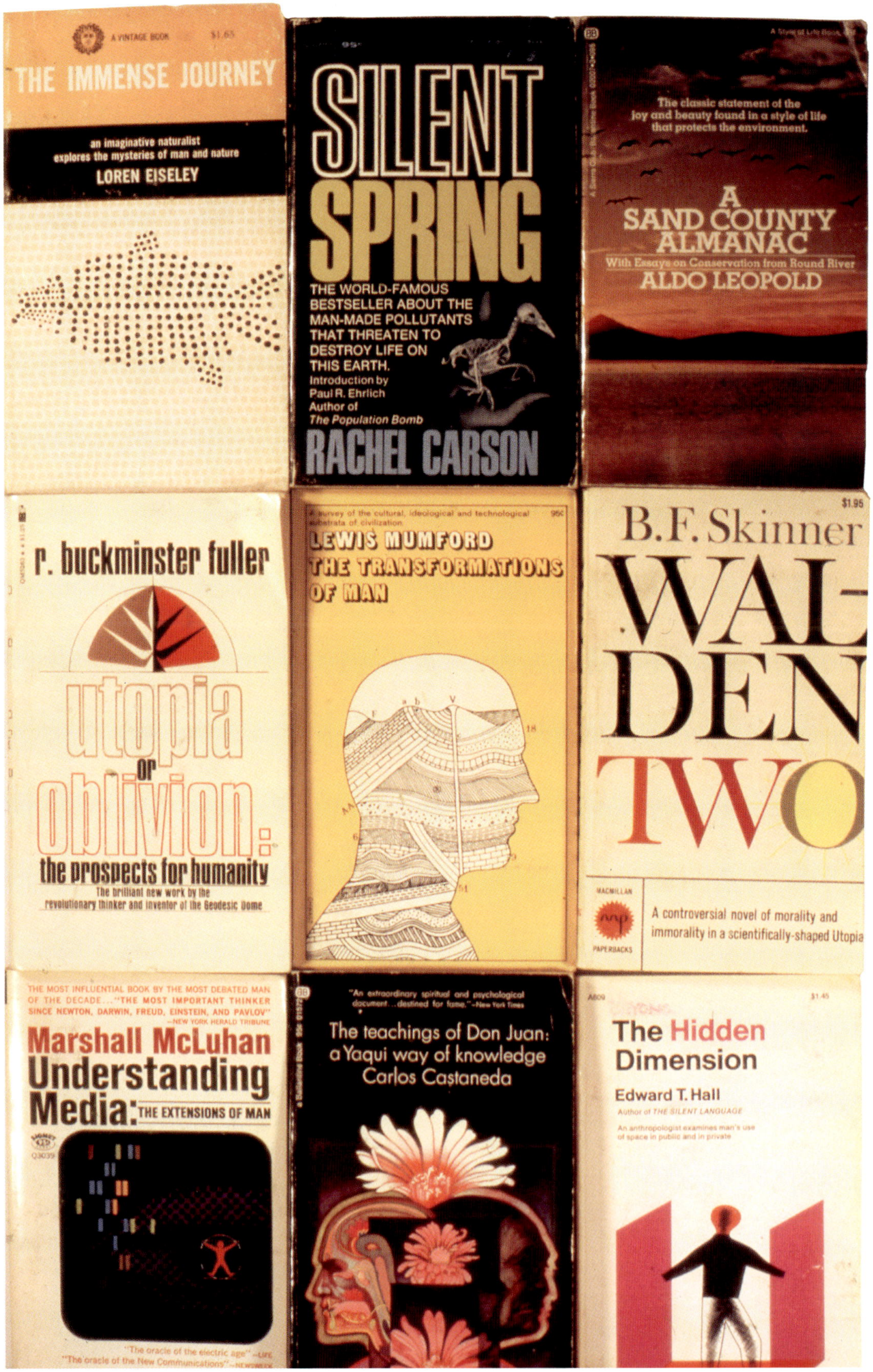

The titles shown here encompass many of the reading requirements for the elective courses that I took alongside the masterclass studio. Environmental concerns, human behavior, and social issues sparked many intense discussions in these courses.
P. O. Fjeld.

strong research-oriented knowledge base concerning the relationship between the human and space. His position was certainly at odds with Kahn's intuitive approach—and it was a vexing corrective, since again we were left to work out the contradictions on our own. Lang stressed that architecture should support human behavior; but for him it was important to be solution-oriented more than problem-oriented. He believed that spatial insight alone was too shallow without a more scientific understanding of behavioral criteria. This was about as far away from Kahn's volume zero as possible. Lang, who worked from set premises and intentions, offered guidelines that were simple to follow but that also took creativity as a given. Sometimes late at night in the masterclass studio, when both my creativity and my wonder seemed to have evaporated under stress, Lang's teachings surfaced as a reflective pause.

Reflections

Inside the changing academic environment of the early 1970s it was easy to overlook Kahn's contribution. His studio was often criticized for not dealing with "real" architecture and "real" programs, and as lacking in content that reflected professional attitudes and goals. There was a concern that Kahn's students relied too much on intuition and their individual naive perceptions; that we were not able to justify in an effectual way the line of reasoning behind our projects; and that we lacked flexibility, teamwork skills, and the ability to connect to other professionals in the building field. For these reasons the value and future of the masterclass were continually questioned. To attack Kahn's built work outright was difficult, but his masterclass was an easier target. In all the criticism, it rarely came up that most of the students in the class had completed a professional degree previously, that a number had already worked professionally for several years, and that a few already had established practices.

Kahn's strong belief in the intuitive as an essential energy source within the creative act and his trust in a nonlinear process were difficult for some faculty to take seriously. Some argued that Kahn and teachers like him were apprehensive to put their process into a measurable framework because their approach was ultimately only valuable to them. They asserted that if our masterclass projects were to be regarded as experimental research in a traditional sense, they had to be connected to previous research to allow for comparison. Yet if all this had been forced into the teaching plan, it is very doubtful that the content of the masterclass would have been open enough to hold the interest of its three teachers. Kahn's studio had another, more important, agenda: one directed toward a stronger search into the core essence of architecture as a means to discover and revitalize human institutions.

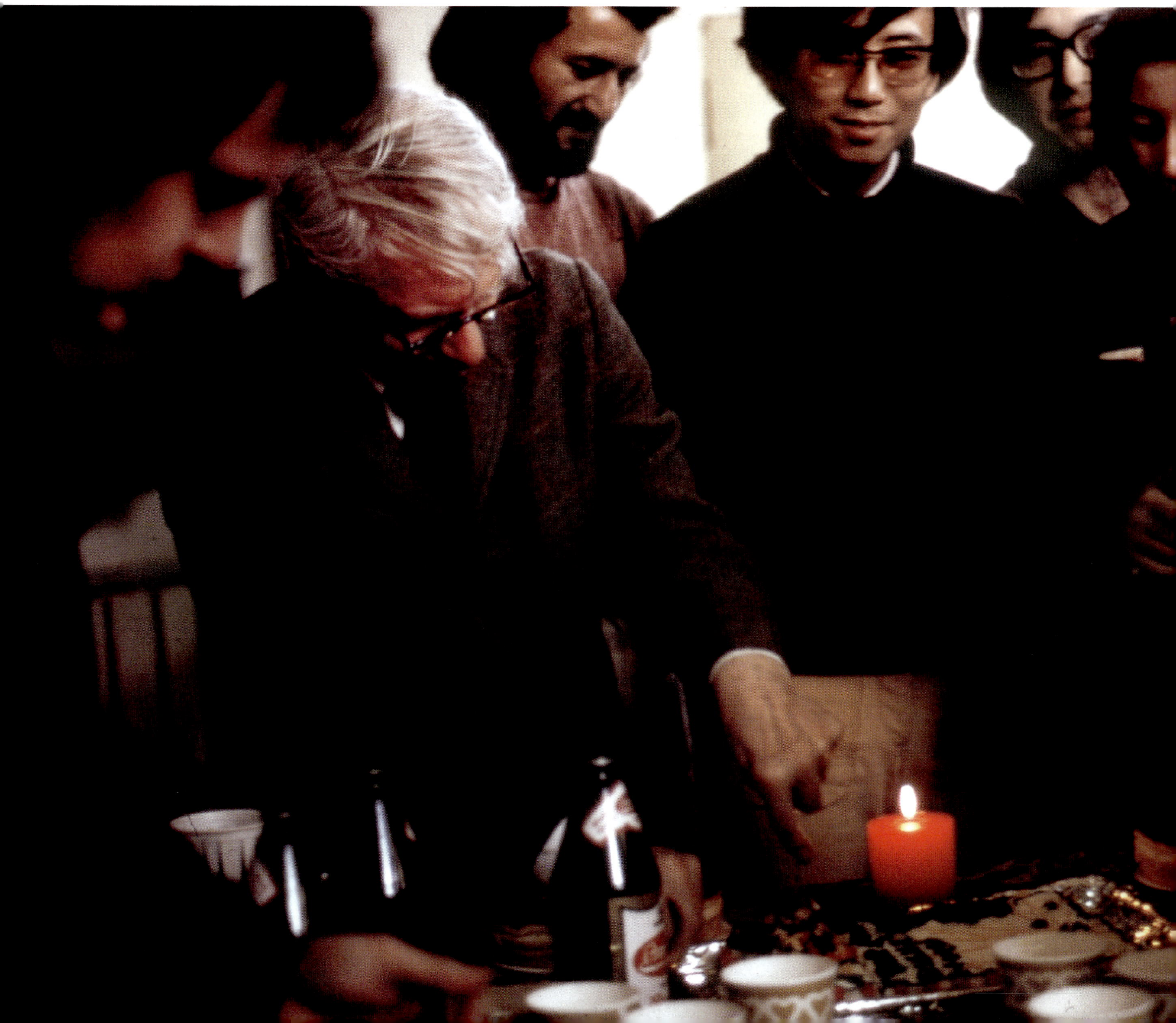

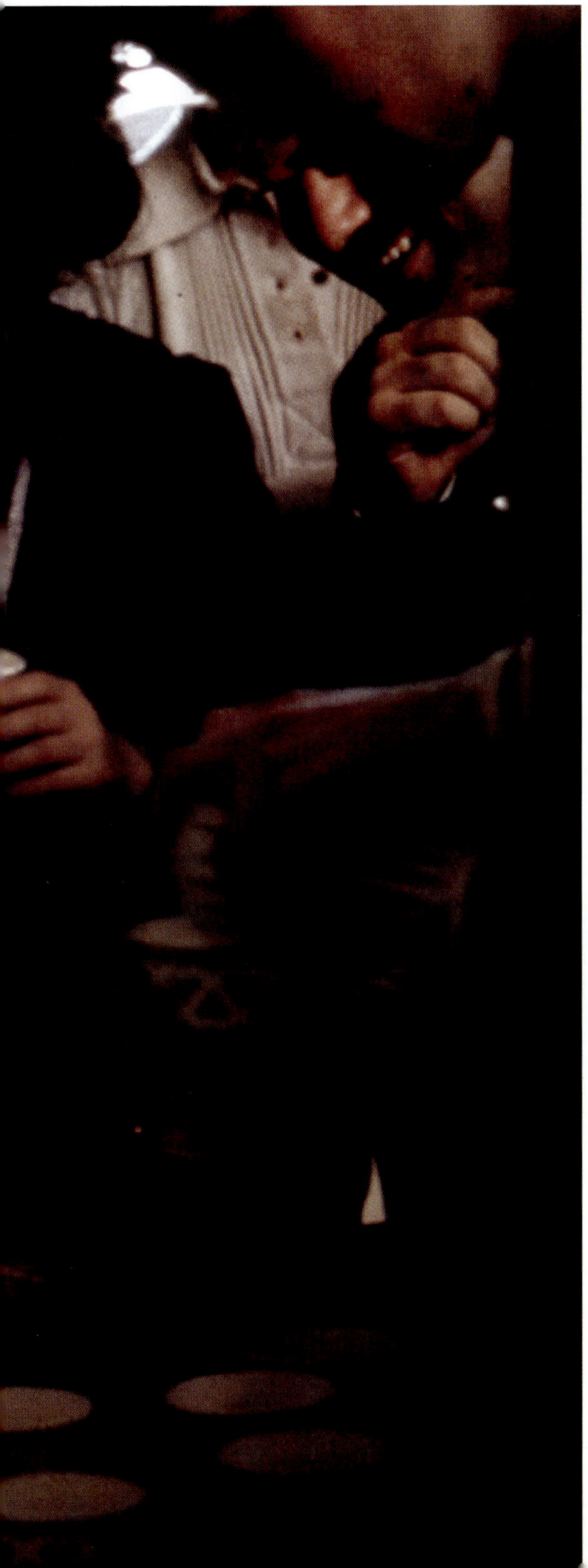

The last ten years Kahn ran his masterclasses at the University of Pennsylvania were a time of political change and unrest. Everything was under scrutiny: institutions, including the university system; human rights, social rights, and politics; and, not least, the Vietnam War. This was a period in which architecture, along with the other arts, questioned its identity and role in regard to social and political challenges. Even the most entrenched architectural curriculum inside well-established schools was challenged both by students and young teachers. Sometimes the confrontations that resulted seemed to put the institutions themselves at risk; but from this tumult arose the belief that architecture and its pedagogy needed renewal. Many students were caught between the profession's established traditions and new pedagogical strategies—pulled between contradicting notions regarding both how to become an architect and the responsibilities of the profession to society.

In Kahn's studio, the importance of architecture was never in question. He believed that the nature of architecture should be based on human values, whereby individual capacity and social responsibility gain deeper meaning and direction beyond the realm of a professional or commercial agenda or private ambition. Kahn believed that through architectural means we could make the world a better place to live in—and he saw this as not only our opportunity but also our destiny.

Kahn impressed upon us that everything is on one level incomplete. That the actual physical work is always less than the dream that inspired it. That need is something quite different from desire. He continually reminded us that as architects we were all servants of architecture. When a work was finished it did not really belong to us but rather to the spirit of architecture. The deeper a work was embedded within the immeasurable, the greater its lasting value. He regarded joy as the essence and force of creativity—the beginning. He taught us that all creative work should spring from joy, although even for him finding this energy was sometimes a struggle. As his students, we saw his strength and passion—and the uncertainty that would occasionally surface in the midst of these—from a privileged angle.

One of the few studio breaks: Kahn preparing to cut his birthday cake. My classmate Chiaki Arai is to his left. *Robert Couch Private Collection.*

Louis I. Kahn as Teacher

Architecture is not a Science but an Art. In other words, an accepted way of conveying an expression or desire of the Architect, with respect to rules and conventions.

Louis Kahn's attitude, in general, in his teaching obligations, was never dogmatic. Often, in his strategy, he succeeded in making the student believe he was teaching the teacher whilst he was being taught.

It was interesting to note that students imitating the master's style made no impression upon him. Louis Kahn's architecture belongs to no other than Louis Kahn, and it was up to the student to find the mode of expressing himself.

The wonder of his critiques was his patience and relaxed human feeling, together with the most rigorous and keenest sense of values.

Even the victims of his irony were proud of being heroes of the sacrifice, because beyond castigation there was stimulation.

—Robert Le Ricolais, February 1975 [4]

Louis I. Kahn as Teacher

The qualities of Louis Kahn's teaching grew from his nature, his sensibilities, his visions, his abilities and experience. These qualities were inseparable elements, proportioned, composed and integrated in a constitution of one singular man. In words, one quality is cited after another, but the reader must compose them as a unified picture wherein all are seen together and at once.

Kahn's fame in the latter years predisposed many to come and listen with already open, receptive ears and hearts; that eased the teacher's task.

Students and others sensed that he expressed with utter sincerity his innermost convictions on architecture and life, founded on a longtime search. He said he spoke his convictions and beliefs, and if any of it rubbed off on students that was the extent of his teaching. He disdained the didactic and the school-marmish. Totally in love with architecture and dedicated wholly to it, he was often a charismatic missionary generating for others visions that could be fulfilled.

Through deep insights he distilled many first principles and essences, and discovered the natures of architectural elements and buildings. He not only revealed these to students but also inspired them to do likewise, sometimes with amazing results gratifying to student and teacher. In the open, informal, lively seminars held at every meeting in the loft studio, students were encouraged to discover and to realize, through their architect's sensibilities, the essential nature of a projected building, and thus to become architect of its nature as well as of its configuration and structure. Merely to accept a ready-written program was not worthy of a good architect. Hence, explanations of his own projects fascinated students.

His language and style of speech were of the highest order, and became poetic when expressing a poetic insight. More and more he came to musical analogies with architecture. Humor was ever present. Even foreign students with limited English caught on very quickly.

Critiques were always objective and constructive, usually extending student ideas and often revealing facets unrecognized by the student. "I don't like it" or "I like it" were considered too personal, narrow comments, not educational or stimulating.

These qualities as teacher, coupled with his great abilities as architect, encouraged and inspired nearly all students to the highest self-realization and achievement, often higher than many believed themselves capable.

—Norman N. Rice, February 1975 [5]

poemS
introduction to architecture 800.the university of pennsylvania. fall 72.
per olaf fjeld.

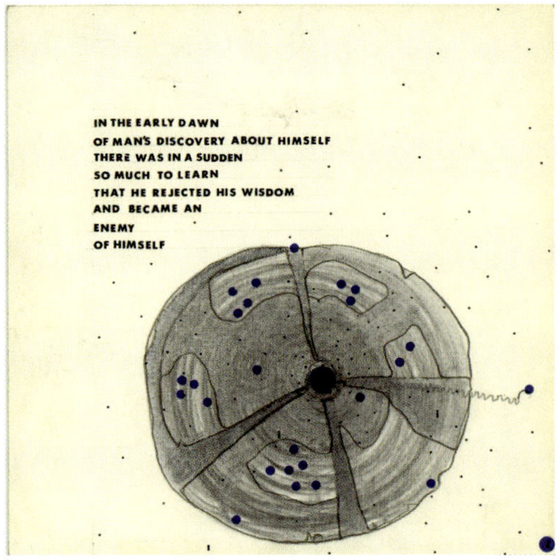
IN THE EARLY DAWN
OF MAN'S DISCOVERY ABOUT HIMSELF
THERE WAS IN A SUDDEN
SO MUCH TO LEARN
THAT HE REJECTED HIS WISDOM
AND BECAME AN
ENEMY
OF HIMSELF

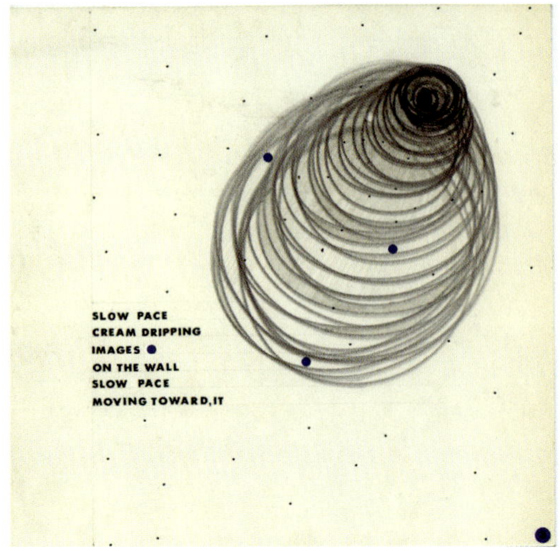
SLOW PACE
CREAM DRIPPING
IMAGES
ON THE WALL
SLOW PACE
MOVING TOWARD,IT

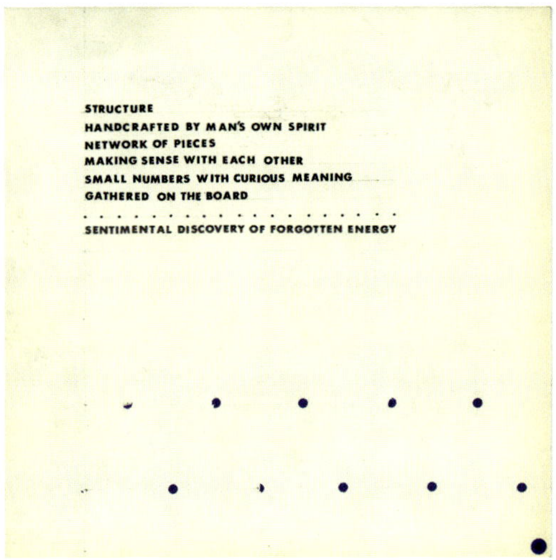
STRUCTURE
HANDCRAFTED BY MAN'S OWN SPIRIT
NETWORK OF PIECES
MAKING SENSE WITH EACH OTHER
SMALL NUMBERS WITH CURIOUS MEANING
GATHERED ON THE BOARD
SENTIMENTAL DISCOVERY OF FORGOTTEN ENERGY

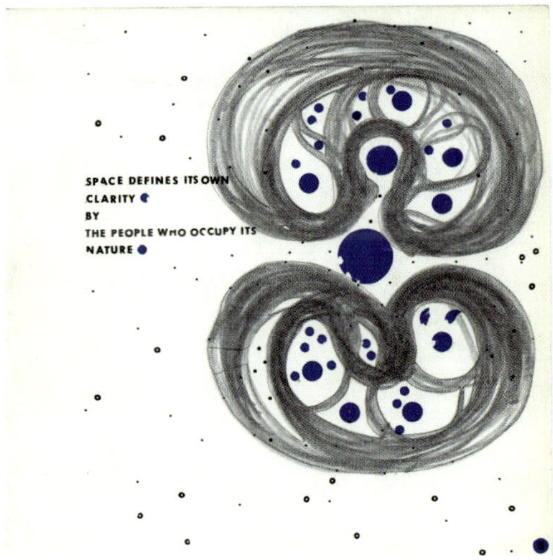
SPACE DEFINES ITS OWN
CLARITY
BY
THE PEOPLE WHO OCCUPY ITS
NATURE

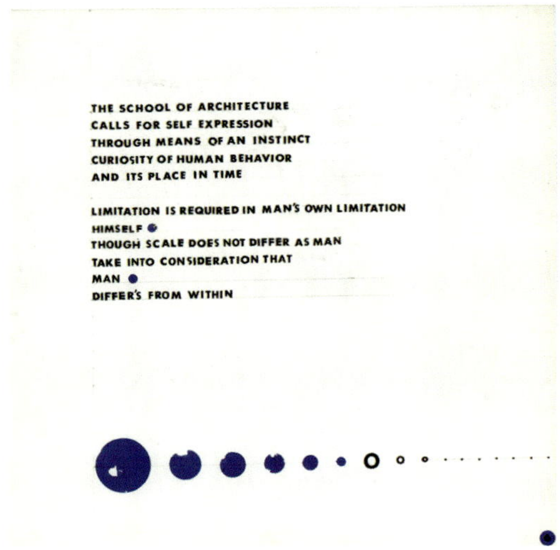
THE SCHOOL OF ARCHITECTURE
CALLS FOR SELF EXPRESSION
THROUGH MEANS OF AN INSTINCT
CURIOSITY OF HUMAN BEHAVIOR
AND ITS PLACE IN TIME
LIMITATION IS REQUIRED IN MAN'S OWN LIMITATION
HIMSELF
THOUGH SCALE DOES NOT DIFFER AS MAN
TAKE INTO CONSIDERATION THAT
MAN
DIFFER'S FROM WITHIN

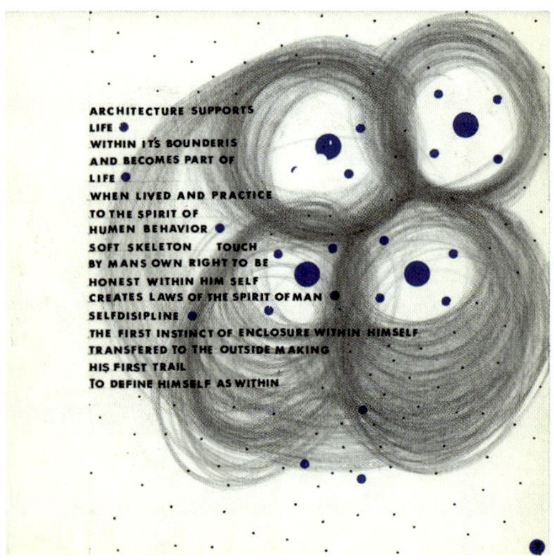
ARCHITECTURE SUPPORTS
LIFE
WITHIN IT'S BOUNDERIS
AND BECOMES PART OF
LIFE
WHEN LIVED AND PRACTICE
TO THE SPIRIT OF
HUMEN BEHAVIOR
SOFT SKELETON TOUCH
BY MANS OWN RIGHT TO BE
HONEST WITHIN HIM SELF
CREATES LAWS OF THE SPIRIT OF MAN
SELFDISIPLINE
THE FIRST INSTINCT OF ENCLOSURE WITHIN HIMSELF
TRANSFERED TO THE OUTSIDE MAKING
HIS FIRST TRAIL
TO DEFINE HIMSELF AS WITHIN

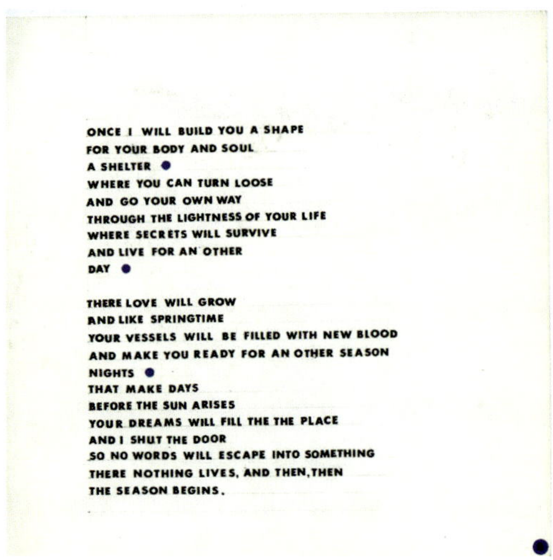
ONCE I WILL BUILD YOU A SHAPE
FOR YOUR BODY AND SOUL
A SHELTER
WHERE YOU CAN TURN LOOSE
AND GO YOUR OWN WAY
THROUGH THE LIGHTNESS OF YOUR LIFE
WHERE SECRETS WILL SURVIVE
AND LIVE FOR AN OTHER
DAY
THERE LOVE WILL GROW
AND LIKE SPRINGTIME
YOUR VESSELS WILL BE FILLED WITH NEW BLOOD
AND MAKE YOU READY FOR AN OTHER SEASON
NIGHTS
THAT MAKE DAYS
BEFORE THE SUN ARISES
YOUR DREAMS WILL FILL THE THE PLACE
AND I SHUT THE DOOR
SO NO WORDS WILL ESCAPE INTO SOMETHING
THERE NOTHING LIVES, AND THEN,THEN
THE SEASON BEGINS.

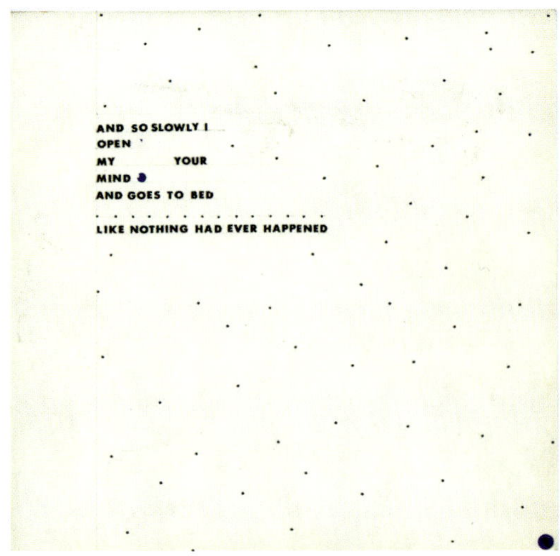
AND SO SLOWLY I
OPEN
MY YOUR
MIND
AND GOES TO BED
LIKE NOTHING HAD EVER HAPPENED

The Project Assignments

THE INTRODUCTORY TASK

Our first individual task in the masterclass studio was to present a personal reflection related to architecture—something that deeply engaged or inspired us, that filled us with wonder and made us ask questions. Kahn made it clear from the outset that honesty in relation to our own desires was an important factor. We were asked to open up, to be personal without guise. This was the start of an individual creative process that would continue for the rest of the year.

THE FIRST PROJECT: ORPHANAGE AT GIRARD COLLEGE

Our first project assignment was an orphanage for children in institutional care up to the age of sixteen. When Kahn introduced the task to us, he provided his own improvised interpretation of what he considered to be its primary challenges. Then a representative from Girard College, where the orphanage would be located, presented the brief and the rural site that was part of an old orchard bordering a cornfield. In his role as an imaginary client, he gave a detailed description of both the project's content and context, and it became apparent that the site as a vital part of a larger landscape would require meticulous attention.

After the client's presentation, Kahn appeared restless and began to downplay the representative's heavy emphasis on the brief. As the day progressed, it became apparent that we were being tasked to redefine in our own terms—as well as in the terms of a deeply shared humanity—the nature of an orphanage. Kahn directed us to reflect on our personal understanding of the given information, to not rely blindly on secondhand experience, and to keep in mind that the human aspect was seldom emphasized in a brief. To search for the nature within each given task was our primary responsibility. He asked us to work in relation to impulses, to give new meanings to old institutions. What is this particular home and what can it be? How can we trigger a reaction and a deeper understanding of our own motivations, and at the same time find the strength to be independent from earlier expressions? He regarded the search for a harmonious relationship between the individual and the collective as an essential challenge of this effort.

Kahn was adamant that the school should embody "the institutions of man," and thereby support learning, well-being, and community. He emphasized the importance of understanding

My output for the first assignment in the masterclass: nine reflections placed within a black, bespoke cardboard box. *P. O. Fjeld.*

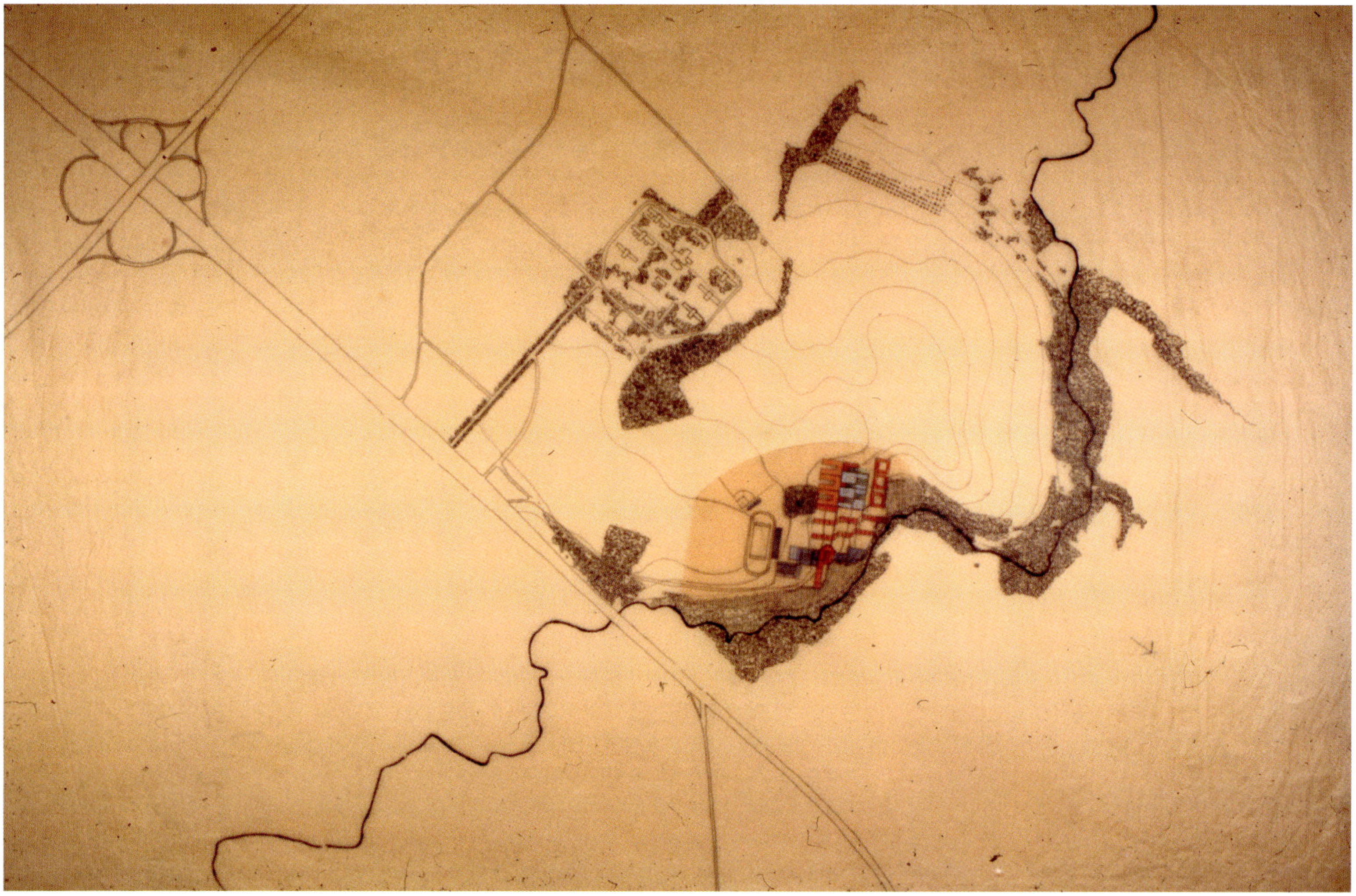

ABOVE: Girard College site plan by Robert Couch.
Robert Couch Private Collection.

OPPOSITE: Girard College site plan by Tim Spelman.
Tim Spelman.

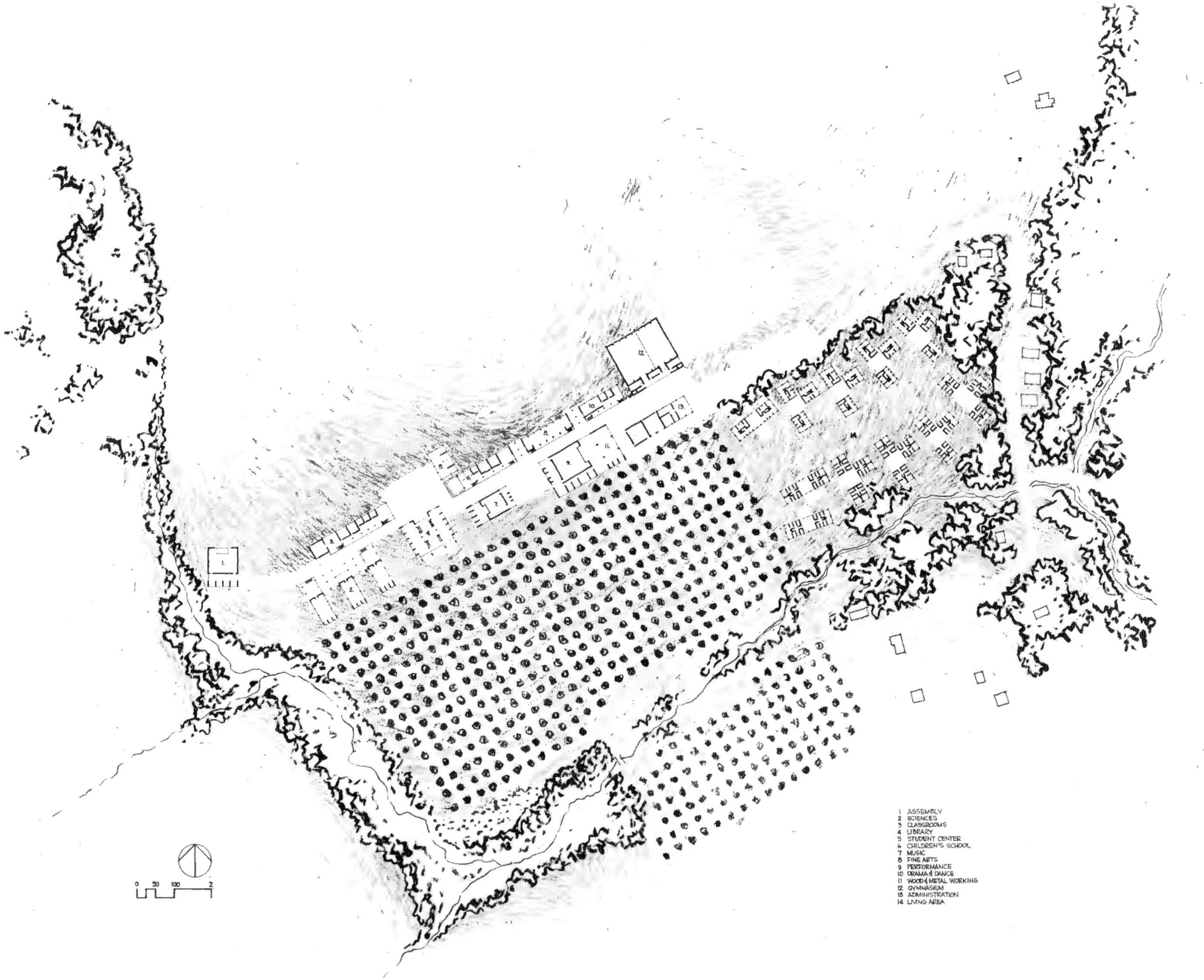
1 ASSEMBLY
2 SCIENCES
3 CLASSROOMS
4 LIBRARY
5 STUDENT CENTER
6 CHILDREN'S SCHOOL
7 MUSIC
8 FINE ARTS
9 PERFORMANCE
10 DRAMA & DANCE
11 WOOD & METAL WORKING
12 GYMNASIUM
13 ADMINISTRATION
14 LIVING AREA
0 50 100 2

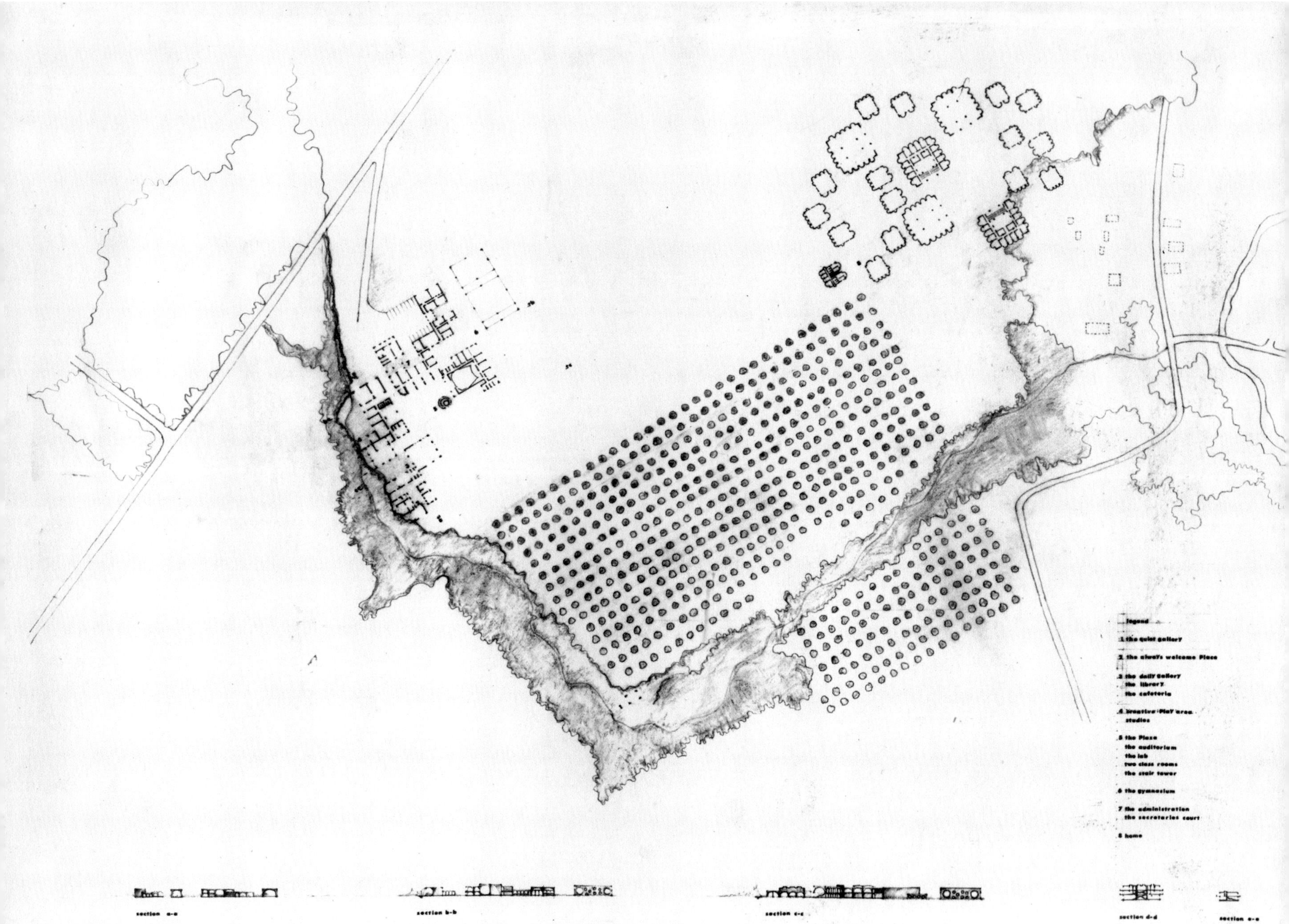

Girard College site plan by Per Olaf Fjeld. As I noted in my class notebook at the time, “The site works like a pocket. I am fascinated with the orchard and its straight rows of trees, which give a strong pattern to the site along with the cornfield and the creek.” *P. O. Fjeld.*

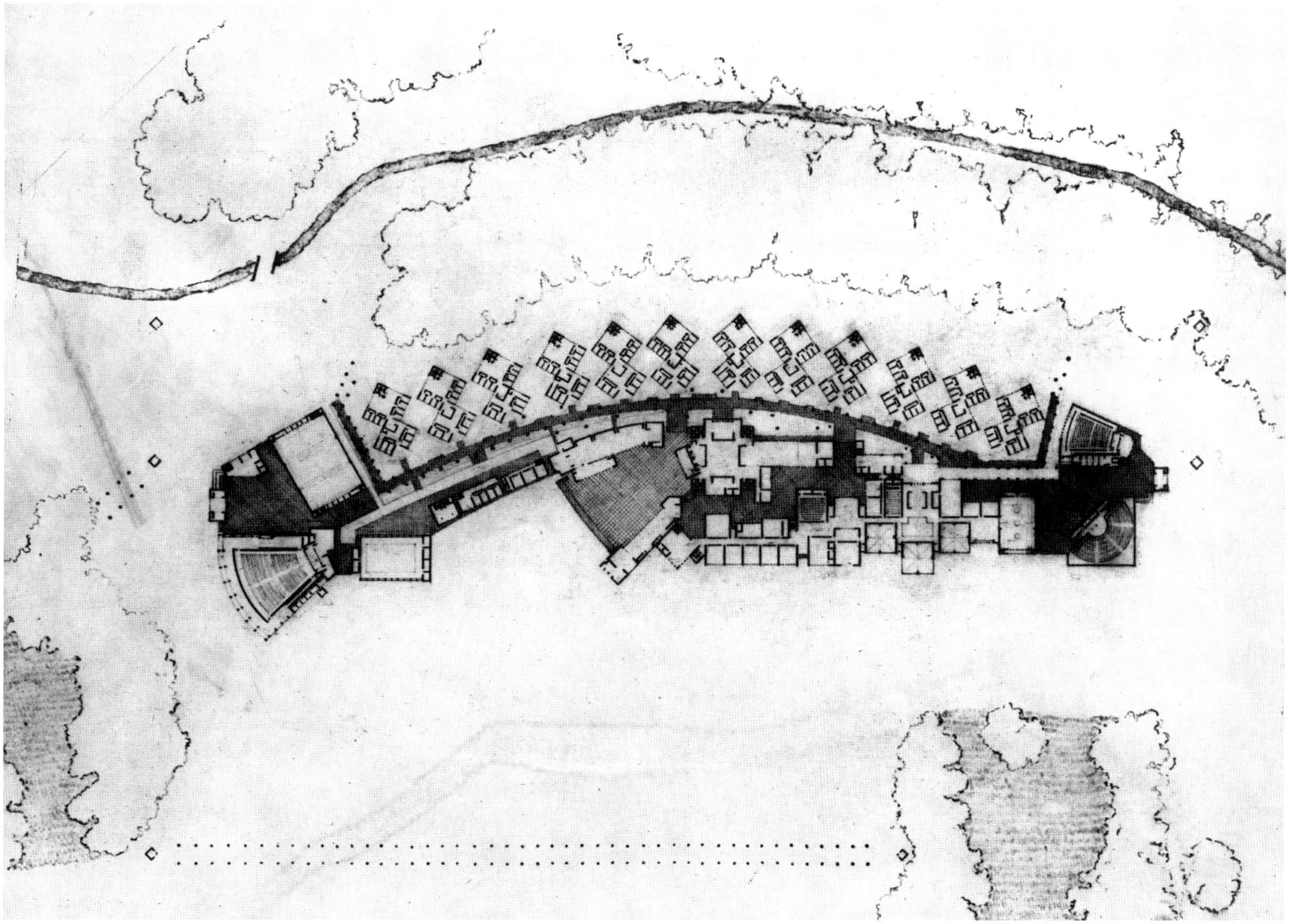

Girard College master plan by Chiaki Arai. Arai's scheme connects the college as a built street to the adjacent landscape and creek. *Chiaki Arai.*

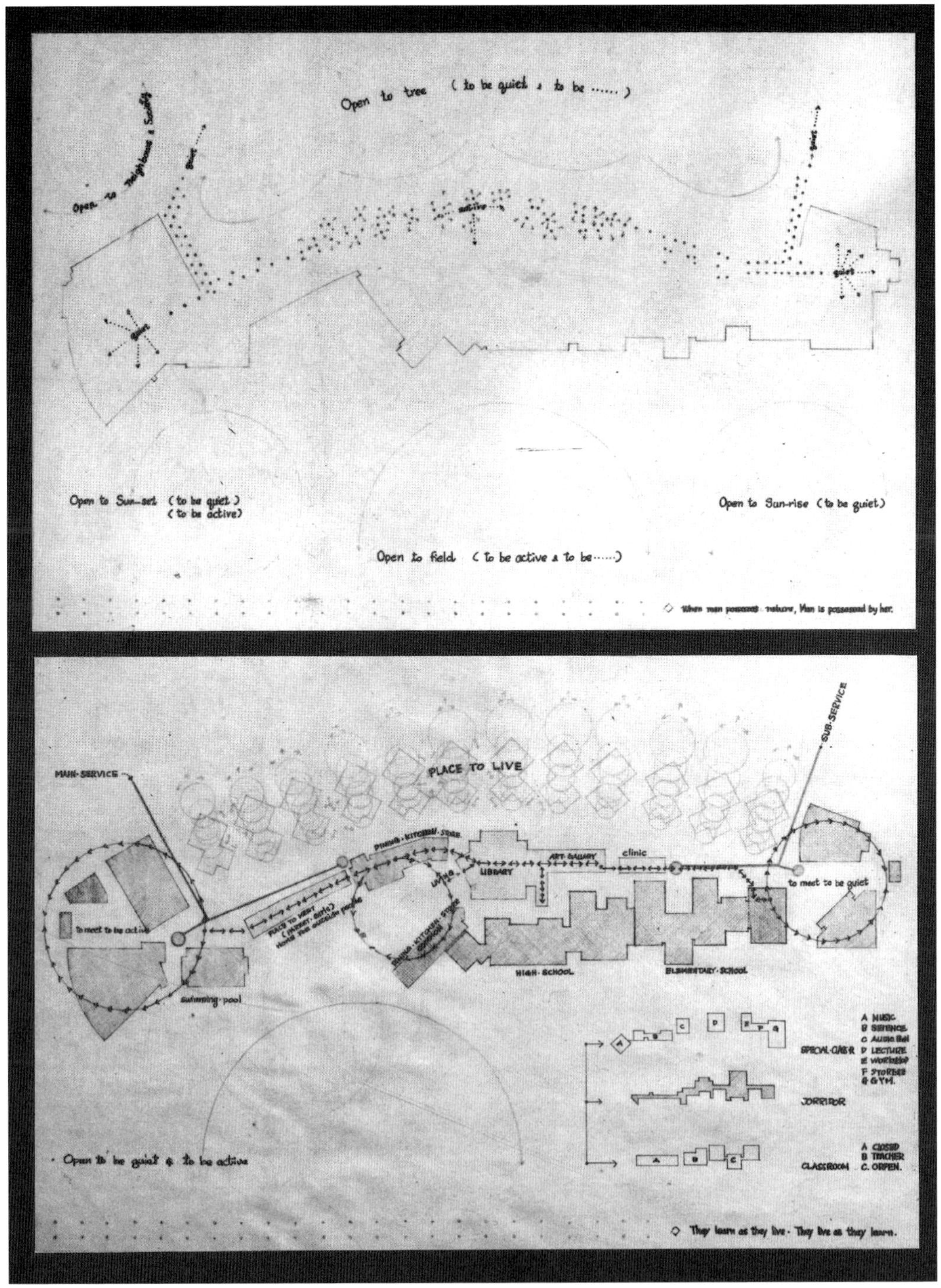

THIS PAGE AND OPPOSITE: Girard College plan diagrams by Chiaki Arai. *Chiaki Arai.*

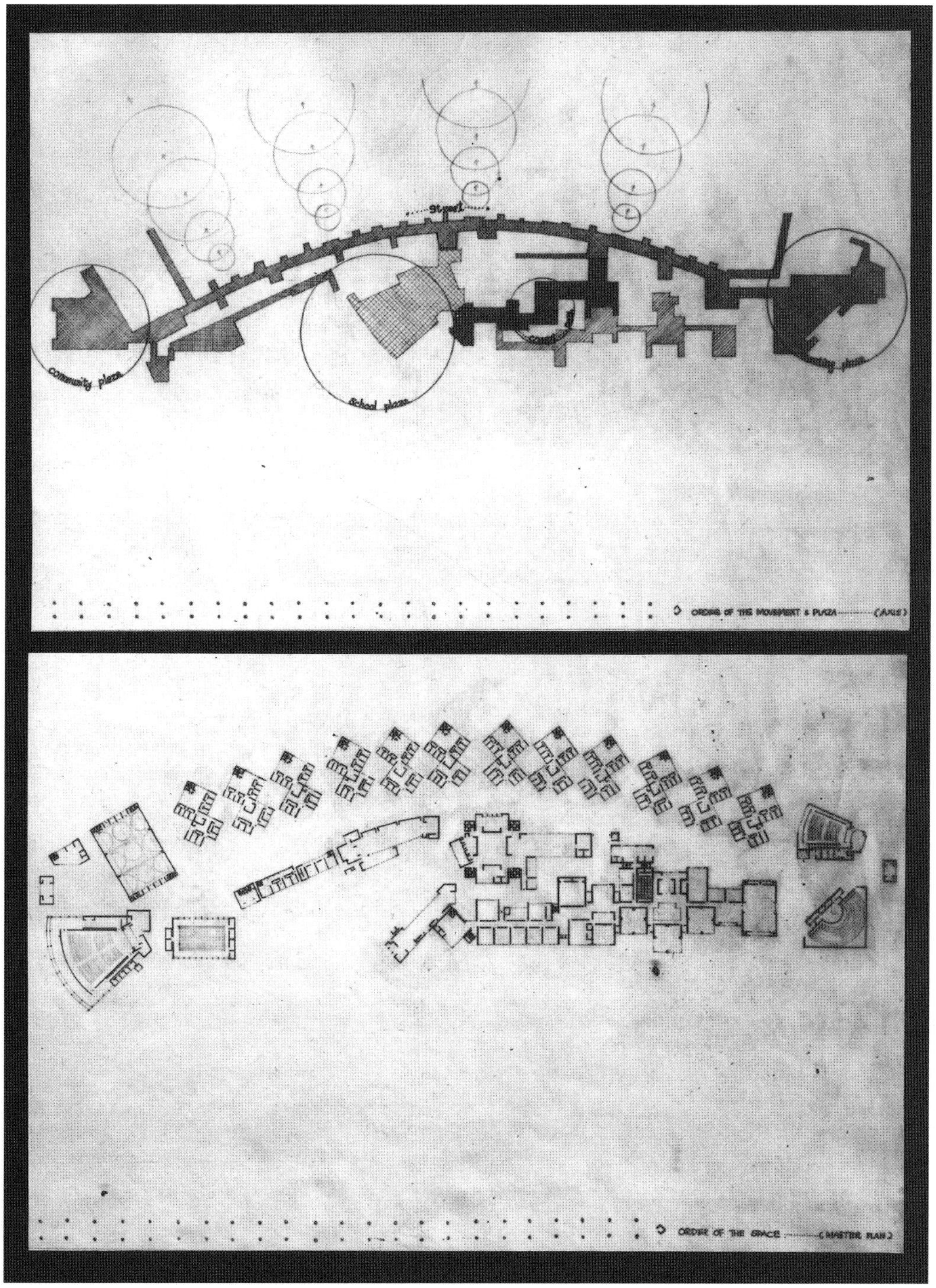
street
community plaza
school plaza
ORDERS OF THE MOVEMENT & PLAZA (AXIS)
ORDER OF THE SPACE (MASTER PLAN)

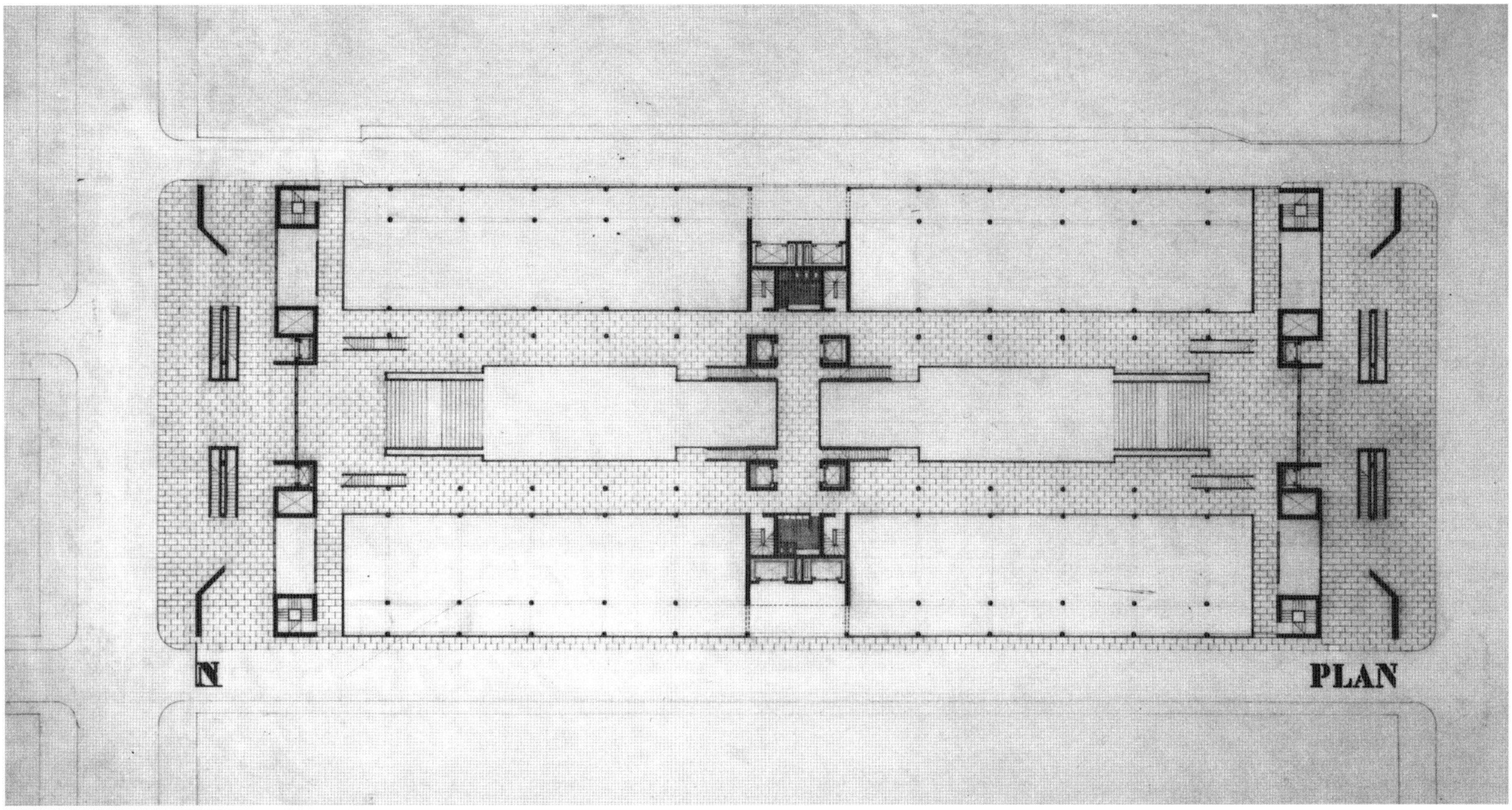
N
PLAN

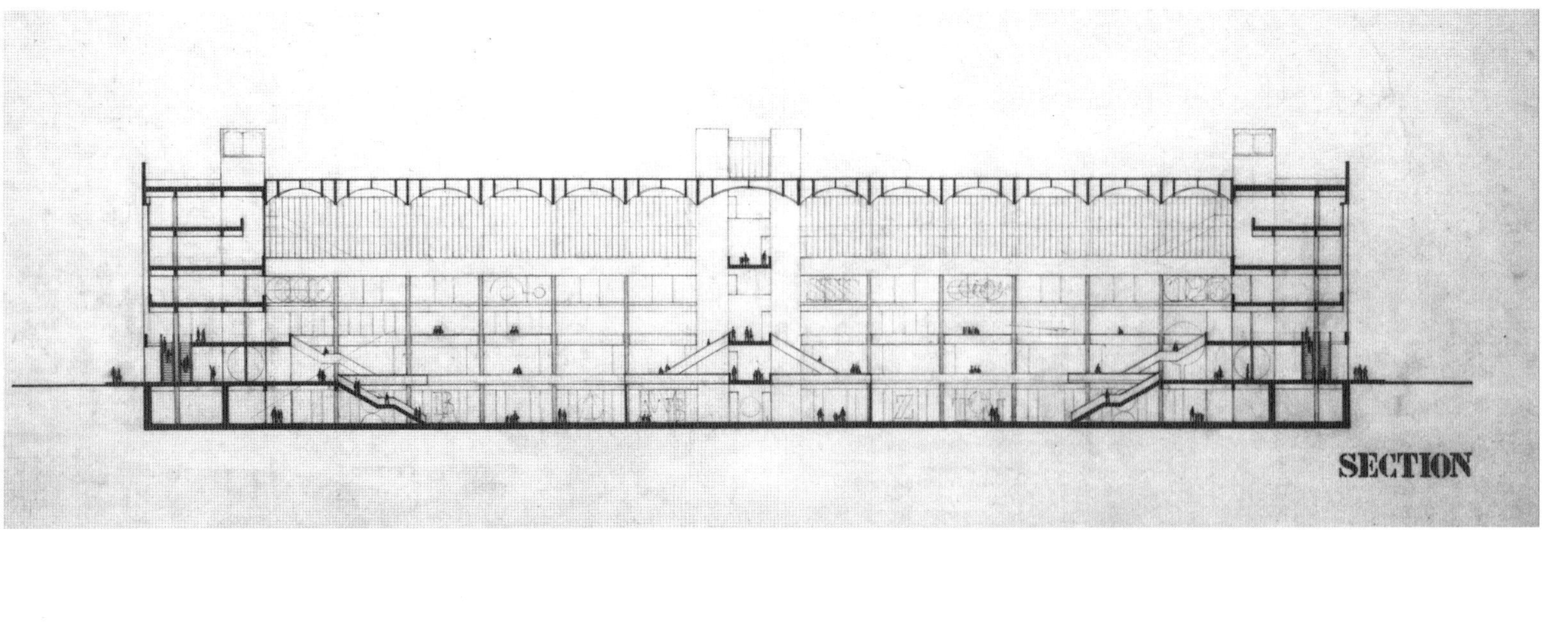
SECTION

the interactions between the school- and dormitory-related spaces of the orphanage. He advised that we should focus on the relationship between the human and the room, rather than on such issues as flexibility or efficiency regarding use. He also believed that a child's response to how a building is made should inform the learning process in some dimension.

To further encourage us at the outset of this project, Kahn remarked that we should be amazed at our willingness and capacity to work. From the start, he stressed that any creative process contains struggle and that this should be harnessed as a stimulus. Felix Candela visited the studio when we were working on the orphanage project. He discussed the necessity of material economy and efficiency related to the making of an architectural object, and his lecture seemed to release some pressure. Just the same, he emphasized the importance of retaining the kind of open-mindedness that Kahn championed. Candela was adamant about one thing regarding our working process: we could not focus on everything, only the essential things.

One of Kahn's remarks from the beginning of that first semester made a strong and lasting impression on me: "Those who work best are those who try to perfect themselves." Learning is not enough in itself without a sharpened inner dialogue with oneself—the drive to explore deeper into what one thinks, feels, and truly expects out of life. Kahn's reflections on life and work were more than enough for most of us to handle that fall.

A few years after returning home, I visited Aldo van Eyck's Amsterdam Municipal Orphanage for the first time. In a shot I was transported back to my first semester in Philadelphia, back to all my questions and uncertainties of that time, back to Kahn persistently dragging us through our individual creative process. Wistful, and at the same time full of joy, I asked his question once again: "What is an orphanage?" Standing there in what was left of the building, I understood what Kahn had once asked and why.

THE SECOND PROJECT: A SHOPPING CENTER

From the start of our second project, Kahn asked us to put aside our possible disdain for shopping centers, to distance ourselves from their negative connotations and instead focus on their role in the community. He suggested that if we began optimistically, with joy, then the project would soon become part of us. Our point of departure was to be a form of inner concentration, a device that was intended to free us from any doubts and prejudices that we might otherwise bring to the project.

To help us gain clarity about the program topic and at the same time retain an open curiosity, he asked us to jump straight into the task. Our project site was located in the center

OPPOSITE TOP: Shopping mall plan at the street level by Chiaki Arai. *Chiaki Arai.*

OPPOSITE BOTTOM: Shopping mall section by Chiaki Arai. *Chiaki Arai.*

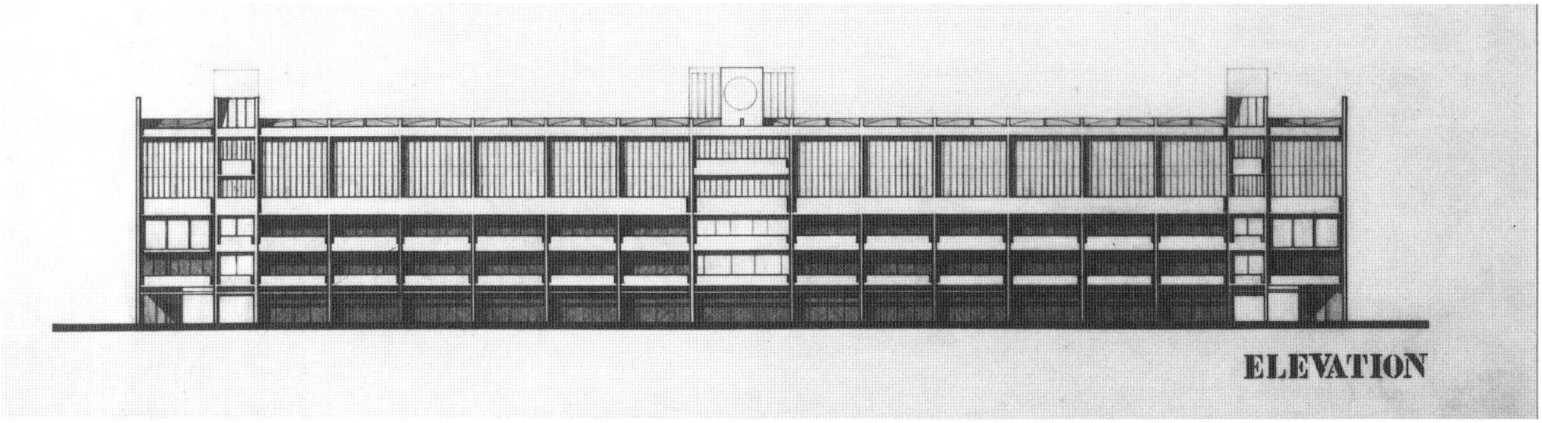

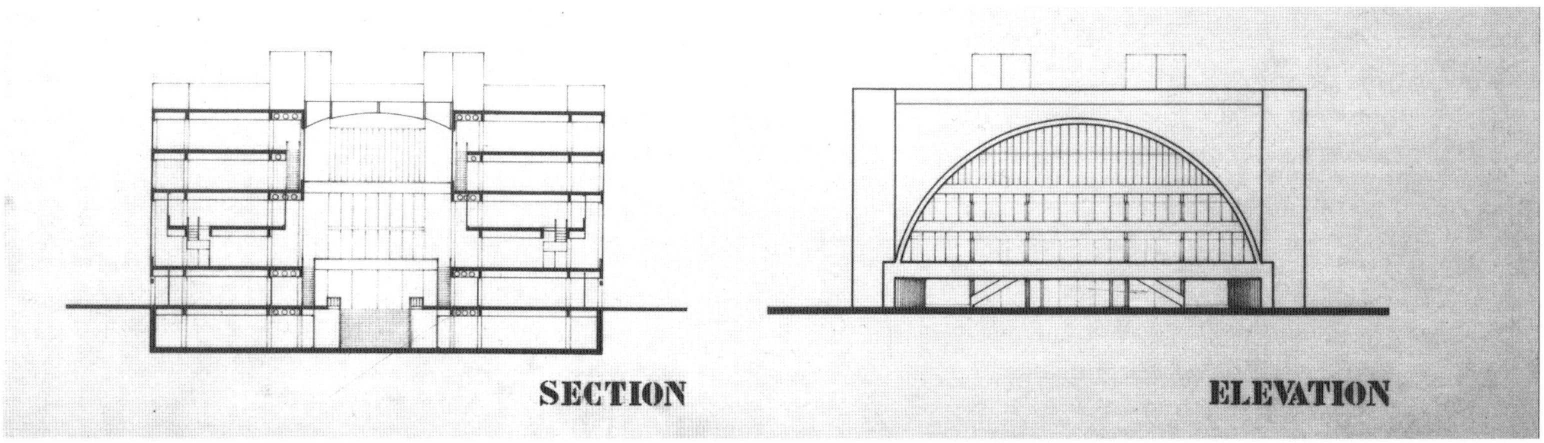

TOP: Shopping mall elevation by Chiaki Arai. *Chiaki Arai.*

BOTTOM: Shopping mall section and elevation by Chiaki Arai. *Chiaki Arai.*

OPPOSITE: Shopping mall plans and sections by Per Olaf Fjeld. *P. O. Fjeld.*

of Philadelphia, now a familiar testing ground for us. From day one, Kahn stressed that we should not regard the shopping center as an isolated built object, but as a public space belonging to the street. Its responsibility was to give positive energy and activity to the city. It could be a building *as street*, but it needed a clear spatial identity of its own. In the end, few of us truly managed to design a project that fulfilled all of these criteria, especially because it was difficult to break away from our preconceptions about the building type. This assignment brought the idea of the institutions of man into contact with a program that was both in transformation and constrained by commercial considerations.

What was the core identity of a shopping center? This question sparked many discussions. We talked about the act of buying as a preference stemming from both reason and the personal sphere, concluding that in order to fully materialize a shopping center we needed to find a spatial expression for the opportunity of choice. We hoped that comprehending the

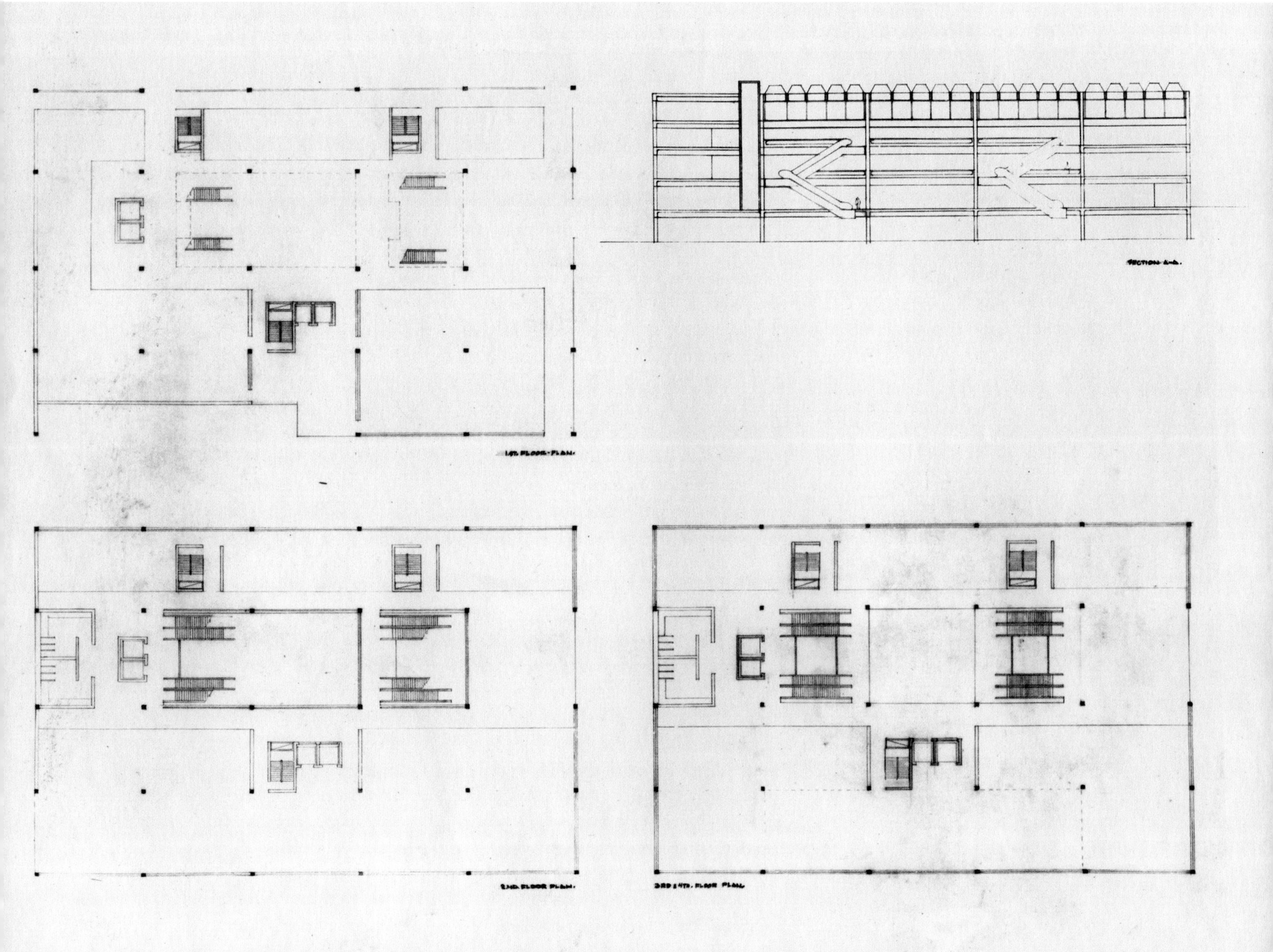
SECTION A-A.
1ST. FLOOR-PLAN.
2ND. FLOOR PLAN.
3RD & 4TH. FLOOR PLAN

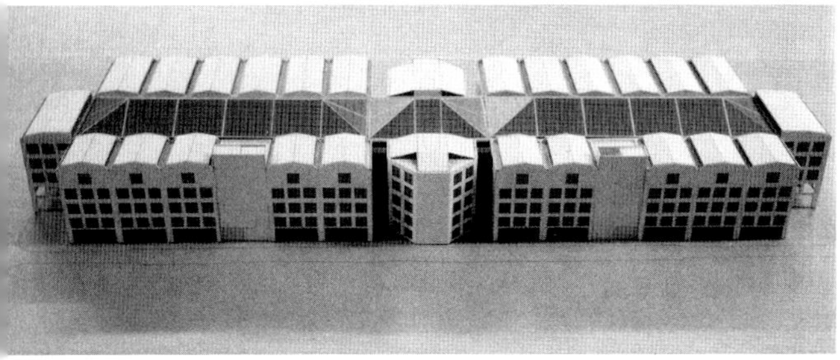

Shopping mall model by Robert Couch.
Robert Couch Private Collection.

differences between choice and opportunity at a fundamental level would bring us closer to understanding this type of institution.

Kahn prioritized the user over the client in these discussions, but he also emphasized the necessity to find a balance. He underlined the role that daylight should play in indicating to users what type of institution they had entered: though daylight would not necessarily be that important to the shops, it would be essential for public areas where people moved about and for spaces with close contact to the street. The order of movement set by structure therefore surfaced as the major theme in many of our discussions. We were asked to regard the stairs, escalators, elevators, and ramps as unique spatial elements within themselves.

Our discussion focused on the urban dwellers who lived in the city center; the idea of the city as a pulsating workplace; and the relationships between the collective and the individual that were transforming and activating the city constantly. To bring all of these elements together was not easy, but urban life in downtown Philadelphia occupied many planners and architects at the time, so there was no lack of ideas. As students, we were drawn to Kahn's proposals for parking in the city and his city movement diagrams. These drawings played a role in our nightly discussions after class, but in the end they had little impact on our own work, as our final presentations tended to focus more on the object, the shopping center, than the surrounding city.

During this project, we encountered Kahn's sometimes confusing push to strengthen our awareness of the creative process. Quite often, this effort ended in our simply coming to terms with dualities within Kahn's approach, as we were only able to interpret portions of his critiques and, at times, lost some crucial nuance of meaning along the way. In one session he asked us to search for the beginnings of things—and then he commented that we could not depend on the trueness of things. In the next session he argued that we could not start a project without having a deliberate sense of purpose—and then he asserted that architecture could not be invented through process. He went on to say that the beginning of a creative act sits in the mind of the artist, not as something that belongs to that individual but to everyone, and that to understand this difference would make one a better person. One of his comments about the gardens that appeared in some of the shopping center projects epitomizes, for me, the ambiguities that animated his instruction. He suggested that the gardens "should not be directly connected to a shop, but carry a more general feeling as if they came out of the shop." Sometimes during a session one of us would instantly understand what he was trying to convey, but that understanding was usually an individual experience rather than a collective discovery.

The shopping center at first seemed out of character with what we had envisioned as

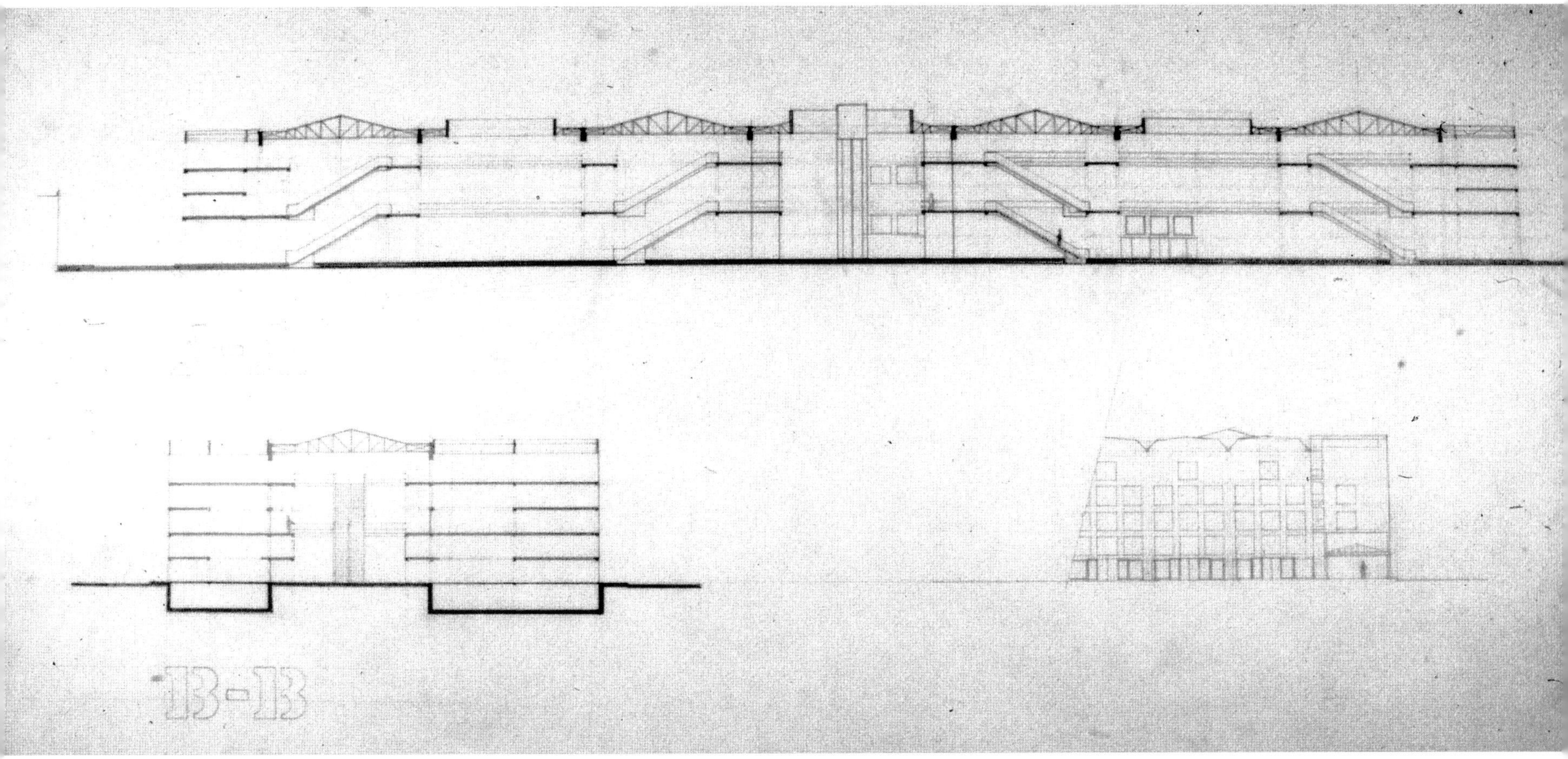

Shopping mall section by Robert Couch.
Robert Couch Private Collection.

likely subject matter for the masterclass, and many of us intuitively felt that Kahn had assigned this project with some reluctance. All the same, his office was then working on the Baltimore Harbor project and the Yale Center for British Art, which included shops on the ground level. Both projects had commercial elements in the brief, so our task was not so distant from the design challenges Kahn faced at the time. He envisioned the shopping center as an active institution in constant transformation. Unfortunately, commercial design today tends to be governed by developers' immediate economic priorities, which tend to work against the public's long-term inclinations. Kahn referred to this situation as "approval" and regarded it as an alibi for short-term thinking. Our second assignment therefore touched on an architectural complexity that is still unfolding and unresolved.

"Start something and it immediately becomes part of you"—Kahn's comment has stayed with me ever since. Each semester I encounter at least a few students who hesitate, waiting

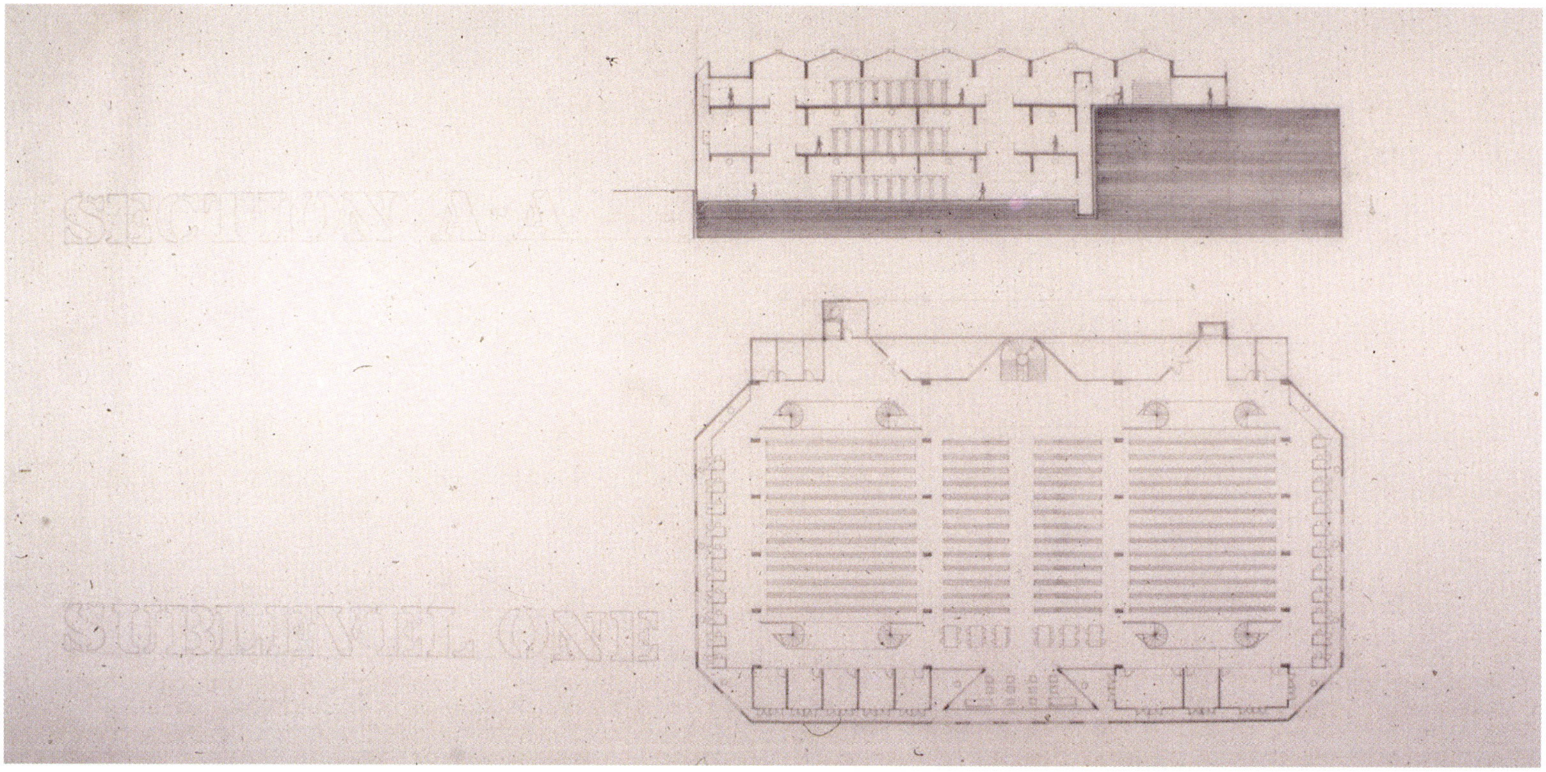
SECTION A-A
SUBLEVEL ONE

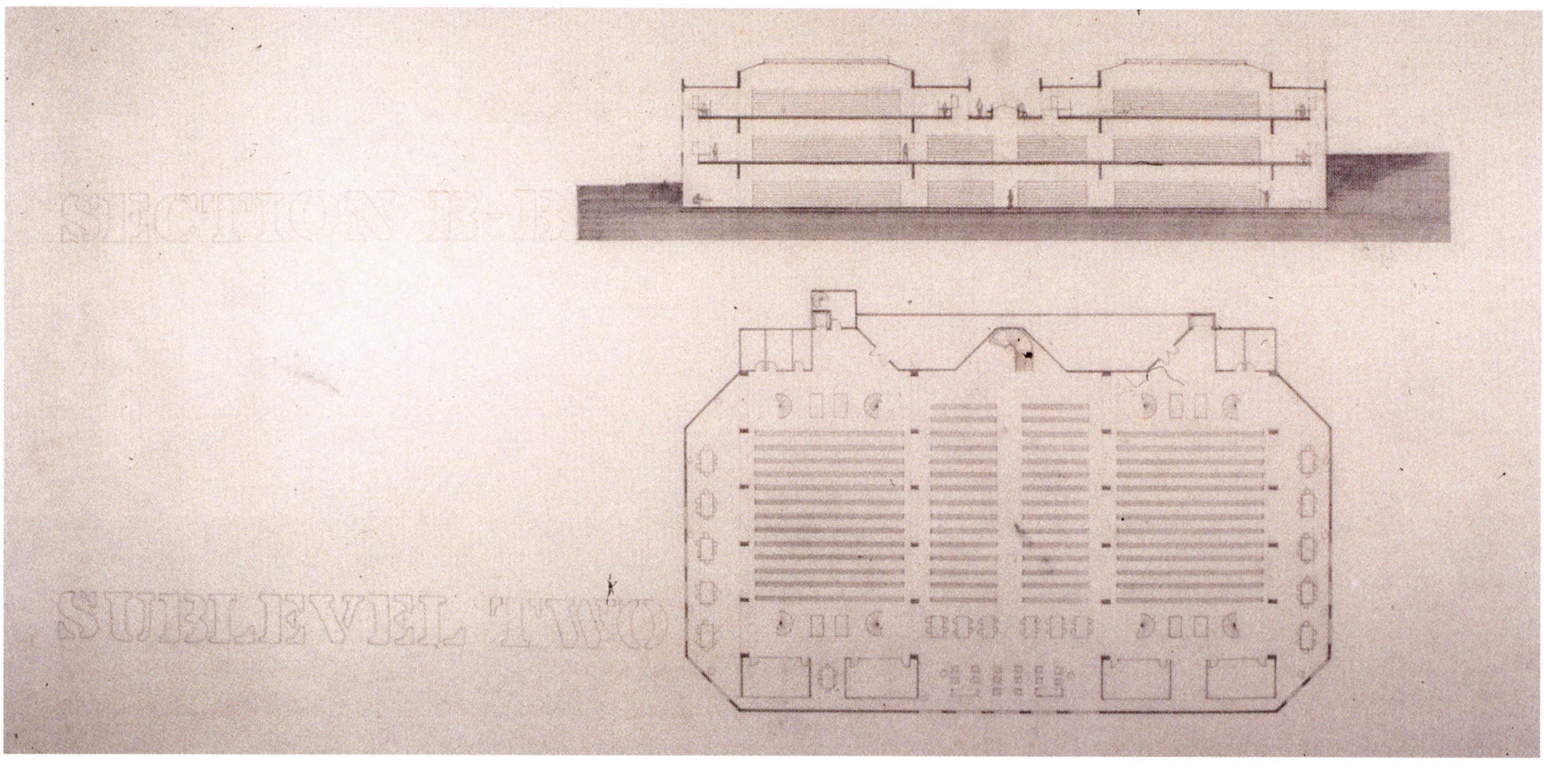
SECTION B-B
SUBLEVEL TWO

for the right pencil, the right table, a new program, the best information, all the facts, the perfect moment. When I say "just start and it will become part of you," the effect is no less than it was for us that first semester.

THE THIRD PROJECT: A THEOLOGICAL LIBRARY

Judging from my notes at the time, by our third project the class seemed to be more comfortable and familiar with Kahn's teaching approach and vocabulary. The first semester had not only been intense but also required that we adjust our past working processes, ambitions, and goals. In assigning a theological library as our third project, Kahn continued to stress that the aim of our work was not to solve a problem or directly address the program text. Rather, we were to search for the nature of the library and thus to think fundamentally about meeting and learning. He again asked us to dig deeper, to acknowledge what we were striving toward and to go beyond personal preference and established images. He could become quite irritated when one of us presented a "Kinder Egg"—an idea with no core architectural base—or when we elaborated on our schemes in purely aesthetic terms. Throughout this phase, we were asked to distinguish between need, desire, and whatever knowing we brought to the table. Kahn wanted us to rely on our senses and concentrate on the human aspects of the library as an institution.

As I mentioned earlier, the library at Exeter was just completed at the time of our masterclass and influenced all of us on some level. Meanwhile, Kahn's office was working on the Graduate Theological Union Library at Berkeley, a commission very much aligned with our assignment. As in earlier projects, for this assignment Kahn stressed the relationship between structure and daylight. He was interested in the weight of the books relative to the dimensions of the different reading rooms and how the differences indicated individual spatial layers, structure, and light. He was steadfast that each room needed an identity of its own set by structure as mass, yet that each space should be understood within its larger sequence of rooms, as part of a plan that constitutes a "society of rooms." He believed that if a project were in need of a connector, this spatial device should be part of the order of the building itself, and only then could the connector enrich the core spatial intentions. In class he vigorously attacked the lightweight partition wall, arguing against the impulse to cut up a space that had already been given its identity through structure. He believed that the kind of spatial flexibility that partition walls created should be avoided, because such flexibility ultimately signaled a lack of identity and spatial precision.

OPPOSITE TOP: Library section and plan (sublevel one) by Robert Couch. "There is nothing more degrading to the mind than to call a library an information center," Couch recorded Kahn saying during our library project. *Robert Couch Private Collection.*

OPPOSITE BOTTOM: Library section and plan (sublevel two) by Robert Couch. *Robert Couch Private Collection.*

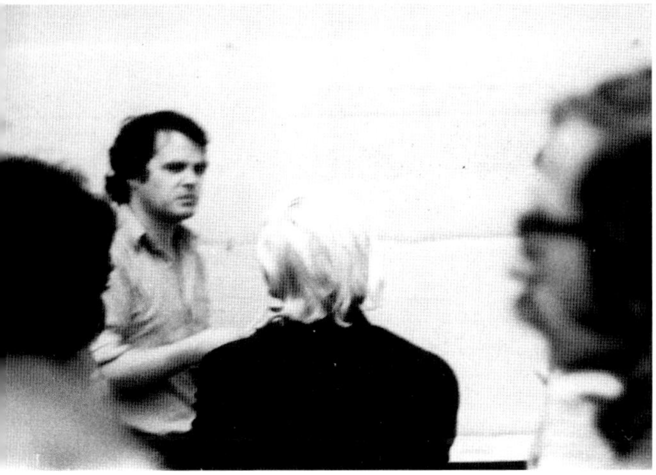

Kahn and Robert Couch during a critique.
Robert Couch Private Collection.

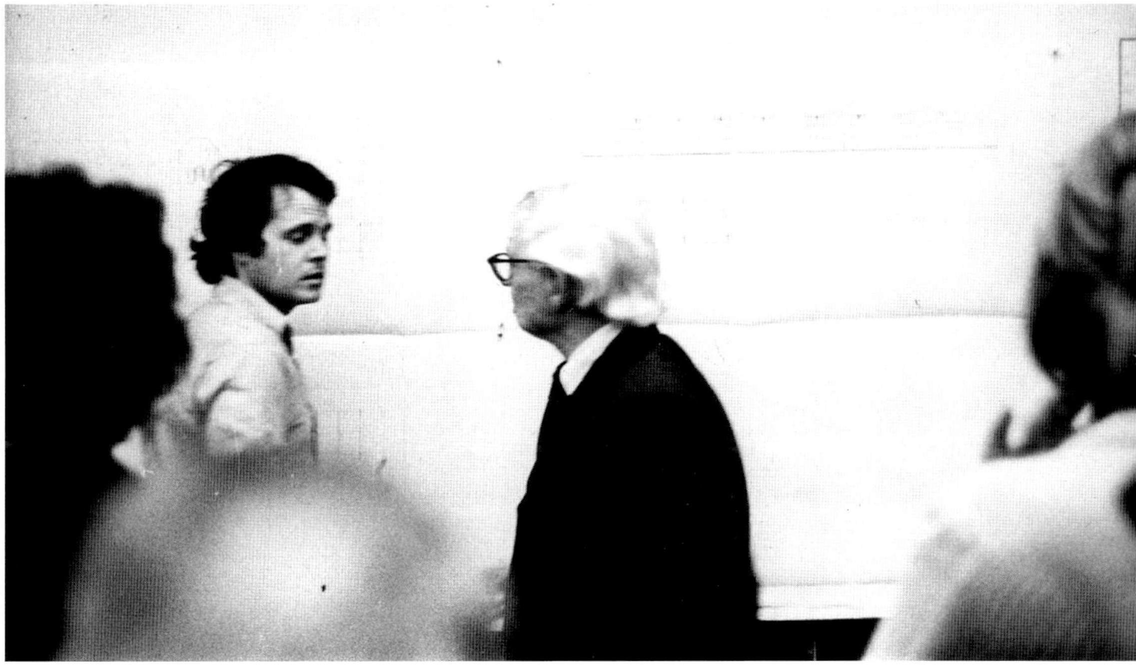

To Kahn's dismay, this project revealed our class's shaky relationship with materials as well as our conventional, catalogue-oriented attempts at detailing. He pressed us to overcome these shortcomings through more direct experience with materials, to recognize both potential and resistance forces, and to record how things are made. Le Ricolais's course and feedback in the studio were an important corrective for the deficiencies Kahn identified in these discussions. Just the same, our capabilities and experience with materials usually fell short of our ambitious project aims.

At one point during this project we had an intense discussion about art and architecture: Could they be compared? Did we see differences? Kahn, who had become more and more agitated with this talk, declared that creativity could not be subject to comparison: it was either there or it wasn't. He concluded with the assertion that "Not believing in art is believing in no expression whatsoever, and it should never be considered a subject." There was a slight sense of division within the class as the day of this debate ended.

Our questions during this project prompted Kahn to give several memorable small talks about literature and his admiration for writers. He regarded the poet as holding the highest

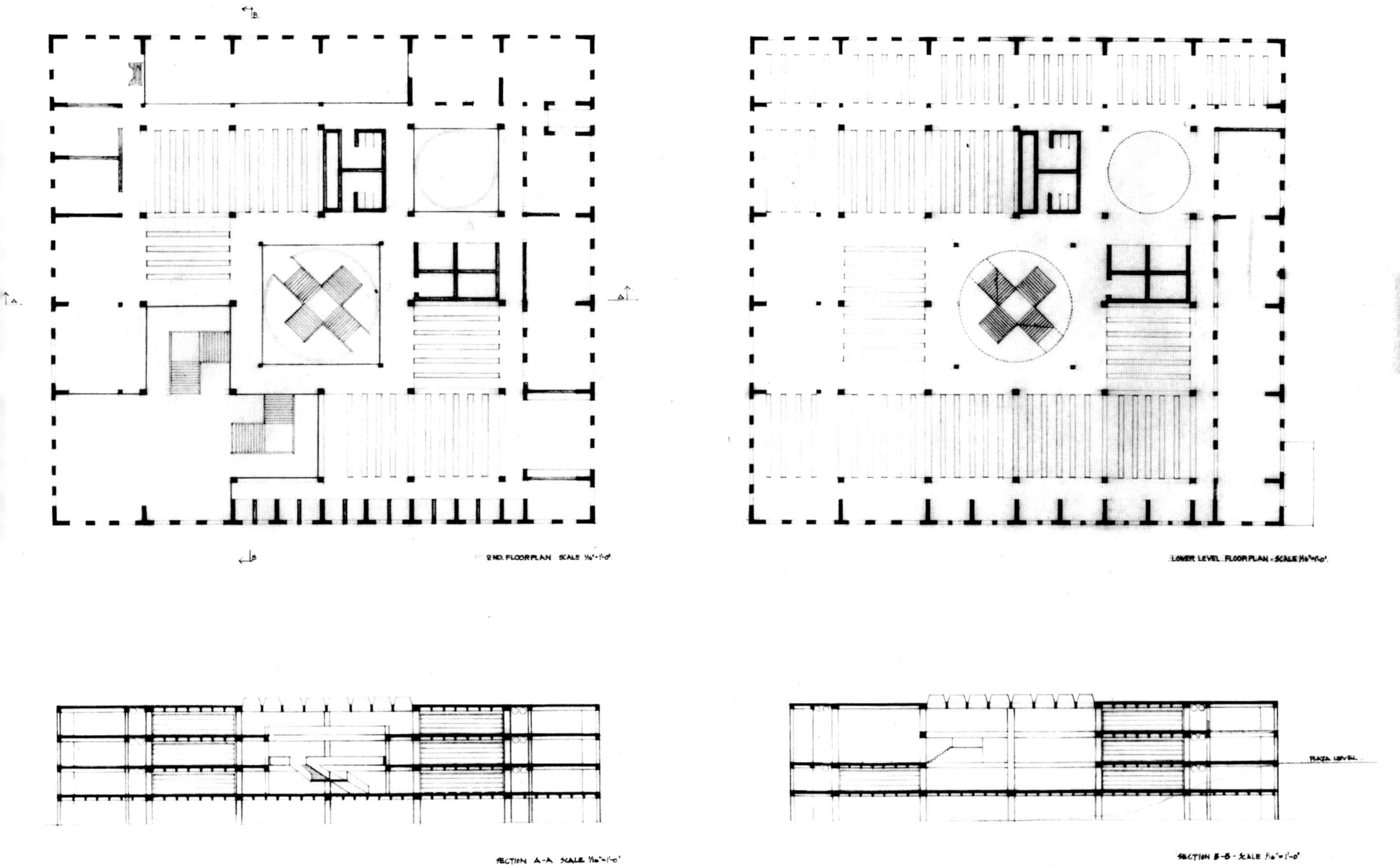

Library section by Per Olaf Fjeld. *P. O. Fjeld.*

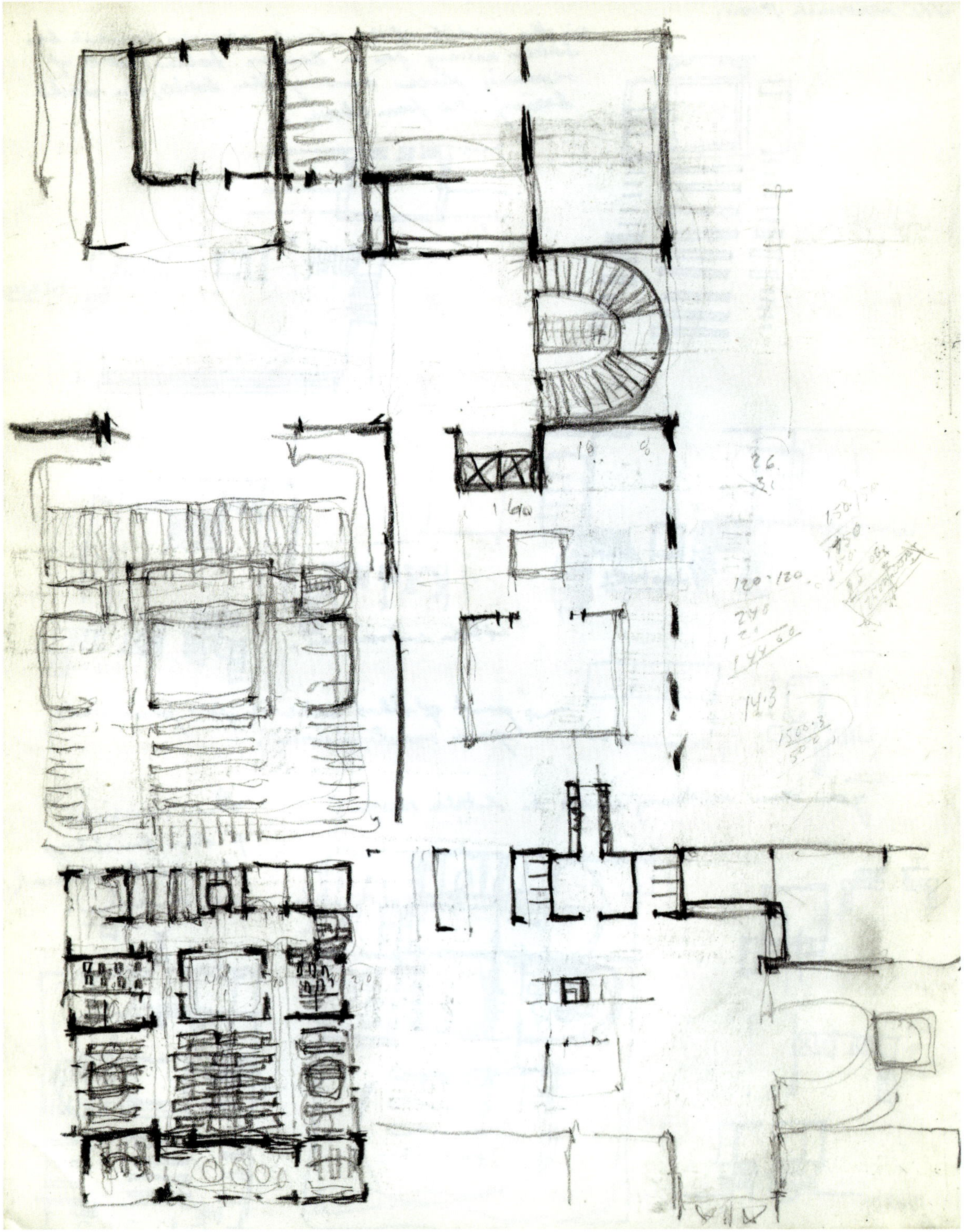

Some of Per Olaf Fjeld's initial sketches for the library project.
P. O. Fjeld.

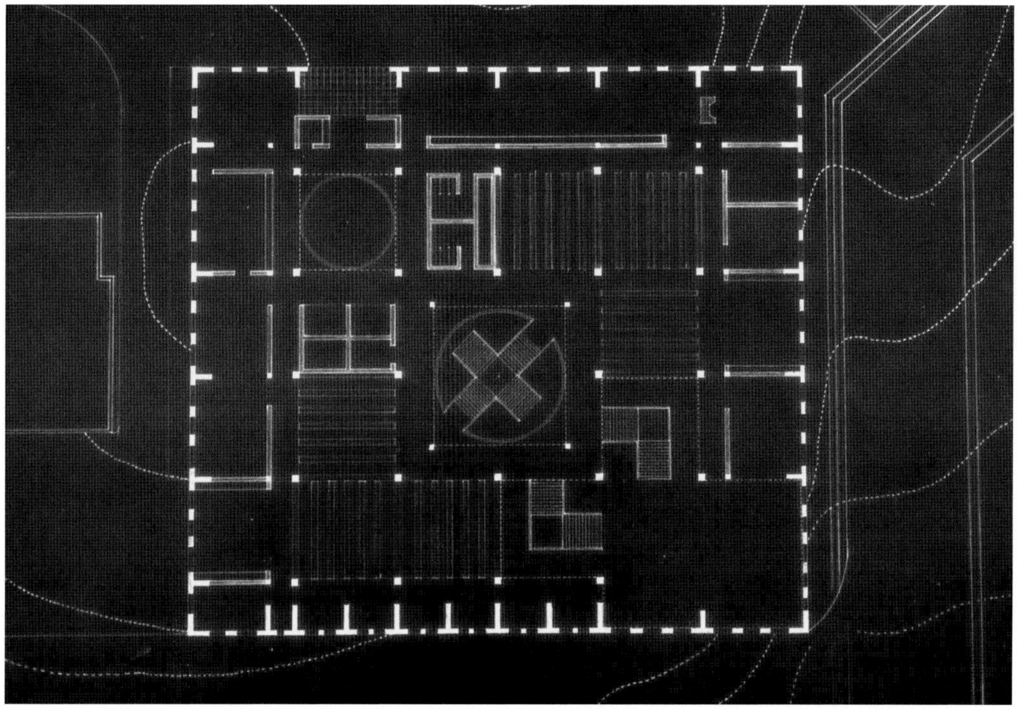

Second-floor plan for library by Per Olaf Fjeld. Escaping the influence of Kahn's Exeter library was a challenging task, as this plan demonstrates. *P. O. Fjeld.*

position among writers. He put the poet first because he or she was compelled to write for existence. I also remember the class went completely quiet when he talked about Nikolai Gogol. He asked us to search for our own words and understand their inherent meanings in relation to what was said before, as each word is already embedded in some form of human agreement.

The term "joy" also surfaced throughout our library discussions. In the face of the struggles and frustrations we experienced during the creative process, Kahn asked us to find joy in our work because projects need positive energy and inspiration. It was only much later that I would discover that several prominent Nordic architects used the term "joy" in much the same way: first in writings by and about Gunnar Asplund, and then in the diary where Arne Korsmo recorded his observations about the 1928 trip during which he met Kahn.

Years later, when reminiscing with some of my classmates, we remembered the library assignment as our best and most rewarding project. Much of what surfaced in the discussions about this project has remained with me throughout my teaching career. One particular statement from Kahn that I recorded then I often return to: "Teachers belong to their beliefs." I have interpreted this to mean that teachers must stand up for what they believe in, not necessarily combatively, but with a passion capable of advancing clarity. Strangely, I am still proud of my library project. It shares similarities with the library in Exeter, yet it has an identity

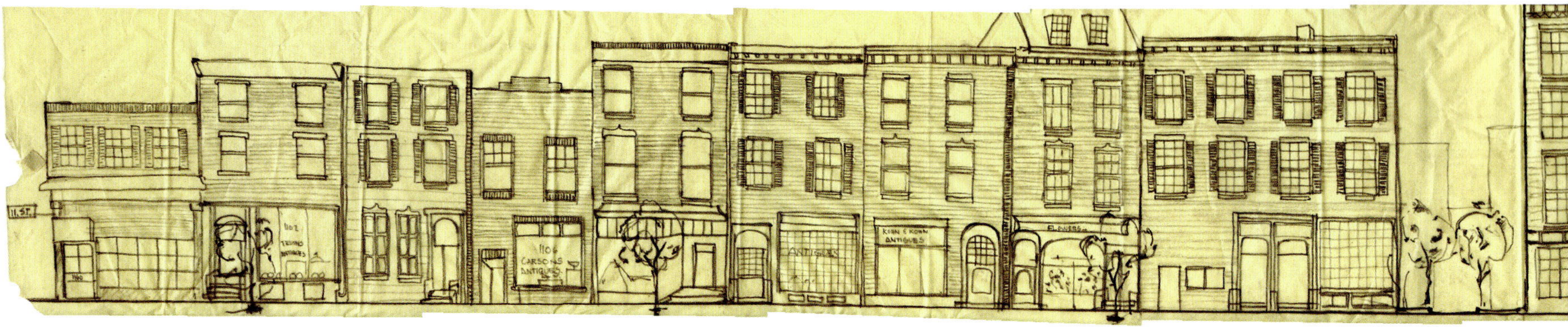

Urban project in Philadelphia: A long sketch of Pine Street on tracing paper by Per Olaf Fjeld. Measuring the intersection of Pine and Broad Streets using a yardstick in the middle of the night with Emily was not easy. *P. O. Fjeld.*

of its own. In retrospect, it tells its own story about my understanding of Kahn and how his teaching strongly influenced my work at the time.

THE FOURTH PROJECT: URBAN INTERVENTION IN PHILADELPHIA

Kahn introduced the final project assignment—an urban intervention in Philadelphia—by declaring his love for the city and urging us to respect it and all it contained. Here again issues with the car surfaced almost immediately; we discussed the significant amount of wasted or inactive space parking created and how this endangered the city's identity. We talked about the relationship between the street and what was considered a road, and the sidewalk as land where the car is not. He asked us to question the position and impact of the car and joked that the car needed an identity too. These were topics that truly engaged Kahn at the time. The impasse between Venturi and Kahn during a class discussion also influenced the discourse.

We were tasked with devising an urban intervention that would make an impact and that would be accepted by the community it was intended to serve. Kahn was not asking for a large-scale planning project, but a contribution that was more than just a repair or a local design idea. He stressed the growing lack of communality and pressed us to work toward a stronger clarity between the served and serving spaces related to an urban context and challenged us to comprehend this relationship anew. At times he talked about these issues from his personal experience and reminded us to be aware of the power of circumstance, in that one could have a great proposal but sometimes circumstances could rip it apart.

In the middle of the assignment Kahn became anxious about our progress. He stressed the importance of producing more material, and came straight to the point: he was tired of words and wanted to see drawings, different drawings, not all with the same general type of information! From now on it was not enough to talk about potential; such talk had to be transformed into physical space. He reminded us about the power of form drawings, expressing

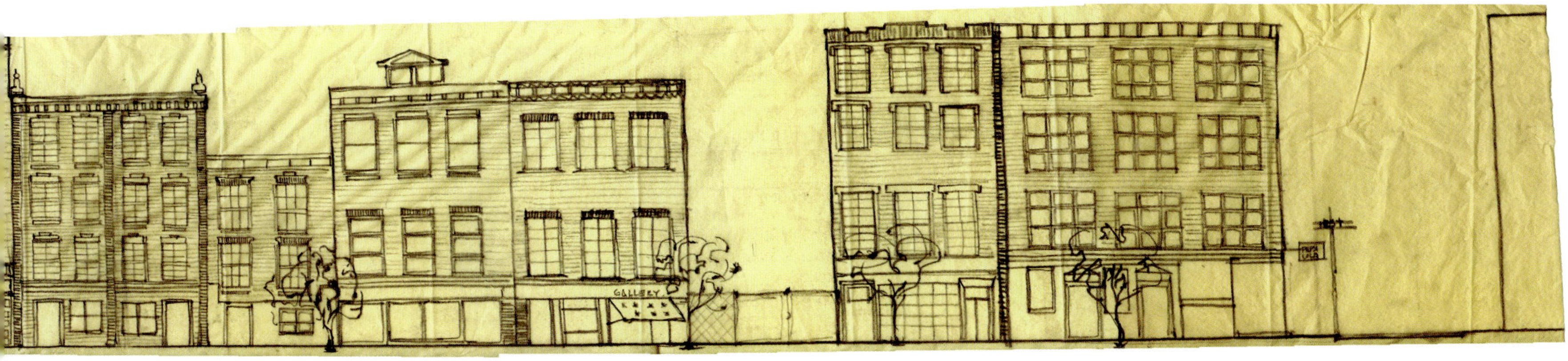

core content not as a utopian idea, but rather as an inspiration toward realization. He not only wanted us to produce more drawings but also to ensure those drawings were more precise and provided greater detail; if, for example, the site had trees, the drawing should indicate which were old and which were not. For us students, the challenge was again to go beyond our established tastes and ideas, to achieve a consensus based on the strength of our proposals. We explored a multitude of scales and touched on simple as well as complex urban situations. I think he liked my last project, but it did not reach beyond a good idea, as its order of movement was too contrived. At the end of my final presentation Kahn gave me one compliment: "You spoke from your heart."

Again, I think it is interesting to consider projects that were in Kahn's office at the time of our project—in this case, the master plan for the Bicentennial Exposition and the redevelopment plan for the Independence Hall area, both of which were based in Philadelphia and addressed similar issues to those we were exploring in class.

When Kahn declared his love for cities, he put it very directly. He even went so far as to claim that a city has a biological purpose. He was an urban dweller, at home in a hectic urban working environment, busy on the weekdays and weekends—and that is how I saw him as a student. He loved the city because it was shaped through human agreement and its institutions were directly contingent on these agreements.

After Graduation

My allotted time in Louis Kahn's masterclass came to an end in the early summer of 1973. He made an indirect invitation to work in his office on the last day—but a little shy, and not quite understanding that the offer was at all a possibility, I did not follow up, though several of my classmates did. Occasionally during my first years after returning home, I contemplated if I had made the right decision.

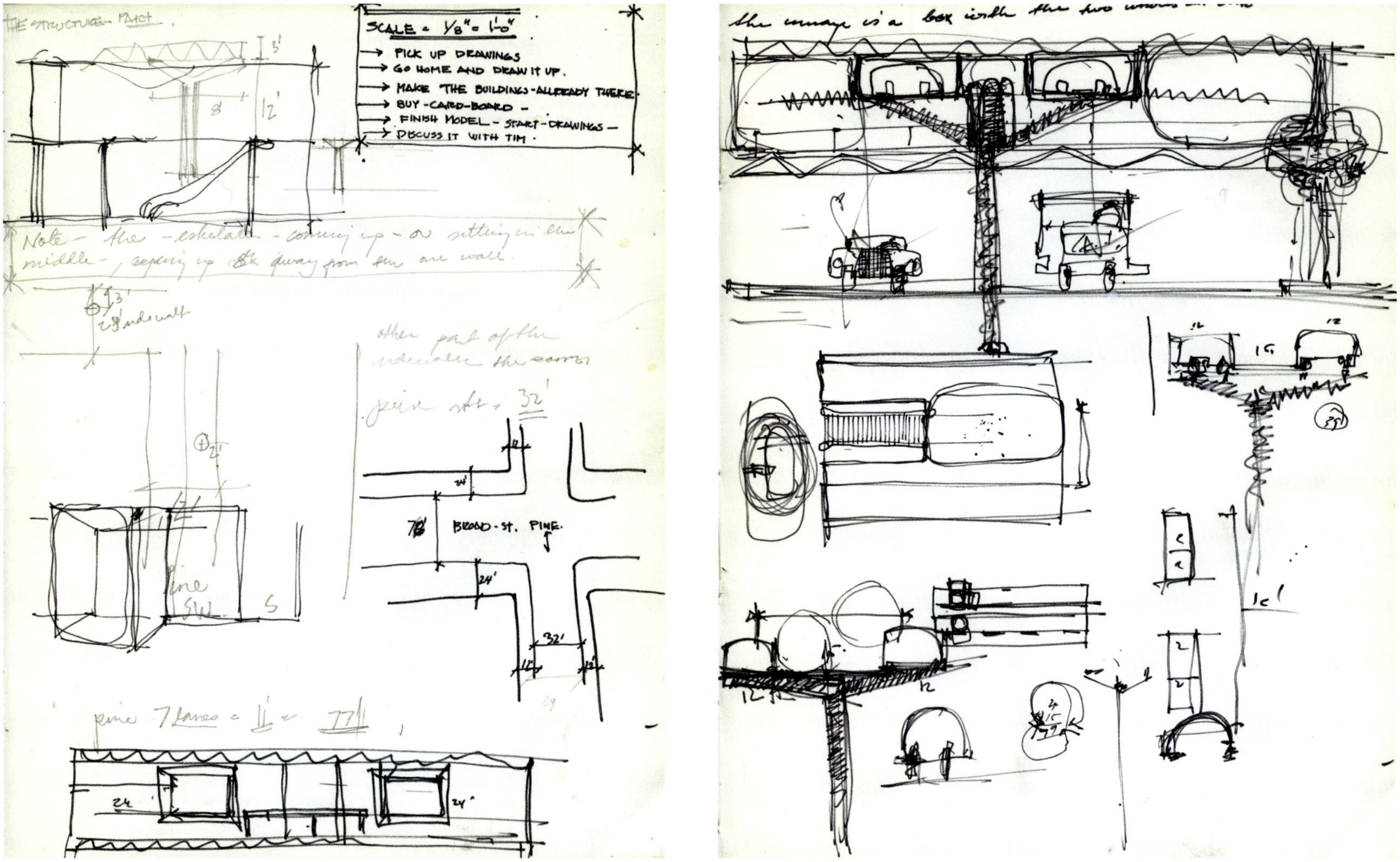

Urban project: working sketches by Per Olaf Fjeld concerning the intersection of Pine and Broad Streets and various section attempts. *P. O. Fjeld.*

An old friend from Washington State who had just finished his studies at Haverford College was planning to drive home, so I tagged along, convincing him to visit a number of Kahn's buildings along the way. After a short stay in Seattle I flew home to Norway. By August, I was already working for the architect Sverre Fehn in Oslo. If I had stayed in Philadelphia and returned a half year later, Fehn's office would not have been in the position to hire me. This window of opportunity was open for just a few months, and I was able to climb through it just in time.

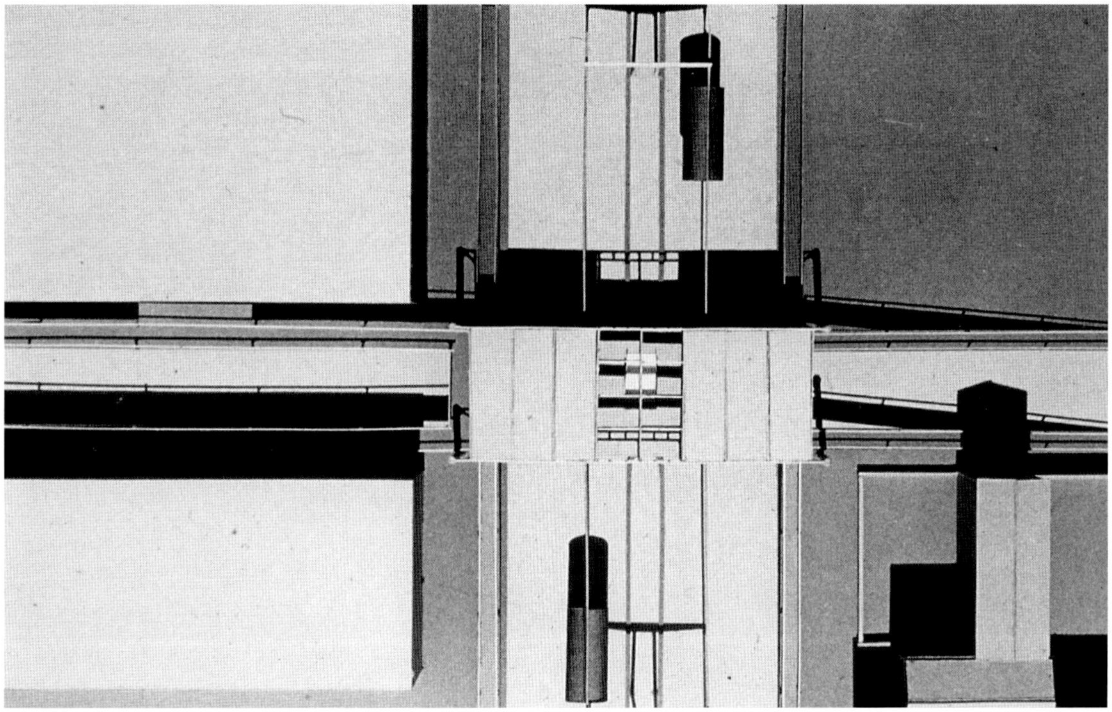

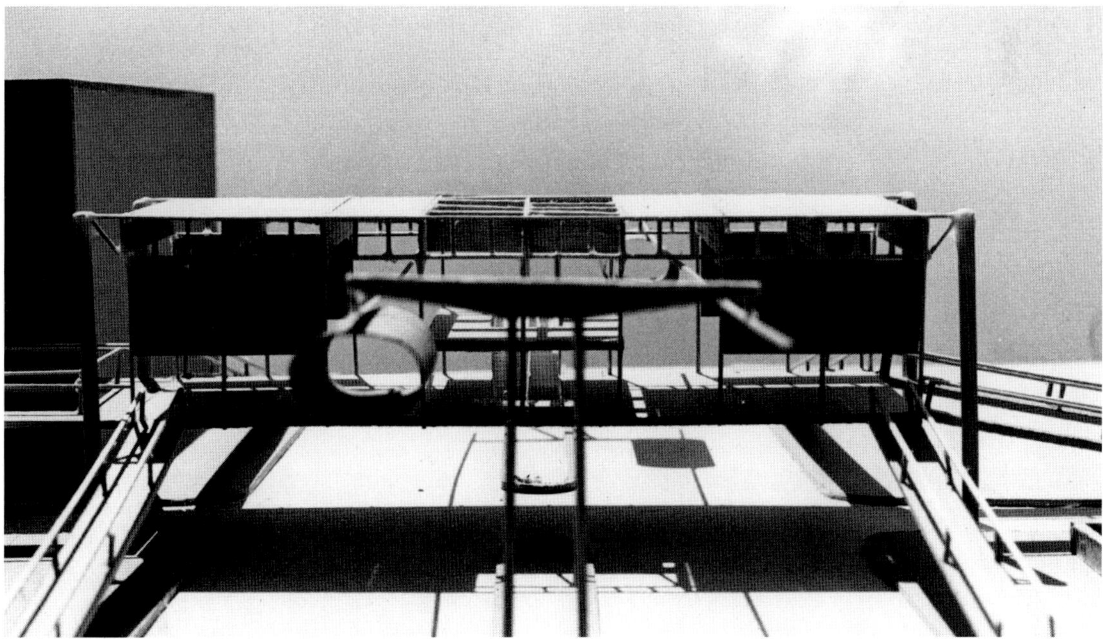

TOP: Final project model of Broad Street Crossing, as seen from above, by Per Olaf Fjeld. *P. O. Fjeld.*

RIGHT: Final project model of Broad Street Crossing, facing south, by Per Olaf Fjeld. In reviewing this model Kahn remarked, "You spoke with your heart." *P. O. Fjeld.*

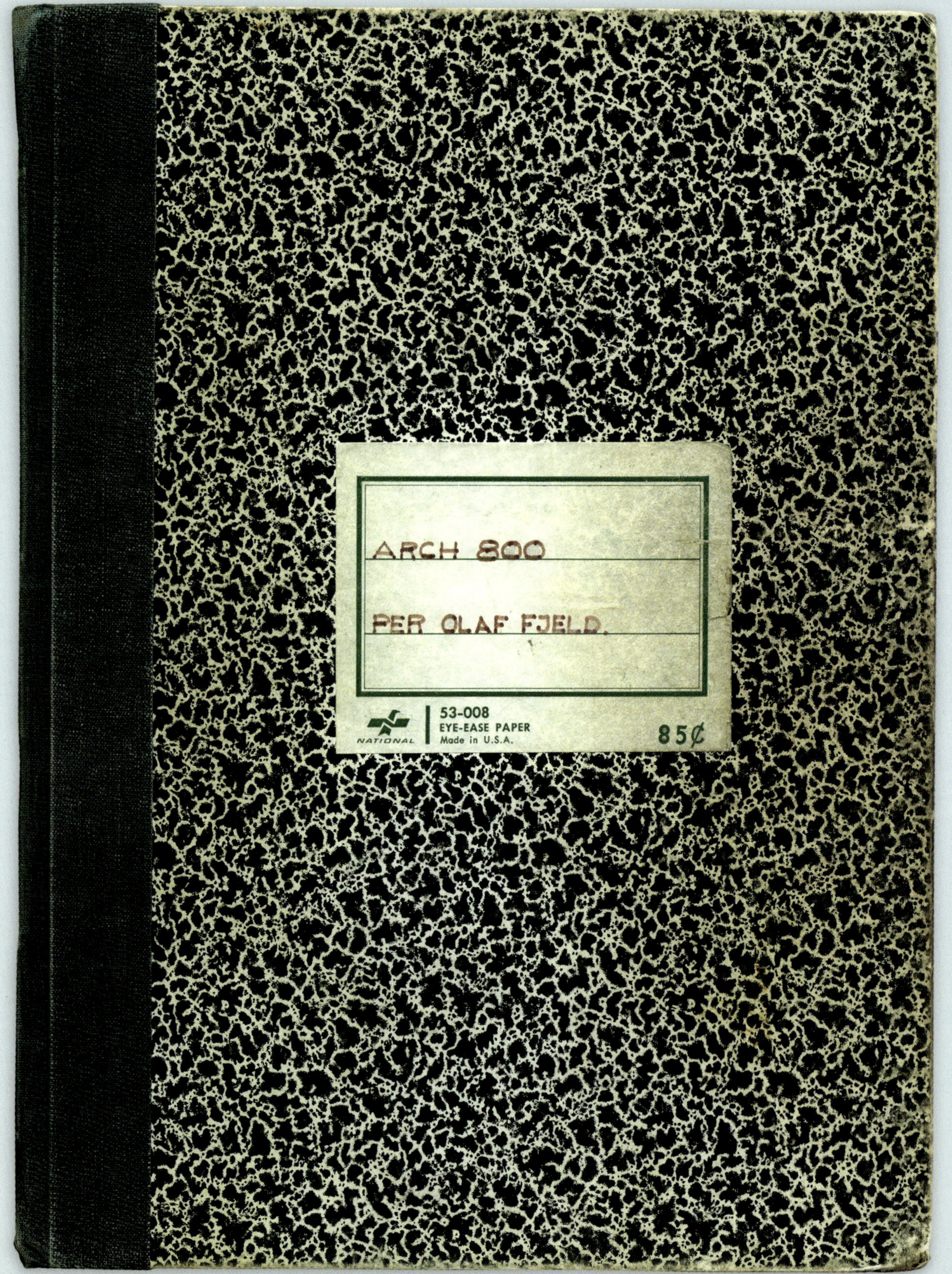

Cover of my class notebook for Arch. 800, fall semester 1972. *P. O. Fjeld.*

3 MY MASTERCLASS NOTEBOOKS

Kahn's own search into architecture was tightly linked to his teaching. His studio was a testing ground both to clarify and inspire his own thoughts as he initiated an architectural search together with his students over and over again. My class notes—which testify to all of this—are a record of studio lectures, critiques, and personal conversations I had with Kahn at the drawing table. While much of their content can be found in Kahn's earlier writings and lectures, my notebooks stand as a complete journal, compiled week after week—a personal log of what was discussed and emphasized during the year. Perhaps equally important, the notes are a record of how a student from abroad experienced Kahn's pedagogical approach and the studio in general. After each class, I reread my notes and recounted the day's events. For me these were working notes that formed a mental picture of the day, Kahn, and the class—and which therefore served as not only a record but also an inspiration. A simple sentence, or even just a word, could keep me going for days.

To be sure, in my efforts to record Kahn's insights from the masterclass, I missed some words. Some of my notations are unclear or somewhat disconnected, and my entries sometimes comprise a strange mixture of Norwegian and English. But my entries nevertheless record what I considered the most important issues and sensibilities within the classroom. In the interest of clarity, here I have gathered some of the essential insights that Kahn made, and that I in turn recorded, during the 1972–73 academic year. They are reproduced here in the sequence in which I noted them.

Search through the problems that trouble you, problems that go beyond yourself, not necessarily the problems of today, not just everyday problems. What do you really think architecture is? It is here. Then the attitude towards your problem is born. The solution is a matter of learning, but it is incomplete outside of yourself. Knowing is personal. Knowledge is learning. You can only convey the singularity of yourself, in that you are pretty much alone in confronting just how different you are from other people. The profession is one thing, and the spirit of the profession another. The way one says things does not belong to oneself; only the way one makes things belongs to oneself. Sometimes the beginning is not even recognizable.

A town has a lot of different spaces, some small and others large, but they should all be livable.

You must feel like studying in a place where you feel like working. A place where light comes in the way you want it to. It is the light of a particular room which is important.

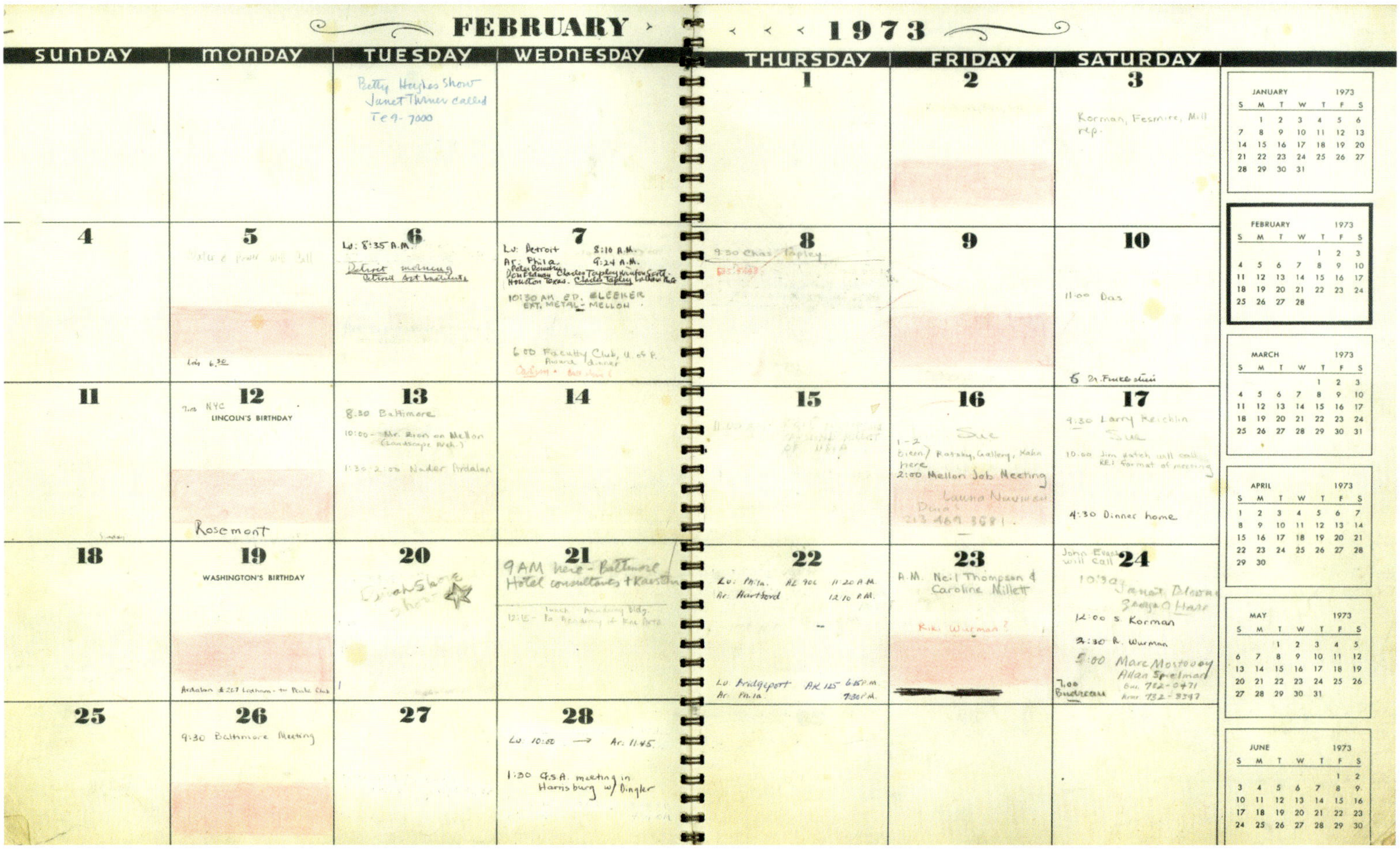

Pages from Kahn's calendar, February and March 1973. *Sue Ann Kahn Collection, The Architectural Archives, University of Pennsylvania.*

It is the individual who belongs to the individual. Those who work best are those who work to perfect themselves. It's the one who feels the greatest pain offering something to you. How do I know? In a symphony, I can understand in depth that the man in the profession is a man who through his work gives a starting point for somebody else's work. Gaudi—his buildings become landscapes, a retranslation about what was done.

Concept, philosophy, and reality—we need to have a more fundamental beginning in our minds, relate to something more fundamental. Where can you find those things before you proceed in your design?

The reconditioning or coming to the realization of truth does not make me seek the truth, because it cannot be found in the wonder of a single act.

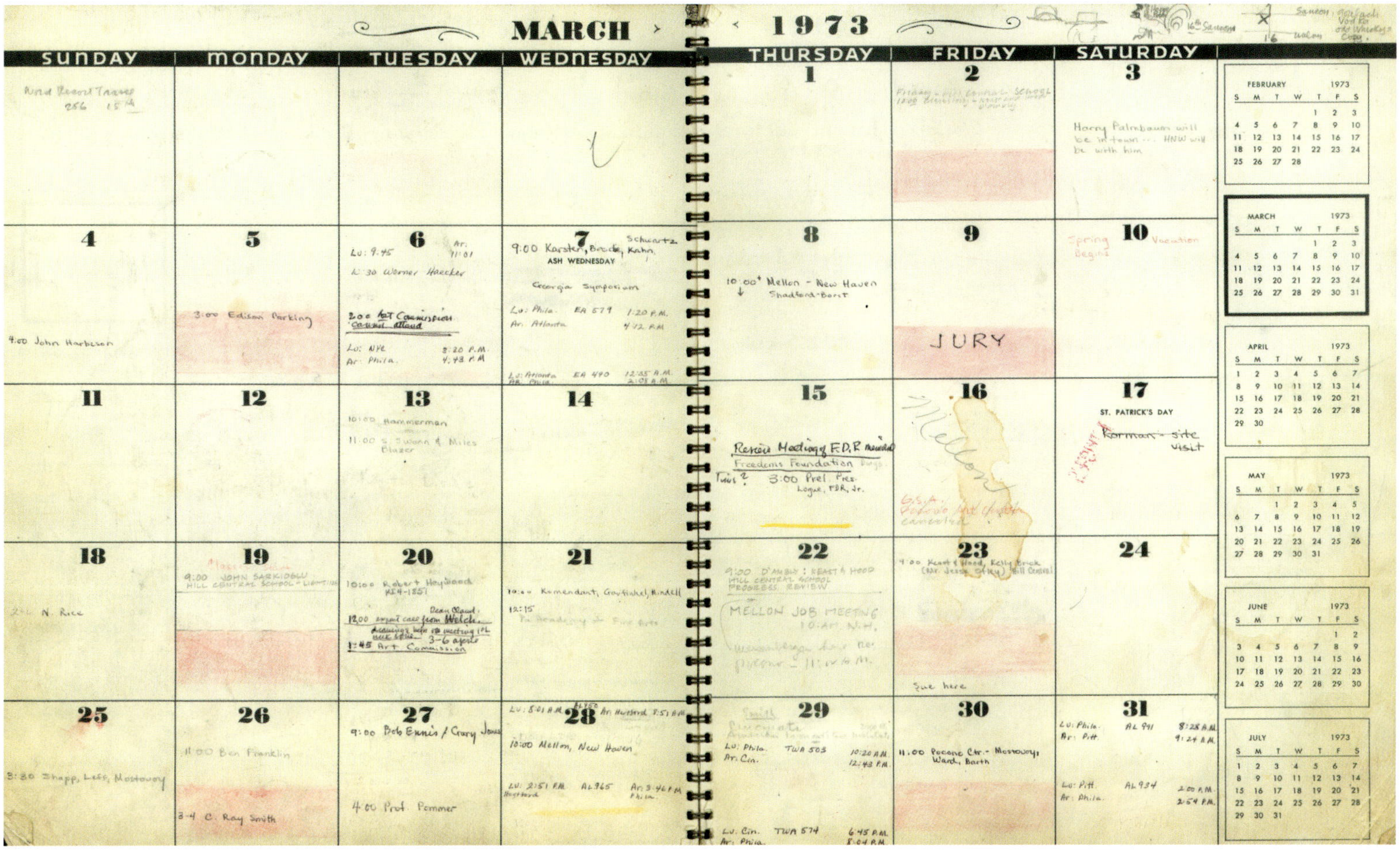

Methods of making decisions: you are looking for answers, but you are accepting the question's mathematical arrangement of the problem.

Rooms communicate with other rooms. Circulation is the image of the circulation of how swiftly your thoughts can enter another person.

A bathroom always needs natural light.

I don't like connectors, spaces, or rooms divided by cabinets. This has never been a wall. This is a room because I can see how it was made. For me, if it is not that way, it is only an area.

The energy of that wall [. . .] Why bother with that great energy and then divide it? [. . .] See the importance of the position in the room. Don't try to cut up great spatial energy. It must be done more consciously, done through the laws of nature.

August 12 | Kahn leaves for Bangladesh to attend a meeting about the National Assembly Building in Dhaka.

September 8 | First day of masterclass for the 1972–73 academic year.

September 11 | Kahn has eye operation (and is therefore absent from the masterclass for ten days).

You cannot wait for the technology to come. The longer you wait, the better the technology will be, but the greater the difference between the means and the making of something. If you take from the means first, you are trapped. The machines are brain things, not mind things. Houses don't lend themselves much to the machine.

The wall cried when they put a hole in it: "Why did you put a hole in me—I, who have protected you for such a long time?" "I made an opening to get breezes from outside." But when the opening got an arch and a crown on the top, even the wall realized the opening was a great thing.

Highly developed programs are a very dangerous thing. One has to realize the human aspects of a program, but not as a chemical formula.

The rooms that are intended to be made—the connecting rooms, the rooms without names—in the broadest terms of thinking, they are not just a single house, but they are a kind of mannerism. There are surprising spaces due to the nature of the project.

The design belongs to you, but the nature of the problem belongs to everybody.

You have to have great trust in the power of a space.

Keep your words sweet because you may have to eat them. [. . .] Illuminate what the mind feels, and the will to express meets the exception, the goal.

Tradition exists, and it exists everywhere. Keep in touch with this energy; this is what we have to work with.

The whole idea of a hospital is that you want to leave as soon as possible—a place for the elderly, a vertical graveyard.

Patterns, textures, rhythms, and different types of walls—you have different dreams from other men's dreams.

The house—just what kind of house? What kind of spaces make things happen, things that couldn't happen somewhere else?

There are two ways of making the project: from the inside to the outside, or the other way around. It is an attempt at form and a definition of form. If you take one away, you don't have anything.

Can you tell me what you have to do to destroy everything? Where are the in-between places you don't have to define? The meaning has to be so strong that if you take one thing away, it will destroy everything.

October 2 | Opening of Kimbell Art Museum.

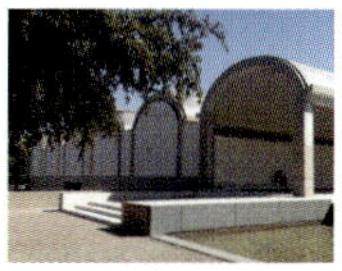

Main entrance of the Kimbell Art Museum. *Frida Johansen.*

October 27 | According to his calendar, Kahn visits Luis Barragán in Mexico with Richard Saul Wurman.

October 28 | According to his calendar, Kahn hosts Peter Smithson in his office.

November 20 | Kahn meets with the board of directors of the upcoming Bicentennial Exposition regarding his master plan for the event.

Society is always you—what and the way you feel. I must be society in man, and that is only two. I think nature and man are the same, so then it is only one. You can't separate man and nature.

It is tedious to listen to your way of doing something, but it is not tedious to talk about something that is of interest for all of us. Take a chance to find which things connect themselves [to everyone]. The validity of what you choose depends upon being common for everyone. This is the beginning of the nature of something, and it can grow.

The way the street senses what the land wants and then what the land becomes.

A new time—can it be done? If you are able to come up with a new sense of time, everybody would love it at once. It is the same with architecture. The mind is always ready for something that has never been said or seen before.

Inspiration is an undeniable force, but it is not always in the middle. The shorter the distance you are to it, the better you grasp the problem.

Even a darkroom has a flaw in its construction: When you flip the switch, the light is always the same.

Silence can be said to be the will, to be, to express, but I don't think anything followed anything. I feel everything started at the same time. Silence has no measurement, yet quietness already has a measurement.

That a stream has no wonder—that is the worst thing you can say, even if the stream is polluted. *It has wonder.*

You must feel tremendous freedom in the expression. Understanding is only a weak part of nature.

It is like the idea of building an old-age home and putting a sign, "Old Age Home," on the outside. One loses the idea there. And one won't find what he is searching for, and if he did, the sign would never have entered his mind.

Gaudi and his church are like a glass. He had come a long way and wanted to give it to heaven.

Knowing how to start, what is the starting point, a sense of beginning—a person has these things in him. It is a question of how selective you are, that you know what you know and how much you do not know.

Structure is the giver of light—and you need a lot of light. When you need little light, you have more enclosure.

The concrete wants to be granite.

Every time you have a column, you have a beam.

Be aware of the environment structure gives you.

Believe in a terrace, if you have a flat room.

If you think in terms of what is a room, there will be lines that truthfully tell you the way it was made. You start with a room and its association with other rooms—not a statement of the eye.

The joint was the beginning of ornamentation and the beginning of a sense of what is an enclosure.

Is it exciting to make free shapes? Accept the way they form themselves.

In a brick construction, when the choice of material is decided, you can immediately draw the building.

I cannot say enough about the meaning of windows, the qualities in the rooms where people are in need, or the invention of rooms towards the garden. Decide what should be the center of where people gather. This gives you a kind of thread and you hang things up with it. It takes the parts you already know and [connects] to rooms [. . .].

Consider entering a room without going through another, or the room in connection with other rooms it serves. The corridor should be a kind of hall that makes you look for a garden and that leads you to your room, which is not labeled the way a room usually is, but the way [the corridor] serves tells you the plan.

Some things belong to windows; other things should be in the middle where the rug is placed.

You have to start with the small things. Natural light is good all the time.

As we write poetry, the words get smaller. It is a unity. It is a celebration. Corbu's best buildings are on stilts, and narrow. There is still light coming under them.

A great thought actually gives you freedom.

It is in the music itself where the difference is, not the color or size of a brick. The discussion comes from knowing the nature of materials.

Repeating does not necessarily make something more powerful.

A room is made for the mind.

Illustration is a way to paint a view.

Geometry is the shape of things. In the end, buildings can be very simple, but it is places that illuminate things that are of importance. Architecture is not geometry. It is not a program. It is the meaning behind the space.

A teacher whom you like can take the role of a parent.

You design the orchard in a way that you know it will die. That is, now when it is alive, you put your whole power into it, knowing, however, that it will die and something else will replace it. [*Here Kahn was discussing the orchard in one of the class projects.*]

What type of places establish happiness? Not a place for playing games that have already been played, but a place that creates play, creates new play.

The room cannot take any type of shape—architecture is not arbitrary shape making. There must be a feeling of structure; the structure will iron things out.

The true color within a building is in the shadow—and a shadow is where the sun is not. You cannot read under a skylight; you cannot read where the sunset starts.

By overexpressing things you usually isolate them.

A greenhouse has communication with the sun. What a conversation they have!

In the beginning, relate to things you know are good, the nature of it. Think about it in terms of the characteristics of a room.

You can't make your geometry force the shape of a garden. It isn't in its nature.

School is a place you go to and not from. You need more area at home than you do at school.

Living in a more compact environment is an indication of being free.

What is happening in a space, if the space doesn't talk at all?

[In a drawing,] lettering within a space destroys the space. Never place a letter in the middle of a room. Put it aside, as a piece of furniture. It must be read as a thing in itself.

What do we walk out of in an auditorium during intermission?

Never build a park within a park. Let it all be park. The park is not free in this sense, so let it come into the land and be part of it.

And the concrete said, "Instead of using the stone, why don't you use me? Put a vase inside of me."

Bring out the symphony with the use of materials. In a large space, you naturally think about beams and columns, but as a single building, space does everything to be connected.

Any cement applied to concrete looks bad. Cement and concrete are too much the same thing.

Put [a mechanical plant . . .] in a building like a heart, just like an organ that belongs in the middle, or a little bit on the side. It should be expressed properly, due to its cost.

Do not look upon a boundary as something that is always working against you.

If you can bring a measurable quality into reality, you can find your place very easily.

Images are not easily committed to form.

When I see a building attached to another building—there are only a few cases where I will do that. Glued to another building, it will lose its personality.

You must ripen your harvest of suggestions without naming them.

The living space has to be something more than just a living unit.

Never try to imitate the color of a photograph.

To give birth to an idea and express it, find the right piece of paper.

Everything that nature does is perfect. The materials that are its making exist already, and its structure.

I can put whatever I feel like into the concrete, but I still have to go to nature and say, "Give me a loan." [. . .] The loan can never make you build something you do not believe in.

Structure is the giver of light.

Set aside what disturbs us for the moment. What do you think about the problem? As soon as you start something, it immediately becomes part of you.

Just because it has not occurred to you before, it does not mean it has not been done before. Everything has its own beauty: it lies in a sense of order to which it belongs. Consider the birth of certain new elements.

How does a person see the beginning and ending of something? [. . .] The circumstances that take you from beginning to end go in many strange ways and are always changing.

Priorities are often mixed up by what you know.

The tracks of trucks are all over the world, and the railroads died because of this.

The hitching post has become the [parking] garage.

Area is an important aspect of the problem [of designing a shopping center]. There is only one space you have to measure: the rentable space. Man makes a plan: the general subsistence, an escalator, the cost of something, impulse buying, arrival points. Understand how you get to a place, or how the ground floor becomes a pedestrian level to a theater. You should think before you do it. Do you put parking right outside the building? Where does the car belong? It belongs to the street, the shaded area, and then there is the black area called "parking." [. . .] If you have a corridor street on both sides, the light will come in where you walk—the street. [. . .] Shops have to be close together. If you want natural light, how do you get it? It has to be taken as a highly concentrated thing. You begin with the discipline of the lot. You respect the fact that you have been given this piece of land. The shops need all the company they can get, so get the variety you need inside [the building]. Nobody wants to look at the underside of a building.

The store does not need natural light; the circulation, however, does. You go into a place where you sense the street goes around, and the little spots of light will never give you the feeling of light.

The more the street becomes a place with meaning, the more potential the street has to serve.

There are things of others that you just can't get into but just accept as the artist's hand—the things you appreciate, the things that do not have to belong to you. Get this straight in your head and you will be a better human being, [and] you will also learn a lot more. [. . .] A thing that belongs to everyone you don't have to understand, but understand those particular relationships that belong to everyone.

The garden: It must respond to the general feeling and not just part of it. Can it ever exist in this dream of human acceptance? It is a new validity, but is it valid? Capturing a tree within a building is a crime.

No matter what height the roof is, the chimney must be higher.

The limits of architecture are its beauty.

The ultimate reality seeks personal knowledge. There are no categories: personal knowledge is knowing, not knowledge.

When you say that a man is creative, do you mean that one man is creative and another is not? You can't say it that way. You are acting on your personal naturalness, not distinguishing being creative. But the man who does what he does, looks for a better way, a greater sense of continuity, he does something that comes from evidence.

You can say I constructed something. It is an uncalculated calculation. It implies that it is possible to make even if you have not approved it: a kind of organizational sense that applies structure without knowing the structure, unfolding qualities that can only be helped through criticism by sensing what others feel.

Order, the maker of all presence [. . .] The sense of order does not lie in preferences, but it does lie in choices.

You must always be ready before the engineer. Have everything exposed: this will add something to the building. Also by exposing it, you will have to perfect it, because the ventilation ducts are not made for exposure. It requires care in the assembly. Free yourself from the point of view of supporting the building. The building should stand on its own within its structure.

You are never coming to the center: you are going by it.

I believe it is a bad thing to give too many choices of where to go up and down. Circulation is not enough to give activity to those areas.

You can't depend upon the trueness of a thing.

The idea is to become a monk when you build a monastery.

You look for clarity first. Give it to me hard: I look at the light like an eye. This is the part that works with the gods. It almost has to be done through its clarity, because a person sees the whole damn thing as he walks in. The structure, the movement, and the light must all show what kind of place it is [. . .].

The spatial environment and the way in which you get to it should never be dull. The entrances can never be the same, because their paths are in different places. The whole thing is not only done for the variety of places, but for the nature of places. Nothing is just done for the variety of things.

You always have to start a project with a deliberate sense of purpose. It is just like a service station: you know exactly where to go.

You invent the building, but the [users] are the ones that make something for you.

Drawing is sort of a religion, the sensitiveness in a drawing.

Consider the importance of your priorities. You make two handles in case you forget the first one.

Always look for an inborn sense of balance.

The tendency for people to choose spaces that have odd shapes in a stupid way.

Your building, ending it, don't present it as a conclusion, but as a direction of thinking.

Understand the rhythm in a building.

Charming angles, the movement, are usually due to the nature of the ground or site. It is not just charming alone.

1973

January 12 Kahn attends meeting about the Yale Center for British Art.

January 16 Kahn departs for Venice.

February 15 Kahn attends meeting about the Yale Center for British Art.

February 24 Kahn attends meeting about the Korman House.

February 26 Kahn attends meeting about the Baltimore Harbor project, begun in 1969; the project is terminated.

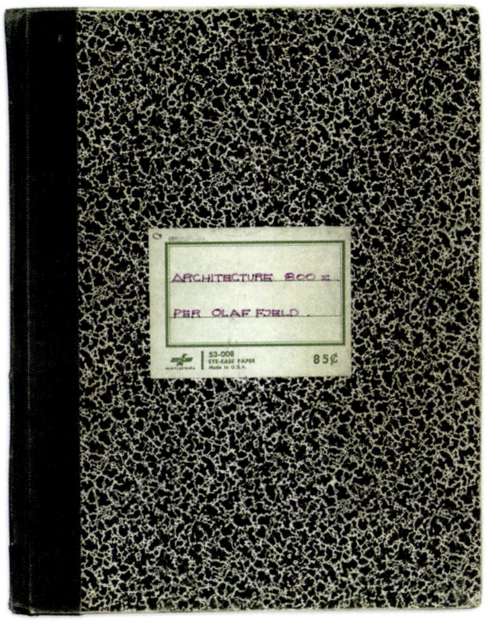

Cover of my class notebook for Arch. 800–2, spring semester 1973. *P. O. Fjeld.*

The Greek air and sky [light] are so sharp it knocks the corners off buildings. Therefore they have to be sharp.

Every man proportions things his own way.

The discipline of necessity is the rule of survival.

From a distance, you feel the sound of hammering like a musical instrument.

The wall is a dynamic organism; it breaths like our body.

You are in doubt—that's part of the interest.

You don't have to think about anything that is not really human.

To give it a name does not mean you distinguish it.

"I don't believe in art" is believing in no expression whatsoever.

The most sympathetic response for other people is the one that finds no answer, just the most superb question.

Every word you say is a symbol, but it does not mean what you say becomes a symbol.

You can sense a quality from within, what a room is able to generate.

The intention of the program is very important. The parts that you believe in are always worthwhile considering. It is essential to distinguish need from desire. Never give nature more than it needs. You can't give it too much: rather take it or disregard it. Think of early Greek theaters. When you write a play you have a theater in mind—Ibsen or Shakespeare. It is the same with a room: places where there is light and where the light is not. There will be different activities in the dark than in the light.

Teachers belong to their beliefs.

Art should never be considered a subject. We are not looking for scientific answers that are completely measurable.

Study the carrel: reading and slumbering go together. There are various ways to read. The book itself can be given attention in a better way.

If you could only recognize the individuality of a room as related to the society of rooms. Consider the feeling of the spaces before the intentions are with you. Now you have great spaces, but you can feel the programming of it—spaces and the association of these spaces to each other.

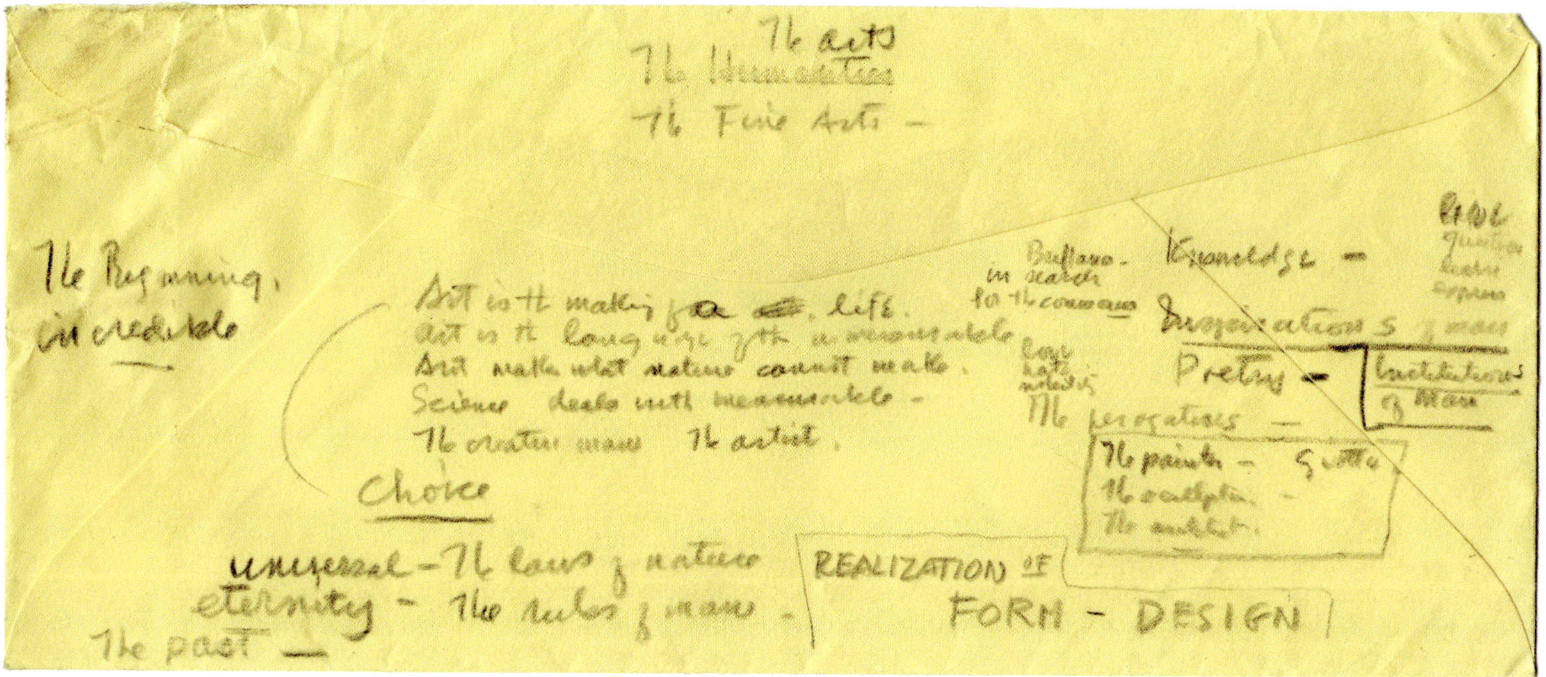

The back of an envelope is as good as anything for recording thoughts: "Art is the making from life. Art is the language of the unmeasurable[.] Art makes what nature cannot make."—Louis Kahn. *Louis I. Kahn Collection, The University of Pennsylvania and the Pennsylvania Historical and Museum Commission.*

You make a room, and that is the end of it. I wish I could see the validity of cutting up spaces. The partition wall—the feeling of structure that isn't actually there.

The structure of the building sets the size required. You cannot be very far away from the source of light.

Everybody can make a container. What is the space that can inspire a room? One must appreciate this idea. You feel the interior so much more when you can look outside.

Books should be taken care of and regarded as a piece of art. You have to be reasonable with what you expect a library to be, but its treasure is where the rare books are. [. . .] When you go into this treasury it should feel completely different from other rooms.

The glow of a book—not everyone can see it.

The central space: see how it swells on one floor and reduces itself on another floor. Its organic center is the books. Something nuclear, that's what a library should be.

Mies is interesting, but not fundamental. I would rather be right than interesting.

The eye, the ear, and touch must all belong to the library, because it is in the nature of the library itself.

Great people never think they accomplish anything.

April 17 | Kahn attends meeting about the Yale Center for British Art.

April 26 | Kahn presents his model for the Franklin D. Roosevelt Four Freedoms Park planned for Roosevelt Island in New York.

April 30 | Final class critique.

May 3 | Kahn travels to Israel for the Hurva Synagogue project planned for Jerusalem.

May 11–14 | Kahn stops in Paris and Casablanca on his way back to Philadelphia.

June 22 | Kahn leaves for London.

The quality of man is contained in his nature.

You don't have an idea unless you know how to make it.

A room has a distinct character within itself. It is not a flower arrangement! The solution is a personal thing.

Man never knew how rich he was before he faced the sun.

It is not silence just because there is an absence of sound.

The pyramids have a voice due to the strong presence of self.

A place can become as big as the world itself.

If a library is just a place where you pick up a book, it will become a supermarket and you will not read there either.

Rooms have definition by reason of their construction. The structure is the making of the light. You find a sense of order from another sense of order.

The stoa is so generous—given to people as a place to meet. There is a sense of non-programing, a human agreement.

Some things can be prefabricated—the bathrooms, mechanics—but not the air. That goes around.

The quality of the city is in what way human inspiration is met.

The mind has to do with a single person—not a computer. We are here because the mind has been able to record what we have experienced. You put a thought into a computer—an intelligent person will never doubt the difference.

If the architect gives you exactly what is in the program, you will not be happy. What we want to see is something nuclear. It is something you want to see in the beginning of every project.

An idea is nothing without the comprehension that comes before. What you are doing is not an idea. It is a realization. Realization is the opening of the mind.

Look at yourself in full-length. If you are in a cave you have to sit down or bend your knees, but this is circumstances. If you stand up, that is the whole self. It is the same with a building: it starts with the whole thing, just like you. That is the nature of the problem. That's where you start, the site. Everything else is so far away. It is the nature of things we are looking for.

Working should be like living in your house.

[Corbusier] did not have a golden rule. He just had a sense of proportion, but he had the golden rule within him.

Always think about the project as a dream. I could fly just to stretch my legs, but it is the question of coming down again. It is just a matter of will.

Books from the outside: that is just advertising.

To expose the interior is to ruin the interior. You are weakening its image. It is a complete world within itself. The universe is made up of multiple interiors.

Consider using things that are not made, or a right thing applied the wrong way.

It is not about the way you want it, it is just the idea around your thinking.

A library can grow downward instead of upward.

I love things you cannot love.

I say to myself, "What is the reality of the project? The idea of now and how do I bring this out? The structure as a maker of light?" An understanding of light is essential. Except I have not been aware of it that much. Architects should take a closer look at this problem. It is always fundamental to see the area of light between the columns. Instead of choosing rooms that have a little bit of light, give them light instead and use devices to control it.

The program is given to you in the way the client understands it, in a way someone else has told it to him. Here you have to let a dream world come in. [. . .] What is the thing in your scheme that will make us jealous?

The idea of putting up a wall instead of a window because there is no view in a way is a very cruel decision, because you are not honoring the light that can come into the room. Do you have the right to do this? Is it in the nature of light to block it out, just because you don't want any view there?

The differences in structure are due to the load.

Two points on architecture: 1. Never force the dream of your idea. 2. [The dream] needs to be translated.

The sense of a garden inside or outside a building is a very difficult problem.

You should always think of light as a strength. Some countries need light, others not so much, but to sense where the light is coming from, this need is the same.

[In a library, the] carrels should be where one senses the most is on offer: a room of architecture, a large lounge, whatever it is.

The sense of the room has something to do with its nature.

The periphery is a place somewhere else.

A man is for living the desire to be. Desire is something individual, not anything general.

You want the central idea, not the solution. The solution has no interest in anybody, but the nucleus of the idea belongs to everyone. Consider the nucleus as the most important factor. Take the personal out of it. What is undeniable about it? What is the nature that you are serving?

[*About libraries*] The place to read honors the book. Man is there as a property owner, but he is not alone. [. . .] When everyone is gone, the books are having a party.

To make a show of the view is not a good idea. I will never make a building around the view. It is not the point.

The connections should be included within the order. If not, they belong to another building. They are something that adds to and enriches the building from within.

Nature cannot be jealous of another nature.

Columns make non-walls possible. The discipline of supports is very important. It is realized through the strength of an army of columns

The monk had a cell, which had a garden and an arcade, just like the city. Today we have the prefab cell and we put a flower in it.

As in an orchestra, a tempo is in the spaces designed for reading.

Away from but also *in*, there is a sense of being close to something.

Sense being in a living space occurs because life is not absent—all the answers of things are there.

The room that has a personality invites somebody and says, "Can't you stay forever?" Architecture has to have such a binding requirement, so you can never go away from it. "Leave me if you want, don't like me, but never use half of me. Make me into something that is not even me." This has its own beginning. It's as fresh as any building with an idea behind it. There is something very nuclear about this.

Do not make an imitation of the day. The night room is different than a day room, so when I go into a night room I feel fine. Some people light up the trees—it is terrible. Trees want to rest at night. That is why they die so fast too. Night is different from day, and each one should not imitate the other.

Words—they were [once] written for a few people, not for everyone. I think the world lived this way. Books are prostitutes: everyone can buy them.

I'm always thinking in terms of rooms. In the midst of all of this, there is a little bit of chaos that is so marvelous.

You go by the reasoning of your own connections. You will not be able to predict the future. Poets will exist forever, because when a poet is born he has no choice. From all the words possible, he is drawing and painting for his own existence, for himself.

It is not what works one way or another; it is a matter of what is the nature of the thing.

Never use a shape just because you like to make it.

If you don't use the roof, you might as well not see it.

You call it "spiritual" before you make it. That is like striking the walls and then they come down.

Discover yourself as a desire to express. You must suffer in order to surrender a quality that belongs to everybody else. It is not a matter of changing the world; it is an internal thought of wanting to change something.

The city is still understood as a common agreement, but the notion of communality no longer exists.

Instead of solving a problem, state it instead.

Zone the street, not the land.

Think in terms of the order of movement—the horse, the car, but not the air. It doesn't belong to you.

Design is the act of calling upon nature about how to make something. The nature of the thing is already there. The design is very personal.

Change cannot be predicted—it is governed by circumstances—but you can prevent total destruction.

The difference between a column going down or up is nature.

Beethoven was not an aesthete. If he made the "columns" bigger than needed, he always had a particular reason for it.

One thing can be realized by another thing, but the limit is its order.

The roof is a demand that should never be forgotten.

You know how to design something, if you know its nature, its limits.

Prepare your mind for something to happen, for poetry that is not as yet written. The fullness of the state of your mind is before you make a drawing.

To judge you are assuming that you belong to eternity. Whatever is taught is one singularity to another singularity. Make something, an offering beyond criticism. What is offered must be received as part of you.

The sidewalk is all the land where the car is not. You don't build it on the ground. The car comes to the place where it serves. There is not just a physical aspect to this. People who love cars should live in Los Angeles. The automobile is very much part of the road, and not the house. The car might have to be designed for two purposes: one to the house and the other to the interior. Consider the car that arrives at a house, and the scale that changes. The entrance for a car is sort of a corridor.

Houses and their location are much more important than the car.

The rock you throw in a stream modifies the stream's path. The city gives it direction.

You can never hide potential, but its power has to be transformed.

When it is a necessity, it is already too late.

To touch communality, to touch agreement, gives the inevitable quality of approval.

How powerful is the grass without the tree?

Should you open up an illuminated manuscript? If you use a word, it should be one of your instruments.

How do we realize a district based on the phenomena of the mind?

You put a tree down [on paper], but you cannot depend upon it. You should be able to tell from the drawing which trees are old and which are not.

You have a great prospect, but sometimes circumstances rip it apart.

When you are making something, you are really obeying nature. The idea has to go beyond a common trick. The idea has to find the nature of the thing—don't start with the trick. No one likes others' designs, but they like the way they can borrow from them.

All buildings want to come together.

Places for people to be protected from the rain—doorsteps, arcades, bridges—must belong to the street.

Going to a place is something or somewhere due to the nature of the thing.

A bridge over a river needs the river's permission.

In what way can you reconsider where a building could be? Where the car is dead? Where the car is alive?

A cultural center is not a building; it is a whole town.

Nature who has been so good to you, what are you doing to it?

Consider the park as a city trust.

A quiet place near the river is more in the realm of art than putting an artist down there. A poet does not go down there to write poetry: he sits in a bar half drunk.

A room is different than a space.

In an architectural sense, life belongs to any city, not just a beautiful city.

A strong idea before the making is terribly important, and you have to adjust the making to that. You don't have an idea unless you can exercise it. The drawing must include what is possible. It is not an idea. Consider ingredients which you have not as yet thought about. The form drawing should include those parts you cannot be without. Consider the unfulfilled aspects which introduce aspects you see as possible.

Consider architecture as a life-giving thing: you make something in a way you sing because it is so quiet.

Buildings come about because of the reasons behind why the lands are used. Redefine the streets and the zoning of the streets—you define the exterior.

A room does not continue and continue. Most of the time it is surrounded by four walls. To arrive at its potential, an idea has to be created. To change the situation, you have to put up new walls.

Do you wait for everything to die out before it can happen? You can't leave the whole thing for somebody else to do.

I don't want to hear words, I want to see drawings!

Maybe building over or under a street is a convenient argument for building in the street.

September | Korman House, begun in 1971, completed.

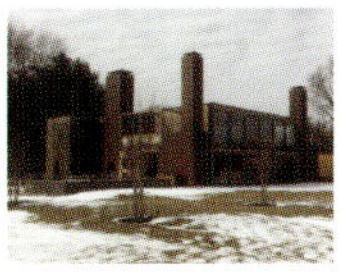

Korman House. *P. O. Fjeld.*

October | Arts United Center in Fort Wayne, Indiana, completed.

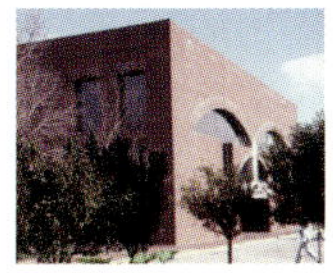

Arts United Center in Fort Wayne. *P. O. Fjeld.*

1973 | Skidmore, Owings & Merrill's Sears Tower (Willis Tower), Charles Moore's Leland Burns House, Richard Meier's Douglas House, Jørn Utzon's Sydney Opera House, and Sverre Fehn's Hedemark Museum completed.

Some streets are not necessary, and other streets have more freedom. Some streets are strictly service; others, walkways and paths that free the eye.

In medicine there is architecture. Its beauty lies in its limitations. Its limits are its conditions.

The periphery is very rich in its capacity.

The sense of the structure must be present in any drawing. It's a great feeling that you need such a thing.

It is so cruel to build a symphony hall with no orchestra [. . .]. It is just like an empty can at a beer party.

Putting a pool in is like taking an aspirin.

The river wants the sun—it wants to be out in the open.

The reality of a thing is everything about it.

The mega-structure came to the baker on the second floor.

It takes a long time to make yourself meaningful.

Make a drawing of the heart and a drawing of the mind.

Would a man naturally choose the lifestyle indicated by your proposal? You must find a life-giving proposal.

A building wants to look fat under and slender above. That is also the way the wind works on it.

You can't just try a thing, it has to work.

You have to have a realization of the nature of things, because even nature should not be asked to do more than it can do.

The imagination is something that is never satisfied, and it is brought forward by an idea. Architects should have an idea of what is feasible and what is not. Consider the sense of responsibility in what you are doing.

Watch out for any type of regularity in any building. You should be careful with any architectural machine. A skyscraper cannot be prefabricated, because every place has a different moment. The thickness of the cord varies according to the height. The framework is much more important in a prefab than the unit itself.

What are the indicators that inspire architectural work? Many times you get tired of a solution, but you never get tired of those things that can inspire you. An idea just has to be so great that nothing else comes to your mind.

The beginning is the time of belief in Form. ~~The realization~~ of an existence without material without shape or dimension, Design serves this belief into being, and places the maker in harmony with order and being,
When the work is completed the beginning must be felt.

Belief is the beginning of form.

~~Form is the beginning of belief~~

~~The beginning is the time of belief in form~~, an existence without material without shape or dimension.
Design serves this belief and places the maker in harmony with order and being.
The work completed reflects [illegible] ~~belief~~.

~~Art has its~~ ~~Belief is the~~ beginning of form. It is feeling as religion as dream and thought as philosophy. Its exists without material without shape or dimension,
Design is the maker in harmony with order and being.
A work inspired by form renews belief. The aura of transcendence commonness.
One feels the work [illegible] in

4 GROUNDING THE VOCABULARY

"The beginning is the time of belief in form, an existence without material, without shape or dimension. Design serves this belief into being by placing the maker in harmony with order and being. When the work is completed, the beginning must be felt.

"Belief is the beginning of form, an existence without material without shape or dimension. Design serves this belief and places the maker in harmony with order and being. [. . .]

"Beginning is the belief in form. It is feeling as religion, and thought as philosophy. It exacts material without shape or dimension. Design is the maker in harmony with order and being. . . . "

A page dated 1959 from Louis Kahn's notebook that shows him working to find language for the interrelationships among belief, form, design, and other entities. *Louis I. Kahn Collection, The University of Pennsylvania and the Pennsylvania Historical and Museum Commission.*

In the masterclass studio, Kahn spoke openly about his working process. He laughed and admitted that he was not a researcher in the common sense of that term. Instead, he gathered impulses from numerous sources into a new, personal amalgam that would motivate and challenge him. For instance, using the catalogues in the library was not always a straightforward process; searching the shelves for a particular book, he often discovered something else that he would also integrate into his approach to the matter at hand. He liked to keep certain books within reach, but he very seldom read a book page by page; instead he would fixate on a particular sentence or paragraph. Insights from philosophers, scientists, poets, and artists filtered into his vocabulary. While particular thinkers are sometimes identified as the likely sources of some of his statements, he configured his beliefs into something truly personal. As a student, penetrating Kahn's terminology was an ongoing struggle, but the process was also very seductive and inspiring. Each time Kahn's fundamental concepts were invoked in the studio it seemed as if the subject matter was new for Kahn as well, thus as students we felt we were taking part in his discovery. These shared moments were a unique experience for us and also appeared to be important to Kahn.

His terminology offered alternatives to the established pedagogy, and this clearly influenced our thinking and long-term approach to life and work. In the studio it was easy to incorporate his terms into the general discussion, as they were presented as ongoing discoveries rather than foregone conclusions. (In the middle of a critique or discussion, Kahn sometimes admitted that "I cannot in any way practice what I just preached.") None of his concepts were constrained by a single definition or suggested a finalized, universal solution. Instead, they called for imagination and numerous interpretations.

Each of us absorbed his vocabulary in different ways, but for most there was common ground in that he connected his ideas about individual creative capacity to a broader notion of shared human responsibility and "the laws of nature." He moved freely from discussing personal experience, to philosophy, to poetry, to people, to the built object, considering whatever topic might bring clarity to his search. Kahn's deliberations in the studio, however expansive, always concerned the realm of architecture. Although for some his talks were perhaps unintelligible and frustratingly difficult to follow, for Kahn the content always pointed in one direction: to the "institutions of man."

Kahn's iconic phrases, most of which originated in his lectures and notes, are frequently referenced in architectural discourse. But their specific content and the relationships between the terms that comprise them can often be difficult to comprehend. Some of his writings from the beginning of his career offer possible clues about the gradual development of his architectural language; it seems feasible that much of his thinking was in place by an early age and it simply took time for him to find the personal language to express it. His early written work tended to focus on the role of architecture and on social issues of the time, while the philosophical base that undergirded his work as a mature architect relied on a few key words and phrases with both personal connotations and a strong visual component. By the time these words and phrases entered into his teaching and lecture vocabulary, he was clearly interested in retaining their openness to interpretation. On one level, with regard to philosophical content, he was rehearsing the same thoughts over and over. However, several terms transformed over time. Below I explore some of Kahn's most important phrases and terms and how they interconnect.

Wonder

Kahn was deeply motivated to uncover the core "beginnings of things," in the belief that an awareness of this core could enable a collective understanding of the essential—of "what a thing wants to be." He strove to uncover a pristine state of beginning. He stressed in class that every beginning must start from wonder and that our ability to wonder is one of the most precious and immeasurable dimensions of human life. He regarded wonder as a state of humanness without obligation, an immediate response to the intuitive, a condition before realization and knowledge.

In his vocabulary, "wonder" has its own singular position, but in order to give it a more comprehensible substance, he connected it to a duality between "thought" and "feeling." In his view, feeling could connect to an intuitive beginning (wonder), while thinking connected to the rational (objective reasoning). At first, Kahn considered feeling more important, but gradually he came to regard the two modes as equals that were both necessary to the creative process. Feeling drew on the desire to create, while thinking was essential to the envisioning of physical expression. He believed these modes were linked by a process of "realization," and he thus regarded realization as the meeting of thought and feeling.

Nature / Order / Form / Design

Kahn referred to various kinds of "nature"—and it was not always easy to distinguish which kind he was referring to in a particular case. Often he was alluding to a physical nature—including such phenomena as wind, sun, and rain—whose existence is unwilled. For him, this

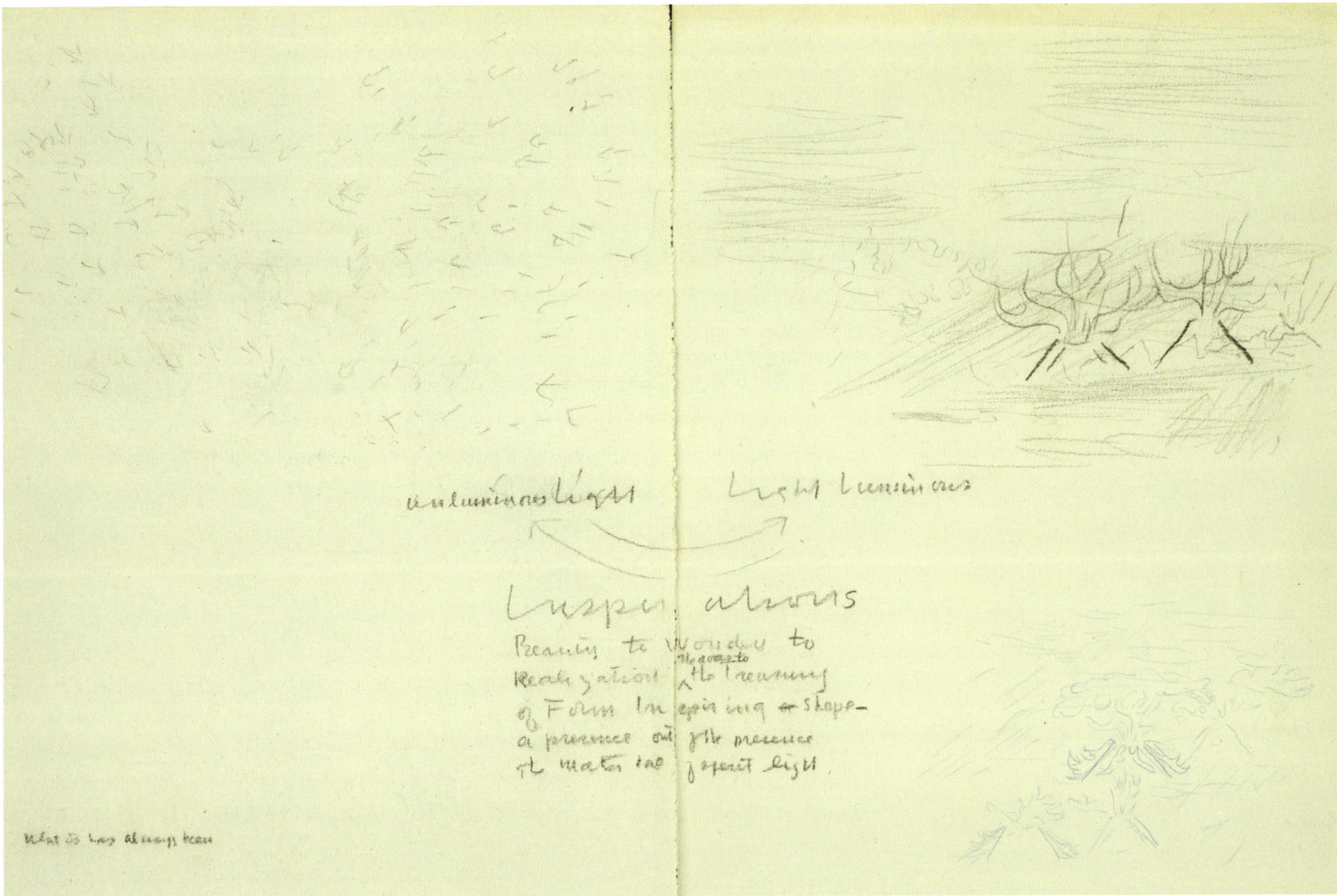

Kahn set "unluminous Light" and "Light Luminous" on opposite pages in this 1968 creative act drawing. The text centered beneath them runs across the page break: "Inspirations / Beauty to Wonder to / Realization. The door to the Treasury / of Form Inspiring shape— / a presence out of the presence / The material of spent light." *Louis I. Kahn Collection, University of Pennsylvania and the Pennsylvania Historic and Museum Commission.*

nature follows the law of action and reaction, as its parts work together in an overall harmony within the parameters of their own immutable laws. In Kahn's view, nature could not make anything that the human makes, but the human could not make anything physical without knowledge of "nature's laws"—the laws, in his words, "that bind all material together." In the studio, he often brought up the necessity of acknowledging nature's laws, while emphasizing that in the making process these laws should be regarded not as an obstacle but rather as a way to challenge physical possibilities and discover new opportunities. Though often disregarded in analyses of Kahn's thinking, a deep respect for the laws of nature was a fundamental part of his teaching, as he impressed on us the need to keep these laws in mind from the start, before opinions and knowledge could enter the creative process. This deep respect surfaced during our project for an urban intervention in Philadelphia when he noted that the Schuylkill River "may be polluted, but it is still a river and its course has to be respected."[1]

In exploring the relationship between nature and human behavior, Kahn made a clear distinction between "the laws of nature" and what he called "the rules of man." He regarded the rules of man as changeable, temporary, and an outcome of our interpretation of nature's laws. To clarify this connection, Kahn asserted that man is not "nature," but "made by nature," thus distinguishing between "man the species" and "man the human." He explained this relationship simply: What we do as a species can be studied and modulated with the same tools as any other natural phenomena, because "man the species" is tied to the laws of nature. By contrast, "man the human" possesses immeasurable properties that cannot be investigated with quantitative tools. This duality affects the core essence of our human behavior. As Kahn saw it:

> The humanness of man is not subject to cultural or evolutionary changes, neither is it subject to racial or aesthetic differences between men. The way a man walks, talks, dresses or conducts himself all comes from his being human, and everything that man does is somehow tied to his desire to express the nature of his being.[2]

Kahn also talked about "the nature of an object" as the source of its beginning. By his account, each object has a direct connection to its embodiment, which in turn indicates a particular identity—what it wants to be by way of its nature. In classroom discussions, Kahn sometimes used the terms "the nature of an object" and "form" interchangeably to describe the origin of things. This could be confusing, as most of us already had highly ingrained associations with the word "form." Thus when Kahn first talked about "form" as being independent of shape, scale, and material, we were mystified until we understood his use of the term. As Kahn saw it, "Form is a psychic predisposition to be and consists of inseparable abstract elements which invoke a nature, 'what a thing wants to be.' Being immeasurable in essence, it is never completely realized in concrete terms, and thus it has infinite potential for expression."[3] Kahn firmly believed that each time a new form was discovered its identity would be intuitively accepted. From then on, we understood form as having a presence, of being out there, somewhere inside "volume zero."

While Kahn's application of the term "form" was unrelated to the physical, he made a connection between form's infinite potential for an expression to the physical realization of a specific expression through what he termed "design." For him, "design" signified something physically specific that possessed materiality and scale. Unlike form, design is personal and

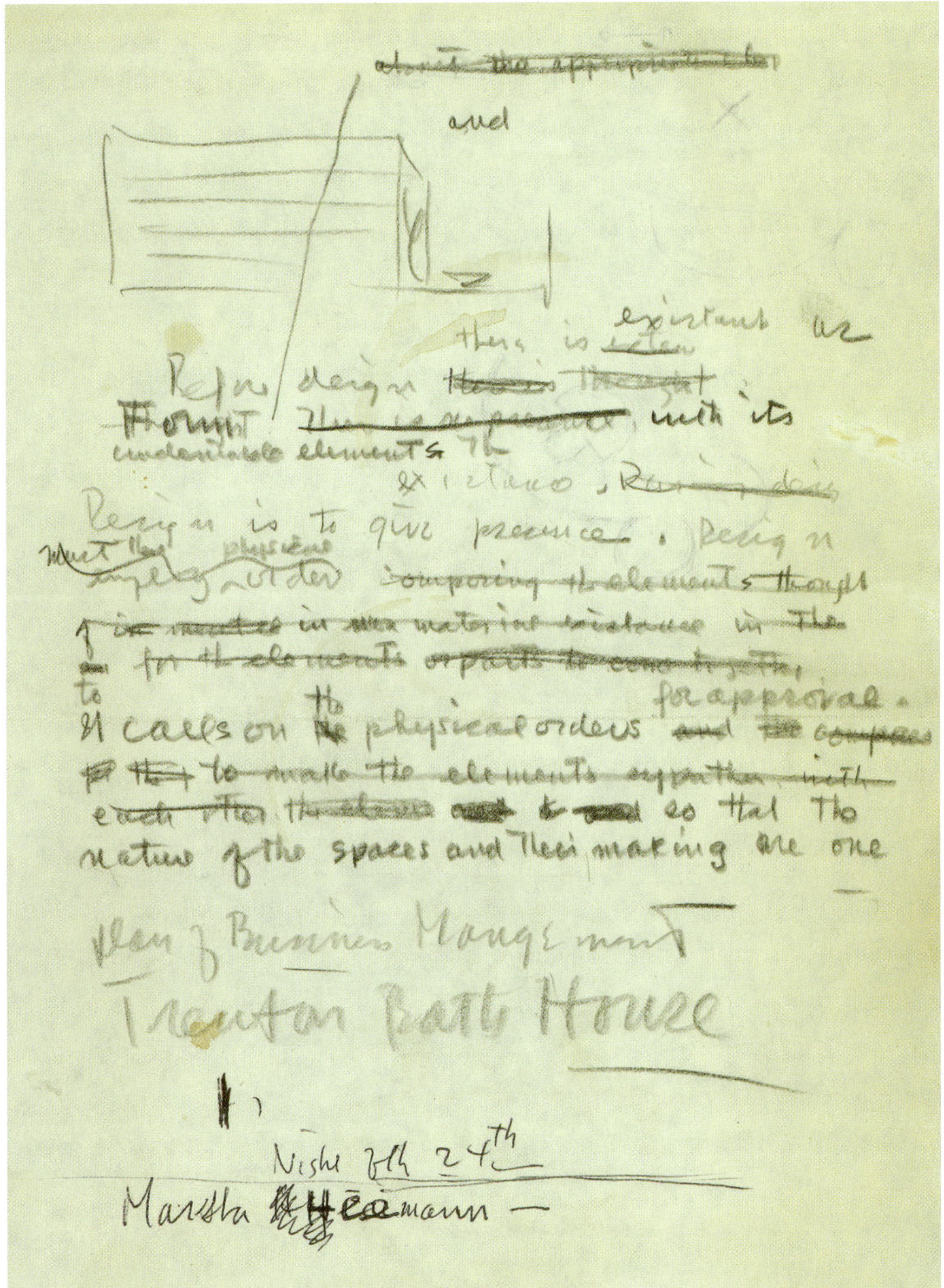

A page from Kahn's notebook that shows him working to find language for the relationship between form and design: "Form with its undesirable elements. [. . .] Design is to give presence. Design is physical. It calls on the physical orders for approval, so that the nature of the spaces and their making are one." *Louis I. Kahn Collection, The University of Pennsylvania and the Pennsylvania Historical and Museum Commission.*

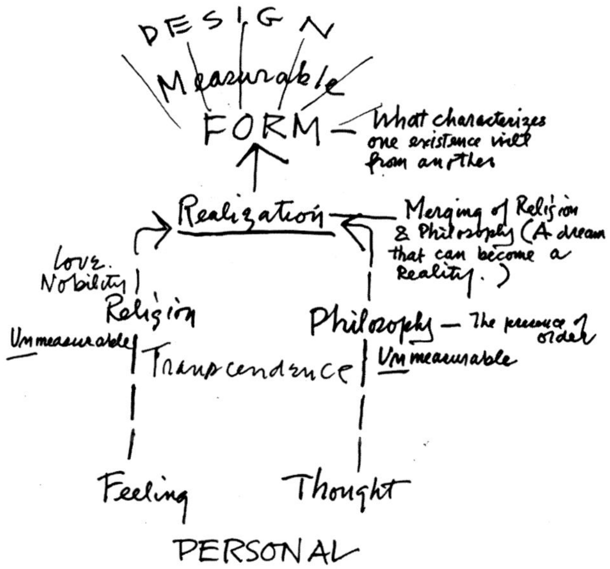

The creative process as diagrammed by Kahn in 1960. He starts at the bottom of the page with "personal" and ends with "design," which emanates from "form," at the top. *Louis I. Kahn Collection, The University of Pennsylvania and the Pennsylvania Historical and Museum Commission.*

influenced by circumstances and local conditions. When differentiating between form and design in class one day, he used the example of a spoon: a shared form is common to all spoons, but design is specific to each particular spoon.

All of this brings up the question of how Kahn's notion of form related to his notion of the laws of nature. He struggled to find a concept that linked these, but by 1955 he landed on the term "order." By his definition, "order is a maker of all existence but without will." Order is implicit within the nature of an object—its "form"—and therefore in the physical making it is inextricable from the laws of nature, since "order is the embodiment of all the laws of nature." An idea has no physical presence until one calls upon nature to exercise its order. Within this constellation that unites form, order, and the laws of nature, one finds each object's fundamental physical specificity and limitations.

Perhaps even more essential to Kahn's creative approach was comprehending the gap between the laws of nature and man's expression, which were never in complete balance. By his account, it is impossible to copy, compete with, or completely understand nature, so in reaching an agreement between nature and a desired human expression some contradiction will inevitably arise in relation to nature's order. The perception of beauty emerges from this contradiction or discrepancy. As Kahn often noted in class, "Order does not imply beauty." Kahn asserted several times that to express, one must follow nature's laws (in speaking of this dynamic, he occasionally replaced the word "follow" with "consult" or "refer to"). The closer we came to order—to what a thing wants to be, its form—the clearer our ability to sense which laws were necessary to release a project's potential into a physical expression.

Knowing and Knowledge

Throughout the masterclass, Kahn repeated his statement that "you can only learn that which is already within yourself." This assertion embodied his concept of "knowing," which referred to the personal, lived experience rooted in the character of the individual. He saw knowing as an essential component of the creative process because it related to intuition and the capacity for wonder, and he further connected "knowing" to the more complex notion of "the way we are made." According to Kahn, at birth every individual is directly confronted with "nature and its laws," hence these laws are embedded in our initial perceptions of life. Here Kahn identifies a link from our inherent knowing to the laws of nature. As Kahn put it:

> the institution of learning actually stems from way back, the nature of nature. Nature, physical nature, records what it makes, how it was made, and from this sense which is the

> sense of wonder comes a quest to know, to learn, and the entire quest, I think, will add up to only one thing; how we are made. I think our entire quest for knowledge is only that; how we were made.[4]

Kahn stressed that with our inherent "knowing" established at birth, we are equipped to have a direct dialogue with nature. Thus he regarded "knowing" as more important than "knowledge." However, he did stress that "knowledge" is important to our own awareness of our "knowing," which is individual and not necessarily either clear or relevant to others. By contrast, "knowledge" reflects nature's laws and belongs to everything related to the universe; and for this reason, "knowledge" could not be connected to his idea of eternity as a human construct—an essential difference for him.

Consciousness: Silence and Light

In the studio, Kahn occasionally used the term "the sense of man" to further differentiate between his concepts of "man the species" and "man the human." In this discussion, the word "consciousness" was never far behind. Nature and its laws have no cognizance of being, no consciousness, but man the human does, and Kahn envisioned this as a gift outside of physical nature, as something beyond time and circumstantial events. At first he related "consciousness" to spirit, calling it "pure consciousness." He defined this as the state of mind that precedes the "will to express" and as a spirit present in all life forms—not just humans, but everything living. Trees, grass, animals, insects—everything for him possessed a form of "pure consciousness," a spiritual beginning. Kahn's second application of the word relates to the "existence of will," which in his view differentiates each life form from any other.

In a 1959 letter to Harriet Pattison, Kahn introduced the acronym "INA" (in nature all), but this soon disappeared from his vocabulary because the term was without any visual content. In the same way, Kahn's personal notes reveal that he struggled with the word "consciousness" and that he searched for supporting words to give it more substance, similar to the way he tied "wonder" to "thought" and "feeling." In using the adjective "pure" with "consciousness," he believed he could express a connection to spirit, to the non-luminous. This connection is an important key to Kahn's "Silence and Light" diagram, where "light as the giver of all presence" figures prominently. Finding the language to connect human will with consciousness seemed to pose a greater challenge. As Kahn put it, "consciousness can be without will, but there is no will without consciousness." In continuing to try to illuminate the relationship between consciousness and will, Kahn began to combine "consciousness" with "silence."

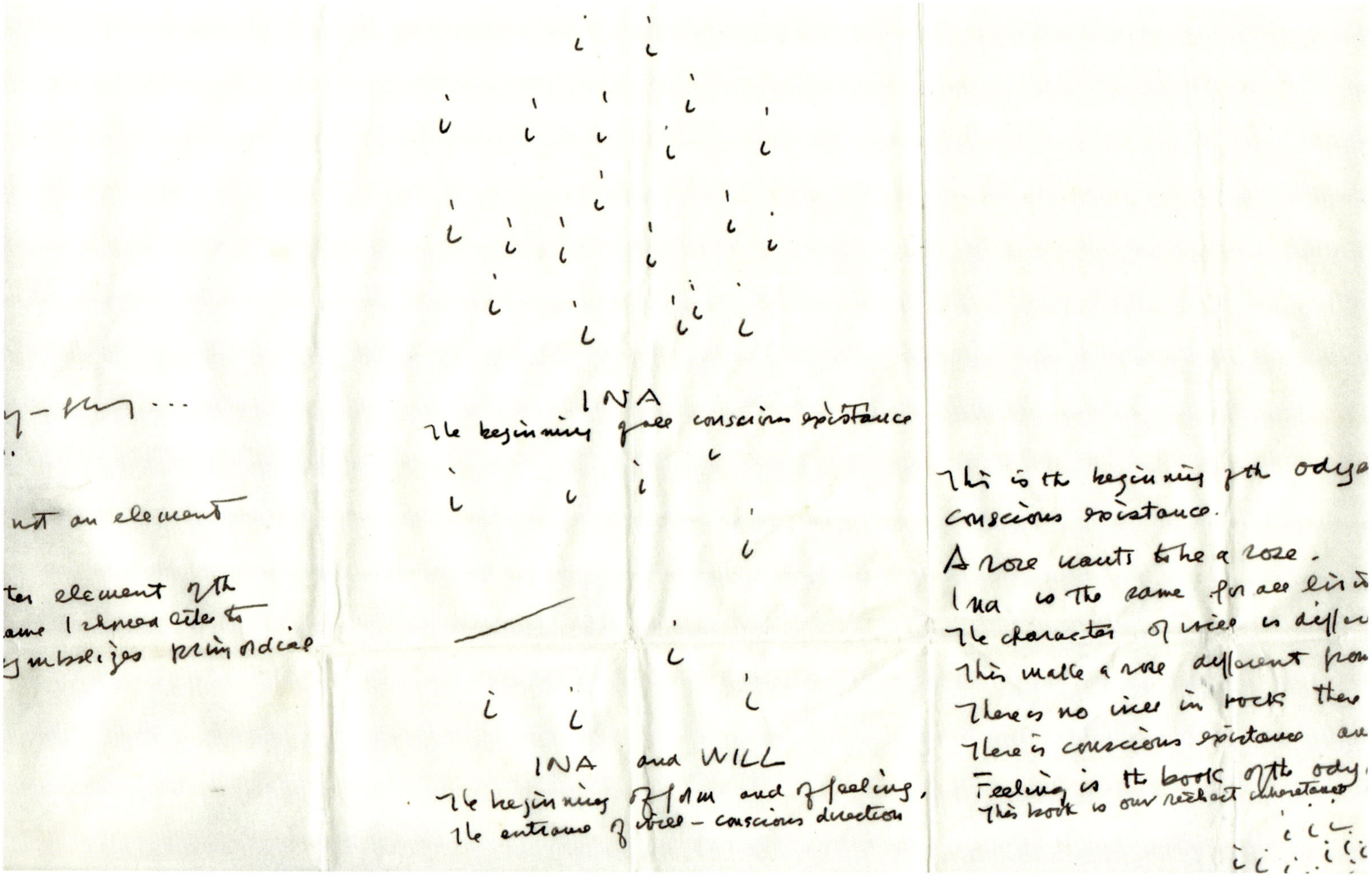

"INA [in nature all]: The beginning of all conscious existence." Creative act drawing by Louis Kahn, 1959. *Nathaniel Kahn Collection.*

(For instance, he noted that "the humanness of man lies in his consciousness, in his silence, and in the consciousness-silence is the will to express.") Together these words contained a visual energy that seemed to satisfy him for some time.

What then connects the will to express to the physical act of making in Kahn's view? Here his use of the term "light" offers some insight. While in the late 1950s Kahn expressed interest in the interplay between built mass and daylight, by the mid-1960s light figured prominently in his personal interpretation of the creative act. By that time he clearly envisioned a relationship between consciousness, silence, and light—and this connection would engage his thoughts until the end of his life.

Kahn believed that "we are all spent light." In class Kahn asserted that light was the "very

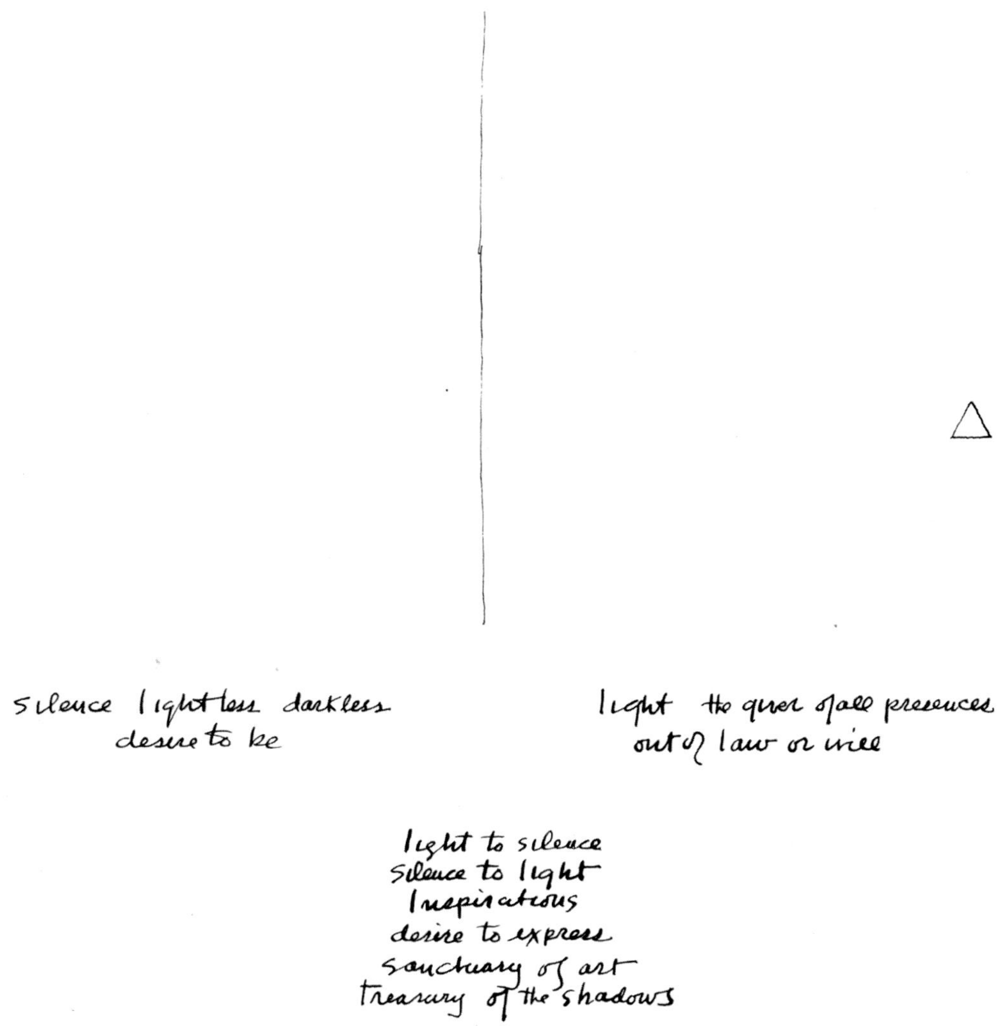

A vertical boundary line separates "Silence" from "Light" in this creative act drawing by Louis Kahn, 1968. *Louis I. Kahn Collection, The University of Pennsylvania and the Pennsylvania Historical and Museum Commission.*

source of matter itself"; that "light that has ceased to be light becomes material"; that "all material casts shadow, thus it belongs to light." Though light lacks the will to express, within its potential to become material Kahn associated light with "the will to make." In his descriptions of the creative act, "consciousness-silence" became, simply, "silence." Between the will to be ("silence") and the will to make ("light"), he envisioned a kinetic relationship: a dynamic time lapse before "realization" as the will to express moves closer to the means to express. In the movement from silence to light, and from light to silence, this relationship passes through a threshold, the moment when inspiration releases an expression.

This pairing of "the will to express" and "the will to make" set the base for his "Silence and Light" diagrams, which he continued to alter until the end of his life. In a 1968 diagram,

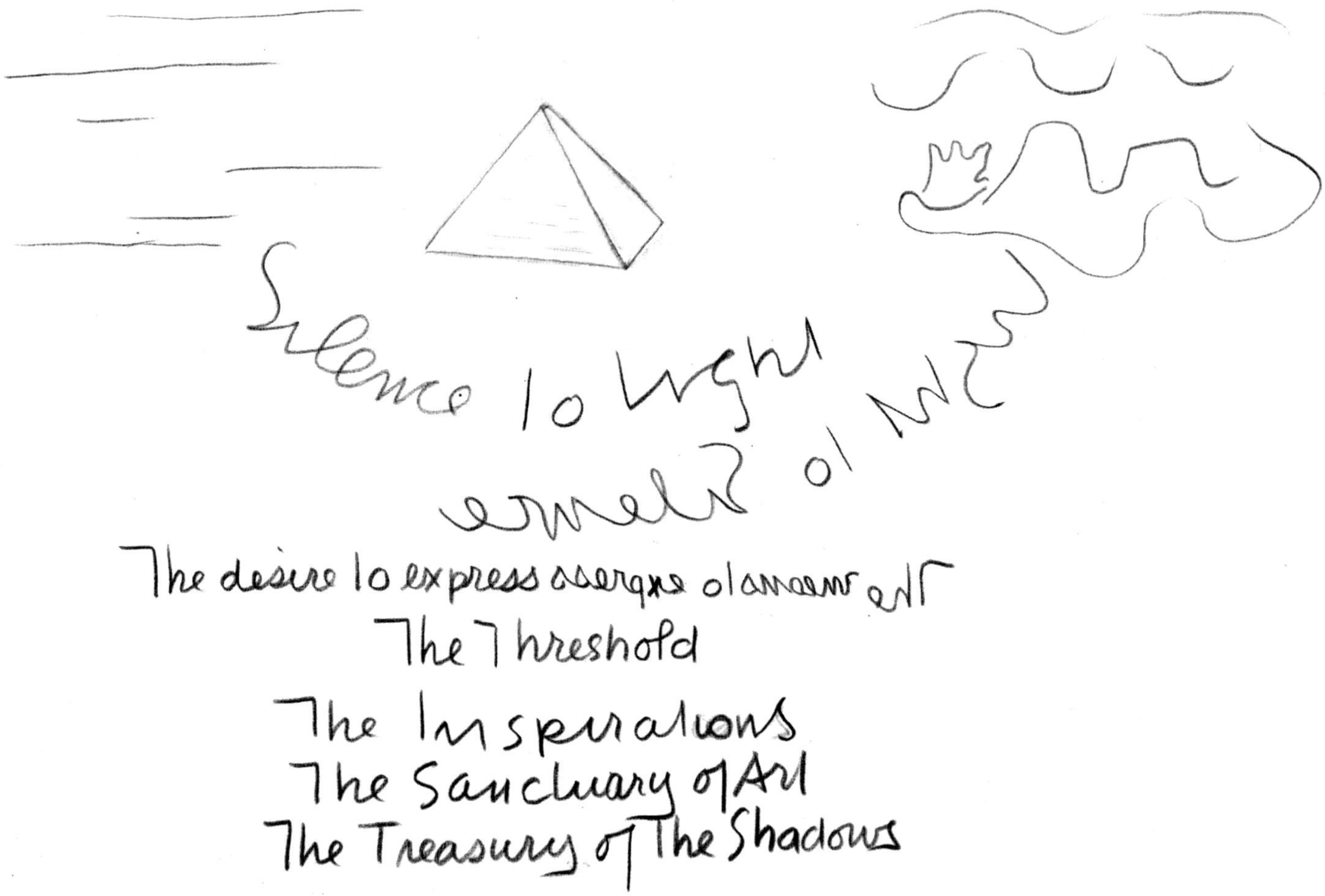

In this drawing, "Silence" and "Light" are no longer separated by a line, thus suggesting a greater integration. Here Kahn has mirrored his script for "Silence to Light" with "Light to Silence." This technique serves to further underline the fluidity between the two entities. Creative act drawing by Louis Kahn, 1969. *Louis I. Kahn Collection, The University of Pennsylvania and the Pennsylvania Historical and Museum Commission.*

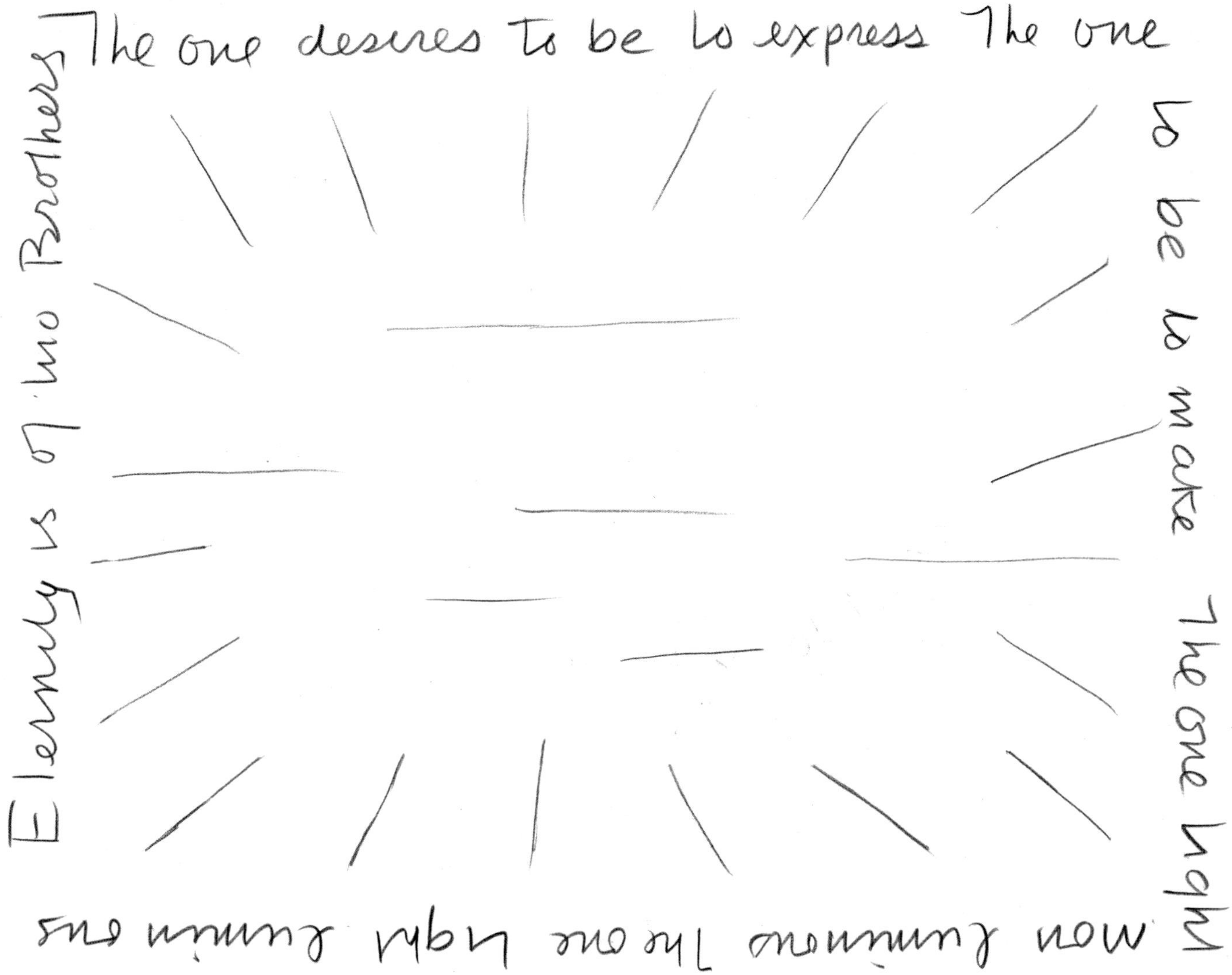

Kahn struggled to find a way to visually erase the boundary between the "non-luminous" and the "luminous," as his Silence and Light drawings indicate. In one drawing from 1972, he cast this pair as two brothers: "Eternity of Two Brothers / The one desires to be to express / The one to be to make / The one light non luminous / The one light luminous." *Louis I. Kahn Collection, The University of Pennsylvania and the Pennsylvania Historical and Museum Commission.*

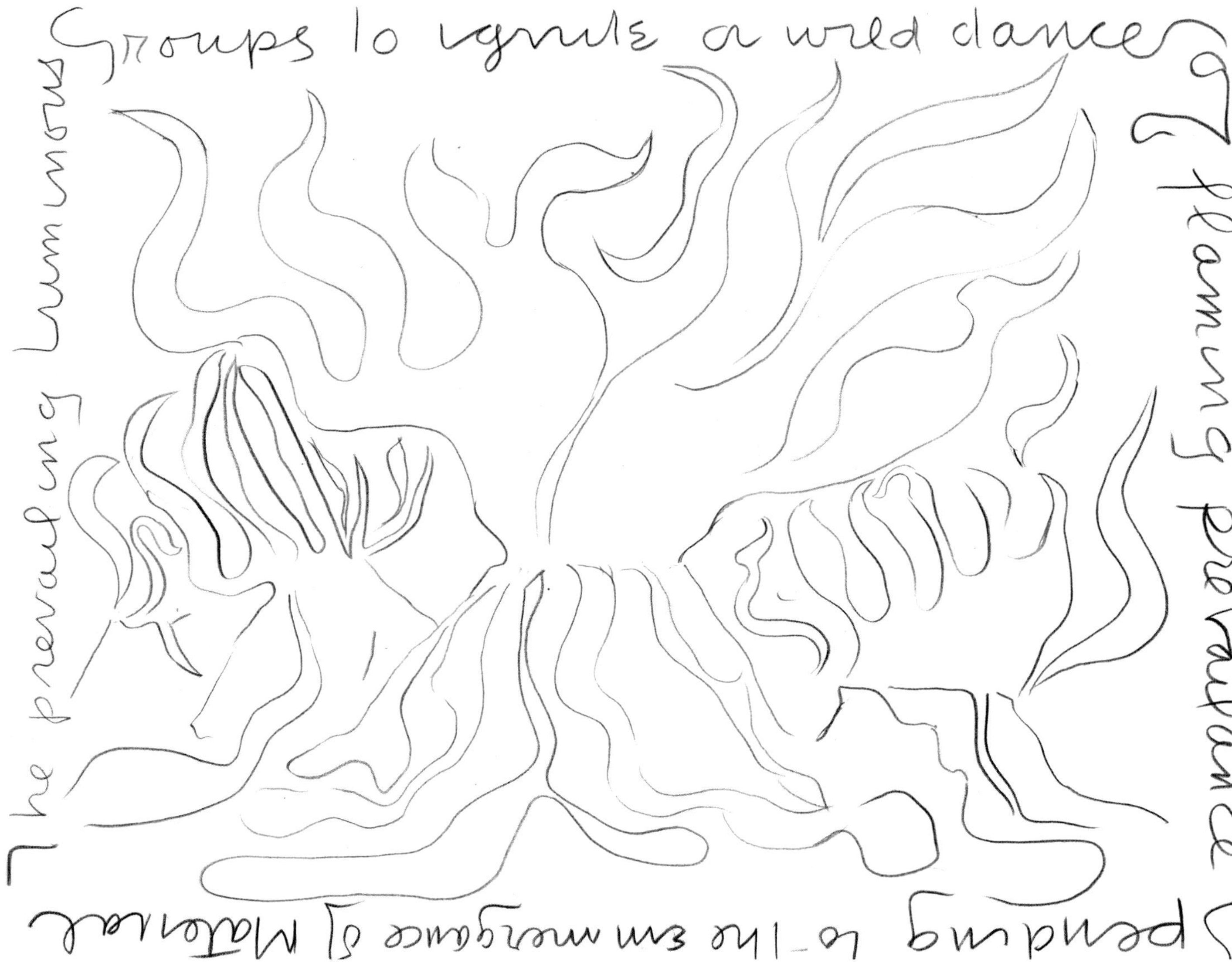

"Eternity of Two Brothers 1972": "The prevailing Luminous / Groups to ignite a wild dance of flaming prevalence / Spending to the emergence of Material." *Louis I. Kahn Collection, The University of Pennsylvania and the Pennsylvania Historical and Museum Commission.*

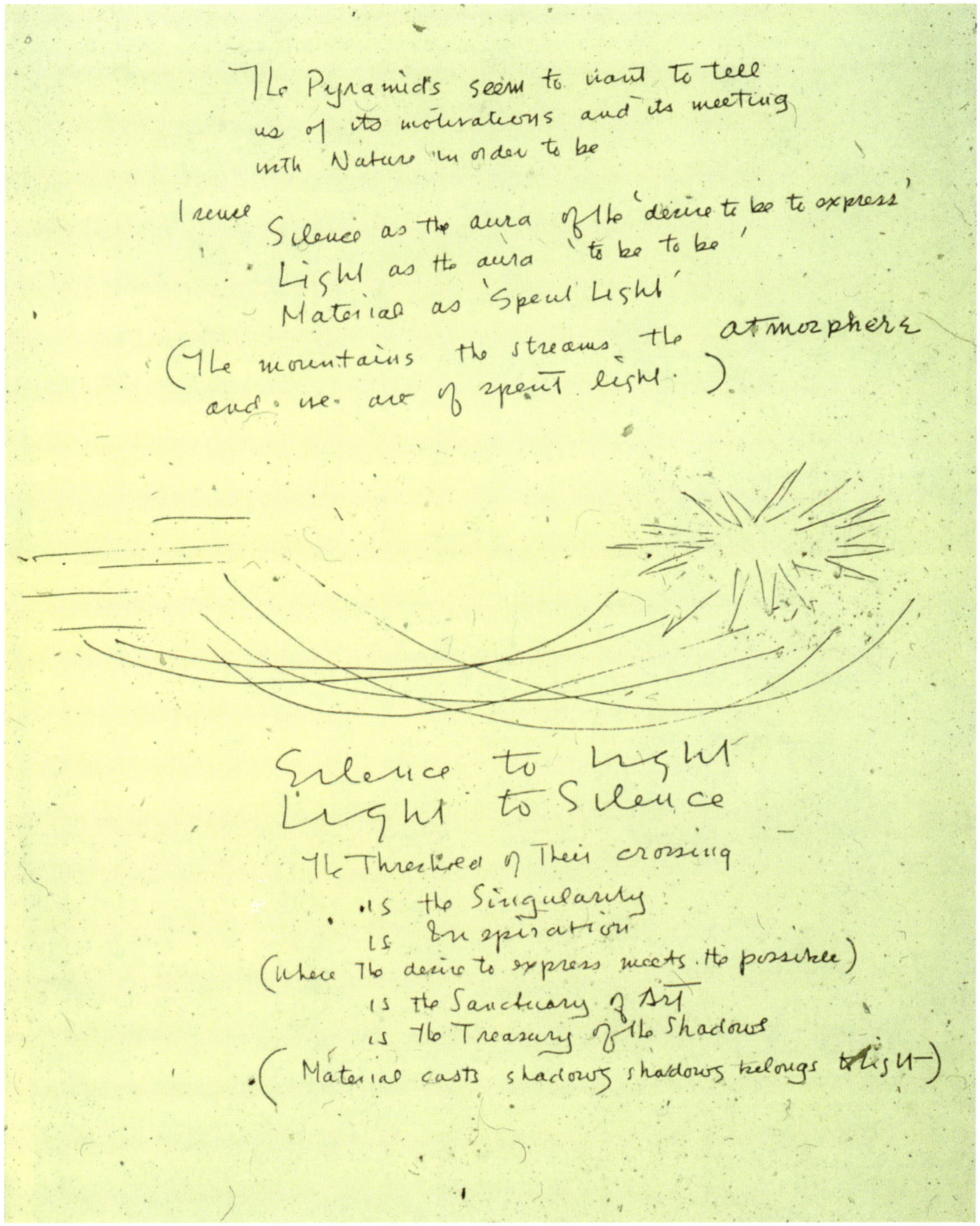

A creative act drawing from 1972 in which Kahn continued to explore the threshold between silence and light. Here he writes, "The Threshold of their crossing / is the Singularity / is Inspiration." *Louis I. Kahn Collection, The University of Pennsylvania and the Pennsylvania Historical and Museum Commission.*

I wanted to illustrate Silence and Light.
Silence I felt ___ this way about.
Light? — how could I do better than accept the whiteness of the paper itself?
Looking at an illustration of the Waverly Tales by Cruikshank I noticed his lines followed the direction of the source of light. I realized that the stroke of the pen was where the light was not.

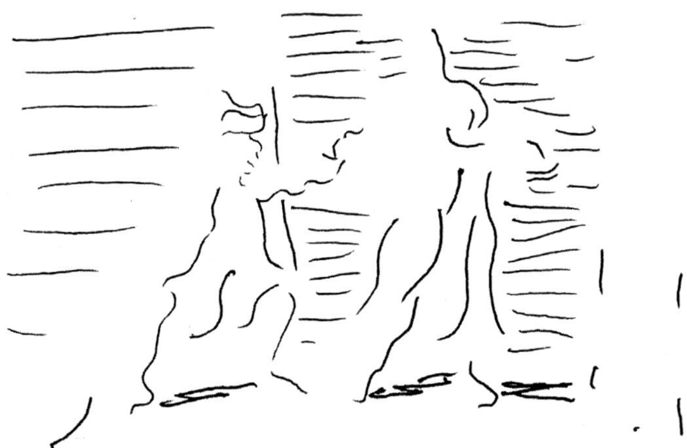

This was the clue to the illusion
My remark that structure is the giver of light is here by recalled. The column in the Greek Temple is where the light is not.

Louis I Kahn June 15 '73

Kahn sketched this Silence and Light drawing in June of 1973, a month after my graduation. It is a strong reminder of our class discussions. *Louis I. Kahn Collection, University of Pennsylvania and the Pennsylvania Historical and Museum Commission.*

the movement from silence to light and from light to silence passes through a threshold—the "inspirations," the "sanctuary of art," the "treasury of the shadows"—which he envisioned as the melting point of singularity. At times his diagrams became far more abstract and unintelligible, and it seems almost as if the faintly sketched vertical line separating "Silence" from "Light" irritated him. Later diagrams show a blurred line between the two regions, and in one of his last diagrams, the line seems to have been replaced by a pyramid-like object. In a 1972 diagram he drew Silence and Light as two brothers: one is the desire to express; the other, the desire to make. One brother is light non-luminous, and the other, luminous. Kahn regarded them as one, inseparable, since for him both brothers represent eternity. In this diagram the movement between them generates a "fire dance" that represents a material reality. The brothers were an attempt to eliminate two different images, but at the same time retain the concept of luminous and non-luminous.

In a 1973 diagram, the dividing line reappeared. In comparison with the 1968 diagram, this drawing is more abstract and more open to interpretation, but the text has changed only slightly. "Silence" and "Light" have remained the same, but "a will to make" is now "to be to be." During the "Silence and Light" lecture he delivered to my class, Kahn drew a version very close to the original 1968 diagram: the border between "Silence" and "Light" was a thin line, and the two brothers were not illustrated.

Institutions of Man

When Romaldo Giurgola and Jaimini Mehta published *Louis I. Kahn* about a year after Kahn's death, they wrote that the most important contribution their friend and colleague had made to architecture was related to the institutions of man. Within Kahn's vocabulary, each form of institution supported an individual identity—whether that of a house, a street, or a school. Over time, I have come to believe that it is not possible to fully understand Kahn's teaching—or, for that matter, the fundamental concerns that guided his built work—without understanding this concept.

While most architects were asking *how* a project could be resolved, Kahn was asking *why,* and *what* approach to the project could inspire humanity's shared activities and aspirations. For him, the institutions of man embodied a collective recognition of essential human values, a consensus that is intuitively apparent long before the more circumstantial material demands of life begin to have an impact. His search for a core meaning within each task revolved around architecture's capability to strengthen "humanness" and the importance of creating spatial environments of human consensus.

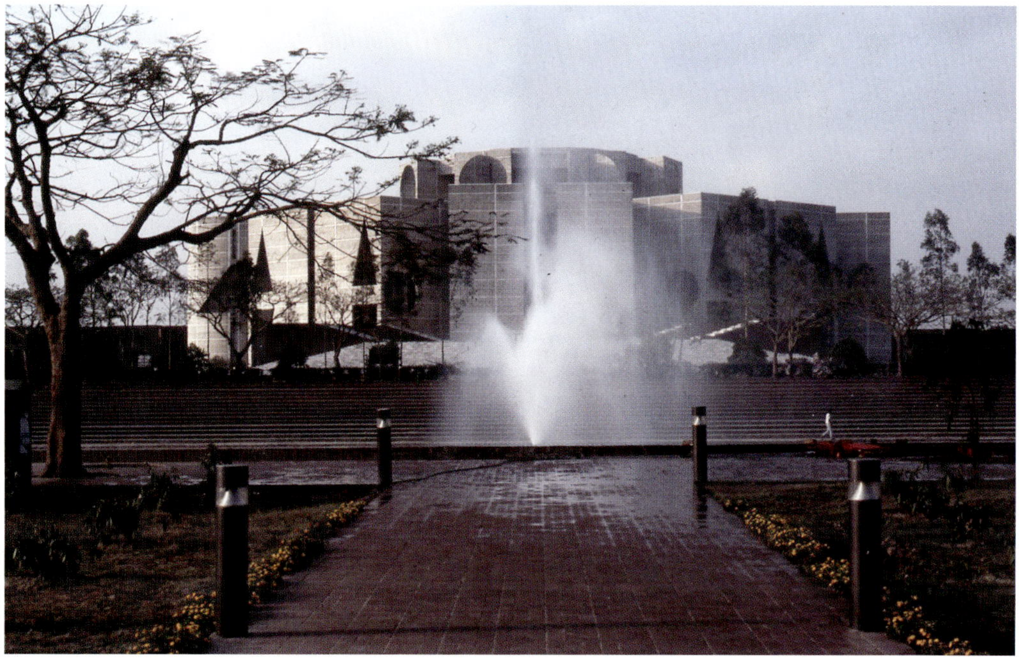

National Assembly Building of Bangladesh, Dhaka, 1962–73. Kahn rejected the notion that contemporary society had no shared image of itself strong enough to sway architecture toward a collective sensibility. *P. O. Fjeld.*

Kahn's focus on the institutions of man emerged at a time when new technologies, an array of new materials, and the growing influence of the media were impacting the architectural profession. However, this focus appears to have been influenced by his personal experience more than by the state of the architectural profession at the time. His perceptions of the world were no doubt tied to a tough inner-city childhood in which he observed his parents struggling with the challenges of life in a new country. Such experiences gave substance to his concepts of "the way of life" and "living," which undergirded his ideas regarding the institutions of man. In relation to this, Kahn would comment on our abilities to accumulate what he called "expressive instincts," which were, in a sense, one's available intuitive moments of "knowing." For Kahn, the gathering and retaining of these moments were essential to the individual creative act. At the same time, he felt that through "knowing" the individual expression carries a collective agreement. Thus Kahn believed that the institutions of man as a shared human expression originated from an individual creative act rather than from preconceived plans, designs, or images.

He stressed that collective understanding embedded in the institutions of man relies foremost on the continuity of human behavior's "content" rather than its "context"—meaning that human content always precedes context, as context evolves from circumstantial, changeable conditions. Toward the end of his life, Kahn worried that increasingly image-oriented architectural trends would enable context to override content, and that an overreliance on an

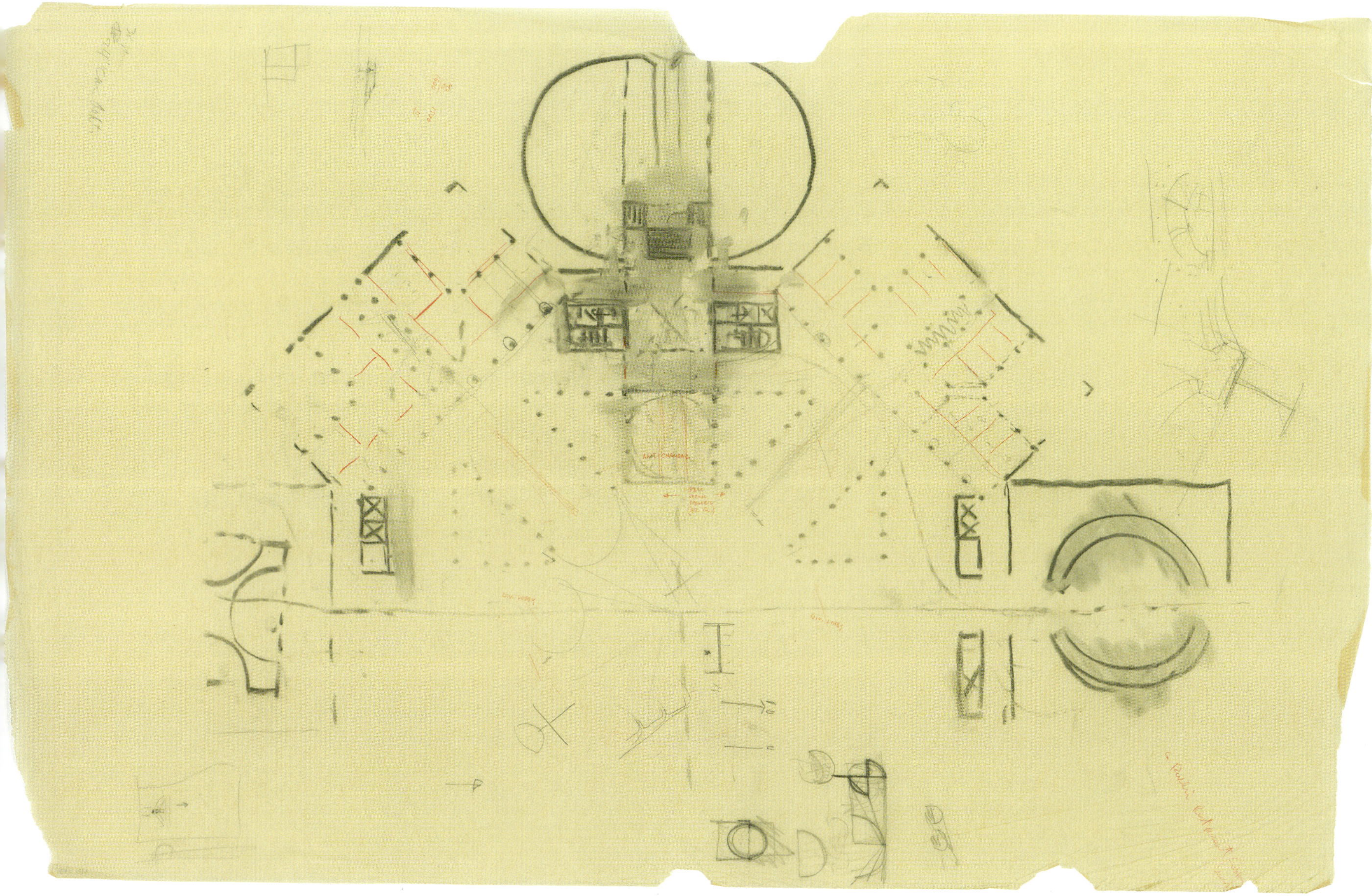

One of Kahn's plan sketches of the National Assembly Building of Bangladesh, which shows the entrance hall and offices on both sides. *Louis I. Kahn Collection, The University of Pennsylvania and the Pennsylvania Historical and Museum Commission.*

ever-changing context would in turn shorten the lifespan of built work. If an architect envisions a new public building principally in terms of current program relevance, this would be at the expense of core human content. In addition, Kahn argued that under the influence of modernism, architecture's role in creating a collective awareness had been downgraded. As early as 1951, he argued that "institution was on trial because the inspiration that had called it into being was no longer felt." Yet he strongly rejected the idea that contemporary society had no shared image of itself strong enough to sway architecture toward a collective sensibility. In fact, Kahn ultimately regarded this shared understanding as a permanent condition. In April 1965 at the National Conference of Church Architecture, Kahn stated:

> It cannot be so meagerly made as to rely on just changes or the modern way of making candlesticks or painting a painting so that you can read it, or sign things and say it is modern . . . not at all. It is a new form that simply must be there in such a way that it inspires in all directions because it has a new ingredient.[5]

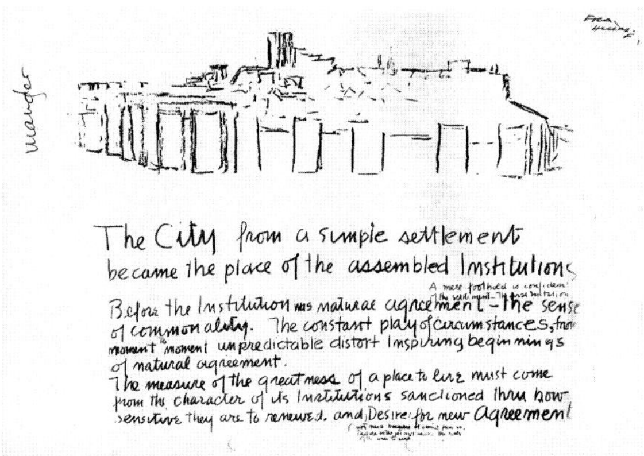

Sketch by Kahn: "The city from a simple settlement became the place of the assembled Institutions . . . " *Louis I. Kahn Collection, The University of Pennsylvania and the Pennsylvania Historical and Museum Commission.*

Each institution of man has its own evolution, but in the absence of a collective awareness it is far more difficult to comprehend or envision such transformations.

The Way of Life

Kahn talked about two human realities: "the reality of belief" and "the reality of means." In regard to "institution," the difference between the two realities is important. He felt that much built work was not generated from belief but rather from means, and therefore was able neither to convey a strong collective sensibility nor to revitalize established institutions. Unlike "means," which acquires short-term authority from the circumstantial or the specific, "belief" has an "aura" that is answerable to all. In Kahn's terms, "the whole reality is not there without the reality of belief," thus "means" is answerable to "belief." By making a distinction between "means" and "belief," he gives insight into his differentiation between "life" and "living."

His term "life" refers to the universal, immeasurable, and the nature of existence; while his "living" refers to the circumstantial and pertains to behavior, events, and his idea of the rules of man. As he put it, "The garden—to see it and love it is life, but to care for it, which you might hate, is living."[6] He had a firm belief in architecture's potential to mold "living." Illustrating this, Kahn noted that:

> The strongest and finest is not the Pantheon realized, but the Pantheon before it was realized. One day there was no dome, and then there actually was. This one day, before

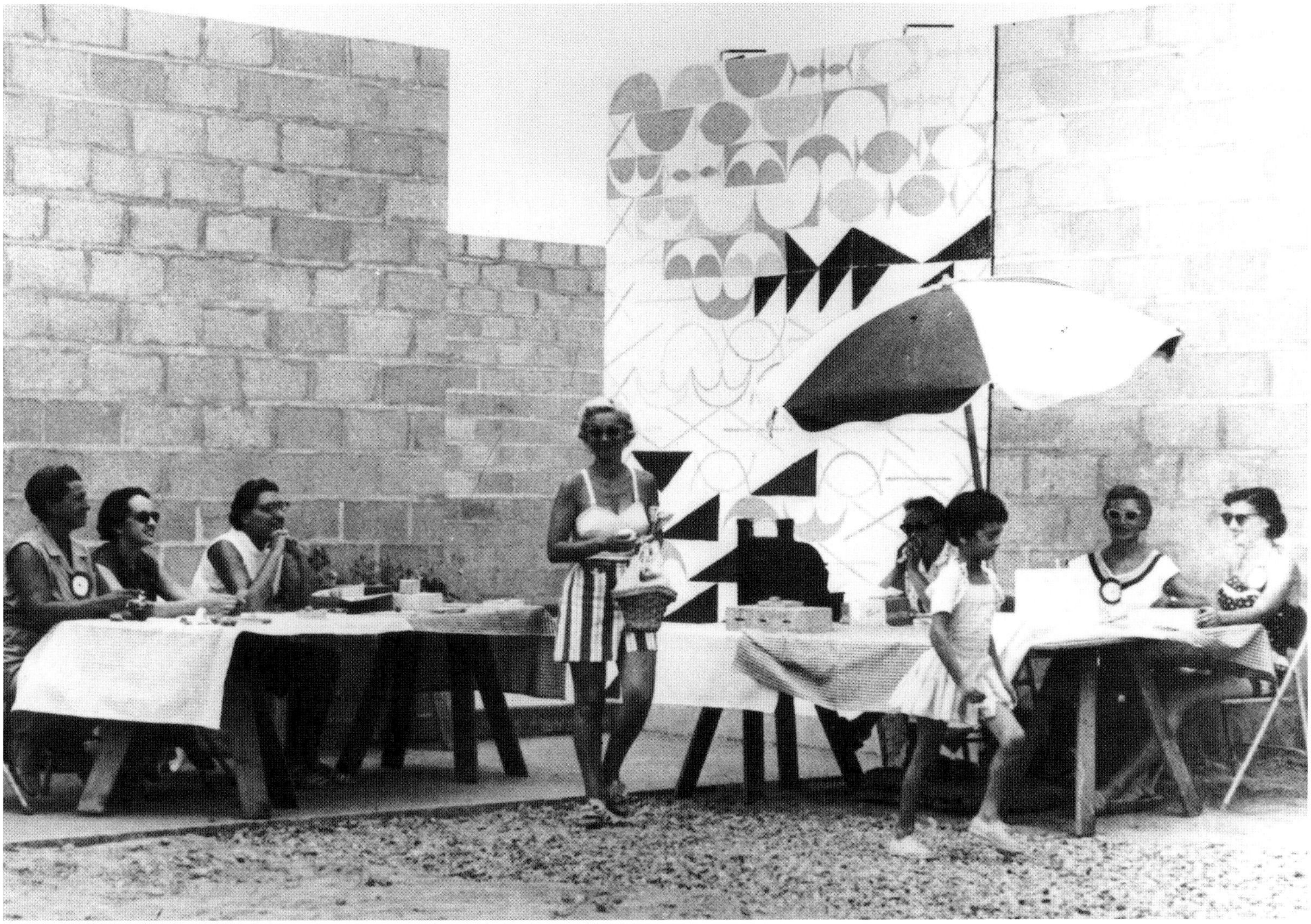

The Trenton Bath House (1955–56) pictured before its pyramidal roof was finished. In considering possible application methods for the mural at the building's entrance, Kahn noted that "the person looking at the painting should feel the struggle within the way it was made." *Susan G. Solomon Collection, Louis I. Kahn Collection, The University of Pennsylvania and the Pennsylvania Historical and Museum Commission.*

> the Pantheon was built, has changed all men in their way of living. The Pantheon came from Life, but ended in the realm of Living, and what it came to change was Living.[7]

In class Kahn stressed that the content embedded in these terms had to be guided by one's own knowing, as well as knowledge.

Served and Servant Spaces

Kahn's early collaboration with Anne Tyng is important to consider, particularly in light of her structural and geometrical insight. During her time in the office, Kahn's work achieved a heightened spatial and structural awareness, as both the Trenton Bath House and the Yale University Art Gallery revealed new architectural strengths and strong promise for work to

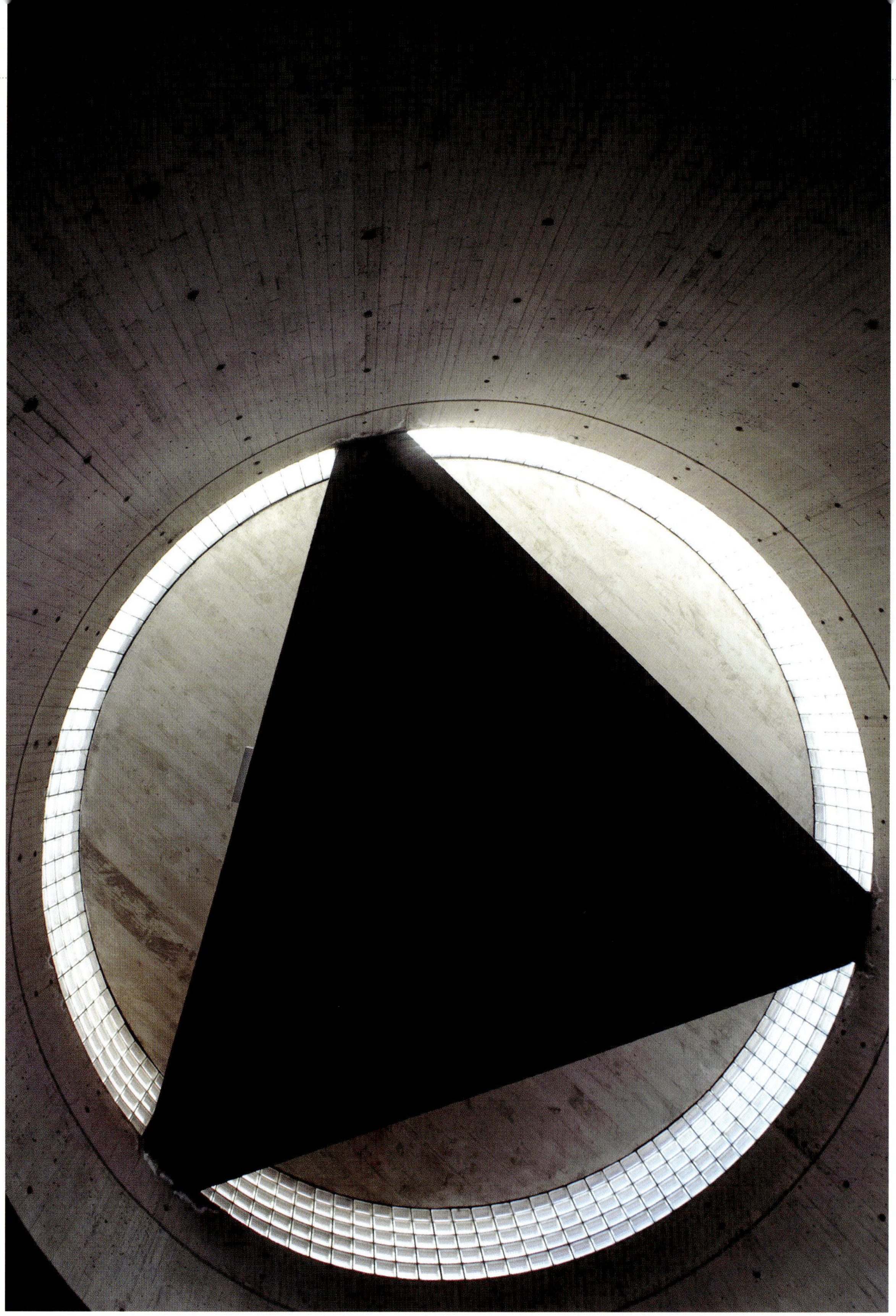

RIGHT: Yale University Art Gallery, New Haven, Connecticut, 1951–53. In the stairwell looking up. *Jon Reksten.*

OPPOSITE: At the Yale University Art Gallery, the tetrahedral space-frame ceiling houses the mechanical utilities. *Pietro Sala.*

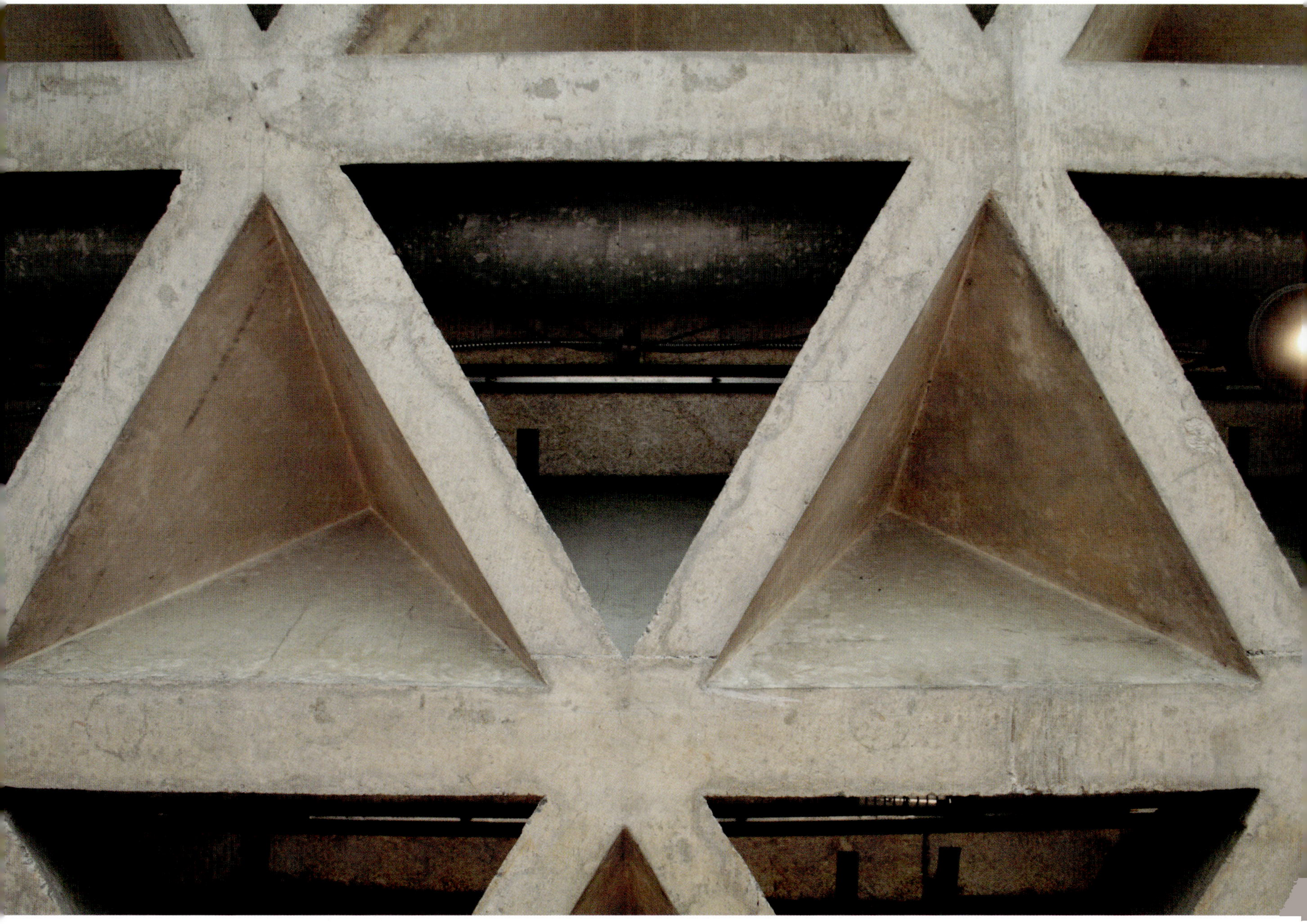

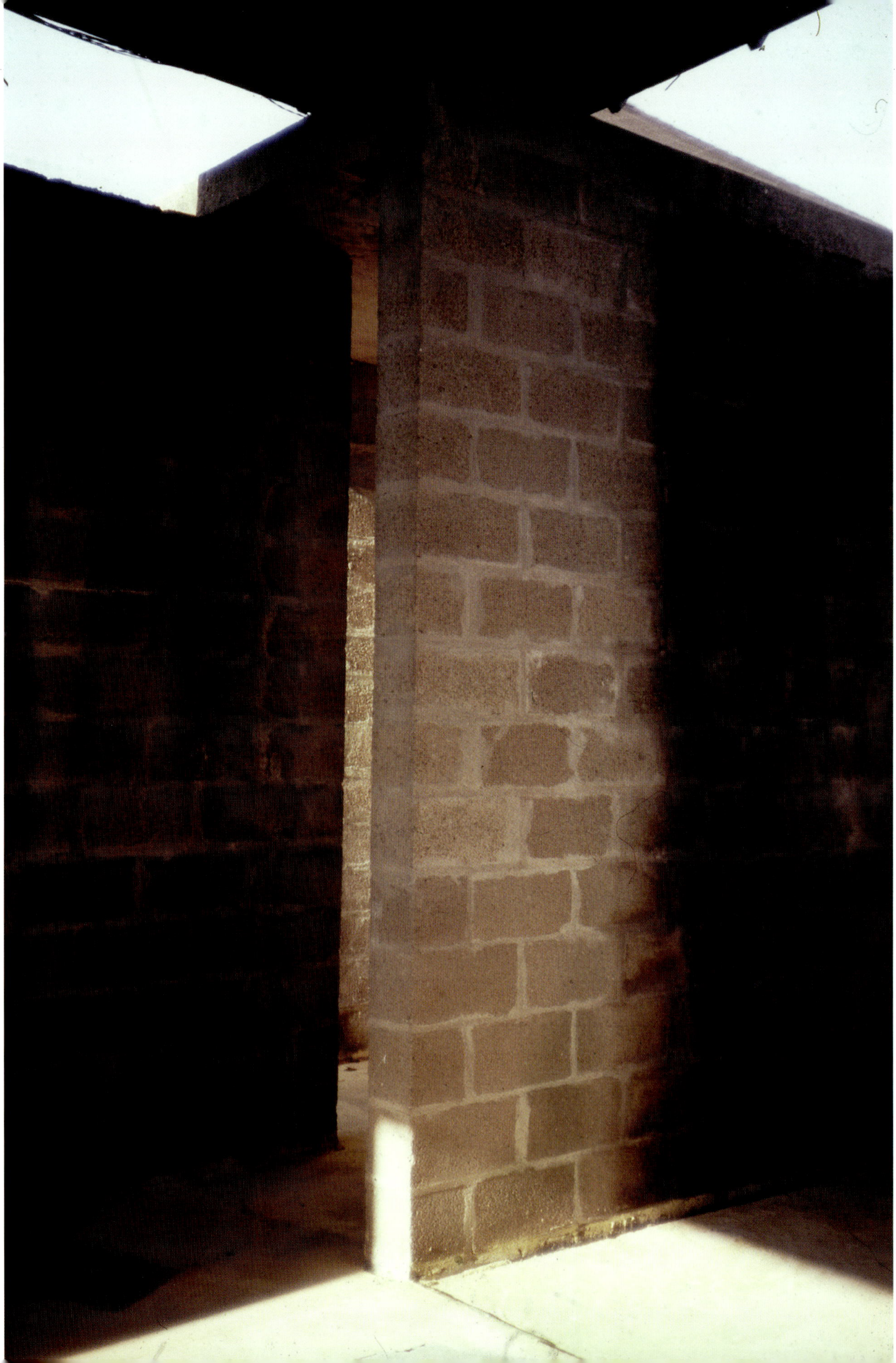

Hollow column at the Trenton Bath House, Jewish Community Center, 1956. To experience the hollow column for the first time was an event. *P. O. Fjeld.*

come. Tellingly, Kahn's notion of "served and servant spaces" emerged during these projects. In the studio we discussed the relationship between rooms with the capacity to serve and those that were served. We were aware that a number of architects were skeptical of this concept. Their critique arose from an interpretation of spatial hierarchy directly related to human activity and understood through a perceived social status or the valuing of one space over another, which was at odds with Kahn's thinking. For him, the idea about "served and servant spaces" was far more about defining and understanding each room's architectural potential and the role of specificity and position within a total spatial sequence.

The Hollow Column

The idea of the "hollow column" understood as a room was first realized in the Trenton Bath House, and it reappeared in Kahn's later work, including the project for the Mikveh Israel Synagogue. The hollow column was part of a provocative shift in Kahn's work that saw interior spatial sequences achieving a new and more varied relationship between structure and light. In the synagogue, for example, each hollow column as a circular room housed an activity of its own, while at the same time offering its light to the sanctuary, thus freeing this main room from the responsibility of providing daylight within its spatial domain. As students, we were familiar with Kahn's idea of the hollow column, and for their uniqueness we admired the projects that incorporated it. Nevertheless, we were somewhat reluctant to test the idea in our own projects. Unfortunately, Kahn never talked about the synagogue in the studio. I do not think it was for lack of interest, but rather because the project was unfinished, without a conclusion, and the possibility of its being realized was still oddly present.

Geometry, Structure, Material, and Light

The First Unitarian Church is considered by many to be a turning point in Kahn's work. During this project, Kahn shifted his focus to daylight as an integral part of architecture. This concern wasn't new for him, but it now carried a spiritual dimension: there could be no room without daylight. In consequence, Kahn began to see a strong connection between geometry, material, structure, and light; and he felt the need to go deeper into the relationships between these four elements, to investigate their individual properties as well as each element's potential for interaction. He was by no means alone in this search. Influences from Le Corbusier's postwar built work and writing can be discerned, but as mentioned earlier, Kahn's approach

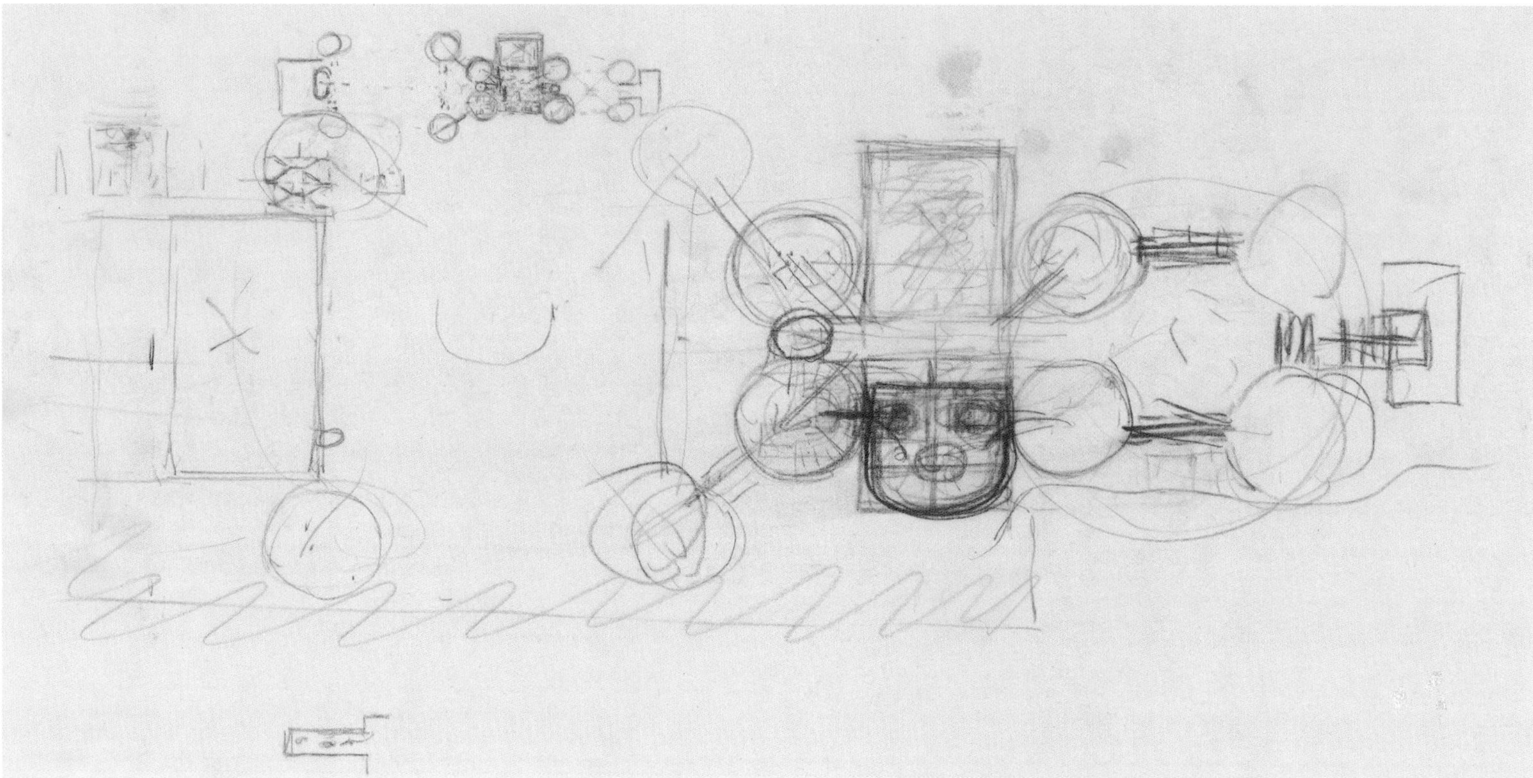

ABOVE: Plan sketch for the Mikveh Israel Synagogue in which Kahn explored the relationship between the hollow columns and the rooms required by the program. *Louis I. Kahn Collection, The University of Pennsylvania and the Pennsylvania Historical and Museum Commission.*

RIGHT: One of Louis Kahn's sketches of the unbuilt Mikveh Israel Synagogue, 1961–72, which was to be located in Philadelphia. Hollow columns, which carry an identity of their own while bringing daylight into the main sacred room, feature in this rendering of the project. *Louis I. Kahn Collection, The University of Pennsylvania and the Pennsylvania Historical and Museum Commission.*

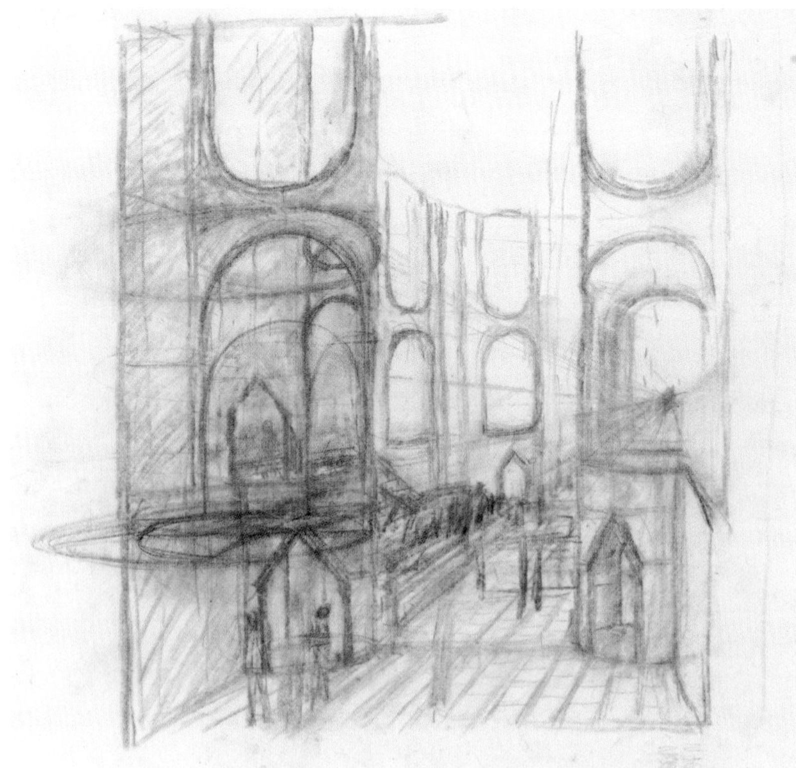

was closer to that of a number of important Nordic architects and teachers from the first half of the twentieth century. They likewise understood the connection between geometry, material, structure, and light, but as vital to addressing the Nordic climate and way of living.

For Kahn, in the development of a plan, geometrical identity seemed to work as a guideline, as part of nature's structure and order, and thus recognizable to everyone. For this reason, geometry conveys a collective understanding—but the creative thought behind Kahn's use of geometry is far more complex. In Kahn's working process, tellingly, geometries would emerge rather late—after the "form drawing" was conceived and perfected. When looking at the plan of the Assembly Hall in the National Assembly Building of Bangladesh, one is struck by its geometrical order, but it is the integrity of its sections—how Kahn cut the distinct geometrical shapes with the sharpness of a scalpel—that makes the individual rooms and the sequence of spaces unique. His use of geometry was an operative tool that guided his cuts and determined where daylight entered; here geometry and daylight crossed paths. Daylight as material was inseparable from architectural presence, thus it was also an integral part of conveying a sense of "institution."

Form Drawing

When Kahn abandoned the traditional program while working on the First Unitarian Church, he turned to what he called a "form drawing," which was not a drawing of design intentions, but rather a condensed sketch capable of conveying the essence of a project. In his teaching Kahn actively applied his concept of the form drawing as an important tool to explore spatial potential in advance of final design decisions. First the form drawing had to be discovered and explored—a challenging task. We struggled to conceptualize the essence of a project in an expression of its own, and at times we employed geometry as a shortcut to realize intentions in relation to "institution." Exhausted, we argued for our geometric scenarios, as they seemed to confer an immediate collective expression. I think this irritated Kahn, since he could not flatly deny geometry had this capacity, and yet he saw that this effort could finalize our search prematurely. One of the critiques that Alison Smithson leveled at Kahn's work around the time of the Otterlo meeting was somewhat justified: She pointed out that Kahn's use of geometry could blind students to the spatial complexity and precision found in his work, enticing them to naively rely upon the use of geometry as a method to give spatial identity.

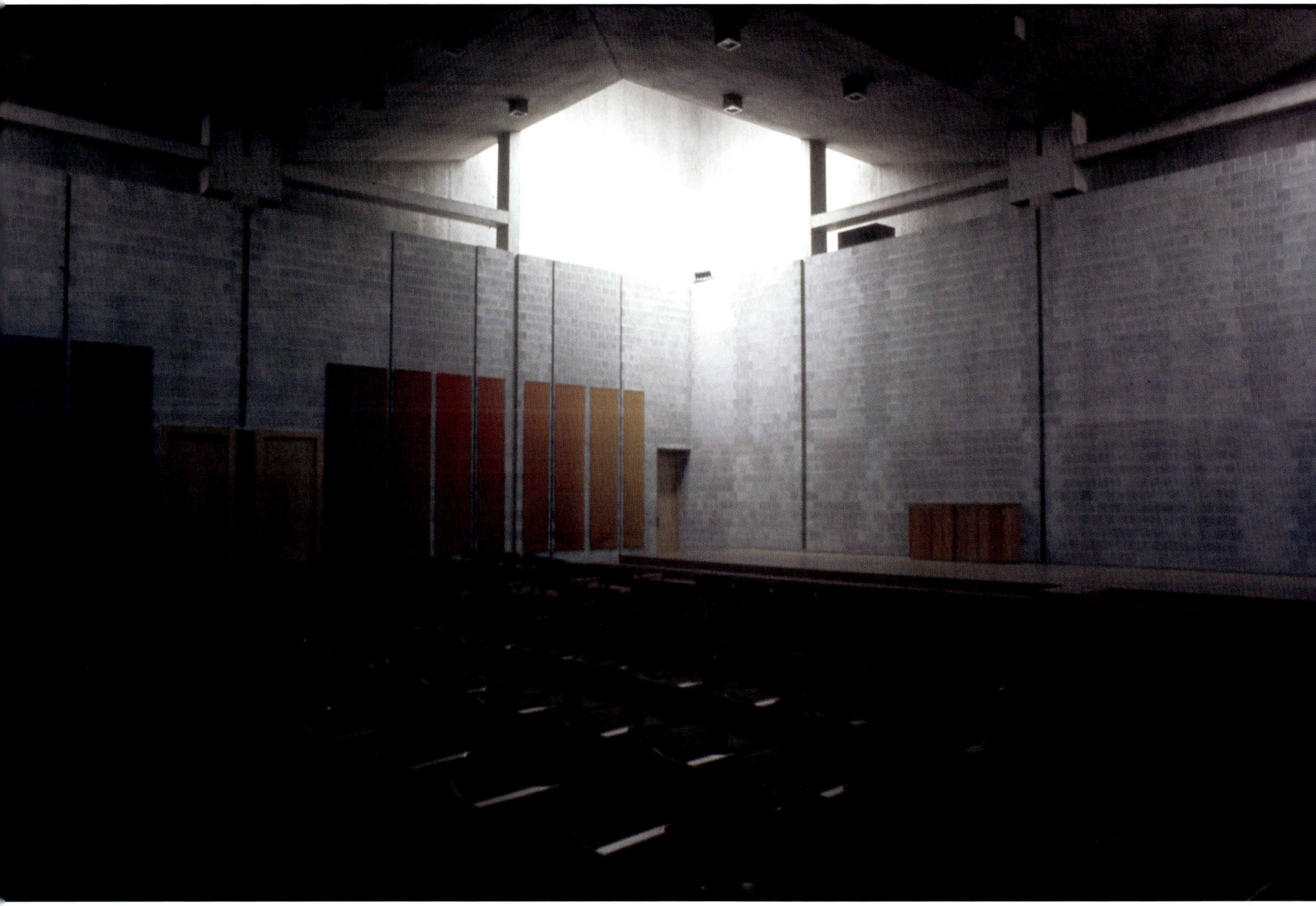

Silence and light brought into architectural presence: the meeting room of the First Unitarian Church of Rochester, Rochester, New York, 1959–69. *John Dorio Nicolais Collection, Architectural Archives, University of Pennsylvania.*

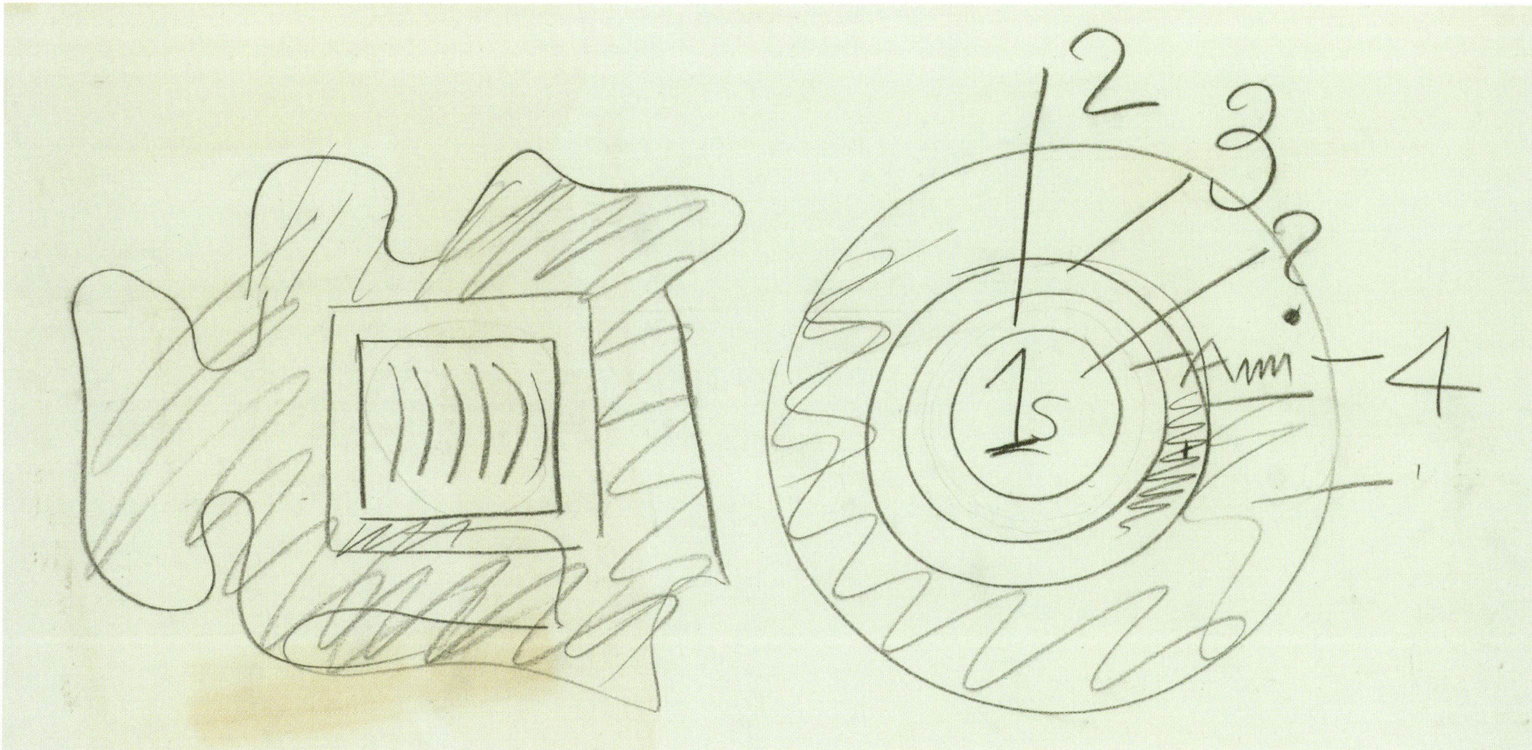

Kahn's form drawing of the First Unitarian Church of Rochester. As Kahn described it: "I made a square center in which I placed a question mark. Let us say I meant it to be the sanctuary. This encircled with an ambulatory for those who did not want to get into the sanctuary. Around the ambulatory, I drew a corridor, which belonged to an outer circle enclosing a space, the school. It was clear that school which gives rise to questions became the wall, which surrounded questions. This was the form expression of the church, not the design." *Louis I. Kahn Collection, The University of Pennsylvania and the Pennsylvania Historical and Museum Commission.*

Material and Materiality

Kahn's approach to materials also changed during the First Unitarian Church project. At the same time that he began to investigate materials' specific identities, he began to disengage from some aspects of modern technology, including its emphasis on efficiency and lightweight materials. Bearing in mind his 1944 article on monumentality, this was a definite turnaround from his earlier position. By the late 1950s it appears that he simply rejected steel as a primary building material, believing it did not have a strong enough collective identity to attain "institution." This was difficult to come to terms with as a student. A quote from his class in 1960 gives some insight. "Mies is concerned with technology, but expects more of it than he gets," Kahn noted. "He is clearly disturbed and upset by this, and he even has to sand down his steel to make it clearer than what he gets. The way of life of steel is within concrete."[8] Eschewing steel, Kahn turned to brick. Made of earth, with a size and weight that was universally understood, brick carried material's potential in relation to "institution." He embraced concrete for yet another reason: its surface conveyed how it was made. I can remember him commenting that travertine was a good complementary material to concrete; though different in nature, the two materials had something in common: their pores. As a consequence of these attitudes and his belief that “all materials are spent light,” Kahn now clearly equated material with mass in his work. Thus structure and mass could not be separated. It was not a matter of using the most optimal materials—ones that favored rational or efficient structure for the sake of structure—nor of satisfying regulations. Instead, Kahn considered which materials embodied the specific institution and how architecture could convey the way it was made.

In the studio Kahn challenged our acceptance of the popular stances of the time regarding both material and structural rationality. Kahn made clear that the emphasis on structural efficiency and spatial flexibility that we brought with us from our previous education was not a primary issue for him.

The Brief

During the last two decades of his life, Kahn gave greater attention to the “rooms outside the brief.” In these non-programmed spaces, which were unconstrained by a preconceived image or assigned role at the start of a project, Kahn sensed great opportunity to search for new possibilities or to revitalize existing spatial content. Here he could look unhindered for a core beginning. Some of the most beautiful and timeless aspects of his work evolved out of this type of search. In the studio he argued that a sign of a good architect was his ability to bring forth the non-programmed spaces. Their spatial energy could strengthen the building as a whole with their unique capacity to release pressure from rooms with assigned activities.

In relation to the brief, the term “function,” understood as referring to space more concerned with use than spatial quality, would come up in class discussions. For Kahn, talk of “function” was more often an irritation than a real platform for debate; it was obvious that a building must function. For him, the form drawing and the plan as a society of rooms constituted the proper starting point. “Function” in his vocabulary was not a static or finite spatial state, but rather one altering, transforming, and rediscovering itself through time. In the search to revitalize the content of “institution,” traditional concepts of program and function had to be challenged.

Connections

In the plans for the Erdman Hall dormitory at Bryn Mawr College and the Fisher House, the rooms connect directly to one another. The projects’ almost interstitial plans show

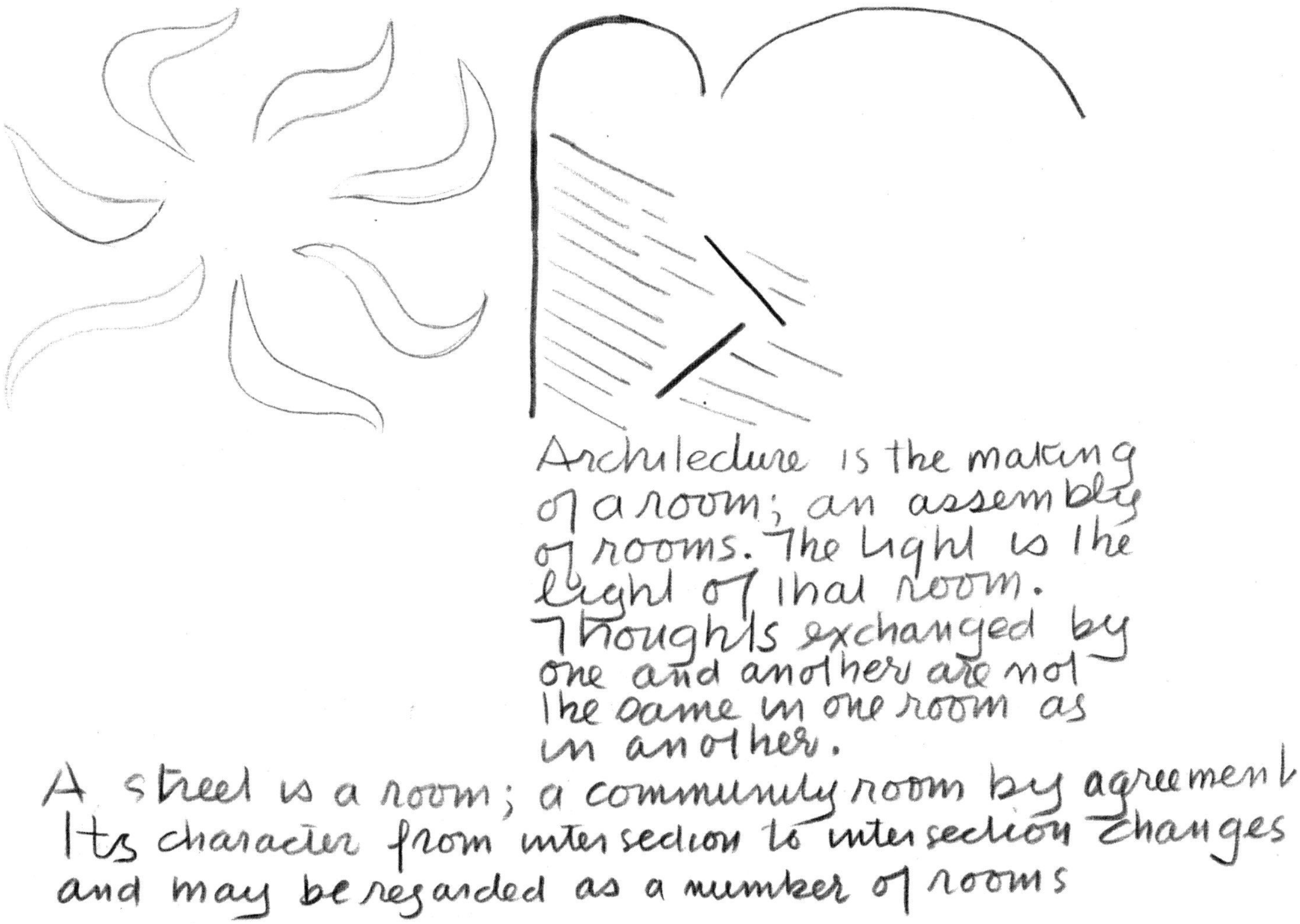

Sketch by Louis Kahn: "Architecture is the making of a room; an assembly of rooms. The light is the light of that room. Thoughts exchanged by one and another are not the same in one room as in another. A street is a room; a community room by agreement. Its character from intersection to intersection changes and may be regarded as a number of rooms." *Louis I. Kahn Collection, The University of Pennsylvania and the Pennsylvania Historical and Museum Commission.*

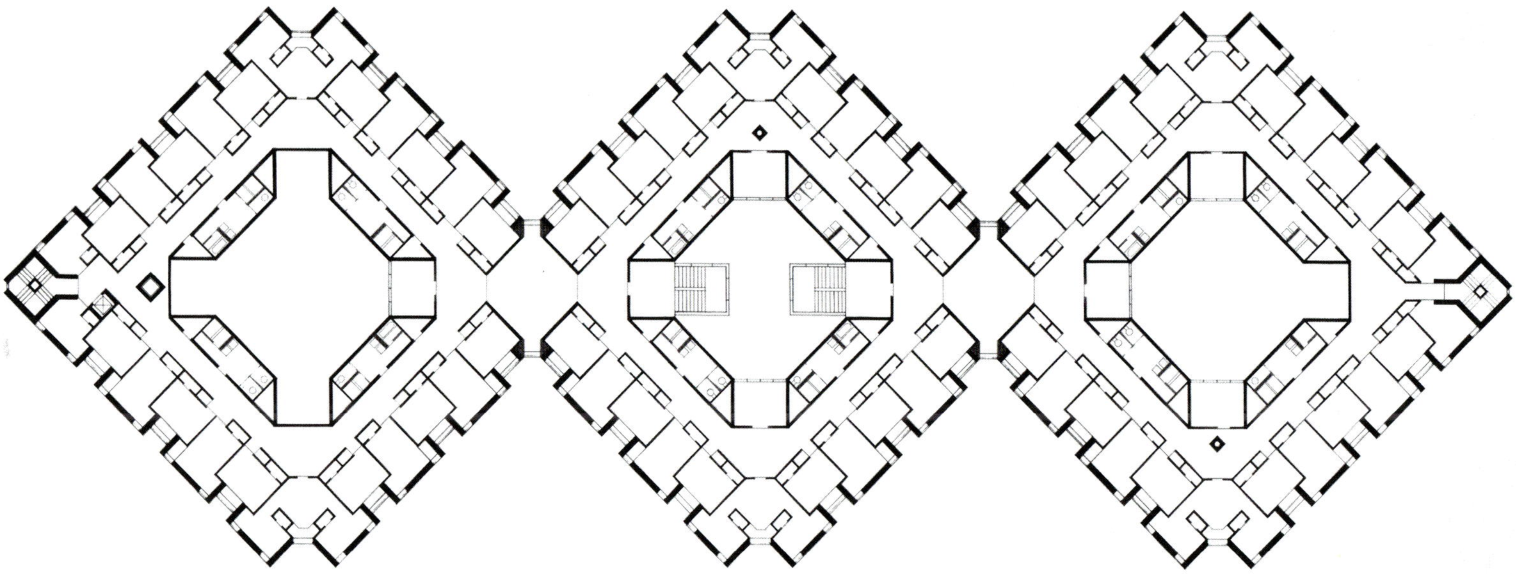

ABOVE: The plan for the Erdman Hall dormitory building at Bryn Mawr College, 1960–65, showing how its rooms connect directly to each other. Kahn once remarked in class that he hated corridors. *Louis I. Kahn Collection, The University of Pennsylvania and the Pennsylvania Historical and Museum Commission.*

RIGHT: The living room of Erdman Hall. The room's bare materiality and light demand a direct dialogue with its users. *P. O. Fjeld.*

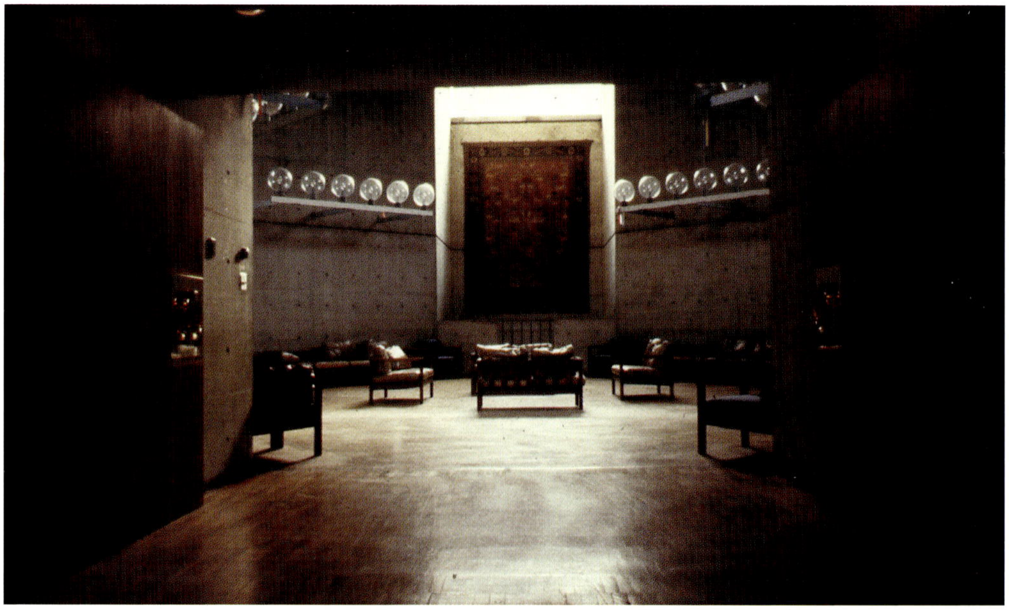

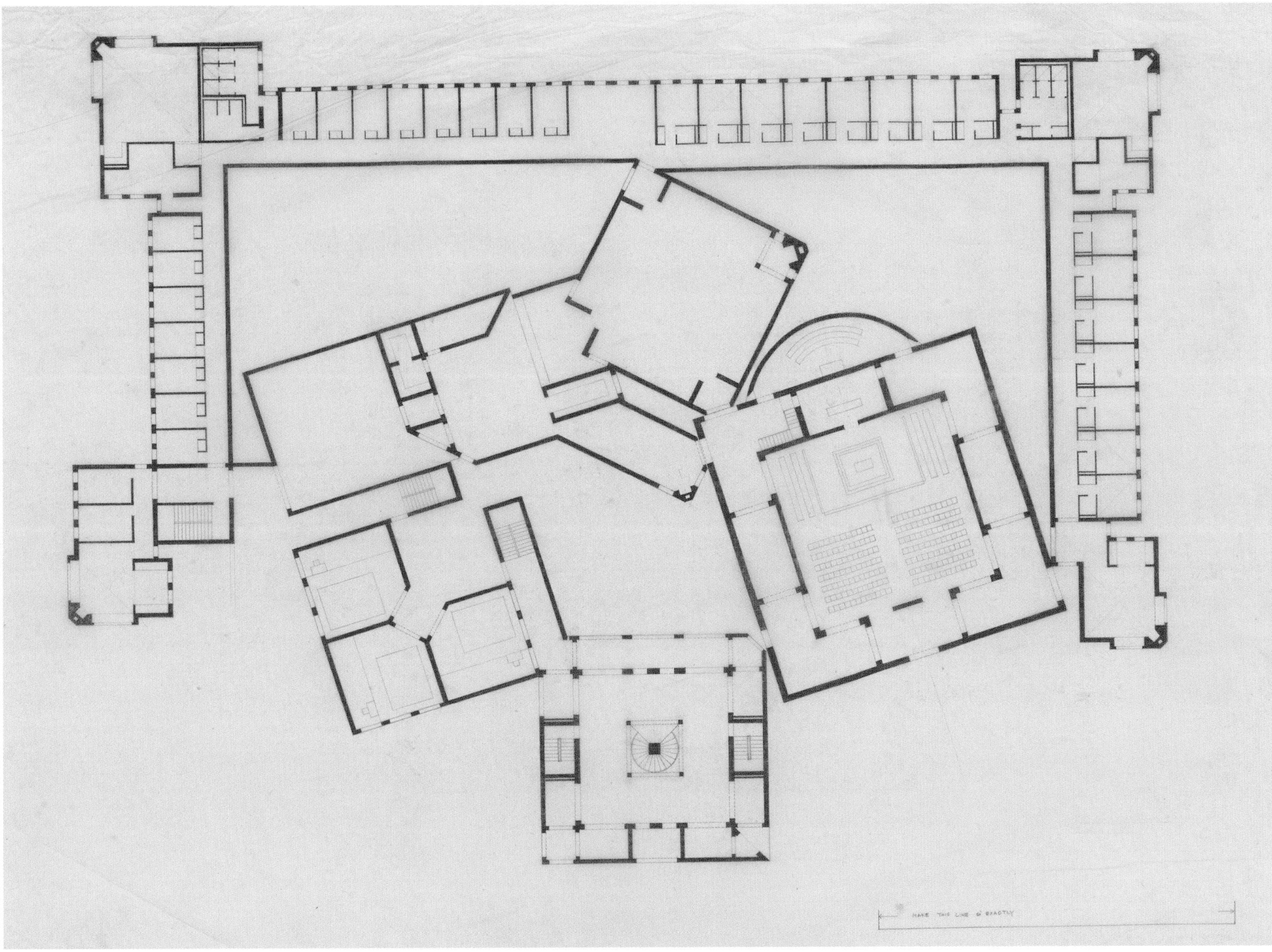

Louis Kahn's plan drawing of the Dominican Motherhouse of St. Catherine de Ricci, Media, Pennsylvania, dated April 22, 1968. Here one room connects directly to another, allowing spatial energy to flow actively between them, even as each space retains an identity of its own. *Louis I. Kahn Collection, The University of Pennsylvania and the Pennsylvania Historical and Museum Commission.*

direct spatial connections activating each specific room while at the same time energizing the whole. At first glance, the connecting spaces merely appear sequential, but in fact they set another threshold, thus altering the spatial hierarchy and, by extension, generating new social arrangements. From this perspective, there are many spatial elements that echo Aldo van Eyck's work of the same period. In class Kahn talked about how he hated corridors. He commented that he never really understood the true nature of such a space except as a rational link from one room to another, thus he deliberately tried to avoid them in his own work. I

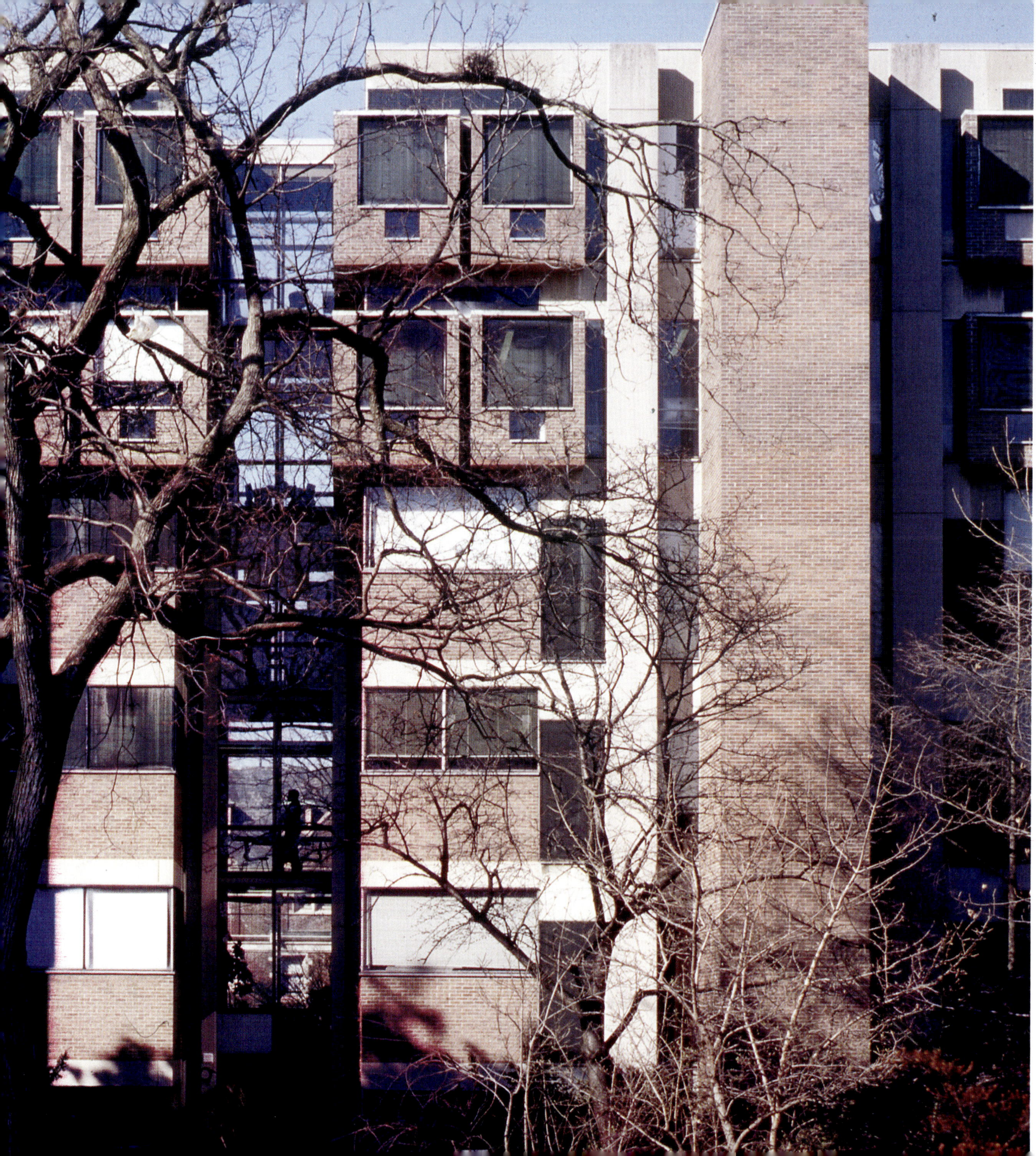

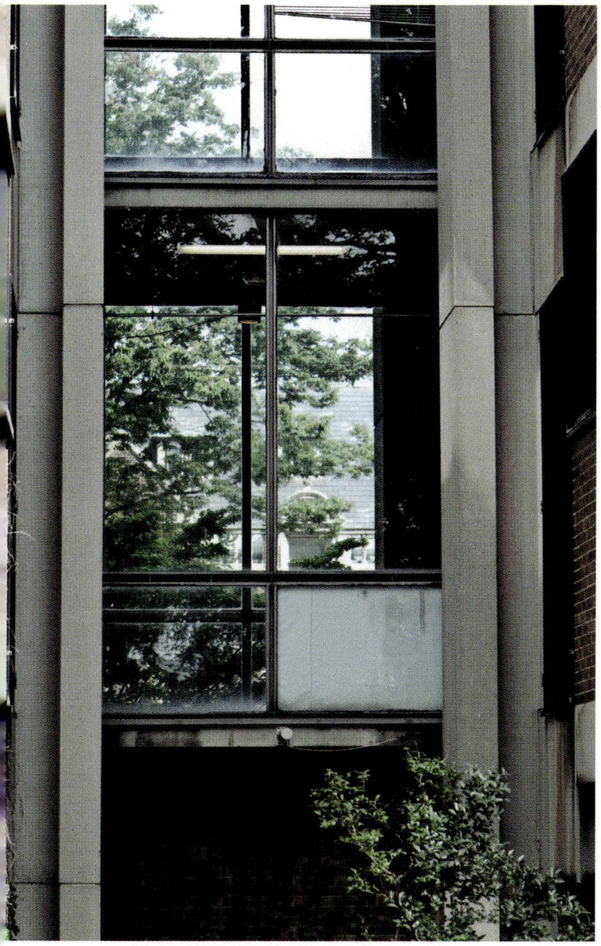

OPPOSITE: The Richards Medical Research Laboratories, Philadelphia, 1957–65. The laboratories are expressed as rooms that directly connect to the garden. *P. O. Fjeld.*

ABOVE: A spatial connection forms a relationship between two outside areas, the campus walk and the garden. *Jon Reksten.*

remember that after class a few of us looked at his plan for the Dominican Motherhouse of St. Catherine de Ricci, which sparked an all-night discussion. We tried to comprehend its spatial complexity—not just in the plan, but also in how one room invites itself to be part of another room and in the process transforms both spaces. This project introduced a spatial sequence that was both new and intriguing for most of us. Foreign in its expression, this work was deemed irrational by many architects who embraced the current methods of structure and prefabrication. Kahn felt very strongly about this project, but it would take some time before its strengths were widely acknowledged and linked to a larger international architectural discourse that included the work of van Eyck, among others.

Local

The "local"—understood not as a blind reliance on tradition but as a means to understand the local resources and work skills necessary for a project to be realized—was also important to Kahn's idea of "institution." Balkrishna Doshi, who had worked with Kahn on the campus for the Indian Institute of Management in Ahmedabad, described to me how Kahn's work gradually shifted ownership from the architect to the local community. Kahn's creative capacity would set a community's dream in motion, and for the local inhabitants it was through the building's making that it became their own work. In the masterclass, Kahn dwelt on this subject a number of times; in particular, he detailed the engagement and efforts of the local community in Exeter during the library project. He described how students, teachers, and friends carried the books into the new building, strengthening the library's identity as a collective institution.

The building of the Richards Medical Research Laboratories engaged the local in Kahn's more technically oriented sense of the term. The project was informed by the capacity of the construction crane and its position on the challenging site, and in turn, this influenced choices about the size and weight of the labs' prefabricated structural members. Kahn did not often dwell on anything mechanical in class, but the parameters and possibilities presented by the crane undoubtedly intrigued him. He emphasized the importance of retaining a balance between the size and the impact of the crane and its capacity and its relationship to the existing site—in this case, the garden and the university. Kahn understood "local" as a complicated and sensitive element within the creative process, as it could so easily be guided by context alone.

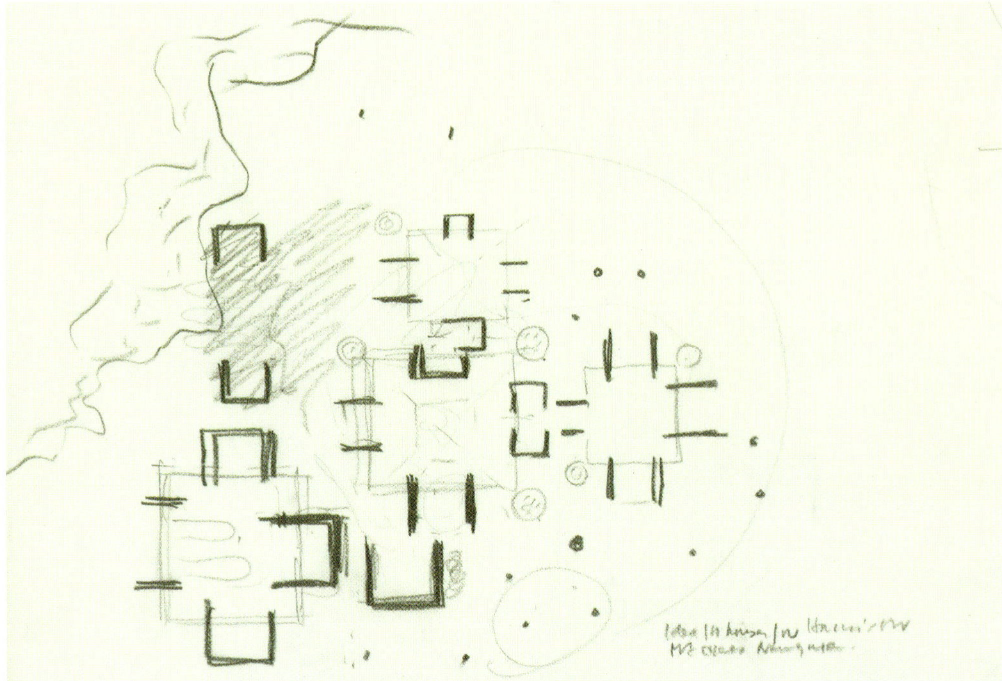

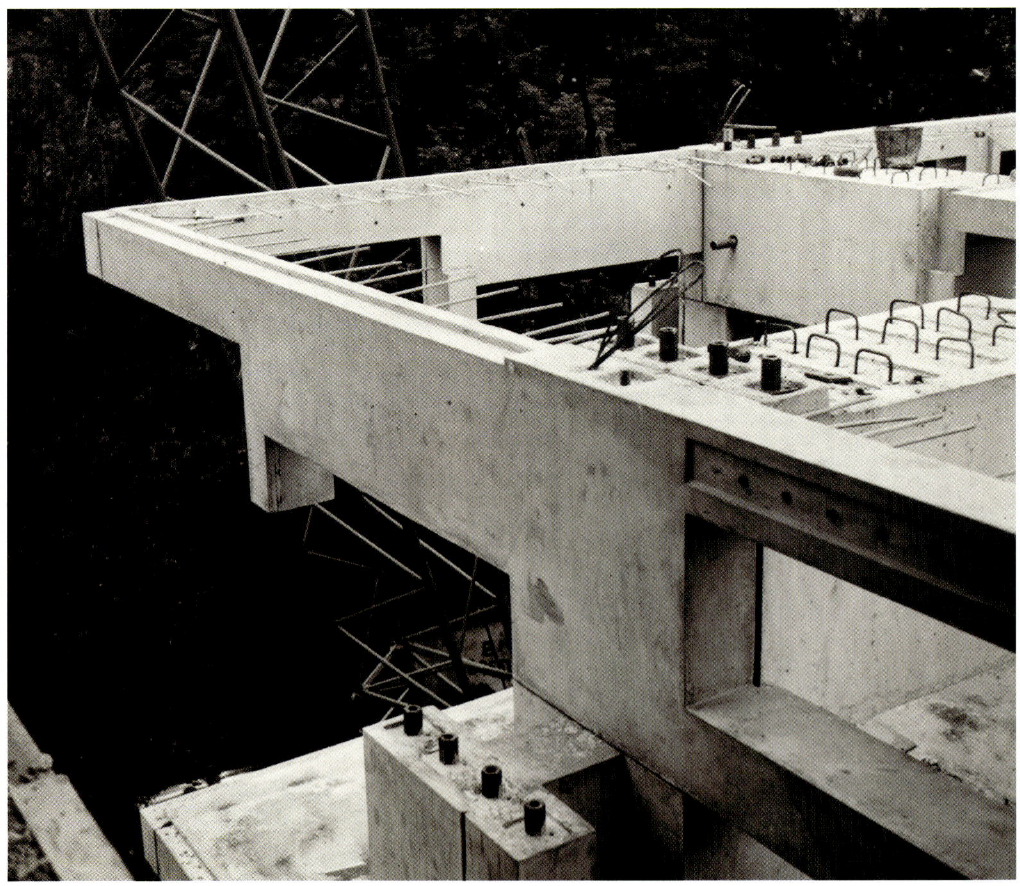

TOP: This early plan sketch of the Richards Medical Research Laboratories sheds light on how the project developed. *Louis I. Kahn Collection, The University of Pennsylvania and the Pennsylvania Historical and Museum Commission.*

RIGHT: Prefabricated structural members set in place by a crane. The crane's role in the construction of the labs came up in our class discussions. *Marshall D. Meyers Collection, The Architectural Archives, University of Pennsylvania.*

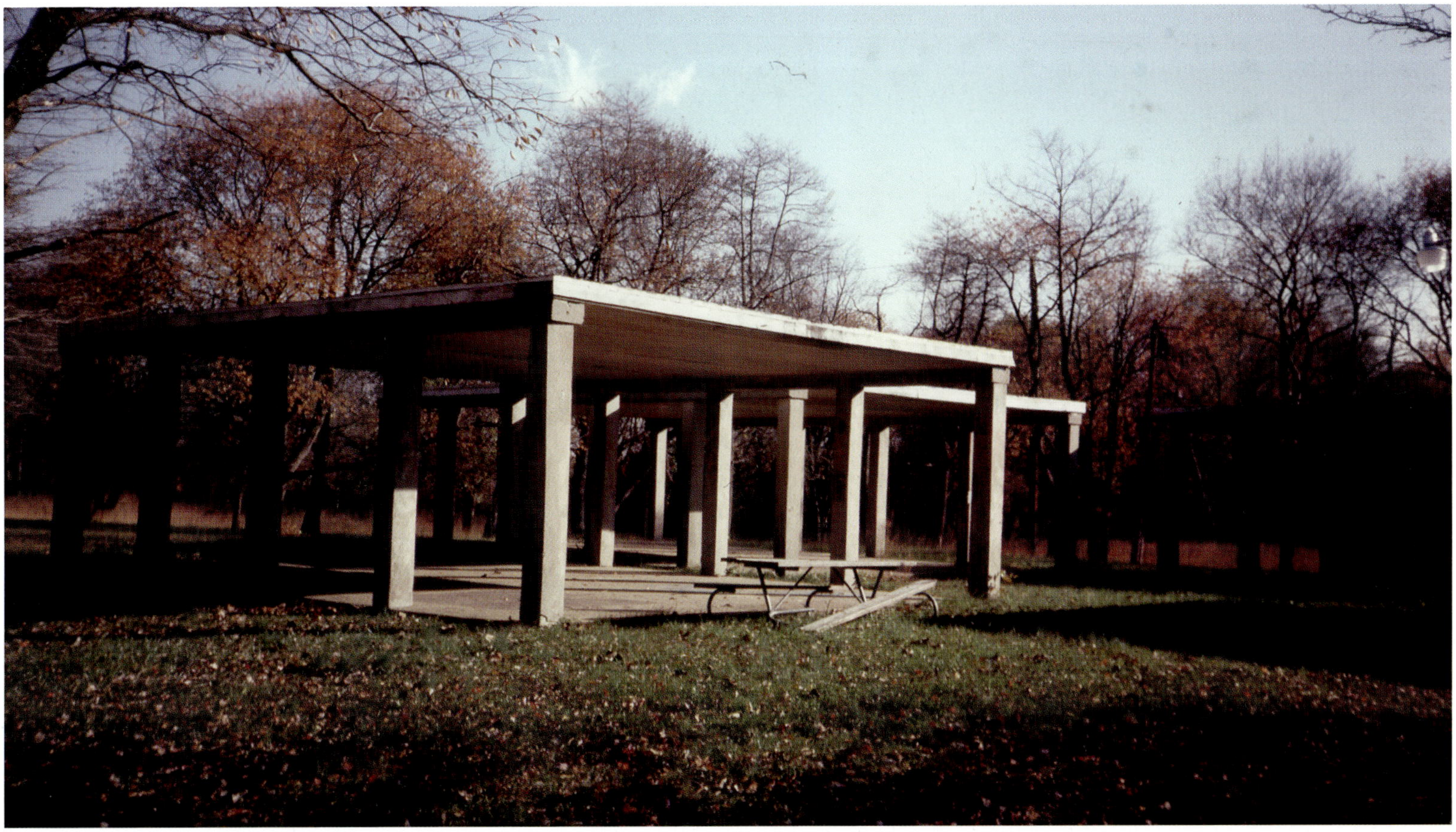

Abandoned structure at the Jewish Community Center, Trenton, N.J., 1955. This picture was taken in 1984 just before the center was put on the National Register of Historic Places. *P. O. Fjeld.*

Connecting Experience to "Knowing"

My first truly moving experience of the institutions of man in Kahn's work occurred while revisiting the Trenton Bath House in 1985. After many years of neglect the building looked like an abandoned ruin. The entrance mural had been painted over and the sandstone-block walls and the wood roof needed repair. Even in this sad state, however, the building seemed to exude a strong presence that existed beyond the memory of an earlier time. The hollow column, with its distinct light, served as the link between the communal, shared space and the more private areas, and the pyramid roof still gave identity to the central room and surroundings. After several hours of exploring the building, I left with the feeling of having lived my first meeting with Kahn all over again. The spatial energy that once permeated the bath house was still present, but it was holding on for dear life, waiting to be discovered anew.

On my way back to Philadelphia I grappled with how this of all his buildings could be so

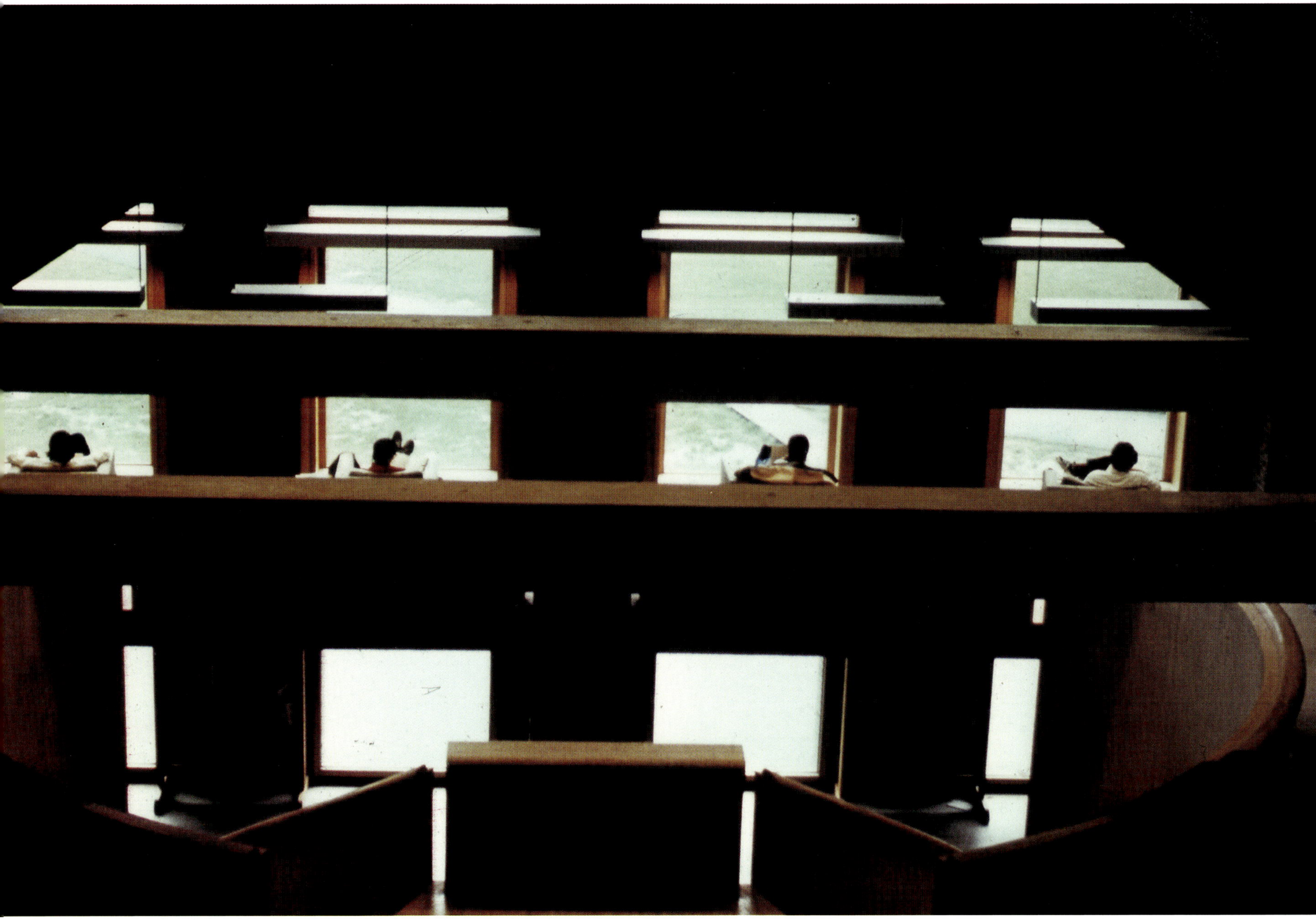

Phillips Exeter Academy Library, Exeter, New Hampshire, 1965–72. "A man with a book goes to the light. A library begins that way."—Louis Kahn. *P. O. Fjeld.*

thoroughly abandoned—and yet its present state was not out of line with Kahn's thinking that a building must fight for its existence over time. Back at the Kahn Collection, I went through the Trenton Bath House drawings again, and I wondered if the optimism that I detected in them was still embodied by the building I had just visited. I recalled that many young postwar architects regarded this modest institution as a breakthrough. Over the years, several of my older colleagues in Oslo had noted how this modest project had generated such enthusiasm at the start of their careers.

My first visit to the Phillips Exeter Academy Library took me through Kahn's idea of "institution" step-by-step. Reserved from the outside, the library nonetheless tells its story—the way it was made and what it can offer—beginning with its exterior. The open-arch space that encircles the exterior of the building serves as an introduction to the main entrance, but once inside, each structural layer generates different social conditions. Upon entering you climb the central staircase and quickly become aware of others, as the spatial sequence allows for numerous relationships between the individual and the collective. In facilitating this, the architecture does not force social interactions but enables them to unfold. The dramatic central space, the position of the librarian's office with its direct contact to the atrium, and the fireplace—none of which was part of the brief—embody all the insights that Kahn shared with us in the studio. The hidden music room overlooking the central space, the second-floor shelves lined with large picture books that skirt the atrium, the reading carrels with sliding shutters that allow users to control the amount of daylight on their desks—all are invitations to inhabit the building not as a to-and-from place, but as a place to dwell, as an extension of home. In this building all of my student notes concerning Kahn's architectural vocabulary are activated.

I visited the Salk Institute just weeks after graduation and stayed to observe it over several days. It simply felt good to be there. Although I was alone and did not have access to the interior of the buildings, spending time in the institute's outdoor spaces made me feel like I was part of a collective much larger than myself. The courtyard defined by concrete walls, with its particular light and open view to the sea, has neither program nor strategy. Altogether, it seems to blur time, sublimely encompassing both past and present with its abstract physicality. It is an architecture that draws its meaning from something much more enduring and human than mere commerce and entertainment. The Salk Institute belongs to the institutions of man, as it is truly collective and at the same time specific to each individual. Its spatial energy triggers moments of collective experience and shared inspiration.

Perhaps my most direct experience with Kahn's architecture of "institution" occurred

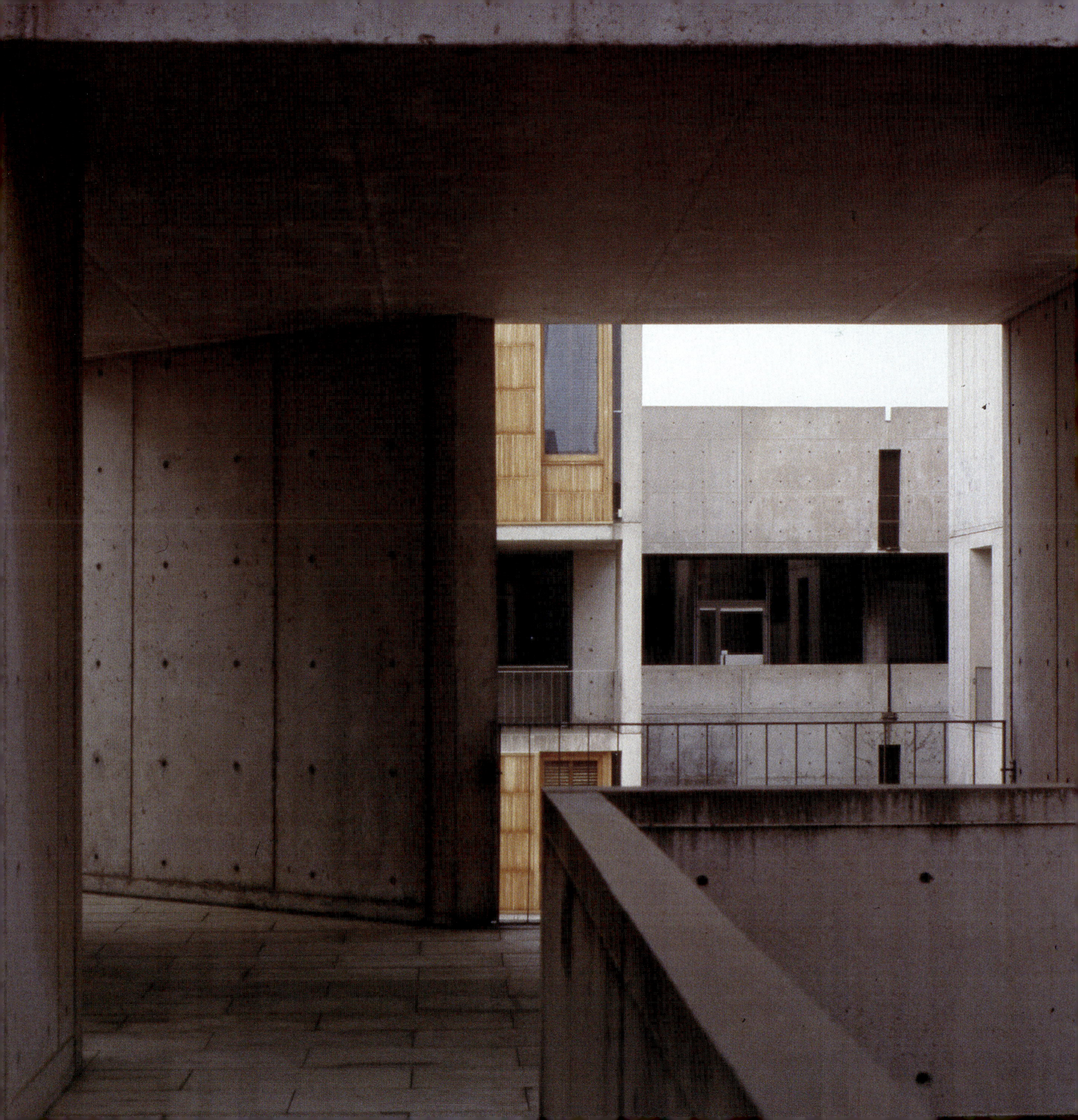

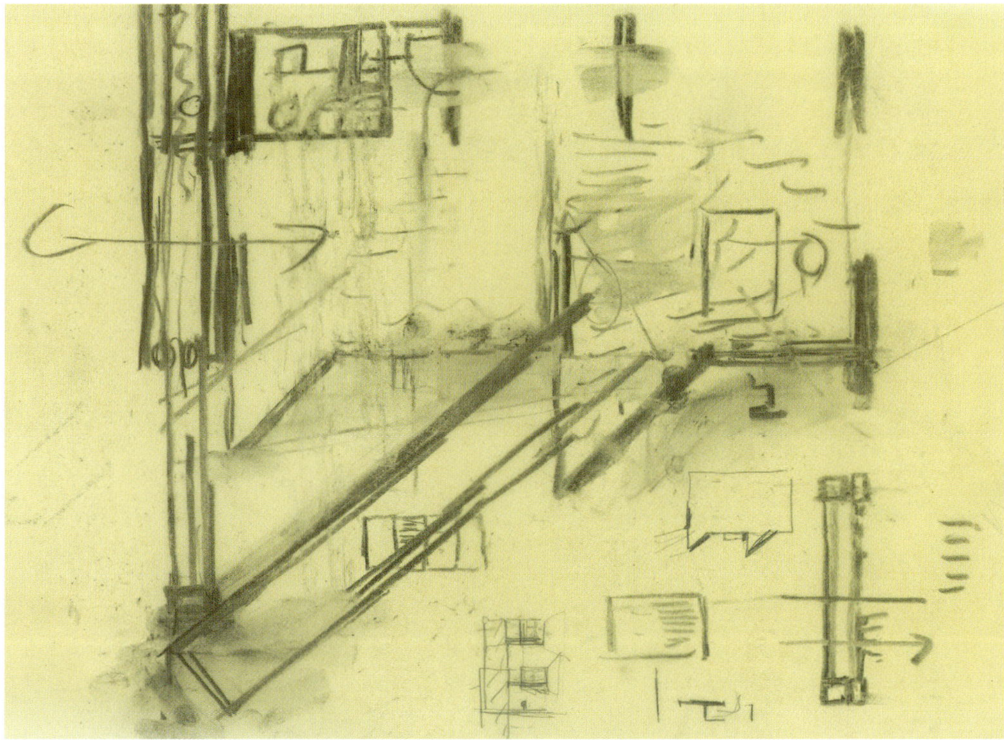

OPPOSITE: Entrance sequence to an individual studio cell at the Salk Institute for Biological Studies, La Jolla, California, 1959–65. *P. O. Fjeld.*

RIGHT: Kahn's sketch of an individual studio cell for the Salk Institute. As he described it: "The light of the exterior wall would modify the light in the interior, and you can look through the opening and see without drawing your blinds, so you can freely look through what's in back of it. This was a forerunner of what I did in the synagogue, and Dhaka and all the rest, the realization of this." *Louis I. Kahn Collection, The University of Pennsylvania and the Pennsylvania Historical and Museum Commission.*

during my initial trip to the First Unitarian Church of Rochester. I had prepared for my visit in the Kahn Collection—going over the drawings and reading many related notes and articles along with everything about Kahn's Silence and Light diagram. Expecting a reflective, sacral experience, I was taken by surprise: That day the church was transformed into a bazaar. Enthusiasm, laughter, and joy filled the central room—and I experienced a humanness that deeply moved me. All of Kahn's comments about circumstance seemed to fall into place, as the building's inherent capacity accommodated various activities and social gatherings. The following day, a Sunday, I entered that same central room, now a quiet, sacral room, and yet the architecture had not changed. I met the light and the same people as I had the day before.

Each fall semester over the past fifteen years, my studio class at the Oslo School of Architecture and Design has taken a study trip to New York, and quite often we make a side trip to visit Kahn's two museums at Yale University. The closed exterior wall of the Yale University Art Gallery, with its come-along entrance and the busy street and sidewalk pressed up against its long facade, always takes my students by surprise. Although they anticipate the much-published ceiling inside, the interior spaces likewise take them by surprise.

Then we cross the street to the Yale Center for British Art and gather in the large room

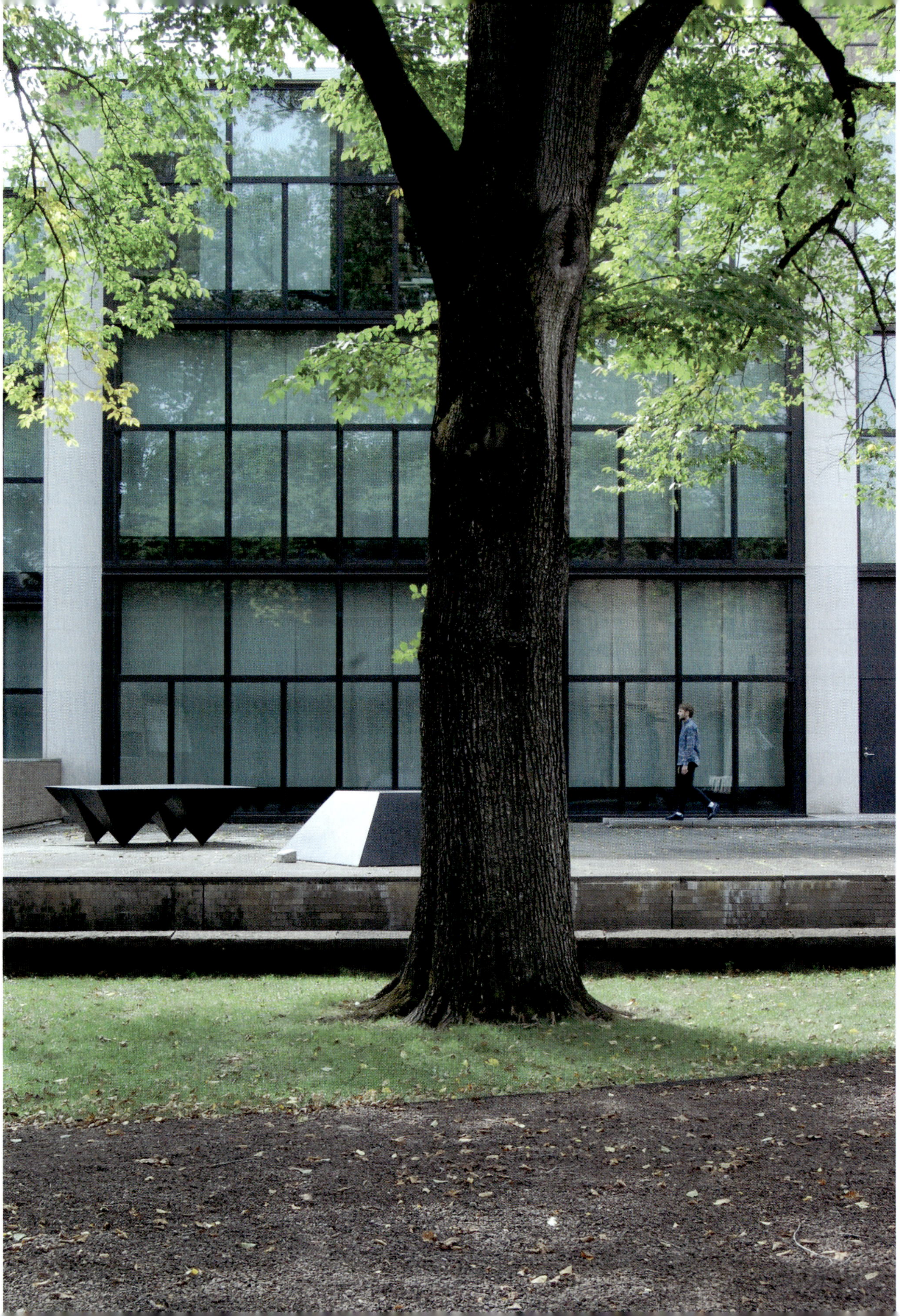

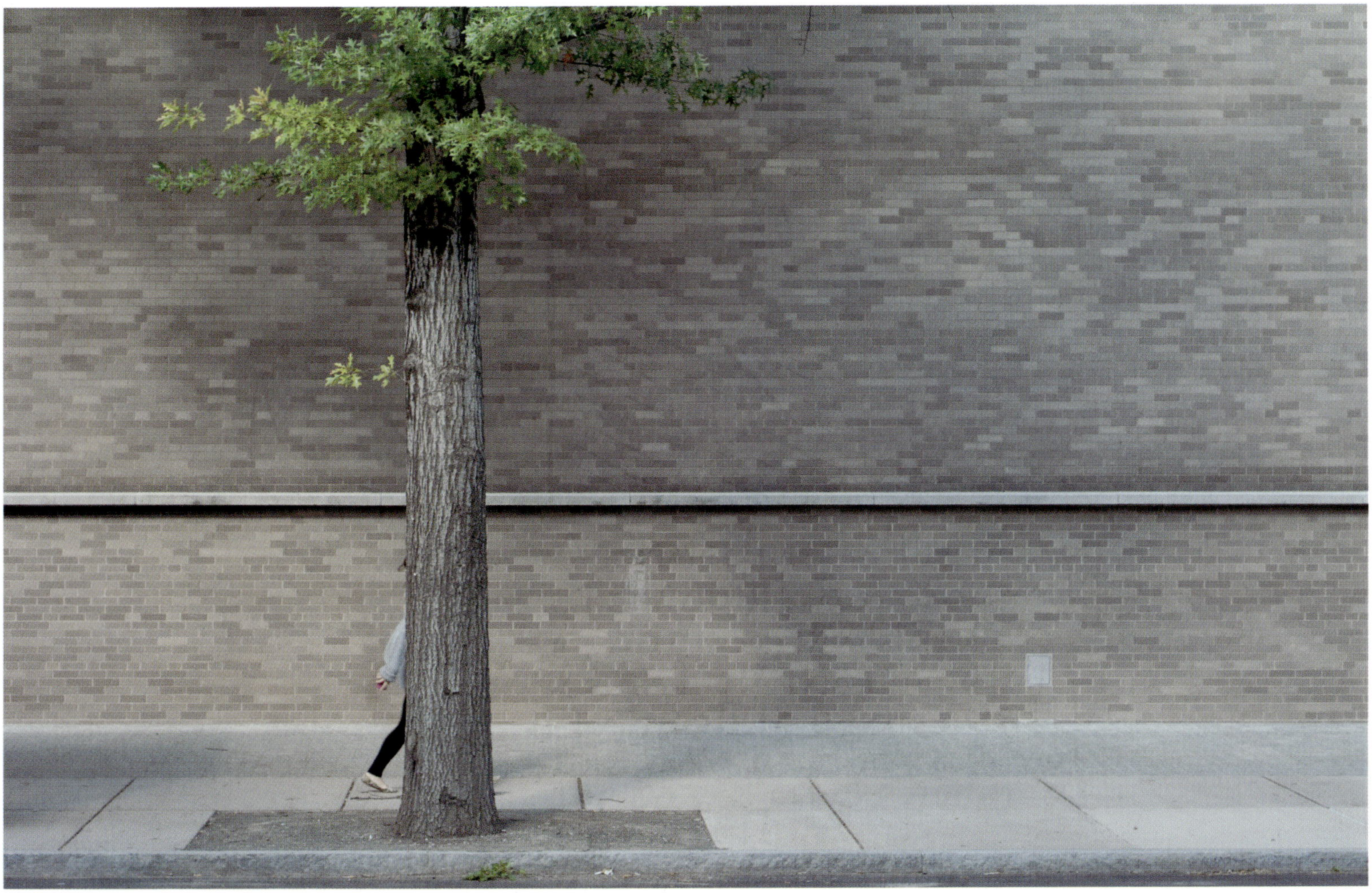

OPPOSITE: View of the interior court looking on to a glass wall of the Yale University Art Gallery. *Daniel Aarset Loe.*

ABOVE: The Yale University Art Gallery's closed facade facing the street reinforces the directional activity of the sidewalk and the adjacent street. *Rolf Gerstlauer.*

facing the hollow column for a short talk. The students, half asleep in the large leather sofas, pretend to be listening, but more importantly, a sense of calm overcomes the group and my enthusiastic talk about the fine concrete work and Kahn's standard cut grooves in the wood panels. The room slowly cuts out my teacher's voice and draws us into the immeasurable part of architecture.

In my dreams I envision the plan from the air, and hardly anything is there. When I stepped into the Kimbell Art Museum, the dream as a physical structure, *architecture*, was the only thing there—with me everywhere. For those who have visited, no further description is necessary.

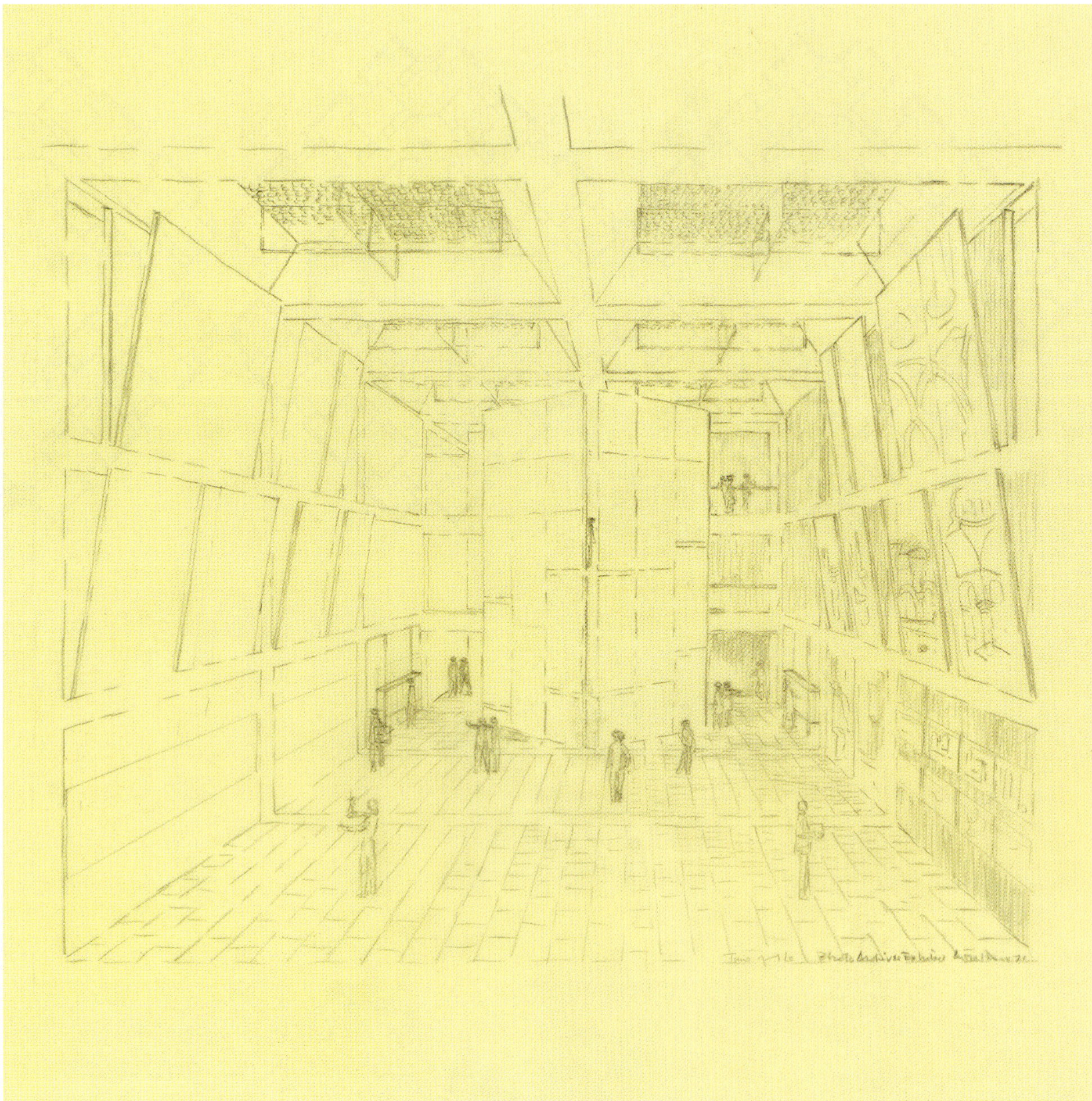

RIGHT: A drawing by Louis Kahn showing the main exhibition space at the Yale Center for British Art. In it, Kahn proposes an active relationship between the room, the paintings, and the visitor. *Louis I. Kahn Collection, The University of Pennsylvania and the Pennsylvania Historical and Museum Commission.*

OPPOSITE: Top-floor entrance to the large hollow column at the Yale Center for British Art. *Jon Reksten.*

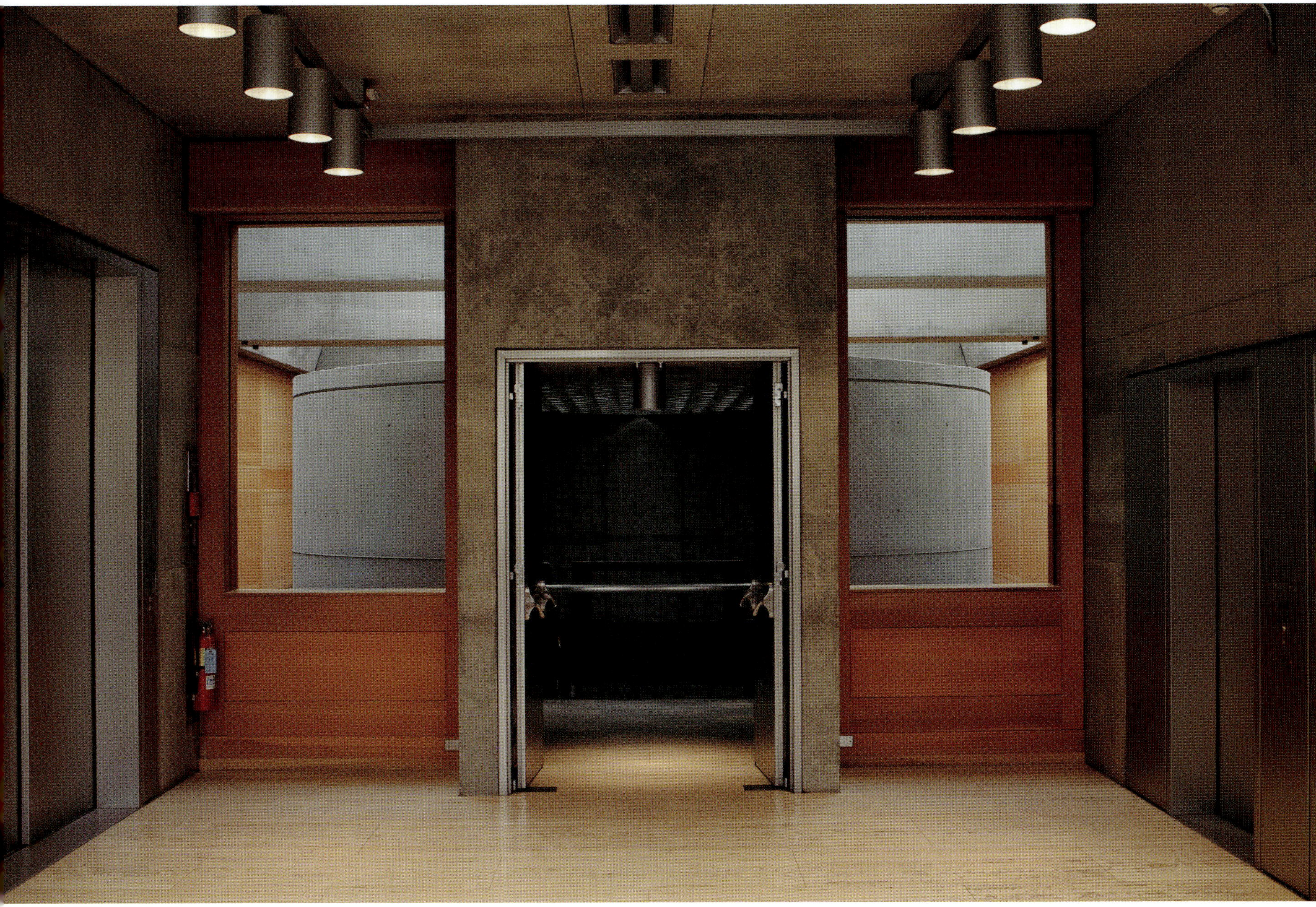

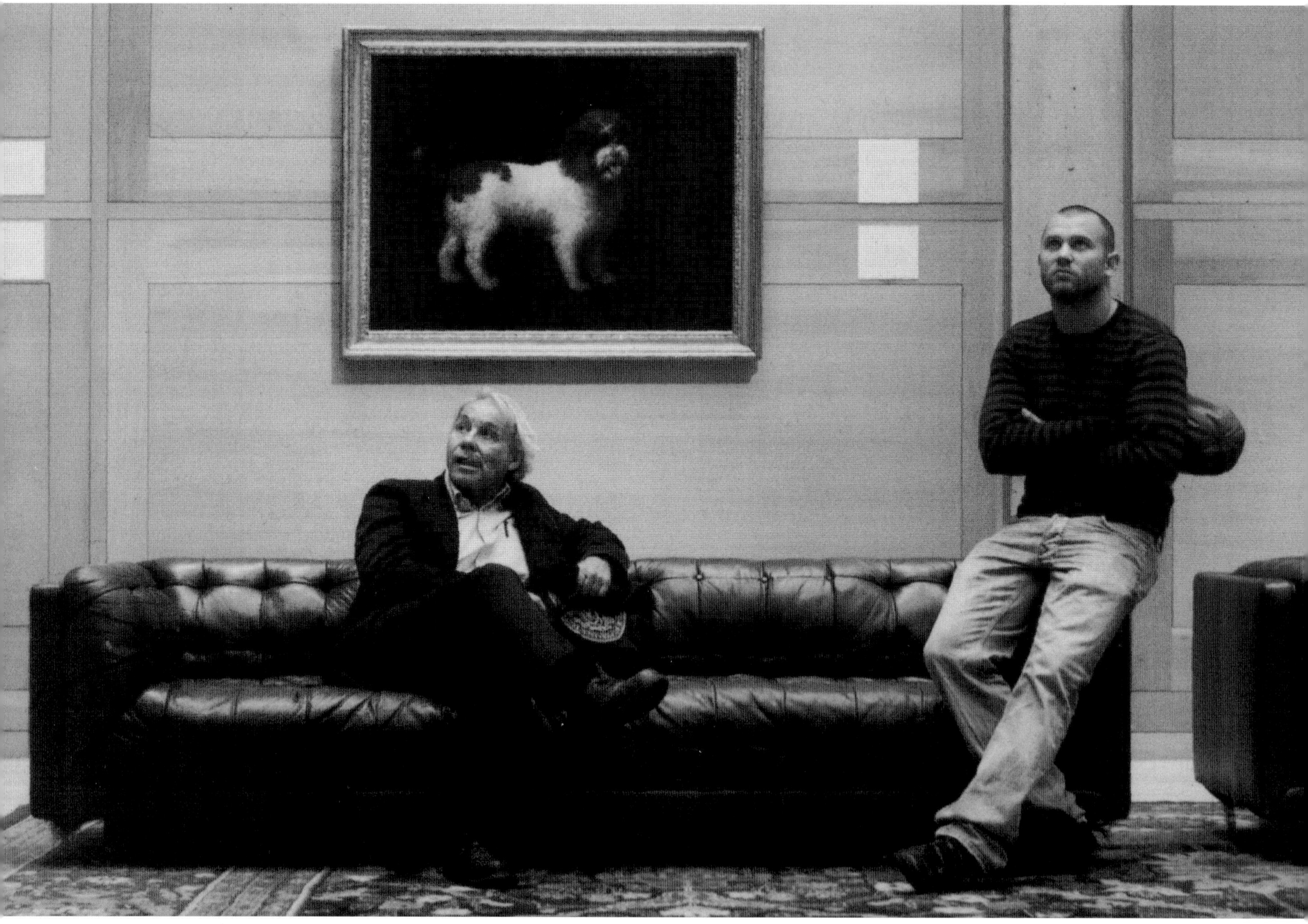

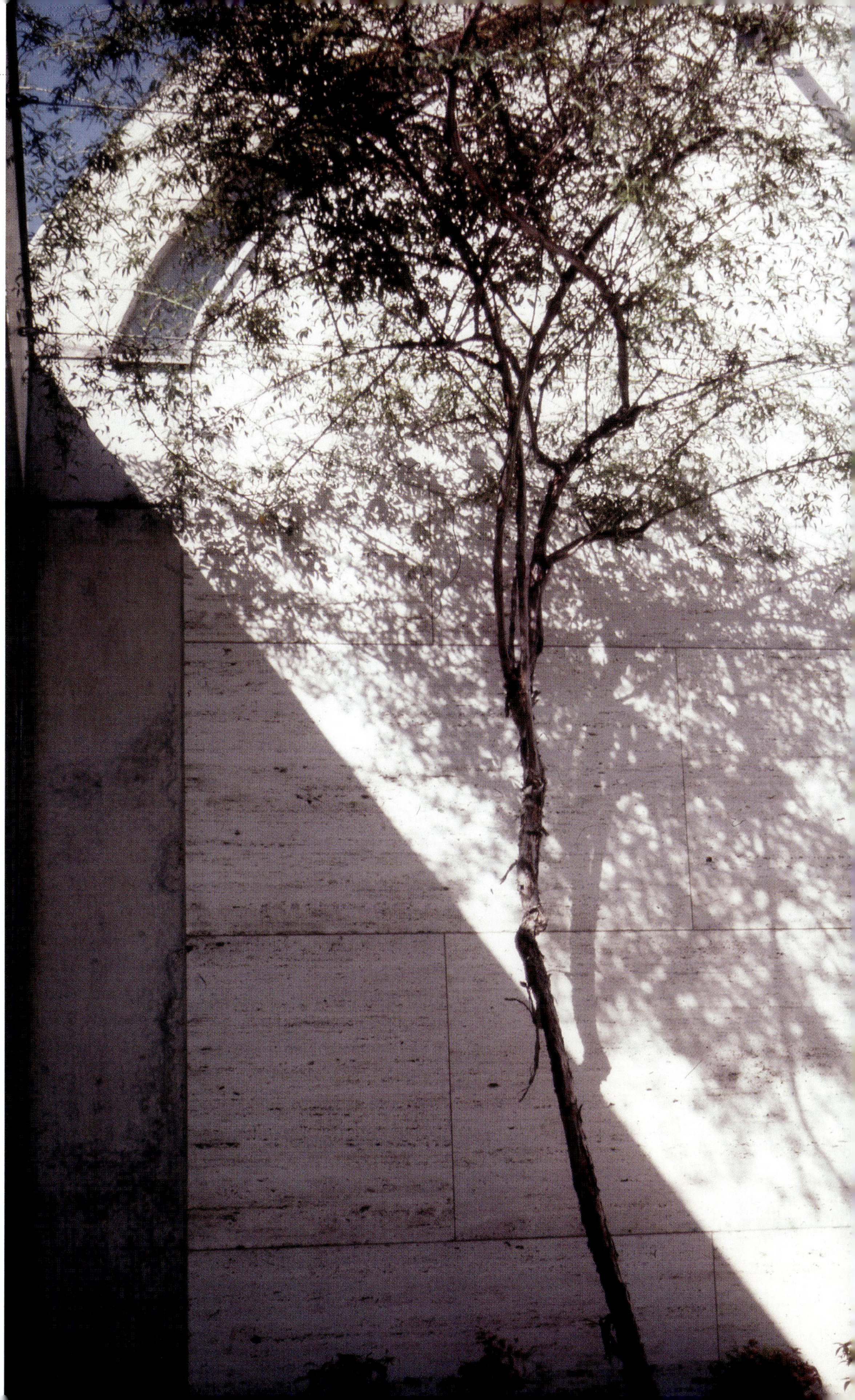

OPPOSITE: Per Olaf Fjeld pictured on one of the sofas at the Yale Center for British Art admiring Kahn's craft along with a student. *Annette Apold.*

RIGHT: A courtyard at the Kimbell Art Museum, Fort Worth, Texas, 1966–72. Kahn named each of the courtyards—Yellow Court, Blue Court, and Green Court—according to a principal aspect of their daylight or natural conditions. *P. O. Fjeld.*

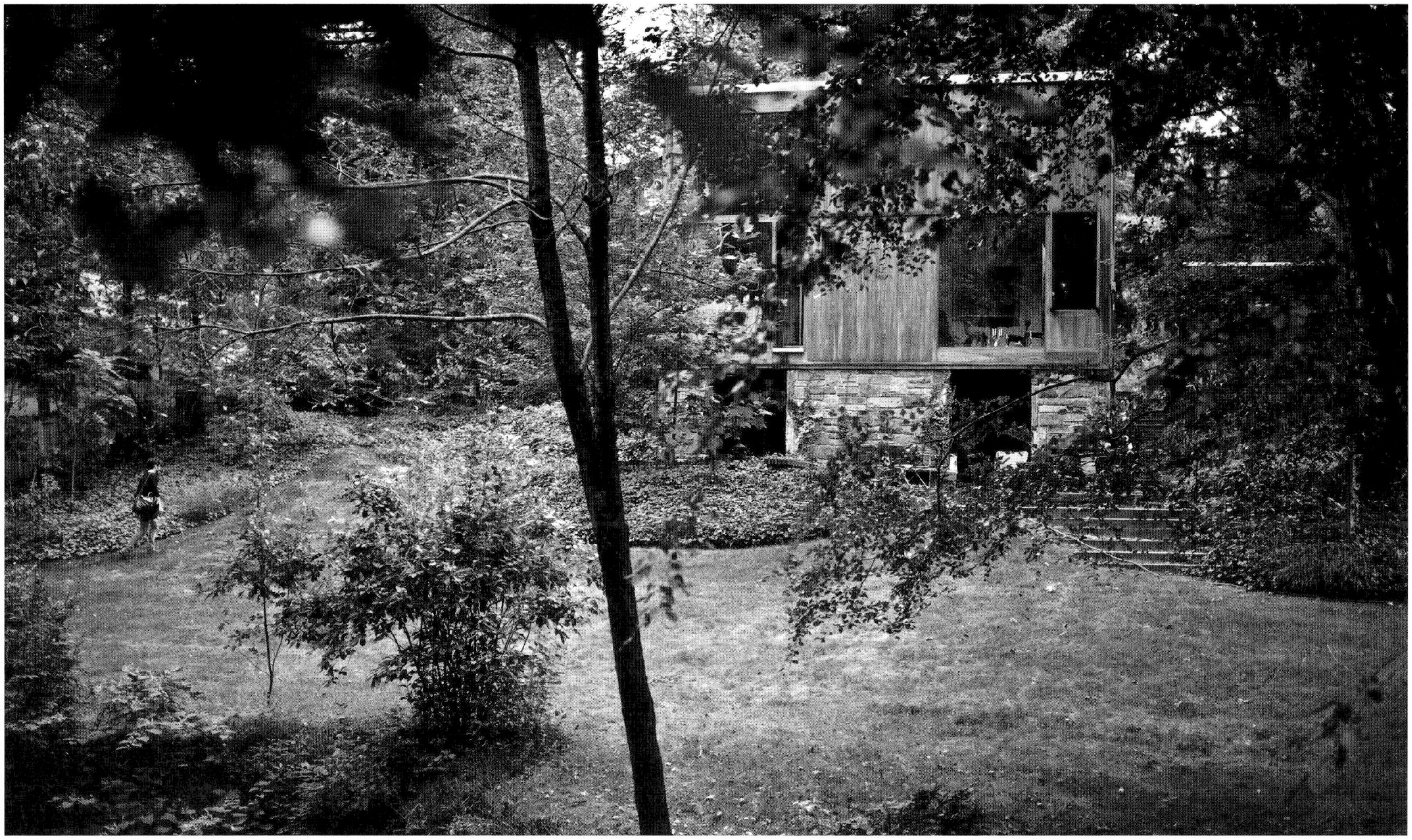

ABOVE: Exterior of the Fisher House, Hatboro, Pennsylvania, 1960–67. *Jon Reksten.*

OPPOSITE: Interior detail of the Fisher House living room looking out to the wooded site. The red sticker indicates an object on its way to a new home. *P. O. Fjeld.*

I will end this journey of personal experiences that illuminated Kahn's concept of "institutions" for me with the Fisher House, which I visited most recently a few years ago. I had been in the house earlier with a group, but this time I visited it alone with Bill Whitaker, the curator of the Kahn Collection at Penn. The house would soon be up for sale: Mrs. Fisher had moved out and her daughters were there to pack. This was an emotional experience I will never forget. As the day went on, the sisters told me about their home, their hidden in-between places, each room gently rekindling memories of things that had once shaped their lives, as more and more boxes with red tags filled the van outside. "Living" and its journey were packed up that day, and the red tags indicated a new destiny. Soon the house would rely on its sense of "institution" anew, and within this moment of transformation I saw the house as neither old nor new. For the first time in fifty years, the Fisher House as a home seemed to rehearse its form drawing once again.

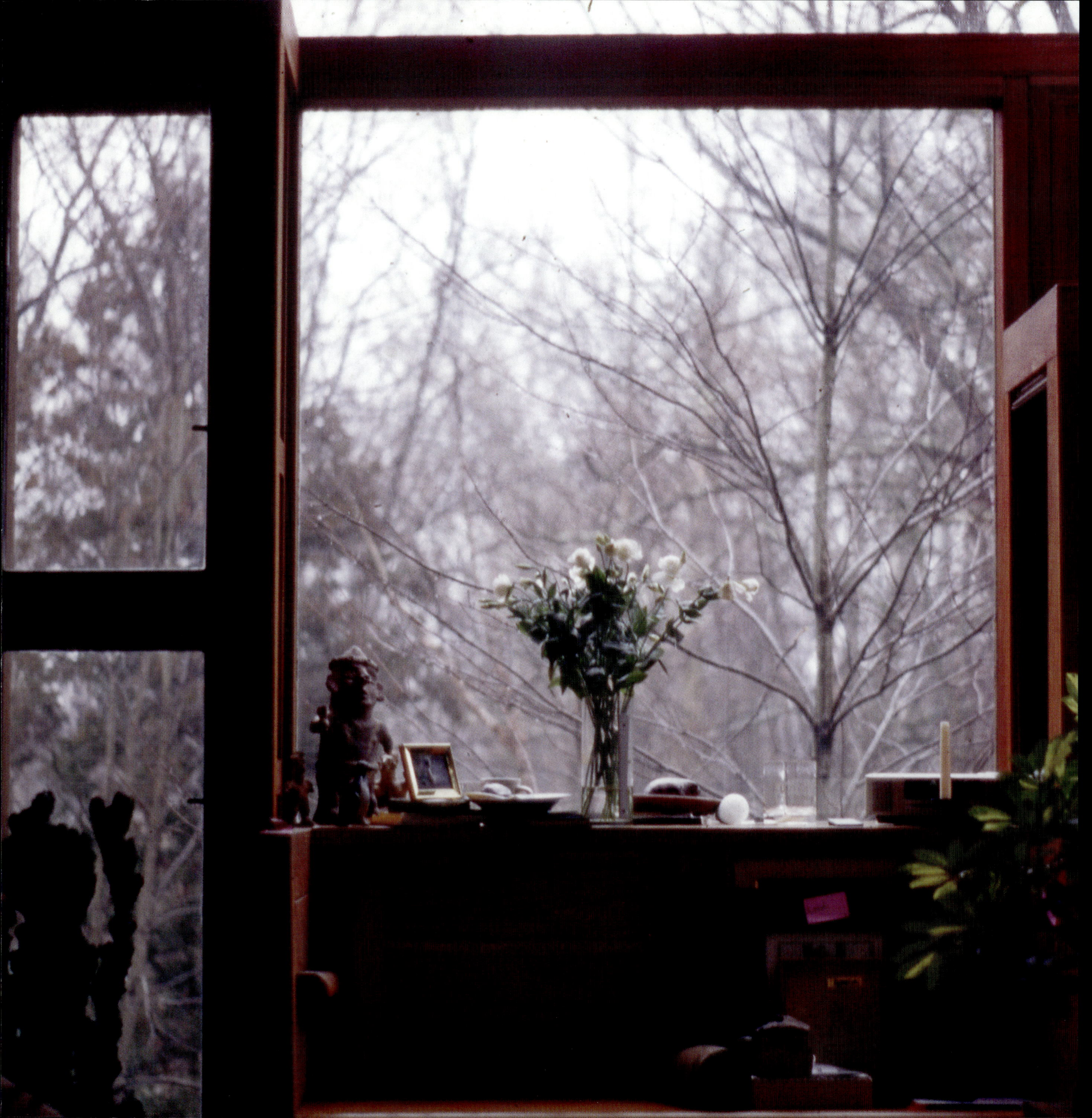

THE WAY THE EARTH MOVES

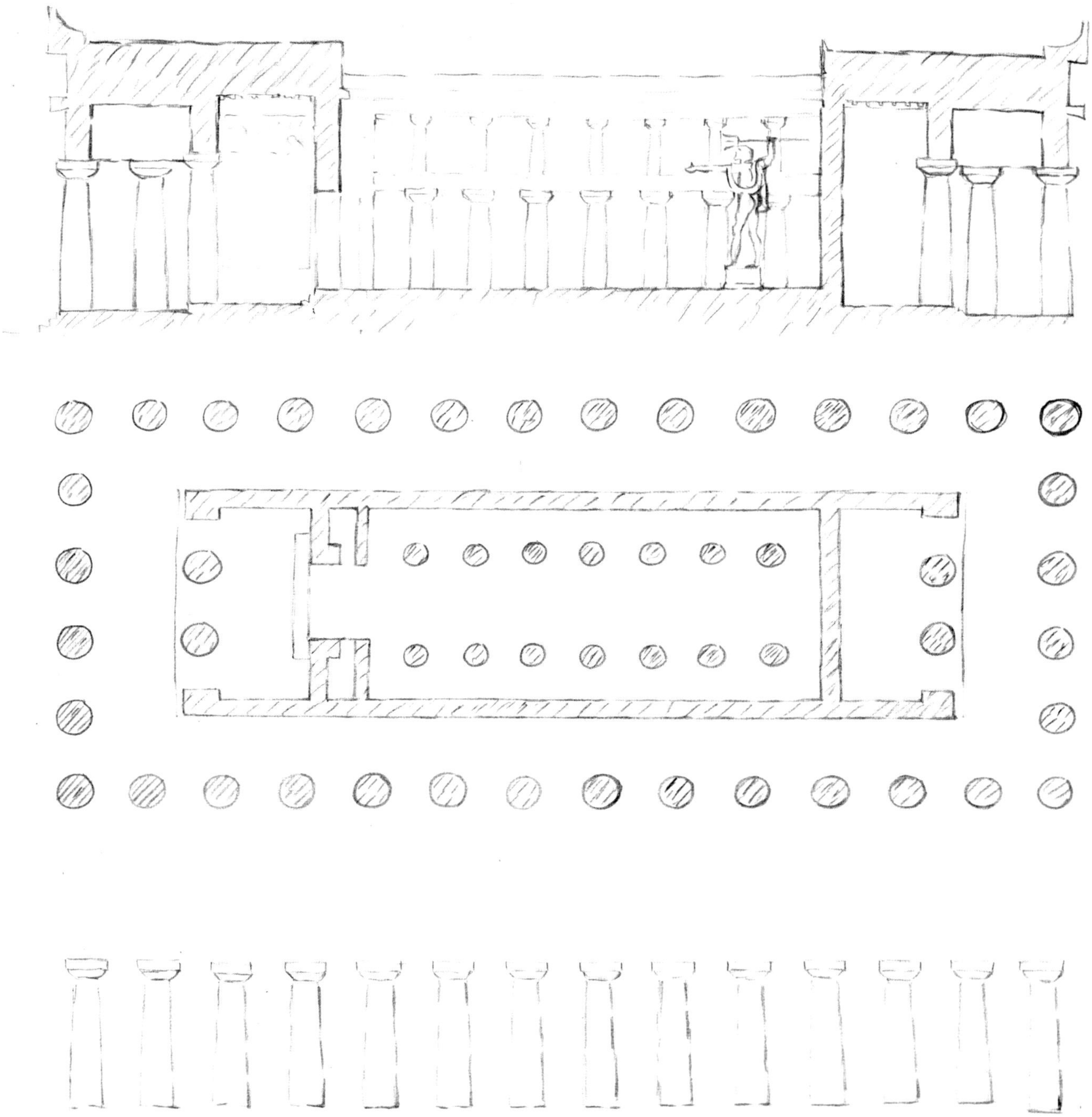

5 TEN YEARS LATER: INVESTIGATIONS INTO MASS

Kahn's plan and section sketches of the Second Temple of Hera, Paestum, 1969. "How marvelous it was when the wall parted and how column became how the rhythm of the decision of what is a void and what is solid. We are still living under the marvel of that wonderful creation that came completely out of nothing."—Louis Kahn. *Louis I. Kahn Collection, University of Pennsylvania and the Pennsylvania Historical and Museum Commission.*

After several years of my working in Sverre Fehn's office, there was a slump in the Norwegian economy, and his office had only a few small projects in the works. Emily and I decided that the best course forward for us was to open our own studio, where she could concentrate on her artwork and help me with architectural work as needed. Our start was challenging, and with only a few small commissions on the table, it meant freelancing in other offices to make ends meet. The slow transformation of my six-and-a-half-year American education into a Nordic mind-set was still ongoing, and my so-called foreign education (Kahn or no Kahn) was not regarded as an advantage at this time. In addition, some elements of the first wave of international postmodernist thinking had marginally entered Nordic architectural discourse, and Kahn's work was, to its detriment, at times associated with it.

On many levels, my friendship with Ingrid and Sverre Fehn played an important role during these years, notably in expanding my knowledge of European architecture and in helping me retain the core essence of what I had learned from Kahn. My first visits to works by Asplund, Lewerentz, and van Eyck were all inspired by Fehn. Undoubtedly, for Fehn these works brought to mind his teachers Arne Korsmo and Knut Knutsen; but for me they evoked Kahn. During this interval after graduation, I began to work on my first book on Fehn, *Sverre Fehn: The Thought of Construction.* Our weekly sessions for that undertaking brought our two small families close together. During this time, teaching in Fehn's studio class at the Oslo School of Architecture turned from an occasional freelance opportunity into an important part of my life.

Despite all this activity, I longed for the opportunity to study Kahn's creative approach in depth and, in a sense, to come to terms with my own direction as an architect and teacher. Postmodernist thinking was then affecting many schools' curricula on some level, and the conflicting perceptions of Kahn's architectural legacy were unresolved. Happily, in late 1983 I received a Fulbright–Hays grant to study Louis Kahn's work through the Kahn Collection at the University of Pennsylvania.

A few weeks before my departure, Fehn and I spent five working sessions on an article titled "Has a Doll Life?" for *Perspecta 24: The Yale Architectural Journal.* Fehn was aware of my ambitions for my upcoming trip, so in preparation for the article we talked about his recent visits to Philadelphia and New Haven, as well as his teacher Arne Korsmo. We agreed from the start that materiality and the notion of mass should be the central topic of our piece, but as always with Fehn, the conversation took its own course. Thus it jumped energetically from a focus on "material as mass" to the spirit of an object (hence the article's title).

In reviewing the notes from these five sessions many years later, I was struck that Fehn's understanding of mass touched on many of the same issues that concerned Kahn—in terms

1974 | Kahn dies in New York following a work trip to India.
Kahn's Indian Institute of Management completed.
Kahn's Project Palazzo dei Congressi terminated.
Charles Moore, Donlyn Lyndon, and Gerald Allen's *The Place of Houses* published.
Willem Dudok dies.

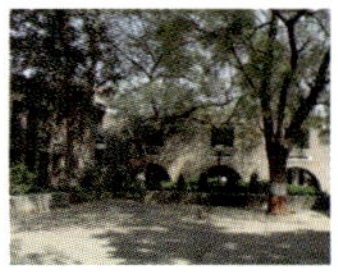

Indian Institute of Management. *Herman Neukermans.*

1975 | Vietnam War ends. Romaldo Giurgola and Jaimini Mehta's *Louis I. Kahn* published.
Ricardo Bofill's Walden 7 housing complex completed.
Sigurd Lewerentz dies.

1976 | ILAUD founded by Giancarlo De Carlo.
Jørn Utzon's Bagsværd Church completed.
Alvar Aalto dies.

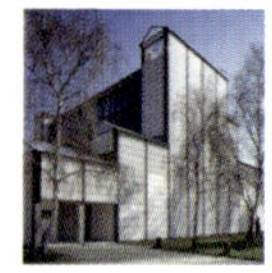

Bagsværd Church. *P. O. Fjeld.*

not just of a material discussion, but also of how material as mass alters the relationship between nature and architecture. During these sessions, Fehn expressed positions closely aligned with Kahn's idea of the institutions of man, especially regarding their role in urban life. In addition, he elaborated on some of the urban proposals put forward by Danish architect, historian, and theorist Steen Eiler Rasmussen. (Later I discovered that Rasmussen had served as a guest professor at Penn in 1958. It is possible that Kahn had met him before that time, when Rasmussen was a guest professor at Yale in 1954. Regardless, Kahn was certainly familiar with Rasmussen's writing much earlier than both of his stints as a visiting professor.)

The summer following my Fulbright research in Philadelphia, I befriended the Swedish architect and professor Bengt Edman. In a very precise and direct manner, Edman expanded my understanding of the relationship between Nordic culture and its architecture. I recently rediscovered an old letter that he wrote to me at the time. Enclosed with it was his rough draft for an article about Sigurd Lewerentz's St. Mark's in Björkhagen and St. Peter's in Klippan for the magazine *Spazio e Società*. Lewerentz's work was often a topic of conversation between the two of us, and on several occasions during our ILAUD years Peter Smithson also took part. These were enlightening discussions, as Edman had firsthand knowledge of Lewerentz and his buildings. He interpreted the churches as direct, lived experience as well as embodiments of Kahn's concepts of "the laws of nature" and "man the human."

Visiting St. Mark's and St. Peter's was a priority in Fehn's studio class; if no visit was scheduled during a particular year, he encouraged his students to make the trip on their own. Very early in our friendship, Fehn lent Emily and me his car to visit a house he built in Norköping, Sweden; he suggested we also stop by St. Peter's, the Malmö Eastern Cemetery, and the Flower Kiosk.

In recognition of the importance of Lewerentz's St. Mark's and St. Peter's to the Nordic region, here I am including Bengt Edman's article in its original rough-draft form—almost as a Nordic bridge from Kahn on mass to Fehn on mass, from one generation to the next.

I will first explore Kahn's ideas about mass before sharing my notes from my sessions with Fehn and the letter from Edman, which illuminate their own ideas about mass.

Kahn on Mass

Early in his career, Kahn was fascinated with modern technology and the performance of cutting-edge materials. He believed that the new structural opportunities these presented could revitalize architecture and give it new direction. At the time, many engineers and archi-

1977 Yale Center for British Art completed. Renzo Piano and Richard Rogers's Pompidou Center completed. Charles Jencks's *The Language of Post-Modern Architecture* published.

Robert Le Ricolais, Uno Åhrén, Franco Albini, and Gregor Paulsson die.

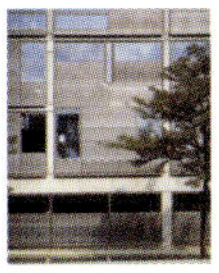

Yale Center for British Art. *P. O. Fjeld.*

1978 Aldo van Eyck's Hubertus House completed. Charles Moore's Piazza d'Italia built in New Orleans. Berlin State Library by Hans Scharoun and Edgar Wisniewski completed. Carlo Scarpa's Brion Tomb and Sanctuary completed. Rem Koolhaas's *Delirious New York* published.

Charles Eames dies.

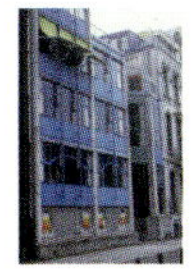

Hubertus House. *Margrethe Dobloug.*

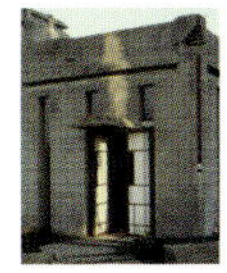

Brion Tomb and Sanctuary. *P. O. Fjeld.*

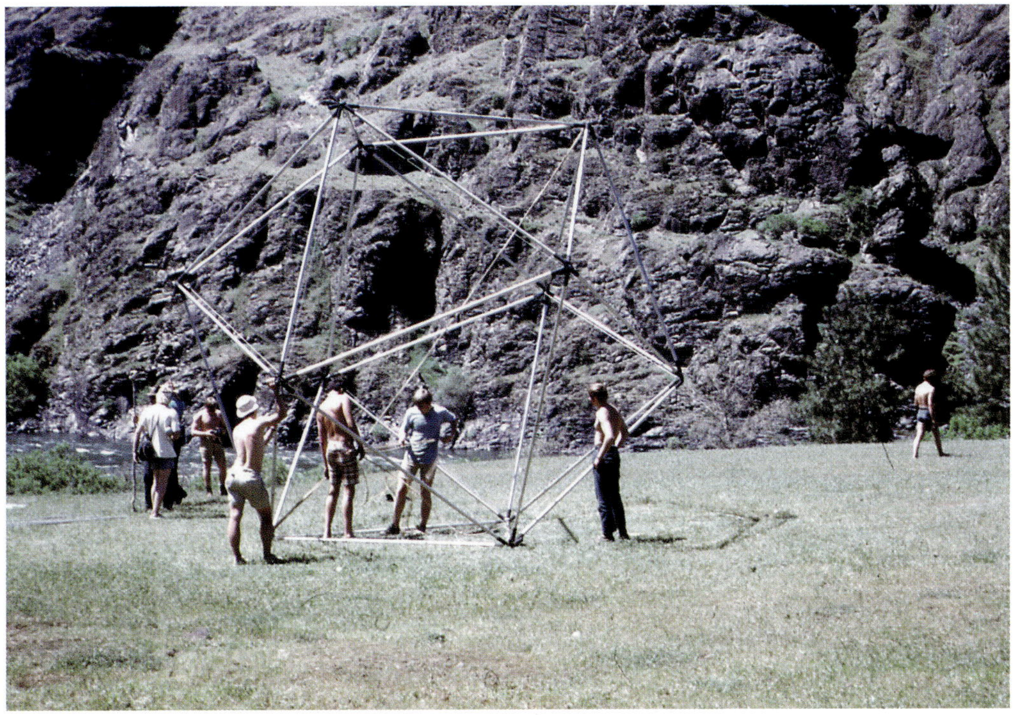

In line with the trends of the time, my fellow classmates at Washington State University and I built this lightweight structure in 1969. Hells Canyon was our testing ground. Each student team developed its own prefabricated structure, which we inhabited as geometric tents. At night, we projected images on the nearby mountainside. *P. O. Fjeld.*

tects were working to achieve the most rational and effective structures with less material—with less weight or mass. Buckminster Fuller, with his geodesic dome structures and investigations into mass-produced housing, was a strong promoter of this new direction.

Prefabrication and standardization became key topics of discussion both within education and the profession, which led to some interesting experimentation. Well into the late 1960s students at many architectural schools were building their own full-scale geodesic domes and other lightweight structures—works that embodied a radical social shift between generations. Thus to build, inhabit, and finally destroy your own lightweight structure was seen by many as emblematic of a new agenda. In discourse that favored the temporary and the prefabricated, Kahn's work was usually sidelined.

However, Kahn showed an interest in lightweight structures and materials in his early work. In the unbuilt 1944 project for a civic center, Kahn used a steel structure in testing a new form of monumentality. That same year he developed an experimental project for the Knoll Associates Planning Unit, the Parasol Houses, which consisted of square roof slabs

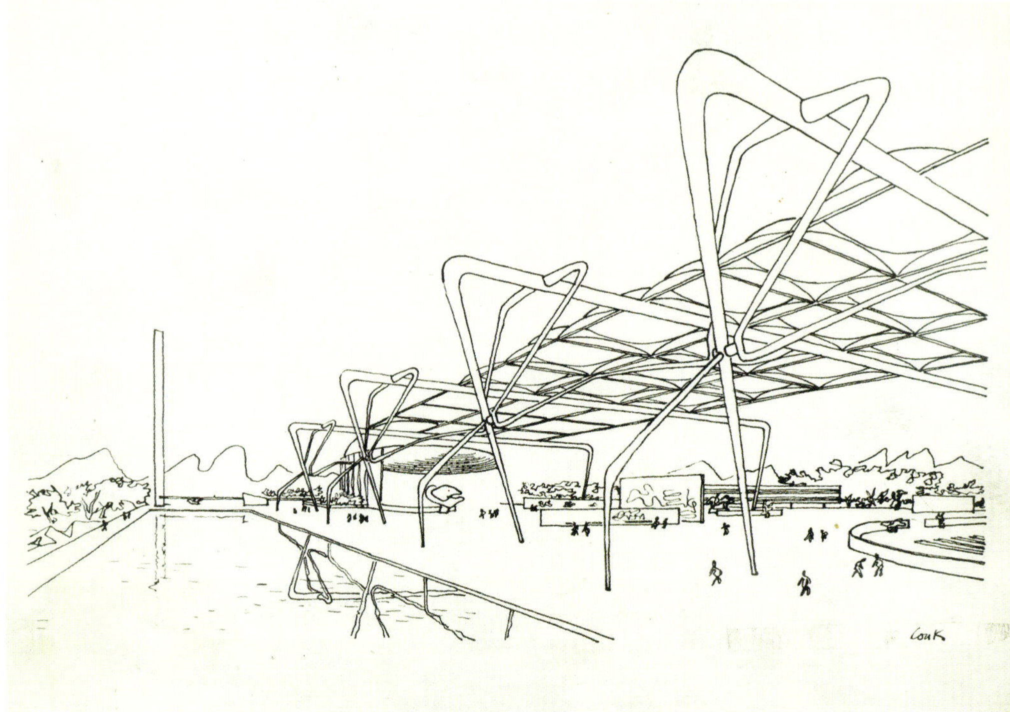

TOP: Louis Kahn's illustration of part of his unbuilt Civic Center proposal for Philadelphia, 1944. With this project Kahn tested the possibility of achieving monumentality through materials such as steel, a material direction he later abandoned. *Louis I. Kahn Collection, The University of Pennsylvania and the Pennsylvania Historical and Museum Commission.*

OPPOSITE: Louis Kahn's sketch of the experimental Parasol House, a collaboration with Oskar Stonorov. The project's square concrete roof slabs were to be balanced on a single central column supported by a grid-like steel structure. Each square slab was to serve as a shelter canopy for one- or even two-story houses. Below the "parasols," the living units could take on individual programs and expressions of their own. *Louis I. Kahn Collection, The University of Pennsylvania and the Pennsylvania Historical and Museum Commission.*

resting on a large steel grid. Each grid was supported by a single column, and together these "parasols" formed an open tent-like canopy that hosted spatial programs under its shelter. To some degree, the project suggests Kahn testing the ongoing developments in postwar modernism, but this interest did not last. In his ability to disconnect from the pressures of style and fascination with newness, Kahn returned to a spatial search where material as mass, independent of technological advances, played a vital role. This pivot was not unlike Gunnar Asplund's situation after the completion of the Stockholm Exhibition in 1930. Asplund then seemed to fluctuate between the new modernist style and expressions and concerns found in his earlier work; even as he mastered the new direction, he held steadfast to what he perceived as architecture's primary concerns. To some critics, Asplund appeared to waver when in fact he was investigating and testing modernism's visual and spatial properties. He finally concluded that in relation to the Nordic landscape and climate and core human issues, modernism as practiced at the time was not entirely satisfying.

Similar insights characterized Kahn's search for direction in his work. The highly articulated concrete space-frame structure that Kahn developed for the proposed City Tower project in Philadelphia (1956–57) in close collaboration with Anne Tyng intrigued him, but he realized that his spatial focus related to human concerns was not at home inside such a structure.

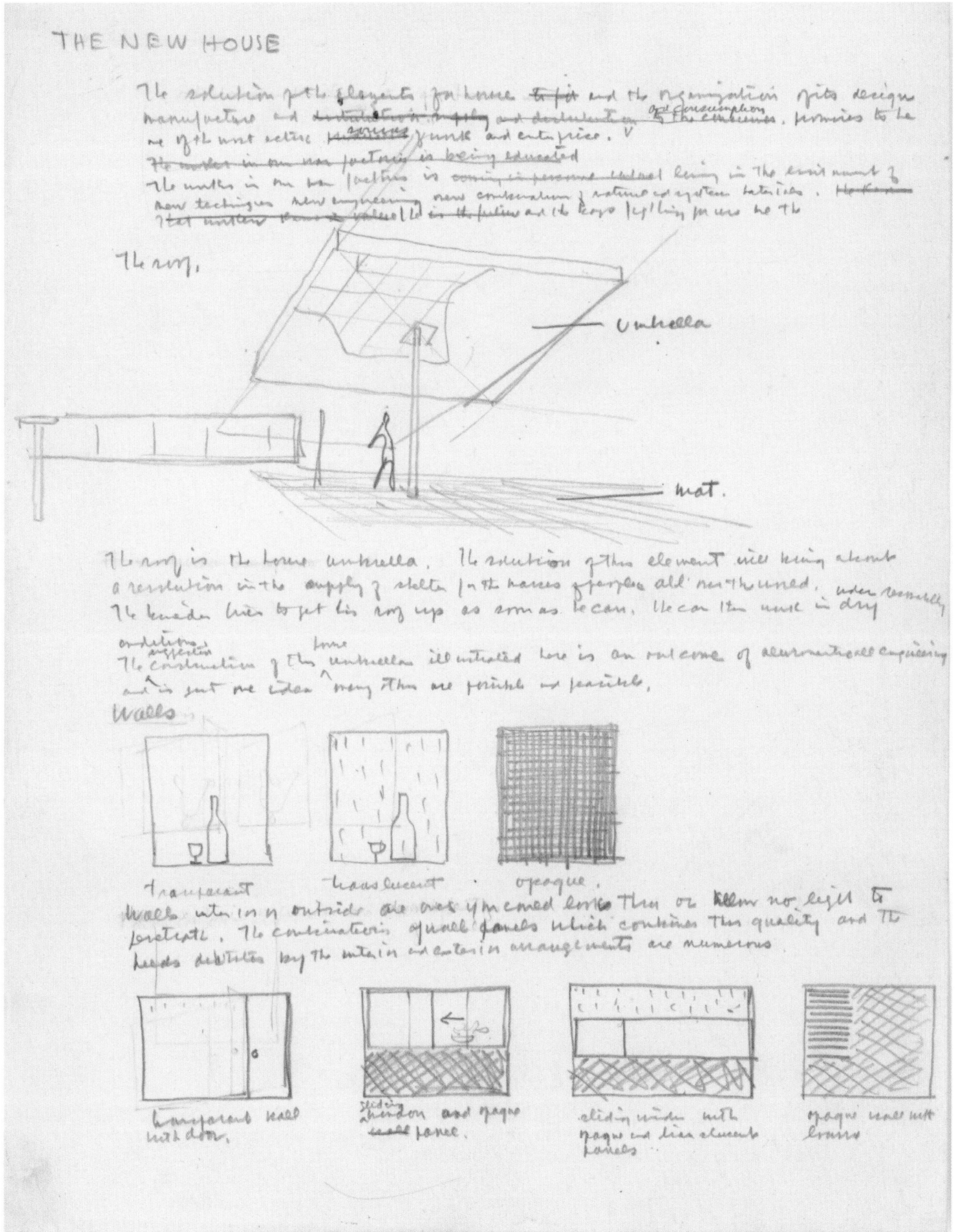
THE NEW HOUSE
umbrella
mat.
Walls
transparent
translucent
opaque.

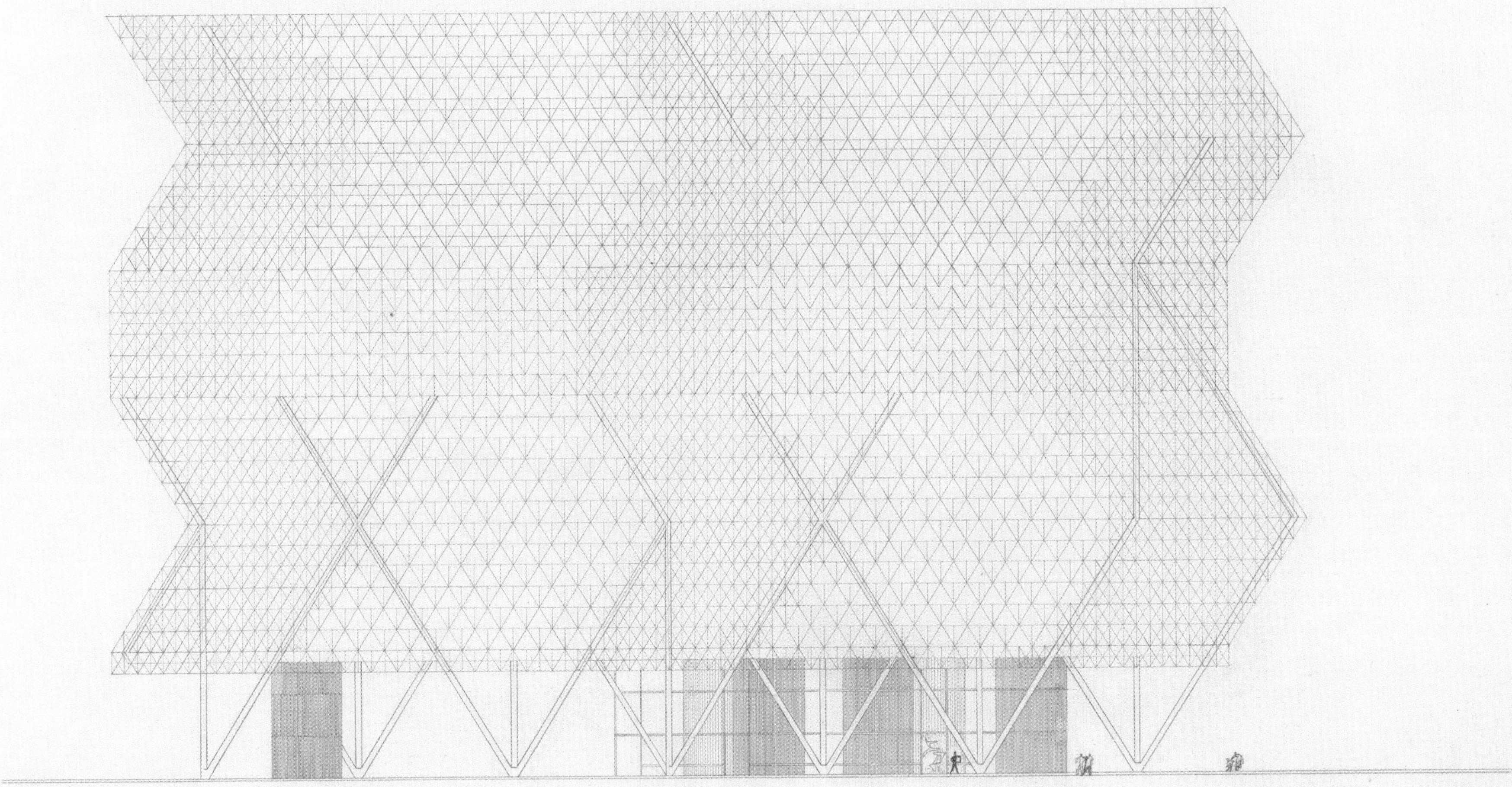

A rendering of the proposed City Tower project in Philadelphia that Kahn designed in collaboration with Anne Tyng. The 616-foot-tall concrete structure, trussed by cross-framing, explored the possibility of extending a triangular space-frame system in a vertical direction. *Louis I. Kahn Collection, The University of Pennsylvania and the Pennsylvania Historical and Museum Commission.*

Instead of embracing the trends of advanced structural possibilities, lightweight materials, and simple shelters, he soon began to build with materials that within their very nature carried weight and a sense of gravity. Brick, concrete, and stone as "materials of mass are not out to charm gravity," he would say in the studio. He was not interested in minimizing the appearance of gravity, but rather in expressing each material's meeting with the ground—a celebration of nature, a connection understood by all. Kahn once noted in class that "after a fire, it is only materials of mass as a ruin that are left, and these remains reflect the core of the building."

I also remember Kahn asserting in class that "material should not be used as infill or in

1979 | Aldo Rossi's Teatro del Mondo and Arch built for the Venice Biennale.

Aulis Blomstedt, Gio Ponti, and Luigi Nervi die.

1980 | Christian Norberg-Schulz's *Genius Loci: Towards a Phenomenology of Architecture* published. Balkrishna Doshi's office and home completed.

Marshall McLuhan dies.

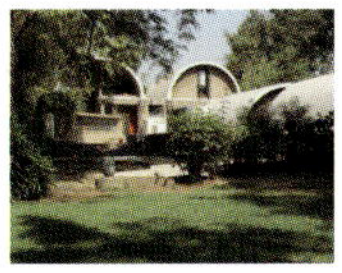

Balkrishna Doshi's office and home. *Tom Wike.*

1981 | Tadao Ando's Rokko Housing I completed. Bernard Tschumi's *The Manhattan Transcripts* published.

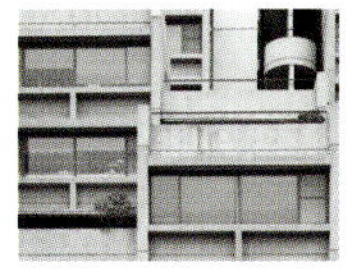

Rokko Housing Complex 1. *Jon Reksten.*

service to another" and that "in each material through its limitations is also its specific identity." In Kahn's view, the search for space was simultaneously a search for material, not an effort independent from its making. To respect and find beauty in a scaffolding that enabled the making of a brick arch or a concrete wall, or in what made the bleeding of the concrete, was essential to highlighting each material's specificity. Kahn believed that the formwork as prestructure should be both respected and regarded as linked to a material's mass identity. As he put it, "the formwork is an instrument in the making of the music called concrete, and the violinist does not burn his violin after a concert."[1] His work in India and Bangladesh, whose final expression was enhanced by local materials and local formwork, constitute strong examples of this viewpoint.

Kahn did not regard making in itself as clearly connected to the creative act, but rather as a process far more related to knowledge. In class, he would argue that you do not have an idea before you know how to make it; but then he would go on to say how the experience and knowledge required to make something are not that instinctive to humans. This quote from 1965 illustrates this duality in his position:

> I think man knows what and why. How to do it is really not natural. It takes experience to know how to make something. Some people do—just tend to know how to make it and believe that is what you rely on. I believe you cannot get a great building [that way]. It is impossible, the why and what must be constantly present to guide. The how is always tangible. In the end it must be unmeasurable.[2]

In a creative search, volume zero must come first, before the means, how it is made:

> An architecture must transcend the means, just as one must forget the construction, one must forget the little things that you have to consider in making a great building. It must hit you somewhat without the means. One needn't point out that it takes so many bricks to make a building or we had such hardships. No, it must be completely unmeasurable, therefore the number of bricks means nothing.[3]

Kahn's primary notion of mass relates to the wall and how he envisioned its different structural capabilities. The possibility of an opening immediately changes the size and mass of a wall—and the opening may grow so large as to diminish the wall to a column or a set of columns. For this reason, the column as traditionally understood was not really part of Kahn's structural vocabulary; rather, he developed the hollow column, which in a sense converts mass into a room. He saw the wall as the beginning of all structures, and always understood

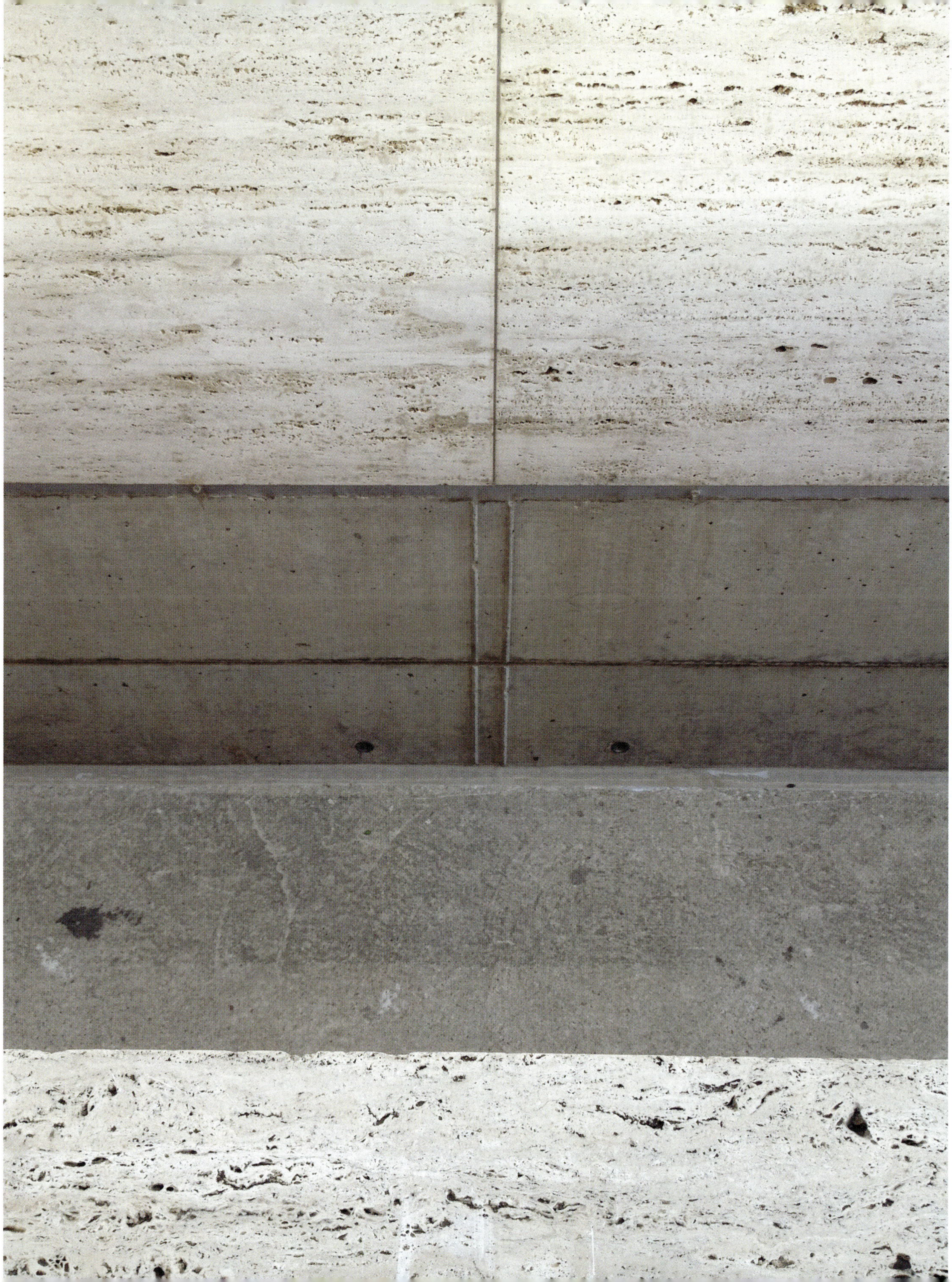

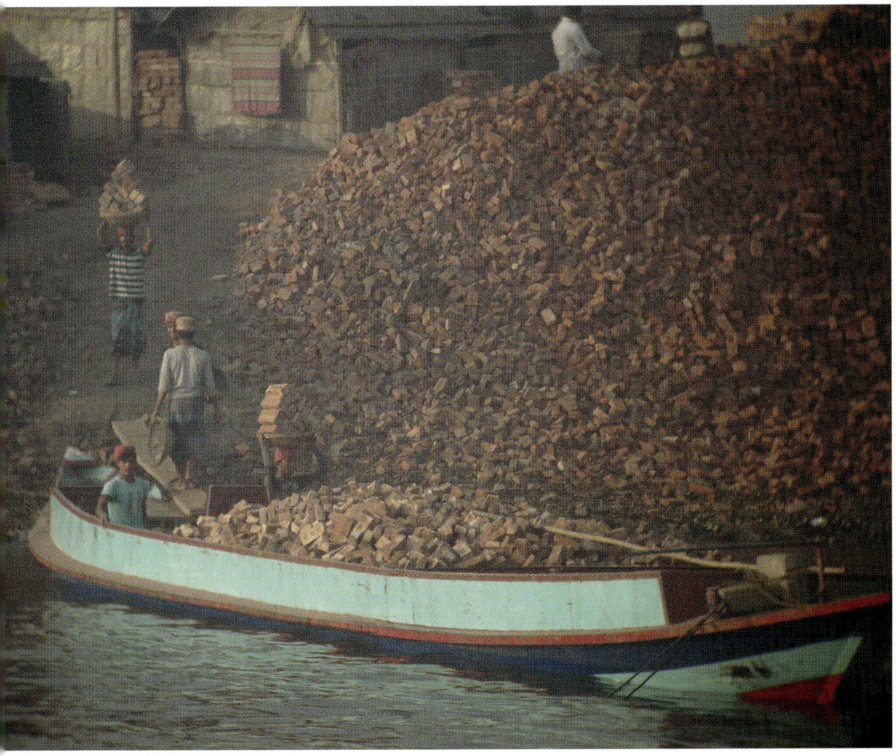

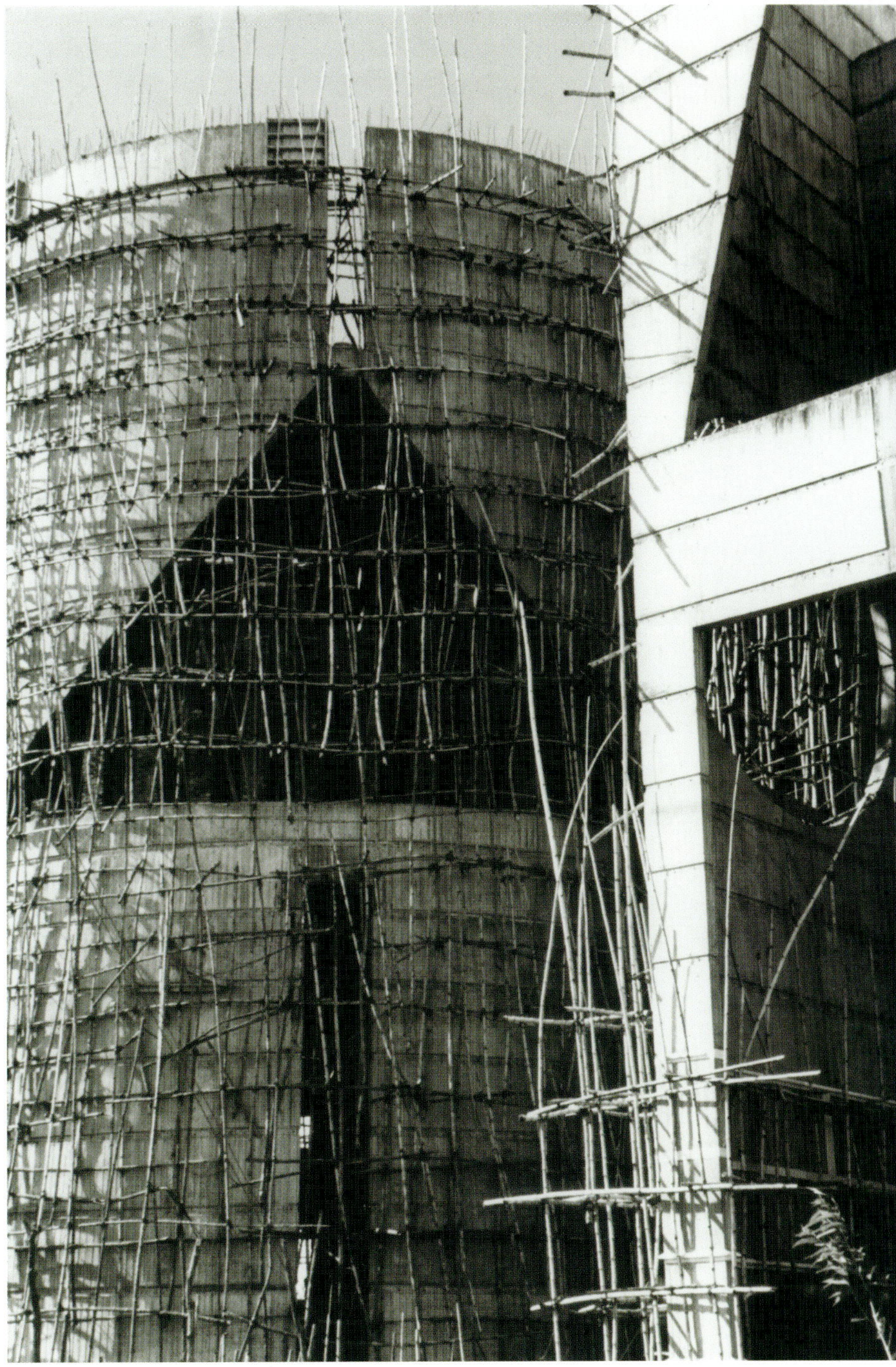

OPPOSITE: Detail of the bleeding of concrete at the Kimbell Art Museum. As Kahn saw it, "The form is made so that the concrete comes out. This is very helpful because the concrete bleeding out takes its nature making, no honeycombing at all. This wasn't touched. This was poured in place, and remained just the way it was. I think you work with the nature." *Frida Johansen.*

ABOVE: Bricks on the move from the local factory to the construction site of the National Assembly Building via Bangladesh's Dhaka River. *Herman Neuckermans.*

RIGHT: Construction photo of the National Assembly Building in Dhaka showing local bamboo scaffolding in use. Kahn understood the importance of using local materials not only in the building itself but also in its making. *Original photos: Lawrence Halprin Collection, Architectural Archives, University of Pennsylvania.*

1982 | Michael Graves's Humana Building completed.

Abel Sørensen dies.

1983 | Kahn's Sher-e-Bangla Nagar, capital of Bangladesh, completed. Venturi, Rauch, and Scott Brown's Gordon Wu Hall completed. Kenneth Frampton's *Towards a Critical Regionalism: Six Points for an Architecture of Resistance* published. Per Olaf Fjeld's *Sverre Fehn: The Thought of Construction* published.

R. Buckminster Fuller dies.

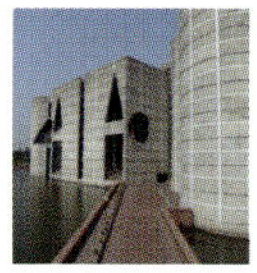

Sher-e-Bangla Nagar, capital of Bangladesh. *Herman Neukermans.*

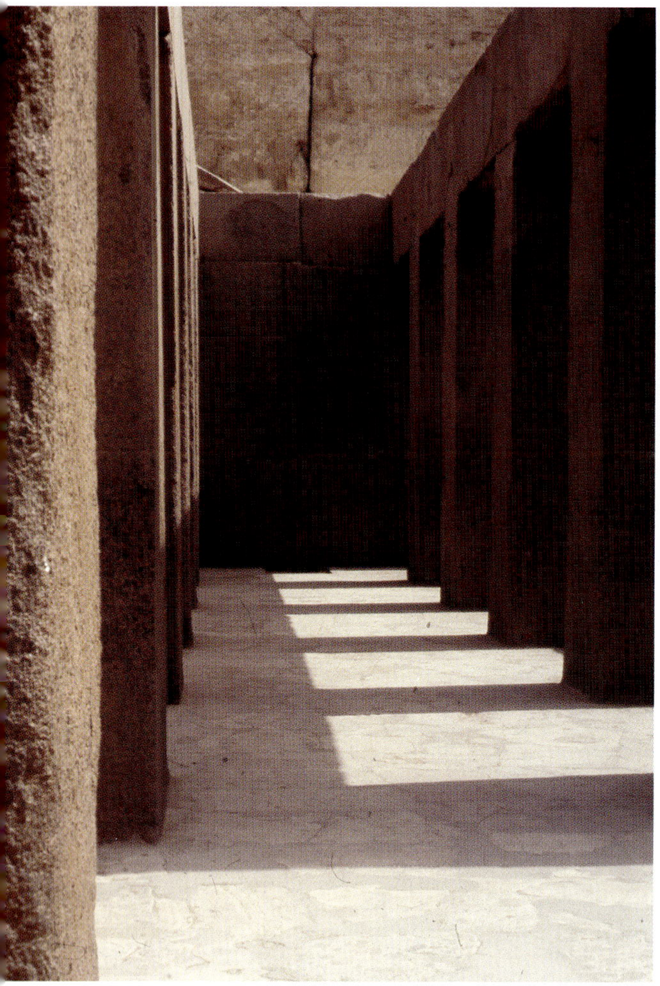

The Columnar Hall in Chephren's Valley Temple, Egypt. Kahn's travels throughout the Mediterranean strengthened his conviction that architecture has an eternal quality and that materiality is essential to this. As Kahn put it, the architect "must answer to gravity, he can't fool around with that, and he has got to realize that a column is a light making thing—it brings light into being." *P. O. Fjeld.*

mass as construction and not material alone. The wall could initiate an inside-outside relationship, but not as an absolute, as mass has the potential to split and, in its division, open up for new layers of inside-outside.

In reviewing Kahn's sketches, one can see he was always investigating how light traveled through a structural depth before entering the room, and how this depth shaped the intensity of the light. In class he commented that light—inseparable from mass within the process of making—should enter a room as a surprise, thus revealing light's true capacity. He drew a plan as the relationships between void and mass, light and no light. His approach seemed to underline his belief that "structure is the place where light is not." I believe his plans communicate his concurrent search for the section: the creative moment when his plan and section became one entity was crucial.

Kahn's second trip to Europe in 1951, during which Rome served as a base while he visited Greece and Egypt, strengthened his conviction that architecture has an eternal quality and that materials of mass as earth-bound weight play an important part in achieving this. How did site play into this thinking? Kahn argued, for instance, that the Parthenon has an architectural autonomy distinct from its site, even though it is at the same time a contextual work. To clarify this position, the Paestum was never far behind in Kahn's thoughts when the Parthenon came up in class: "Some people think that the Paestum is less great than the Parthenon, but the Paestum has a sound from which grew the Parthenon; already in the Paestum there exists a Parthenon."[4] Here Kahn indicated that the Paestum is closer to the "beginning of things," thus also closer to his idea of form as independent of context. This pull between architectural autonomy and site as part of context informed both his work and teaching. As with the plan and section, I believe he was constantly searching for the connection between these two entities during a given project.

Kahn's approach to site was not separate from his concerns about mass. In his writings, the words "site" and "context" are almost nonexistent, in that these are embedded within his terms "nature," "form," and "order." Distinguishing one part of a site for its picturesqueness or potential views was not a primary motivation at the start of his architectural search. Instead, as he stressed in class, he believed that we should regard all parts of the earth as equally beautiful and important. It was up to architecture to meet the earth—to contribute beauty and human joy to it, not subtract from it.

Often one must search for the entrance in Kahn's buildings; the point of entry is far more a matter of choice and discovery than an announcement. In such buildings, all directions are granted equal importance, meaning each opening set by structure is treated with the same

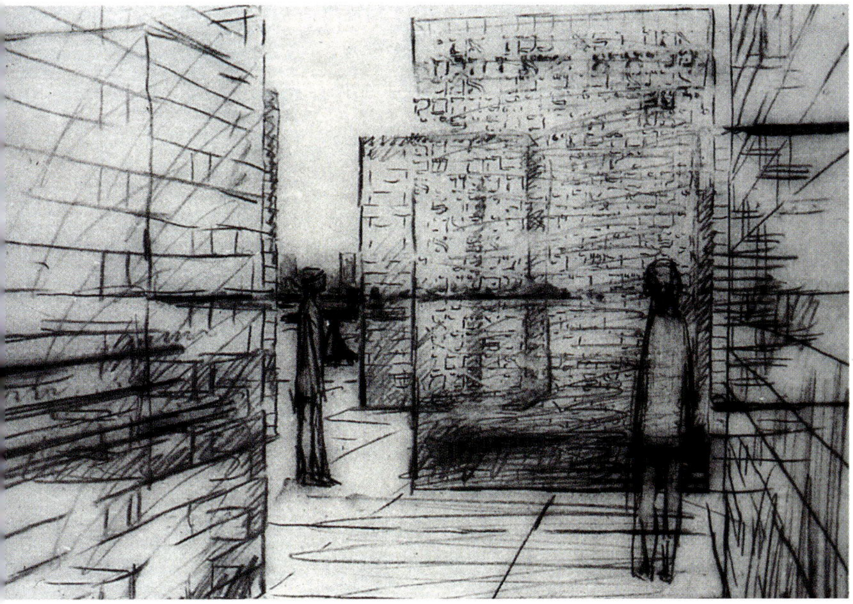

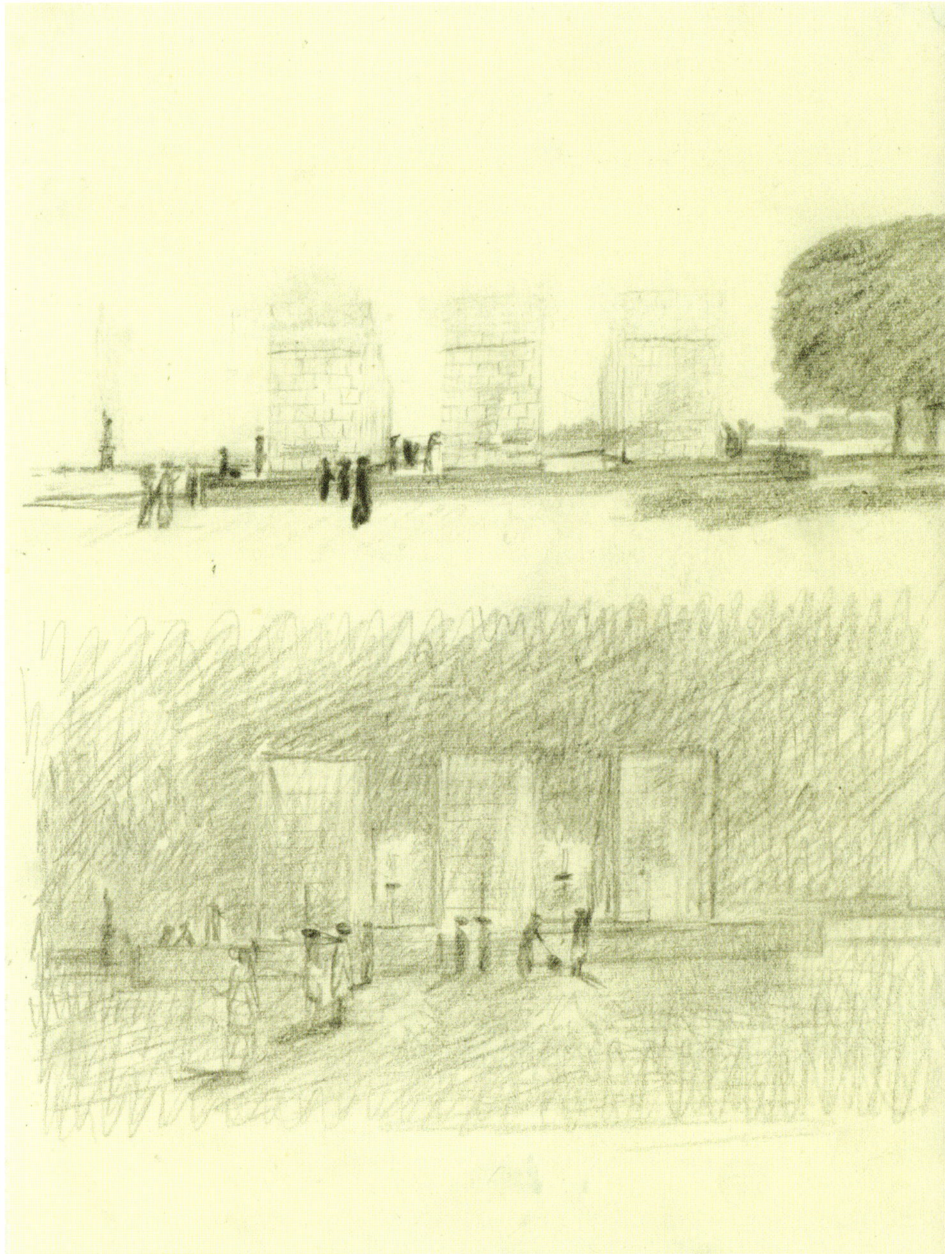

Louis Kahn's sketches of his proposed Memorial to the Six Million Jewish Martyrs. Its glass blocks removed the separation between material and light in an attempt to reach the shadowless. *Louis I. Kahn Collection, The University of Pennsylvania and the Pennsylvania Historical and Museum Commission.*

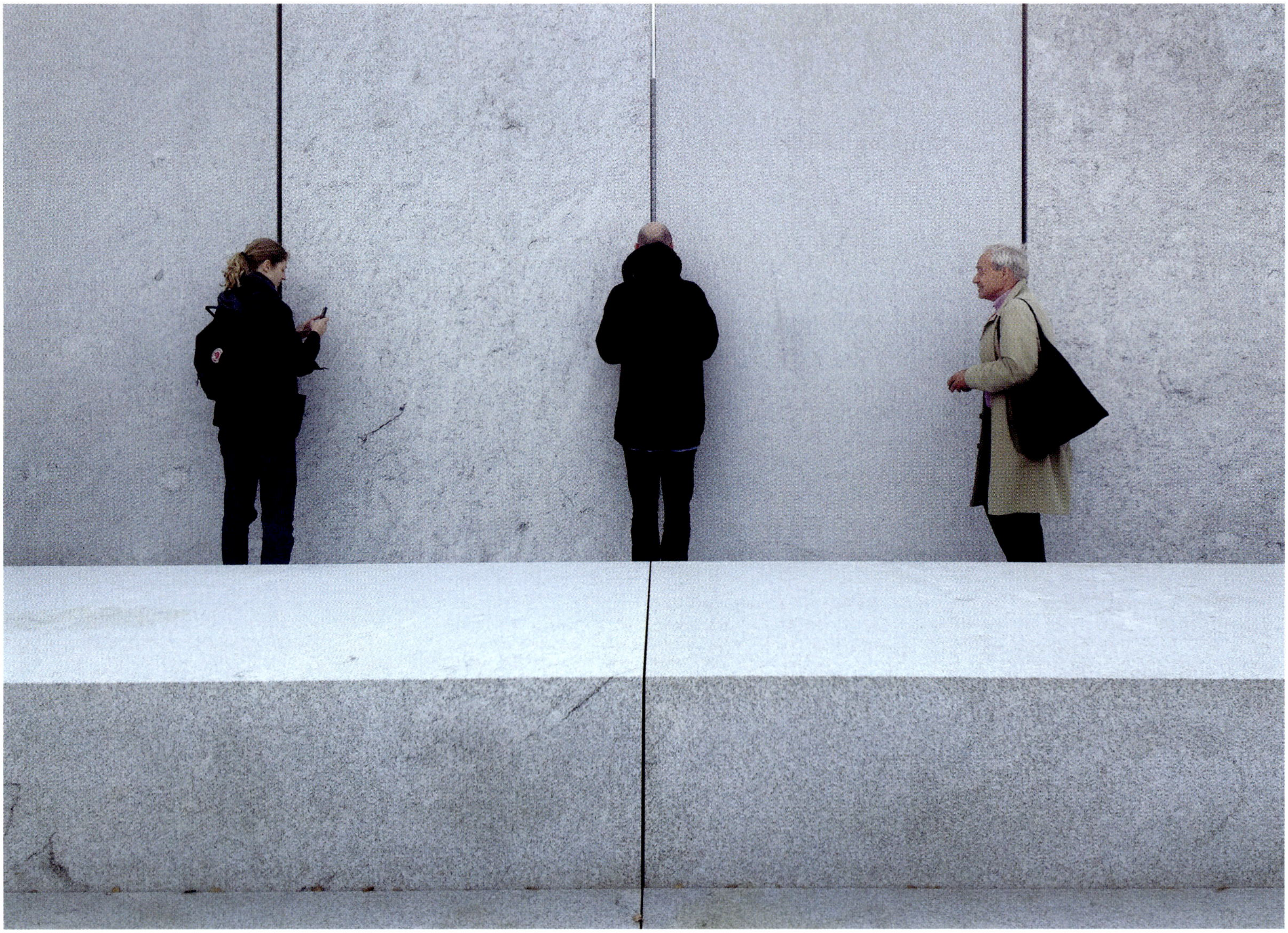

Looking into the spatial moment where the wall parts at Kahn's posthumous Franklin D. Roosevelt Four Freedoms Park on Roosevelt Island, New York City. *Kaia Opstad Sæbø.*

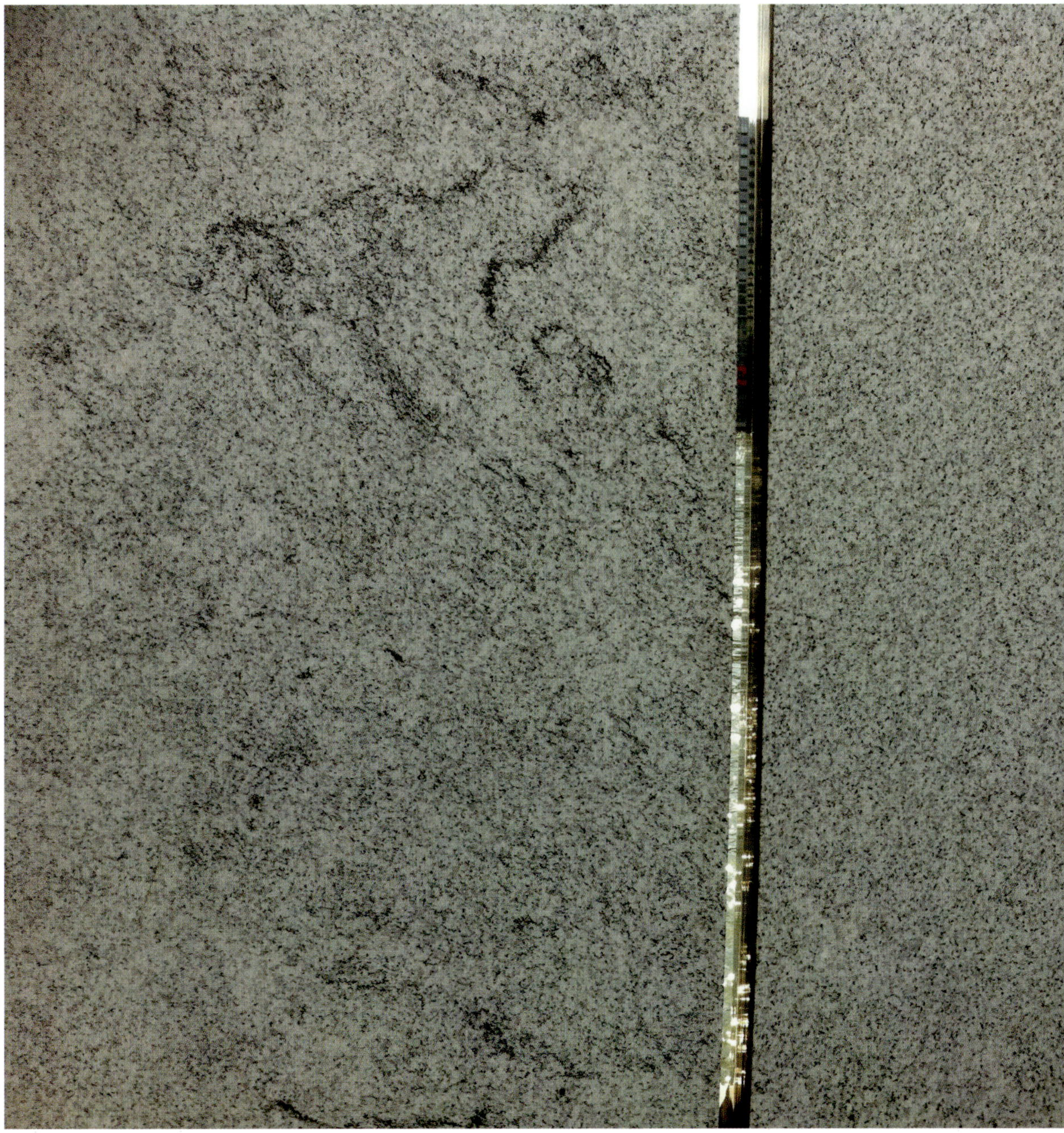

Light reflected by the East River captured in the interstitial space between the Roosevelt memorial's granite blocks. *P. O. Fjeld.*

precision in relation to light. It is in the meeting between the earth and the architectural autonomy inspired by form—the moment the physical object adjusts to nature's laws—that the clarity of site is revealed.

In his proposal for the Memorial to the Six Million Jewish Martyrs, Kahn used glass as if he were building with stone, since the solid glass blocks are both the structure and the space. In meeting the ground, each glass block performs as mass carrying an identity of a large transparent stone with an internalized energy that radiates into the context. Anchored to the earth as a transparent room, technology is simply mass.

Quite differently, although informed by the same thinking, the heavy granite blocks of the Roosevelt memorial bring its outdoor room and the surrounding city into one unique spatial configuration. The memorial's large stair connects the garden to the sky, and this garden as nature connects to the single room. Almost seamlessly, the room as a landing sets the horizon, a platform that meets the river as the sea.

Fehn on Mass

Just before I left Oslo for the University of Pennsylvania, Fehn gave me a notebook from his first trip to the United States that included sketches of and notations about Kahn's work in Philadelphia and New Haven. Unfortunately, Fehn and Kahn never met, but it is easy to see why Fehn had a natural affinity for Kahn's creative approach. The notion that the human is inescapably part of nature but never able to fully comprehend or command it runs through the vocabulary and teaching of both of these architects.

In our five conversations in preparation for the article for *Perspecta 24*, Fehn asserted that humans gradually lost the "animal in man" and thus the instinct to spatially read and behave within the given aspects of nature—a loss critical to how we understand our relationship to place. Fehn was also occupied with the importance of retaining and stimulating our natural instincts within the individual creative process, particularly when applying or heavily relying on scientific knowledge, as this reliance can easily restrict and alter the early stages of the process. Many of his reflections and sketches deal with the relationship between man and nature, how this connects material to mass, and how modern technology is influencing this connection.

Below I have gathered Fehn's comments about mass that were not included in the published article. The five sessions that produced these observations took place in Fehn's own home, Villa Dammann, the house that Arne Korsmo designed not long after he returned home from the 1928–29 study tour where he first met Louis Kahn. Over a hectic two-week period beginning in late August of 1984 we met five times.

SESSION ONE

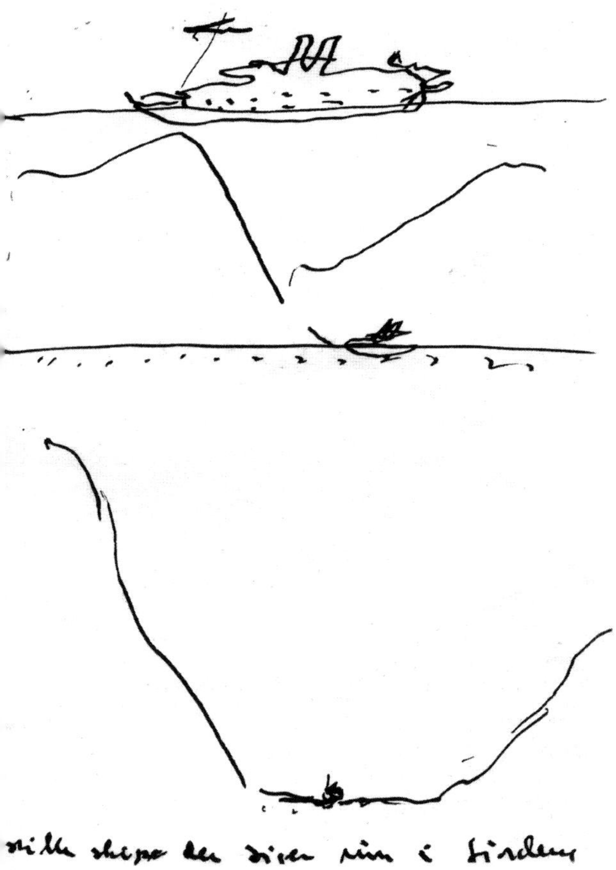

Sketch that Sverre Fehn produced during a work session with the author: "The boat penetrates mass and the movement defines a mass concept where there is no separation between static and movement." *The National Museum of Oslo.*

When thought penetrates mass it creates a defined space.

The physical space is constant; we are in fact in a mass. You cannot get out of it, but you can edit it. When an object generated by thought penetrates mass, it is also a mass that requires its own place. Place is a point on earth that carries a spiritual mass. [. . .] A plane, a boat, a house, or a pair of shoes are all mass spaces generated by spiritual thoughts.

The boat penetrates mass and the movement defines a mass concept where there is no separation between static and movement. The ship as an object gives a precise dimension to the large mass of water. We move inside the mass. The light, the wind, the rain, the clouds are all elements we move through as mass. It is light together with time that sets mass in motion.

Two mass concepts: the movement through mass as one, and mass itself.

Technology changes our perception of mass: all the forests are glued together [with wood lamination], and iron as a heated mass flows over the earth.

It is the human spirit that gives the material as mass an order. It is the same spirit that gives it form and puts the mass on stage. Is there a difference between you and the object? Is spiritual mass like life? Through the human spirit, the mass comes to life. It moves mass in relation to thought, but if you kill the spirit, only the mass is left behind. Humans' true material is the spirit; it is the spirit that holds everything together.

A puddle is filling an existing hole, and one mass builds another mass. The water meets the earth and builds a new figure. As a human, you pull back and allow nature to play on its own. Nature can teach you all constructive things. You replace water with a thought that is to meet another mass. When the column hits the earth it finds its dimension.

SESSION TWO

For the cave dweller, mass is absolute. He sits there with his thoughts inside his cave. The sky enters and fills the heavy mass with air. Outside, the heaven as mass is infinite. The cave increases the heaven.

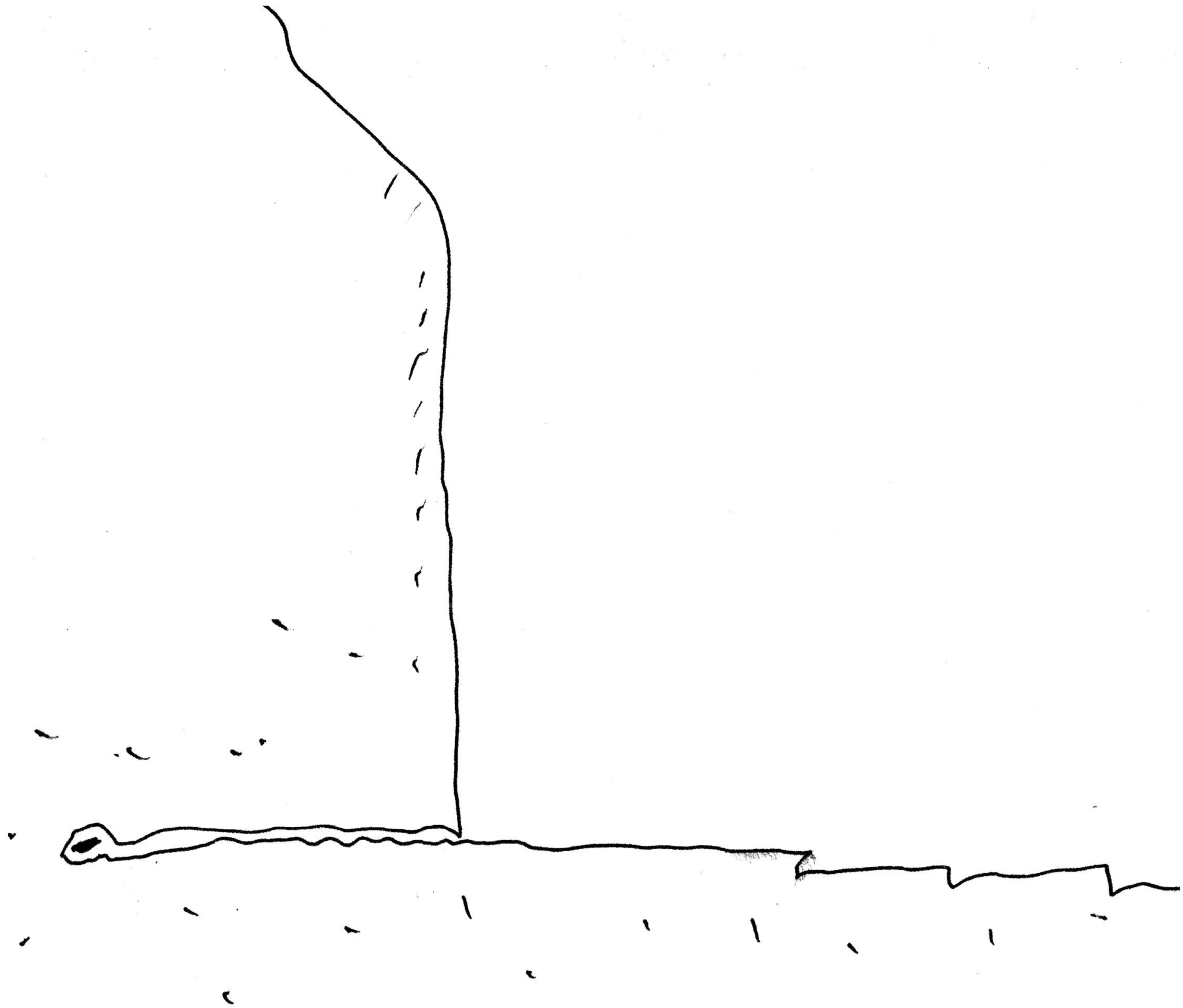

Drawing from Sverre Fehn's notebook, 1992.
Fehn made many cave drawings, as he envisioned the cave as the beginning of architecture.
The National Museum of Oslo.

It is the stone that gave the first opening. You have a mass construction you are able to remove.

The mass is absolute in a shadowless world. In death, mass surrounds you without definition; in this world, there is no shadow. The only way to grasp light is to regulate mass. Kahn had a unique understanding of this.

Today, what happens with the mass we take out? It does not disappear from the concept of mass. We move mass and its energy, but in this new relationship we do not understand that in a sense this is the beginning of a new architectural space. The large architectural expressions—the Great Wall of China, the large fortresses, burial mounds, the aqueducts—all had a strong awareness towards this relationship.

Outside the cave, a tree grows up from the earth and fills the open space with its mass. It gives protection, a roof-shade, and thus removes part of the heavens. In the Sahara you have no other construction other than sand. My own shadow is a marker of my mass. The shadow is a visual understanding of a mass concept. The wind moves mass, blows away dust. Sand is the wind's architect.

The city is a concept of mass. It seeks a mass identity more than it searches for form. It gathers physical presence and becomes a mass. The city is the largest human mass concept that belongs to the spirit, as the city offers a broad enough variation and openness as an inspiration for the spirit. Yet the city as a mass is out of control. One is not able to sort out the different mass concepts—and modern technology supports this uncontrolled growth; you can just call for the endless beam. There is only one limitation—economy—which is the most primitive of all mass concepts. And with money in control of all of the other mass concepts, we are in trouble. Money is not the earth, nor has it any relationship to the ground. In just choosing and consuming, and having no idea how things are made or where they are coming from, we no longer have a technology that serves as mass limitation. This is the key to the city's uncontrolled growth.

We have not been able to find or define limits, but in every earlier spiritual construction, we have managed this. We were offered greatness through limitation. Today, it appears as if our philosophical or spiritual presence is not strong enough to release an understanding of a new concept of mass: one that has limitations in all this chaos. Growth is still out of control. It is not regulating itself in relation to anything.

Even in the Renaissance, each material was embedded in its own limitations, one that called for an internal technology. You could not imagine at that point an endless laminated wooden beam. Though impressive, the pyramids were an example of stone's limitations. Even the modern materials such as steel and concrete cannot be regarded as unlimited—but then came plastic, and everything was unending.

The fight is how we will be able to redraw from numbers. We have too much baggage and believe that our collaboration with nature is based on numbers. Instead, it is in fact a dialogue, an understanding of nature with nature that tells you how mass should be formed.

The absolute mass—death—has no light. In Kahn's monument for six million Jews, he strives for a shadowless object.

And—what about the mass of the sky and the sea? If we had conquered the sky before the sea, the sea would have been our heaven today. The sea had been our unknown.

Kahn's use of concrete and brick relates to a strong awareness of materials as mass.

Pietilä said a blind person draws the difference between materials through an understanding of material's different weights.

Niemeyer: in his work the heaviness of concrete appears light.

Utzon: in his unusual treatment of the Sydney Opera House, very heavy building forms also appear light. It does not belong to material, but to the spirit of architecture.

Material says to itself, "Oh my god, didn't I manage this OK? Bricks made an opening, and I can become air. You can walk through me." Material's poetry lies here.

Had you calculated the tree, the tree would have been forbidden. I can make a little tree for a bird to land, a dialogue with the wind, a mass concept's extreme poetic point. Modern architecture lacks this dialogue.

SESSION THREE

Light belongs to a mass concept. Light belongs to eternity. Look at Kahn's glass block: he offered minimal shadow as a sign of eternity.

On the North Pole, one runs after one's own shadow because it is full of light.

The Greek in his bathtub—the moment when mass is described as a volume, one leaves weight. The mass as a volume is free from material. Philosophically, one becomes a transparent shadow. One is involved in a beautiful definition of mass; you leave behind weight, material, flesh, and blood. The object becomes a sort of circumference or outline. Earlier, one thought about weight and material, and never of volume. When material/weight begins to disappear, mass becomes a transparent shadow. It does not materialize.

A pyramid has limits in comparison to a laminated beam that has no stop. Technology ruins topography's earlier limitations—a mass concept out of control. It can no longer regulate itself, as it lacks the nature of a resistance force.

The earth has become a measurable concept just like the man in the bathtub. As a mass understood in relation to other mass concepts in the universe—the sun, the moon, the stars are no longer mysteries.

Man presses a weight down into the earth and up comes a mass. What does he do with this? This is very little discussed, as we have lost our dialogue with nature and therefore also our spirit. St. Peter's dome in Rome came about through the desire for a spiritual construction. Today, it is money which generates the wish for the large domes and towers. The relationship to nature is no longer part of the main motive. Again, money has substituted nature; this is where the main mass concept is today.

Unfortunately, our new technology is not as yet in harmony with nature. The rock has disappeared; the brick is gone; and I am just left with concrete, glass, and steel. To work with wood has also changed as lamination has taken over.

The landscape has all dimensions, from the small rock to the large mountains, but there needs to be a balance of what one places in this landscape and what one takes away. What we are doing is making the landscape small; it is shrinking as it does not really receive any positive input. The calculated numbers as our dialogue are only limited to size. No conversation has really taken place.

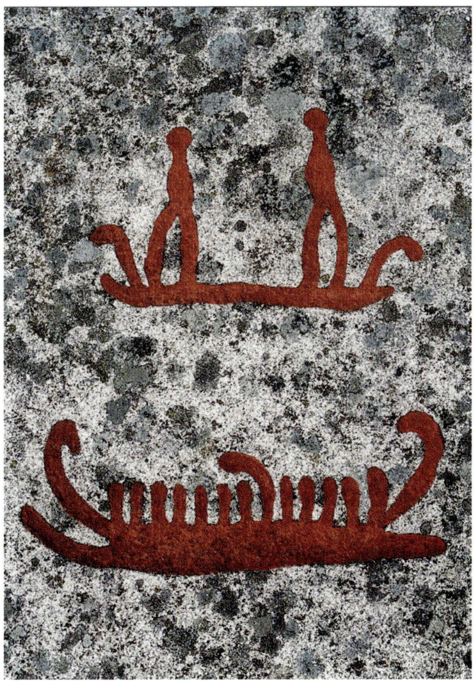

A petroglyph picturing two ships and their crew from Vitlycke, Tanum, Sweden. Fehn noted, "The little cut in the rock. You take away mass and you get a shadow, a hieroglyph." *Carla Media Lysekii.*

SESSION FOUR

The Egyptians wrote on the walls and discovered mass in transformation. This has to do with visualization of material. The little cut in the rock. You take away mass, and you get a shadow, a hieroglyph. The shadow drew the symbol and developed as a mass. If one worked out from this principle, mass in the North should be totally different. Our carvings are on the ground. In the dark one doesn't see anything.

Why has our architectural ideal been to minimize mass? This can only end in glass, the shadowless. Why do we seek materials that cannot give silence and darkness a feeling of safety? Why are we doing this and at the same time maximiz[ing] technological complexity? You can pour a concrete desert, and with wood lamination build a cave out of trees.

Old architecture had a trust in maximizing mass. They loved weight. We love weightlessness. One builds in relation to what one sees as a weight quality. It does not only create emptiness, but also a silence without symbols, a doubling of the absolute silence.

The thick wall is no longer comprehendible. By minimizing mass, one has also minimized the shadow. This is no place for a cat.

We no longer wander between distinct arranged masses articulating their weight, and the rock as earth loses its importance.

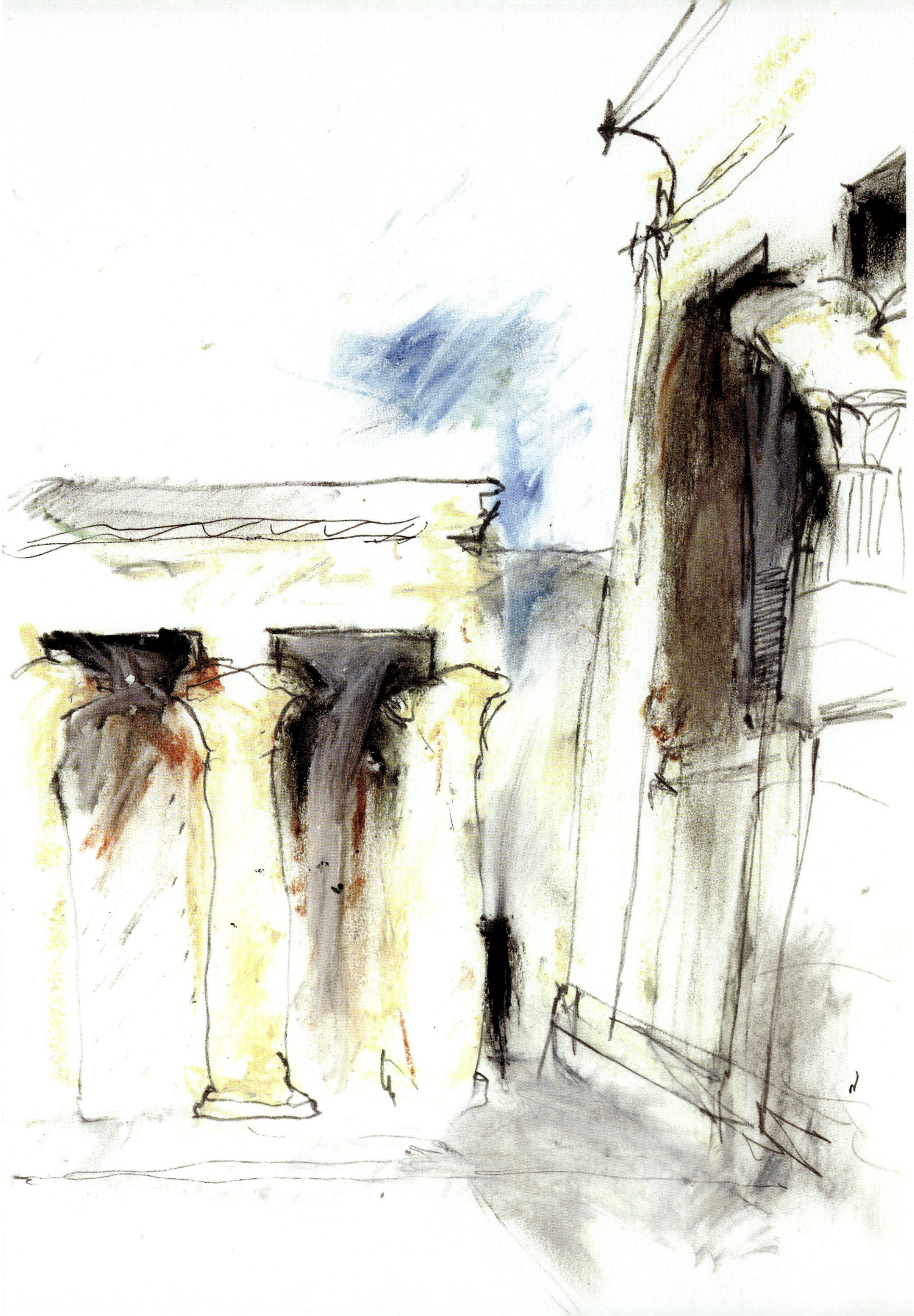

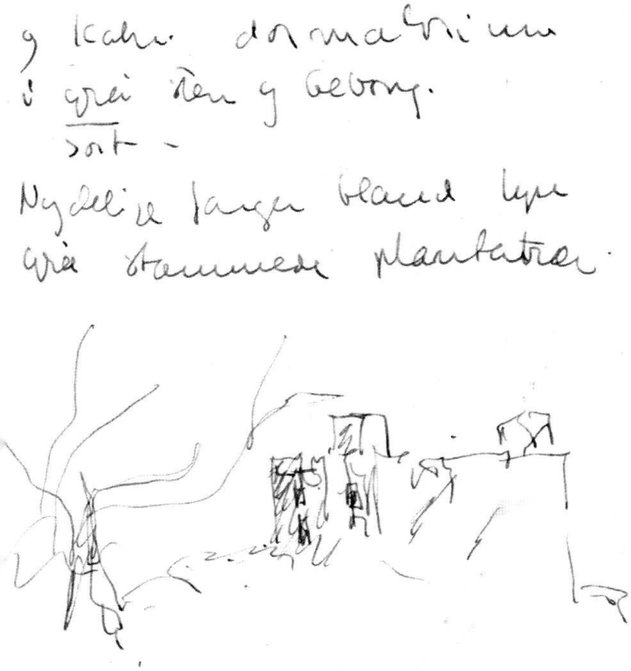

ABOVE: Sketch of Kahn's Eleanor Donnelley Erdman Hall at Bryn Mawr College that Sverre Fehn made during a trip to the United States in March 1980. Fehn described it as "the dormitory in grey-black stone and concrete. Beautiful colors among the light grey trunks of planted trees." *P. O. Fjeld Private Collection, gift from Sverre Fehn.*

OPPOSITE: Sketch of the funerary temple of Ramesses II by Sverre Fehn, 1992. *The National Museum of Oslo.*

SESSION FIVE

[During this meeting, we reviewed our notes from our previous sessions.]

When the earth was comprehended as unending, the built mass was seen as finite. The moment the earth was regarded as finite, as a measured and calculated volume, our built mass was infinite. Once the earth was regarded as a measured object, its relationship to other masses changed. The more we define the earth, the more fluid becomes the mass concept of material.

To work with mass while the earth was still infinite must have been a blast. You could work without stop and with the safety of form as a defined mass on earth. You had no competition. To place a stone on a surface that is infinite was to manifest a point in infinity. You could trust the earth as mass and build your cathedral—and the contest between the sea and land was an absolute line. Out there, the wind and the boat explored the mass, both aware of the horizon. Aalto discovered the line between the land and the earth.

To make something upon a defined mass is an entirely different situation. This gives no feedback, as it is already related to a dimension. The game must be played for higher stakes. It has to be inspirational. A great quality within Kahn's work is that he always builds a base for his buildings. They are not standing alone. He prepares his structures to enter a dialogue with the earth. He always builds some sort of plateau for them. The same with Mies and his terraces—and that takes us back to Palladio.

In Villa Rotunda, Palladio made a fantastic platform; the entire landscape is reworked to meet the house. This is an architecture that is almost forgotten. This has an effect: overdimensioning. If you look for minimization, it will choose material. This is wrong, because then you have no freedom in choosing material; it is already decided. If you want to reach a thick column, you must first offer the thought of its material, the freedom to be inspired towards a mass identity. Minimization justifies the materials that give you the minimum, like glass and steel, and that stops everything.

One must find weight in shadow, to reinvent the shadow. We do not have the shadow of the fortress with us anymore. We have lost a dialogue with the earth, a dialogue of mass, light, and sound. A great deal of architecture's resistance force is no longer present in our work. We have lost our hiding places behind a great column or as part of their [the columns'] endless repetition.

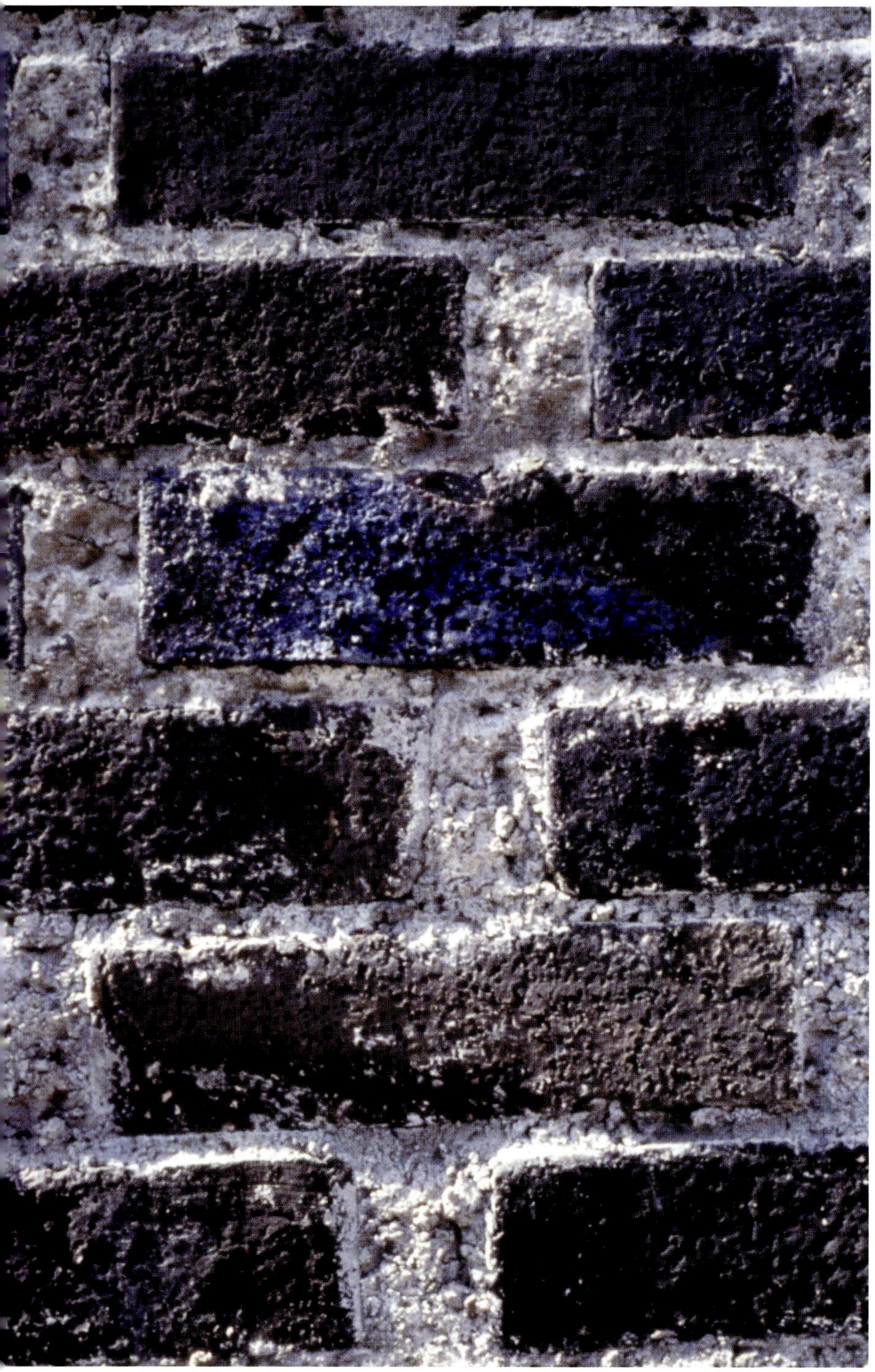

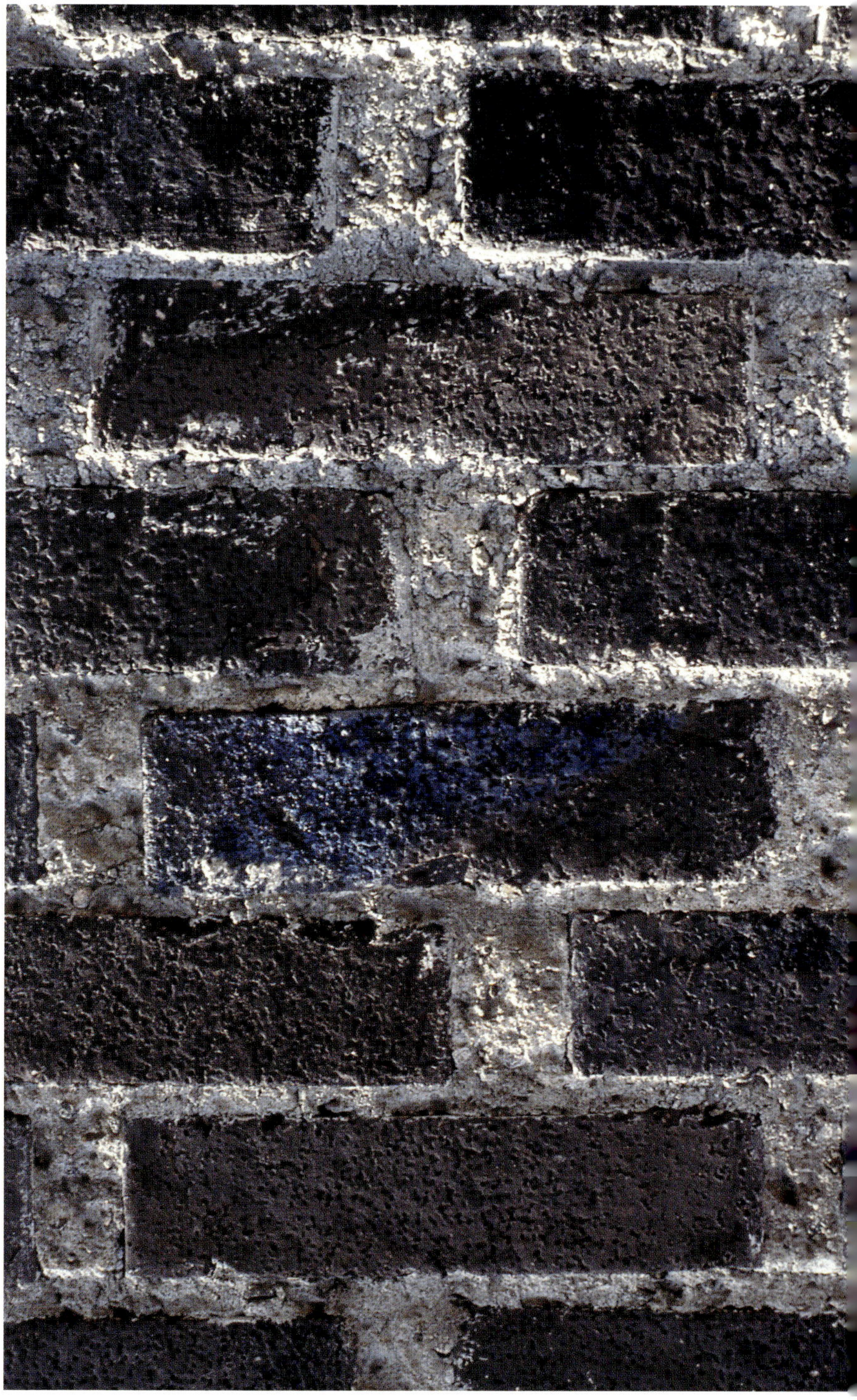

The Letter from Edman

To close these investigations into mass, I will turn to the letter about the work of Sigurd Lewerentz that I received from my late friend Bengt Edman, professor at the Royal Technical College in Stockholm. I was quite familiar with Lewerentz's churches in Björkhagen and Klippan when Edman sent me this letter in 1989, but just the same, my knowledge of Lewerentz was limited, and I had not then met anyone who had known or worked with him. Edman's article touches on concerns not just in Lewerentz's work but also in Kahn's later work, as well as core issues in much of the great midcentury Nordic architecture. Ultimately, it is about mass.

Here I have chosen to reproduce Edman's original draft rather than the final version published by *Spazio e Società*, correcting only clear translation mistakes and adjusting punctuation for readability where necessary.

Lewerentz the Bricklayer

The masonry walls of the Björkhagen and Klippan churches have something in common. Both tell us about the very moment when brick was put into the mortar, and how that piece of wall, from being nothing, suddenly and without return is ready for generations. Any finishing like cleaning or jointing did not take place.

In such a situation the architect is working on purpose under certain premises. The skill of the bricklayer, irregularities in deliveries of material, frost and sunshine—everything is recorded. The goal here is evidently not a conventional neatness but rather the demonstration of building activities under given local circumstances. It is like baking bread. The bricklayer is present.

The joints seem to play an important role in the construction . . . two roles if you like. Somewhere the mortar keeps the bricks apart . . . mortar is the filling material. In that way the sloping edge of the roof is built . . . not cut! Elsewhere mortar keeps the bricks together, and the bricks are the filling pieces. In this way the altar and the table in the wedding chapel are cantilevered. These elements are concrete constructions like many other parts of the building where scaffolding and reinforcing irons are used.

So now we suddenly see the building as a concrete building . . . a masonry concrete building. But these aspects probably did not bother the architect at all. He

Detail of a brick wall in Sigurd Lewerentz's St. Peter's Church (1963–66) in Klippan, Sweden. Each individual brick together with the mortar performs as mass. Despite Lewerentz's advanced age and poor health at the time of the project, he often visited the church during construction, making decisions and numerous revisions on-site. *P. O. Fjeld.*

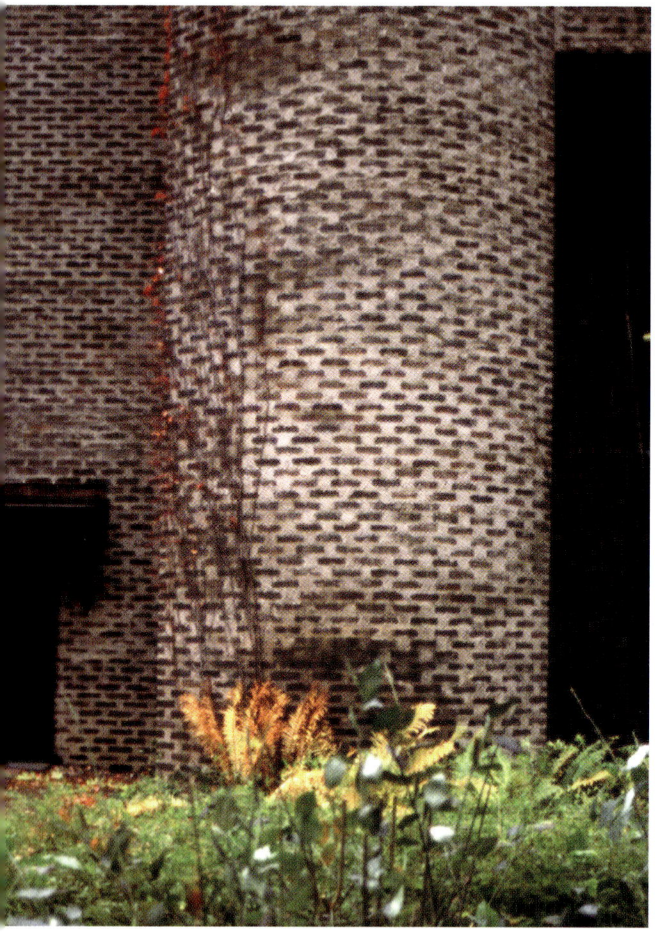

The brick wall as mass stops and shapes an opening at Lewerentz's St. Mark's Church (1956–59) in Björkhagen, Sweden. *P. O. Fjeld.*

simply used his experience and knowledge about material and construction in order to build the space he wanted. But his passion for joints is obvious.

Ceramic tiles and bricks seem to swim around in mortar, somewhere, to manage the geometry around the baptismal font, or to enrich the pattern of joints in the parish office. There the joints swell up when the tiles are pressed down into the mortar. The architect's argument was to make the floor less slippery, but he probably also had other silent arguments.

Again the moment of construction and the bricklayer are present and so is the blacksmith who welded the fence, the hinges and the grafted (giraffe) lampposts. Lewerentz asked him not to grind down the beads on the joints but to work carefully. The blacksmith was proud. Maybe we cannot expect a building culture again until the worker takes some steps backward, saying . . . "This is good. I am proud!"

A kind of directness is also expressed in the way a window glass is fixed to the wall . . . four brackets . . . pang, pang! . . . and the roof ridges to the wall; two irons and nails . . . pang, pang, and the electrical wires and lamps. It is strange that the window glass appears more like a block than a slab. Maybe we see it that way because there are other blocks around; the doorframe and door make a block, the altar and the wedding table are blocks, the skylight chimneys, and even the void of a window . . . is a block of light. Sharp edges make us see it that way. Many volumes meet the sky, knife-sharp, and suddenly the whole building can be seen as a block . . . a block of blocks. The details might be seen as brutal and ignorant by some, but also essential and poetic by someone else.

Sven Ivar Lind, a well-known Swedish architect, in his announcement [opening speech] for Klippan church explains it like this:

> Lewerentz's way of expression is harsh, unsentimental and straight on. But, everyday language becomes poetry. How? [. . .] What happens when the everyday language sometimes is exalted to poetry and we experience it with overwhelming intensity . . . when poetry comes into an electric cable or into a gutter? Maybe the artist, the observer of reality is successful in bringing to us the intensity of his observation, bringing us indirect touch, sweet or shocking to the world surrounding us blind and deaf. [. . .] The artist wants to unveil the reality beyond the conventional image of it. This passionate, patient realism has to watch and question everything—question ready-made formu-

> lations, be open to all possibilities, test and retest. Such an attitude releases from prejudices, doctrines, systems, routines and leads to a supreme but uncomfortable freedom. For this attitude there are not small or big questions. All are essential but they exist on different steps of the scale, like problems of the universe and the atom, organism and cell, building and detail. Primary and secondary depend on where the observer is, paradoxically free floating above the analysis of systems. For such a passion the work is a newly opened room, and reality is the big illusion.

Thus, it can happen that a new room is opened even to us "blind and deaf." St. Mark's Church stands in a forest of birch trees. I have to admit that I never saw a birch tree so sharply before.

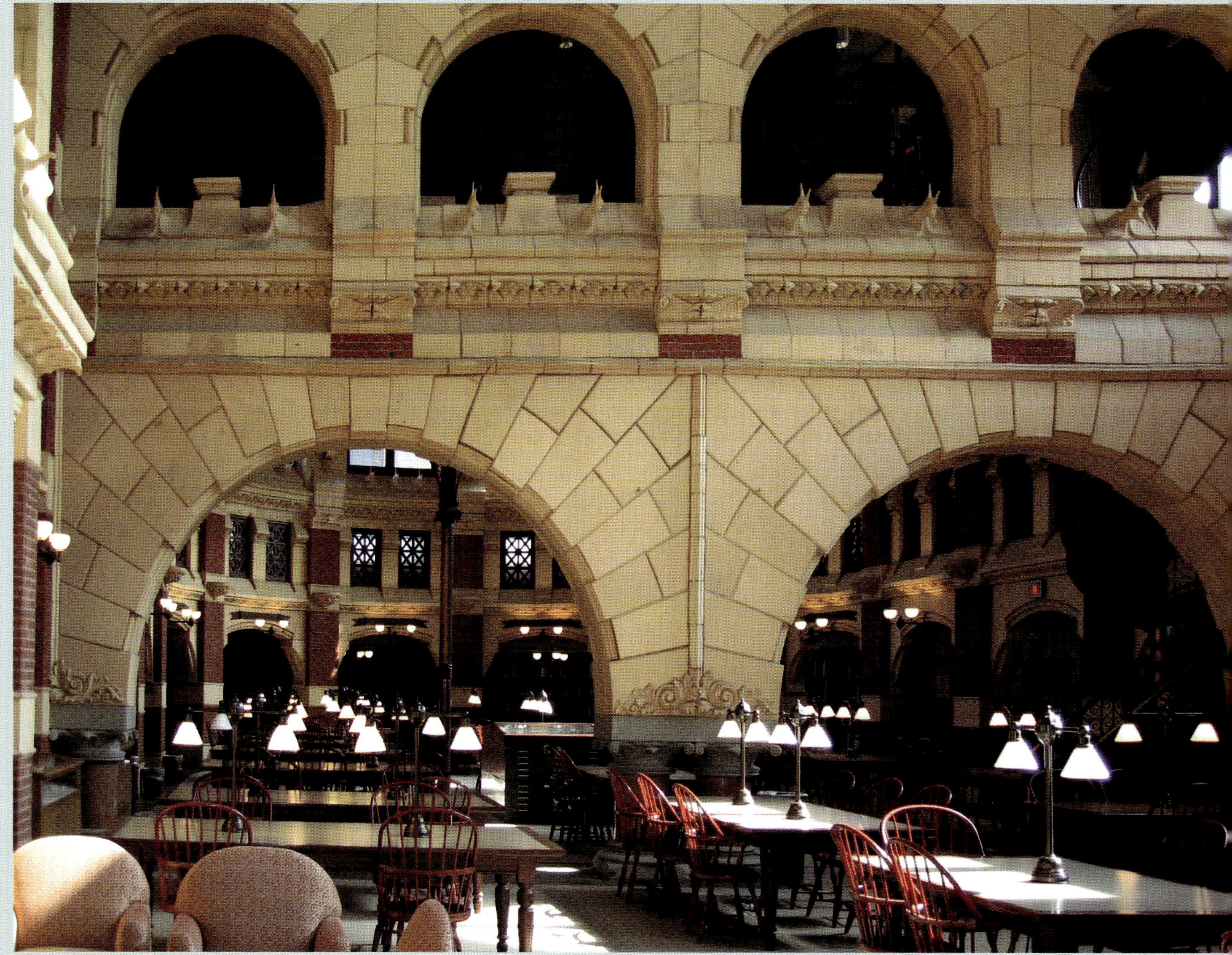

6 TEN YEARS LATER: ENCOUNTERS AT THE KAHN COLLECTION

Soon after my last session with Fehn about the article, I arrived in Philadelphia with the notes from our sessions and a new notebook for my stay. What unfolded was an unforgettable and inspirational visit. Among my notes on the materials from the Kahn archive and the Fehn article I was poring over at the time, I recorded three encounters—with Gabor, Esther Kahn, and Dean Holmes Perkins. In a sense, for me these three conversations concluded a chapter of the education that had begun with Kahn's masterclass.

Gabor

Two months into my stay at the Kahn Collection I ran into Gabor. Below are my diary entries recording our two meetings.

November 11, 1984
From an alcove in Furness's library building I caught a glimpse of Gabor as he came through the entrance door. I recognized him immediately despite the eleven-year lapse since the last time. Once in the main room, he climbed the spiral stair to the second floor and sat down close to the railing. From here he had a great view of the main library space, but restless, he did not stay long. After a few puffs on a cigarette, he stood up, surveyed the room and promptly went down the stairs and out of my sight. "That was Gabor," I thought to myself. His hair was grey, but he seemed the same, just as I remembered him. I contemplated saying hello but hesitated, and when I turned around he was gone.

I saw him again, and just as the day before, he took the spiral stair up to the second floor, sat down in the same alcove, lit a cigarette, and the smoke drifted up into the open air and into the light. Suddenly I missed the Kahn studio and felt sentimental. After a few puffs he got up, looked out over the library, then went straight down heading towards the entrance, but stopped at the counter and started an animated conversation with the librarian, supporting his argument with a roll of yellow tracing paper. I could not hear what they were discussing, but even from a distance it appeared to be an intense conversation. The librarian was not saying much, just shaking or nodding his head, laughing, and trying to keep up with the words that hit him. After a few minutes they departed, leaving the yellow tracing paper at the desk by the door. It was as if another piece of my experience and memories as a student in Kahn's masterclass ended unresolved. But Gabor returned to the library that afternoon. He performed the same routine all over again: the spiral stair, some

The main reading room in Frank Furness's Fine Arts Library at Penn. Alcoves on the mezzanine level look into the space. *P. O. Fjeld.*

puffs followed by coughing, and a quick surveillance of the room. I was still at work in the same alcove as in the morning, but this time I sensed he was looking directly at me. He came over and asked if I was the Danish guy from Kahn's class many years ago. Instead of correcting him, I reached for his hand and expressed my pleasure and surprise to see him again after such a long time.

We stood there surrounded by books and old images, adjusting memories to fit the present, and agreeing that a great deal had changed over the years. Gabor started to talk about the "terrible America," a land without values and a sense of civilization. He said it was hard to be a man [referring to human values]. Then he adjusted his critique: perhaps it was not that bad after all, but he felt a frustration with Penn. It was as if a floodgate of a past state of mind had opened up and everything came to the surface unsorted, raw. I had a feeling this outbreak was a mixture of frustration, reminiscences of past times [and perhaps a premonition of architectural and technological challenges just becoming apparent at this time]. He continued in a sense to update me on issues that concerned him and the university, mentioning that Aldo van Eyck had been at Penn and had come into conflict with the dean and resigned. Gabor intimated that van Eyck returned home telling everyone that Penn Architecture was a madhouse and advising prominent architects in Europe to stay away. "I do not see Europeans here anymore," he said.

I invited him for a cup of coffee and something to eat. Gabor suggested the university coffee shop, and we went downstairs to the main dining hall. It was crowded, we stood in line, but after a while it was apparent we were in the wrong queue and had to start all over again. By this time Gabor had changed his mind; he did not care for coffee, but rather wanted a cup of hot water. I was very hungry, having spent the entire day in the library, but as we passed along the food counter he pointed out that everything was full of fats and starches, not healthy food for students. Well, I ordered Gabor's water and a cup of coffee, and as the food seemed out of the question, a small orange juice was added to the tray. In the meantime, Gabor showed me two pills in a tiny silver box. A friend in Japan had introduced him to the pills, which contained a particular type of healthy grass, and he added that he liked rice but the two pills satisfied everything he needed. We settled into a corner of the large room. By this time, I became more aware of the way in which Gabor was dressed. He wore an old brown jacket, blue pants, a white shirt, and a red tie. His shoes were of an army type, black and shiny. It was an unusual combination, but it fit him, almost elegant.

The following notes record fragments from conversations that Gabor and I had that day, November 11, and the next. This chance meeting was the beginning of conversations that I will never forget. The first lasted non-stop for more than four hours, accompanied by that glass of hot water, the two Japanese pills, the coffee, and the orange juice. Gabor did the talking; I just listened. I did not take notes as he was speaking; I jotted down everything I could remember late that same night.

He talked about Kahn, but left out how his personal relationship figured in his memories. It was not part of the conversation. "Kahn never gave up," he said. His work was never good enough for him. Gabor continued to say that all the project drawings could be finished, ready to be presented, but just talking to a taxi driver on his way to a meeting could suddenly shift his intentions. A trip from the office to a meeting could be fatal for both the project and the office. He could ask the driver to return, and then he would pull apart the drawing set. The gesture was clear for everyone: it was just to start all over again. The amount of work put into a project, its time schedule and financial status were at that moment secondary for him. His only focus was towards the immeasurable in architecture. Once, an architect in the office—a friend for many years—advised Kahn to stop the changes; the drawings had to be cleared and delivered because the engineers were waiting. He didn't stay with the office long after this outbreak of frustration. Kahn had no limitations in relation to his own working process. He was never really satisfied with any of his projects. Sometimes late at night the office could look like a battlefield. Working on the Venice project, Palazzo dei Congressi, he pressed the charcoal so hard that it ripped the original drawing. This often happened: the dust, "the gun smoke from the charcoal," as Gabor called it, "filled the room and no one dared talk before the chalk smoke had settled on the floor."

Gabor said Kahn was a very powerful man with a brilliant mind. He could stay up for several nights in a row. Tired and half-dead at 1:20 in the afternoon—but when the secretary said he was supposed to be in class in ten minutes, all the problems were gone. Working with young people always cheered him up. He loved his students and was seldom tired in the classroom.

We talked about the realization of our dreams. For Gabor, it was to search for truth in every sense of the word, and that the only thing that really mattered was to search for the truth from within, the realization of a particular internal thought or idea. "Some work is eternal and has a life of its own once released from its maker," he said.

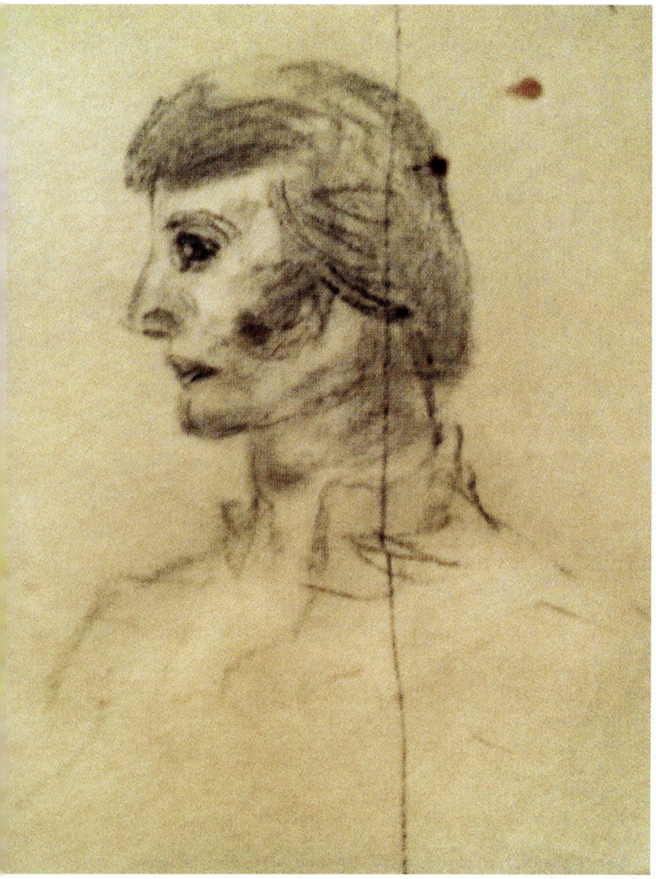

Sketch of Gabor by Louis Kahn. *Nathaniel Kahn Collection.*

My intention with the stay at Penn is to study and read whatever is available on Kahn's thoughts and writings about light, but Gabor did not want to talk about daylight. He responded with, "Real light comes from within oneself; the sun must also get its light from somewhere. Your built work has to be so strong that the sun asks for permission to enter instead of you asking for the sun. The real light comes from within. [. . .] Natural light, how unnatural can you be? Light comes from within. The sun is only an instrument."

Gabor was always searching for a deeper meaning in words, or reinventing words to establish a revised understanding of old words. He is a poet that does not write. Gabor has a unique capacity to put together phrases that in the right situation would set off a chain reaction of thoughts in others. In the middle of our conversation he set up a hierarchy of words as follows:

GOD
GRACE
SPIRIT
SELF

We talked loosely around them and agreed that "grace" was the most beautiful word of all. He also mentioned that another set of words had come to him recently and impacted his stature and appearance. He said just thinking about this set of words gave him energy. [I could not remember all the words when I later tried to record our meeting.]

RESPECT
AWARE
REALIZATION
RELIANCE

Gabor said he had thought about these words over and over again until one day he realized that he should add "self" to the list. This was such a revelation that he felt it changed his body posture and made him walk differently, with more grace and dignity. Gabor said that for a long time after Kahn's death he had been looking for some sort of sign, a kind of recognition, and for him the discovery of "self" was a sign of grace. After so many years, he finally felt as if Kahn had given him a sign. From this point he shifted the conversation slightly, commenting on Kahn's ancestors from the Baltic countries, and then on how after the move to the United States his father was suddenly without a language and job, so he opened up a candy store. Gabor mentioned something about picking candy in the air, but I said that to sell candy, no language was needed. I think he was puzzled by this remark, as he began to elaborate about the room with the man and his candy. After this, the Roosevelt memorial project entered the conversation.

Gabor said that after Kahn had finally completed the Roosevelt memorial project he was always humming in the office. The memorial was a room with a garden—that was all. The staff in the office also noticed a change. He continued to say that the memorial was first of all a place for mankind, for all, and even Roosevelt, whom Kahn greatly admired and respected, was just another human being in this room. He had finally accomplished a project which fulfilled his idea of institution. He was ready, and Gabor considered this a great moment in an artist's life. After the completion of the memorial project, Gabor sensed that Kahn lost some of his intense interest in other projects, or they became more complicated and unclear. He was constantly referring to the one room and the garden.

Gabor went on to comment on the Kimbell Art Museum. He said that Kahn never let go of the project, even towards the end when it seemed perfect. It could not be better, but just the same, he continued to work on it. He could have built that museum out of everything or anything, so strong was his belief in the project, he simply had to get that structure up in the air. When someone in the office suggested travertine, Kahn was at first hesitant, having never had a commission that allowed for such expensive materials. But it was not long before the idea gained acceptance. A man was sent to Italy, and upon his return Kahn looked at the material samples, and with a glimmer in his eyes he said, "Let's go. The war is on."

I mentioned that Kahn told our class of the love he felt when his son held on to his pant leg in order to stand up. Gabor responded immediately with, "Different from all we know, the world is still OK. It is still fine."

From these introspective thoughts, the conversation returned to more everyday topics: the love and care for other people, outside oneself. He felt the country was losing its sense of these things, and children were hurting the most, and that social empathy was a clear mark of a mature civilization.

I commented that I felt close to Kahn as a student. I didn't elaborate because I felt that many, many students sensed a special connection. Gabor replied that Kahn was puzzled that I didn't apply for a job in the office at the end of the year, but quickly added that he never outright asked anyone to apply.

Gabor commented that Mario Botta had visited the campus, and after his lecture was depressed, since he had not been able to communicate with the audience. Botta felt the

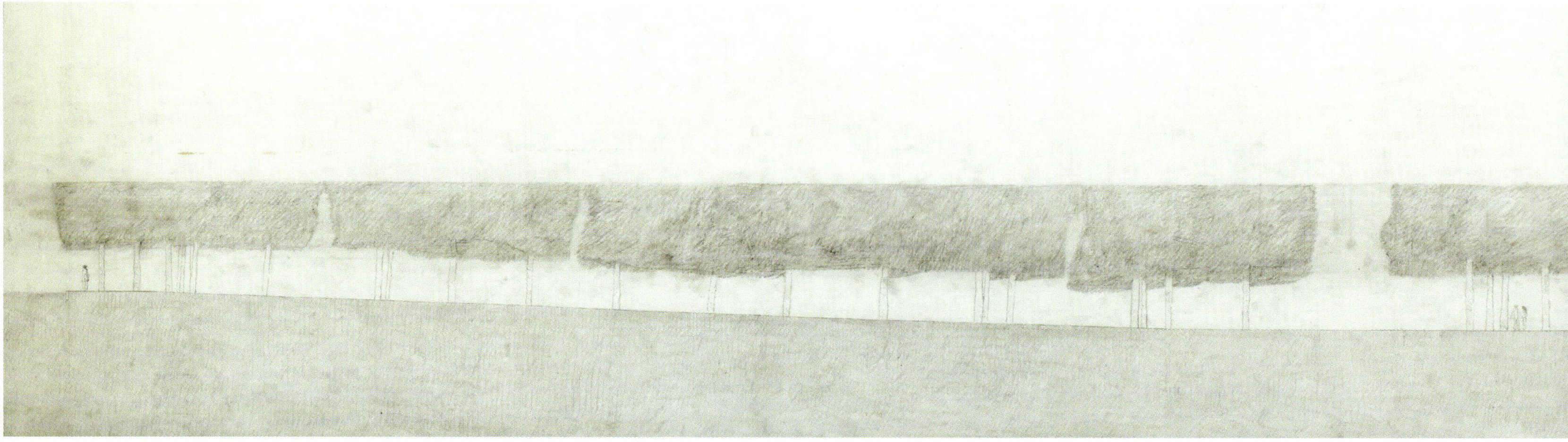

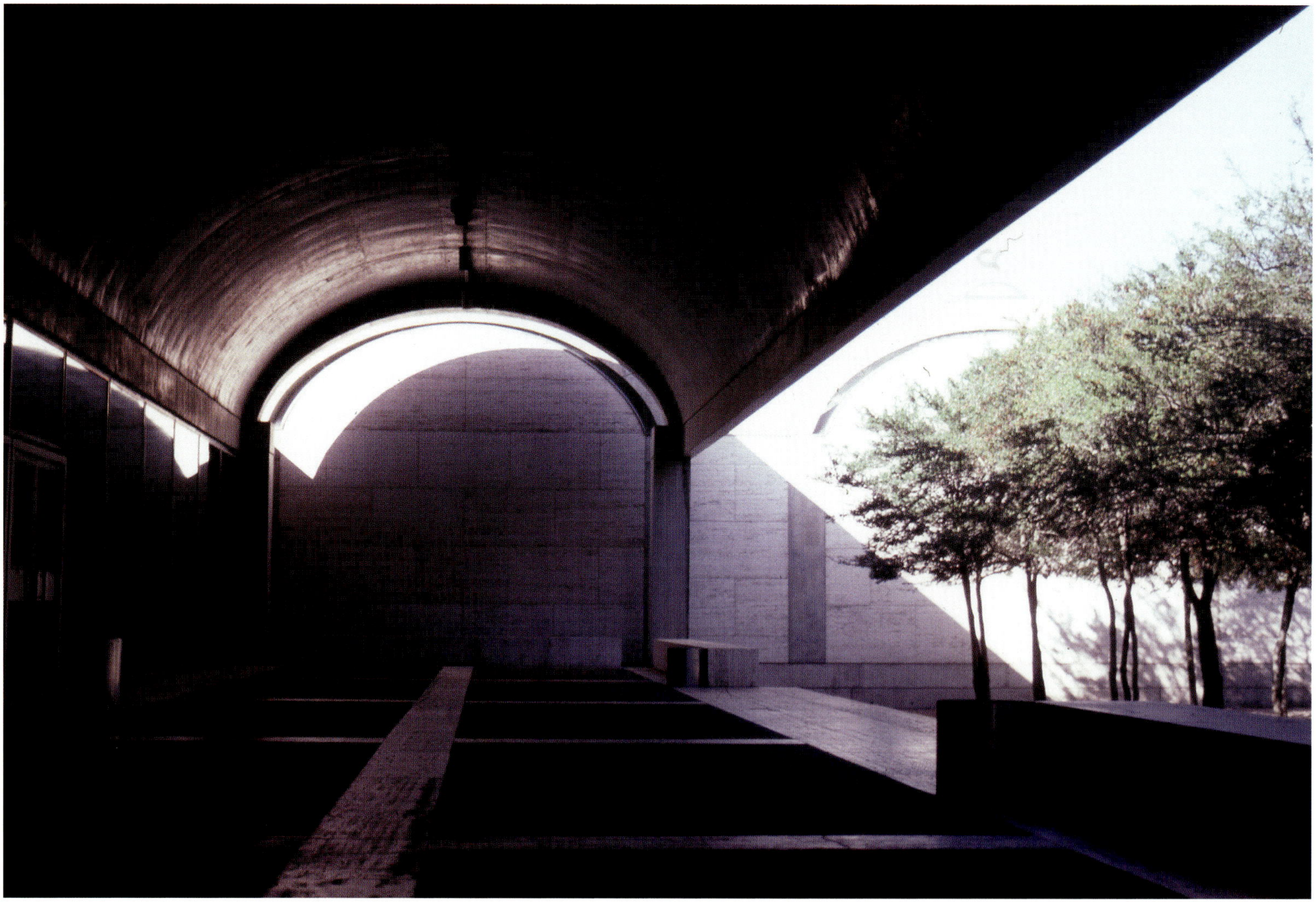

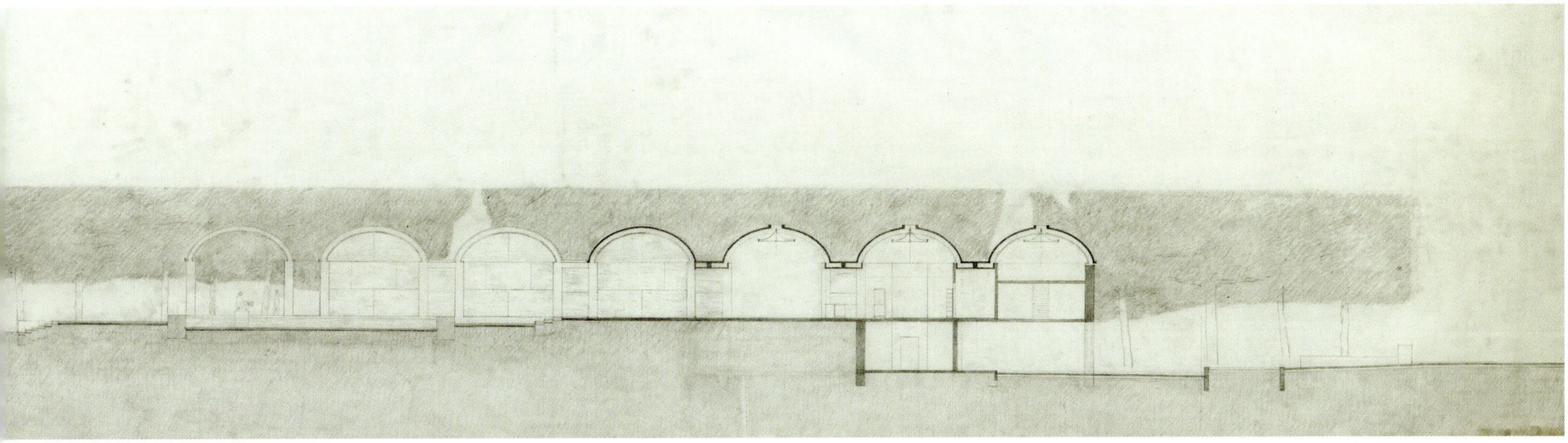

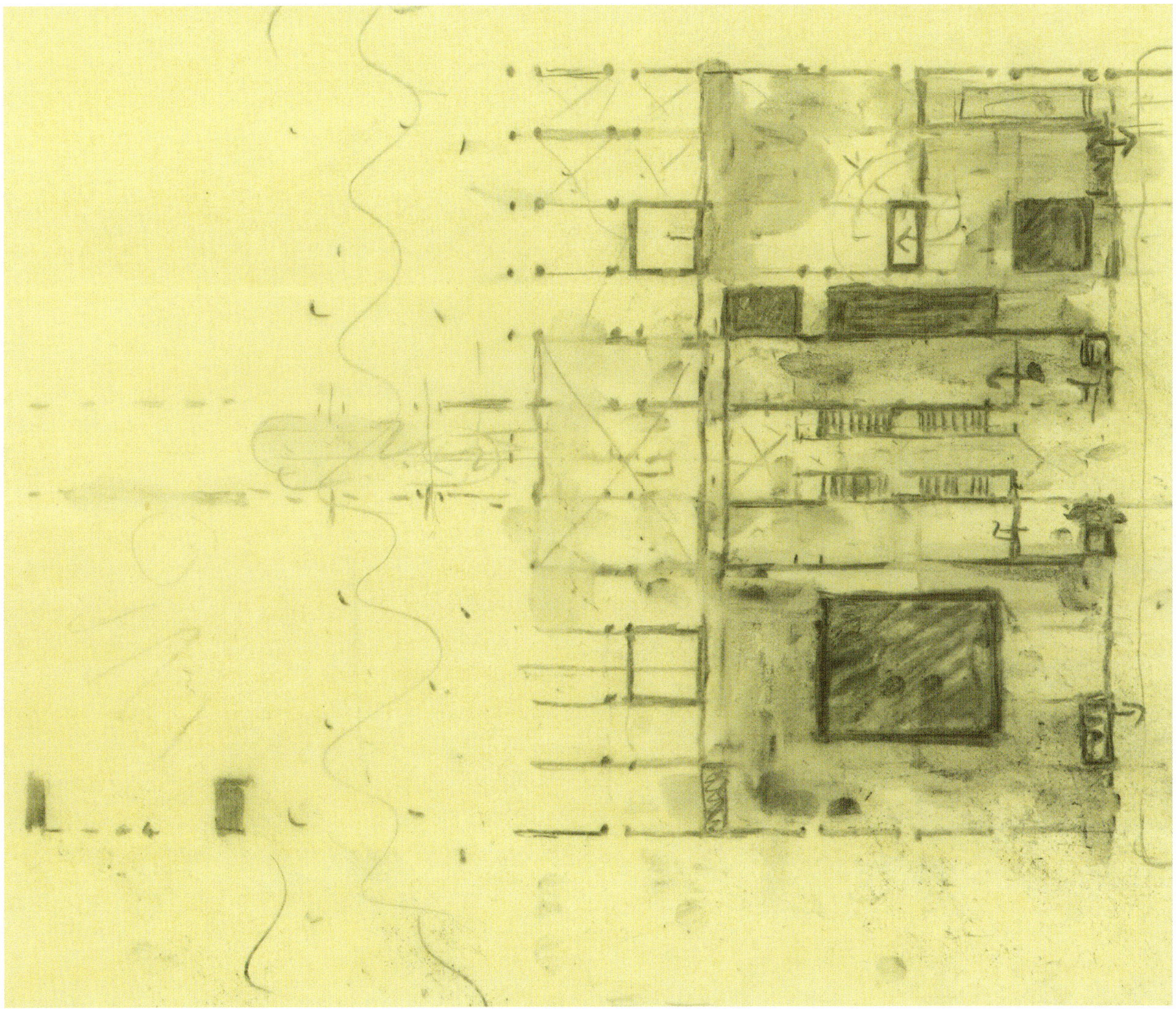

TOP: Section drawing of the Kimbell Art Museum (1966–72) by Louis Kahn. *Louis I. Kahn Collection, The University of Pennsylvania and the Pennsylvania Historical and Museum Commission.*

OPPOSITE: Entrance portico at the Kimbell. *P. O. Fjeld.*

RIGHT: Kimbell plan sketched by Kahn. *Louis I. Kahn Collection, The University of Pennsylvania and the Pennsylvania Historical and Museum Commission.*

audience just wanted him as an actor, a performance, so that they could lean back and enjoy the speech, a light head massage. Botta wanted a dialogue, a conversation. He never got it and felt disappointed. “I will never come back,” he said upon departure. I replied that he is still young as an architect and he knows what day it is tomorrow, alluding to his awareness of the commercial aspects of architecture and its challenges. I knew this remark would probably trigger Gabor. He laughed and agreed, but said Botta had talent. He just needed someone to talk to. He then remarked that the best thing that could happen to him was to be ill for a time. This would mature his architecture.

[At some point late in the conversation, I told Gabor that I had just published a book, *Sverre Fehn: The Thought of Construction*. At the time, few were familiar with the work of Fehn. Gabor was intrigued by the book’s title, and he seemed to taste every word of it, and then sorted it out the way only Gabor could do.] “The construction that gives strength to the thought. What a beautiful way of putting it, to reverse the order.”

“It is hard, reality,” he said. “But it is all worth it. At times you must walk with your head; you have to do it.” He asked if I was familiar with the work of Palladio. I said that Fehn was a very good friend of his, and that they had daily imaginary conversations. I told him that Fehn had written several stories about their meetings, and I went on to relate a few. Suddenly I felt Gabor was jealous, very jealous. He hoped Palladio one day would be his friend too. “Palladio is a true friend of architecture,” he said. And from there we went on to talk about teaching.

“I am not a social person,” he said, “and I am too free to be polite. I do meet a lot of young people and I have no intention of lying. Learning is to meet a person who has something to give.” He said if I felt this in my heart I had an obligation to teach. I related how I ended up in Sverre Fehn’s office almost immediately after leaving Kahn’s studio, and from this, to some part-time teaching. Gabor then said, “Kahn liked you. He talked about you and now I understand more of it. Norway is a good place to be for you. The place ‘North’ is like the small paper boats that always make their route downstream.” Towards the end of this first meeting, he said the reason he stopped in the library was not just to say hello. He had a feeling he knew me from inside, and it was the inside person he wanted to meet. “I am not trying to be friendly,” he nodded.

This evening while jotting down the day’s events, I reflected over all that has passed during the last eleven years. After graduation, I left for home almost immediately and was never able to thank Kahn. I thought there was still time.

November 12

I saw him across the room in the library looking at some of the Scandinavian architectural magazines and decided to go over and say hello. I believe he was glad to see me, since he took up the conversation exactly where we left it the day before. He said talking to me had made him warm inside, but on the outside, he had felt the wind coming from the North, and it was very, very cold.

Gabor then shifted the topic and went directly to the word "apartment." He commented that it was not the right word; rather, it should be "togetherment." He wanted to build a togetherment instead of an apartment: "The world has been apart for a long time. It's time to come together in a togetherment." Inhabitants would still have their "apart" (their privacy) but this apart would also belong to a togetherment. With this word he sensed the idea of dwelling would change.

He then turned to the predominance of horizontal and the diagonal axis: "Now is the time for an upward axis, the axis that could complete the three-dimensional diagram. The idea of scale has to be understood anew." I nodded and added that Kahn made the column into a room of light, a room that also could be inhabited by people. He replied that in the village of togetherment the room would inhabit the wall and through this the idea of scale would change. The village of togetherment is not one building, but a society of buildings with a presence inside the wall. Togetherment should start from the ground in a normal way, but from this point it should possess the vertical axis, gaining its true identity, its spirit, and scale. The village of togetherment should indicate a new type of scale, capable of enhancing social issues.

[He said that in earlier times] a man who took part in building railroad tracks could go home to his family after a hard day, and when the children asked their father what he had been doing he could say, "Oh, I am making something that never stops, but goes on and on and on. The kids were very proud of their father building something that never stopped."

He said the village of togetherment should serve the poor, not just the middle class. The poor are living in the street, and by just making them a little bit happier, it creates a sense of belonging, and not "apart." Everybody would have to approve of togetherment, including the middle class, and they are exhausted, as they have to work very hard just to stay middle class; that is their problem.

He wondered whether Norway had a site for such a structure and asked me to draw the topography of Oslo. He also wondered whether it was possible to form a team that could develop a togetherment into reality. "Architects should never wait for a job, for someone to come to them, but intuitively search for places and people that are waiting for an architect to express concerns."

By intuition, I dropped the following remark into the conversation: "In the Viking Ship Museum in Oslo there is a little piece of wood, a stick, and on it is written in runes 'man knows little.' That is the North." I could see a reaction, and for a moment Gabor forgot the village of togetherment. He then continued with: Let us build something that honors the North. Let us build a gate to the North, as an offering to Norway, to the people of the North. Let the gate be of two boxes of ice or glass to simulate the idea of light and water, and let one be the symbol of the soul and the other of hope, a symbol of spring. The symbol of the soul and the symbol of spring should have a similar character. The soul belongs to man, and hope belongs to spring. Gabor was really excited about the idea to build at a place where the light was on vacation half the year, to build a gate that could bring the people of the North even closer together.

He had to get some cigarettes, and we walked over to the cafeteria and sat down in the same place as the day before. I asked if he wanted coffee this time, but the answer was again no. I returned with two cups of hot water, with a lot of sugar in mine, as I expected the conversation to go on for a while. Gabor, not interested in his water, reached for his cigarettes and started to talk about the brain.

It became a very emotional conversation, an abstract and complicated story about the brains of the people living close to the North Pole. For Gabor that day, it was Norway. He started to explain his understanding of the brain in a very personal way—in particular, about the oil in the brain. He had a theory that the Nordic oil was like a chamber for all brains, and that the drilling for oil was a danger for such a chamber. It is important that the chamber is not disturbed but kept at all times in equilibrium, he said. When the drill head starts to vibrate, it sends the human being a certain warning. He said that it would take time, but it certainly would influence the way the signals from the cosmos reach our bodies. He felt that Norway had a unique location in relation to these signals, but he was concerned, as we were actually taking up the brain fluid from our ancestors. He said all people have the same antennas in relation to the cosmos, but they are hooked up and respond differently. The people of the North respond differently than the people living in the South. This again reflects on how you see things, and how you construct your environment.

From this point on, our conversation dwelled upon the relationship between life and death. He had no fear of dying; rather, he had more problems with life, the fear of life. "Life is the last fear," he told me. "The last fear is life." He constantly came back to the idea of the North gate, saying he felt good just thinking about the idea. By this time it was late in the evening. He suggested we go and have a dinner together. I had given up any hope of food so this came as a surprise, and even more so when he said he had a car outside. I never imagined Gabor could drive. He was wearing the same clothes as the day before, except he was also wearing a leather hat formed like a helmet. A truly unique experience just to see him in that hat. The car was a fairly new BMW, but the glass in one of the side windows was gone, replaced with a transparent material; and the doors from the inside had been stripped down to their structure. With Gabor beside me in his leather hat, I felt as if I were in a car race—but our conversation belonged somewhere else. We talked about the respect for the Orient. He took me to a small Japanese restaurant in the middle of the city.

He ordered a maki. I ordered a dinner. He stayed with the maki, the same plate, three times. It was a good place to sit, and from here unfurled a very personal story. He came to Kahn's office in 1965, but Kahn never allowed him to work full-time. Gabor commented that he was often sent home to sleep when the rest of the office was working through the night and that this at times would cause some jealousy. His drawings and notes would disappear, and even his desk was moved around at times. More or less unknown to Kahn, the competition within the office was fierce, especially concerning the older members who had been in the office for some time.

At times Kahn was completely exhausted and would lean over his drawing board in search of some rest. He would take short breaks, go out for an hour, and then come back to his desk. Another thing Gabor mentioned was how he would look at his drawing and say the same sentence to himself every time—"Oh no, Lou, it is not that easy"—and then he would start all over again. When he worked with charcoal, it was like war; every line was a matter of life and death.

Gabor mentioned that Kahn suffered a lot. His intense commitment also generated a form of asceticism. Every situation he could think of to make his life harder for himself seemed to attract him. Gabor said it was a way of life for him. All his life he refused to sit in a good chair. "Oh—that is too good for me, I don't deserve that," he used to say, and if somebody finally got him down he would only sit on the edge. "Who deserves—who deserves to live?" Gabor said looking at me. "Gabor . . . I'm still alive. Who am I? Who deserves to live?" In everything he did, Kahn took the hardest route possible. He continued to say that Kahn usually had a bottle of aquavit in his office and that he drank from a big glass but filled it only slightly. He would take the glass to his mouth and drink the few drops, as if it was filled to the top. He loved smoked herring and always had some tins in the office together with hazelnuts. He used to put three nuts on his table and crack them between samples of marble and say, "This is my breakfast, lunch, and dinner—and now back to work."

Kahn met Gandhi once in India, and when he returned from the trip Gabor found him extremely happy in the office. He asked what was cooking, and Kahn had explained, "I am so proud of myself—for the first time I acted like a businessman. I told them how much money they had to have in order to make my project." Gabor continued: Kahn could lose any big job, any job in any meeting. He would start to talk about the spirit of architecture, the realization of room, and the only thing the men around the table could think about was lunch. You know they were businessmen, they did not care about the spirit of architecture, they just wanted to earn a fast buck and have lunch. There is Kahn taking it all very seriously, as if the project was a matter of life and death, saying that the only thing they had to be concerned about in architecture is room.

He went on to talk about education, about Mies and how he became an architect. Recounting the story of how his father threw an axe at him and how in that moment he saw the play of light flickering in the steel before it hit the ground, Mies knew what architecture was all about. He used to lecture by just coming into the class, sitting, and not saying a word. He was sitting in a way that made the class uncomfortable, and they became aware of the act of sitting.

He talked about poetry, that it could have inspirational meaning in architecture, but it could only inspire the plan, not the section. The section had to come from something else; it has a life of its own. Gabor then said that there are two kinds of people that live in a cell—a cell which is the beginning of a room. One is the monk and the other is the prisoner. The first has movement in the mind that is upward; the other has a downward direction. It is up to the people again to choose what kind of direction will guide the room of architecture. Architecture needs a long period of preparation.

It was about midnight when I paid the bill. For eight hours Gabor had been going full speed, and he showed no sign of being tired. As we were leaving the waiter asked his name. Blushing, he said, "My name is Gabriel."

Esther Kahn

Toward the end of my stay, I ran into Esther Kahn and recorded the encounter in my journal:

> Today, I ran into Esther Kahn, who was working in the collection. Whether the curator Julia Converse had remarked earlier that a former student was visiting the collection or Mrs. Kahn actually remembered me, I will never know. But she appeared to recognize me and used my name. Unfortunately, I interrupted her by shaking her hand and saying, "I am only here to study the work of Mr. Kahn." This seemed to make her very happy. What I remember the most about this short encounter was the way she looked at her husband's drawings on the table and seemed to know every line and notation. There was one sketch the collection just received, and the curator could not place it. Mrs. Kahn recognized it immediately and added: "I can remember this drawing very well. Lou was in bed with some sort of flu, and I had to bring all kind of things up to him. You know it was three floors up! Lou made the drawing in bed." Later in the conversation, she talked about her many activities serving on all kinds of committees, and said that she was glad that once in a while someone asked about her age. She went on to say she was trying to raise money for the restoration of the Furness building [where the collection is now located]. Mrs. Kahn talked about her husband in a very loving voice, commenting that she missed him, but that she was very happy so many remembered him. For some time after his death, she was afraid that he would be completely forgotten.

By the time of my research in the Kahn Collection in 1984, it was clear that Kahn's work would not be forgotten, but the future of the archive was nevertheless somewhat uncertain. The collection was largely brought together through the efforts of Kahn's family, office, friends, and university colleagues, but at this early stage it felt somewhat informal and precarious. During my stint, for days I was often the only researcher there, which must have been frustrating to the curator, considering the importance of the collection and the efforts so many had made in saving Kahn's drawings and papers.

Dean Holmes Perkins

Just before leaving the university, I had a conversation with George Holmes Perkins, who had served as dean of the Penn architecture department during most of Kahn's tenure there. I recorded my impressions of this conversation, which took place in his office, in my notes.

Dean Perkins is probably a man of knowledge. I am puzzled by everything after our meeting. He is very kind, yes, but every time I talk to him, it always seems as if I am disturbing him. His strength is really the way he depresses you, making you feel somewhat uncomfortable. Though at the same time, he gives you strength such that you really want to prove to him that you also know a little bit of something.

Mr. Perkins was the dean during Kahn's period at Penn, but what happened between them there, and what kind of relationship they had, I do not know. He talked somewhat negatively about Kahn, which might be OK, but it is the way he does it that puzzles me a little. Difficult to accept his success? He said it was only during certain periods in his career that Kahn talked about light. He was not always possessed by it. Perkins sensed that in his early work Kahn was more occupied with achieving a workable plan, and that it is in the plan that his architecture is strongest. He never understood Kahn's relationship to the land. He was puzzled by Kahn's orientation towards his buildings, and he felt that some rooms were luckier than others in that sense. I mentioned that Kahn had an orientation that belonged more to the cosmos, a higher hierarchy of orientation, and Mr. Perkins agreed with that. [Considering my young age and enthusiasm, he probably let this comment slide.]

I said that my aim was to go deeper into Kahn's work, but Perkins replied that he did not know what I had to add. Well, that is what I am trying to figure out. Perkins reminded me that architecture can never be based on light alone, as it has to rely on everything else that goes into its making. I really do not think that he was very interested in the subject, but, anyway, he was generous and we continued.

He said that very little had been written about Kahn in relation to his city and urban planning work, but that Kahn never really participated in the urban scene and in those discussions. This puzzled me. He was probably never asked or invited into the discussions. Perkins said he had a work relationship with a man named Bacon, but they were never able to communicate with one another. Kahn wanted to do the total plan at once; Bacon wanted to do a little bit at a time. They never met in their conversations, and Kahn was left out. Perkins said that Kahn's plan was absolutely unrealistic at the time—it would not work.

He said that the lighting in Kahn's Yale University Art Gallery was really bad. You can hardly see the paintings in there, he said, but added that when the building was first finished, it got a lot of publicity and everyone liked it. I had nothing to say. The building has, in my opinion, very distinct natural light in its interior, different in every room, and it is certainly a building that understands the importance of daylight.

Well, I sort of tried to say that, after all, Kahn was occupied by light and his buildings show an intensity of light that is remarkable. I mentioned that I had just visited I. M. Pei's new art gallery [his extension to the National Gallery of Art in Washington, D.C., which had just opened at that time] and said that its main space had lots of natural light, but that it didn't seem to affect the space itself. Mr. Perkins said that he supported that building due to its large, generous open spaces. I did not make any more comments. I was afraid to go any further, and our meeting ended.

Looking back, it was not a great conversation, but it was not such a bad one either. He reminded me that if I was going to work on a book on daylight in relation to Kahn, the man's personal development must also be part of that story. Kahn's history of light is the history of himself and his architectural development.

A short time after this conversation, I left to travel around the United States. I visited a great deal of Kahn's built work, and by early spring I returned home to Oslo.

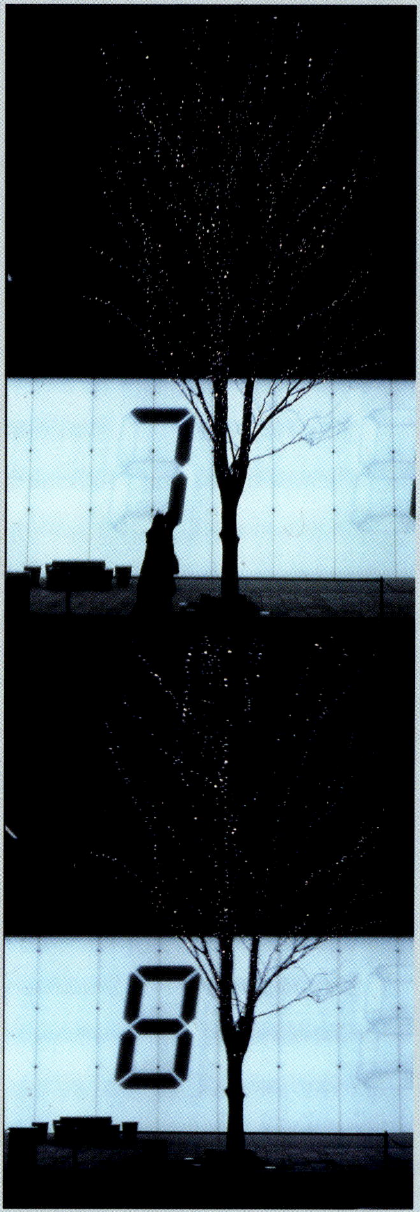
7
8

7 THE WAY THE EARTH MOVES

As our masterclass came to a close in the spring of 1973, we entered a profession at the start of a profound transformation. Although we did not fully anticipate all this would entail, we could sense that a general change of mood was unfolding. The early postwar generation of architects were now well established in their practices and influential through their teaching and writing, and their architectural focus seemed far more directly project-oriented than our comprehensive approach in the masterclass. Thus after graduation many of us faced the dilemma of finding balance between the work culture inside the practice and the more personal creative search that Kahn had introduced to us.

Many areas of the building industry were then becoming large corporate entities, multinational and interconnected. The process of producing building parts locally or regionally that had prevailed at the beginning of the century was being supplanted by a large-scale industry that privileged prefabrication. This change had significant consequences, as the new global scale of production, the growing demand for increased profits, and the minimization of economic risk promoted different expectations within the building industry.

Many architects who had initially supported greater standardization now found their work restricted by a multiplicity of preapproved options more or less set by large-scale manufacturing. The American building industry had been moving toward greater standardization for some time, but the slow economy of the period just after my graduation fanned an even greater dependence on new technologies and prefabrication—and the European building industry quickly followed suit. One consequence was that focus shifted heavily to a predesign strategy, in which a project's visual communication to the user and its economic viability were now major factors. Meanwhile, expanding building codes and regulations impacted the working process and competencies within most offices, and this in turn gave rise to changes within architectural education. But even among the socially oriented architects who vigorously questioned the impact of increasing regulation and commercial influence there was not consensus about the best way to confront these transformations.

By 1980 detailed regulations and codes were in place in many countries. Despite all the good intentions that initially motivated greater regulation, this coordination proved first and foremost profitable for large businesses and questionable in relation to deeper architectural concerns. To address this transformation, many offices expanded in size, offered more specialized services, and increased their strategic focus on publicity. The architectural client was also changing—from the strong individual representing a firm or governmental agency to a committee format. This new client expressed its ambitions and functional requirements differently

A clock in Tokyo, 2012. *P. O. Fjeld.*

1984 | Jean Prouvé dies.

1985 | Norman Rice dies.

1987 | Kahn's Graduate Theological Union Library completed after his death by Esherick, Homsey, Dodge & Davis, Peters and Clayberg & Caulfield. Michael Graves's Walt Disney World Dolphin Hotel inaugurated.

Henry-Russell Hitchcock dies.

1988 | Mario Botta's Mediatheque in Villeurbanne completed.

Ray Eames dies.

1989 | Tadao Ando's Church of the Light completed. Peter Zumthor's St. Benedict Chapel completed.

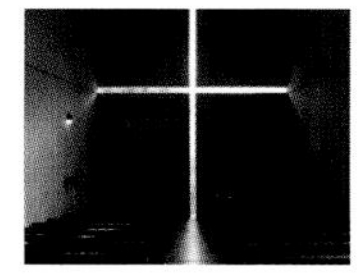

Church of the Light. *Jon Reksten.*

and, in turn, altered the program. The brief was now addressing a much larger and stratified building committee, and this resulted in a certain amount of inflexibility. The first stages of the design process were forced to adapt to official procedures in order to satisfy all the various stakeholders. The kind of creative dynamic between an individual client and architect—such as that between Kahn and Jonas Salk—was fast disappearing. The potential for spatial investigation to reenergize human institutions was now threatened by the ongoing transformation within the architectural profession.

Fortunately, some studio offices managed to survive and significantly contribute to architectural innovation and education during this time, but for most it was increasingly difficult to secure larger viable projects except through open competitions. Corporate clients looked more and more to the larger architectural firms to fulfill their needs: these firms had the economic backing and labor capacity to showcase new products, technology, and the latest fads; and they tended to work within the comfort zone of the corporate clients' immediate operative concerns and standard functional brief. On a local level, a business-oriented architectural firm with a good grasp of public relations made sense for the strategic client. Such a firm could sell the public on their design proposals by pronouncing that they addressed certain "needs"—a convenient and effective alibi for masking architectural mediocrity. Meanwhile, "teamwork" and "consensus" became the new bywords for obtaining work. The new fast-track building production strategically observed the codes and laws to ensure speed and a means of control, thus there was little outside incentive to question the core motivations behind these regulations. As firms adjusted to and behaved in accordance with the new rules, they more or less gained a free pass in developing cities, suburbs, and countryside.

Though this transformation unfolded simultaneously in North America, Europe, and Asia, there were key differences. In Europe the various climates, cultures, politics, population densities, and economic environments slowed and differentiated the process. Meanwhile, faster and easier communication was beginning to have clear ramifications, and practicing in an influential country whose language was international conferred definite advantages. The increase of this "international" communication—first through cheap publications, and later through the internet—also affected education faster and on a broader cross-cultural scale than previously.

Many architects of the early postwar generation were well versed in Marshall McLuhan's writings concerning communication and technology, but they were not prepared so late in their careers for the full impact of the changes that McLuhan had anticipated. It was one thing

1990 | Steen Eiler Rasmussen and Lewis Mumford die.

1991 | Herman Hertzberger's *Lessons for Students in Architecture* published.

1992 | August Komendant and Alison Smithson die.

1993 | Charles Moore and Reima Pietilä die.

1995 | Shigeru Ban's Paper Dome (Takatori Church Rescue Center) completed. Dominique Perrault's National Library of France completed.

1996 | Peter Zumthor's Therme Vals completed. Juhani Pallasmaa's *The Eyes of the Skin* published. Esther Kahn dies.

to master new skills—but to survive seismic changes within the profession, quite another. Experienced senior architects soon fell behind in many offices, losing some of their earlier standing and control, since most junior colleagues were the fastest and most technically equipped to produce the final project material. By the late 1980s it was clear there would be no escaping these changes, as government agencies and large companies came to expect digital working drawings along with lavish presentations from their architects. Many schools adapted to these demands without any deep reflection on how this would impact the curriculum or on the challenges of teaching new technological competencies without compromising earlier architectural knowledge. These technological advances unleashed both immediate and unforeseen complications within the profession as well.

Many new graduates faced a changing landscape for employment. Architectural firms' hiring now tended to hinge on whether an applicant possessed the latest computer-programming skills and on how quickly that applicant could apply these to an ongoing or upcoming project. The notion of employment as a reciprocal investment was on the decline. As the informal talk around the drawing table grew increasingly static, and as newly hired recent graduates were permitted only limited access to physical building sites, the sharing of information between older and younger architects diminished. This was the start of a serious generation gap—a development applauded by many as it altered the traditional office hierarchy. Meanwhile, architectural discourse was deeply impacted by an almost uncritical admiration for the capabilities of the new tools, thus technology more than architecture guided the discussion.

During this period, Kahn's creative approach and vocabulary were interpreted by many as merely idiosyncratic, and thus questionable as guiding principles. His form drawing was regarded as an ill-conceived method for starting a project; and his insistence on the importance of discovering the essential substance of the beginning—"volume zero"—before embarking on a given program was shrugged off as unrealistic rather than embraced as a tool for renewal and clarity. Surprisingly, and far more injurious to architectural discourse, his concerns about the institutions of man were partially dismissed. For Kahn, architecture had had one unremitting objective: to recognize and strengthen shared essential human values. He was convinced this could not be achieved through context or circumstantial decisions alone, as this would allow fundamental values to become secondary to passing trends. Unfortunately, Kahn's approach to both teaching and the practice of architecture faded into the background during this period, as the general discourse moved on to a far

1997 | Frank Gehry's Guggenheim Museum Bilbao and Steven Holl's Chapel of St. Ignatius completed.

Felix Candela dies.

1998 | Construction of SANAA's Gifu Kitagata Apartment Building completed. Steven Holl's Museum of Contemporary Art Kiasma completed. Alvaro Siza's Pavilion of Portugal completed.

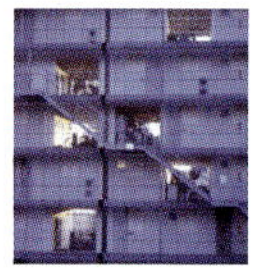

Gifu Kitagata Apartment Building. *P. O. Fjeld.*

1999 | Daniel Libeskind's Jewish Museum Berlin completed. John Hejduk's *Education of an Architect* published.

Aldo van Eyck dies.

2000 | Jean Nouvel's Culture and Convention Center in Lucerne completed.

more short-term-oriented frame of mind. For years, Kahn's aspirations were misinterpreted as romantic ruminations or unrealistic by many, and the impact of his call for a greater awareness of architecture's innate capacities seemed to quickly fade into the background.

In our masterclass we briefly discussed the computer—which of course was instrumental to the many changes described above—in terms of its being a tool, with limitations like any other tool. Considering that one of the most powerful computers of the time took up an entire floor of a building just down the street from our studio, the conveniences of today's small, easily portable instruments seemed very remote. Kahn was open to new technologies, but he carefully balanced these with his architectural beliefs. To imagine how Kahn would have regarded the desktop computer would be pure speculation, but it is an odd fantasy to envision him behind a computer screen.

During this period of technological change, many clients and architects tired of modernism's severity and therefore came to embrace postmodernism's looser visual style and historical references. Although postmodernism constituted another international style, its historic references were specific and essentially Western. Depending on regional cultural differences, a single reference could produce quite divergent interpretations. While it may have been difficult to decode these references in some of the locales where postmodernism cropped up, early postmodernism came to widely represent lifestyle and glamour, which were easier to convey than remote historical meanings. The ease with which this image-oriented style proliferated globally had the unfortunate effect of strengthening the association between the architectural image and authenticity.

The built and written work of Robert Venturi reflected this turn from local to global. His work posed some provocative questions about cultural perception; his texts, for instance, were not easily applicable to Nordic culture. The double coding or referencing that animated many of his projects assumed a shared understanding of a specific history. At the time, though intriguing to some, for many in Scandinavia his work was foremost understood as a reflection of the political environment and the growing consumerism unfolding in the United States. Thus the more important issues that Venturi took on in his early writings were overshadowed by a general perception of their Americanism. Venturi was concerned with the institutions of man, but his interpretation of "institution" was far more situational. He defined social content through a specific regional framework of visual impressions and historic perspectives, and in the wider world this social content was often misunderstood. I recorded an example of this contextual problem in my masterclass notes on the day Venturi commented on the placement of the car in relation to the house. Although we easily understood his references, they were clearly tied to

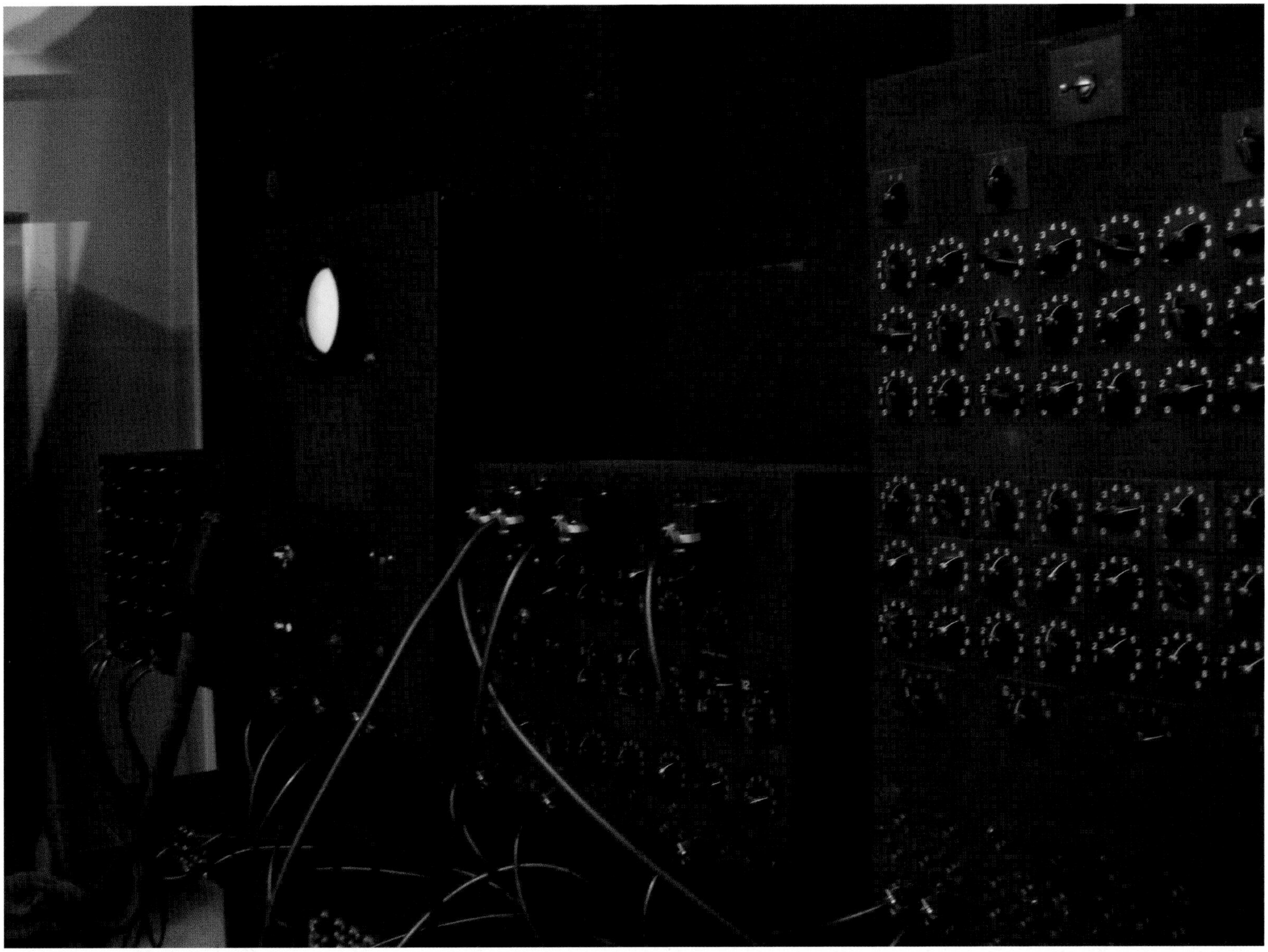

The first computer at the University of Pennsylvania. In class Kahn asserted that the "machine will never take the place of the mind, but it will prove itself as being a marvelous brain." *Herman Neuckermans.*

the context of life in American cities like Philadelphia. In Oslo during this period, a car was still somewhat of a luxury, and Kentucky Fried Chicken (an important point of reference in Venturi and Scott Brown's seminal *Learning from Las Vegas*) had not yet appeared. Despite such incongruities, the attitudes embodied by architecture like Venturi's held sway, casting local cultural references as global while promoting vague lifestyle aspirations.

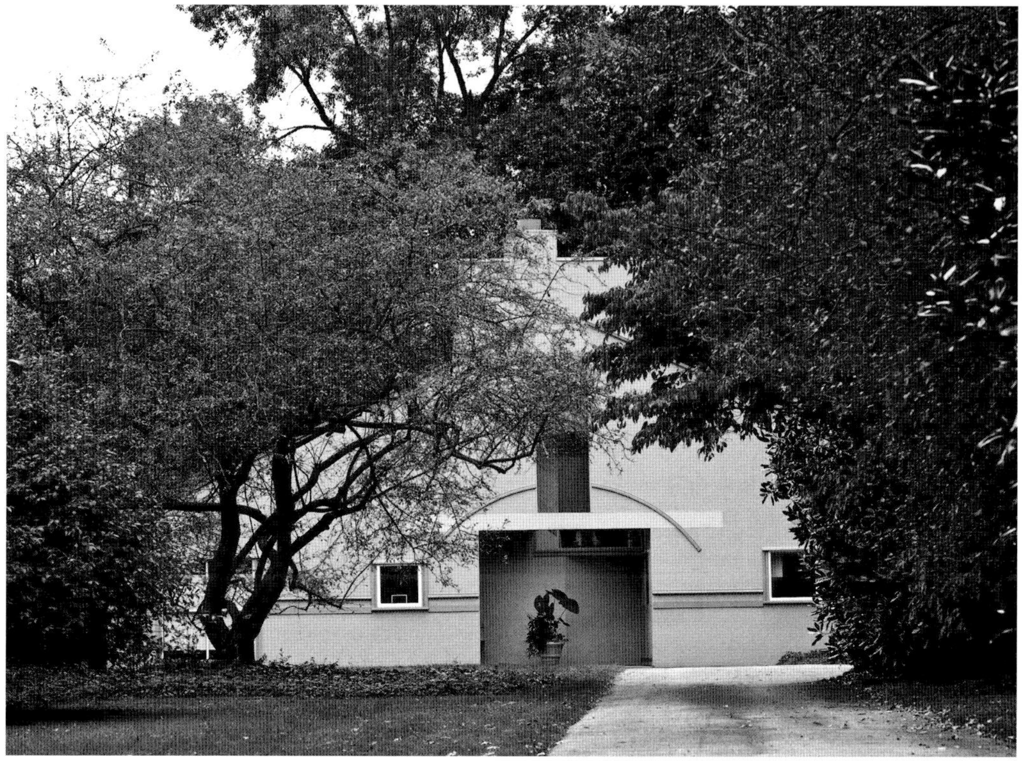

Venturi & Rauch, Vanna Venturi House, Philadelphia, 1962–64. *Jon Reksten.*

ILAUD

By the mid-1980s I had a small practice in Oslo and was teaching full-time at the Oslo School of Architecture. This arrangement was hectic but also had its advantages. Though small, the school had an exceptional professional network, which formed the basis of a lecture program that brought many prominent architects to campus over the years. At the same time, Fehn was frequently lecturing abroad, and he shared his experiences and new contacts with his colleagues in the department. One of his connections abroad was ILAUD, the International Laboratory of Architecture and Urban Design.

The year Kahn died, Giancarlo De Carlo, an early Team 10 member, began organizing ILAUD. In part a response to the difficulties and lagging momentum in Team 10 discussions, De Carlo addressed the need to involve schools in an architectural discourse with a stronger focus on social and cultural concerns. He regarded these issues as a primary challenge for the future of both the profession and education. In addition, he envisioned that a strong international studio workshop could serve as an operative tool for investigating such issues and

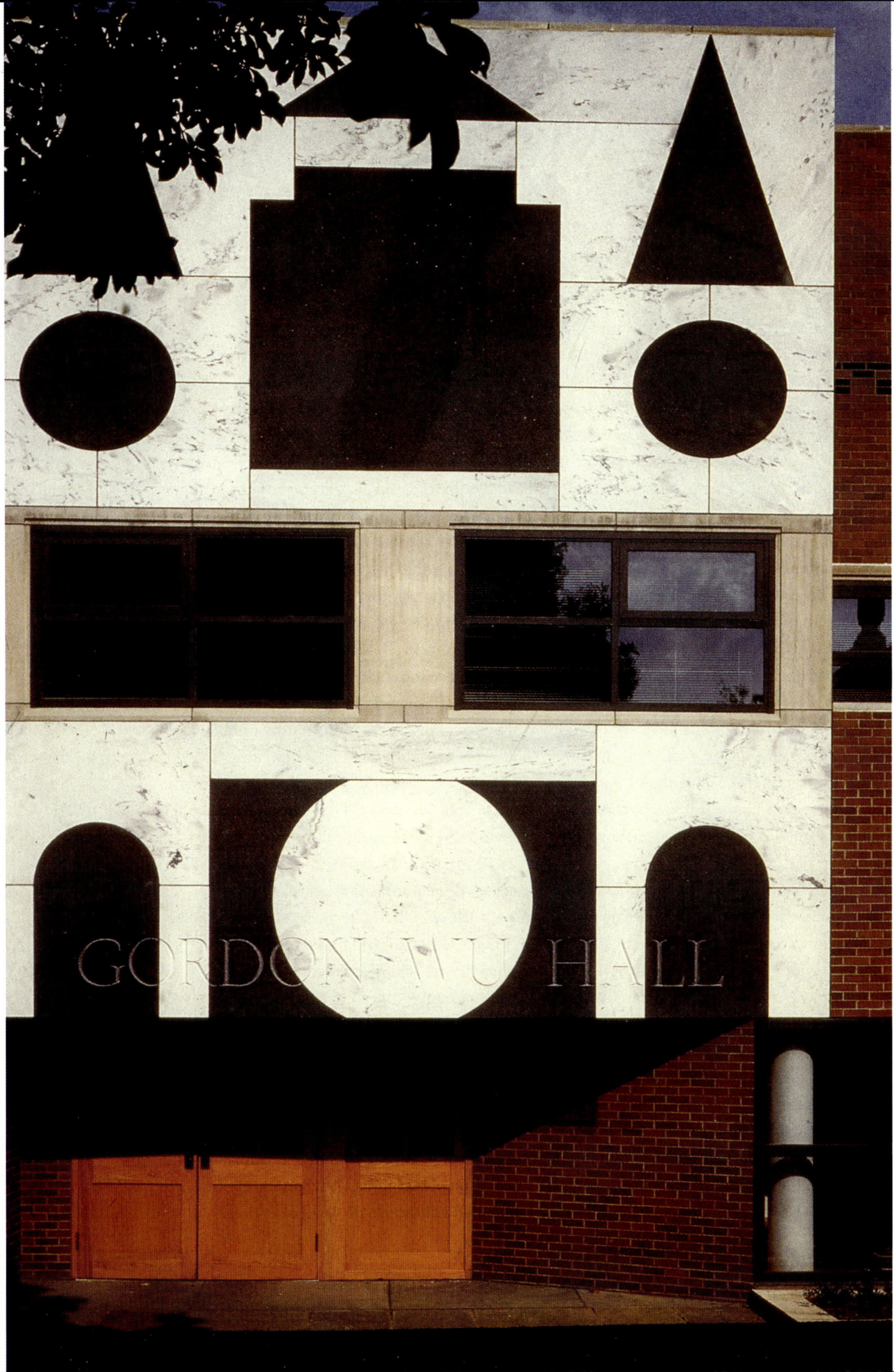

Facade as a visual image: Venturi, Rauch and Scott Brown, Gordon Wu Hall, Princeton University, 1980–83. *Oslo School of Architecture Photo Collection.*

create an environment that expanded and gave depth to discussions about them. In seeking partnerships, De Carlo first approached schools where he had ties or contacts, through either earlier CIAM connections or Team 10 participants. To establish this kind of organization was not an easy task; it would take two years before the summer laboratory and program were in place. The Oslo School of Architecture and the Escola Tècnica Superior d'Arquitectura de Barcelona signed on as some of ILAUD's first partners, and participation soon spread throughout Europe, as did a more informal network between schools. MIT and Berkeley, where De Carlo had previously served as a guest professor, were also involved early on. The University of Pennsylvania participated much later, but only for a short time. In any given year, about eight to ten schools participated in the summer residential course.

The discussions that ILAUD generated over many years were vital, constructive, and sometimes contentious, in that the generational divide, local and global perspectives, politics, and deeply humanistic values were all on the table. Always engaged with actual projects tied to a specific local site, we employed what De Carlo called "attentive design"—a thorough reading of not just a site's physical attributes but also its social and contextual elements. Several Team 10 members supported the laboratory during the summer weeks, and this collaboration altered the group dynamic that had emerged earlier in Team 10 meetings. Here a more fluid and relatively flat hierarchy evolved and De Carlo gave the younger members an equal voice. Strong differences of opinion often surfaced within the assigned groups, which brought together a mixture of teachers and students from the various schools. Strong friendships and cultural respect also grew out of these international groups. At its best, ILAUD facilitated a very open architectural inquiry.

I had my first encounter with ILAUD the summer after my Fulbright grant in Philadelphia—and I remained an active member of the laboratory team for the next seventeen years. I remember arriving in Siena for the first time, excited but also nervous. Fehn had warned me: it was a tough group, made up of strong individuals with a capacity to challenge anything and everything that came their way. But after my introductory lecture I felt accepted. From the start, I experienced the summer laboratory as a unique and invigorating opportunity. I had not traveled around Europe much before leaving to study in the United States, so to work in Italy each summer with such an international group of dedicated teachers and students was truly inspirational.

Meanwhile, what I experienced in ILAUD further strengthened my conviction in Kahn's work both as an architect and teacher. Slowly I gained a new perspective on the depth of Kahn's belief in architecture's ability to convey and support human consensus and his belief that working toward such a consensus must be an architect's priority. Like Kahn's

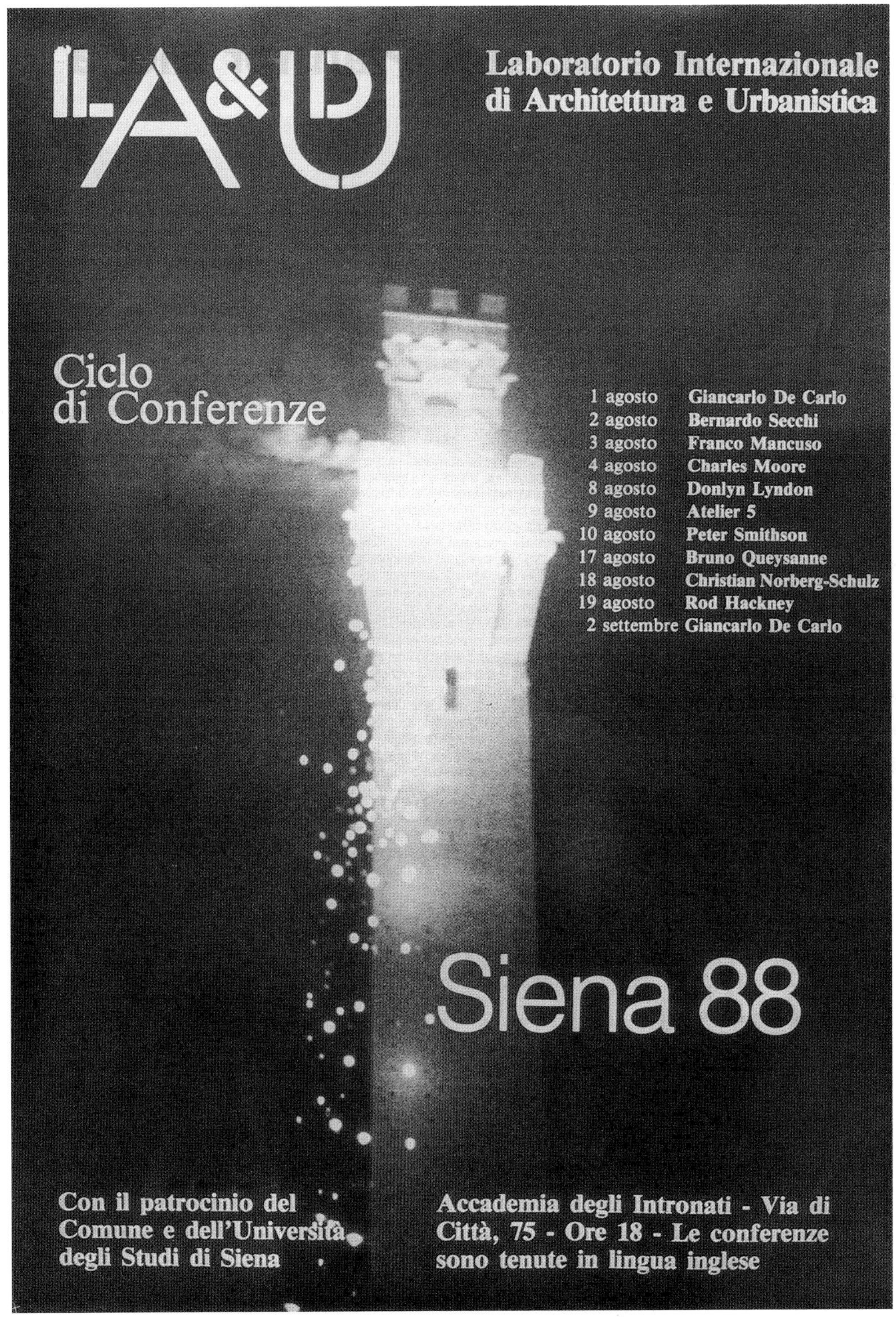

Poster for the 1988 ILAUD summer residential course in Siena, highlighting the year's list of guest lecturers. *ILAUD Archives.*

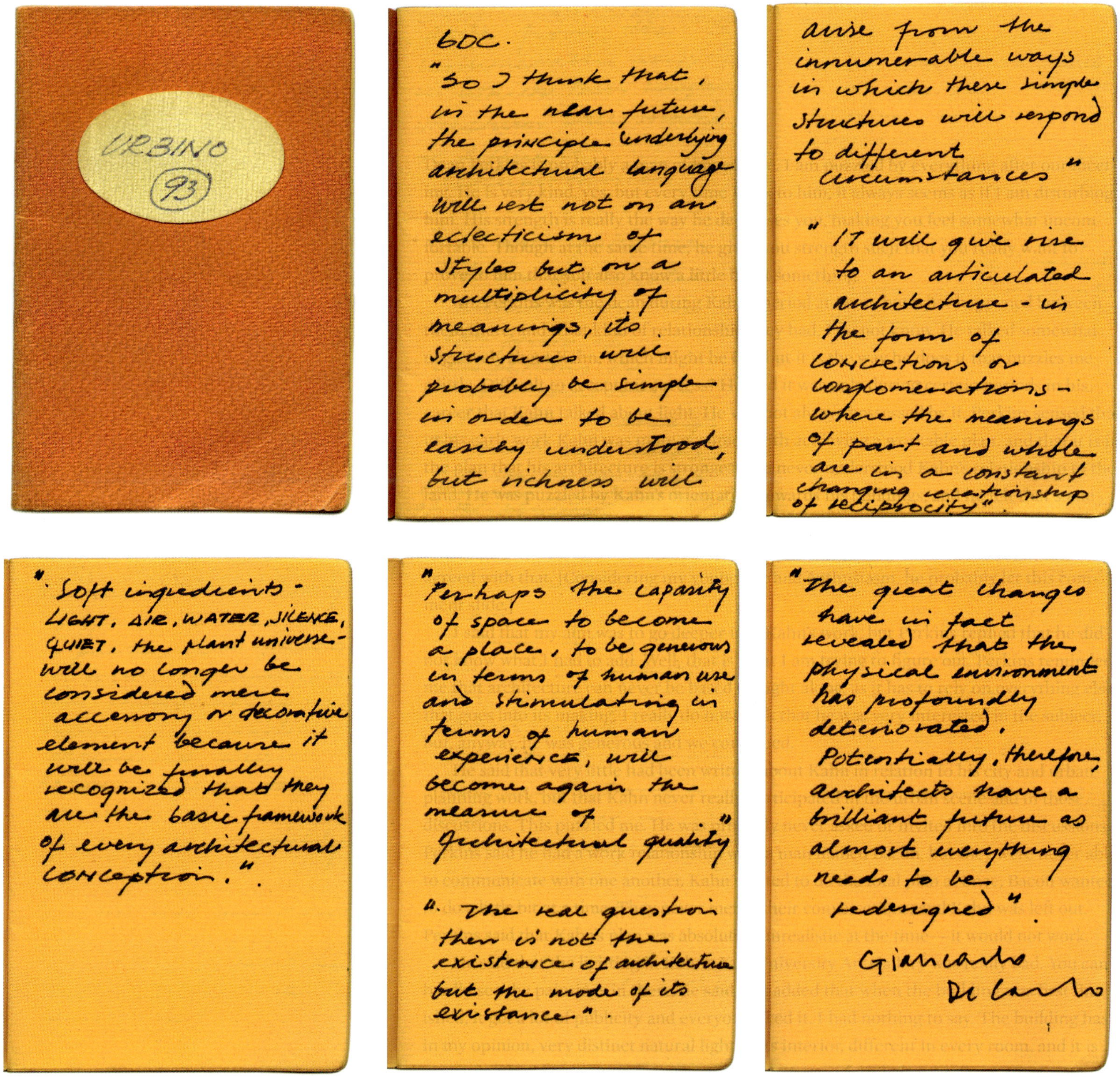
URBINO
93
GDC.
"So I think that, in the near future, the principle underlying architectural language will rest not on an eclecticism of styles but on a multiplicity of meanings, its structures will probably be simple in order to be easily understood, but richness will
arise from the innumerable ways in which these simple structures will respond to different circumstances"
"It will give rise to an articulated architecture - in the form of concretions or conglomerations - where the meanings of part and whole are in a constant changing relationship of reciprocity".
"Soft ingredients - LIGHT, AIR, WATER, SILENCE, QUIET, the plant universe - will no longer be considered mere accessory or decorative element because it will be finally recognized that they are the basic framework of every architectural conception."
"Perhaps the capacity of space to become a place, to be generous in terms of human use and stimulating in terms of human experience, will become again the measure of architectural quality"
"The real question then is not the existence of architecture but the mode of its existance".
"The great changes have in fact revealed that the physical environment has profoundly deteriorated. Potentially, therefore, architects have a brilliant future as almost everything needs to be redesigned".
Giancarlo De Carlo

masterclass, the ILAUD studio relied on a tireless commitment and confidence in the importance of the work at hand. Avoiding anything that could indicate a predetermined answer at the start of each summer session, De Carlo's initial presentation of program intentions, though always inspiring, was only a means to begin a process of discovery.

The laboratory moved to various towns in Italy over the years depending on what kind of project and economic support De Carlo had secured. However, the underlying themes in all our work engaged urban social issues in an effort to strengthen humanness through architecture. Connecting the legacy of Kahn's teaching to my experience in ILAUD was an important step. From its start to its last years at the turn of the century, the laboratory explored some of the essential issues related to Kahn's institutions of man.

Over the years the laboratory investigated themes such as "The Contemporary Town" and "Reading and Design of the Physical Environment." The philosophical depth, commitment, and architectural weight that De Carlo always brought to the discussion were remarkable. He detested architectural fashion for its own sake, and like Kahn, believed the core had to be discovered and defined first, before design or private interpretations could be pursued. For me, De Carlo's approach embodied an early quote of Kahn's that I discovered in the collection at Penn:

> We arrive at shapes too quickly because we take the end products of the creativeness of others and read into them certain appropriateness. Whereas, we should arrive at these forms ourselves through some internal inspirations of the spaces to be read. I believe that we should study the masters of today from the standpoint of how they can make a beginning for us, but not from the standpoint of the buildings themselves.[1]

During the laboratory's active years many prominent architects visited and lectured, staying a couple of days and participating in discussions. While broadening the debates, these guests often heightened the internal temperature and latent polarizations within the studio, and their involvement sometimes impacted our approach to the specific task of the summer. Because the laboratory's international mix of individuals represented a great variety of opinions, it was not unusual for the assigned working groups to be at odds about a project's direction; in some cases, De Carlo was called in to mediate. I often felt that the potential for disagreement was a deliberate step in the unfolding of the working process—and that this stage revealed the depth of what Kahn meant by "the rules of man."

I met Aldo van Eyck for the first time in this intense work environment. Although he did not participate in every summer session, his thinking and terminology emerged in many of

Per Olaf Fjeld's notes from a lecture that De Carlo presented to the studio at ILAUD in Urbino, Italy, in 1993. *P. O. Fjeld.*

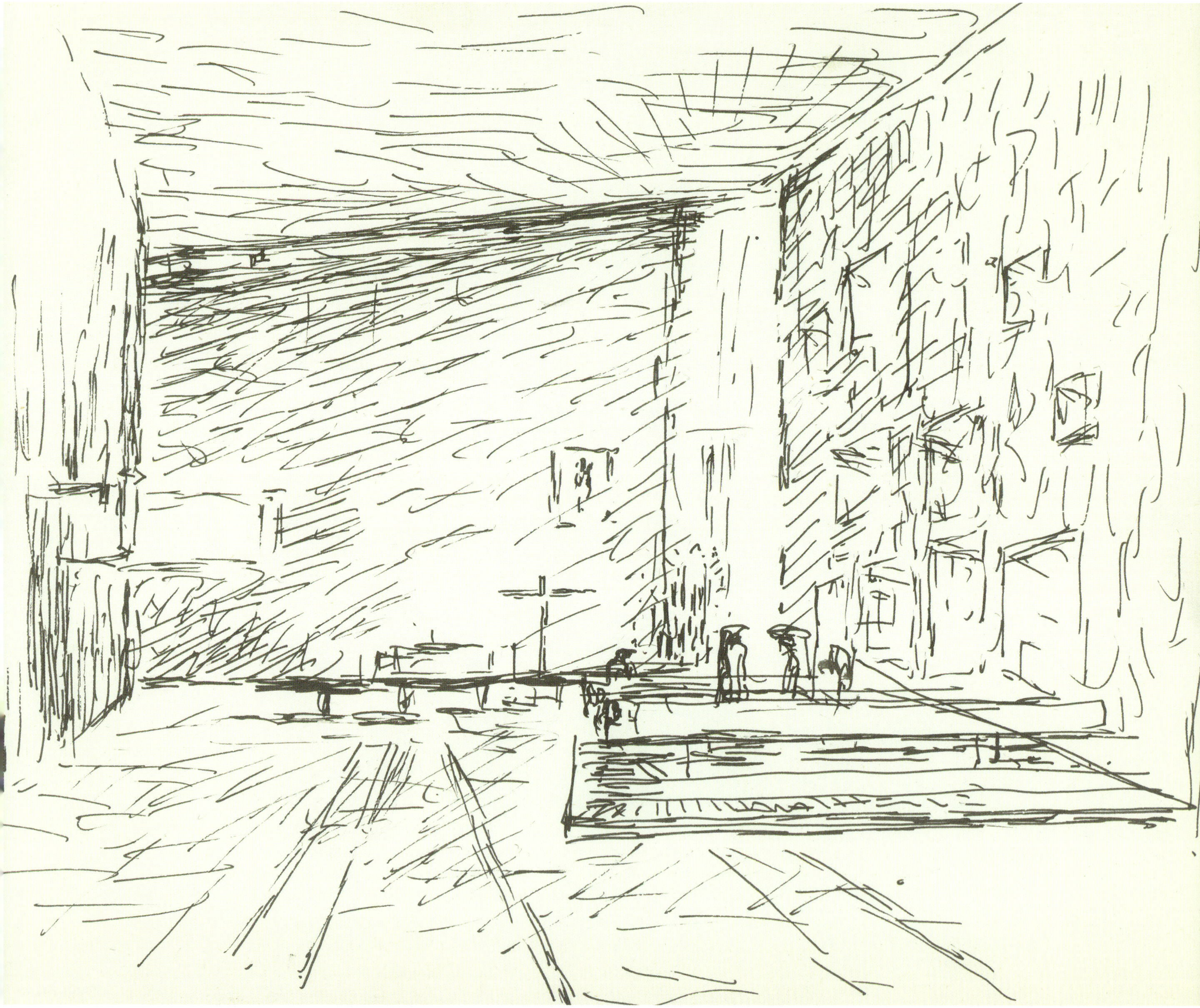

our discussions. Caught within the architectural polarization of the time, ILAUD's mix of committed individuals nevertheless enabled both Kahn's and van Eyck's thinking to lurk in the background of our discussions and thereby sharpen our focus at the start of each task. Many of Kahn's primary concerns from the masterclass were never far away, since understanding the core beginning of things was taken seriously by the ILAUD community. Van Eyck insisted that architectural reality should be understood in terms of relationships rather than functions. During one of his visits to Siena, his "Twin Phenomena," which concerned the potential of an interstitial space between two polarities, was discussed, and though this concept may have initially mystified some of the students, it ultimately influenced our work on Santa Maria della Scala hospital.

In 1989 van Eyck gave one of the principal lectures of the summer laboratory. I remember looking forward to it with great anticipation—with Fehn's praise of van Eyck in mind, and because I thought van Eyck could illuminate some things about Kahn. Unfortunately, I found his lecture, which included an extensive discourse on numbers, enigmatic and hard to follow. Afterward, working to gain clarity on van Eyck's affinities with Kahn, I became entangled in their differences. Now, in hindsight, rereading my notebook from the time, I identify several correspondences I overlooked then—for instance, between Kahn's notion of the plan as a society of rooms and van Eyck's question that evening: "Is the new form in the sequence, or does the sequence give the form?"[2] Van Eyck had talked about the border between inside and outside, as well as the importance of regarding "the edge as facade, but not the facade." He posited that "when the wall parted, a new order of inside and outside was established."[3] Looking back, I am struck by how close this thinking is to some of Kahn's comments in class.

An observation that van Eyck made late during one of his visits has always stayed with me. A group of us were sitting on the edge of the Campo in Siena during a break. It was a hot afternoon, children were chasing pigeons in the center of the Campo, tourists were thronging the central fountain, and trays of food clinked behind us. There van Eyck declared, "The world is around me, not in front of me." Inside the language of both van Eyck and Kahn there are hidden layers of architectural knowledge; to reach their full meaning is a slow, individual discovery akin to what Kahn called "knowing."

Peter Smithson was also an important contributor to ILAUD for many years. Smithson had his routines: he was meticulous in visiting the site in the morning, always in search of precise information to support his own project for the summer. In the afternoon, he would work on his drawings in a corner of the studio or join De Carlo for a desk critique of a team. He also gave a much-anticipated lecture toward the end of each of his stays. Smithson seldom agreed

Sketch by Kahn of the interior of Le Corbusier's Notre Dame du Haut in Ronchamp, France—one of the few sketches of work by a contemporary that Kahn made in later life. Kahn believed "that we should study the masters of today from the standpoint of how they can make a beginning for us." My classmate Robert Couch recorded Kahn remarking on the sweep of the cathedral's roof: "The top—Corbu, after all, mainly made a hat. It had a hat on it. Thank you, big church!" *Louis I. Kahn Collection, The University of Pennsylvania and the Pennsylvania Historical and Museum Commission.*

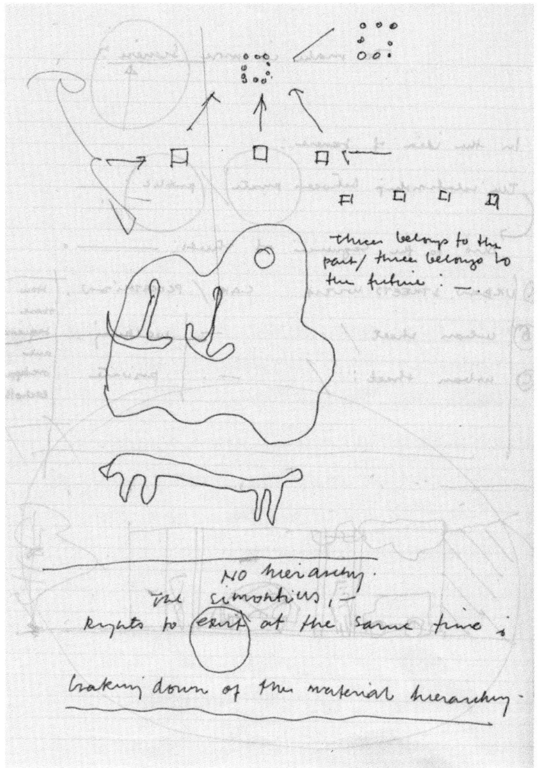

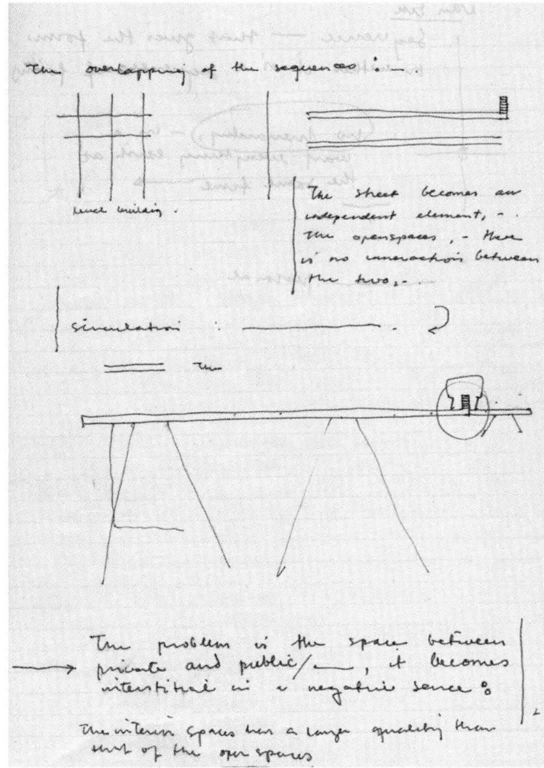

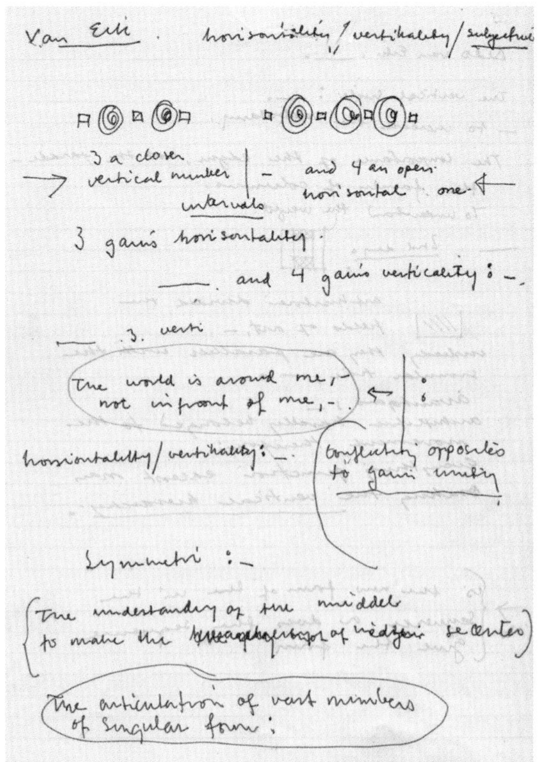

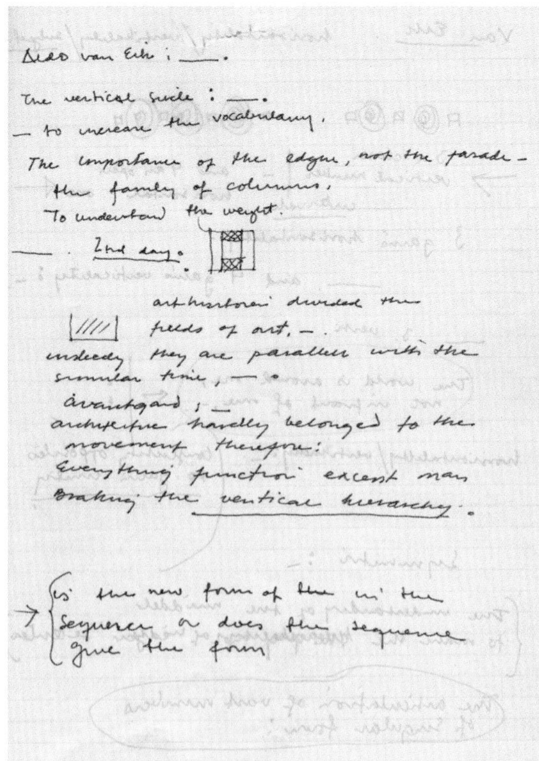

Per Olaf Fjeld's notes from a lecture that Aldo van Eyck presented at the 1989 ILAUD summer residential course in Siena, Italy. *P. O. Fjeld.*

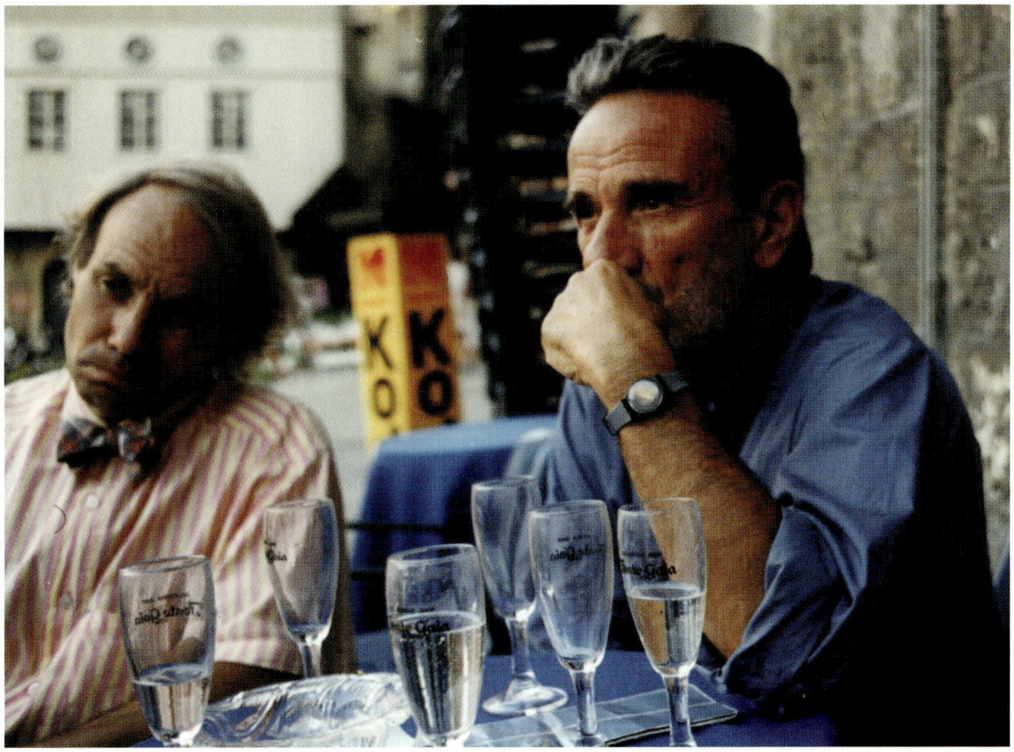

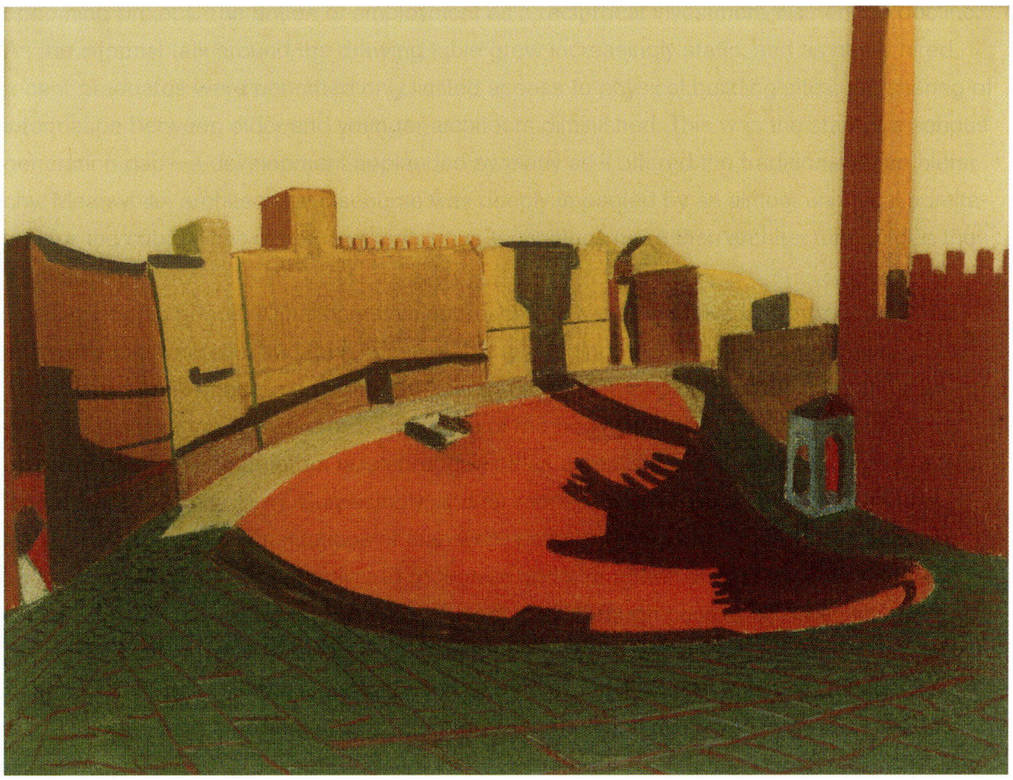

TOP: Giancarlo De Carlo (in blue) and Per Olaf Fjeld at the Campo in Siena during an ILAUD summer residential course. *P. O. Fjeld.*

RIGHT: Painting of the Campo by Louis Kahn, 1951. *Nathaniel Kahn Collection.*

outright with De Carlo, or with anyone else for that matter. However, he had an uncanny ability to reassemble details from the previous day's discussions with nuance and thus enrich our work with his surprising and incisive reflections. While this was important for the depth of discourse in the laboratory, he could sometimes turn the entire discussion on its head.

At the time, I knew very little of his role in inviting Kahn to the Otterlo CIAM meeting, nor about how much contact they had had over the years. (There is an entry in Kahn's calendar for a lunch appointment with Smithson during my fall semester at Penn, but Smithson did not visit our studio.) During the ILAUD summers, Smithson and I occasionally talked about Kahn. Though he spoke positively of Kahn's built work, after some conversations I was left with the feeling that he was testing the strength of my convictions about my former professor.

Smithson's insistence on categorizing some Nordic work and some of the buildings that Kahn designed in the 1950s as New Brutalism was one of the things that rankled me in our conversations. I just remember being irritated over Smithson's need to categorize, as it seemed to cut short an open investigation and spatial interpretation. Considering the 1952 completion date of Le Corbusier's Unité d'habitation—regarded by many as the origin of New Brutalism—this categorization of Kahn's work from the mid-1950s took hold in a remarkably short period of time. Meanwhile, the Smithsons' own early work, such as the Hunstanton Secondary School finished in 1954, was also often identified with this style. In retrospect, Smithson's attribution of this style to some of Kahn's buildings, including the Yale University Art Gallery, could have been a reaction to Kahn's later work being interpreted through a postmodernist perspective.

As a teacher, Peter Smithson had few similarities with Kahn. He often tested and prodded his students, and his reactions were unpredictable. He seemed to enjoy the stir, even though students at times avoided him for fear of being thrown off balance. Then again, he was observant, loyal, and protective of his close friends and family; ILAUD as an organization benefitted from these inclinations. But Smithson's relationship with van Eyck was among the most difficult challenges the laboratory confronted. De Carlo and his excellent field director, Connie Occhialini, managed to defuse most of Smithson and van Eyck's potential conflicts with finesse, but some were clearly not reconcilable.

Donlyn Lyndon—a founder of WLTW, which had designed the widely admired Sea Ranch complex—was another important member of ILAUD. Each summer Lyndon arrived with a positive spirit and a clear position on that summer's project. His focus was squarely on the relationship between people and place. Very committed, he always added a valuable layer to discussions, and his engagement was clearly appreciated by everyone.

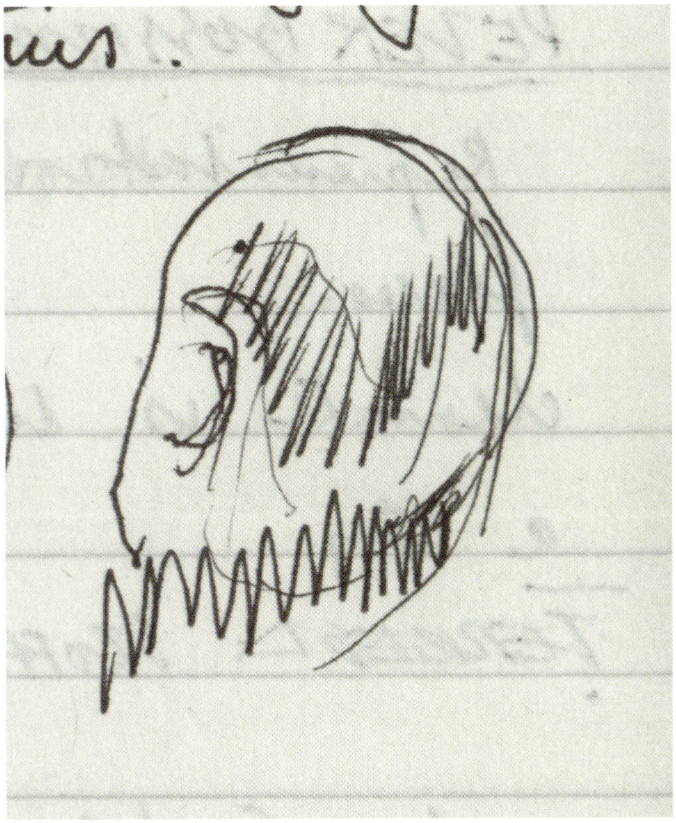

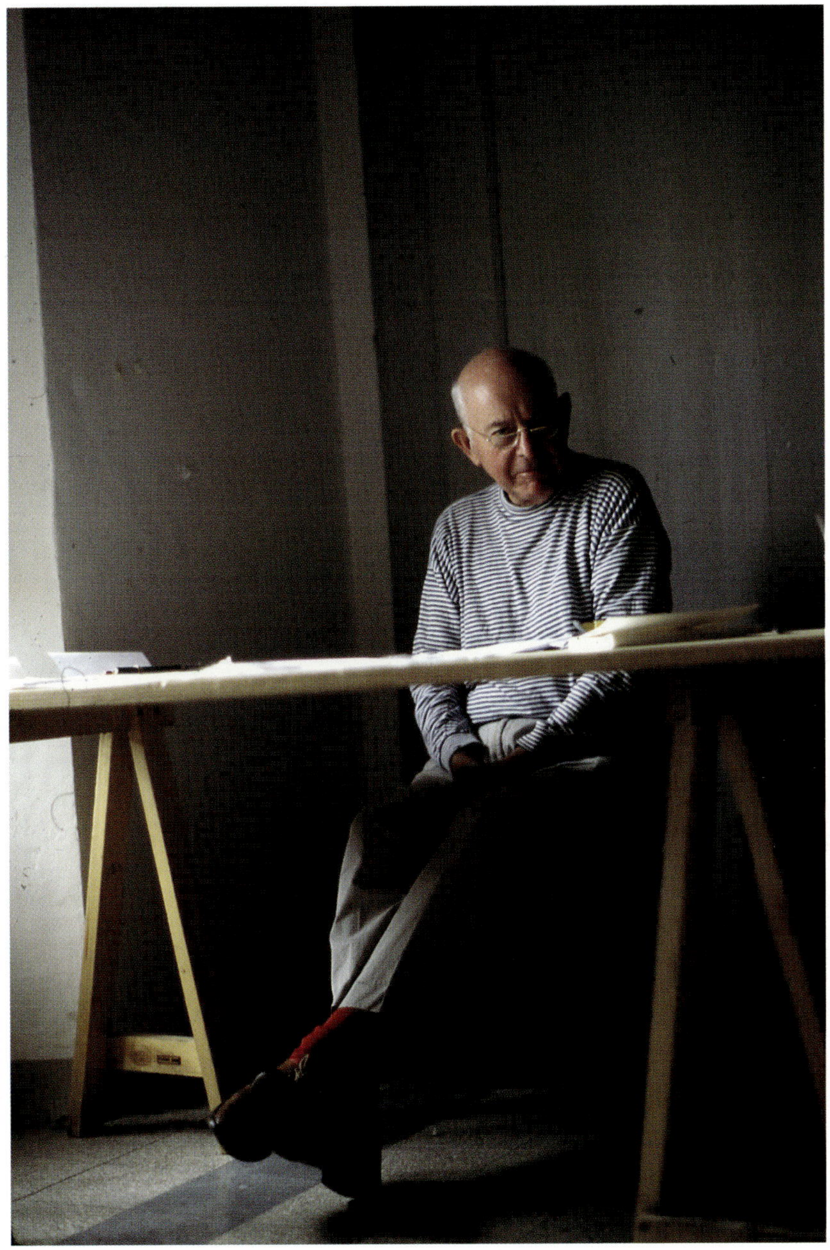

ABOVE: Sketch of the back of Peter Smithson's head by Per Olaf Fjeld, 1998. "If we all whisper, we will hear each other better," Smithson remarked during a critique that summer. *P. O. Fjeld.*

RIGHT: Peter Smithson at his desk during the 1998 ILAUD summer residential course in Urbino. *P. O. Fjeld.*

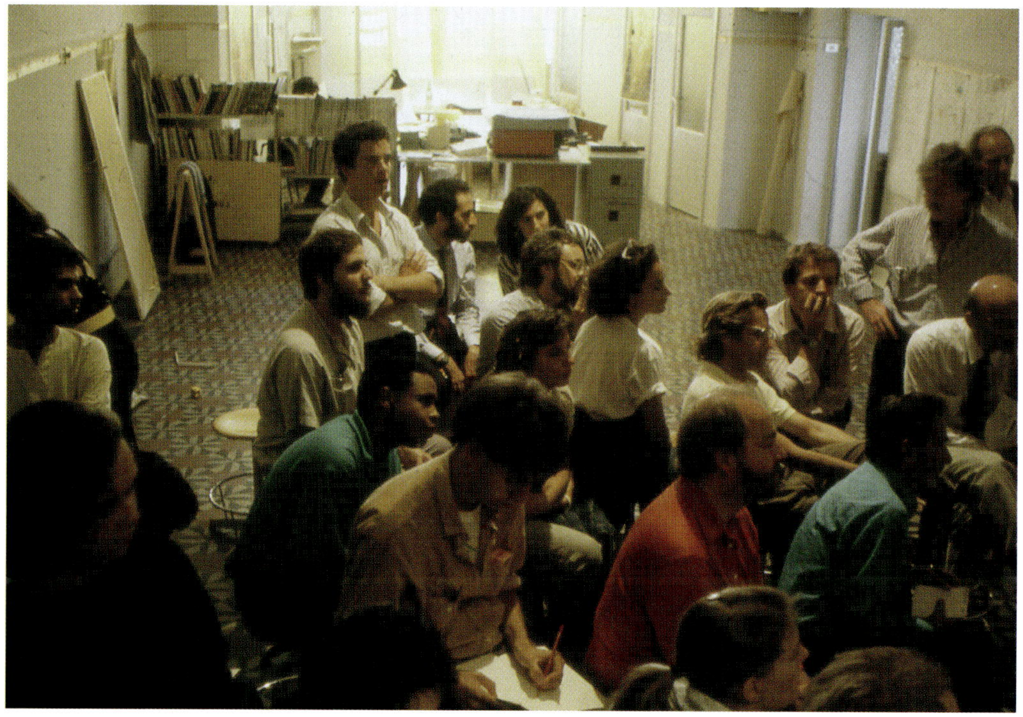

Team review at the 1988 ILAUD summer residential course in Siena. Don Lyndon (in red) is seated beside Giancarlo De Carlo (in blue). *P. O. Fjeld.*

Lyndon's students introduced perspectives that reflected not just their school's pedagogy but also new approaches to visual and media technology that were then emerging from the San Francisco area. We were a little jealous at times of the new methods of presentation that arrived with them from California. Lyndon also constituted an important link to William Wurster, who had served as dean at Berkeley beginning in 1950. Wurster had known a number of Nordic architects, including Aalto and Arne Jacobsen. As dean at MIT, he had promoted the building of Aalto's Baker House dormitory and had endorsed the West Coast architect Pietro Belluschi as his replacement. At Berkeley, Wurster had championed a broad, all-encompassing curriculum that allowed room for a multiplicity of views. He was essentially concerned with what he termed "place" and how it was necessary to draw "inspiration from the land and customs." Wurster had laid the foundations for the Berkeley that Lyndon represented in ILAUD. Lyndon was one of the few in ILAUD to whom I could talk about Kahn without the conversation ending in a muddle of cross-purposes. He shared many of Kahn's central concerns, but his vocabulary and approach were less abstract—supported by his clear voice representing his own generation.

Postmodernism

During these years in ILAUD, the position of postmodernism in international architectural discourse transformed. At its start, it surfaced as a break from prewar modernism's doctrines, clearly unfolding into a new territory. In Italy—a base for some of the earliest discussions about postmodernism—Aldo Rossi talked about the need for a general intelligibility. He asserted that we live not in a world of abstraction but of complex memories, and that archetypes are the essence of architecture. At the time, few questioned which memories and archetypes would be privileged by this new order. Instead, we engaged Rossi's arguments for some time in the laboratory, in reaction both to the perceived emptiness of much of modern architecture and the conviction that architecture had lost touch with its humanness. The desire for a more figurative expression in turn strengthened the reputation of Kahn's work from this vantage point. Thus his work was quickly recast as a link to this movement, while ignoring the underlying issues fundamental to his built work. Unfortunately, many used his architecture as an easy way to bolster the legitimacy of their own strategic use of image.

By 1980 Sverre Fehn and Christian Norberg-Schulz, both professors at the Oslo School of Architecture and Design, participated in ILAUD's summer sessions. Meanwhile, they found inspiration in very different sets of colleagues at home and abroad. Fehn, whose office had little work at the time, taught advanced architecture and maintained some contact with Team 10 participants, such as De Carlo, van Eyck, Herman Hertzberger, Aulis Blomstedt, and Reima Pietilä. Later, he turned his attention to New York and London, serving as a visiting professor at Cooper Union and an external diploma critic at the Architectural Association, which was then under the leadership of Alvin Boyarsky. The dean at Cooper Union, the architect John Hejduk, visited Oslo several times while executing an experimental project in the center of town, and by the time of these visits Fehn and Hejduk had become good friends. Even within his expanding network, Fehn never lost sight of Kahn—of his buildings, of his focus on the core beginning—but his work nevertheless reflected the more image-oriented expressions of the period.

In another corner of the Oslo School of Architecture and Design, Norberg-Schulz chaired the department of theory and history. His influential writings prompted many invitations from schools and institutions abroad. Along with a number of close colleagues and friends in Italy, he championed the postmodernist cause in Europe. He was a member of the committee chaired by Paolo Portoghesi for the first Venice Architectural Biennale (1980), which selected Robert Venturi, among other "postmodernists," as the focus for its first exhibition.

In an article titled "The Way to Figurative Architecture," which he contributed to the

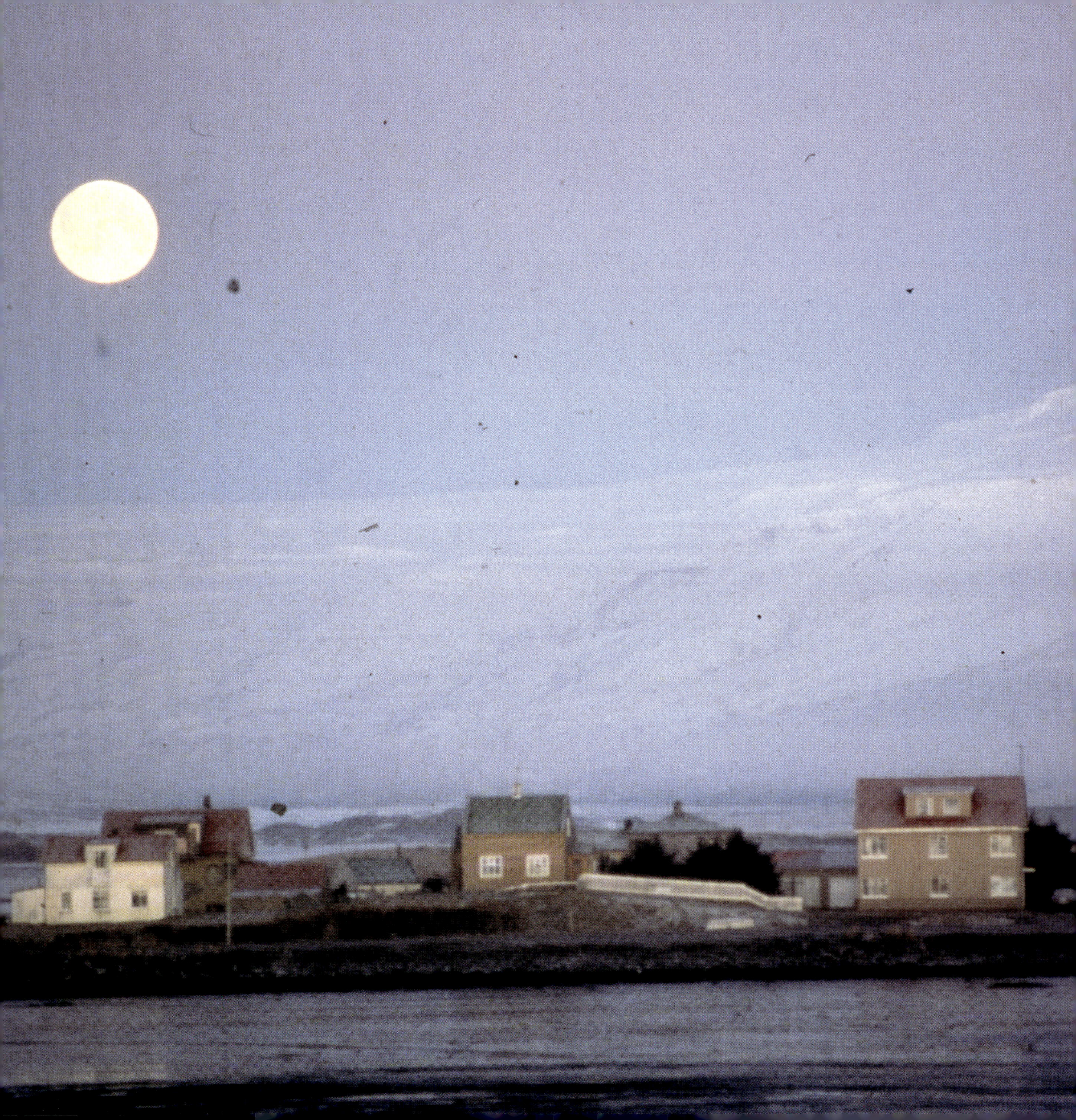

1984–85 *ILAUD Year Book*, Norberg-Schulz cited Kahn as the father of postmodernism, although not in figurative but in structural terms. Unfortunately, Norberg-Schulz gave little consideration to the distance between these two poles—and he suggested that Kahn's architecture had fallen behind Venturi's. Thus image and illusion, not the institutions of man, became primary. Like many, he stressed the importance of recovering a figurative dimension in architecture, but he did not take into account that by this point the "figurative" was fast becoming an arbitrary play of motifs.

When Norberg-Schulz's article was published, a strong backlash against postmodernist thinking was just beginning to surface. Toward the end of his career, Norberg-Schulz shifted focus, returning to basic architectural concerns—in particular, the perception of place and its inherent spatial potential, and the particularities of Nordic sensibilities relative to those of central Europe. His thinking had turned from global to local.

Experiencing the entire span of a movement, its peak and ebb, can only happen a few times in one's professional life. By the summer of 1988, when Charles Moore visited the laboratory in Siena, the debates about the essential ambitions of architecture had intensified. Moore was quite feeble at this point, and as he sat at the table facing us with slides of his latest work, it felt as if the last spark of joy in postmodernism had ended. Confronted with his lecture images and my own reflections on all that had happened to architecture during the turbulent years after my graduation, I was left with the feeling that a preoccupation with the image had sidetracked architecture's focus on room and its specific energy.

In the midst of all these changes, ILAUD had served as a serious platform for discussing architectural intention and responsibility and the creative approach. Much of the conceptual work initiated there had provided a direction from which both theoretical and built projects could later develop. While there were few occasions where Kahn was discussed in any depth, several individuals who participated in ILAUD over the years addressed Kahn's impact as a teacher and architect. Balkrishna Doshi, a friend of De Carlo's, visited the laboratory several times. In a 1991 lecture he gave concerning the challenges facing the architect-planner in India, Doshi touched on many of the issues and attitudes—in particular, about nature and the institutions of man—that Kahn had impressed on us as students. The intensity of ILAUD studio work and the discussions that followed, along with the laboratory's impressive list of visitors, revived my memories of Kahn's masterclass and inspired me to reflect on his Nordic ties.

Van Eyck's insights, just for instance, lead me to reassess Kahn's Korman House, which had been completed just after I returned home after the masterclass. The first time I had seen a photograph of the Korman House I had been left feeling a little puzzled. As an image, the

A Nordic settlement in Iceland: here architecture directly confronts nature's laws. Toward the end of his career, Norberg-Schulz returned to basic architectural concerns, including the particularities of Nordic sensibilities. *Sigbjørn Kjartansson.*

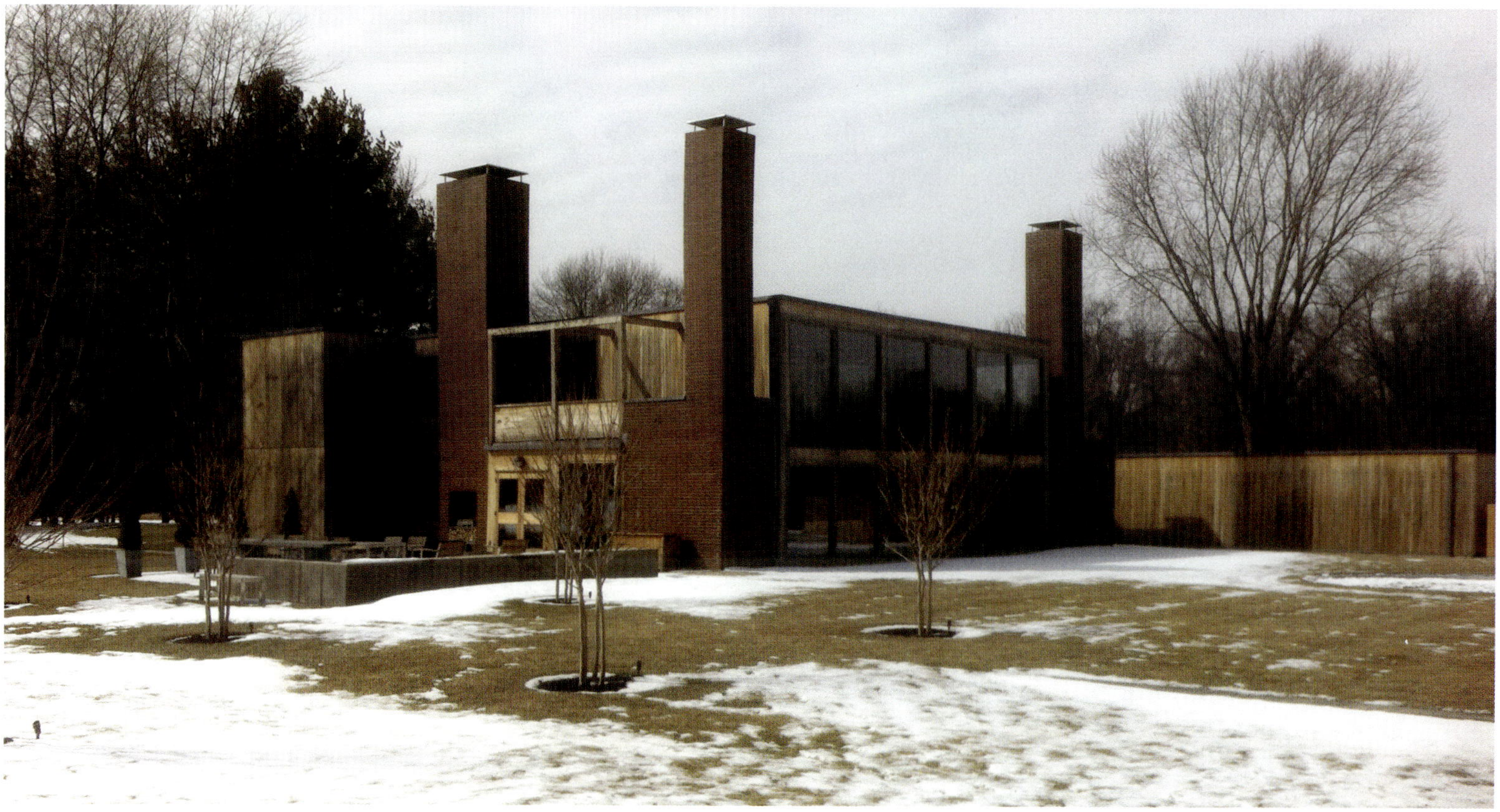

Louis Kahn's Korman House, 1971–73. The house as a body of mass and the immediate landscape face one another directly. *P. O. Fjeld.*

house appeared rather monumental and slightly disconnected from its immediate landscape. I had put the photograph aside and had not returned to it in years. Van Eyck's concept of "the edge as facade, but not the facade"—which both haunted and inspired me, even as I struggled to make sense of it—put the Korman House into another perspective. Here a wall understood as "edge" brings the immediate spaces on either side of it into a unified whole—active, sequential, and balanced. The "edge as facade" directs the contact with the landscape as nature, facilitating a relationship with the surrounding site that exceeds conventional notions of the picturesque. Scale is in turn set by the edge and interpreted through a spatial sequence relative to both the inside and outside. Altogether, this spatial relationship seems to embody van Eyck's concept of "Twin Phenomena." No image of the Korman House is truly able to capture this interaction and fluidity of threshold.

When I finally visited the house, the first thing that struck me was its latent Nordic sensibility, which I imagined as evolving from a synthesis of many life experiences coming together. The house seems to declare, "I cannot be moved," as if it had primed its site with its own

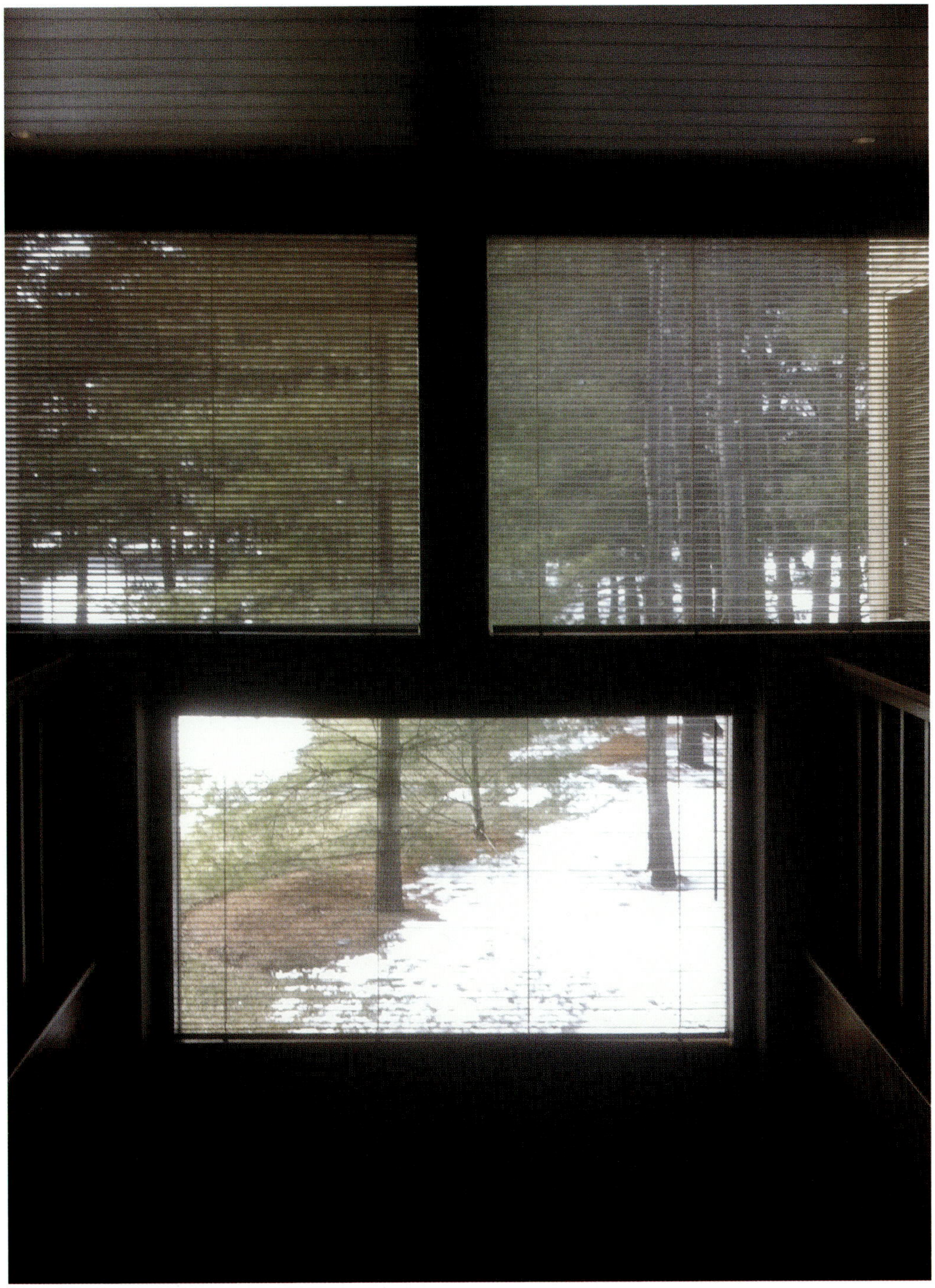

At the Korman House, a wall understood as "edge" brings the immediate spaces on either side of it into a unified whole. *P. O. Fjeld.*

2001 Toyo Ito's Sendai Mediatheque completed.

Ian McHarg dies.

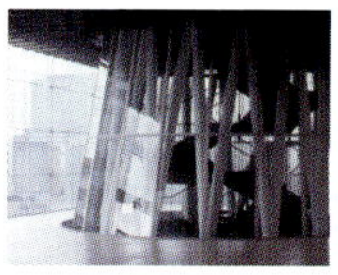

Sendai Mediatheque. *P. O. Fjeld.*

2002 Foreign Office Architects' Yokohama International Passenger Terminal completed.

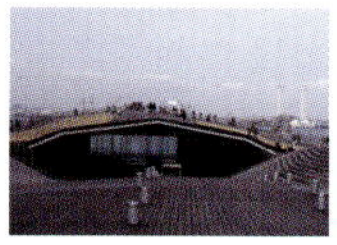

Yokohama International Passenger Terminal. *P. O. Fjeld.*

2003 Peter Smithson dies.

2004 SANAA'S 21st Century Museum of Contemporary Art completed.

George Holmes Perkins dies.

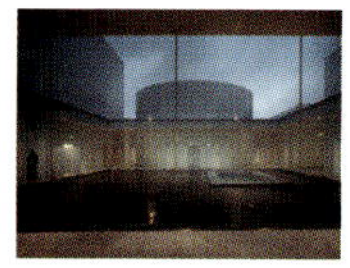

21st Century Museum of Contemporary Art. *Jon Reksten.*

mass and gravity. Though the Korman home is the largest of Kahn's houses, an intimate scale is essential to the spatial precision of its interior. The thresholds between inside and outside, the light, and the materiality of the house feel quintessentially Nordic, yet the house clearly belongs to the Philadelphia area. On the day of my visit, snow covered the ground and the winter sky cast a light without shadow. Inside the house a fire was burning. A grey, Estonian winter light seemed to wait by the window's edge.

The Global Stage

By the turn of the twenty-first century, the international architect had truly claimed center stage. Before the middle of the last century, architects who achieved international stature had generally created work that belonged to a specific culture and place; the influence of their work was therefore somewhat contained. Today this has changed dramatically, as images of architecture can be shared globally with the click of a button and as buildings that attract media attention are widely imitated. Unfortunately, the copycat buildings that proliferate around the globe are often far weaker in addressing the social and cultural concerns that inform the originals they feed off, thus these buildings are environmentally flawed from the start. This has created a global, deracinated architecture that has undermined local customs and building conventions tied to place. This transformation is altering how the human perceives and forges relationships with nature—and the Nordic region has certainly not been spared these changes. The temptation to view nature as a large-scale picture—as a purely visual entity best observed from a place sealed off from the "discomforts" of natural physical forces—is negatively impacting our present understanding of architecture. This is an especially unfortunate trend in my home country, since it oversimplifies our physical relationship with the environment as well as the collective understanding of nature's laws that once undergirded Nordic architecture's precision and specificity.

This current climate reaffirms many of the insights that Kenzo Tange, Kahn and Korsmo's mutual friend, outlined in an article that he wrote following the 1959 CIAM meeting. At that time, Tange questioned technology's prominence in architecture as he affirmed the importance of regionally inflected work. He asserted:

> I do not think of regionalism as an expression of visual language that has been traditionally employed in a given region. [. . .] I think of regionalism as resulting when each region with its own inconsistences and difficulties takes creative means to resolve them. [. . .] I do not believe that tradition as such can either be preserved or converted into creative

2005 Kenzo Tange, Giancarlo De Carlo, Ralph Erskine, and Philip Johnson die.

2006 Renzo Piano's renovation and expansion of the Morgan Library completed.

2007 Toyo Ito's Tama Art University Library completed. Snøhetta's Norwegian National Opera and Ballet completed. Herzog & de Meuron complete Beijing National Stadium.

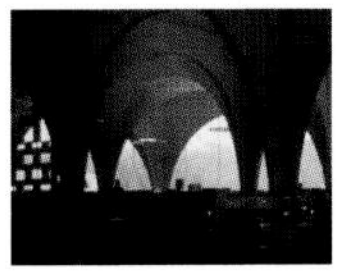

Tama Art University Library. *P. O. Fjeld.*

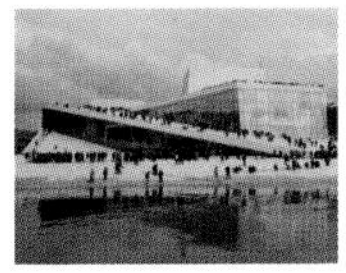

Norwegian National Opera and Ballet. *Snøhetta Archive.*

2008 Junya Ishigami's KAIT Workshop completed. Sverre Fehn's restoration and pavilion for the Norwegian National Museum completed.

Jørn Utzon dies.

> drive. Creative drive today is an association of technology and humanity. The role played by tradition is that of the catalyst, which encourages and stimulates a chemical reaction, but does not remain in the resulting compound. Tradition can play a part in creation but does not itself create.[4]

The latest modes of promulgating architectural trends—and the concurrent political and marketing interests that attach themselves to these—have worked to undermine the very regionalism that Tange advocated.

Meanwhile, new public projects are increasingly planned with the expectation of a short life span, both diminishing long-term investment and undermining our collective understanding of our institutions. This has transformed the built work into a strategic tool whose value depends on the expediency of its economic strategy. Thus public funding is increasingly funneled to projects that will draw tourists, who are courted for the economic potential they represent rather than for any deep commitment to the institutions they visit only passingly. In this scenario, commercial interests collect on what they perceive as architecture's value through a quantitative understanding of the user.

When the short-term life span of a building is the main parameter for investment, where does this leave nature and the relationship between humanity and technology? "Green architecture" and "sustainable building" remain for the most part the province of technology, as Western societies rely heavily on technological improvements to prolong the status quo. Architects have generally neglected the undiscovered potential within physical space itself, since all too often the easy fixes that can achieve immediate results are prioritized first, over those solutions that require the kind of long-term search toward architectural depth that Kahn always emphasized. As he noted in the masterclass, we focus on the how while giving little attention to the underlying what and why. We have not paid enough attention to Kahn's notion of volume zero, and thus have neglected to strip away the layers to reveal the human component in nature. Instead, we have sought more complexity, more layers, distancing ourselves from physical engagement with nature.

With today's rendering technology, it is possible to evaluate a potential space virtually—but this is only possible because we have embraced the status quo. Architecture's ability to transform and enrich will remain restricted by the parameters of this image orientation as long as the core identity of institution is not aggressively questioned. Climate change, migration, competition for resources, and technology will continue to transform our lives—but the architectural challenge lies in how all of this will change our perception of our collective institutions. While social media continues to promote the individual above community in the

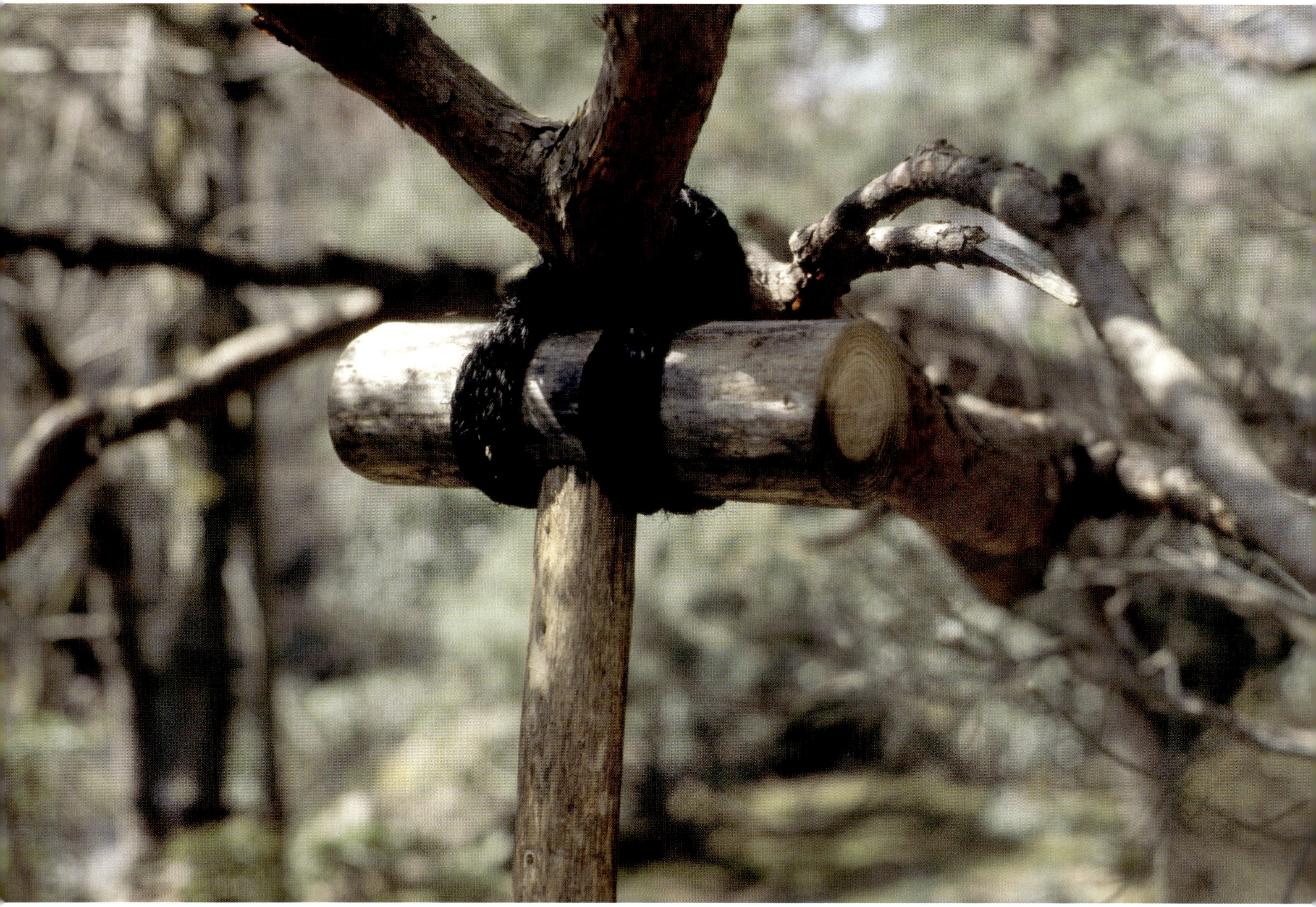

Structural support for a branch outside the temple in the Ryōan-ji garden in Kyoto: Kahn's rules of man and the laws of nature combined. *P. O. Fjeld.*

2009 Kengo Kuma's Nezu Museum completed. Lacaton & Vassal's Nantes School of Architecture completed. Diller Scofidio + Renfro and Piet Oudolf complete New York's High Line park. Per Olaf Fjeld's *Sverre Fehn: The Pattern of Thoughts* published.

Sverre Fehn dies.

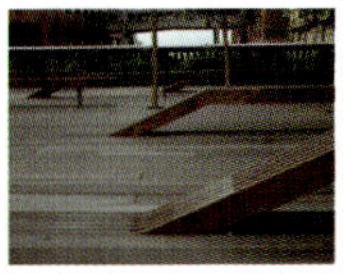

The High Line, New York. *Elisa Grindland.*

2010 Ryue Nishizawa's Teshima Art Museum opens.

Grete Prytz Kittelsen dies.

2011 Anne Tyng and Kiyonori Kikutake die.

2012 Kahn's Franklin D. Roosevelt Four Freedoms Park completed. Tod Williams and Billie Tsien's Barnes Foundation completed. Louis I. Kahn exhibition held at the Architecture Museum in Oslo (in the Fehn-designed pavilion).

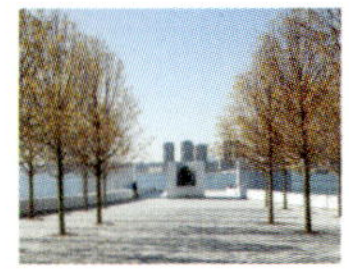

Franklin D. Roosevelt Four Freedoms Park. *Jon Reksten.*

industrialized world, architects must remain committed to exploring the individual's proper role in the collective.

Despite all these recent developments in architecture, including the proliferation of copycat buildings, inspiring works are indeed being built all over the world. Kahn's instruction to focus on the inspiration, the beginnings, of contemporary masters' work rather than the work itself has never been more relevant. Japanese architecture, which of all the contemporary work seems to best embody Kahn's ideals, has especially excelled. For all its technical focus and spatial efficiencies, Japanese architecture still finds inspiration and innovates within the context of a deep respect for nature, whatever form that nature may take. Throughout the technical transformations of the last century, Japanese society retained its relationship with nature, and the laws of nature in turn remained in the cultural consciousness. In this awareness a keen sensitivity to the institutions of man persists. This sensitivity promotes an exploration into the essence of material, both new and traditional, and a search for a spatial and structural identity where technology does not override the deeper human concerns.

Life's Circumstances

So what became of all of us from the masterclass? Kahn did not mold any of us into international starchitects, nor was that his intention—but he did change all of us as human beings on some level. I am left remembering how he admonished us in class: "Don't do what I do. Listen to what I am saying." During all my years as a teacher and practicing architect, one of Kahn's other simply put insights has also stuck with me: "We are all born with a sense of what to do, but we are not born with how to do it." No doubt Kahn's Nordic beginning in some essential way invested him with that original sense of what to do—and that he acquired the skills to do it through all that came his way, the places he visited, and the people he met. What he gave us as a teacher was something deeply complex, and even more relevant today than it was forty-six years ago. Sadly, I was never able to thank him properly—a fact that remains unresolved, without closure.

Over the years we never met again as a class. Kahn's sudden death a little more than eight months after our graduation seemed to loosen our ties to Penn. Many of us have divided our time between practicing and teaching, and probably all of us at some point struggled to balance the architectural commitment that Kahn impressed on us with what life threw at us. I was lucky: Emily followed me to Norway and I landed my first job with Sverre Fehn. Under Fehn's wing I had the privilege of reflecting on all that had happened in the masterclass. For

The desire to express
The Threshold

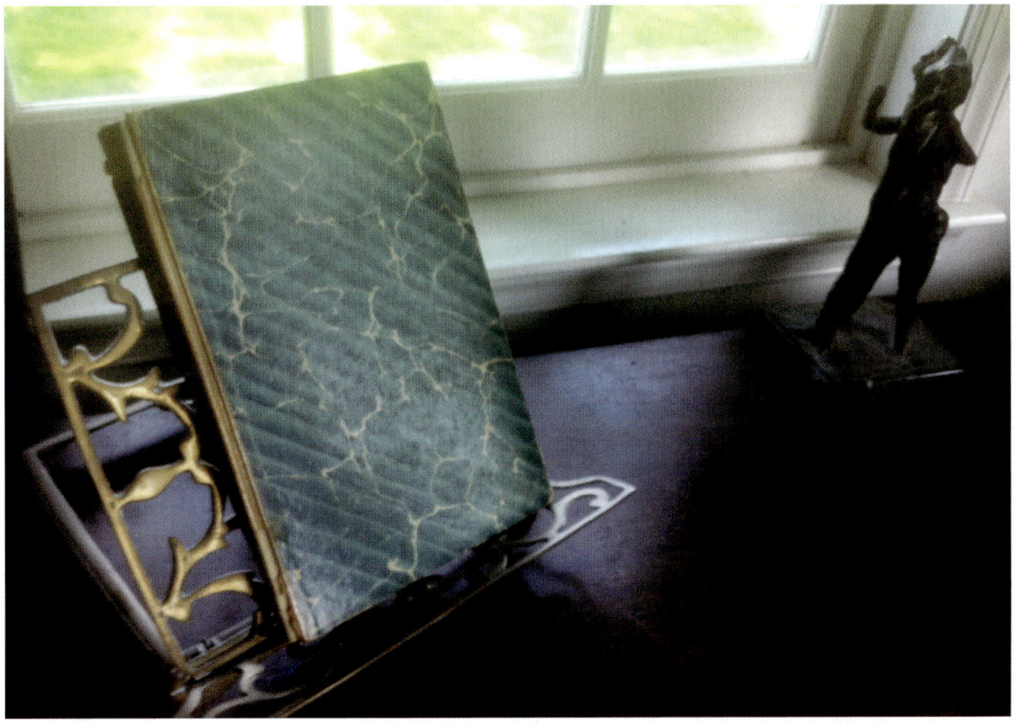

me the years after graduation opened a small window into the personal side of Kahn that had prompted him to ask me that first semester, "Do you know Arne Korsmo?"

Over the years I have been fortunate to meet several people who were close to Kahn or his family. In 2013 I met all three of Kahn's children when they attended the opening of a Vitra exhibition of Kahn's work that was held in the Norwegian National Museum pavilion designed by Sverre Fehn and finished just before he died. In the middle of an introductory speech on that dim late-fall afternoon, I could not help but say, "This light is yours, Mr. Kahn. We have just been waiting for a visit to welcome you back to the North."

A half year later, Emily and I had lunch at Harriet Pattison's home in the country with her son, Nathaniel Kahn, and Susan Behr. The conversation flowed back and forth from drawings and sketches, my class notes, and recollections. In the middle of a sentence, Nathaniel Kahn's attention shifted across the room to a table full of mementos of his father. At its center was a leather-bound book on a stand. Harriet Pattison noted that it was one of Kahn's favorite books: Steen Eiler Rasmussen's *Towns and Buildings*—the same book that Sverre Fehn had given me many years ago with the instruction that "You should probably read this." In class, Kahn had often talked about how chance determines how one perceives the world. Here was such a coincidence—and it strengthened my belief in Kahn's Nordic connection.

OPPOSITE: "The desire to express / The threshold"—a portion of tracing paper preserved in the Louis I. Kahn Collection visualizes one of Kahn's searches for volume zero. *Louis I. Kahn Collection, The University of Pennsylvania and the Pennsylvania Historical and Museum Commission.*

TOP: Life's strange circumstances: Steen Eiler Rasmussen's book *Towns and Buildings*, a favorite of Kahn's, on a display stand in Harriet Pattison's living room. *Nathaniel Kahn.*

NOTES

CHAPTER 1

1. Olavi Pesti, "Kuressaare of a Century Ago," in *Ehituskunst, Estonian Architectural Review*, no. 47/48 (2007): 7–44.
2. Per Olaf Fjeld, notes from a lecture by Christian Norberg-Schultz at the Oslo School of Architecture, spring 1996.
3. Herman Munthe-Kaas represented Norway from 1933 until the last meeting before the war. He studied in Oslo at the same time as Backer and then received his diploma in Stockholm a year after Backer. He then worked in Asplund's office for a time. Göran Schildt, in his book *Alvar Aalto: His Life* (2007), gives a good account of the Nordic build up to the Athens CIAM meeting of 1933.
4. Christian Norberg-Schulz, *Arne Korsmo* (Oslo: Universitetsforlaget, distributed by Oxford University Press, 1986), 36.
5. August E. Komendant, *18 Years with Architect Louis I. Kahn* (Englewood, NJ: Aloray Publishers, 1975).
6. Christian Norberg-Schulz, "Arne Korsmo 1900–1968," in *Byggekunst*, no. 6 (1972): 164.
7. Ibid.
8. Gregor Paulsson was a pivotal figure in the modern movement in Sweden. During the Paris Exhibition of 1925, he accompanied Ferdinand Boberg to see Le Corbusier's pavilion for L'Esprit Nouveau. Boberg, then sixty-five years old and retired from his practice for ten years, commented that this represented the future direction of architecture.
9. Alvar Aalto, "Stockholmsutställinger" [Stockholm Exhibition], in *Arkitektur, Swedish Review of Architecture* (Stockholm), no. 7 (1930): 119–20.
10. Ibid.
11. Franco Albini's exhibit for the Italian pavilion (under Giuseppe Pagano, who was chief coordinator of Italy's exhibits) won a grand prize. This exhibit used many elements from his earlier exhibition in Milan, Mostra dell'Aeronautica (1934). Korsmo may not have met Albini personally by this point, but he must have been aware of this exhibition, as he was on-site working on the Norwegian pavilion. Pagano, along with G. Daniel, wrote the book *Architettura Rurale Italiana* in 1936. Pagano was involved in the Rationalist movement of the time, but the book indicated some of the issues and directions that would surface in the postwar period.
12. Sverre Fehn, "Om Arne Korsmo," in *Byggekunst* (Norsk Arkitekters Landsforbund, Oslo), no. 6 (1985): 304.
13. Per Olaf Fjeld, notes on Sverre Fehn, 1980.
14. Sigfried Giedion, "Arkitekturdebatten" (edited transcript of lecture), in *Byggekunst* (Norsk Arkitekters Landsforbund, Oslo), no. 10 (1948): 135–37.
15. Letter from Kahn to his office, Louis I. Kahn Collection, University of Pennsylvania, Box 6020.
16. On two occasions, Fehn mentioned the friendship between Albini and Korsmo, but I did not follow these conversations up at the time. The first concerned a catalogue from 1979 of an exhibition that I gave Fehn after a trip abroad. He immediately commented that this was a friend of Korsmo. I thought the book would interest him, as he had a number of exhibition commissions at the time, but instead the conversation turned to the impact Albini's work had on Korsmo. The second time began as a conversation concerning Venice and Scarpa, but suddenly shifted to Paris and Albini's design for the Olivetti store, and again Korsmo came up.
17. Frederico Bucci, *Franco Albini* (Milan: Mondadori Electa SpA, 2009): 8.
18. "What is CIAM?" in *Byggekunst* (Norsk Arkitekters Landsforbund, Oslo), no. 6–7 (1952): 94–96.
19. Louis I. Kahn, "Remarks," Perspecta 9/10: The Yale Architectural Journal, 1965.
20. Paul Eisenhaur and Lynne Farrington, eds., *Wharton Esherick and the Birth of the American Modern* (Atglen, PA: Schiffer Publishing Ltd. in cooperation with Penn Libraries, 2010).
21. Louis I. Kahn, "Talk at the Conclusion of the Otterlo Congress," in *Louis Kahn: Essential Texts*, ed. Robert Twombly (New York: W. W. Norton Company, 2003), 37–57. Originally published in *New Frontiers in Architecture* by Oscar Newman.
22. Letter to Kahn from Ralph Erskine, dated December 14, 1959, Louis I. Kahn Collection, University of Pennsylvania, Box 6536.
23. Herman Hertzberger interview in *Louis Kahn: The Power of Architecture* (Vitra Design Museum in cooperation with the Architectural Archives of the University of Pennsylvania and the Nederlands Architectuurinstituut, Weil am Rhein, 2013), 258.
24. Louis I. Kahn, "Talk at the Conclusion of the Otterlo Congress."
25. Per Olaf Fjeld, notes on Sverre Fehn's rendition of van Eyck's brief for the orphanage, 1980.
26. The Japan trip always came up when Korsmo's students from Trondheim reminisced about student days. His students raised money for the trip as a birthday gift and threw a very creative Japanese-themed party in advance of his trip. The Japanese tour guide who appears in many of the pictures Korsmo took in Japan visited Norway later.
27. Korsmo letter dated June 6, 1964, Louis I. Kahn Collection, University of Pennsylvania, Box 6532.
28. From the transcript of Kahn's lecture in Oslo, Oslo Chapter of the Norwegian Architects Association.
29. The full transcript of Kahn's Lecture in Oslo, Oslo Chapter of the Norwegian Architects Association, 1966. Transcription by Per Olaf Fjeld and Emily Randall Fjeld.
30. Transcript of Kahn's address to a planning conference in Helsinki held just days after his lectures in Copenhagen, Oslo, and Stockholm in 1966. Alvar Aalto also addressed this conference. Aalto's speech is printed in *Arkkitehti, Finnish Architectural Review*, no. 5 (1967).

CHAPTER 2

1. Per Olaf Fjeld, masterclass notes, spring 1973. The value of the Schuylkill River despite its polluted state came up in class. Kahn noted that regardless of its state, it was still a river and thus deserved to be treated with respect.
2. Per Olaf Fjeld, class notes, Le Ricolais's first class session, September 1972.
3. Per Olaf Fjeld, class notes, Le Ricolais's class, fall 1972.
4. Robert Le Ricolais, "Louis I. Kahn as Teacher," Louis I. Kahn Collection, University of Pennsylvania, Box 346.1.
5. Norman Rice, "Louis I. Kahn as Teacher," Louis I. Kahn Collection, University of Pennsylvania, Box 346.1.

CHAPTER 4

1. From Per Olaf Fjeld's project notebook, spring 1973.
2. Romaldo Guirgola and Jaimini Mehta, *Louis I. Kahn* (Boulder, CO: Westview Press, 1975), 33–34.
3. Louis I. Kahn, *Louis I. Kahn: Conversations with Students; Architecture at Rice 26* (Houston, TX: Architecture at Rice Publications, 1998), 24.
4. Louis I. Kahn Collection, University of Pennsylvania and the Pennsylvania Historical and Museum Commission, Box 54.
5. Louis I. Kahn, speech for the 1965 National Conference of Church Architecture, Louis I. Kahn Collection, University of Pennsylvania and the Pennsylvania Historical and Museum Commission.
6. From Richard Church's Kahn 1960 masterclass notes, which he gave to Robert Couch just before he entered the masterclass of 1972–73. Robert Couch Private Collection.
7. Ibid.
8. Ibid.

CHAPTER 5

1. From Richard Church's class notes from 1960, which he shared with Robert Couch just before he entered the masterclass. Robert Couch Private Collection.
2. Louis I. Kahn, draft of lecture for the National Conference of Church Architecture, 1965. Louis I. Kahn Collection, University of Pennsylvania and the Pennsylvania Historical and Museum Commission.
3. Ibid.
4. From Richard Church's class notes from 1960, which he shared with Robert Couch just before he entered the masterclass. Robert Couch Private Collection.

CHAPTER 7

1. Princeton conference, Louis I. Kahn Collection, University of Pennsylvania, Box 55.
2. From Per Olaf Fjeld's notes from a lecture that Aldo van Eyck presented at the 1989 ILAUD summer residential course in Siena, Italy.
3. Ibid.
4. Kenzo Tange, "Aestheticism and Vitalism: On Participating in the New CIAM Talks of September 1959," *Japan Architect*, no. 2 (1960): 5.

INDEX

J

K

L

M

O

P

R

T

U

V

W

Y

Z

PER OLAF FJELD is professor emeritus at the Oslo School of Architecture and Design and former president of the European Association for Architectural Education. He was educated at the University of Pennsylvania, where he studied with Louis I. Kahn. He is the author of *Sverre Fehn: The Pattern of Thoughts*, which illuminates the work of the Pritzker Prize–winning architect with whom he once worked and taught. He has a studio practice in Oslo with his wife, coauthor and artist **EMILY RANDALL FJELD**.